Second Edition

Gender

Psychological Perspectives

Linda Brannon
McNeese State University

Allyn and Bacon
Boston • London • Toronto • Sydney • Tokyo • Singapore

Senior Editor: Carolyn Merrill
Series Editorial Assistant: Amy Goldmacher
Vice President and Director of Field Marketing: Joyce Nilsen
Composition and Prepress Buyer: Linda Cox
Manufacturing Buyer: Megan Cochran
Cover Administrator: Brian Gogolin
Production Editor: Christopher H. Rawlings
Editorial-Production Service: Omegatype Typography, Inc.
Electronic Composition: Omegatype Typography, Inc.

A Viacom Company
160 Gould Street
Needham Heights, MA 02194

Internet: www.abacon.com

Library of Congress Cataloging-in-Publication Data

Brannon, Linda
Gender : psychological perspectives / Linda Brannon. — 2nd ed.
p. cm.
Includes bibliographical references and indexes.
ISBN 0-205-27589-3
1. Sex differences (Psychology) 2. Gender identity. 3. Sex role.
4. Feminist psychology. 5. Women—Psychology. I. Title.
BF692.2.B73 1999
155.3–dc21 98-3200
CIP

Printed in the United States of America

10 9 8 7 6 5 4 3 03 02 01 00 99

Contents

Preface **xi**

1 The Study of Gender 1

Headline: "Sizing Up the Sexes," Time, *January 20, 1992 1*
History of the Study of Sex Differences in Psychology 3
The Study of Individual Differences 4
Psychoanalysis 5
Development of Women's Studies 7
The Appearance of the Men's Movement 9
Sex or Gender? 12
Should Psychologists Study Gender? 13
Psychology and Gender Research 15
Different Approaches to Gender Research 15
Gender in the Headlines 17
Summary 18
Glossary 18
Suggested Readings 19

2 Researching Sex and Gender 20

Headline: "The Science Wars," Newsweek, *April 21, 1997 20*
How Science Developed 21
Methods and What They Reveal 23
Descriptive Methods 24
Naturalistic Observation 24
Surveys 26
Correlational Studies 27
Experimental Designs 28
Ex Post Facto Studies 29
Qualitative Research 32
Limitations on Gender Research 34
Criticisms of Science 39

Methodologies for the Study of Gender *40*
Summary *43*
Glossary *43*
Suggested Readings *44*

3 Hormones and Chromosomes 45

Headlines: "Aggression in Men: Hormone Levels Are a Key," New York Times, *July 17, 1990* *45*
"PMS: Is It for Real?" Cosmopolitan, *April 1995* *45*
The Endocrine System and Steroid Hormones *46*
Stages of Differences between the Sexes *48*
Sexual Differentiation *48*
Development of Male and Female Physiology 49
The Reproductive Organs 49
The Nervous System 50
Changes during Puberty 53
When Things Go Wrong 56
Abnormalities in Number of Chromosomes 57
Abnormalities in Prenatal Hormones 58
Hormones and Behavior Instability *60*
Premenstrual Syndrome 61
Testosterone and Aggression 65
Summary *70*
Glossary *71*
Suggested Readings *72*

4 The Brain 73

Headline: "Gray Matters," Newsweek, *March 27, 1995* *73*
The Brain and the Nervous System *74*
The Brain and Sex *74*
Structural Differences 75
The Cerebral Hemispheres and Lateralization 75
Gender Differences in Lateralization 79
Other Gender Differences in Brain Structure 82
Functional Differences 84
What Brain Differences Might Mean *86*
Summary *87*
Glossary *88*
Suggested Readings *88*

5 Intelligence and Mental Abilities 89

Headline: "The Great Debate: Gender Differences," Current Health 2, *December 1995* *89*
Mental Abilities *90*

Verbal Abilities 91
Mathematical and Quantitative Abilities 94
Spatial Abilities 99
Other Mental Abilities 103
Implications of Gender-Related Differences 107
Source of the Differences 109
Summary 112
Glossary 113
Suggested Readings 113

6 Gender Development I: The Psychoanalytic Approach 114

Headline: "Sex and Morality," Omni, *May 1985 114*
The Psychoanalytic Approach to Personality 115
Freud's Theory of Personality 115
Basic Concepts 116
Moral Development 119
Freud and Women 119
Horney's Theory of Personality 120
Women, Men, and Psychoanalytic Theory 123
Effects of Freud's Abandonment of the Seduction Theory 124
Contemporary Psychoanalytic Theories of Personality Development 126
Feminist Standpoint Theory: A Different Voice 130
Gilligan's Theory of Moral Development 130
The Maximalist Approach and Its Implications 134
Summary 136
Glossary 137
Suggested Readings 138

7 Gender Development II: Social Theories 139

Headline: "Sexist Piglets: Studies Show That Sex-Stereotyping Is Part of Childhood," Parents' Magazine, *December 1983 139*
Social Learning Theory 140
Cognitive Developmental Theory 144
Gender Schema Theory 147
Gender Script Theory 151
Developing Gender Identity 152
During Childhood 153
The Sequence of Development 154
Differences between Girls and Boys 156
During Adolescence and Adulthood 157
Which Theory Best Explains the Data? 160
Summary 161
Glossary 162
Suggested Readings 162

8 Gender Stereotypes: Masculinity and Femininity 164

Headline: "The Gender Trap," Ms. Magazine, *November/December 1994 164*
From Gender Roles to Gender Stereotypes 165
Stereotypes of Women and Men 165
The Cult of True Womanhood 166
Masculinities 167
Development of Stereotypes 168
Perceptions of Women and Men 171
Stereotypes about and across Cultures 176
Function of Stereotyping 179
Masculinity, Femininity, and Androgyny 181
Summary 187
Glossary 188
Suggested Readings 188

9 Emotion 189

Headline: "Big Fat Lies about Men," Mademoiselle, *August 1996 189*
Physiological, Cognitive, and Behavioral Aspects 190
Gender and the Experience of Emotion 191
The Myth of Maternal Instinct 194
Maternal Deprivation and Its Consequences for Nurturing 195
Attachment 197
Gender and Caring for Children 198
Prominence of Male Aggression 201
Anger and Aggression 202
Developmental Gender Differences in Aggression 203
Gender Differences in Aggression during Adulthood 206
Expressivity and Emotion 214
Summary 215
Glossary 217
Suggested Readings 217

10 Relationships 218

Headline: "Why Are His Feelings My Responsibility?" Woman's Day, *July 18, 1995 218*
Friendships 220
Development of Styles 220
Friendships over the Life Span 223
Flexibility of Styles 226
Love Relationships 227
Dating 229
Marriage and Committed Relationships 231
Concepts of Love and Marriage 233
Communication between Partners 234

Division of Household Labor 235
Power and Conflict 238
Stability of Relationships 241
Dissolving Relationships 244
Summary 248
Glossary 249
Suggested Readings 249

11 Sexuality 251

*Headline: "In the Dark," *Men's Health*, December 1995 251*
The Study of Sexuality 251
Sex Surveys 252
The Kinsey Surveys 253
Hunt's Playboy Foundation Survey 256
The National Opinion Research Council Survey 257
Gender Differences (and Similarities) in Sexual Attitudes and Behavior 258
Masters and Johnson's Approach 259
Childhood Sexuality: Exploration and Abuse 263
Heterosexuality 268
During Adolescence 268
During Adulthood 272
Homosexuality 277
During Adolescence 281
During Adulthood 282
Bisexuality 285
Summary 286
Glossary 288
Suggested Readings 288

12 School 289

*Headline: "A Room of Their Own," *Newsweek*, June 24, 1996 289*
The School Experience 290
Early School Experience 291
Changes during Junior High 295
High School 296
College and Professional School 301
Achievement 308
Achievement Motivation 308
Fear of Success 308
Self-Esteem and Self-Confidence 310
Attributions for Success and Failure 311
Summary 313
Glossary 314
Suggested Readings 315

13 Careers and Work 316

Headline: "Trouble at the Top: A U.S. Survey Says a 'Glass Ceiling' Blocks Women from Corporate Heights," U.S. News & World Report, *June 17, 1991* *316*

Careers *317*

Career Expectations and Gender Role Socialization 318

Career Opportunities 320

Discrimination in Hiring 321

Barriers to Career Advancement 323

Balancing Career and Family 329

Gender Issues at Work *330*

Gender Segregation on the Job 330

Gender, Communication, and Power in the Workplace 332

Sexual Harassment at Work 335

Summary *340*

Glossary *341*

Suggested Readings *341*

14 Health and Fitness 342

Headline: "Is the Longer Life the Healthier One?" New York Times, *June 22, 1997* *342*

Mortality: No Equal Opportunity *343*

Cardiovascular Disease 343

Cancer 348

Violent Deaths 351

The Health Care System *354*

Gender Roles and Health Care 354

Gender and Seeking Health Care 354

Gender and Receiving Health Care 356

Reproductive Health 359

Gender, Lifestyle, and Health *363*

Eating 364

Body Image 365

Eating Disorders 367

Exercising and Fitness 369

Summary *372*

Glossary *373*

Suggested Readings *373*

15 Stress, Coping, and Psychopathology 374

Headline: "Is It Sadness or Madness?" Newsweek, *March 15, 1993* *374*

Stress and Coping *376*

Sources of Stress for Men and Women 376

Family Roles 376

Violence 378

Poverty 380
Discrimination 381
Coping Resources and Strategies 381
Social Support 382
Coping Strategies 383
Diagnoses of Mental Disorders 385
The DSM Classification System 386
Gender Inequity in the Diagnosis of Mental Disorders 388
Gender Comparisons in Psychopathology 394
Depression 394
Substance-Related Disorders 396
Anxiety Disorders 398
Other Disorders 400
Summary 403
Glossary 404
Suggested Readings 405

16 Treatment for Mental Disorders 406

Headline: "Sex and Psychotherapy," Newsweek, *April 13, 1992 406*
Approaches to Therapy 407
Psychoanalysis 407
Humanistic Therapies 409
Cognitive Therapy 410
Behavior Modification 412
Medical Therapies 413
Accusations of Gender Bias in Therapy 414
Gender Issues in Therapy 416
Feminist Therapy 417
Theoretical Orientations of Feminist Therapy 418
Clients of Feminist Therapy 419
Therapy with Men 422
Gender Aware Therapy 423
Sexual Exploitation in Therapy 425
The Self-Help Movement 427
Support Groups 430
Consciousness Raising Groups 432
Summary 435
Glossary 436
Suggested Readings 436

17 How Different? 438

Headline: "A Peace Plan for the Gender Wars," Psychology Today, *March/April 1996 438*
Multiple Roles Have Become the Rule 439

What Do Women Want? What Do Men Want? *442*
Have Women Become More Like Men? 442
Why Can't a Man Be More Like a Woman? 446
Where Are the Differences? *449*
Differences in Ability 450
Differences in Choices 451
Summary *454*
Suggested Readings *455*

References **457**

Name Index **499**

Subject Index **510**

Preface

This book examines the topic of gender—the behaviors and attitudes that relate to (but are not entirely congruent with) biological sex. A large and growing body of research on sex, gender, and gender-related behaviors has come from psychology, sociology, biology, biochemistry, neurology, and anthropology. This research and scholarship form the basis for this book, providing the material for a critical review and an attempt to generate an overall picture of gender from a psychological perspective.

The Topic of Gender

A critical review of gender research is important for several reasons. First, gender is currently a "hot" topic, and almost everyone has an opinion. These opinions are not usually based on research—most people are not familiar with research findings. Their opinions are strongly influenced by their own experience and also by what they have seen in the movies and on television. Whether these programs are news reports or fictional, both types of presentations make an impact—based on these portrayals, people create images about how they believe women and men should be. In *Gender: Psychological Perspectives,* I present what gender researchers have found, but this picture is neither simple nor complete. Research findings are complex and sometimes contradictory, but I believe that it is important to understand this research rather than draw conclusions based only on popular opinions and portrayals.

Second, research is a valuable way to understand gender, despite the bias and controversy that have surrounded the research process. Although scientific research is supposed to be objective and free of personal bias, this idealistic notion often varies from the actual process of research. Gender research has been particularly plagued with personal bias. Despite the bias that can enter into the research process, I believe that research is the most productive way to approach the evaluation of a topic. Others disagree with this view, including some who are interested in gender-related topics. A number of scholars, especially feminist scholars, have rejected scientific research as the best way to learn about gender.

Although I agree that science has not treated women equitably, either as researchers or as participants in research, I still believe that science offers the best chance for a fuller understanding of gender (as well as of many other topics). Some scholars disagree with this view, but I want to make my point of view clear. This proscience orientation is the reason I have chosen to concentrate on research throughout the book—to examine what gender researchers have found and how they have interpreted their findings.

The book's emphasis on gender is similar to another approach to gender—the psychology of women. The psychology of women approach concentrates on women and issues unique to women, whereas the gender approach focuses on the issue of gender as a factor in behavior and in the social context in which behavior occurs. In doing so, gender research and theory draw heavily from the psychology of women, but the emphasis differs.

By emphasizing women and their experience, the psychology of women approach often excludes men, but gender research cannot. Studying both women and men is essential to an understanding of gender. Researchers who are interested in gender issues may concentrate on women or men, but they must consider both, or their research reveals nothing about gender. Therefore, this second edition of *Gender: Psychological Perspectives* examines the research and theory from psychology and related fields in order to evaluate the behavior, biology, and social context in which women *and* men function.

The gender approach also reflects my personal preferences: I want a psychology of women and men. When I was completing the first edition of this book, I attended a conference session on creating a psychology of women course. Several instructors who had created such courses led a discussion about getting institutional approval for such a course and the problems they had encountered, including resistance from administrators (who were mostly men) concerning a course in which the enrollment would be mostly women. One of them advised trying for approval of a course on gender if getting approval for a psychology of women course was not successful. The implication was that the topic of gender included men and would be more acceptable but less desirable. I disagreed. I wanted to include men, not only in the research but also in my classes. I prefer the gender approach, and I wanted this book to reflect that attitude.

My interest in gender came from two sources—my research and my experience as a female psychologist. The research that prompted me to examine gender issues more carefully was risk perception related to health problems. I was interested in investigating people's perceptions of the health risks they created as a result of their behavior, such as the perceptions of health risks in smokers versus nonsmokers. In this research, I found that women and men saw their behaviors and risks in similar ways. Indeed, I failed to find gender-related differences in risk perception even for the health risks in which gender differences appear. That is, I found that men and women perceive their health risks in similar ways, even when these perceptions do not reflect the actual level of health risks for men and women. My research showed gender similarities rather than gender differences.

In examining the volume of research on gender-related attitudes and behaviors, I discovered that many other researchers' findings were similar. Among psychologists, exploration of gender seemed to show more similarities than differences, and when differences appeared, many were small. I came to doubt the widespread belief that men and women are opposites, and to consider that this view is, at least, overstated—women and men are more similar than different. Gender-related differences exist, but the tendency to concentrate on these differences has obscured the similarities.

As a female psychologist, I was forced to attend to gender issues from the outset of my career. Sexism and discrimination were part of the context in which I received my professional training and in which I have pursued my career as a psychologist. Women were a small minority in the field during my early years in psychology, but the numbers have since increased so that now women receive over half the doctoral degrees granted each year in psychology. This increase and several antidiscrimination laws have produced some improvements in equitable treatment for women in psychology (as well as in other professions and in society in general).

The psychology of women approach came from the women in psychology during the feminist movement that began during the 1960s. Most of the women in psychology have not been directly involved in the psychology of women and some are not feminists, but the presence of a growing proportion of women has changed psychology, making a psychology of gender not only possible but, I think, inevitable.

The "Gendered Voices" Narratives

Although I believe that research is a good way to understand behavior, including gender-related behavior, I realize that some people disagree. One group of those who disagree consists of feminist scholars who believe that science is not the best way to approach the study of women—or perhaps anything—and these scholars have proposed a set of alternative methods (discussed in Chapter 2).

I heard Louise Kidder (1994) speak about not only the advantages but also the dangers of such approaches. One of the drawbacks she mentioned was the vividness of the data generated by accounts of personal experience. Statistical compilations may be more representative, but people are more impressed by personal accounts. These methods of studying people do not lead to a comfortable blurring of the results. Rather, each person's account is sharply depicted, with no averaging to blunt the edges of the story.

The text of *Gender: Psychological Perspectives* consists of an evaluation of research findings—exactly the sort of information that people may find difficult to relate to their lives. I decided that I wanted to include personal, narrative accounts of gender-relevant aspects of people's lives, and I wanted these accounts to connect to the research studies. I evaluated the perils of vividness and concluded that the drawbacks were a minor problem compared to the advantages. I believe that people's personal experiences are distilled in research, but I also know that in the process a lot of the interesting details are lost.

These "Gendered Voices" narratives restore some of the details lost in statistical summaries, allowing men and women to tell about their personal experiences. Telling these stories, separated from the text, was an alternative approach to presenting information about gender and highlighting the relevance of research findings with vivid detail. Some of the stories are funny, showing a light-hearted approach to dealing with the frustrations and annoyances of discrimination and gender bias. Some of the stories are sad, revealing experiences of sexual harassment, violence, and abuse. All of the stories are real, not constructed as good examples. When the stories are based on published sources, I name the people who are presenting their experience. For others, I have chosen not to name those involved to protect their privacy. I listened to my friends and students talk about gender issues and wrote down what they told me, trying to report what they said in their own words. I hope that these stories give a different perspective and add a sense of the reality of gender in personal experience to the volume of research reported here.

Reference Notation

When I wrote the first edition of this book, I decided to diverge from the standard format for citing references that psychologists use in one prominent way—I mentioned names. The standard psychology reference style omits professional titles and first names from its references, leaving authors identified by their last names in the text and by last names plus initials in the reference list. This convention omits cues that would allow readers to know the gender of the authors. Some of my own research (Brannon, 1994) led me to conclude that, in the absence of gender cues, people make stereotypical conclusions concerning the gender of researchers.

To counteract this trend, I wanted to include researchers' first names, which usually give very strong clues about their gender. In addition, I thought that knowing researchers' names would personalize the research for students. Still, some students told me, "All those names are too confusing." In response to their complaints, I have minimized the number of names. When I mention researchers in the text, I continue to use their first names, but I have moved most references to parentheses. Those researchers named in the text are people who are particularly prominent or whose research has been exceptionally influential. This style is similar to other writing in psychology; I hope that it decreases the "name overload" that was the basis of my students' complaints, but I regret parenthesizing so many excellent researchers.

Headlines

Long before I thought of writing a book about gender, I noticed the popularity of the topic with the media. Not only are the sexes the topic of many private and public debates, but gender differences are also the topic of many newspaper, magazine, and television stories, ranging from sitcoms to scientific reporting. I had read warnings about the media's tendency to oversimplify research findings and how the media slant reports to give an incorrect impression about research. I wanted to examine the research on gender to try to understand what the research says, with all of its complexities, and to present the media version along with an analysis of the research findings.

Of particular concern to me was the tendency of the media, and of people who hear reports of gender research, to want to find a biological basis for the behavioral differences between the sexes, as though evidence of biologically based differences would be more "real" than any other type of evidence. As prominent gender researcher John Money (1987a) has discussed, the division of biological from behavioral realms is a false dichotomy. Even genes can be altered by environment, and experiences during a critical period of development can produce changes in behavior as permanent as any produced by physiology. The view that biological differences are real and permanent, whereas experience and culture produce only transient and changeable effects, is widely held yet incorrect.

Unlike several of the other books about gender, several chapters of this book are devoted to examining this biological evidence. As Naomi Weisstein (1982) said, "biology has always been used as a curse against women" (p. 41). I want to present and evaluate this research, because it is the basis of popular assumptions about differences between the sexes and also because people accept these findings without question. I want readers to question the extent to which the "curse" should apply, so biological factors are the focus of several chapters.

To further highlight the popular conceptualizations of gender, I have decided to use headlines from newspapers and popular magazines, thinking that these popular presentations would be a good way to show how gender is presented by the media. Some of the headline stories are examples of responsible journalism that seeks to present research in a way that is easy to understand. Other of the headline stories are more sensational or simplified.

My misgivings about the media were dramatically confirmed by a personal experience. As I was beginning to write about chromosomes, hormones, and sex differences in the brain, a student approached me, wanting to interview me for the student newspaper. She was taking a journalism class in which she had to write a story about the differences between men's and women's brains, so a friend had recommended me as a good interview source. I explained to her that the relationship between brain structures and behavior was complex and difficult to establish and that most of the research was based on rat brains rather than human brains, so making generalizations was tricky. She said she wanted some statistics about differences and that she knew such statistics existed. When I explained that statistics on the frequency of occupations or performance differences between men and women do not necessarily reveal brain differences, she said she was not interested in knowing the truth—she just wanted information for her story!

A journalism student's disregard for the truth does not condemn all journalists; however, the media does sometimes give in to the urge to portray findings in sensational ways, because such stories get attention. Such sensationalism distorts research findings and perpetuates stereotypical thinking about the sexes. At more than one point, I believed that Beryl Lieff Benderly (1989), a science reporter, was correct when she warned about media sensationalism of gender research by writing the headline "Don't believe everything you read . . ." (p. 67).

Acknowledgments

At the completion of any book, authors have many people to thank, and I am no exception. Without the assistance, support, and encouragement of many people, I never could have written this book or completed the second edition. I thank all of them, but several people deserve special mention. My colleagues in the psychology department at McNeese State University were supportive and helpful. Jess Feist, my coauthor on the third edition of *Health Psychology: An Introduction to Behavior and Health,* provided advice and improved my writing on this book, too. Patrick Moreno not only read proposed revisions of chapters but also acted as proofreader and librarian. Their assistance was very important in completing this edition.

Husbands often deserve special thanks, and mine is no exception. My husband, Barry Humphus, did a great deal to hold my life together while I was researching and writing—he kept the computer working and offered me his praise, support, and enthusiasm. I would not have attempted (much less completed) this book without him.

Many people helped me get the materials I needed to complete this revision. Camille Vicent helped me with access to electronic information sources. The staff at McNeese's Frasier Memorial Library was knowledgeable and supportive in helping me locate information. I would like to thank the entire staff, but especially Joanne Durand, Leslye Quinn, Jan McFarlain, Brenda Royer, Kenneth Awagain, Stacy Magedanz, Michele Deputy, Kelley Roberts, Ellen Robinson, Linda Bordelon, Carolyn Schexnayder, Brantley Cagle, and Jeannie Brock. Their patience and skill continue to astound me.

I would like to thank all the people who told me their personal stories for the "Gendered Voices" feature of the book. To allow them their privacy I will not name them, with one exception. Melinda Schaefer deserves special thanks, because her story was so good that hearing it made me realize that others had stories to tell. Without her story I would not have realized how important these accounts are.

The people at Allyn and Bacon have been helpful and supportive. My editor for the first edition, Susan Badger, deserves special thanks; without her I would not have thought of doing a book on gender. Carolyn Merrill, my current editor, has offered her continued support and assistance. Norris Harrell encouraged me, telling me what a good idea it was for me to write this book for Allyn and Bacon. I think he was right.

I would also like to thank reviewers who read parts of the manuscript and offered helpful suggestions in the preparation of the first editions: M. Betsy Bergen, Kansas State University; Judy Bowker, Oregon State Univerity; Patrice Buzzanell, Northern Illinois University; Michael Stevenson, Ball State University; Barbara Winstead, Old Dominion University; as well as those who responded to surveys: Kathryn N. Black, Purdue University; Beverly Kopper, University of Northern Iowa; Gary Levy, University of Wyoming; Marcela Raffaelli, University of Nebraska, Lincoln, and Cindy Struckman-Johnson, University of South Dakota.

Chapter 1

The Study of Gender

HEADLINE

Sizing Up the Sexes

—*Time,* January 20, 1992

A story titled "Sizing Up the Sexes," authored by Christine Gorman, included the subtitle "Scientists Are Discovering That Gender Differences Have as Much to Do with the Biology of the Brain as with the Way We Are Raised" (p. 42). As the subtitle suggests, the article's initial emphasis was the biological basis of differences between women and men, but Gorman did not maintain this emphasis throughout the article. Toward the beginning of the article, she highlighted the role of biology, describing recent research with the summary: "The evidence of innate sexual differences . . . began to mount" (p. 42).

As the article continued, Gorman became more tentative in her discussion of the biological underpinnings for differences between men and women and acknowledged that "most of the gender differences that have been uncovered so far are, statistically speaking, quite small" (p. 44). Before the article was half completed, Gorman wrote that the overlap in abilities of men and women and the flexibility of the brains of each reveal "just how complex a puzzle gender actually is, requiring pieces from biology, sociology and culture" (p. 44). Past the halfway point, Gorman acknowledged that "none of the gender scientists have figured out whether nature or nurture is more important" (p. 46). Toward the end of the article, Gorman's emphasis on differences was tempered by her description of research that indicates shrinking differences between women and men in some mental skills. Her conclusions came close to contradicting the strong initial statements about innate biological differences: "Far from strengthening stereotypes about who women and men truly are or how they should behave, research into innate sexual differences only underscores humanity's awesome adaptability" (p. 51).

This popular article about the differences between women and men illustrates the interest in and confusion about the topic. Which is more important, nature (biology) or nurture (culture and society)? What is the extent of these differences? What types of differences exist? And what is the basis for these differences? These questions have answers that are simple and obvious to many people: Men and women are different by nature. They are born with biological differences that dictate the basis for different traits and behaviors. Indeed, they are so different that women are the "opposite sex," suggesting that whatever men are, women are at the other end of the spectrum. Those who hold this view find the differences obvious and important. Research in psychology, sociology, biology, and anthropology has complicated these simple answers. Not only is gender a complex puzzle, but there is a good deal of disagreement about the relative size of each piece of the puzzle. That is, research has led to a different and more complex question: How important are the various contributions of genetics, hormones, family, culture, and individual factors?

Some people at some times have believed that there are few differences between males and females, whereas others have believed that the two are virtually different species. These two positions can be described as the **minimalist** and the **maximalist views** (Epstein, 1988). The minimalists perceive few important differences between women and men, whereas the maximalists believe that the two have fundamental differences. Many maximalists also hold an **essentialist view,** believing that the large differences between women and men are part of their essential biological makeup. Although these views have varied over time, today both the maximalist and the miminalist views have supporters who are convinced of the validity of their positions.

This lack of agreement coupled with commitment to a position suggests controversy, which is almost too polite a term for these disagreements. Few areas are as filled with emotion as discussions of the sexes and their capabilities. These arguments occur in places as diverse as playgrounds and scientific laboratories. The questions are similar, regardless of the setting: Who is smarter, faster, healthier, sexier, more capable, more emotional? Who makes better physicians, engineers, typists, managers, politicians, artists, teachers, parents, friends? Who is more likely to go crazy, go to jail, commit suicide, have a traffic accident, tell lies, gossip, commit murder? The full range of human possibilities seems to be grounds for discussion, but the issues are unquestionably important. No matter what the conclusions, at least half of humans (and most probably all of them) will be affected. Therefore, questions about the sexes are not only interesting, but the answers are important to individuals and to society. Later chapters explore the research concerning abilities and behaviors, and an examination of this research will allow an evaluation of these questions.

Answers are not lacking to these important questions about differences between women and men, but consistency is. Almost everyone has answers, but not the same answers. It is easy to see how people might hold varying opinions about a controversial issue, but some consistency should exist among the findings from researchers who have studied men and women. Scientists should be able to investigate the sexes and provide evidence concerning these important questions. Researchers have pursued these questions, obtained results, and published thousands of papers. There is no shortage of investigations—or headlines—about the sexes. Unfortunately, researchers are subject to the same problems as everyone else: They do not all agree on what the results are and what the results mean.

In addition, many research findings on men and women are not consistent with popular opinion, indicating that popular opinion may be an exaggeration or distortion of people's experience. Both the past and the present are filled with examples of exaggerations of differences between women and men. Carol Tavris (1992) discussed the tendency for people to think in terms of opposites when only two examples exist, as it does with the sexes. If three sexes existed, people might not have the tendency to draw the comparison to such extremes; they might be able to see the similarities in men and women as well as their differences; they might be able to approach the questions with more flexibility in their thinking. The sexual world may not be polarized into only two categories (as Chapter 3 explores in more detail), but people do tend to see only two sexes. The existence of only two sexes pushes people into thinking of the two as opposites. To maintain oppositional categories, people must exaggerate the differences, resulting in stereotypes that do not correspond to real people (Bem, 1993b). Although these stereotypes are not realistic, they are powerful because they affect the ways women and men think about themselves and how they think about the "opposite" sex.

History of the Study of Sex Differences in Psychology

Speculations about the differences between men and women probably predate history, but these issues were not part of the investigations of early psychology. Wilhelm Wundt is credited with founding modern psychology in 1879 (although there is some debate over the accuracy of this date) at the University of Leipzig (Schultz & Schultz, 1992). Wundt wanted to establish a natural science of the mind to investigate experimentally the nature of human thought processes. Using chemistry as his model, he tried to devise a psychology based on an analytical understanding of the structure of the conscious mind and founded the **structuralist** school of psychology. This structure was based on adult human cognition, and Wundt and his followers believed that psychology could not be applied to children, the feebleminded, or species of nonhuman animals.

Wundt's psychology was concerned with the workings of the mind as unaffected by individual differences among adult humans. The structuralists were interested in investigating the "generalized adult mind" (Shields, 1975a) and therefore any individual differences, including differences between the minds of women and men, were of no concern to the early psychologists who followed Wundt.

This inattention to sex differences did not mean equal treatment of men and women by these early psychologists. Wundt and his followers used a method of investigation called *introspection,* a type of self-observation of one's mental processes. Wundt described introspection as internal perception (Schultz & Schultz, 1992), and Wundt's students were required to undergo training to learn the type of attention and reporting required in these investigations of thought processes. These students (and thus the subjects in this early psychology research) were men, and the "generalized adult mind" on which the findings were based was a generalization drawn from data collected from and by men.

Wundt's psychology spread from Germany to the United States, where it changed focus. Although some U.S. psychologists were interested in following Wundt's definition and goals for psychology, many others found Wundt's views too limiting and impractical. As psychology grew in the United States, it developed more of a practical nature. This change is usually described as an evolution to **functionalism,** a school of psychology that emphasized how the mind functions rather than its structure (Schultz & Schultz, 1992).

Darwin's theory of evolution was a strong influence for the functionalists in the United States. As these psychologists with a functionalist orientation started to research and theorize, they drew a wider variety of subjects into psychological research and theories, including children, women, and nonhuman animals.

The Study of Individual Differences

Among the areas of interest in functionalist psychology were the issues of adaptability and intelligence. From these interests evolved intelligence testing and the comparison of individual differences in mental abilities and personality traits, including sex differences. The functionalists, influenced by the theory of evolution, tended to look for biologically determined differences, including a biological basis for sex differences. Indeed, as Stephanie Shields (1975a) pointed out, these psychologists were hesitant to acknowledge any possibility of social influence in the sex differences they found, and their findings usually supported the prevailing cultural roles for women and men.

The studies and writings of functionalists of this era tended to demonstrate that women were less intelligent than men, benefited less from education, had strong maternal instincts, and were unlikely to produce examples of success or eminence. Women were not the only group deemed inferior: Nonwhite races were also considered less intelligent and capable. (See the Diversity Highlight: "Parallels between Race and Gender.")

These findings of the intellectual deficiencies of women did not go uncriticized. As early as 1910, Helen Thompson Woolley contended that the research on sex differences was full of the researchers' personal bias, prejudice, and sentiment (in Shields, 1975a). However, these studies of sex differences did little to allow women equal opportunities (including the psychologists who were women) for education or careers and tended to relegate women to maternal and domestic roles.

Edward Thorndike was one of the prominent functionalists who believed that women were less intelligent than men. But Leta Stetter Hollingworth, who had been one of Thorndike's students at Columbia University, took a stand against the functionalist view of women (Shields, 1975b). Early in her career, she argued against the prevailing view and criticized the methodology of the studies that confirmed women's inferiority. She contended that women's potential would never be known until women had the opportunity to choose the lives they would like—career, maternity, or both.

The functionalist view began to wane in the 1920s, and a new school of psychology, **behaviorism,** gained prominence. The behaviorists emphasized observable behavior as the subject matter of psychology rather than thought processes or instincts. With the change from a functionalist to a behaviorist paradigm in U.S. psychology, the interest in research on sex differences sharply decreased: "The functionalists, because of their emphasis on 'nature,' were predictably indifferent to the study of social sex roles and cultural concepts of masculine and feminine. The behaviorists, despite their emphasis on 'nurture,' were slow to recognize those same social forces" (Shields, 1975a, p. 751). Rather, behaviorists were interested in the areas of learning and memory. Research on these topics ignored social factors, including sex roles and sex differences. In ignoring gender, psychologists created what Mary Crawford and Jeanne Marecek (1989) referred to as "womanless" psychology, an approach that either failed to include women as participants or failed to examine gender-related factors

DIVERSITY HIGHLIGHT
Parallels between Race and Gender

In addition to their poor opinion of women's intellectual, emotional, and physical abilities, White male scientists often have held negative views of the abilities of some ethnic minorities. Indeed, 19th-century thought held that women and men among "more primitive peoples, notably among blacks" were more similar to each other than men and women in Europe (Sherman, 1978, p. 7). Any similarities to these "primitive peoples" were to the inferior European female rather than the superior European male. These openly racist and sexist opinions were part of the intellectual tradition of that time, and the science of that time confirmed the inferiority of women and non-European races.

These similarities of bias highlight the parallels between the research on gender and race. Both women and people of "inferior races" (that is, people of color) were inferior because of their biological endowment, which was the view of biological essentialism and determinism. According to R. C. Lewontin, Steven Rose, and Leon Kamin (1984), sexism and racism were prominent features of 19th-century biological determinism. They cited Charles Darwin's assertion that the mental traits in which women could excel were similar to the traits that were characteristic of lower races, and they quoted a 19th-century French scientist who maintained that "the Negro resembles the female in his love for children, his family and his cabin…the black man is to the white man what woman is to man in general, a loving being and a being of pleasure" (p. 143).

As Stephen Jay Gould (1996) observed, "'Inferior' groups are interchangeable in the general theory of biological determinism" (p. 135). That is, when making comparisons to the standard set by White men (using themselves as that standard), others often fail to meet this standard (in the assessment of White men). Lewontin, Rose, and Kamin (1984) argued that such biological determinism was directed toward preserving distinctions between the classes in Great Britain and between ethnic groups in the United States, demonstrating the biological inferiority of the less privileged and thus their inability to attain higher levels of intellectual achievement.

Some basis was needed to preserve the superior position of White men, and science was a respected authority that served to substantiate biological determinism throughout the nineteenth and into the 20th century. When psychology and sociology began to confirm that the environment and culture are important in determining behavior, biological determinism became less dominant. However, the belief that biology is an important influence in determining intelligence, emotion, and other important psychological factors has persisted, and those who wish to argue for the inferiority of women and nonwhites often propose biological determinism as this basis.

when both men and women participated in psychological research. During the time when behaviorism dominated psychology, the only theorists who unquestionably had an interest in sex differences were those with a psychodynamic orientation—the Freudians.

Psychoanalysis

Both Freud's theory of personality development and his psychoanalytic approach to treatment appear in more detail in Chapter 6. However, the history of psychology's involvement in issues of sex and gender necessitates a brief description of Freud's personality theory and his approach to treatment.

Although Sigmund Freud's work did not originate within academic psychology, the two are popularly associated. And unquestionably, Freud's work and Freudian theory concerning personality differences between women and men have influenced both psychology and society in general. These influences have made the work of Freud very important for understanding conceptualizations of sex and gender.

In the United States, Freud's work began to gain popular attention in 1909, when Freud came to the United States to give a series of invited lectures at Clark University (Schultz & Schultz, 1992). Immediately after his visit, newspapers started carrying features about Freud and his theory. By 1920, the interest in Freudian theory and analysis was evidenced both by books and by articles in popular magazines. Psychoanalysis gained popular interest, becoming almost a fad. Indeed, the popular acceptance of Freud's work came before its acceptance by academicians.

Freud emphasized the role of instinct and physiology in personality formation, hypothesizing that instincts provide the basic energy for personality and that the child's perception of anatomical differences between boys and girls was a pivotal event in personality formation. Rather than relying on genetic or hormonal explanations for sex differences in personality, Freud looked to early childhood experiences within the family to explain how physiology interacts with experience to influence personality development.

For Freud (1925/1989), the perception of anatomical differences between boys and girls was critical. The knowledge that boys and men have penises and girls and women do not forms the basis for personality differences between boys and girls. The results of this perception lead to conflict in the family, including sexual attraction to the other-sex parent and hostility for the same-sex parent. These incestuous desires cannot persist, and Freud hypothesized that the resolution of these conflicts comes through identification with the same-sex parent. However, Freud believed that boys experience more conflict and trauma during this early development, leading to a more complete rejection of their mother and a more complete identification with their father than girls experience. This difference in strength of identification produces enduring differences in personality between men and women. Consequently, Freud hypothesized that men typically form a stronger conscience and sense of social values than do women.

Did Freud mean that girls and women were deficient in moral standards compared to men? Did he view women as incomplete (and less admirable) people? It is probably impossible to know what Freud thought and felt, and his writings are sufficiently varied to lead to contradictory interpretations. Thus the question of Freud's view of women has been hotly debated. Some authors have criticized Freud for supporting a male-oriented society and the enslavement of women, whereas others have defended Freud and his work as applied to women. In defense of Freud, Carol Tavris and Carole Wade (1984) pointed out that his view of women was not sufficiently negative to prevent him from accepting them as colleagues. Freud accepted a number of women into psychoanalytic training and encouraged his daughter, Anna, to pursue a career in psychoanalysis. Freud's writings, however, reveal that he held many negative views about women and seemed to feel that they were inferior to men. As Michael Jacobs (1992) concluded, "It is difficult to avoid the impression that Freud saw women as less developed than men, genitally, emotionally and in their moral thinking" (p. 107).

Regardless of Freud's personal beliefs, the popular interpretation of his theory represented women as inferior to men, as being less ethical, more concerned with personal appearance, more self-contemptuous, and jealous of men's accomplishments (and also, literally, of their penises). Accepting the feminine role would always mean settling for inferior status and opportunities, and women who were not able to reconcile themselves to this status were candidates for therapy because they had not accepted their femininity.

Freud's theory also held stringent and inflexible standards for the development of masculinity. For boys to develop normally, they must experience severe anxiety during early childhood and develop hatred for their father. This trauma should lead boys to identify with their father and to experience the advantages of the male role through becoming like him. Boys who do not make a sufficiently complete break with their mother were not likely to become fully masculine and to remain somewhat feminine and thus experience the problems that society accords to nonmasculine men.

The psychoanalytic view of femininity and masculinity has been enormously influential in Western society. Although not immediately accepted in academic departments, the psychoanalytic view of personality and psychopathology was gradually integrated into the research and training of psychologists. Although the theory has prompted continuing controversy, interest continues—both in the form of attacks and defenses. This continuing stream of books and articles speaks to the power of Freud's theory to capture attention and imagination. Despite limited research support, Freudian theory has been and remains a force in conceptions of sex and gender. Table 1.1 summarizes psychoanalysis and psychology's theories of women and men. In contrast to these male-dominated theories, some investigators have begun to emphasize the study of women.

Development of Women's Studies

The development of interest specifically in the study of women came as a result of the feminist movement of the 1960s (Ferree & Hess, 1985). This movement was not the first to push for changes in women's roles and legal status. Earlier versions of feminism had pressed for the vote for women, availability of birth control, and other legal changes to improve women's social and economic status. The feminist movement of the 1960s grew

TABLE 1.1 Emphasis and the Importance of Gender in Theories throughout the History of Psychology

Theory	Emphasis of Theory	Role of Gender
Structuralism	Understanding the structure of the human mind	Minimal—All minds are equivalent
Functionalism	Understanding the function of the mind	Sex differences are one type of individual difference
Behaviorism	Studying behavior in a scientific way	Minimal—Behavior varies with individual experience
Psychoanalysis	Studying normal and abnormal personality development and functioning	Biological sex differences and their recognition is a motivating force

out of the civil rights movement and brought about some of the changes that earlier feminist movements had sought.

During the 1960s, 1970s, and 1980s, women entered the workforce in record numbers, producing changes in society that affected the lives of women, men, and children. Although most of these jobs were in clerical or sales work, women also entered the professions in increasing numbers. The women in psychology began to change the field, bringing an interest in gender-related behaviors that differed from the earlier focus on individual differences (Walsh, 1985).

In 1968, psychologist Naomi Weisstein presented an influential paper, "'Kinde, Küche, Kirche' as Scientific Law: Psychology Constructs the Female," which has influenced a generation of psychologists. In this paper Weisstein (1970) argued that psychological research had revealed almost nothing about women, because the research had been contaminated by the biases, wishes, and fantasies of the male psychologists who conducted the research. Although the criticism was aimed mostly at clinical psychology and the Freudian approach to therapy, Weisstein also charged research psychologists with finding what they wanted and expected to find about women rather than researching women as they were. She wrote, "Present psychology is less than worthless in contributing to a vision which could truly liberate—men as well as women" (Weisstein, 1970, p. 231).

Weisstein's accusations came at a time when the feminist movement in society and a growing number of women in psychology wanted a more prominent place for women in the field and sought to create feminist-oriented research. One of Weisstein's points was that psychological research had neglected to take into account the context of behavior, without which psychology could understand neither women nor people in general. Twenty years later, this criticism seems to have contained a great deal of foresight (Bem, 1993a); psychological research on gender began to change in the ways that Weisstein advocated.

Psychologists held no monopoly on this new orientation to the study of sex and gender. Sociologists, anthropologists, ethnologists, and biologists also became involved in questions about biological and behavioral differences and similarities between the sexes. Motivated by the feminist movement, women began to assert their view about the inequity of stereotypical views of the abilities and roles of men and women.

Although the history of studying gender in psychology is lengthy, psychologists' involvement in feminist research is relatively new; the formation of a division of the American Psychological Association (APA) devoted to women's issues and studies did not occur until 1973. Women were admitted as students in doctoral programs from the early years of psychology, but they had to struggle for professional acceptance and had a difficult time finding positions as psychologists. In 1941, a group of women who were psychologists formed the National Council of Women Psychologists to further the work of female psychologists in the war effort (Walsh, 1985). This group attempted to become a division of the American Psychological Association, but it was rejected repeatedly.

Another group succeeded in gaining division status in 1973. Division 35, Psychology of Women, can be directly traced to the Association for Women in Psychology, a group that demonstrated against sex discrimination and for an increase in feminist psychological research at the 1969 and 1970 APA national conventions (Walsh, 1985). Unlike the earlier International Council, Division 35's goals included not only the promotion of women in psychology but also the advancement of research on women and issues related to gender.

The great volume of psychological research on sex and gender that has appeared in the past 20 years is consistent with the Division 35 goal of expanding the study of women and encouraging the integration of that research with current psychological thinking. Indeed, Division 35 members have conducted much of that research, but other disciplines have also contributed substantially. Therefore, not only have psychologists participated in the current plethora of research on sex and gender, but the topic is actively investigated in biology, medicine, sociology, communication, and anthropology.

In summary, psychological research that included women dates back to the early part of the 20th century and the functionalist school of psychology. These psychologists were strongly influenced by Darwin's theory of evolution and viewed the sexes as opposites, with women having inherent biological differences that made them well-suited for motherhood but poorly suited for formal education. This approach emphasized sex differences, searching for the factors that distinguished men and women. After this school's influence faded, the behaviorist school dominated academic psychology. These psychologists were less interested in sex differences, creating a virtually "womanless" psychology. During that same time, Freudian psychoanalysts held strong views on the sexes, and their theories had an impact not only on academic psychology but also on popular opinion. The Freudian view is generally taken to hold that women are physically and morally inferior to men, and this belief in the innate inferiority of women influenced research on women. With the feminist movement of the 1960s, a different type of research arose, producing results that questioned the stereotypes and assumptions about innate differences between the sexes. This research began to examine not only sex differences and similarities, but these researchers also expanded ways to study women and men. This more recent orientation has led to voluminous research in the field of psychology as well as sociology, anthropology, and biology.

The feminist movement questioned the roles and stereotypes for women, and soon the questioning spread to men, who began to examine how the inflexibility of gender stereotypes might harm them, too.

The Appearance of the Men's Movement

The men's movement mirrors the women's movement, beginning during the 19th century women's suffrage movement. During this time, the women's suffrage movement was not the only challenge to men's roles. Men felt increasingly constrained in their masculinity by the change from agricultural to industrial society. An early form of the men's movement was the Boy Scouts, with its emphasis on men and boys involved in outdoor activities (Hantover, 1992). The contemporary women's movement has also aimed questions and challenges men concerning the status quo of legal, social, and personal roles and relationships. Some men failed to see the problem, but other men began to consider that the questions were pertinent to their lives, too. Figure 1.1 shows some important events in both movements and when each event occurred.

During the 1970s, these concerned men sometimes became feminists interested in ending the inequalities in power and privilege accorded to men, because they also saw toxic elements connected to the male sex role. Robert Brannon summarized this view by saying, "I have gradually come to realize that I, with every other man I know, have been limited and

Women's Movement			Men's Movement
First women's rights convention Seneca Falls, New York	1848		
		1870	15th Amendment to U.S. Constitution gives African American men voting right
19th Amendment to U.S. Constitution gives women the right to vote	1920		
National Council of Women Psychologists	1941		
Simon de Beauvoir's *The Second Sex* published	1952		
Betty Friedan's *The Feminine Mystique* published	1963		
The Civil Rights Act prohibits discrimination on the basis of sex	1964	1964	The Civil Rights Act prohibits discrimination on the basis of sex
National Organization for Women formed	1966		
Association for Women in Psychology demonstrates against sexism at APA convention	1969		
APA Division 35 formed	1973		
		1983	National Organization for Changing Men founded
		1990	Robert Bly's *Iron John* published
		1995	APA Division 51 formed
		1996	Million Man March, Washington, DC
		1997	Promise Keepers rally, Washington, DC

FIGURE 1.1 Important Events in the Women's and Men's Movements

diverted from whatever our real potential might have been by the prefabricated mold of the male sex role" (Brannon, 1976, pp. 4–5).

Feminist men formed groups equivalent to the consciousness-raising groups common in the women's movement (Astrachan, 1986). Although these group members discussed their common problems and sought support from each other, their activities usually did not progress to the larger organizations that sought political power, as the women's groups had done. Many of these groups tended to remain small, local-level organizations, but a few became national organizations.

The largest of the national organizations for profeminist men is the National Organization to Change Men. Within psychology, the Society for the Psychological Study of Men and Masculinity succeeded in gaining divisional status in 1995, becoming Division 51 of the American Psychological Association. The goals of this division include promoting the study of gender's role in shaping and constricting men's lives, helping men to experience their full human potential, and eroding the definition of masculinity that has inhibited men's development and has contributed to the oppression of others.

But other national groups within the men's movement are not interested in feminist goals; indeed, these men are interested in restoring the traditional gender roles that they believe have been destroyed by the women's movement. One such group is the National Organization for Men, a group that wants to "throw off the shackles of female oppression" (Gallagher, 1987, p. 39).

Many of these men's rights groups are organized around specific issues, such as changing divorce laws or promoting joint child custody, but some of the groups offer support to men who feel as though they have experienced discrimination. Rather than feminist groups for men, these groups are closer to antifeminist organizations. Their members feel confused and threatened by the changes that have come about during the past 20 years in women's and men's roles and would like to return to well-defined, separate roles for the sexes. Some of these men would like to see a less sharply gendered society in which both women and men have choices not bounded by their biological sex, whereas other men would like a more sharply gendered society in which the changes brought about by the women's movement would be reversed. Men in both of these types of groups consider themselves part of the men's movement.

Yet another variation of the men's movement comes from men trying to find a masculine identity. Authors such as Robert Bly (1990) and Sam Keen (1991) have contended that modern society has left men with no easy way to form a masculine identity. The culture provides inappropriate models, and fathers are often absent, providing no model at all. This deficit produces men who are inappropriately aggressive and poorly fitted to live in society, to form relationships with women, and to be adequate fathers. Bly proposed explorations of masculinity and ceremonial initiation into manhood as a means of overcoming the failure to establish the missing masculine role. These initiation ceremonies have been the subject of much ridicule (Pittman, 1992). In many ways these groups echo the Scouting movement, with the emphasis on male bonding in an outdoor setting. The need to find and affirm a masculine identity is a need that many men feel. Unfortunately, Bly's recommendations for achieving masculinity can be characterized as antifeminist, relying on devaluing women and forcefully rejecting feminine values to help men achieve masculinity.

The Promise Keepers do not share Bly's vision of how to reclaim masculinity, but they believe that men need to bond and to reassert their role as men (Messner, 1997; Wagenheim, 1996). This organization is part of evangelical Christianity and urges men to reclaim their position as head of the family, living up to their roles and keeping their promises to their wives and children. Promise Keepers reject the racism that is often associated with the evangelical movement, but they do not accept homosexuality or equal partnerships with women, making this group among the antifeminists in the men's movement.

Another testament to the pull of the men's movement was the Million Man March held in Washington, DC, on October 16, 1995. Organized by Louis Farrakhan and the Nation of Islam, the march brought African American men from the entire United States to Washington to be together. Five percent of the African American men in the United States attended (Loury, 1996). Farrakhan's agenda includes goals similar to Promise Keepers, with men reclaiming their positions as head of families. His movement also rejects gays, lesbians, and people who are not African American. Even men who disagreed with Farrakhan's religious and political agenda experienced the power of the gathering. The need to be together as men brought them to Washington.

The number of men who have participated in the Promise Keepers weekends and the 400,000 to one million men who attended the Million Man March represent a growing interest in some version of the men's movement. However, none of the versions of the men's movement has exerted the impact of the women's movement in influencing public opinion and changing social policy.

• *Sex or Gender?*

Those researchers who have concentrated on the differences between men and women historically have used the term **sex differences** to describe their work. In some investigations, these differences were the main emphasis of the study, but for many more studies, such comparisons were of secondary importance (Unger, 1979). By measuring and analyzing differences between male and female participants, researchers have produced a huge body of information on these differences and similarities. As Rhoda Unger pointed out, this information was not of primary importance to most of these researchers. When the analyses revealed statistically significant differences, the researchers provided a brief discussion; when no significant differences appeared, researchers dismissed their lack of findings with little or no discussion. Thus, the differences between male and female participants' responses have appeared in many studies but have not been the focus of most of these studies.

What have researchers meant by *sex differences?* One objection to the term is that it carries implications of a biological basis (McHugh, Koeske, & Frieze, 1986). Another objection is that the term has been used too extensively and with too many meanings (Unger, 1979).

> *A major problem in this area appears to be the too inclusive use of the term* sex. *In various contexts,* sex *can be used to describe the chromosomal composition of individuals, the reproductive apparatus and secondary characteristics that are usually associated with these chromosomal differences, the intrapsychic characteristics presumed to be possessed by males and females, and in the case of sex roles, any and all behaviors differentially expected for and appropriate to people on the basis of membership in these various sexual categories. (Unger, 1979, pp. 1085–1086)*

Unger proposed an alternative—use of the term **gender.** She explained that this term describes the traits and behaviors that are regarded by the culture as appropriate to women and men. Gender is thus a social label and not a description of biology. This label includes the characteristics that the culture ascribes to each sex and the sex-related characteristics that individuals assign to themselves. Carolyn Sherif (1982) proposed a similar definition of gender as "a scheme for social categorization of individuals" (p. 376). Both Unger and Sherif recognized the socially created differentiations that have arisen from the biological differences associated with sex, and both have proposed that use of the term *gender* should provide a useful distinction.

Unger suggested that use of the term *gender* might serve to reduce the assumed parallels between biological and psychological sex, or at least make explicit those assumptions. If researchers had accepted and used the term consistently, then its use might serve the function Unger proposed. However, no such consistent usage has yet appeared, and confusion remains. Some researchers use the two terms interchangeably, whereas others have substituted the term *gender* for the term *sex* but still fail to make any distinction.

Douglas Gentile (1993) proposed additional terms, including *biologically sex-linked, gender-linked,* and *sex-correlated* to distinguish between biological and social differences and between differences that are causally linked to sex and those for which the causal link has not been established. Others have objected to the attempt to draw distinctions, saying that distinguishing between the biological and social aspects of sex is not possible (Maccoby, 1988). Still others (Deaux, 1993; Unger & Crawford, 1993) have objected to Gentile's proposed distinctions, pointing out that the knowledge does not exist to make them. As Unger and Mary Crawford (1993, p. 124) wrote, "The problem of distinctions between sex and gender is due to unresolved conflicts within psychology about the causality of various sex-linked phenomena rather than to the terms used."

Therefore, psychologists have attempted to draw distinctions between the concepts of sex and gender to distinguish between those differences that are social and those that are biological. Such distinctions have been elusive, but those who use the term *gender* often intend to emphasize the social nature of differences between women and men. Indeed, the terminology that researchers use can indicate their point of view, with those researchers who are biological essentialists using the term *sex* to refer to all differences between men and women whereas those who use the term *gender* want to emphasize the social nature of such differences.

• *Should Psychologists Study Gender?*

Should psychologists study gender? Does past research merit further research? The history of gender research in psychology is filled with examples of bias, and most current studies do not meet stringent requirements for eliminating such bias. Should gender research expand and change to meet these challenges or should the area be abandoned as too problematic and possibly even too dangerous?

Psychologists have taken both positions. Alice Eagly (1987a, 1997) and Diane Halpern (1994) have taken the position that psychological research on gender differences and similarities is valuable, whereas Roy Baumeister (1988) and Bernice Lott (1997) have voiced their concerns about this type of research. Eagly (1987a) recommended that all psychological research should report on gender if such comparisons were part of the design. Rather than restricting reporting to theoretically meaningful or replicable results, she advocated making gender a routine part of psychological research. Furthermore, Eagly (1997) and Halpern (1994) both have professed a belief that the methods used by psychologists are sufficiently sophisticated to yield credible results.

Both Baumeister (1988) and Lott (1997) have raised questions about the wisdom of continuing gender research. Baumeister argued that Eagly's strategy would result in virtually all research in psychology becoming gender research. He proposed that psychology should go in the opposite direction—away from reporting on gender comparisons. Both Baumeister and Lott pointed out that by reporting and discussing gender differences, psychological research serves to perpetuate the exaggeration of gender differences. When people believe in large gender differences, they find it easier to categorize and treat women and men differently. Baumeister would like to see a gender-neutral psychology of people, which he proposed would serve society and science better than exaggerating gender differences. Lott advocates that gender research go beyond the simple comparisons of men and women to find similarities or differences so that the complexities of human behavior can be explored.

Although these suggestions about how to proceed with gender research are in opposition, all have similar concerns—that research on gender may be misunderstood and inappropriately used to perpetuate stereotypes and discrimination. The suggestion that gender research should be abandoned is not likely to be implemented. As Eagly (1995) pointed out, the area has gained a momentum that is not likely to stop. Although dangers exist in connection with gender research, it will continue.

Other psychologists (Bem, 1993b; Yoder & Kahn, 1993) have expressed an additional concern in connection with gender differences in psychology. They contended that the comparison of women and men places men as the standard, making women appear deficient if the comparison yields differences. Bem referred to this as an *androcentric bias*, contending that this bias has permeated not only psychology and its research but also society in general, putting women at a disadvantage. Whenever research finds a gender difference, that finding is interpreted as a disadvantage for women.

Yet other psychologists (Unger, 1995; Yoder & Kahn, 1993) have voiced a third concern related to gender research. Janice Yoder and Arnold Kahn worried that the same disadvantage resulting from comparing women and men has occurred in attempting to include women from various ethnic groups in psychological research. White, privileged women have become the standard for research with women, and when women from other ethnic groups are included, they are compared to White, usually middle-class, college women. In such a comparison, the dominant group tends to consider its own experience as the standard, and differences can be interpreted as deficiencies (Unger, 1995). Diversity in psychological research is a desirable goal, but Yoder and Kahn (1993) warned that "just as there is no singular male experience, there is no one experience or characterization that can be applied indiscriminately to all women" (p. 847). (See the Diversity Highlight: "When I Look in the Mirror.")

Therefore, the study of gender is likely to continue in psychology, but several concerns exist for this research. Some psychologists have contended that gender research poses dangers in exploring differences while others have argued that such research can be valuable. Others have pointed out that examining differences has continued discrimination by placing men as the standard in gender comparisons, and yet others have warned against extending this disadvantaged comparison to women from ethnic minorities.

DIVERSITY HIGHLIGHT
When I Look in the Mirror

"When you wake up in the morning and look in the mirror, what do you see?" a Black woman asked a White woman (Kimmel & Messner, 1992, p. 2).

"I see a woman," was the White woman's reply.

"That's precisely the issue," the Black woman replied. "I see a Black woman. For me, race is visible every day, because it is how I am not privileged in this culture. Race is invisible to you, which is why our alliance will always seem somewhat false to me" (p. 2).

As Michael Kimmel witnessed this exchange, he was surprised. He examined his own thoughts and realized that when he looked into the mirror, he "saw a human being: universally generalizable. The generic person" (p. 2).

Just as the White woman did not see her gender, the White man saw neither his gender nor his ethnic background. His privileged status as a White man had made him blind to these factors. Rather than thinking of himself as White or male, he considered himself a generic human. The White woman saw femaleness because she was aware of the discrimination she experience as a woman. The Black woman saw both her skin color and her gender when she looked into the mirror due to her experiences of those factors in her life.

As Michael Kimmel and Michael Messner (1992, pp. 2–3) summarized these experiences, "The mechanisms that afford us privilege are very often invisible to us.... Men often think of themselves as genderless, as if gender did not matter in the daily experiences of our lives. Certainly, we can see the biological sex of individuals, but we rarely understand the ways in which gender—that complex of social meanings that is attached to biological sex—is enacted in our daily lives."

Psychology and Gender Research

Research on gender has been of interest to psychologists since the early years of the 20th century and, despite the concerns of psychologists like Baumeister and Lott, such research will continue. Indeed, in the past two decades the amount of psychological research on gender and related topics has increased dramatically (Denmark, 1994). However, the current focus of gender research has changed.

Different Approaches to Gender Research

Psychologists' traditional view of gender, which can be traced to the functionalist movement, has been that differences between the sexes were part of the study of individual differences. That is, gender-related differences are among the factors that contribute to differences among people. The emphasis, as in most psychological research, has been on the individual. Thus, researchers have chosen to compare groups of women or girls to groups of men or boys, looking for differences or similarities between the two. In making such choices of design, these researchers have examined gender as a subject variable; that is, as a characteristic of the subjects in the studies.

In 1974 two psychologists, Eleanor Maccoby and Carol Jacklin, published *The Psychology of Sex Differences,* a review of research-based psychological findings about gender-related differences to that point. These authors collected over 2,000 studies in which gender was a subject variable and organized them around different topics, such as aggression and verbal ability. Maccoby and Jacklin then evaluated the topic, determining how many studies failed to find a difference, how many studies supported a difference, and the direction of the differences for those comparisons that showed differences. Maccoby and Jacklin's book was soon accepted as a classic in this type of research review (Deaux, 1984).

Their conclusions, however, have not gone unchallenged (Block, 1976; Deaux, 1984), but their encyclopedic work highlighted both areas of gender similarities and gender differences. Maccoby and Jacklin's book pointed out gaps in the research and thus prompted additional research within the same framework at a time when psychologists and the media were questioning the traditional assumptions about women (Eagly, 1995), but it did not consider a change in the concept of how gender and gender-related behaviors should be studied. Kay Deaux spoke for many gender researchers when she contended that the gender-as-subject-variable approach may not be the best for developing an understanding of gender.

Since Maccoby and Jacklin's review, another type of research has become increasingly common—gender as a social category (Deaux, 1984, 1987). In this view, researchers consider the gender of subjects not as individual differences (within the person) but as a type of information on which people base judgments and individuals choose actions (within the situation). This approach is more likely to incorporate the context of behavior and the complex factors that can influence any situation. Those who take this approach believe that "traditional conceptions of masculinity and femininity have oversimplified that which is not simple, have unidimensionalized that which is multidimensional, and have conveyed a sense of stability and permanence to that which is inherently flexible" (Deaux, 1987, p. 301).

Researchers who approach gender as a social category investigate how people use information about gender as part of their beliefs and expectations about behavior and how people assimilate information about gender into their own behavior. For example, Janet Swim and her colleagues (Swim, Borgida, Maruyama, & Myers, 1989) presented participants with background information about two people—John T. McKay or Joan T. McKay. These fictional people supposedly wrote a story, and Swim and her colleagues wanted to know if the gender of the writer influenced the evaluation of the story. Therefore, these researchers manipulated information about the gender of the writer to determine the reaction of participants to this information. According to Deaux's (1984) review of this approach, the results indicated that gender is an important piece of information that people use in forming impressions and interacting with people: "The focus is not on how men and women actually differ, but how people *think* that they differ" (Deaux, 1984, p. 110). This approach is especially well-suited to investigating stereotypes, attitudes, and conceptions of gender.

A third approach to gender comes from sociologists Candace West and Don Zimmerman (1987), who suggested that gender is a feature of the situations in which people interact rather than a property of the individuals. That is, they contended that people "do gender" rather than have gender. Gender is an active process created when people interact with others. Researchers who ignore the complex social context of gender-related behavior will fail to understand important aspects of gender.

The view of gender as a social category expanded psychology's research, and the view of gender as a social construction also has research implications. Studying gender as a subject variable may reveal no difference between men and women in a particular behavior, but people may believe that men and women differ and behave according to the differences they expect. A study of women and men in a naturalistic context may reveal results that a laboratory study with gender as a subject variable fails to show.

Psychologists, then, have taken several different approaches to the study of gender: as a subject variable, as a social category, and as a social construction. These approaches ask different questions and therefore are destined to give different—but not necessarily incompatible—types of answers concerning gender. The research that considers gender as subject variable has concentrated on differences and similarities in gender-related behaviors. That research focusing on sex as a social category has examined the cognitive categories that people form around gender and how they use this information in constructing views of women and men and react on the basis of these views. The research that focuses on gender as a social construction examines the social context of gender and how social situations and institutions affect people's gender-related beliefs and behaviors. Research of all these approaches appears throughout this book.

Gender in the Headlines

This book approaches the psychological study of gender through portrayals in the popular press. Media coverage can be revealing in several ways. As M. Junior Bridge (1995, p. 19) commented,

> *In a free society such as the United States, the way the media cover the news provides an excellent cultural looking glass. The attitudes, values, biases, strengths, and weaknesses of the society covered by the media are reflected in the media mirror. Simultaneously, the media, by the way they report the news and by the way they define what is newsworthy, influence the society they cover.*

Gender has become such a "hot" research topic that news stories appear frequently on television, in newspapers, and in magazines. These stories often present less technical versions of research findings than those appearing in research journals, and these popular versions of research results are easier to understand. However, some important details and limitations of research findings can be lost in the simplification process, or the urge to write an eye-catching story can lead to sensationalizing research results. Simplistic, unidimensional, and oppositional ways of thinking about women and men are common in our culture, and media portrayals are part of the process. Indeed, they can be part of the problem, forming the type of mirror that Bridge (1995) described. Media reports can distort research findings through the lens of sensationalism and in doing so, promote stereotypical thinking, which in turn, entrenches stereotypes in popular belief and can lead men and women to strive to measure up to these portrayals.

Headlines along with the image they present and the research on which they are based form the unifying theme for this book. Each chapter begins with a headline from a story about the sexes, providing a starting point for an evaluation of the theory and research evidence that contributed to the headline story. This evaluation will delve into the research and examine the popular story and the popular stereotypes. By examining how the media presents information about women and men and by contrasting these headlines with the research in psychology, biology, sociology, and anthropology, an evaluation of these popular views of the sexes is possible. Through this evaluation process, readers can develop an understanding of personal and societal beliefs and attitudes as well as a view of what psychological research has revealed about the sexes.

Summary

A child's sex is typically the first thing that parents learn about the child, and this situation highlights the importance of sex and gender. Beliefs about gender differences are common, but opinions vary, with some people believing in minimal differences and others holding that the differences are maximal and part of essential biological differences.

Gender research in psychology can be traced to the functionalist school of the late 1800s, which held that men and women differ in ability and personality (a view that received criticism at that time). With the transition to the behaviorist school, interest in gender differences faded from academic psychology but persisted in psychoanalysis. This latter view held that differences in anatomy produce personality differences in women and men, with women being inferior in a number of important ways. The feminist movement of the 1960s produced a resurgence of interest among psychologists concerning questions about gender differences, and research tended to question stereotypes about the sexes.

One issue concerns the traditional terminology—namely, the use of the term *sex differences.* By proposing the use of the term *gender,* psychologists have tried to clarify the difference between socially determined and biologically determined differences. However, both terms continue in use, and the proposed differentiation between sex differences for biological differences and gender differences as socially determined differences has not yet come into consistent use.

Baumeister and Lott have taken a different view than Eagly concerning the prevalence of gender research, with Baumeister and Lott advocating a decrease and Eagly an increase in such research. Psychological research on gender reflects different approaches: gender as a subject variable, gender as a social category, and gender as a social construction. The first approach is historically the most common, and its goal is to investigate gender-related differences and similarities. The second approach considers gender not as an individual trait but as a type of information that people have and use in making decisions and judgments, and the third considers the social context of interaction in which gender appears.

Research on gender often appears in media reports. These popular reports sometimes reflect complex research findings in a simplified form, and this simplification can perpetuate misconceptions. An evaluation of the headlines and the stories behind them will allow an examination of the media images of women and men, and the research that the headlines summarize shows what areas researchers have investigated and what they have found.

Glossary

behaviorism the school of psychology that emphasizes the importance of observable behavior as the subject matter of psychology and discounts the utility of unobservable mental events.

essentialist view another term for the maximalist view.

functionalism a school of psychology arising in the United States in the late 1800s that attempted to understand how the mind functions. Functionalists held a practical, applied orientation, including an interest in mental abilities and in gender differences in mental abilities.

gender the term used by some researchers to describe the traits and behaviors that are regarded by the culture as appropriate to men and women.

maximalist view the view that many important differences exist between the sexes.

minimalist view the view that few important differences exist between the sexes.

sex differences the term used by some researchers (and considered to be inclusive by others) to describe the differences. between male and female research participants.

structuralist a school of psychology arising in Europe in the 1880s that attempted to understand the workings of the conscious mind by dividing the mind into component parts and analyzing the structure of the mind.

Suggested Readings

Bem, Sandra Lipsitz. (1993). *The lenses of gender.* New Haven, CT: Yale University Press. Bem contends that gender provides a lens, and people view the world through the distortion of this lens. She discusses three lenses of gender: androcentrism, gender polarization, and biological essentialism. Bem argues that viewing the world through these lenses provides the basis (and biases) for organizing gender knowledge.

Eagly, Alice H. (1997). Comparing women and men: Methods, findings, and politics. In Mary Roth Walsh (Ed.), *Women, men, and gender: Ongoing debates* (pp. 24–31). New Haven, CT: Yale University Press.

Lott, Bernice. (1997). Cataloging gender differences: Science or politics? In Mary Roth Walsh (Ed.), *Women, men, and gender: Ongoing debates* (pp. 19–23). New Haven, CT: Yale University Press. This debate reflects the two discrepant views concerning the study of gender differences, with Eagly taking the position that such research is important, and Lott taking the view that the research is dangerous.

Shields, Stephanie A. (1975). Functionalism, Darwinism, and the psychology of women: A study in social myth. *American Psychologist, 30,* 739–754. This lively article details the history of early psychologists' research on gender differences, with all of the biases showing.

Weisstein, Naomi. (1970). "Kinde, küche, kirche" as scientific law: Psychology constructs the female. In Robin Morgan (Ed.), *Sisterhood is powerful: An anthology of writings from the women's liberation movement* (pp. 228–245). New York: Vintage Books. (Also reprinted in 1993 in *Feminism & Psychology, 3,* 195–210.) Weisstein's article has been reprinted many times and appears in many anthologies, a testimony to its influence. Originally a presentation, this angry criticism details tendency in psychological research to distort the view of women and describes this failure to study women in an unbiased way. Psychological research is no longer as inadequate as Weisstein charged, partly because of her charges.

Chapter 2

Researching Sex and Gender

HEADLINE

The Science Wars

—*Newsweek*, April 21, 1997

> *Scientists worship at the shrine of objectivity, but even the pious occasionally lapse. A century ago archeologists who discovered the great stone ruins of Zimbabwe went through all sorts of contortions to prove that the magnificent oval palace and other structures were built by the Phoenicians of King Solomon's time—or by anyone other than the ancestors of the Bantus. In the 1960s biologists studying conception described the "whiplashlike motion and strong lurches" of sperm "delivering" genes required to "activate the developmental program of the egg," which "drifted" along passively. The model portrayed sperm as macho adventurers, eggs as coy damsels. And throughout the 1970s and later, ornithologists gathered sheafs of data proving that, in birds, a female's success laying eggs and rearing hatchlings was always enhanced by the presence of a male.*
>
> *These acolytes of scientific objectivity were spectacularly wrong. The Bantus' ancestors did build the great stone complex. The human egg does play an active role in conception. And in some bird species, particularly the eastern bluebird, the father's presence makes little or no difference to the survival of hatchlings. But why did scientists get it wrong in all three cases, and many others? (Begley, 1997, p. 54)*

According to Sharon Begley (1997), this question is the basis of a major battle in contemporary science. The heart of the battle is the question of objectivity in science. The defenders of science see science as a process of discovering the natural principles that govern the functioning of the world. Although objectivity is not easy to attain, this position holds that through careful research design, it is possible to conduct objective scientific research.

The critics claim that science, like all other human activities, is a reflection of the values (including the biases) of the society in which it functions. These critics argue that science is a process of constructing a view of the world. These **constructionists** believe that "we do not discover reality, we invent it" (Hare-Mustin & Marecek, 1988, p. 455). That is, science does not lead researchers to map a realistic picture of the world but to construct views of the world in ways that reflect their personal perceptions and biases. In this view, science is a process of invention rather than one of discovery. Bias is inevitable, the constructionists argue, because all humans are tied to their perceptions and actively try to organize and interpret all information, including scientific data. To disconnect perception to the point of objectivity is impossible, so science must always contain the influence of subjective perceptions.

Although the constructionist position may sound like a minor modification that acknowledges the limitations of human perception, it is a more fundamental criticism of science because it challenges the philosophies that underlie science (Gergen, 1985). According to science, the only way to legitimately gather information is through observing objective facts and rejecting information gathered from other sources. Constructionists argue that objective facts do not exist, and anything presented as fact is personal and subjective perception. Therefore, science cannot be free of values, nor can it be socially or politically neutral (Hare-Mustin & Marecek, 1988).

This controversy has produced extremes on both sides, but each position has influenced the other. Begley reported that she interviewed more than 20 of the critics of science, and all acknowledged that science is "the best game in town" in generating useful knowledge. Scientists have also had to acknowledge their critics' arguments. Physicist Kurt Gottfried conceded that "Cultural and other extraneous factors are more important in the creation of science than most people realize" (in Begley, p. 55). (See the Diversity Highlight: "Other Ways to Knowledge? Science in Nonwestern Cultures.")

The "science wars" relate to gender research more strongly than to many other scientific fields because gender issues are among the most controversial in science and society. In addition, scientists have a long history, to paraphrase Judith Lorber (1997), of seeing because they believe rather than believing because they have seen in studying gender-related topics.

Criticisms of science apply to the various disciplines that have explored gender issues, including psychology, sociology, medicine, biochemistry, biology, and anthropology. Researchers in these disciplines may vary in their viewpoints and approaches, but their methods of investigation usually do not—most researchers adhere to a set of methods that are part of traditional science. The alternatives to traditional science offer different ways to approach gender research. An understanding of the traditional approach to research is necessary before examining the alternatives.

How Science Developed

Modern science arose in the 16th and 17th centuries and came to prominence during the 19th century, bringing about radical changes in ways of knowing and understanding the

DIVERSITY HIGHLIGHT
Other Ways to Knowledge? Science in Nonwestern Cultures

The activities identified as science arose in 16th- and 17th-century Europe, but all cultures over the world and throughout history have developed some understanding of physical, biological, and social existence. Some of these conceptualizations have been close to the views of modern science, yet many have differed substantially. The cultures that did not develop this type of science took an alternative path due to their view of the world and how it operates. Several prominent cultures have existed within civilizations that have not adopted the positivist, materialist, empiricist traditions essential to European science.

For example, Chinese culture developed some sophisticated technology and engineering but not much science. This omission reflected a Chinese outlook (Ronan, 1982) that regarded the entire universe as a vast unified organism, with humans and the physical world as part of this unity. This view prompted the Chinese to develop an understanding of some aspects of the world but to ignore others. Their understanding of the world was influenced by those who followed either the Confucian or the Taoist philosophy. Followers of Confucius tended to make no division between the physical and social world and to concentrate on promoting social harmony rather than intellectual understanding about the physical world. Taoists had an interest in nature, but their view was not one of domination of humans over nature, a view basic to Western science. Rather, the Taoists strove to gain knowledge as a path to inner peace. Neither of these views prompted the development of a science comparable to Western science, with its emphasis on objectivity and the separation of the observer to the object observed.

The theme of the unity of nature and humanity was also part of the two religions that dominated India—Hinduism and Buddhism. Neither of these views was conducive to the development of science (Ronan, 1982), so the science that existed in India largely was borrowed from the West.

The dominance-oriented, objective, rational approach that is basic to Western science differs from the African view (Harding, 1986). The African conception is one of connection rather than opposition, with a reluctance to divide the world into nonoverlapping categories, including a split between self and nature. Such a split is essential to the type of objectivity required by science, but African philosophy found such divisions impossible. Furthermore, the African view is curiously similar to that of Native Americans and many feminist scholars, being one of connection and interrelatedness with an emphasis on relationships to the world rather than an analysis of it.

All of these nonWestern views of the world are similar in their conceptualizations of nature as intertwined with humanity rather than as describing the two in dynamic opposition (Fee, 1986). These views of nature did not prevent these cultures from developing a formal understanding of the world, including engineering, agriculture, medicine, and astronomy. However, none of these cultures developed the kind of science that arose in Europe, and the science that developed in Europe has spread to all countries and dominates modern knowledge, perhaps to the exclusion of other world views.

world (Caplan & Caplan, 1994; Riger, 1992). Instead of looking to religion and the Bible for knowledge and wisdom, the new science looked to knowledge gathered through observation. This view represented a radical departure from ancient and religious thought. This new scientific view assumed that the world works by a set of natural laws and that these laws can be discovered by careful, objective investigation. Humans can understand the laws of nature if they use the correct methods of investigation. During the 18th and 19th centuries, science proliferated in Europe and spread throughout the Western world. Research in chemistry, physics, biology, and medicine produced findings that changed the world and the lives of most people. New products, medicines, and industries came into existence because of the research of scientists. The success of science created an enthusiasm that fostered the development of more sciences, including the social sciences of psychology, sociology, and anthropology. These social sciences held to the same assumptions and methods as the natural sciences—that is, the laws of human behavior and society were also subject to discovery through **empirical observation** and objective investigation.

Empirical observation requires collecting information through direct observation, and objective investigation necessitates removing personal feelings and biases from the process of research. Critics of science contend that objectivity is not possible, whereas proponents believe that it is necessary for good science. What steps do these proponents believe are necessary to ensure careful and objective investigation? What makes scientific investigation different from other ways of gaining knowledge? What techniques do scientists use to accomplish these goals? The following sections explore these questions.

• *Methods and What They Reveal*

Science is not just a set of methods; it is also a process of gaining information, an activity (Ray, 1993). By performing this activity, researchers gain information, but that information must meet certain criteria. One of those criteria applies to the type of information, which must be open to empirical observation. Scientific information must be observable not only to the person doing the observing but also to anyone else; that is, it must be publicly observable. By restricting information in this way, the observer's perceptions and biases can be minimized, and scientific observation can attain some level of objectivity.

Another restriction on gathering information in science is that scientific observation must be systematic: Scientists must follow some plan or system to gather information. Everyone makes observations, but most people in most circumstances do so in a nonsystematic, personal way rather than according to a systematic plan. This lack of systematicity can lead people to notice certain things while ignoring others—a selection process that can result in distortion and bias. Scientists strive to be systematic in their observations in order to gather information that more accurately reflects the situations they have observed. This is not to say that scientists are free of personal biases; as humans, they are subject to the same perceptual distortions (and even biases) as other humans. However, acting as scientists, they strive to treat the information fairly, although they cannot avoid personal opinions (Gould, 1996). Working with observable information according to a systematic plan can help researchers to minimize bias.

Thus, science is an activity that is restricted to gathering information through observation and by forming systematic plans. The care such observation requires has led to an erroneous impression about science—namely, that science is precise. The use of numbers for **quantification** of observations further contributes to this mistaken impression. People tend to believe that numbers lend precision when actually numbers are only a way to summarize certain characteristics of a situation. Scientists do work with numbers, and they strive to make exact measurements based on their observations, but neither of these activities makes science precise.

All measurements are subject to error, and researchers need to find ways to eliminate as much measurement error as possible. However, they never succeed in eliminating all measurement error, so the measurements of science are representations rather than exact replications of the observations. That is, scientists collect **data,** which are usually quantifications of their observations. These data are not the same as the observed phenomenon but rather are representations of some facet of the phenomenon the researcher considered important.

For example, a researcher who is interested in cross-gender interactions in preschool children might choose to study how many times children approached a child of the other gender in play situations. The researcher would observe children of the appropriate age and count the number of such interactions, perhaps both by girls and by boys. The data would consist of the number of times such interactions were initiated by girls versus by boys. These data capture one aspect of the play situation but omit many others. Thus, when this study is finished, the researcher will have a collection of data—in the form of numbers—that can be analyzed to determine the results of the study.

An additional narrowing of the observations in science comes from the specification of a **variable** or several variables in research studies. A variable is the factor of interest in a research study. The term comes from the notion that the factor varies, or potentially has more than one value (as opposed to a constant, which has only one value). Most things vary, so finding a variable of interest is not nearly as difficult as restricting a study to only a few variables. For example, variables include factors such as time of day, family income, level of anxiety, number of hours of practice, gender of participants, and so forth. Thousands of variables are of interest to researchers, yet studies typically include only a few.

The systematic plans and measurements in science include many different specific techniques or methods, each of which has the power to reveal different types of information. In addition, each method has it own advantages and disadvantages. Rather than consisting of an unorganized assortment of techniques, scientific methods fall (but not neatly) into two types: descriptive and experimental. Different methods exist within each type, but descriptive research techniques have limitations and advantages that experimental techniques do not, and the reverse is also true. Therefore, one approach to understanding research methods is through an examination of these two approaches.

Descriptive Methods

Descriptive research methods help investigators answer "what" questions. That is, descriptive research can tell what types of things exist, including great detail about those things and even the extent of relationships among various things. Descriptive methods include naturalistic observation, surveys, and correlational studies. All of these designs allow researchers to gather information about phenomena that already exist, and none of these methods involves manipulation of existing conditions or the introduction of change by the researcher.

Naturalistic Observation

Naturalistic observation involves just what the name implies—observation of a naturally occurring situation. Like all scientific observation, this gathering of information must be of publicly observable phenomena and according to a systematic plan. In making these observations, the researchers must not change the situation. If researchers make any change in the situation, it is no longer naturalistic; the phenomenon may change when researchers become part of the situation. Therefore, naturalistic observation is not a particularly easy method. Researchers must find ways to gather their data without influencing the situation.

For example, if a team of researchers wanted to study the gender-stereotypical versus gender-atypical toy choices of 3-year-old children through naturalistic observation, these investigators would have several tasks. First, they would have to define what they considered gender-stereotypical and gender-atypical toy choices so that observers could classify the toy choices the children make. Researchers might choose to specify an **operational definition,** a definition of the concept in terms of the operations used to obtain it rather than the concepts underlying it. For the study on toy choices, the researchers would need to specify which choices would count as gender stereotypical and which would count as atypical.

Second, the researchers would have to find a way to observe 3-year-old children playing with toys. In addition, the children could not come in contact with or see the investigators lest their presence change the children's behavior. In such a study (Lloyd, Duveen, & Smith, 1988), 3- and 4-year-old children were observed playing with gender-stereotyped toys to examine the different toy choices according to situation and play partner. These young children tended to use gender stereotyped toys, especially in action play and to a lesser extent in pretend play. That is, the situation was an important factor in children's gender stereotypical toy choices.

How do researchers become unobtrusive? One common method is to make observations through one-way mirrors. These devices consist of a mirror on the wall of a room that faces an observation room on the other side. Observers can see through the mirror, but those who are observed see only the mirror. Such observation facilities exist in many university laboratory schools and day care centers to aid researchers in doing naturalistic observations. These observation facilities can be arranged for this type of study, but creating opportunities for naturalistic observation in other situations can require innovation as well as flexibility. Researchers may have to hide or use binoculars to gather their information.

What can researchers learn through naturalistic observation? In the above example (Lloyd et al., 1988), the researchers were interested in knowing what types of toys children chose in different play situations. Other similar studies might investigate toys children bring with them to day care, how long the children play with each type of toy, which toys children are willing to share and which they are not, or many other such questions. Indeed, many possibilities exist for even this single topic, and other investigators must do as Barbara Lloyd and her colleagues did in both choosing a question and finding a way to make their measurements in the naturalistic situation.

The information that researchers can determine from naturalistic observation is limited to descriptions of what occurred. This information may be exactly what the researchers wanted, and therefore this limitation may not be a disadvantage. An advantage of this method is its lack of artificiality, which is a problem for laboratory research. The specification of the behaviors under observation and the decisions concerning how to collect data narrow the focus of the research to certain aspects of the naturalistic situation. Thus, naturalistic observation is not a recording of a situation but a choice of which data to collect from a complex environment. The complexity of the naturalistic situation results from many factors that make simple interpretations of this type of research nearly impossible.

Although researchers may gain some insight into the important variables in a situation, naturalistic observation lacks the power to allow researchers to determine causal relationships.

Surveys

Surveys are a second method of descriptive research. In surveys researchers construct questionnaires, choose a group of people to respond to the questionnaire, collect the data, and analyze the data to yield results. This method sounds deceptively simple—almost anyone can think of questions to ask. However, the method is filled with choices. For example, researchers using this method must decide about the wording of questions ("Do you agree . . ." versus "Do you disagree . . ."), the answer format (respondents reply versus respondents choose from a set of answers), the appearance of the questionnaire (number of pages, size of type, page layout), the choice of people responding (representative of the entire population versus a select group, such as registered voters or first-time parents), the number of people needed (what number will give a good estimate for accuracy), and the method of administration (face-to-face interview, telephone interview, mailed questionnaire). Unwise choices on any of these decisions may result in a survey that does not allow the researcher to answer the question that prompted the research or, worse, may give the researcher an answer that is misleading.

The main limitation of the survey method is inherent: Surveys pose questions rather than make direct measurements. That is, surveys typically rely on self-reports rather than direct observations of behavior. Researchers ask people to respond to a series of questions either in person or through a mailed questionnaire or telephone survey. In many surveys participants are asked to share their opinions and attitudes, but in some surveys participants try to report on past behavior. The responses that people give may not accurately reflect their beliefs or behaviors. Even if people are honest about their beliefs, they may not always behave in a way that is consistent with reported attitudes. Indeed, people may lie, withhold the truth, or simply not know or remember the information.

Replies to survey questions are open to bias due to participants' beliefs about social standards and their tendency to present themselves in a favorable way. This bias can invalidate a question or even an entire survey, and information obtained through self-reports is generally not considered as strong as information obtained by direct observation. Despite the wide variety of information that can be obtained through the survey method, that information is limited not only by its descriptive nature but also by its potential inaccuracy.

Despite the disadvantages, surveys offer the advantages of allowing researchers to ask people about things that the researchers could not easily (or possibly ethically) observe directly. Thus, the method is flexible and useful in a variety of situations. Surveys are a very common method for measuring people's attitudes. Psychologists, sociologists, market researchers, and political pollsters all use this method to help decide how people feel about a wide variety of issues.

For example, survey of over 1,500 college students in the United States, Russia, and Japan questioned students' experience concerning token resistance to sex and consent to unwanted sexual intercourse (Sprecher, Hatfield, Cortese, Potapova, & Levitskaya, 1994). Token resistance to sex is defined as saying "no" when the person actually wants to have and later consents to have sex. One focus of the study was the stereotype that only women engage in token resistance, and the survey showed that this stereotype is incorrect—the behavior occurs in both men and women. Indeed, men in the United States reported this behavior more often than men in the other two cultures and, surprisingly, more often than U.S. women. Consent to unwanted sex occurred in all three cultures, but women in the United States reported higher frequency of this behavior than women in the other countries.

Correlational Studies

If researchers want to know about the relationship between two specific variables rather than information about several variables, researchers will do a **correlational study,** another type of descriptive method. Correlational studies allow researchers to determine both the existence and the degree of relationships between the variables under study.

To do a correlational study, researchers must choose two variables for study, operationalize and measure these variables, and then analyze the relationship between them. To perform this analysis, researchers calculate a correlation coefficient, the results of a statistical test that reveals the strength or magnitude of the relationship between two variables. The correlation coefficient is described by a formula, and researchers must apply the formula to their data. A number of variations on the correlation coefficient exist, but the most common is the *Pearson product-moment correlation coefficient,* symbolized by the letter r. The results of the analysis yield a number that varies between $r = +1.00$ and $r = -1.00$. Correlations that are close to $r = +1.00$ indicate a strong, positive relationship: As scores on one variable increase, those on the other also increase. Correlations that are close to $r = -1.00$ indicate a strong, negative relationship: As one measurement increases, the other decreases. Correlations that are close to $r = 0.00$ indicate little or no relationship between the two variables.

For example, Bernard Whitley, Jr. (1988), conducted a study to investigate the relationship between people's reports of their degree of masculinity or femininity and their masculine and feminine behaviors; that is, he studied the degree of relationship between traits and behaviors. Whitley administered two different tests—one that measured the traits of masculinity and femininity and the other that asked people about their behaviors related to recreational activities, vocational interests, and social activities. These two tests yielded scores, and Whitley then used the correlation coefficient to analyze these scores.

The correlational study by Whitley yielded a number of correlation coefficients indicating relationships between the personality measurement of masculinity or femininity and the participants' reports of behaviors, but few of these correlations indicated strong relationships. For example, the relationship between the trait of masculinity and men's reports of their masculine behaviors was $r = +.32$. This correlation indicates a fairly low relationship between the personality measure of masculinity and the measure of masculine behaviors. For women, the correlation between the feminine personality trait and feminine behavior was $r = +.17$, a low correlation. These correlations indicate a low but positive relationship: As masculine personality score increased, reported masculine behavior shows some increase, and as feminine personality score increased, feminine behavior also tends to increase. However, the correlation coefficients of $r = +.32$ and $r = +.17$ indicate a low relationship for two factors that logically should be highly correlated. The magnitude of these correlations would suggest that the personality measures of masculinity and femininity reflect relatively few of the qualities that contribute to masculine and feminine behavior. Indeed, the distance from a perfect correlation of $r = +1.00$ indicates that other factors omitted from the measures of masculine and feminine personality contributed much more to masculine and feminine behaviors. In addition, the low correlations between the measured traits of masculinity and femininity and behaviors cast some doubt on the validity of the measurement of masculinity and femininity. If these traits do not have a strong relationship to behaviors, how can they be labeled masculinity and femininity?

Correlational studies, like other descriptive methods, do not reveal why the relationship exists. That is, correlations do not indicate causality. However, such a deduction may be very tempting. Indeed, a causal relationship may exist between two variables that have a high correlation, but the method does not allow the conclusion. Even a high correlation would not allow a researcher to know the source of the relationship: Did changes in one variable produce changes in the other, or vice versa? Another possibility is that both variables may be causally related to a third variable that has not been part of the study. In any case, a conclusion of causality is not legitimate on the basis of the evidence from a correlational study. Thus, the information that researchers obtain and the conclusions that they may draw from correlational studies exclude causality but include information on the existence and strength of relationships.

Experimental Designs

To obtain information about cause and effect, researchers must do **experiments.** This type of design allows researchers to answer "why" questions—questions with answers that involve explanations rather than descriptions. An experiment is a method that involves the manipulation of one factor, called the **independent variable,** the measurement of another factor, called the **dependent variable,** and the need to hold all other factors constant. By manipulating the independent variable, the experimenter tries to create a change. Detecting change requires some basis for comparison, so the simplest version of an experiment requires two conditions to provide this comparison. These two conditions consist of two different levels of the independent variable, with all other factors held constant. The manipulation may be more elaborate, consisting of three, four, or more levels of the independent variable, and experiments may include more than one independent variable.

The dependent variable is the one that the experimenter measures. Choosing and quantifying dependent variables can also be complex. In psychological research, dependent variables are always some type of behavior or response. By using such dependent variables, psychology is placed among the sciences that require empirical subject matter—behavior and responses that can be observed and measured.

The logic of experimental design holds that the manipulation of the independent variable should produce a change in the value of the dependent variable if the two are causally related. If the experimenter also holds other factors constant, the only source of change in the dependent variable should be the manipulated change in the independent variable. Thus, in a well-designed experiment the changes in the value of the dependent variable can be entirely attributed to the manipulation of the independent variable. That is, the changes in the independent variable caused the changes in the dependent variable.

Although the logic of experimental design is simple, creating conditions to effectively manipulate one factor while holding all other factors constant is far from simple. Such a situation would be almost impossible in a naturalistic setting, because any one change would result in many others. Therefore, almost all experiments take place in laboratories.

These settings offer the possibility of the necessary control, but they open experiments to the criticism of artificiality. Despite the validity of that criticism, scientists highly value experiments because of their potential to reveal cause-and-effect relationships, a type of information that other methods cannot show.

In an experiment by Stephanie Shields and Pamela Cooper (1983), participants rated women who had made three different childbearing choices to determine people's attitudes toward these choices. The independent variable was the childbearing choice and the dependent variable was the attitude rating. The three levels of the independent variable were represented by the three choices: The women in one description were pregnant and happy about the pregnancy; women in a second description were pregnant and unhappy about the pregnancy, and women in the third version were childless by choice. Except for their childbearing choice, the women were similar: All were the same age, married the same length of time, happy in their marriages, and pursuing careers with flexibility that would allow them to have a child and resume their career later. Therefore, any differences in participants' ratings of these women should reflect their different attitudes toward the childbearing choices.

The happy pregnant woman received significantly more positive evaluations than the unhappy pregnant woman, a finding that indicated an endorsement of a cultural stereotype for motherhood. Surprisingly, they found that the childless woman received evaluations almost as positive as the happy pregnant woman. These results allow a conclusion that a woman's childbearing choices can prompt people to have different attitudes about them.

No other type of scientific method allows conclusions concerning causality, and if the experiment is not done carefully, interpretation of causality can be in error. In addition, the laboratory setting differs from a natural social setting. The participants in Shields and Cooper's study may have behaved differently in the lab than they would have in a more naturalistic situation—evaluating descriptions differs from evaluating people.

The laboratory situation provides a social setting of its own and may prompt different behavior than would occur in a more realistic context. Because participants are always aware that their behavior is of interest, they may behave differently than they otherwise would. Thus, the laboratory experiment takes place in an situation removed from its typical context and may alter behavior. This possibility limits the extent to which researchers can generalize their results to other situations. The artificiality of the situation and its limitation in generalizing results to other situations are drawbacks of the experimental method. Researchers have a prejudice in favor of experiments, leading them to prize experiments above other methods (perhaps inappropriately), and scientists do experiments when they can. Table 2.1 presents descriptive and experimental methods with their advantages and limitations.

Ex Post Facto Studies

Scientists cannot always do experiments. Some variables of interest are beyond possible manipulation, either for practical or ethical reasons. For example, researchers might want to know about the effect of brain damage on memory. To do an experiment, researchers would be required to select a group of people and perform the surgery that would cause brain damage in half of them while leaving the other half with undamaged brains. Obviously, this research is unethical, but the question that prompted it—Does brain damage influence memory?—is still of interest.

TABLE 2.1 Advantages and Limitations of Descriptive and Experimental Methods

Method	Advantage	Limitation
Naturalistic Observation	Looks at behavior in a natural setting	Cannot distinguish among many variables that can affect a situation
Survey	Can examine a variety of topics without being intrusive	Relies on self-reports and not direct observation of behavior
Correlational Study	Allows strength and direction of relationship between two variables to be determined	Cannot reveal any information about causality
Experiments	Allows cause and effect relationships to be determined	Conducted in laboratory situations that are artificial Can only investigate a few variables at a time

Researchers interested in the question about brain damage and memory have at least two choices. They might choose to do the experiment with nonhuman subjects (although some people would object to the ethics of this research, too), but the problems of generalizing the findings to people would be a severe limitation. Another choice would be the **ex post facto study.** In this type of study, researchers might select people who have suffered brain damage in the area of interest and enlist these individuals as research participants, contrasting them with a group of people who have not experienced brain damage of any sort or those who have damage in some other area of the brain. Both groups would participate in the assessment of memory. Therefore, the presence of brain damage would be the **subject variable**—the characteristic of interest in the subjects—and the scores on the memory test would be the dependent variable.

Such an ex post facto study would not be an experiment, because the researchers did not produce the brain damage while holding all other factors constant. Instead, the researchers entered the picture *after* the manipulation had been performed through accidents (hence the term *ex post facto*—after the fact of the creation of differences). With no opportunity for precision in creating the values of the independent variable or in holding other factors constant, the ex post facto study lacks the controls that would allow researchers to draw conclusions about cause-and-effect relationships (Christensen, 1997).

The ex post facto study seems very much like an experiment, including the presence of contrast groups and a dependent variable measurement. These similarities can lead to misinterpretations of these studies and incorrect attributions of causality. Researchers are usually careful to use the correct language to interpret their findings from ex post facto studies, but people who read the research may not be appropriately cautious, leading to misunderstandings of research findings.

Gender of participants is a subject variable, a characteristic of the subjects that exists prior to their participation in a study but one that can be the basis for division of subjects into contrast groups. The studies that approach gender as a subject variable are ex post facto studies, with all of the limitations of this method. That is, these studies do not and cannot reveal that gender *causes* differences in any behavior. This caution is difficult for many people to keep in mind, and those who are not familiar with research methods have a tendency to believe that gender-related differences in behavior have biological sex as the underlying cause. This reasoning contains two errors: (1) incorrectly attributing causality to a research method that cannot demonstrate cause-and-effect relationships and (2) reducing the many variables that coexist with biological sex to the variable of subject gender. Therefore, an erroneous interpretation of such studies can lead people to conclusions for which there is no research evidence.

An exploration of gender differences in sense of humor used an ex post facto design in which men's and women's senses of humor were contrasted (Crawford & Gressley, 1991). Rather than presenting jokes or cartoons that the experimenters found funny and testing gender differences in appreciation of humor, the researchers measured the different dimensions of humor. In contrasting women and men, more similarities than differences appeared. However, men scored higher on appreciation of hostile humor, jokes, and slapstick humor, whereas women scored higher on appreciation of anecdotal funny stories.

Figure 2.1 illustrates some of the differences between experimental and ex post facto designs, using gender as an example. In the experimental design, researchers often randomly divide the participants into groups in order to keep individual differences equal among the groups. Therefore, the groups in an experimental design would not consist of one group of men and another group of women, because random assignment would be very unlikely to yield such a configuration. The ex post facto design, on the other hand, assigns participants to groups on the basis of some factor that the participants already possess, such as gender. In this type of design, the researcher might have one group consisting of women and another of men. Indeed, thousands of studies use this design to study gender-related differences and similarities.

An experimental design can use gender as a variable if the researcher manipulates the gender of some target person whom the participants rate, evaluate, or react to, but this

Experimental Design — Gender as a Social Category

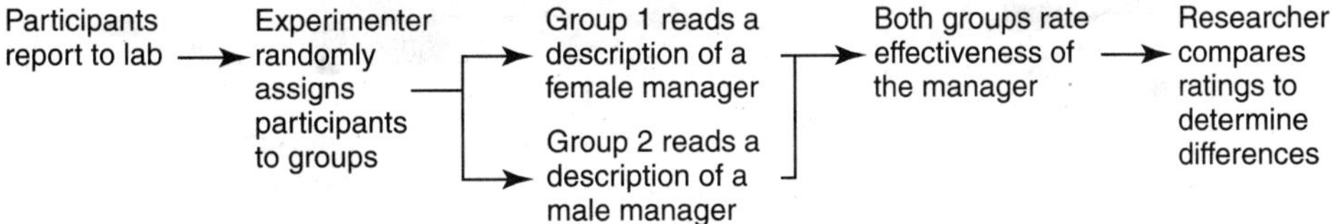

Ex Post Facto Design — Gender as a Subject Variable

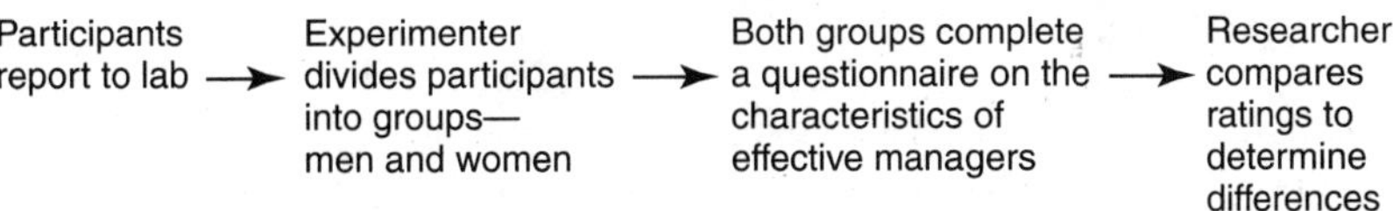

FIGURE 2.1 Two Designs with Gender as a Variable

approach makes gender a social category, not a subject variable. Further, the subject variable of gender can be included in a study that manipulates an independent variable to study each variable as well as the variables in combination. Therefore, ex post facto designs can examine gender as a subject variable, experimental designs can study gender as a social category to which participants react, and studies can use gender as a subject variable combined with additional, manipulated independent variables. These approaches are not equivalent, and each yields information that requires careful interpretation of findings.

In summary, different research methods yield different types of information. Descriptive research methods include naturalistic observation, surveys, and correlational studies. Such studies help to answer questions about *what* occurs; that is, they describe what exists. Experimental research, on the other hand, allows researchers to explain *why* a relationship exists between independent variables and dependent variables. Because it yields information about cause-and-effect relationships, this method is highly prized. A quasi-experimental method, the ex post facto study, is similar to an experiment in the designation of variables (called subject variables) and dependent variables, but these designs differ from true experiments in using the values of the subject variable rather than creating the values of the independent variable through manipulation.

Qualitative Research

Descriptive and experimental research methods are usually quantitative; that is, these research methods involve the process of collecting data in terms of numbers. As previously mentioned, researchers must choose some aspect of the situation to measure, and these measurements almost always result in numbers that can be analyzed by statistics. Some scholars have raised objections to this process, claiming that quantification fails to capture important aspects of the situations under study.

An alternative to the quantitative approach is qualitative research. Qualitative researchers focus on the complexity of the situation rather than trying to manipulate and control different variables. They also reject the notion that researchers should be detached and impartial; instead they accept the subjectivity of the research process. By interacting with research participants as equals, they try to understand the meaning and context of what they study.

Qualitative research has been more common in anthropology and sociology than in psychology, but the interest in qualitative methods has grown among psychologists in recent years. **Ethnography** is one of the most common qualitative methods, and this method has a long tradition in anthropology. Researchers using this method spend time becoming immersed in the situation they are studying. For anthropologists, this situation is typically another culture; for psychologists and sociologists, the situation may be a school, company, or hospital. By becoming part of the situation, the researcher can gather and interpret information.

Barrie Thorne (1993) conducted an ethnographic study in which she observed students in middle school to understand how children of this age behave with children of the same and the other gender. She sat in their classrooms, ate in the lunchroom, and observed activities on the playground. Although she did not become one of the children, her status was unlike that of the other adults. Her presence for over 8 months allowed her to make in-depth observations and interpretations of the gender interactions among these preadolescents and to describe and classify these interactions.

Case studies and **interviews** are additional qualitative methods. A case study is an intensive study of a case—that is, a single person (or a small sample of people). The choice of a case for study may occur for several different reasons. The person may be typical and thus reflective of many other people, or unusual and thus of interest. Researchers conducting case studies often spend days or months interviewing or observing the person in order to write a case study. Miguel, a gay Mexican American man, was the subject of such a case study (Carrier, 1997). The case study told of Miguel's sexual life history, contrasting the sexual behaviors and cultural attitudes of Mexican American and European American gay men. In addition, the case study described Miguel's relationships with women, his career, and his problems with alcoholism.

Interviews can take many forms, but qualitative interviews differ from interviews conducted as part of survey research in both format and goals. Survey interviews are quantitative, including a specified and uniform set of questions to which all respondents reply. The uniformity of responses allow statistical analysis, but such analysis is not the goal of qualitative interviews. These interviews can take the form of oral or life histories, or the interview may be oriented around a narrower topic. An interview study of convicted and imprisoned rapists helped clarify their motivations and attitudes toward women (Scully, 1990). The interviews varied in length, with some lasting only a few minutes and others lasting for hours. This procedure did not yield a uniform set of data, but an analysis showed some common patterns of motivation and attitudes among the rapists' responses.

Therefore, qualitative research offers alternatives to traditional quantitative research methods. A comparison of the two approaches appears in Table 2.2. The philosophy of qualitative research includes an emphasis on the context and an acknowledgment that subjectivity is part of the research process. Qualitative researchers become involved in the research situation, interacting with participants in order to understand the patterns of their behavior.

TABLE 2.2 Comparison of Quantitative and Qualitative Research

Quantitative Researchers	Qualitative Researchers
Often work in laboratories	Rarely work in laboratories
Strive to detach themselves from the situation to attain objectivity	Immerse themselves in the situation and accept subjectivity as part of the process
Attempt to study a representative group of individuals to be able to generalize	May seek unusual individuals because they are interesting cases
Create a distinction between researchers and subjects	Treat participants as equals
Collect data in the form of numbers	Collect information that is not reduced to numbers
Attempt to control the influence of variables other than the independent variable(s)	Attempt to understand the complexity of the situation as it exists
Use statistics to analyze their data	Do not use statistics to analyze their information

Limitations on Gender Research

The type of research design limits the conclusions that researchers can validly draw. Each method has inherent limitations concerning the permissible conclusions, and when these limitations are exceeded, errors of interpretation occur. The mistakes in interpretation often involve the evaluation of research studies, especially the concept of statistical significance. Although researchers tend to be knowledgeable about design and statistics and careful in interpreting their research, such caution may be lost in media reports of scientific research. These can, and often do, lead to widespread misunderstanding of the meaning of certain results and their practical implications.

As the study on humor showed (Crawford & Gressley, 1991), gender is often an subject variable in psychology research. In such studies, gender is part of an ex post facto design rather than an experimental design. Gender of the participants is a variable that cannot be manipulated in an experimental design. Researchers do not choose a group of people who have no gender and make them male and female as part of the study. Instead, researchers select groups of men and women and form two groups in an ex post facto design. Thousands of such studies exist, but *not one* of these studies is an experiment, and *not one* of them allows conclusions about the causal role of gender in the behaviors these studies have measured. However, people who are not very knowledgeable about research design can mistake an ex post facto design for an experiment and may interpret such studies as indicating causality. This error can lead to serious misunderstanding about the meaning of gender-related differences, with the implication that gender is the cause of these differences.

No method that researchers can actually perform will reveal the *cause* of gender differences. Those studies would be experimental, and such experiments are impossible to perform. Any study that uses women and men, or even the youngest infant boys and girls, is an ex post facto study that has that methodology's limits. This methodological limitation should restrict conclusions about the nature of gender differences, but such discussions still exist. These assertions and discussions are speculation—perhaps with some research finding as a basis, but speculation nonetheless. Both those who speculate and those who read the speculation should be aware of their nature.

Scientists are certainly allowed to speculate. Indeed, the speculations that they can weave into coherent, integrated explanations become theories, and theories guide much scientific research. Such theories are important, powerful, and influential but are not the same as observations or findings. When a discrepancy arises between a theory and a finding, the scientist should discard or revise the theory rather than ignore or question the finding. However, the opposite often happens. According to Thomas Kuhn (1962), scientists tend to cling to theories and find ways to reject their findings rather than the other way around. Although such behavior calls into question the objectivity of scientists, the history of science is filled with examples. Kuhn gave many examples of such bias, including the insistence that the earth was the center of the universe despite a growing body of evidence that was inconsistent with this view.

The study of gender is also full of examples of situations in which speculations and theories have attained a status in which they are mistaken for results. Freud's theory is probably the most prominent example, with its emphasis on the importance of biological sex differences in building personality. Although research has not supported this theory (see Chapter 6 for more on Freud), the theory claims an authority it has not earned.

Additional bias in research on gender (and many other topics) comes from the procedures involved in planning studies and evaluating results. Researchers' values enter the research process as early as the planning stage of studies, influencing the choice of problem to investigate and the questions to ask (Wallston, 1981). Publications place too much emphasis on results and too little on the conceptualization of the questions underlying the research process. The answers that researchers find depend on the questions they ask, so the planning and questioning aspect of the process is critically important.

When researchers formulate their studies, they ask questions and choose methods of gathering information that will allow them to answer their questions. Most researchers know what they expect to find when they ask their questions, so research is not free of the values and expectations of the scientists, even at this stage of the research. These expectations lead to the formulation of a **hypothesis,** a statement about the expected outcome of the study. Researchers test hypotheses by gathering data and analyzing it to obtain results. They can then decide if the results support or fail to support their hypothesis.

Table 2.3 shows the stages of research and how bias can enter at various points in the process. The possibilities for gender bias listed in the table are only examples, and the history of gender research is filled with too many other examples.

To evaluate the data collected from studies, researchers often use statistical tests. Many different statistical tests exist, but all of those used to evaluate research data have a common goal—to allow researchers to decide whether or not the results are statistically significant. A **statistically significant result** is one due to other than chance alone. If researchers are careful in the design of their studies, then they can attribute significant results to the factors they have identified in their studies. The procedure for determining the statistical significance of a result involves choosing the appropriate statistical test and analyzing the data from the study using that statistic. If the analysis indicates significant effects, then the researchers can conclude that their results were not due to chance alone; that is, the study worked as hypothesized. If the analysis does not indicate a significant effect, then the researchers cannot claim that their results are due to anything but chance or that their study worked as hypothesized.

Researchers are constrained from making claims about factors that do not produce significant results, because these results are not considered "real," and researchers have no confidence in the validity of nonsignificant results. When researchers obtain statistically significant results, they have confidence that their research has revealed effects that probably are not due to chance. However, the term *significant* can be misleading, because people who are not sophisticated in the logic of statistical evaluation may believe that statistically significant means *important.*

The concepts of statistical significance and practical significance are not the same. A result is statistically significant when it is unlikely to have occurred solely on the basis of chance. A result has **practical significance** when it is important to everyday life. For example, a low correlation ($r = 0.20$) can indicate a statistically significant relationship if the number of people participating in the study was sufficiently large (what constitutes a large sample varies with the design and statistic), but this magnitude of correlation does not

TABLE 2.3 Stages of Research and Potential for Bias

Stage	Ways Bias Can Enter	Gender-Related Example
Finding a problem to investigate	Allowing personal and societal values to influence choice of topic	Studying heart disease rather than breast cancer in middle-aged populations
Selecting variables	Using inaccurate, incomplete, or misleading definitions	Defining rape as vaginal penetration accompanied by force or threat of force (excludes other forced sexual acts and excludes men as victims)
Choosing a design	Choosing a design that would not allow for the evaluation of context	Testing participants in a situation that is anxiety-provoking for women but not for men
Formulating a hypothesis	Failing to consider the validity of the null hypothesis; following a theory that is biased	Always hypothesizing gender differences rather than similarities; following Freudian theory to hypothesize that women have weak superegos
Collecting data	Permitting personal bias to influence measurement, leading to mistakes in the direction of researchers' prediction	Failing to record some cases of playground aggression in girls because the observer does not believe that girls are as aggressive as boys
Analyzing results	Allowing personal values and expectation to guide the choice of which factors to evaluate	Failing to make a comparison of female and male participants
Interpreting results	Failing to report effect sizes	Interpreting a gender difference in a way that makes it seem large when it is not
	Interpreting gender differences as due to biological factors with no biological data	Claiming that boys' advantage in math is biological when no biological data have been collected
Publication bias	Publication of findings showing significant gender differences	Publication and media attention for findings of gender differences but no attention for findings of similarities

reveal a strong relationship between the two variables in the correlation. That is, this correlation would have little practical significance. People who hear about significant results may believe that the results have practical significance when the researchers have reported statistical significance. Such misunderstandings can lead people to believe that results mean more than they actually do.

The development and use of a statistical technique called **meta-analysis** allows researchers to evaluate results from several experimental studies and thereby determine the overall size of various effects. This information is related to practical significance because it can reveal which results are small and which are large. Janet Hyde (1986) explained that meta-analysis allows "the synthesis or integration of numerous studies on a single topic and a quantitative or statistical approach to that synthesis" (p. 3). She contended that meta-analysis is preferred over evaluations that count the outcomes or combine probabilities from various studies because meta-analysis allows similar studies to be combined and statistically evaluated.

This analysis technique allows researchers to simultaneously combine the results from many studies in order to determine the overall size of the effect of a variable of interest. The

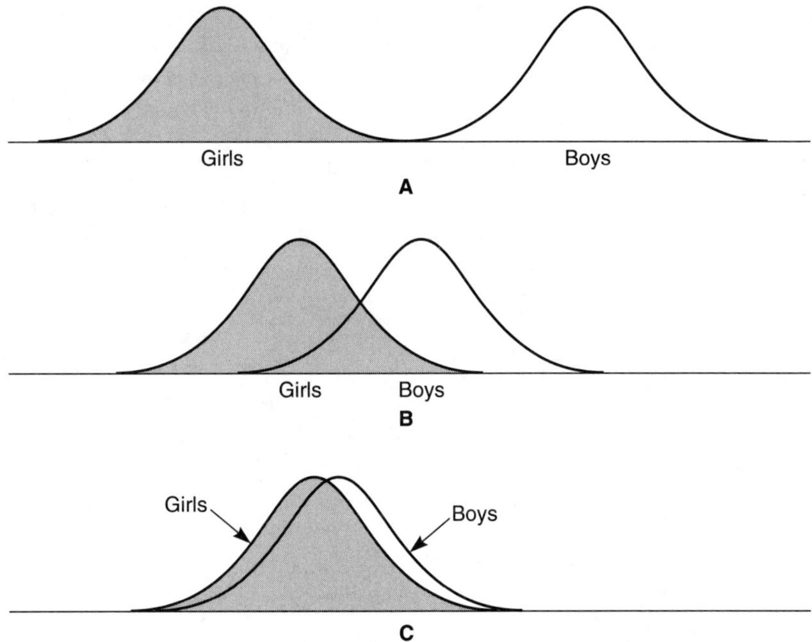

FIGURE 2.2 Distributions with Varying Degrees of Overlap

size of this effect is called *d,* which represents the mean of one group subtracted from the mean of the other divided by the pooled standard deviation. Combined across studies, *d* values reflect the size of group differences. Effect sizes of .2 or less are considered small, those around .5 are considered medium, and .8 or larger are considered to be large differences (Cohen, 1969). These levels are somewhat arbitrary, but many researchers have accepted them as a metric to evaluate the growing number of meta-analytic studies.

For example, one common finding of a gender difference is performance in mathematics. Many studies have found that boys score significantly higher than girls in high school and college mathematics courses (Maccoby & Jacklin, 1974). (This difference does not appear before junior high school age, so no general statement is correct about better math performance at all ages.) How much better are boys at math? Do all boys do better than all girls? How much do math scores of boys and girls overlap? Figure 2.2 shows some possibilities for the distributions of math scores for boys and girls. Group A of this figure shows two distributions with no overlap. If this figure represented the mathematics performance of boys and girls, then all boys would do better than all girls. Group B shows the performance of boys and girls overlapping slightly. If this figure represented the performance of boys and girls, then most boys would do better than most girls. A few girls would do better than a few boys, but no girls would do better than boys with the highest performance. Group C shows a lot of overlap between the performance of the two. If this figure represented performance, all boys would not do better at math than all girls, and many girls would do better at math than many boys.

Hyde (1981, 1986; 1994) contended that the upper range of difference between men and women is no more than 1% in mathematical ability, reflecting a *d* of .15. That is, only a small percentage of the distribution of math scores for boys and girls fails to overlap, and most of the scores for the two are in the same range. Group C comes closer to this distribution of math ability than the other parts of Figure 2.2. Gender-related differences in math performance are sufficiently large to show a statistically significant difference, but this difference does not have any practical significance when applied to the performance of most boys and most girls. This magnitude of difference would not lead educators to create different math classes for boys and girls because their abilities were so dissimilar, nor would counselors advise girls to avoid math courses because of their lack of ability.

This gender difference in mathematics achievement after junior high school age may be due to many factors other than biological sex. Parents have expectations that their daughters will be less mathematically inclined than their sons and treat each gender accordingly. Teachers treat boys and girls differently in the classroom. Girls complete fewer math courses during high school and college. (See Chapter 5 for more about mathematics ability of girls and boys and Chapter 12 for more about classroom treatment.) These differences in experience and expectancy make it impossible to conclude that the gender difference in mathematics achievement is due to biological sex.

Finding statistically significant differences is the goal of both experimental and ex post facto designs. When researchers plan studies, they typically look for differences and draw their hypotheses accordingly. Such researchers do not look for similarities. If researchers find the expected differences, they report and discuss these differences. If they fail to find differences, such results do not typically lead to a discussion of the similarity of the groups. Instead, researchers will often dismiss a study (or this part of a study) as a failure and gloss over the absence of statistically significant differences as unimportant.

Studies that do not find the hypothesized differences in outcomes are less likely to be published than studies that succeed in supporting their hypotheses. A strong prejudice exists in favor of findings that show differences rather than findings that do not succeed in showing differences; that is, there is a prejudice against findings that show similarities (Greenwald, 1975). This tendency to report and publish findings of significant differences therefore prompts researchers to highlight the differences they find and to dismiss the similarities. Indeed, researchers may omit any mention of failure to find a difference, such as a gender-related difference, but researchers who find statistically significant differences will always mention the differences and the level of statistical significance. Researchers cannot discuss an effect they have failed to find and must discuss effects that they have found. However, the omission of some information and the mention of other information can lead to a distorted view of overall findings by magnifying differences and obscuring similarities.

In summary, the limitations on gender research come from the type of studies that researchers must conduct and the ways their results are interpreted, both by the investigators and by others. All studies with gender as a subject variable are ex post facto studies rather than true experiments. Although these studies may appear to be experiments, no manipulation of conditions occurs, and experimenters do not have control over the subject's characteristics. This limitation restricts researchers from drawing conclusions from these studies about cause-and-effect relationships. Therefore, none of the studies with gender as a subject variable reveal the cause of the differences, although differences, not similarities, are the focus of the studies. Researchers look for statistically significant differences in their studies, often considering their studies failures if the results do not reveal such differences. However, studies that show statistically significant differences still may not demonstrate differences of such a magnitude to indicate practical significance. In the case of gender, statistically significant differences may still not reveal much about differences in behavior between women and men.

Criticisms of Science

The traditional view of science holds that by using empirical, objective methods to gather and evaluate data, scientists can understand the underlying laws of the natural world. As scientists gain more and more information, their view of the world becomes closer and closer to the "truth." Begley's headline article, which opened this chapter, pointed out that critics have questioned the notion of objectivity and the view that science shows an orderly progression toward "truth."

An early criticism came from Thomas Kuhn (1962), who analyzed the history of science. He concluded that science does not proceed in an incremental, orderly way; instead, he argued that science, like politics, progresses through a series of upheavals (revolutions) and periods of orderly progress (normal science). During the periods of normal science, the research is organized around a prevailing theory, a paradigm, and this paradigm defines the types and content of investigations. During the times of revolution, very little scientific research takes place, because no ruling paradigm exists to guide and order the work. Thus, Kuhn presented evidence that science is neither orderly nor incremental in its progress.

The philosophers whose work spurred the founding of science were all men, and Evelyn Fox Keller (1985) has argued that they introjected a masculine bias into the very conceptual foundation of science. She has interpreted the emphasis on rationality and objectivity in science as masculine values, and she has contrasted those masculine elements of science with the feminine elements of nature—feeling and subjectivity. Thus, Keller discussed what she interpreted as the gendering of science and nature: masculine for science and feminine for nature. She also analyzed the interaction of the masculine–feminine dichotomy in the view of one influential philosopher, Francis Bacon, who proposed a metaphor of a marriage between Nature and Science. In his metaphor Nature is the bride and Science is the groom. Keller took Bacon's metaphor as particularly significant in its gender and sexual connotations. She argued that this metaphor has influenced contemporary views of science as a masculine activity that strives to bring rationality and to dominate unruly feminine nature. Thus, even at its inception, science carried connotations of maleness, rationality, and dominance. According to Keller, not only have women been discouraged from the pursuit of science as a profession, but the activity of science itself suggests masculinity.

Keller's analysis draws on the symbolic and unconscious images of science in modern culture, and other critics have attempted to replace the gendered terminology of masculine and feminine with the terms *agency* (or *agentic*) and *communion* (or *communal*). Philosopher David Bakan (1966) originated these terms, explaining that "agency manifests itself in self-protection, self-assertion, and self-expansion; communion manifests itself in the sense or being at one with other organisms. Agency manifests itself in the urge to master;

communion in noncontractual cooperation" (p. 15). Although Bakan also connected these terms to masculinity and femininity, many gender researchers have adopted his terminology as a less overtly gendered way to describe these two dimensions.

Some feminist scholars have questioned much more than terminology or symbolic issues within science. Indeed, the methodology for investigating sex- and gender-related behaviors is the source of heated controversy, as Begley's (1997) headline article discussed. The constructionists deny the possibility of objectivity and thus reject the basic tenets of science. A sizable group of feminist scholars has advocated rejecting traditional quantitative methodology for studying women, gender, and gender-related behaviors and has proposed alternative qualitative methods for such investigations.

Qualitative methods do not include the assumption of objectivity, one of the key points of dispute in the current controversy over science. As Begley's headline article discussed, scientists have trouble distancing themselves from the values of the society in which they work, leading to bias that critics find inevitable. A growing group of scholars advocates replacing or supplementing traditional science with alternative methods, whereas others argue that scientists must try harder to do good science.

Despite the long history and success of science, some modern scholars have questioned its assumptions and procedures. One criticism is that science grew from not only the activities of men but also from a gendered, masculine bias that is part of science. According to this view, this masculine bias affects our modern conception of science, including the men and women who do scientific work. Another more concrete criticism of science has come from the constructionists, who contend that science is incapable of revealing an objective picture of the natural world. This inability stems from the inevitable bias within the perceptions of scientists, who are influenced by their personal and societal prejudices. Scholars who take this view have used the study of gender as a particularly good example of the distortions and misrepresentations of science.

Methodologies for the Study of Gender

Whereas the charges of bias in scientific investigations have led some feminist scholars to call for a more objective study of gender, others have rejected science or called for radical changes in scientific methodology: "Ever since the scientific method became a way of learning about nature, including ourselves, some people have hailed science as the only way to comprehend natural phenomena, while others have questioned whether it is an appropriate road to knowledge" (Hubbard, 1990, p. 9).

Those scholars who advocate a more objective study of gender can be termed *feminist empiricists* (Riger, 1992). In contrast, scholars who claim that research should center on women are *feminist standpoint epistemologists.* Scholars who take this latter view claim that women have a unique point of view and different cognitive processes that have been ignored. These researchers believe that the analytical categories that are appropriate for men may not be appropriate for women and that research should remedy these shortcomings by devising methods to study the unique experience of womanhood.

Several scholars have argued that feminist research has the power to transform research with women and even the discipline of psychology. Research on issues important to women, such as incest and sexual abuse of children, rape and sexual assault, sexual harassment, spouse abuse, and achievement by women, has increased dramatically within the past 25 years (Worell, 1996). In addition, extending research to understudied populations has been a force in expanding psychology research beyond White middle class college students (Worell & Etaugh, 1994).

As a way of gaining additional information about women and their experience, the feminist standpoint epistemologies have considerable value and appeal. Some feminist scholars have rejected traditional quantitative research as impoverished in capturing the female experience and have opted for more qualitative approaches. Such methods allow researchers to be subjective and interpretive, which qualitative researchers believe is important in studying behavior.

A demonstration of the value of widening research methods came from a study (Landrine, Klonoff, & Brown-Collins, 1992) that approached the same problem with two methodologies: one quantitative and behavioral and the other qualitative and based on personal perceptions. The study focused on self-perceptions of African American, Hispanic American, Asian American, and European American women concerning several gender-stereotypical behaviors. The quantitative analysis showed no differences among these groups of women, but the qualitative evaluation revealed ethnic differences by allowing participants to express feelings that the more traditional approach failed to find. This study demonstrated that more diverse methods of investigation have the potential to enrich traditional science.

Other feminist researchers have argued that the development of a feminist methodology will not benefit research on women and gender-related behaviors. "A distinctive set of feminist methods for psychological research are not only futile but dangerous" (Peplau & Conrad, 1989, p. 380), and "any method can be misused in sexist ways." This view rejects the notion that methodology is gendered or that feminist research must be conducted by women or exclusively on women. Instead, the use of diverse and appropriate methods will be most appropriate for the study of women and gender-related behaviors.

To adequately study gender contrasts, research must include men (or boys) as well as women (or girls). Such comparisons are the subject matter of gender similarities and differences, and this research cannot include only one sex or the other. However, the necessary research must differ from much prior research, because so much of the existent research concerning gender is filled with serious bias. Diane Halpern (1995) contrasted the feminist empiricist position with previous research:

> *The fact that research has been used to justify discrimination and support the prevailing social view is precisely why sound empirical research is needed. If researchers find that society consistently values those traits that are associated with being a man and devalues those traits that are associated with being a woman, then the fault lies in the society in which researchers are participants, not in the research that demonstrates that there are gender differences. (p. 79)*

Several groups of feminist empiricist researchers have made suggestions that can improve traditional research on sex and gender; they have alerted researchers to the potential for inadvertently introducing sexist bias into research and have presented some suggestions for conducting nonsexist psychological research. McHugh et al. acknowledged that psychology research has included biases, some of them unintentional, and an unwarranted confidence in traditional research methods can lead to bias (McHugh, Koeske, & Frieze, 1986), In addition, bias can come from explanatory systems, and both inappropriate labeling and definitions can result in bias.

Unwarranted confidence in traditional research methods occurs, for example, when psychologists accept that observations of behavior are objective. Observations are not necessarily free of sexist (or other) biases, because the observer may be biased and the *context* of the observation is rarely included in the analysis of the situation. Gender may be part of that context yet go unmentioned in the study. For example, the gender of the participants may be a variable in the study, but the gender of the experimenter is usually not. Yet, the gender of the experimenter may affect the behavior of participants, and researchers rarely consider this factor.

Bias in an explanatory system occurs when researchers use broad terms (such as hormones or modeling) to explain specific behaviors. Appropriate explanations should take into account many factors, including social, cultural, biological, and situational factors. Inappropriate labeling and definitions occur in gender research when differences exist and one variation is labeled in a derogatory way. For example, women's attention to the context of behavior has been labeled as "dependence," a term that carries negative connotations. Researchers should avoid value-laden labels on behaviors before they either have evidence of the value, consider the context of the behavior, include both women and men in research on gender-related behaviors, or give appropriate emphasis to topics of interest to both men and women (McHugh et al., 1986). It may not be possible to eliminate gender bias in research, but such bias can be decreased. Nonsexist psychological research can reveal more about gender than biased, sexist research.

Other critics have enlarged the list of criticisms and offered further suggestions for conducting nonsexist research. Critical thinking can lead to an appropriate skepticism and a reformulation for gender research that includes a step-by-step consideration for how bias can enter the study of gender at any point (Caplan & Caplan, 1994). Analysis and reporting results also require changes (Hyde, 1994). Researchers should conduct all appropriate significance tests and report all (even nonsignificant) findings and sizes of effects, exercising caution in interpreting results so as to make appropriate conclusions, and applying appropriate scientific standards to assure that findings are not misused. All of these suggestions are intended to make the research on sex and gender more scientifically rigorous and thus eliminate the biases that have been so common in this area, creating a feminist empiricism.

The feminist standpoint epistemologies have the disadvantage of departing radically from accepted methodology, and such departures are difficult for mainstream science to accept (Riger, 1992). The growing interest in qualitative research and its increasing frequency in psychology journals speaks to the possibility of including these changes in research.

Less radical changes, however, are easier to accept and enact. Thus, the recommendations by McHugh et al. and Hyde, which are within traditional science, are more likely to have a wider impact. Such careful design might be appropriate for any psychological research but is particularly important for the study of gender.

Summary

A "science war" is currently under way, with critics maintaining that traditional science is not (and cannot be) objective. This criticism has prompted scientists to examine the extent to which societal values are included into the process of research, producing biased and inaccurate results. The history of gender research is filled with examples of the bias of scientific research in studying gender issues.

Scientific methods of gathering information can be traced back to the sixteenth century and rest on philosophical traditions that assert the advantages of an objective, observation-based understanding of the world. By using descriptive methods, such as naturalistic observation, correlational studies, and surveys, researchers gather and evaluate information that leads them to understand the world. By using the experimental method, researchers can develop an understanding of the cause-and-effect relationship between an independent variable and a dependent variable. Although the ex post facto method resembles experimentation, it differs in procedure and in the type of information it yields: Ex post facto studies do not involve the manipulation of independent variables and do not allow the determination of causality. All studies with gender as a variable are ex post facto designs, and none have the ability to reveal the cause of any differences they might show. In addition, studies that reveal gender-related differences may show a difference that is statistically significant—that is, not due to chance. Yet the difference may not have any practical significance; for instance, it may not reveal important differences between women and men.

Although the scientific method rests on objectivity, the constructionist movement holds that any observation is biased and that researchers can never escape their own personal feelings and beliefs when they do scientific research. An extreme version of this belief calls for the abandonment of research, but acknowledges that the possibility of bias can make researchers more careful. Those researchers who advise taking care to avoid sexist bias in research can be described as feminist empiricists. On the other hand, some researchers advocate abandoning the traditional scientific method and adopting alternatives that center on women and that use different methods of gaining information, especially qualitative research methods such as ethnography and interview studies. The term feminist standpoint epistemologists applies to those who want to create a woman-centered approach to researching the female experience. In psychological research, the former are more numerous than the latter, and some psychologists have considered the problems and proposed solutions for carrying out nonsexist research. Feminist standpoint epistemologies can add new dimensions to the study of both women and men, but abandonment of traditional scientific methods is unlikely. In addition, some feminist scholars have argued against excluding any method and proposed a more objective feminist empiricism.

Glossary

case study a qualitative method that focuses on gathering extensive information about a single person.

constructionists a group of critics of science who have argued that reality is constructed through perception and is inevitably subject to bias. Included in this bias is all scientific observation, thus excluding science from its claim of objectivity.

correlational study a descriptive research method that requires researchers to measure two factors known to occur within a group of people to determine the degree of relationship between the two factors.

data representations, usually in numerical form, of some facet of the phenomenon that the researcher observes.

dependent variable the factor in an experiment that the experimenter measures to determine if the manipulation of the independent variable has an effect.

descriptive research methods a group of research methods, including naturalistic observation, surveys, and correlational studies, that yield descriptions of the observed phenomena.

empirical observation collecting information through direct observation.

ethnography a type of qualitative research in which the researcher becomes immersed in a situation to make observations and interpretations of that situation.

experiment a type of study in which a researcher manipulates an independent variable and observes the changes in a dependent variable; only through experiments can researchers learn about cause-and-effect relationships.

ex post facto study a type of nonexperimental research design that involves the comparison of subjects, who are placed in contrast groups, on the basis of some preexisting characteristic of the subjects.

hypothesis a statement about the expected outcome of a study.

independent variable the factor in an experiment that the experimenter manipulates to create a difference that did not previously exist in the participants.

interview a type of qualitative study in which respondents are interviewed in order to determine patterns or commonalities among their responses.

meta-analysis a statistical analysis that allows the evaluation of many studies simultaneously.

naturalistic observation a descriptive research method that requires researchers to collect information about a naturally occurring situation without changing the situation in any way.

operational definition a definition of the concept in terms of operations rather than concepts.

practical significance an important result with practical implications; different from statistical significance.

quantification the process of turning observations into numerical data.

statistically significant result a result obtained by analysis with statistical tests and found unlikely to have been obtained on the basis of chance alone.

subject variable a characteristic of the subjects, such as gender, that allows researchers to form contrast groups in quasi-experimental studies.

survey a descriptive research method involving the measurement of attitudes through the administration and interpretation of questionnaires.

variable a factor of interest to researchers; something that can have more than one value, as opposed to a constant, which has only one constant value.

Suggested Readings

Caplan, Paula J.; & Caplan, Jeremy B. (1994). *Thinking critically about research on sex and gender.* New York: HarperCollins. Caplan and Caplan critique the history and current research on sex and gender, including specific guidelines concerning what to look for to determine the types of bias in gender research. Their book is easy to read and contains critiques of specific content areas as well as a general evaluation of the research process.

Peplau, Letitia Anne; & Conrad, Eva. (1989). Beyond nonsexist research: The perils of feminist methods in psychology. *Psychology of Women Quarterly, 13,* 379–400. Peplau and Conrad criticize the concept that a feminist methodology is necessary for feminist research in psychology, contending that any method can be sexist or feminist. They instead argue for the use of a variety of methods.

Riger, Stephanie. (1992). Epistemological debates, feminist voices: Science, social values, and the study of women. *American Psychologist, 47,* 730–740. This excellent article outlines the different positions and ongoing debates about the scientific method. Although the article is not easy reading, Riger does a fine job of stating the complex issues in clear terms.

Chapter 3

Hormones and Chromosomes

HEADLINE

Aggression in Men: Hormone Levels Are a Key

—New York Times, July 17, 1990

PMS: Is It for Real?

—Cosmopolitan, April 1995

> *Right before her period, Cheryl, an otherwise bubbly twenty-nine-year-old account executive, gets irritated with her boyfriend. She may throw things at the wall, even threaten to end the relationship. "He just rolls his eyes," she says, "because he knows: It's that time of the month."*
>
> *Jamie feels sad and incompetent for a couple of weeks each month. Negotiating with clients at a business meeting not too long ago, the thirty-four-year-old computer analyst burst into tears, then skipped dinner with colleagues because she couldn't decide what to wear.*
>
> *Both Cheryl and Jamie attribute their behavior to being premenstrual. (Murray, 1995, p. 209)*

The story, "PMS: Is It for Real?" (Murray, 1995) evaluated the evidence about premenstrual syndrome (PMS), beginning with the examples of the two cases above. These two women described their symptoms in ways that are consistent with popular thought. Although few people question the reality of PMS, this story did, and the conclusions were very different from most popular reports on this topic in the press.

The story "Aggression in Men: Hormone Levels Are a Key" (Goleman, 1990) described the results from several research projects that investigated the relationship between testosterone and aggression. Although the title of the story suggested that hormone levels are a key to aggression, the story included both evidence of such a relationship and some failures to find a relationship between these two factors. Among the skeptics quoted in the article was Robert Rose, a researcher who cautioned against overemphasizing the role of hormones in human behavior. Rose contended that many other factors influence aggression and that a search for a simple relationship would be unsuccessful.

Both these popular articles implicated the role of hormones in a wide variety of behaviors. Are these views correct? If so, what role do hormones play in physical development and ongoing behavior? Are hormones the key to the differences between male and female? Or are chromosomes the key? To answer these questions, this chapter examines development from an individual's conception, exploring the contribution of chromosomes and then tracing the effect of hormones throughout prenatal development and again during puberty. When hormonal or chromosomal abnormalities occur, individuals do not follow the pattern of developing into women or men. Instead, these individuals develop characteristics of each, providing interesting examples of the roles of chromosomes and hormones in the development of sex and gender. Finally, this chapter examines the role of hormones in adult behavior, including the relationships claimed by the headlines between hormone levels and the behaviors associated with premenstrual syndrome and with aggression.

The Endocrine System and Steroid Hormones

Hormones are substances released from **endocrine glands** to circulate throughout the body. Receptors on various organs are sensitive to specific hormones, which produce many different actions at various sites. Although the body contains many endocrine glands that secrete many different hormones, **steroid hormones** relate to the differences between the sexes and reproduction. The reproductive organs, the ovaries and testes, are the **gonads.** These organs are obviously among the physical characteristics differentiating the sexes and are also essential to reproduction, but the ovaries and testes are not the only endocrine glands that are important for sexual development and functioning.

The **pituitary gland** is located within the brain and is often referred to as the master gland because its function controls the production of many other hormones. The pituitary produces many **tropic hormones,** which stimulate the release of other hormones. Thus, the action of the pituitary controls many hormones. Gonadotropins are one type of hormone produced by the pituitary. These hormones circulate through the bloodstream and stimulate the ovaries and testes to release their hormones.

The action of the pituitary is affected by a nearby brain structure, the hypothalamus. The complex action of the hypothalamus results in the production of a class of hormones called **releasing hormones.** The action of releasing hormones is necessary for the pituitary to release its tropic hormones. Therefore, the hypothalamus acts to produce releasing hormones, such as gonadotropin-releasing hormone, which stimulates the pituitary to release its gonadotropins, which in turn stimulate the gonads to produce their hormones. Figure 3.1 summarizes the action of these glands and hormones.

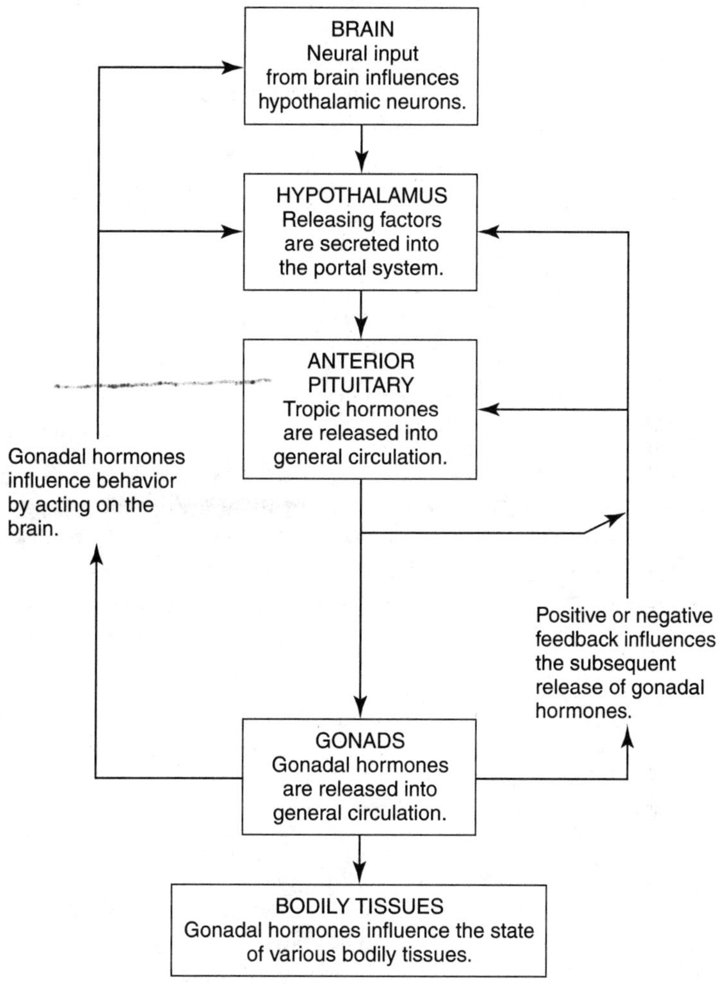

FIGURE 3.1 A Summary Model of the Regulation of Gonadal Hormones

SOURCE: From John P. J. Pinel, *Biopsychology* (2nd ed.). Copyright © 1993 by Allyn and Bacon. Reprinted by permission.

Gonadal hormones are of the steroid type; that is, all these hormones are derived from cholesterol and consist of a structure that includes four carbon rings. The two main classes of gonadal hormones are **androgens** and **estrogens.** Although people tend to think of androgens as "male hormones" and estrogens as "female hormones," that belief is somewhat inaccurate—each sex produces both types of hormones. The most common of the androgens is **testosterone,** and the most common of the estrogens is **estradiol.** Men typically produce a greater proportion of androgens than estrogens, and women typically produce a greater portion of estrogens than androgens.

The gonads also secrete a third type of hormone, the **progestins.** The most common progestin is progesterone, which plays a role in preparing a woman's body for pregnancy. Men also secrete progesterone, but its function for them is unknown (Pinel, 1997). The chemical structure of the androgens, estrogens, and progestins is similar.

The gonads are not the only glands that produce steroid hormones; the adrenal gland also produces them. Although the amounts of hormones produced by the adrenal glands are smaller than the amounts produced by the gonads, the types are the same.

Stages of Differences between the Sexes

Humans (and most other animals) are sexually dimorphic; that is, they come in two different physical versions—female and male. This **sexual dimorphism** is the result of development that begins with conception and ends at puberty, resulting in men and women who are capable of sexual reproduction. Sexual dimorphism can be conceptualized as the product of five stages: genetic, gonadal, hormonal, internal genitalia, and external genitalia (Kaplan, 1980). The *genetic stage* refers to the inheritance of the chromosomes related to sex. The *gonadal stage* includes the development of the gonads, the reproductive organs. The *hormonal stage* begins prenatally, with the secretion of androgens and estrogens. Hormonal development also occurs at puberty, producing mature, functional gonads. The stage when the *internal genitalia,* the internal reproductive organs develop, occurs prenatally and affects not only the ovaries or testes but also the other internal structures relating to reproductive functioning. Therefore, the **internal genitalia** consist of the internal structures related to reproduction: ovaries, Fallopian tubes, uterus, and upper vagina in women and testes, prostate gland, seminal vesicles, and vas deferens in men. The **external genitalia** are the reproductive structures that can be seen without internal examination: clitoris, labia, and vaginal opening in women and penis and scrotum in men. These developments result in differences that are apparent at birth. The stage of developing the *external genitalia* occurs later during the prenatal period than the development of internal genitalia.

In the development of physical gender characteristics, prenatal development is critically important. For the doctor to be able to pronounce, "It's a boy" or "It's a girl," a great many prenatal events must occur in a coordinated sequence. These prenatal events occur within a complex set of stages that result in a girl or a boy, but sometimes things go wrong. When things go wrong, the result is a baby who has some developmental abnormalities as a result of the combination of the female and the male patterns of development. These mistakes are rare, but these cases are clinically interesting and also provide a means of understanding the necessary elements of normal development.

Sexual Differentiation

The development of sexual differences is a complex process. The physical differences between men and women start at conception—the fertilization of an ovum by a sperm cell. Most of the cells in the human body contain 23 pairs of chromosomes, but ova and sperm carry half the normal amount of chromosomal material. In the fertilized ovum, the full amount of genetic material is present, with half coming from the mother's ovum and half from the father's sperm.

Of the 23 pairs of human chromosomes, pair number 23 is the one that is critical in determining chromosomal sex. Although most chromosomes are X-shaped, only those in pair 23 are called **X chromosomes.** An individual who inherits two of these X chromosomes (one X from their mother and the other X from their father) will have the genetic patterns to develop according to the female pattern. Individuals who inherit one X and one **Y chromosome** (the X from their mother and the Y from their father) will have the genetic information to develop according to the male pattern. Therefore, normal girls and women have the XX pattern of chromosome pair 23, and normal boys and men have the XY pattern.

The presence of the XY chromosome constellation is only the first factor that produces male physiology, and its presence is not sufficient to produce a normal male. Other configurations are possible for pair 23, but those patterns are abnormalities, discussed later in the section titled When Things Go Wrong.

Development of Male and Female Physiology

After conception the fertilized ovum starts to grow, first by dividing into two cells, then four, and so on. The ball of cells becomes larger and starts to differentiate; that is, they begin to form the basis for different structures and organs. Within the first six weeks of prenatal development, no difference exists between male and female embryos, even in their gonads. Both the embryos with the XX pattern and the XY pattern have the same structures, and this duplication gives both types of individuals the potential to develop into individuals who look like and who have the internal reproductive organs of either boys or girls.

The Reproductive Organs

Both male and female embryos have a **Wolffian system,** which has the capacity to develop into the male internal reproductive system, and a **Müllerian system,** which has the capacity to develop into the female internal reproductive system. During the third month of prenatal development, two things typically happen to fetuses with the XY chromosome pattern that furthers the developing male pattern.

The first involves the production of androgens, which begin to be produced by the fetal testes during this period. The presence of androgens stimulates the development of the Wolffian system. The growth of the testes further increases production of testosterone, which further stimulates development along the lines of the male pattern. The second event that prompts male development is the production of Müllerian-inhibiting substance, which causes the Müllerian system to degenerate.

Therefore, one type of secretion prompts the Wolffian system to develop into the male internal reproductive organs, and the other causes the female Müllerian system to degenerate. One action produces a masculinization and the other a defemininization of the developing fetus, and both actions produce male internal reproductive organs in the fetus. Figure 3.2 shows how the male reproductive system develops from the Wolffian system, resulting in testes, vas deferens, and seminal vesicles. This figure also illustrates how both male and female reproductive structures originate from the same prenatal structures.

The development of the female reproductive system requires no surge of fetal hormones. The fetal ovaries produce few estrogens. In female embryos the Wolffian system degenerates and the Müllerian system develops, resulting in ovaries, uterus, Fallopian tubes, and the upper part of the vagina. Figure 3.2 also shows how the female reproductive system develops from the Müllerian system.

GENDERED VOICES

Beyond Hormones, There's Very Little Room for Movement

A male engineer told me of his belief in a strong biologically deterministic view of behavior: "I don't think that there are any real differences in intelligence between men and women, but I think that both are overwhelmed by hormones. Beyond hormones, there's very little room for movement, very little chance for people to exert any effort toward behavior that is genuinely adaptive. People can't depart from those hormonal influences. It deprives both of any real intelligence, making their behavior restricted to what their hormones allow."

He expressed the belief that men's shorter average life span was due to hormonal influences on their behavior and that they have little choice in actions. He said, "I think that men harm themselves due to the influence of their hormones. Women have many advantages over men, benefiting from men's behavior, but it's not that women force men to do the difficult things while women take it easy. I think that men's choice to do things like go to war is due to their hormones and not to their desire to protect women. Men have little choice, and they are harmed by their hormones. Women's behavior is also fixed by their hormones, but they live longer, so it must not be as much of a disadvantage for them. I don't think that people have much free choice in their behavior. It's all hormones."

Six weeks after conception, the external genitalia of male and female fetuses are also identical. The structures that will become the penis and scrotum in males and the clitoris, outer and inner labia, and vaginal opening in females have not yet formed. The fetal structures that exist at this point have the potential to develop into either male or female external genitalia, depending on the presence of androgens, especially testosterone.

Figure 3.3 shows the development of the external genitalia for both the male and female pattern. Notice that the structures are identical at six weeks after conception but start to differentiate into the two different patterns during the third and fourth months of gestation.

Prenatal production of androgens produces the male pattern, and the absence of androgens results in an incomplete version of the female pattern. If few or no hormones of either type are present, a fetus will develop external genitals that appear more like the female than the male structures, suggesting that the basic pattern for development is female (Pinel, 1997). These prenatal hormone effects organize developing fetuses around the female or male pattern, resulting in permanent changes in the ability to produce hormones and also in the existence and function of reproductive organs.

The Nervous System

Organizing effects of hormones influence the development of the brain and nervous system as well as the organs that relate to reproduction, and the presence of different amounts of androgens and estrogens during prenatal development account for these differences. Chapter 4 explores the details of brain development and gender differences, but a brief consideration of hormonal influences on nervous system development is in order here.

With rats, the differences between male and female nervous systems and the course of these developments are easy to investigate, but due to practical and ethical limitations on experimentation with humans, similar investigations are difficult. Thus, many of the findings about brain differences come from studies with rats or other nonhuman subjects, and generalizations to humans should be done with caution.

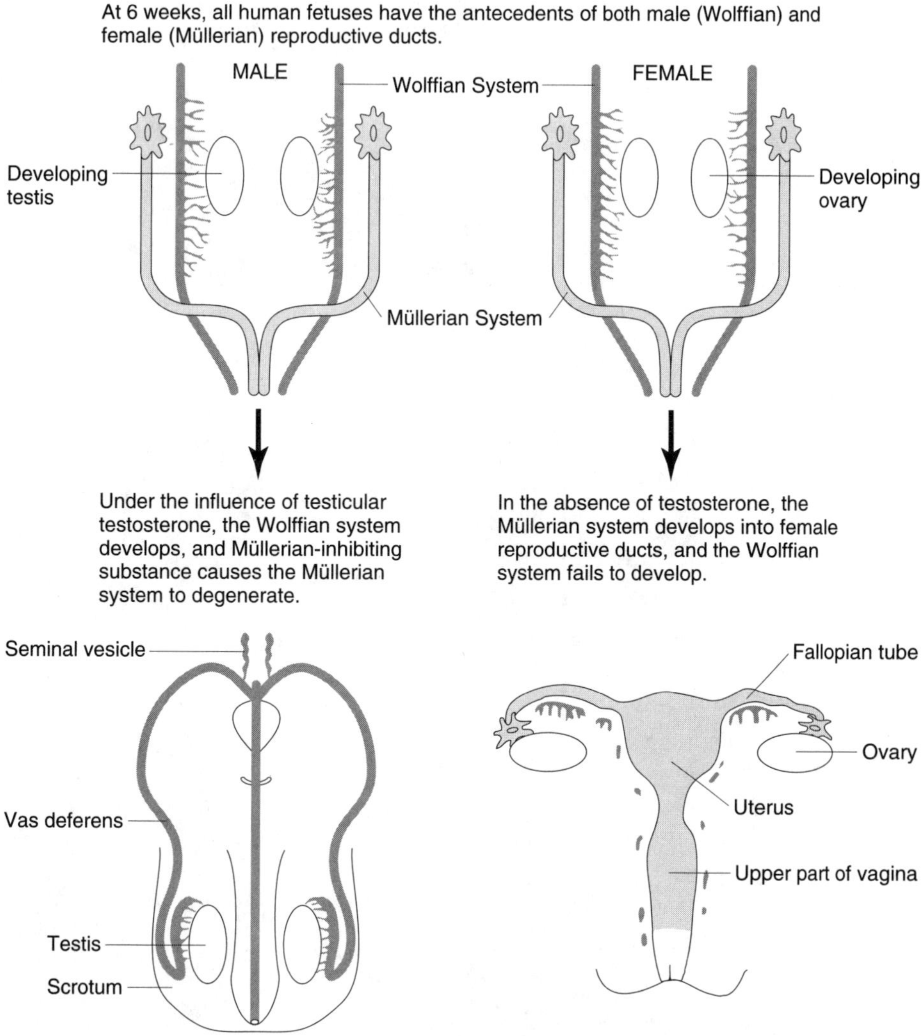

FIGURE 3.2 Development of Internal Reproductive Systems

SOURCE: From John P. J. Pinel, *Biopsychology* (2nd ed.). Copyright © 1993 by Allyn and Bacon. Reprinted by permission.

For example, one of the nervous system sex differences is in the **spinal nucleus of the bulbocavernosus** (Breedlove, 1994). The spinal nucleus of the bulbocavernosus is 25% larger in men than in women. These spinal neurons aid in the ejaculation of sperm in men and constrict the opening of the vagina in women. These neurons are present in both male and female rats at birth, but the neurons die in female rats. In male rats, the presence of androgens allows these neurons to survive. Therefore, there is a larger difference between the nervous systems of male and female rats than male and female humans, and a simple generalization from rats to humans would be invalid.

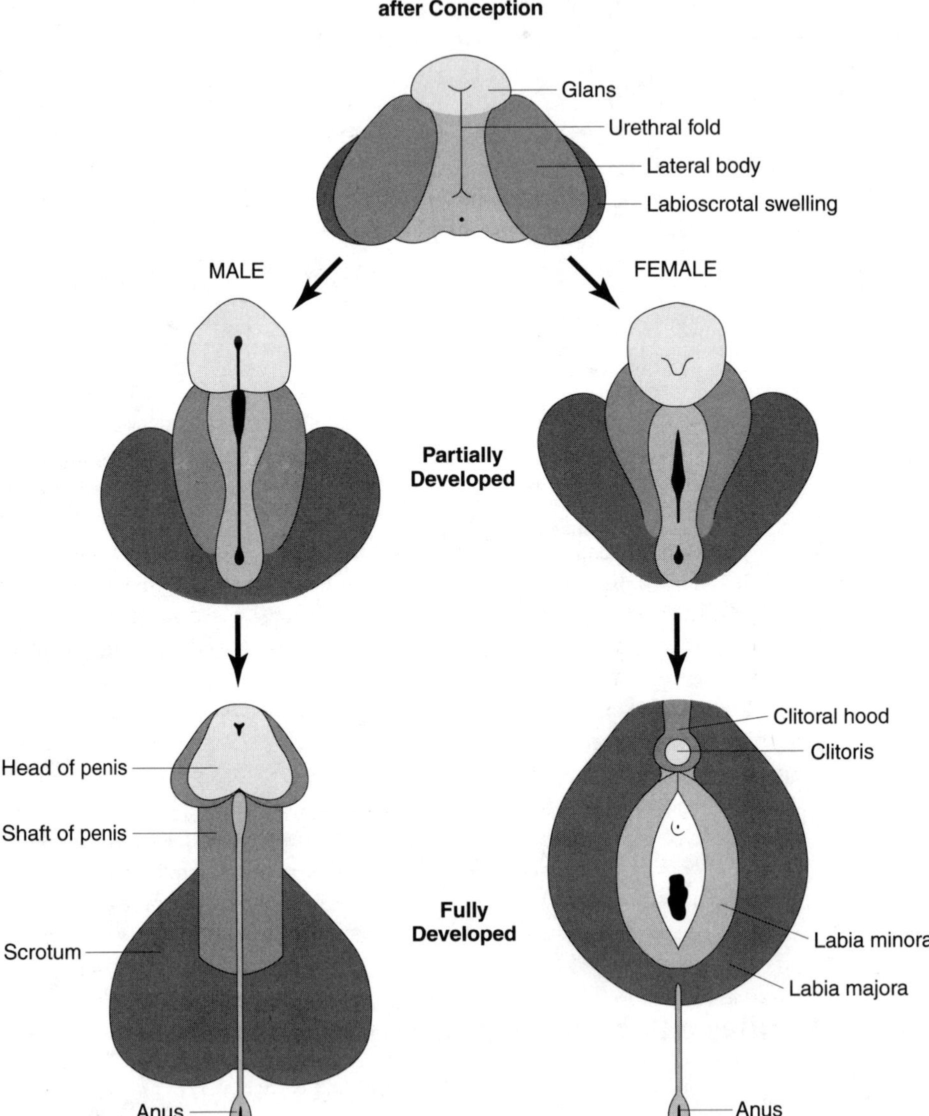

FIGURE 3.3 Development of Male and Female External Genitalia

SOURCE: From John P. J. Pinel, *Biopsychology* (2nd ed.). Copyright © 1993 by Allyn and Bacon. Reprinted by permission.

Another caution is related to interpretations for sex and gender differences in understanding hormonal versus social factors. The tendency exists to see a one-way chain of causality in which genetic and hormonal influences produce physiology, which in turn, produces behavior. As S. Marc Breedlove (1994) pointed out, this reasoning is false because it is impossible to separate biological from social influences and because the causality goes both ways. He contended that it is possible to concentrate on either biological or psychological measurements, but because biologists and psychologists are studying the same phenomena, any distinctions they make are illusory. In addition, social influences can affect behavior, which can alter the brain. For example, any change in the number, size, or connection of neurons in the structure of the brain constitutes a biological measurement, but such alterations will have psychological implications in terms of behavioral changes. Conversely, behavior can alter brain chemistry, which can alter brain structure, resulting in biological changes. Breedlove warned against confusing biological measures and biological influences, claiming that psychological and biological influences are impossible to separate.

Psychological and social influences are least likely to contribute to differences during prenatal development, when the uterine environment can produce changes to the developing fetus, but no social interactions occur. As soon as a child is born and labeled male or female, the social environment must be considered as a factor in brain development.

The organizing effects of hormones take place in human fetuses during critical periods within which the stimulation from these hormones results in structural and functional changes. In addition to the spinal nucleus of the bulbocavernosus, differences exist in the hypothalamus and possibly in other brain structures as well. (Chapter 4 explores these differences in more detail.)

What is not clear is whether these differences develop prenatally as a result of hormonal influences or whether they develop as a result of social forces. Some researchers (Reinisch, Rosenblum, Rubin, & Schulsinger, 1997) have argued that prenatal hormonal differences are the building blocks for gender differences that appear during childhood, adolescence, and adulthood, whereas others (Breedlove, 1994; Carli, 1997) have argued that the different treatment and expectations associated with being male or female, when ignored, leads to an invalid reliance on biological explanations. As Breedlove pointed out, few gender differences in the nervous system exist at birth in humans, and the social environment from infancy onward diverges on the basis of gender. Therefore, it is not possible to clearly attribute brain differences between women and men to hormonal influences.

Gonadal, hormonal, genital, and brain organization are not sufficient to produce sexually interested and sexually active people capable of reproduction. Such changes depend on the activating effects of hormones during puberty.

• *Changes during Puberty*

The levels of circulating hormones are low during infancy and childhood, but these levels increase during puberty, the onset of sexual maturity. The changes that occur during this period include not only fertility but also the characteristic adolescent growth spurt and the development of secondary sex characteristics. These characteristics include the differences between male and female bodies other than reproductive ones and appear in Figure 3.4. Both sexes experience the growth of body and pubic hair and the appearance of acne. Young men experience the growth of facial hair, larynx enlargement, hairline recession, and muscle development, whereas young women experience breast development, rounding of body contours, and menarche—the beginning of menstruation. All of these changes are prompted by changes in the release of hormones.

The adolescent growth spurt is the result of muscle and bone growth in response to increased release of growth hormone by the pituitary. Increased production of tropic hormones by the pituitary act on the adrenal glands and the gonads to increase their production of gonadal and adrenal hormones. As puberty begins, the pituitary starts to release two gonadotropic hormones into the bloodstream—**follicle-stimulating hormone (FSH)** and

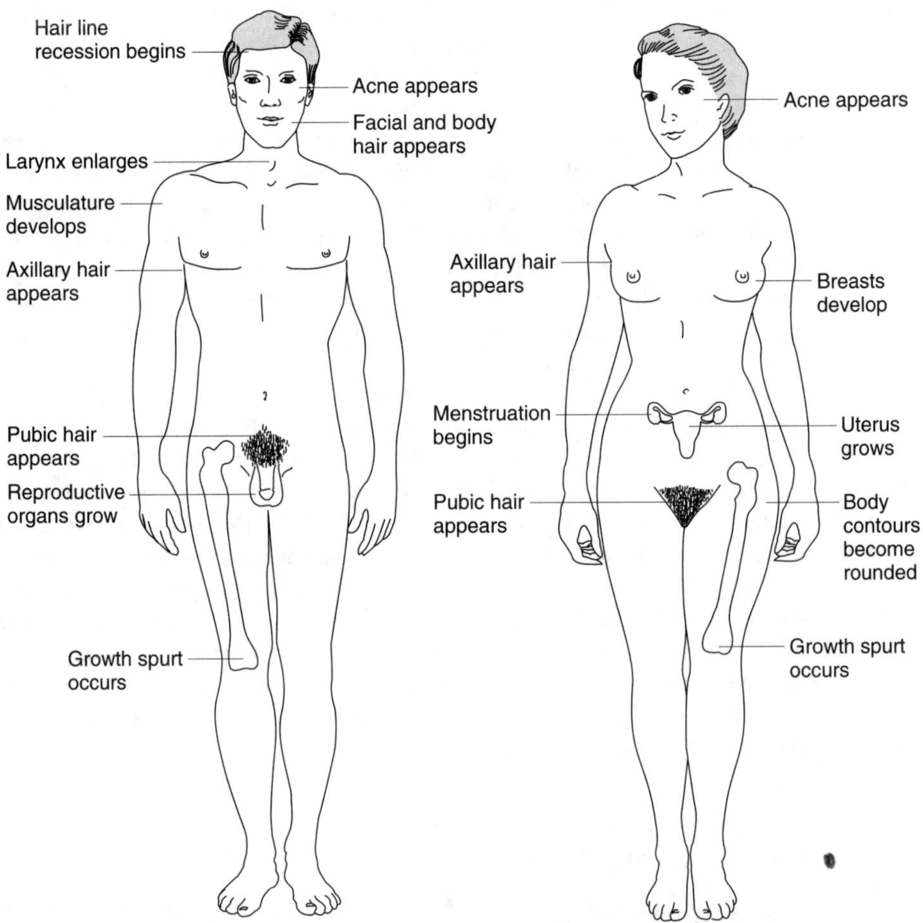

FIGURE 3.4 Changes Occurring in Males and Females during Puberty

SOURCE: From John P. J. Pinel, *Biopsychology* (2nd ed.). Copyright © 1993 by Allyn and Bacon. Reprinted by permission.

luteinizing hormone (LH). These hormones stimulate the gonads to increase their production of estrogens and androgens. Increased circulation of these gonadal hormones results in maturation of the genitals, that is, the development of fertility as well as the development of secondary sex characteristics.

In adolescent boys and adult men, the production of androgens is proportionately higher than their production of estrogens; in adolescent girls and in women, the production of estrogens is proportionately higher than their production of androgens. Again, it would be inaccurate to think of androgens as "male" hormones and estrogens as "female" hormones. An example of the influence of one hormone on both sexes comes from the growth of pubic and underarm hair: One of the androgens results in the growth of pubic and underarm hair in both boys and girls.

LH and FSH, the hormones that initiate puberty, are also important for reproduction. In girls and women, the production of these two hormones varies cyclically, whereas in boys and men, their production is not cyclic (but neither is it entirely steady). The cyclic variation of LH and FSH produces the menstrual cycle as it begins an increase in the production of luteinizing hormone-releasing factor and follicle-stimulating hormone-releasing factor by the hypothalamus. As with other releasing factors, these two cause the pituitary to produce LH and FSH. Follicle-stimulating hormone stimulates follicles, a group of cells within the ovaries, to mature an ovum. Luteinizing hormone causes the follicle to rupture and release the ovum, which begins to travel down the Fallopian tube toward the uterus. The remainder of the follicle starts to produce the hormone progesterone, which prepares the uterus to receive and implant the ovum, if it happens to be fertilized. Then all of these hormone levels begin to decline. If the ovum is fertilized, pregnancy will produce an increase in estradiol and progesterone, but if the ovum is not fertilized, the prepared lining of the uterus is shed in menstruation, and the cycle starts again.

In boys puberty causes the maturation of internal and external genitalia, including growth of the penis, seminal vesicles, and prostate. The maturation of seminal vesicles and prostate is necessary for ejaculation of seminal fluid, and sperm production is necessary for fertility. Follicle-stimulating hormone and luteinizing hormone are involved in the production and maturation of sperm. FSH is involved in the production of sperm, and LH contributes to the maturation of sperm, but its main function is to stimulate the production of testosterone. Testosterone is controlled by feedback to the hypothalamus that can inhibit or prompt the production of LH and FSH, which can affect the production of sperm.

The role of hormones is essential in the regulation of fertility, and the role of hormones for sexual activity is very clear in some animals. In rats, for example, the cyclic production of hormones by the females relates to sexual receptivity or level of interest in sexual activity. Female rats are receptive during the time in their cycle that they are fertile, and male rats respond to that receptivity. Hormone levels are also important for the development and maintenance of sexual interest. Rats that have their gonads removed before puberty fail to develop any interest in sexual activity. If their gonads are removed after puberty, their sexual interest fades. In humans, the relationship between hormonal levels and sexual interest is less clear-cut, but some activating effects exist for hormones on sexual interest.

Individuals who do not undergo puberty generally fail to develop much interest in sexual activity (Meyer-Bahlburg, 1980), so hormones seem to be important in the development of sexual interest in humans as well as in other animals. However, the relationship is far from simple, with puberty necessary but not sufficient for development of sexual interest. No single measure of sexual interest or activity correlates very well with the onset of increased hormone levels in humans during puberty, but conditions that prevent this increase seem to result in a failure to develop sexual interest and activity.

The story is even more complex concerning the maintenance of sexual activity in humans who experience a decline of hormone levels. Such declines can occur for a number of reasons, including removal of the gonads or decreased hormone production associated with aging. For men, removal of the testes tends to produce a decrease in sexual activity, but the extent and rate of decrease varies enormously from person to person. Some men experience the significant and rapid loss of either ability to get erections, ability to ejaculate, or both, whereas other men experience a slowly decreasing interest in sexual activity, followed by difficulty in ejaculating, and then by loss of ability to achieve erections. Few men remain unaffected by loss of androgens, though replacement testosterone can reverse the decline in sexual interest and possibly in sexual performance. Testosterone replacement therapy has increased with the creation of the testosterone patch, but its cost and availability only by prescription has limited the widespread use of this treatment (Cowley, 1996).

On the other hand, women's sexual interest seems less affected by the removal of ovaries. Indeed, some women report increased sexual motivation after such surgery. One possibility is that the hormones that are important for the maintenance of sexual interest in women are androgens, so a decrease in estrogen is not critical. Adrenal androgens may be sufficient to maintain sexual interest. Another possibility is that humans are so little controlled by their hormones that drastic physical changes in sexually mature adults are mediated by experience and expectation. Additionally, some combination of hormones and expectancy may account for the variations of sexual motivation in men and women without gonadal hormones.

In summary, luteinizing hormone and follicle-stimulating hormone produce the changes in reproductive and secondary sex characteristics associated with puberty. In girls, these changes produce cyclic variations in hormone levels that are associated with the maturation and release of an ovum approximately every month. If this ovum is fertilized by a sperm, the fertilized ovum will implant in the uterus and pregnancy will occur. If no fertilization occurs, the lining of the uterus is shed in menstruation, and the process will reoccur. In boys, the changes during puberty produce growth of the penis and maturation of the internal reproductive system, which will allow them to produce and ejaculate sperm. In addition to the physical changes associated with boys' bodies and reproductive systems, raised levels of gonadal hormones seem to be related to the development of sexual interest. Individuals who do not undergo puberty do not develop motivation to participate in sexual activity. Also, the maintenance of sexual interest in humans is not directly related to the levels of hormones but instead depends on experience and expectancy.

When Things Go Wrong

A number of events relating to the development of the reproductive system can, but usually do not, go wrong during prenatal development. These mistakes can originate even before conception, with the formation of the mother's ovum or the father's sperm. Yet other problems arise when the prenatal hormones are not consistent with the genetic configuration of the developing fetus.

Abnormalities sometimes occur in the assortment of chromosomes carried by the sperm and ova. Instead of the normal 23, sometimes chromosomes are missing or extra chromosomes appear. Several types of chromosomal abnormalities have direct effects on the development of the internal reproductive system, the external genitalia, or both. Beginning with the single cell consisting of fertilized ovum, males differ from females in their chromosomes, but the presence of the normal sex chromosome pattern does not guarantee the development of a normal boy or girl.

Abnormalities in Number of Chromosomes

Turner's syndrome (sometimes identified without the possessive as *Turner syndrome*) occurs when the fertilized ovum has only one chromosome of pair 23—that is, one X. This syndrome is usually described as X0, where the 0, a zero, stands for the missing chromosome. Although many embryos with this chromosomal configuration spontaneously abort (Mittwoch, 1973), some do not. Less than 1 in 10,000 individuals are born with this abnormality. Individuals with Turner's syndrome appear to be female at birth, because their external genitals develop according to the female pattern. However, the internal reproductive organs do not develop normally. Their prenatal development begins normally, but their Müllerian systems degenerate and do not continue to develop, producing individuals with no functioning ovaries. At birth they are identified as girls because of the appearance of their external genitalia, but without ovaries, they produce no estrogens, so they do not undergo puberty or produce ova. They will not experience puberty without hormone supplementation and are not fertile, even with hormone supplements.

Another mistake in chromosome number is the presence of an extra X chromosome—the XXX pattern. Extra chromosomal material typically produces problems in development, often in intelligence. Individuals with the XXX pattern develop prenatally as female, but their development may not be entirely normal. Women with the XXX pattern may be either retarded or of normal intelligence. They may have menstrual irregularities or amenorrhea (absence of menstrual periods) that results in sterility (Mittwoch, 1973), but they may not. It is possible for women with this chromosomal pattern to have children. Individuals with the XXXX pattern and XXXXX pattern have also been identified. These individuals tend to have more severe developmental problems and are very likely to be seriously developmentally disabled as well as sterile.

Klinefelter's syndrome is the most common of the sex chromosome abnormalities; these individuals have an XXY pattern. This problem occurs in 2 cases per 1,000 male births (Mittwoch, 1973). Individuals with Klinefelter's syndrome have male internal and external genitalia, but their testes are small and cannot produce sperm, resulting in sterility. They may also develop breasts and a feminized body shape during puberty. Like other people with extra chromosomal material, individuals with Klinefelter's syndrome have an increased chance of mental retardation. Other configurations of chromosomes are similar to Klinefelter's syndrome, including XXXY and XXXXY. These individuals typically have more severe deformities of the reproductive and skeletal systems as well as a higher probability of severe mental retardation.

The XYY chromosome pattern has been the subject of a great deal of publicity. In the early 1960s, articles appeared linking the XYY gene pattern to "aggressive tendencies" and "criminality" (Hubbard & Wald, 1993). These studies were based on the estimate of this gene pattern among men in the general population compared to men in prison, who were more likely to have the XYY pattern than the estimates for men from the general population.

These sensational reports, however, were largely unfounded. When measurements were taken from the general population, the results showed that the large majority of XYY men were not aggressive or criminal. Individuals with the XYY pattern of chromosomes are men who tend to be very tall, and some research (Witkin et al., 1976) indicated that these men were more likely than normal men to be in prison. This further examination of XYY men in prison failed to confirm the notion that these individuals are more violent than other criminals.

Indeed, the XYY inmates were no more likely to be imprisoned for violent crimes than other inmates, although they were significantly taller than other men. XYY individuals are also more likely than other men to be mildly retarded, which studies have shown to be linked with having extra chromosomal material. Thus, their height and their lower intelligence, or a combination of the two, may be the reason why a disproportionate number of XYY men are in prison: They are not very adept criminals, and witnesses may find a very tall man easy to identify, making their apprehension more likely than other offenders.

In summary, missing or extra sex chromosomes often affect the development of the sexual organs but more often affect other areas of development, especially intelligence. Although some individuals with missing or extra chromosomal material have normal intelligence, there is a tendency for these people to be mildly to severely retarded. Both missing chromosomes (Turner's syndrome) and extra chromosomes (Klinefelter's syndrome) cause sterility, but individuals with the XXX pattern and the XYY pattern may behave sexually and socially as women or men, respectively.

Abnormalities in Prenatal Hormones

The presence of the XY chromosome pattern is not essential for the development of either internal or external genitalia of males; the hormone testosterone is the key to these developments. Therefore, a fetus that is genetically female (XX pattern) can be masculinized by the addition of testosterone during the critical period of the third and fourth months of prenatal development. Normally, female fetuses would not produce testosterone during this critical period of developing the genitalia, but prenatal exposure to androgens can occur, either through the action of tumors in the adrenal gland or through the pregnant woman's inadvertent or intentional exposure to androgens.

The **adrenogenital syndrome** occurs when the adrenal gland decreases its production of the hormone cortisol, which produces an increase in production of adrenal androgens. For a male fetus or for a boy, increased androgen production is not a very serious problem, except that it accelerates the onset of puberty. For a developing female fetus, however, the presence of excessive androgens produces masculinization of the external genitalia. Although their internal genitals are usually normal because the excess androgens are produced too late to affect this stage of development, these girls are born with a clitoris that may look very much like a penis. If their genitals appear abnormal at birth, their parents and physicians often recommend surgical correction to produce a more normal female appearance. These girls usually receive oral doses of cortisol, which reduces the levels of circulating androgens and allows them normal physical development.

These girls have also been of interest because their brains were exposed to androgens prenatally, leading researchers to study their behavior and sexual orientation. The early medical and parental attention focused on their genitals makes these girls different from others, so any differences may be attributable to sociocultural factors rather than hormone exposure. However, adrenogenital syndrome is associated with play activities more typical of boys than girls; that is, these girls are more likely to be "tomboys" (Berenbaum & Snyder, 1995). As adults, most are heterosexual, but bisexuality is somewhat more common among these women than among women with no prenatal androgen exposure (Ehrhardt & Meyer-Bahlburg, 1981).

A more serious problem is **androgen insensitivity syndrome.** This disorder occurs in normal XY male fetuses whose body cells are insensitive to androgens; that is, the androgens produced by their fetal testes will not induce masculinization because the androgen receptors in their bodies do not function normally. These fetuses will develop as though no androgens were present, and at birth the XY fetus will appear to be a girl. The internal genitalia are not female, however, because the production of Müllerian-inhibiting substance proceeded to cause the normal degeneration of the Müllerian system. Thus, these individuals do not have the internal genitalia of either males or females but their external genitalia appear female.

Individuals with androgen insensitivity syndrome (and their families) can be completely unaware of the disorder until they reach the age at which puberty should occur. Complicating the diagnosis further, their testes produce sufficient estrogen to prompt breast development, increasing their feminine appearance. As they have no ovaries, Fallopian tubes, or uterus, they will not reach **menarche,** the beginning of menstruation. Nor will they grow pubic hair, a characteristic under the control of the androgens, to which they are insensitive. No amount of added androgens will reverse this problem, because their body cells are insensitive to it. Indeed, their levels of circulating androgens are within the normal range for men, but their bodies cannot respond to these hormones.

Individuals with androgen insensitivity syndrome are identified as girls at birth, raised as girls, and have no reason to doubt their gender identification for years. At puberty they grow breasts and begin to look like young women, giving them no reason to imagine they are anything but women. Typically, few suspicions arise concerning any abnormality until they fail to grow pubic hair and fail to reach menarche. Even then these symptoms may be discounted for several years due to the variability of sexual development.

When gynecological examination reveals the abnormality of their internal genitalia, these individuals and their families learn that they are, in some sense, men. This information contradicts years of gender role development, and these individuals often have a difficult adjustment to their new status. No treatments exist to masculinize these individuals, so no attempt is made to change their gender identification. Individuals with androgen insensitivity syndrome continue in the female gender role, and most seek sexual relationships with men. Although they cannot have children, surgical alteration can lengthen their vagina so that they can have sexual intercourse. Despite their male chromosomes, these individuals are women in terms of gender identification, physical appearance, and behavior.

Through a variety of mechanisms, a person can be born with characteristics of both sexes. The traditional diagnosis for these individuals is **hermaphroditism,** but a more modern term is **intersexuality,** and both terms continue in use. True hermaphroditism is extremely rare, with no more than 60 cases being identified in Europe and North America within the last century (Money, 1986). Hermaphroditism occurs when an individual has both ovarian and testicular tissue—either an ovary on one side of the body and a testicle on the other side, or both types of tissue combined into a structure called an ovotestis. However, pseudohermaphroditism—in which individuals have some of the structures of both sexes—occurs much more frequently. Those with adrenogenital syndrome would be considered pseudohermaphrodites, as would those with androgen insensitivity syndrome.

A provocative example of pseudohermaphroditism comes from individuals with a genetic enzyme deficiency that prevents chromosomal males from developing male external genitalia during the prenatal period. Like individuals with androgen insensitivity syndrome, these babies appear more female than male at birth and are often identified as girls. The appearance of their external genitals is ambiguous, neither truly female but definitely not male. Unlike people with androgen insensitivity syndrome, these individuals respond to androgens during puberty and develop masculine characteristics. That is, their voice deepens, their muscles develop, their testes descend into the scrotum, and they grow a penis (Herdt, 1990). If these children had been identified as girls, they no longer fit into that category.

However, these individuals do not clearly fit into either the category of male or female. Despite an early report of the ease of their transition from female sex role to male sex role (Imperato-McGinley, Guerreo, Gautier, & Peterson, 1974), later research (Herdt, 1990; Rubin, Reinisch, & Haskett, 1981) has indicated that these individuals may never fit comfortably into either category. Whereas the majority of the pseudohermaphrodites in one study (Imperato-McGinley et al., 1974) were judged to have made at least fairly successful transitions to the male role, none of those in the later study (Rubin et al., 1981) did so. Indeed, the New Guinea culture (Herdt, 1981) acknowledged the existence of these individuals by devising a third category of sex to describe them. (See the Diversity Highlight: "A Culture with Three Sexes.")

Although hermaphrodites and pseudohermaphrodites have genitalia that are ambiguous, these people may identify themselves unambiguously as either male or female and, with hormones or surgery or both, lead lives that fit one pattern or the other. On the other hand, these individuals may not be able to clearly identify with one gender or the other, and they may not conform to the expectations associated with the male or female gender role.

These instances in which chromosomal, hormonal, gonadal, and genital sex are not consistent are not only fascinating cases but also provide tests of what factors are essential to sexual and gender development. These cases show that complete consistency is not necessary for personal gender identification: Individuals who are not chromosomally, hormonally, or reproductively normal may still have a clear personal gender identity. For example, individuals with Turner's syndrome are not female in their chromosomes, hormones, or internal reproductive organs, but they are identified by others and by themselves as female. Indeed, they are often stereotypically feminine, preferring to wear dresses rather than jeans and to play with dolls rather than other toys. They are female in their own opinion and in the opinion of society.

These possibilities for variations within development of the reproductive organs led gender researcher John Money (1986) to reject the dichotomy of sexual dimorphism and to accept the many criteria that determine sex, gender, gender identity, and sexual orientation.

Hormones and Behavior Instability

In addition to their role in sexual development and activity, hormones are widely considered to affect other behaviors. The concept of premenstrual syndrome has received wide public-

DIVERSITY HIGHLIGHT
A Culture with Three Sexes

Most people develop unambiguously according to the male pattern or the female pattern, and cultures have a word for each classification. Although English includes many words to describe variations in sexual interest and behavior, we have no word for people who do not fit one of the two patterns of sexual development. However, anthropologist Gilbert Herdt (1990) contended that some cultures do; that is, some cultures name a category for a third sex.

These cultures tend to have a factor in common—the relative frequency of the hereditary enzyme disorder that produces pseudohermaphroditism. This disorder is the result of a deficiency in the enzyme 5-α reductase, which prevents prenatal testosterone from producing a boy with normal external genitals. These individuals are chromosomally normal males with normal internal genitalia, but they are born with external genitals that more strongly resemble a girl's than a boy's—a clitoris-like penis, an unfused scrotum that resembles labia, and undescended testes. At birth these babies are sometimes identified as boys but are more often identified and reared as girls. At puberty they produce testosterone and become "masculinized": Their penis grows, their testes descend, they grow facial hair, and their musculature increases. That is, they change from individuals who look more like girls to ones who look more like boys.

This disorder is very rare but is more common in the Dominican Republic and New Guinea than in most other parts of the world. Herdt contended that these two cultures have a term for a third sex, one that is neither male nor female but that starts out as female and becomes male. Indeed, the literal translation of the word used by the Sambia of New Guinea, *kwolu-aatmwol,* is "male thing-transforming-into-female thing," but they also use a slang word "which refers to 'turning into a *man*' " (Herdt, 1990, p. 439).

In his evaluation of both cultures, Herdt concluded that individuals with this disorder fit into neither the male nor female category and that their cultures acknowledge and respond to these differences. Acknowledgment is not the same as acceptance, however, and neither culture accepts these individuals as normal. Even after they had developed masculine characteristics, the Sambia culture did not grant them full male status.

Herdt argued that the acknowledgment of some other possibility in addition to male and female allowed these individuals an opportunity that our culture does not—a third possibility. He wrote, "And these poor souls in turn were spared the dualistic ultimate dilemma of having to be what they were not; unambiguously male or female" (Herdt, 1990, p. 441).

ity, and estrogens and progestins may be involved in the mood and physical changes that have come to be known as premenstrual syndrome (PMS). Another of the possible influences of hormones is the effect of testosterone on aggression. If these hormonal effects occur, then hormones may be involved in some undesirable behaviors: "Raging hormones" might be one cause of unstable, problem behaviors in both men and women.

Premenstrual Syndrome

A pamphlet available in doctors' offices (Murray, 1995, p. 210) proclaimed, "Every month, millions of women unwillingly ride the emotional roller coaster knows as PMS. . . . Experts suggest 70 to 90 percent of all women undergo a similar crisis each month." These figures, however, may not be true. Both women and men use PMS to explain women's emotions. Nonetheless, diagnosis and treatments exist for the disorder of PMS.

As one of this chapter's headline articles (Murray, 1995) mentioned, recent, more careful research has suggested that the experience of PMS may be more closely associated with expectation than with hormones. That is, PMS may be a way of labeling some behavior rather than explaining the underlying cause of symptoms, and the concept's overuse has made it inaccurate as a diagnosis.

Recall that the cyclic variation of luteinizing hormone and follicle-stimulating hormone produces the menstrual cycle by affecting the release of estrogens and progesterone. In the middle of the cycle, the follicles produce larger amounts of one of the estrogens (estradiol) than during other times of the cycle, and this increase produces a surge of luteinizing hormone and follicle-stimulating hormone. This surge causes the release of the matured ovum, and the remainder of the follicle then starts to produce progesterone. Therefore, during the ovulatory phase of the cycle, estrogen levels are higher than progesterone levels. During the premenstrual phase of the cycle, both estradiol and progesterone are falling, and progesterone is at a higher level than estradiol. During the menstrual phase, the levels of both hormones are relatively low. Figure 3.5 shows the levels of hormones during the different phases of the cycle.

The notion that women's reproductive systems affect their lives is ancient (Fausto-Sterling, 1985), but the concept of the premenstrual syndrome can be traced only to the 1960s. During this time, Katharina Dalton published research (reviewed by Parlee, 1973) suggesting that women experience a wide variety of negative emotional, cognitive, and physical effects due to the hormonal changes that precede menstruation. These effects became known as a *syndrome,* although the list of symptoms extended to over 150, and some of the symptoms were mutually exclusive (such as *elevated mood* and *depression*).

The symptoms associated with the premenstrual phase of the cycle include headache; backache; abdominal bloating and discomfort; breast tenderness; tension or irritability; depression; increased analgesic, alcohol, or sedative use; decreased energy; and disruption in eating, sleeping, sexual behavior, work, and interpersonal relationships (Blechman, Clay, Kipke, & Bickel, 1988). The most common among these symptoms are tension and irritability.

All of the hormonal changes that occur during the menstrual cycle have been candidates for the underlying cause of premenstrual syndrome (Rubin, Reinisch, & Haskett, 1981). Several possibilities have been suggested, including an excess of estrogens, falling progesterone levels, and the ratio of estrogens to progesterone. However, research has failed to show that hormonal differences vary according to the experience of PMS (Rubin, Reinisch, & Haskett, 1981). This failure to tie hormonal changes to the experience of PMS is a major problem for the concept of PMS.

Other problems come from the changing pattern of research findings on PMS. Inconsistency is one problem (McFarlane, Martin, & Williams, 1988). Until the mid-1970s, researchers tended to find that mood is highest during the ovulatory phase of the cycle and lowest during the premenstrual and menstrual phases. Beginning in the late 1970s, researchers no longer found this pattern, which may have been because methodological problems existed with menstrual cycle research. Such problems include the bias that expectation can introduce into studies in which the participants know that the research is about the menstrual cycle, a reliance on participants' memories of symptoms, and the failure to use appropriate comparison groups. Indeed, later research indicated that most women do *not* report problems associated with menstrual mood fluctuations (McFarlane et al., 1988).

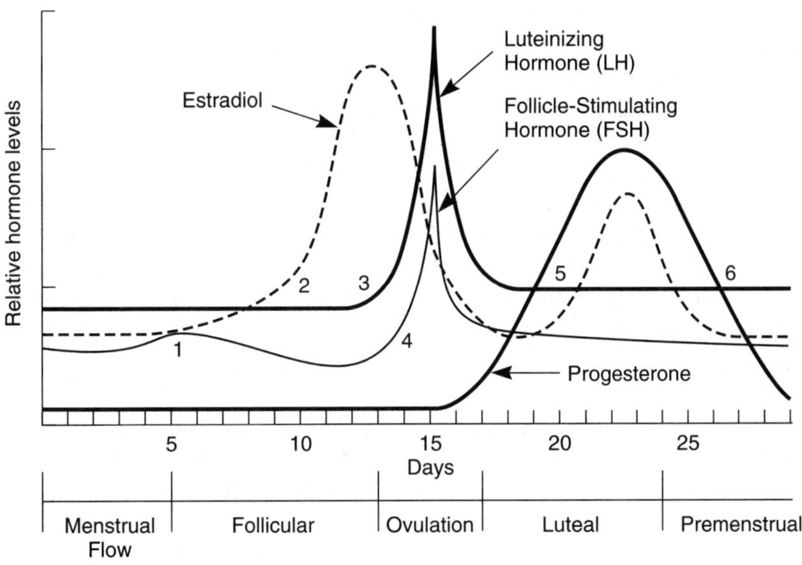

Phases of the human menstrual cycle

1. In response to an increase in FSH, small spheres of cells called ovarian follicles begin to grow around individual egg cells (ova).
2. The follicles begin to release estrogens such as estradiol.
3. The estrogens stimulate the hypothalamus to increase the release of LH and FSH from the anterior pituitary.
4. In response to the LH surge, one of the follicles ruptures and releases its ovum.
5. The ruptured follicle under the influence of LH develops into a corpus luteum (yellow body) and begins to release progesterone, which prepares the lining of the uterus for the implantation of a fertilized ovum.
6. Meanwhile, the ovum is moved into the Fallopian tube by the rowing action of ciliated cells. If the ovum is not fertilized, progesterone and estradiol levels fall and the walls of the uterus are sloughed off as menstrual flow and the cycle begins once again.

FIGURE 3.5 Hormones during the Menstrual Cycle

SOURCE: From John P. J. Pinel, *Biopsychology* (2nd ed.). Copyright © 1993 by Allyn and Bacon. Reprinted by permission.

Jessica McFarlane and her colleagues (McFarlane et al., 1988; McFarlane & Williams, 1994) have conducted two longitudinal studies that avoided the methodological problems from other studies. Both studies involved having women and men keep records of their daily moods without knowing that the menstrual cycle was the focus of the study. Both studies included women who were cycling normally, women who were taking oral contraceptives and thus not cycling normally, and men.

The main result of the study by McFarlane et al. (1988) was that no differences in mood stability appeared when comparing the young men and the young women who participated in the study. All participants experienced similar mood changes within a day as well as from day to day. Also, the men and women reported similar variability in mood during the 70 days of the study.

A second study (McFarlane & Williams, 1994) recruited participants who were older than the typical college student participants and lasted at least 12 weeks to cover more menstrual cycles. The analysis for this study included an evaluation of each participant's cyclic mood variation compared to the individual him- or herself. This study also revealed that people experienced cyclic mood variations but that these changes did not conform to the PMS pattern.

In comparing women who were cycling normally to women taking oral contraceptives and to the men, the women who were cycling normally reported *more pleasant moods* during and immediately after their periods than in the ovulatory or premenstrual periods (McFarlane et al., 1988). The male and female participants experienced cyclicity as the norm, but few reported emotional symptoms consistent with PMS (McFarlane & Williams, 1994). Neither of these studies found evidence to support the concept of PMS, but both studies showed that cyclic variations in mood occur for both men and women.

McFarlane et al. (1988) asked participants to fill out a questionnaire at the end of the study in which they had to recall their moods. They reasoned that if PMS is influenced by biases in memory, then the memory of moods might conform to PMS, whereas the daily reports would not. Their analysis supported that hypothesis: When the female participants remembered rather than recorded their moods, they reported symptoms of PMS that, according to their daily reports, they had not experienced. This finding strongly suggests that the mood changes associated with PMS may be a product of expectation and labeling rather than of hormones.

The studies also demonstrated the power of labeling. About half the women who met and about half who failed to meet diagnostic criteria consistent with PMS reported that they had it. That is, regardless of symptoms, some women will believe that they have PMS.

These studies have not been alone in questioning the existence of PMS. Another study also measured mood and physical symptoms without letting participants know the purpose of the study (Slade, 1984). No evidence appeared to show that negative emotional symptoms were associated with the premenstrual or menstrual phases of the cycle, but some evidence appeared for physical symptoms, such as premenstrual water retention and menstrual pain. Physical symptoms and the dread of menstruation may be the basis for premenstrual complaints rather than a premenstrual syndrome (Blechman et al., 1988).

Why do people believe in PMS? The syndrome is certainly well accepted and even medically treated (Tavris, 1992; Murray, 1995), yet the research that has supported the concept seems flawed. Better research has failed to either find a hormonal explanation for PMS or to demonstrate the variety of mood and behavioral symptoms associated with it. A possible explanation comes from the willingness of both women and men to attribute moody behavior to PMS (Koeske & Koeske, 1975). That is, when furnished with information about a woman's cycle, both men and women tended to use this information to partly explain the woman's emotional behavior. The more irrational the behavior, the more willing the participants were to attribute it to PMS. As Murray's (1995) headline story suggested, women who experience problems, stresses, and irritations to which they respond emotionally may explain their reactions by their phase of the menstrual cycle. If they believe that these symptoms are associated with the premenstrual period as well as menstruation, they can apply this explanation about half the time—the week before and the week during menstruation. When they experience the same situations and reactions at other phases of their cycle, they seek other explanations. In this way, premenstrual syndrome can become a self-perpetuating myth for the women who react to problems, stresses, and irritations in their lives as well as for the people who observe the reactions.

Murray (1995) suggested that many women's "PMS" may be other problems that women (and those around them) label and accept as PMS. Unhappy marriages, poor working environments, and depression can produce symptoms on the list for PMS. For example, Jamie, one of the cases in Murray's story, was actually depressed. Her symptoms increased in severity, and she sought treatment for depression. As her treatment for depression became effective, her supposed "PMS" disappeared.

In summary, PMS has received wide publicity and wide acceptance, but much of the research supporting this concept suffers from flaws in methodology. The results from more careful studies have indicated that premenstrual syndrome is difficult to define on a biological level and does not appear as emotional symptoms except as a function of expectation. The moods of both women and men vary cyclically, but not according to the pattern consistent with PMS.

Testosterone and Aggression

The article "Aggression in Men: Hormone Levels Are a Key" (Goleman, 1990) included a summary of several research projects about testosterone and men's behavior. As the title suggests, these research projects all investigated the role of the hormone testosterone in various types of aggression. Testosterone activates fighting behavior among males of many mammalian nonprimate species (Pinel, 1997), but its effects on primates (including humans) are less clear. In the various research reports summarized in this article, investigators used different approaches to study the actions of testosterone on various behaviors and the reaction of testosterone levels to various experiences. All of the studies found some relationship between testosterone and behavior, but the relationships were very complex. Research on human subjects does not confirm a clear cause-and-effect relationship between hormone levels and aggressive behaviors.

One study (Booth, Shelley, Mazur, Tharp, & Kittok, 1989) examined the relationship between testosterone level and winning versus losing in athletic competition. Participants were the six members of the University of Nebraska varsity tennis team who agreed to provide saliva samples throughout the season so that the researchers could analyze testosterone levels. These players were measured four times in relation to each of the season's six matches—the day before a match, about 15 minutes before each match, immediately after they had finished playing, and one or two days after each match. The researchers predicted that winning players would experience increased testosterone levels compared to losing players. The carryover effects of winning on testosterone level were also a topic of the study.

This study was a test of a biosocial theory of status (Mazur, 1985). Testosterone level is part of a feedback loop in which testosterone and assertiveness are interrelated. When an individual's testosterone level rises, that person is more willing to compete in contests for higher status. Winning such competitions produces a rise in testosterone or helps to maintain a high level of testosterone, which will sustain the willingness to compete. Conversely, losing produces a drop in testosterone, which deters the willingness to compete. Thus, "losing streaks" and "winning streaks" in competitions are sustained by the feedback loop's relationship with testosterone level. This theory also holds that testosterone level and behavior influence each other rather than a unidirectional cause-and-effect relationship between the hormone level and behavior.

In the study with tennis players (Booth et al., 1989), the researchers compared the changes in testosterone level before and after matches. They expected winners to have higher testosterone levels than losers, but their findings were more complex. Players showed increases of testosterone on days when they played, but their hormone levels were highest before the game. Winners showed rises in testosterone across the matches and losers showed declines, but no significant differences appeared in the average levels of testosterone when comparing winners and losers before and after the matches.

The tennis players also rated their feelings about their overall performance. The players who felt positively about their performance tended to have higher testosterone levels. Therefore, winning and losing did not appear to be simply related to testosterone levels, but rather, some emotional or mood factors might have mediated the hormonal effects. That is, winning might produce positive moods that in turn might heighten testosterone levels. This research was consistent with the biosocial theory (Mazur, 1985), because the findings demonstrated that testosterone levels affected and were affected by competition. Rather, the study suggested that the effects of testosterone on performance and responses of players to high levels of testosterone follow complex rather than simple patterns related to competition.

According to research by James Dabbs and his colleagues, hormone levels play a role in aggression in men and in women. One of these studies (Dabbs, de la Rue, & Williams, 1990) investigated differences in testosterone levels for men in various occupations, including physicians, football players, salesmen, actors, ministers, professors, and firemen as well as unemployed men. Although their analysis showed a significant difference among the different occupations, an additional analysis revealed the greatest difference for the actors and football players, who had higher testosterone levels than the ministers. This finding puzzled Dabbs and his colleagues. They had reasoned that salesmen might be high in testosterone due to their need for assertiveness, firemen due to their sensation seeking, and physicians due to their status, but none of these differences appeared.

Nor could these researchers immediately understand what actors and football players have in common (and how they differ from ministers) that would produce elevated testosterone. Two additional studies (Dabbs et al., 1990) confirmed the differences between actors and ministers and explored possible reasons for this difference in testosterone levels that might relate to personality differences. Despite the similarities between preaching and performing, the factors of competition and antisocial tendencies might differentiate the two groups. Ministers' lives have little competition compared to actors' lives; actors experience a constant need to seek employment and win roles. As for antisocial tendencies, Dabbs and his colleagues reasoned that ministers and actors differed in selfishness. They noted that "ministers tend to be self-effacing and actors self-aggrandizing. Ministers praise the glory of God, whereas actors keep the glory for themselves" (Dabbs et al., 1990, p. 1264).

Research on the relationship between testosterone level and occupational achievement (Dabbs, 1992) showed that men with higher levels of testosterone have lower-status occupations. He interpreted this finding to indicate that high testosterone levels are related to antisocial behavior, and such behavior makes success in white-collar occupations less likely. An additional study (Heusel & Dabbs, 1996) confirmed that engineers with high testosterone levels were more likely to quit or be fired than engineers with lower testosterone levels working in the same company.

The interpretation that antisocial tendencies are positively related to testosterone level is consistent with other research by Dabbs and his colleagues. For example, little relationship appeared between testosterone and personality in the college students, but veterans showed a positive relationship between testosterone level and drug and alcohol abuse, antisocial behavior, and affective disorders (Dabbs, Hopper, & Jurkovic, 1990). Among U.S. military veterans, high testosterone levels were related to problem behaviors (Dabbs & Morris, 1990). Men whose testosterone levels fell within the upper 10% of testosterone had a history of trouble with parents, teachers, and classmates as well as a history of drug use and more instances of going AWOL while in the military.

A comparison of college students and young men who were delinquents showed higher testosterone levels in the delinquents (Banks & Dabbs, 1996). An assessment of the testosterone levels in two college fraternities showed that men in the "rowdy" fraternity had higher testosterone levels than the men in the fraternity with a reputation for academic success and social responsibility (Dabbs, Hargrove, & Heusel, 1996). These behaviors can cause problems, but they are not necessarily examples of aggression or violence.

A more specific example of the relationship between testosterone and violence appeared in a study of male prisoners (Dabbs, Carr, Frady, & Riad, 1995). Those prisoners who had committed crimes against individuals that involved sex and violence had higher testosterone levels than prisoners who had committed property crimes. The prisoners with higher levels of testosterone also were more likely to be involved with rule violations and personal confrontations while in prison.

Testosterone levels in men seem to be related to a greater variety of behavior problems, but this pattern is not consistent across all socioeconomic groups. (See the Diversity Highlight "Socioeconomic Status, Testosterone, and Antisocial Behavior.") Table 3.1 summarizes the findings from research by Dabbs and his colleagues.

In addition, the size of the group allowed the researchers to find significant differences when these differences were of a small magnitude. That is, with so many participants, even very small differences will be statistically significant, but as Chapter 2 emphasized, such differences may not be of much practical significance. Although the differences were not due to chance, neither would these differences allow precise predictions about antisocial behavior according to testosterone level.

The various research projects attempting to relate testosterone levels to personality factors, such as aggression and competition, in men have been partly successful. Competition seems to be related to elevations in testosterone levels but not in any simple way. Dabbs and his colleagues have found a relationship between high testosterone levels and a variety of antisocial behaviors, but the relationship is complicated by the factor of socioeconomic

DIVERSITY HIGHLIGHT

Socioeconomic Status, Testosterone, and Antisocial Behavior

James Dabbs and Robin Morris (1990) looked at the role of testosterone level and socioeconomic status (SES) in antisocial behavior, hypothesizing that SES might interact with hormone levels to produce different behaviors in men from different social classes. They found that men who were both high in education and in income were significantly less likely to be high in testosterone than men who were low in both education and income. For the men with low SES, high testosterone levels heightened their risks for problem behavior, including adult delinquency and drug use. Socioeconomic status seemed to play a role in the negative consequences of high testosterone: Men with high SES and with high testosterone experienced fewer negative consequences than men with low SES and with high testosterone. Dabbs and Morris interpreted this finding as evidence that men high in testosterone who are high in both education and income have learned to cope with their antisocial tendencies so as to avoid physical confrontation and to conform to the educational system. Thus, their behavior differs from men with lower SES and with high levels of testosterone who get into more trouble. An alternative possibility is that men who are wealthy and well educated might not get in as much trouble for the same antisocial behaviors as men who are poor and less educated.

Dabbs, Ruback, Frady, Hopper, and Sgoutas (1988) also studied the relationship between testosterone level and antisocial behavior in women by measuring the testosterone levels of inmates in a women's prison and contrasting them with testosterone levels of female college students. Within the prison group, they found some indication that testosterone levels related to violence: Women with the highest levels of testosterone had the highest incidence of unprovoked violence. They found that testosterone levels differed among inmates convicted of unprovoked violence, defensive violence, theft, drugs, and other crimes. The inmates who had committed acts of unprovoked violence had the highest testosterone levels. For these female inmates, testosterone was related to the number of prior charges and to prior parole board decisions about length of time they should serve before being granted parole. Women who had committed violence in protecting themselves, such as those who had murdered an abusive spouse, had the lowest levels of testosterone in the prison group.

Interestingly, the mean levels of testosterone were similar for the inmates and the college students, and both averages fell within the normal range for women. These results provide some support for the notion that testosterone is related to aggression, as the inmates who had committed the most violent crimes—those involving unprovoked violence—also had the highest testosterone levels. However, the failure to find differences between women convicted of crimes and female students indicates that aggression and violence are influenced by factors other than testosterone level, including socioeconomic status, which Dabbs and his colleagues found moderated the relationship of testosterone and problem behavior in men.

class. In addition, the high testosterone levels in these men might be the product of their aggressive behavior rather than the cause of it.

Women also produce testosterone, and some researchers have studied the relationship between this hormone and women's behavior. Two of these studies have been analogous to the studies done with men: One has measured the relationship of testosterone to occupations, and the other has related testosterone to antisocial behavior in women. The Diversity Highlight: "Socioeconomic Status, Testosterone, and Antisocial Behavior" discusses one study showing a relationship between testosterone and criminal behavior in women.

TABLE 3.1 Relationship of Testosterone to Various Behaviors in Men and Women

Associated with Higher Testosterone Levels	
In Men	In Women
Occupations of actor and football player	Professional, managerial, or technical occupations
Lower status occupations	Unprovoked violence among prisoners
Job loss	
Drug and alcohol abuse, antisocial behavior, and affective disorders among veterans	
Trouble getting along with parents, teachers, and classmates among veterans	
Delinquent behaviors while young	
Membership in a "rowdy" fraternity	
Incarceration for crimes involving sex or violence	
Rule violations and personal confrontations among prisoners	
Not Associated with Higher Testosterone Levels	
In Men	In Women
Occupations of salesmen, firemen, professors, physicians, or the unemployed	Violent criminal acts
Personality traits among students	Prisoner versus student
	"Butch" role in lesbian relationships

Other studies have explored the relationship between testosterone and other behaviors in women. Women's levels of androgens show some variation according to occupation (Purifoy & Koopmans, 1979). The mean levels of testosterone were significantly higher in women with professional, technical, or managerial jobs compared to women who had clerical jobs or who were housewives. This study did not demonstrate that high testosterone levels cause women to pursue certain occupations. The possibility exists that levels of androgens might influence career choice and also that career stresses might influence androgen level.

The role of androgens in gender role behavior in couples has also been studied (Pearcey, Docherty, & Dabbs, 1996). This study focused on lesbian couples, investigating the relationship of testosterone levels with the "butch" and "femme" roles. Rather than finding that "butch" lesbians were higher in testosterone than "femme" lesbians, the results showed that lesbian couples were similar to each other in testosterone levels.

The influence of androgens on behavior turns out to be complex, bidirectional, and influenced by a multitude of factors. Rather than testosterone producing aggression, the role of the hormone in influencing behavior is less straightforward. There is some evidence that men *and* women with high testosterone levels are more likely to commit violent crimes than people whose testosterone levels are lower. But socioeconomic status is a moderating factor in men, and possibly research will demonstrate this relationship in women. People with high testosterone levels are also more likely to commit crimes that do not include violence and to exhibit antisocial but legal behaviors, such as heavy drinking. Conceptualizing all of these behaviors as aggression would be inaccurate. Furthermore, behavior can influence hormone levels as well as being influenced by hormone levels, a situation that may account for some of the differences Dabbs and his colleagues have found.

This chapter's headline story (Goleman, 1990) cited provocative evidence concerning the effects of hormones on aggression. But the story also noted that "scientists emphasize that the effects of hormones on human behavior are small relative to social and psychological factors, showing up most clearly in studies of large numbers of people" (1990, p. C 1). Therefore, hormone levels probably play a relatively small role in aggression in humans. Testosterone is not the factor that accounts for the violence that is associated with men's behavior.

Summary

Several steroid hormones are important to sexual development and behavior, including the androgens, the estrogens, and the progestins. All normal individuals produce all of these hormones, but women produce proportionately more estrogens and progestins, whereas men produce more androgens. The prenatal production of these hormones affects the brains of fetuses to organize along the male or the female pattern. During puberty these hormones activate the internal genitalia to develop fertility and prompt the development of secondary sex characteristics, such as beards for men and breasts for women.

The role of hormones in the activation and maintenance of sexual interest and activity is less clear in humans than in other species, but humans who do not experience the pubertal surge of hormones tend not to develop much interest in sex. Testosterone, one of the androgens, plays a role in maintaining sexual activity in men and possibly in women as well.

There are five stages of sexual development—genetic, gonadal, hormonal, internal genitalia, and external genitalia—all of which usually proceed according to either the male or female pattern. The first stage in sexual development is genetic, the inheritance of either XX or XY chromosomes of pair 23. Although the inheritance of chromosomes is the beginning of the pattern, embryos are not sexually dimorphic until around six weeks into gestation. Those with the XY pattern start to produce androgens and Müllerian-inhibiting substance during the third month of gestation. These hormones masculinize the fetus, prompting not only the further development of the testes but also degeneration of the Müllerian structures and development of the Wolffian structures that form the other internal genitalia. Shortly thereafter, external genitalia develop, and this development also depends on androgens.

The female pattern is not as dependent on the presence of estrogens as the male pattern is on androgens, but some estrogen is necessary for the development of normal ovaries, other internal genitalia, and external genitalia. During the third month of pregnancy, those individuals with the XX pattern of chromosomes start to develop the Müllerian structures, which become the ovaries, Fallopian tubes, uterus, and upper vagina. In addition, their Wolffian structures start to degenerate. An absence of all steroid hormones will allow the feminization of external genitalia, but some estrogens are necessary for normal development of internal and external genitalia.

Things can go wrong at any stage, beginning with the inheritance of the chromosomes that determine sex, the X and Y chromosomes. A number of disorders exist that create individuals with too few or too many sex chromosomes, and some of these configurations produce problems with the development of internal or external genitalia. In addition, several of these disorders produce individuals with developmental disorders, especially lowered intelligence. Individuals with Turner's syndrome (X0) appear to be female but lack ovaries; individuals with Klinefelter's syndrome (XXY) appear to be male, often with feminized body contours, but have nonfunctional testes; XXX individuals are female and may be otherwise normal; XYY individuals are tall males who may be reproductively normal but are often mentally retarded.

Even normal chromosomes do not guarantee normal development in subsequent stages, and several types of hermaphroditism and pseudohermaphroditism exist. These cases of individuals with physiology of both males and females suggest the inadequacy of two categories of sex and provide examples of the complexities of sexual development.

The headlines have contained stories that indicate a role for hormones in two areas of problem behavior—premenstrual syndrome (PMS) and aggression. Careful research has indicated that the premenstrual phase of the cycle may include some physical symptoms, but it also suggests that expectation, not hormones, is the major cause of the emotional symptoms associated with PMS. Both women and men may attribute behavioral symptoms to PMS when those symptoms may indicate other problems.

Research on the role of testosterone in aggression has revealed that the relationship is not a simple cause-and-effect one. Testosterone has an influence on and is influenced by competition in complex ways. Men in different occupations differ in their testosterone levels, with actors having higher levels than ministers. Men with higher than average testosterone levels tend to engage in a wide variety of antisocial behaviors that include (but are not restricted to) violence. The complex interaction of testosterone and competition also extends to women, whose testosterone levels vary according to several occupations. For women as well as for men, testosterone levels differ for people who have committed violent crimes, with higher testosterone levels found in the criminally violent. However, testosterone is not a very accurate predictor of criminal violence, as both male and female inmates do not differ in testosterone levels from male and female college students. Such findings highlight the inadequacy of testosterone level alone as an index of aggression.

Glossary

adrenogenital syndrome a disorder that results in masculinization, producing premature puberty in boys and masculinization of the external genitalia in girls.

androgen insensitivity syndrome a disorder in which body cells are unable to respond to androgens, resulting in the feminization of chromosomal males.

androgens a class of hormones that includes testosterone and other steroid hormones. Men typically produce a greater proportion of androgens than estrogens.

endocrine glands glands that secrete hormones into the circulatory system.

estradiol the most common of the estrogen hormones.

estrogens a class of hormones that includes estradiol and other steroid hormones. Women typically produce a greater proportion of estrogens than androgens.

external genitalia the reproductive structures that can be seen without internal examination: clitoris, labia, and vaginal opening in women and penis and scrotum in men.

follicle-stimulating hormone (FSH) the gonadotropic hormone that stimulates development of gonads during puberty and development of ova during the years of women's fertility.

gonads reproductive organs.

hermaphroditism a disorder in which individuals have characteristics of both sexes.

hormones chemical substances released from endocrine glands that circulate throughout the body and affect target organs that have receptors sensitive to the specific hormones.

internal genitalia internal reproductive organs, consisting of the ovaries, Fallopian tubes, uterus, and upper vagina in women and testes, seminal vesicles, and prostate gland in men.

intersexuality a more modern term for hermaphroditism.

Klinefelter's syndrome the disorder that occurs when a chromosomal male has an extra X chromosome, resulting in the XXY pattern of chromosome pair 23. These individuals have the appearance of males, including external genitalia, but they may also develop breasts and a feminized body shape.

Their testes are not capable of producing sperm, so they are sterile.

luteinizing hormone (LH) the gonadotropic hormone that prompts sexual development during puberty and also causes a maturing ovum to be released.

menarche the first menstruation.

Müllerian system a system of ducts occurring in both male and female embryos that form the basis for the development of the female internal reproductive system—ovaries, Fallopian tubes, uterus, and upper vagina.

pituitary gland an endocrine gland within the brain that produces tropic hormones that stimulate other glands to produce yet other hormones.

progestins a group of steroid hormones that have the function of preparing female bodies for pregnancy and have a unknown function for male bodies.

releasing hormones hormones produced by the hypothalamus that act on the pituitary to release tropic hormones.

sexual dimorphism the existence of male and female bodies, including differences in genetics, gonads, hormones, internal genitalia, and external genitalia.

spinal nucleus of the bulbocavernosus a collection of neurons in the lower spinal cord that control muscles at the base of the penis.

steroid hormones hormones related to sexual dimorphism and sexual reproduction that are derived from cholesterol and consist of a structure that includes four carbon rings.

testosterone the most common of the androgen hormones.

tropic hormones hormones produced by the pituitary gland that influence the release of other hormones by other glands, such as the gonads.

Turner's syndrome the disorder that occurs when an individual has only one of chromosome pair 23, one X chromosome. These individuals appear to be female (have the external genitalia of females) but do not have fully developed internal genitalia. They do not produce estrogens, do not undergo puberty, and are not fertile.

Wolffian system a system of ducts occurring in both male and female embryos that form the basis for the development of the male internal reproductive system—testes, seminal vesicles, and vas deferens.

X chromosomes one of the possible alternatives for chromosome pair 23. Two X chromosomes make a genetic female, whereas genetic males have only one X chromosome in pair 23.

Y chromosome one of the possible alternatives for chromosome pair 23. One X and one Y chromosome make a genetic male, whereas genetic females have two X chromosomes in pair 23.

Suggested Readings

Breedlove, S. Marc. (1994). Sexual differentiation of the human nervous system. *Annual Review of Psychology, 45,* 389–418. Breedlove's article is not easy reading, but it is a thorough and careful review of the research. Breedlove is also careful to acknowledge the interaction of biology and experience in the development of gender differences in the nervous system.

Fausto-Sterling, Anne. (1985). *Myths of gender: Biological theories about women and men.* New York: Basic Books. Although this book does not have the most recent research, the chapter titled "Hormonal Hurricanes" contains a readable, critical review of the role of hormones in women's behavior.

Pinel, John P. J. (1997). *Biopsychology* (3rd ed.). Boston: Allyn and Bacon. For more details about the action of the endocrine system, the brain's involvement in endocrine function, sexual development, and some of the things that can go wrong, see Chapter 11 of this biological psychology textbook.

Chapter 4

The Brain

HEADLINE

Gray Matters

—*Newsweek,* March 27, 1995

> *With new technologies... researchers catch brains in the very act of cogitating, feeling or remembering. Already this year researchers have reported that men and women use different clumps of neurons when they take a first step toward reading and when their brains are "idling." And, coming soon to a research journal near you, provocative studies will report that women engage more of their brains than men when they think sad thoughts—but possibly, less of their brains when they solve SAT math problems. (Begley, 1995, p. 48)*

In 1995, Sharon Begley wrote a story for *Newsweek* that described the results of these research studies, concentrating on the differences between male and female brains. Her story focused on the recent technological advances that have allowed brain researchers to study the functioning of living human brains, including **positron emission tomography (PET)** and **functional magnetic resonance imaging (FMRI).** These techniques allow researchers to study the activity of various sites in the brain, and some of those studies have compared the activity of men's and women's brains during various tasks.

Begley contended that this research has shown dramatic differences between women's and men's brains. In examining the findings of the studies, however, Begley discussed how the gender differences in these studies were sometimes unclear. In the study in which participants were asked to think of nothing while their brains were PET scanned, the typical pattern of activity varied for women and men. This variation did not apply to all participants, however, and some men's and women's brains showed patterns of activity typical of the other sex. As Begley (p. 54) pointed out, "the overlap between men's and women's scores on just about every psychological test is huge," indicating that though gender differences exist, this does not mean that women and men are very different.

Any gender difference is not only interesting but also potentially controversial. Begley reported that when brain researcher Raquel Gur told doctoral students about her research, some of the female students asked her to stop publicizing her results out of fear that women would lose the career opportunities they had gained over the past 20 years. Their fear was not unfounded. The history of brain research is filled with examples of finding differences that have been interpreted as deficits, and almost always as female deficits.

Indeed, researchers, reporters, and people in general have been too eager to interpret even the most meager evidence of structural differences between men's and women's brains as the basis for women's disadvantage in achievement and social status. The convenience of explaining discrimination by brain structure or function may appeal to those who want to rationalize discrimination, but brain research does not support such a position. The PET and FMRI research does not reveal how men and women come to be different, and experience affects the brain just as the brain influences behavior. As Begley pointed out, "the scans probe adults, whose brains are the products of years of living, feeling, thinking and experiencing" (p. 54). Thus, it is impossible to know the origins of brain differences; brain research has simply shown that differences exist in both the structure and function of female and male brains.

The Brain and the Nervous System

In order to understand the research on gender differences in brain structure and function, some information on the brain and nervous system is necessary. The brain and nervous system provide the body's internal communication and furnish a link to the outside world. Internal communication allows the rapid relay of messages throughout the body. The sensory and motor systems link the body to the outside world. The sensory system allows the body to receive stimulation from the outside world of light, sound, taste, smell, pressure, heat, cold, and pain; the motor system provides the pathway for physical reactions and movement.

The brain and nervous system are comprised of billions of **neurons,** or nerve cells. These neurons function by way of a complex electrochemical action, and the action of neurons provides the basis for internal communication as well as for the sensory and motor functions of the nervous system. When neurons are stimulated, a neural impulse forms, and if the impulse is sufficiently strong, this electrochemical message will continue through a chain of neurons to the brain, where it will be processed through additional interconnections of neurons.

The brain itself contains an estimated 100 billion neurons (Pinel, 1997), most of which have from dozens to hundreds of synapses, that is, interconnections with other neurons. The enormous number of connections makes an almost incomprehensibly complex system. Indeed, the brain is such a complex structure that neuroscience is far from a complete understanding of its functions and the relationship between its structures and functions.

The Brain and Sex

Sexual dimorphism of the brain is not as obvious as the differences between female and male bodies would suggest. During prenatal development, changes occur that result in dimorphic internal reproductive organs and external genitalia. During puberty, surges of hormones produce additional changes. During prenatal development, the hormones that produce sexual dimorphism in the body also affect the brain, making it possible for the brain structure and function to vary by sex.

Establishing gender differences in the brain is not easy because the brain is difficult to access for the purpose of study. Examining the structure of the brain is much easier than studying its function. Researchers can dissect brains through autopsy studies to learn about their structure, but investigating brain function requires a living brain that continues to operate during the course of the study. Therefore, information about brain structure is much more plentiful than information about brain function, but researchers using some of the new technologies mentioned in Begley's headline article are making progress toward understanding brain function.

• *Structural Differences*

Investigations of structural differences between the brains of women and men have concentrated on several specific structures, but a gender difference exists concerning the entire brain: The brains of men are larger than those of women. Unlike many of the gender differences, this one is present at birth (Breedlove, 1994). The meaning of this difference, however, is unclear. The history of brain research is filled with attempts to interpret differences in brain size, as the Diversity Highlight: "Brain Capacity and Race" discusses.

Most (and perhaps all) of the difference can be explained by differing body size. That is, the brain weight to body size ratio may be virtually identical for women and men. Some authorities believe that gender differences in brain size remain, even with the adjustment for body size (Ankney, 1992).

Except for this difference in brain size, the other structural differences do not exist at birth. Thus, any differences might be a result of experience rather than biological development. The identified structural differences have been small, but some researchers have interpreted these differences as very meaningful.

The Cerebral Hemispheres and Lateralization

Much of the research concerning sexual dimorphism of the brain has concentrated on the anterior (toward the front) part of the brain called the forebrain. The forebrain contains several structures, including the cerebral cortex, the outermost part of the brain. Figure 4.1 shows the exterior of the brain as it would appear with the skull and protective membranes removed. The folds, or fissures, are quite regular from person to person and divide the cortex into different sections, called lobes. Although many of the cerebral cortex's functions are not completely understood, knowledge about areas in the different lobes that receive the sensory input from the body is well established.

The occipital lobe at the back of the brain contains the sensory area that receives visual input. To be able to see, an animal not only needs eyes but also must have intact pathways of nerves that relay neural stimulation about visual information to the occipital lobe, and the occipital lobe must process and interpret the visual input information. The temporal lobe lies under the temples and receives auditory information. The parietal lobe contains a map of the skin's surface, receiving information about touch, pressure, heat, cold, and pain from the neurons in the skin. The frontal lobe contains the motor cortex, where the neural

DIVERSITY HIGHLIGHT
Brain Capacity and Race

The discoveries of the 19th century concerning lateralization of brain functions occurred during a period of intense interest in the capabilities of the brain. As information about the brain accumulated, researchers held firmly to their assumptions about sexual and racial differences in the brain's capacity. According to Stephen Jay Gould (1996), these scientific findings provide a good example of the influence that culture can have on research findings. These 19th-century neurology researchers believed that the male European brain was superior to all others: "The white leaders of Western nations did not question the propriety of racial ranking during the eighteenth and nineteenth centuries" (Gould, 1996, p. 66).

During the 19th century, the main technique for measuring the capacity of the brain was craniometry, measurement of the capacity of the skull (Gould, 1996). These researchers believed that the skull's capacity was a direct reflection of the size of the brain and that the size of the brain was a measure of intelligence. From the 1820s until 1851, Samuel George Morton collected skulls from many parts of the world so that he could measure their capacity and rank the races according to relative intelligence. Of course, he found the evidence he sought, which matched "every good Yankee's prejudice—whites on top, Indians in the middle, and blacks on the bottom; and, among whites, Teutons and Anglo-Saxons on top, Jews in the middle, and Hindus on the bottom" (Gould, 1996, pp. 85–86). White women's brains were more like the brains of these "primitive" races than like White men's.

Gould (1996) reanalyzed the data from Morton's skull collection and found no differences among the cranial capacity of different races. He concluded that "Morton's summaries are a patchwork of fudging and finagling in the clear interest of controlling a priori convictions" (p. 86). However, Gould noted that Morton had apparently not consciously cheated but had been so influenced by his prejudice that he had misread and misinterpreted his own data.

The last half of the nineteenth century saw no decrease in racism or sexism connected with assessing the brain. During this time measurements changed from cranial capacity to the configuration of the skull. One measurement of skull configuration was based on the facial angle, the jutting forward of face and jaws. Another popular measurement was the cranial index, the ratio of maximum width to maximum length of the skull. Jaws that did not jut forward too much and relatively shorter skulls indicated intelligence (Gould, 1996). Of course, non-European races had skulls that indicated less intelligence. Indeed, these races were considered apelike and not as fully evolved as the White races.

Gould's (1996) analyses indicated that body size and age influence the estimates of the size of the brain more strongly than race or sex. With these factors taken into account, no differences in brain capacity exist. However, the racism and sexism in neurology has only begun to fade during the twentieth century and, as Gould has argued, remnants of these biases still exist in science.

impulses that result in voluntary movement of muscles originate. Therefore, part of the function of the cerebral cortex is to receive and interpret sensory information from the outside world and to send neural impulses that result in movement of the body.

Figure 4.2 shows two views of the brain, one view as seen from above and another view as seen cut down the middle. The view of the brain from above shows that the cerebral cortex is divided down the middle into two halves, or hemispheres. This division forms a left cerebral hemisphere and a right cerebral hemisphere. The view through the midsection shows some of the structures in the brain beneath the cerebral cortex. These structures—the anterior commissure, the massa intermedia, and the corpus callosum—are all structures

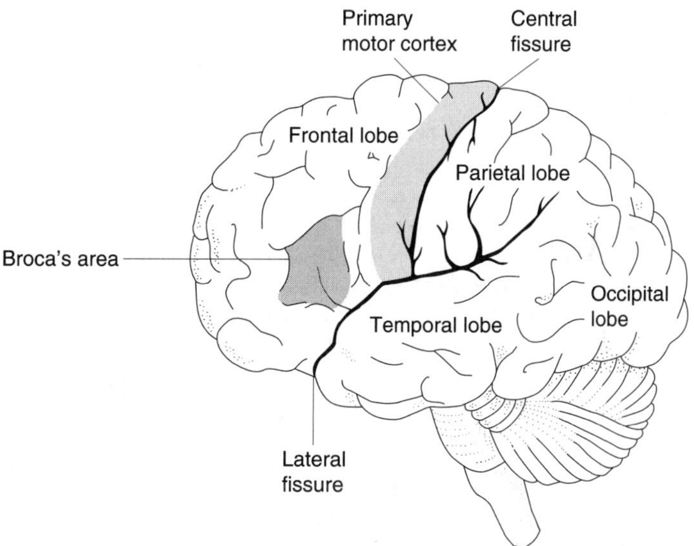

FIGURE 4.1 Location of Broca's Area in the Left Cortex

SOURCE: From John P. J. Pinel, *Biopsychology* (2nd ed.). Copyright © 1993 by Allyn and Bacon. Reprinted by permission.

that, according to some researchers, are sexually dimorphic. In addition, the left and right cerebral hemispheres may also differ in men and women. However, a more prominent difference in the two cerebral hemispheres is the one between the left and right hemisphere, which differ from each other in almost all humans.

The differences between the two cerebral hemispheres were unknown until the middle of the 1800s (Springer & Deutsch, 1998), and in many ways the two hemispheres appear to be mirror images of each other. Early neurology research revealed that left hemisphere strokes produced loss or impairment of the ability to speak, whereas comparable damage to the right hemisphere did not. Interest in the left hemisphere and its capabilities was intense. In the 1930s, research on the right hemisphere began to reveal its unique abilities (Springer & Deutsch, 1998). Patients with damage to the right hemisphere showed different patterns of impaired function when compared to patients with left hemisphere damage. Those with damage to their right hemisphere tended to perform poorly on nonverbal tests that involved manipulating geometric figures, assembling puzzles, completing patterns and figures, as well as performing other tasks that involved form, distance, and spatial relationships among objects. Growing research evidence about the different abilities that seemed to be directed by the two hemispheres led to the concept of **lateralization;** that is, that the left and right hemispheres are each specialized for different functions.

Additional evidence of lateralization came from research on patients who had undergone brain surgery to control seizures. Although surgical treatment has never been a common choice for the control of seizures, during the 1950s and 1960s several hundred patients in the United States and Canada received such surgical treatment (Springer & Deutsch,

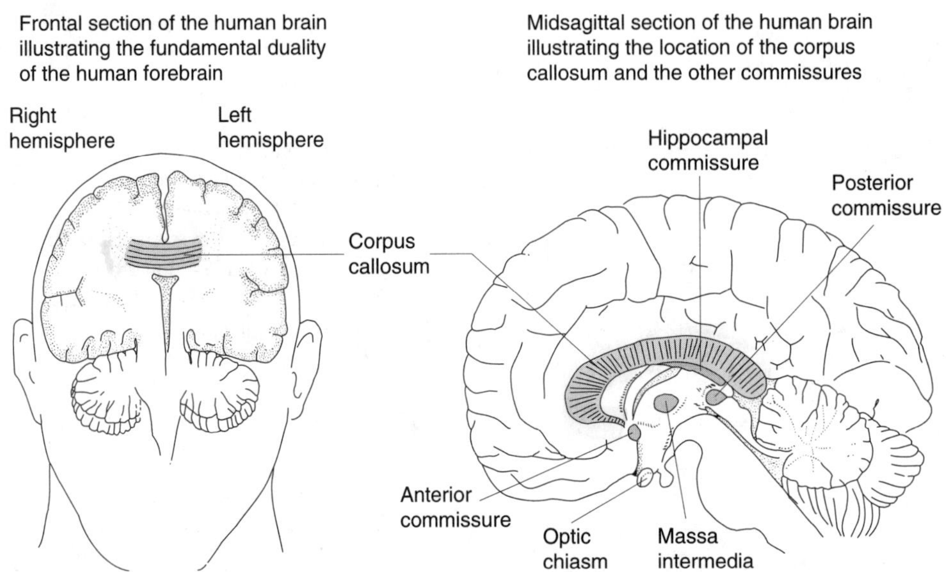

FIGURE 4.2 Cerebral Commissures and the Hemispheres of the Human Brain

SOURCE: From John P. J. Pinel, *Biopsychology* (2nd ed.). Copyright © 1993 by Allyn and Bacon. Reprinted by permission.

1998). Many variations existed, but the preferred type of surgery involved cutting the **corpus callosum,** a band of nerve fibers connecting the right and left cerebral hemispheres. Figure 4.2 shows the corpus callosum as the major connection between the two hemispheres. Research on these patients (sometimes referred to as 'split-brain' patients) has elaborated what the research from brain damage studies suggested: The two hemispheres have different capabilities.

Speculations about the implications of lateralization have captured the attention of people in many fields. Psychologist Robert Ornstein (1972) proposed that the different functions of the hemispheres are associated with different modes of thought: The left hemisphere is capable of logical and analytical thought, but the right hemisphere is capable of more intuitive, holistic thought processes. Ornstein also suggested that education in Western societies fosters left hemisphere functioning, whereas the abilities of the right hemisphere are fostered by Eastern societies; the latter may remain undeveloped in Western cultures. In extending the dichotomy of the two hemispheres to the East–West contrast, Ornstein laid the foundation for hemispheric differences to be extended to other dichotomies, such as rational–metaphorical, intellectual–intuitive, abstract–concrete, realistic–impulsive, objective–subjective, and analytical–holistic (Springer & Deutsch, 1998).

Included in many lists of such dichotomies is the labeling of the left hemisphere as "masculine" and the right as "feminine." This formulation describes the left hemisphere as masculine, rational, intellectual, abstract, objective, and analytical, whereas the right hemisphere is seen as feminine, metaphorical, intuitive, concrete, subjective, and holistic. These

GENDERED VOICES
Will I Be Smarter?

Male brains are larger than female brains, and this situation has been the topic of debate regarding the relative intelligence of women and men. The relationship between brain weight and intelligence is not entirely clear and has been the topic of research and debate for over a century. The initial belief that larger brains make for greater intelligence has been abandoned—under that metric, elephants would be smarter than humans. The measurement of the ratio of brain weight to body size puts humans at the top of the scale, and thus it has been accepted (by humans, at least) as the standard.

Although the variation of brain weight to body size between species is an index of intelligence, the variations within species are difficult to interpret. The differences in brain weight between men and women fall into this debate. When considering the ratio of brain weight to body size, the gender difference changes: Some authorities argue that this gender difference is reduced, others contend that it is eliminated, and some even claim that it is reversed (see Breedlove, 1994, for a brief summary of this argument). The division of opinion may reflect a controversy regarding what measurement to use to define body size. Should the measurement be body weight, height, or skin surface? Each of these measurements has both advocates and opponents.

When I explained these arguments and problems to one of my classes, a student listening to this lecture posed a question that frames the problem: "If I lose weight, does that mean that I will be smarter?" She wasn't serious, but her question highlights the obvious absurdity of using individual body weight in the calculation of intelligence.

associations are not unique to the brain research on lateralization but represent stereotypical descriptions of masculine and feminine traits that have appeared throughout history (Keller, 1985). Do differences exist between the cerebral hemispheres of men and women, and does this stereotypical dichotomy reflect the differences between the two cerebral hemispheres?

Gender Differences in Lateralization

Almost a century of investigation of cerebral lateralization had passed before anyone noted gender-related differences (Springer & Deutsch, 1998). From the 1860s to the 1960s, no one had noticed any differences in the effects of stroke between women and men. When researchers began looking, they found that women were much less likely than men to experience loss of speech abilities after left hemisphere damage. That is, similar brain damage did not seem to cause similar impairment in men and women.

Additional research on normal women and men suggested differences in lateralization: Men had more lateralized language and spatial functions, whereas women seemed to have these functions more equally represented in both hemispheres. Not all studies have found these gender differences in lateralization, and the size of the difference is small. After reviewing hundreds of studies on laterality, Merrill Hiscock and his colleagues (Hiscock et al., 1994; Hiscock et al., 1995) concluded that the gender differences in laterality are small, accounting for 1–2% of the variation in lateralization. This magnitude of difference means that other individual factors are much more important than gender in understanding variations in lateralization.

Gender differences in lateralization are among those that develop rather than appear at birth. A review of the research on laterality in children (Hahn, 1987) led to the conclusion that no gender differences exist in cerebral lateralization in children. In addition, the evidence suggests that cerebral lateralization continues throughout development. Confirmation for this view has come from a study of aging brains (Cowell et al., 1994). This study compared young to older men and women and found that reductions in brain volume as people aged occurred in the frontal and temporal lobes. The shrinkage was greater in men than in women, suggesting that brain lateralization occurs over the lifespan, including during adulthood.

Why should gender differences in lateralization exist? A number of theorists have speculated on the source and reasons for gender differences in brain lateralization. Norman Geschwind and Albert Galaburda (1987) have proposed a complex theory that explains lateralization as well as many other neurological and physiological individual differences. This theory relies on prenatal events, especially the existence of prenatal hormones, to explain gender differences in lateralization. Geschwind and Galaburda have hypothesized that testosterone is the most important agent, acting during critical periods of fetal development to control the rate of development of the right and left cerebral hemispheres. As Chapter 3 discussed, male and female fetuses are exposed prenatally to estrogens and androgens, and these hormones exert prenatal effects on the development of internal reproductive organs and external genitalia. Effects on the prenatal brain also occur, and these influences may relate to gender differences in brain organization.

Geschwind and Galaburda proposed that the effect of hormones on the prenatal brain makes a permanent difference on the organization of the cerebral hemispheres and thus on mental abilities. Part of their theory hypothesized that testosterone slows the growth of the left hemisphere, allowing a more rapid development of the right hemisphere. They proposed that these different growth rates produce different abilities, giving the larger hemisphere an advantage. Even if the two hemispheres eventually grow to equal size, they postulated, the different rates of growth will have permanent effects on brain function and mental abilities.

These theorists hypothesized gender differences in mental abilities. They conjectured that girls and women are more likely to have greater verbal abilities, because their prenatal testosterone levels would not have depressed growth in the left hemisphere. Girls and women would, however, have poorer spatial abilities, because their right hemispheres would not have experienced a growth spurt to compensate for depressed left hemisphere growth. This would leave girls and women more verbally fluent but less capable at tasks involving spatial functions. On the other hand, boys and men should excel at spatial tasks because prenatal testosterone would have depressed left hemisphere growth and prompted right hemisphere development, boosting its function. Boys and men, therefore, would tend to be poorer at verbal tasks than girls and women. Chapter 5 examines these abilities and the existence and magnitude of gender-related differences.

Geschwind and Galaburda's theory extends to factors other than lateralization and is sufficiently complex to be difficult to test (McManus & Bryden, 1991). In addition, their theory assumes a straightforward division of verbal and spatial tasks lateralized into the left and right hemispheres for both women and men. Some research suggests that men have more lateralized brains than women, which does not fit with this theory.

A different view of gender differences in lateralizated brain functions emphasizes growth rates during puberty rather than during the prenatal period (Waber, 1976). This view holds that children who physically mature early would perform better on verbal tasks, and those who mature late would perform better on spatial tasks. Because girls tend to mature earlier than boys, gender differences should exist in verbal and spatial abilities, although gender would be incidental rather than essential for these different abilities. A test of this hypothesis on children with different levels and rates of physical maturation has supported this view. Thus, maturational rate rather than gender may play a role in differences in hemispheric specialization.

Another alternative has emphasized the role of evolution in gender differences in lateralization (Kimura, 1992; Levy, 1969). Following this explanation, different role demands of men and women in the hunter–gatherer societies of prehistory posed different task demands and resulted in different brain organization. Although the logic of these stories may be appealing, these speculations are impossible to confirm or disconfirm—those early societies are gone and can no longer be observed. Also, alternative stories make as much sense. For example, more remote periods in prehistory when prehumans were tree dwellers would present similar selection pressures for spatial abilities (Benderly, 1987). Such abilities would have been very important for both sexes. For example, poor spatial abilities would result in falling out of trees, which would not be conducive to survival and reproduction. Despite the validity of an evolutionary view, the correlation of differential cognitive abilities and different evolutionary pressures is a theory with many possible versions and no way to provide confirmation.

All of these theories about brain lateralization have tried to explain why and how women develop brains that are less lateralized than the brains of men. Doreen Kimura (1992) has questioned the notion that women have less lateralized brain functions than men. She proposed an alternative type of gender difference—that men and women have differences in the cerebral organization of language abilities but that these differences have to do with the front and back of the hemispheres rather than left and right hemispheres. Kimura suggested that women are more likely to suffer from loss of language abilities when the anterior (front part) of their left hemisphere is damaged, whereas men are more likely to experience deficits when the posterior (back part) of their left hemisphere is damaged. She also explained that damage to the posterior portion is more frequent than damage to the anterior, resulting in more men than women with language loss. Although Kimura questioned the concept of different lateralization for men and women, she hypothesized other gender differences in the hemispheres. Her theory replaces the differences in lateralization with the possibility of other differently organized abilities within the cerebral hemispheres of women and men and constitutes a major revision of views on gender differences in lateralization.

In summary, a great deal of research and theory has explored gender differences in the lateralization of the cerebral hemispheres. Early studies neither sought nor found differences between men and women. When researchers started looking, they concluded that women have less lateralized cerebral functions than men; that is, women tend to have both the language and spatial functions more equally represented in both hemispheres, whereas men tend to have language represented in the left hemisphere and spatial abilities represented in the right. Several theories have attempted to explain why the brains of women and men differ. Some theories emphasize prenatal hormones, another postulates that growth rates produce gender differences, yet others claim different social demands during evolutionary prehistory to explain the brain organization of women and men. One recent proposal holds that the cerebral hemispheres are organized differently for genders but that differences between men and women in lateralization do not exist.

GENDERED VOICES
Cerebral Chauvinism

I asked a number of people whether they believed that men's and women's brains were different. Most people said no; some people qualified their answers, saying that they believed in no structural differences in the brains of women and men but that hormonal differences might exist. Several told me that they believed in functional differences in thought but not structural differences in the brain itself.

A substantial minority said that they believed in differences at the level of the structure of the brain, and their beliefs reflected a prejudice in favor of their own gender or against the other, or both. The women said things like, "Yes, I believe there are differences—women's brains are better," or "Yes, I believe in differences—men don't use as much of their brains as women." One man said it very simply, "Yes—men are smarter." Another man reported that he jokes about differences in women's and men's brains, telling the couples he counsels, "Yes, men's and women's brains are different. Men have small penises as one of the structures in their brains; this accounts for many of their differences in behavior."

However, a common view from the research on brain organization is that the brains of men and women differ at the level of the cerebral hemispheres. In addition, other brain structures beneath the cerebral cortex show sexual dimorphism, and some research has suggested that the corpus callosum may also differ in women and men.

Other Gender Differences in Brain Structure

In addition to gender differences in cerebral hemispheres, differences between the brains of men and women may exist in the corpus callosum, the thalamus, and the hypothalamus. Figure 4.3 shows the brain as it would appear if cut down the middle. The massa intermedia and the area of the hypothalamus near the optic chiasm, structures shown in this figure, are two of the brain structures that differ in women and men.

Several of the structures in the brain that connect the left and right sides of the brain show gender differences. The anterior commissure, massa intermedia of the thalamus, and corpus callosum all provide such connections. Evidence for sexual dimorphism of the anterior commissure and the massa intermedia of the thalamus are sketchy, but the massa intermedia is sometimes completely absent—only 86% of women and 72% of men have this structure (Breedlove, 1994). These differences are difficult to quantify, so both the existence and importance of such differences remain to be seen.

Research on differences of the corpus callosum in women and men is more plentiful. Interest in the corpus callosum as a sexually dimorphic structure began with a report (de Lacoste-Utamsing & Holloway, 1982) based on autopsies of 14 brains. The brains of the women showed relative size differences in the posterior (back part) of the corpus callosum, called the **splenium.** The splenium was larger and more bulbous in women compared to its size in men. Another autopsy study of 42 brains (Witelson, 1985) failed to confirm these differences, as did a study of living humans (Byne, Bleier, & Houston, 1988). Subsequent studies have found and others have failed to find gender differences in the splenium

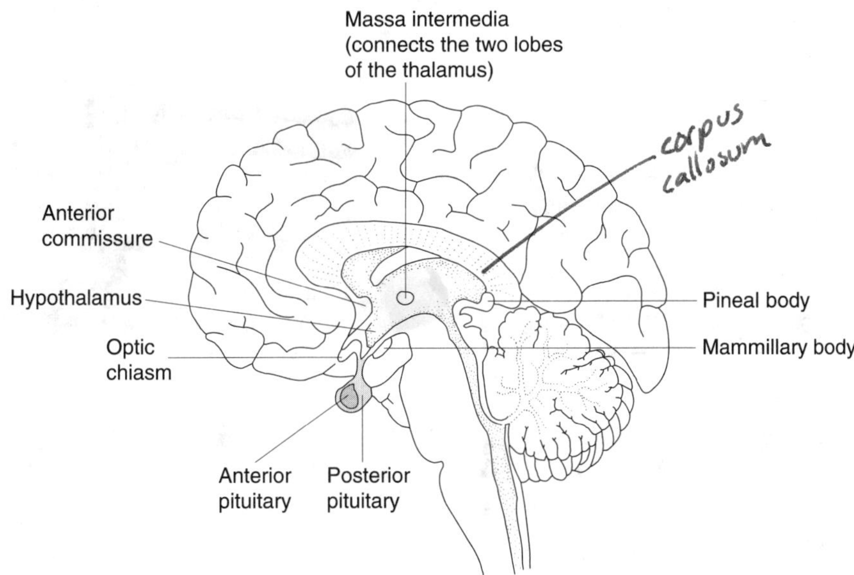

FIGURE 4.3 Midsection of the Brain

SOURCE: From John P. J. Pinel, *Biopsychology* (2nd ed.). Copyright © 1993 by Allyn and Bacon. Reprinted by permission.

(Hines & Collaer, 1993). These discrepant results indicate that if any differences exist, they must be very small.

Another study (Witelson, 1991) showed a difference in the corpus callosum of men and women, but the difference was related to age. The size of the callosum decreased in aging men but remained constant in size in aging women. Thus, differences in the corpus callosum that relate to gender may interact with age, and the corpus callosum may not be one of the brain structures that shows clear sexual dimorphism.

Other than the differences in the cerebral hemispheres, the evidence for sexual dimorphism in the brain is strongest for a section of the hypothalamus called the sexually dimorphic nucleus. This structure is larger in male rats and men than in female rats and women. Though not understood, its function may be related to sexual behavior or gender identity. In the late 1970s, a research team from UCLA discovered that a small area of the hypothalamus called the **sexually dimorphic nucleus (SDN)** is much larger in male rats than it is in female rats (Gorski, 1987). This brain structure consists of about a cubic millimeter of tissue in the area of the hypothalamus near the optic chiasm. This nucleus is very sensitive to testosterone and estrogen, so the presence or absence of these hormones influences its development. Furthermore, hormonal manipulation of baby rats was found to alter the size of the sexually dimorphic nucleus, decreasing its size in male rats or increasing its size in female rats. This study prompted a search for the equivalent structure and the equivalent difference in humans (Swaab & Fliers, 1985) which found that men have a sexually dimorphic nucleus

TABLE 4.1 Summary of Brain Differences between Men and Women

Structure	Difference
Cerebral hemispheres	Men may be more lateralized than women for language and spatial functions
Sexually dimorphic nucleus of hypothalamus	SDN in men is 2.5 times larger than in women
Splenium of corpus callosum	Early studies indicated larger and more bulbous splenium in women; later studies found an interaction with age and gender
Anterior commissure	Evidence for sexual dimorphism is sketchy
Massa intermedia of the thalamus	Evidence for sexual dimorphism is sketchy

that is 2.5 times larger than the same structure in women. In humans, gender differences in this structure do not exist at birth. Between birth and ages 2 and 4 years, the number of cells in this structure increase rapidly (Swaab, Gooren, & Hofman, 1995). The number of cells begins to decrease in girls but not in boys, creating a sexual dimorphism that peaks in young adulthood and middle age (Breedlove, 1994).

An intriguing finding about another nucleus in the hypothalamus has come from Simon LeVay (1991), who claimed that he had found brain-level differences between heterosexual and homosexual individuals. LeVay autopsied the brains of homosexual men and men whom he presumed to be heterosexual and compared them to women (whose sexual orientation he did not know). He found that number three of the four interstitial nuclei of the anterior hypothalamus (INAH-3) averaged twice as large in the heterosexual men compared to the homosexual men and the women.

LeVay interpreted this finding as a biological basis for sexual orientation, and this interpretation provoked a large controversy. Part of the controversy related to the biological essentialism of this position, but criticisms over LeVay's methodology also questioned this interpretation. A large number of the gay men in his study had died of AIDS, creating an uncontrolled factor in the study. Furthermore, the size of INAH-3 differed within the groups as well as among groups, meaning that this nucleus was larger in some gay men than in some heterosexual men, but the averages differed significantly. His finding, however, is intriguing because it suggests that this area of the hypothalamus may relate to sexual orientation.

Therefore, the differences in structure between female and male brains are small. Table 4.1 summarizes the results of studies on structural differences between women's and men's brains. Might the function of male and female brains differ more than their structure? Until recently, answers to this question were more speculative, but as Begley's headline story reported, advances in technology have begun to allow researchers to investigate gender differences in brain functioning.

• *Functional Differences*

Differences in structure may seem to imply differences in function. However, structural differences may or may not produce functional differences. Also, differences in function can exist even in identical structures through varied patterns of activation. Therefore, the study of brain function can supplement the studies of brain structure. This possibility is recent, with the technology necessary to investigate brain function only now developing.

Two techniques are especially useful in investigating brain function: positron emission tomography (PET) and functional magnetic resonance imaging (FMRI). PET can measure glucose metabolism, oxygen consumption, or blood flow, and FMRI detects increases in oxygen consumption that accompany heightened neural activity (Raichle, 1994). Although these techniques are so new that the findings have not yet yielded a complete picture, researchers have applied them to study images of the brain as it responds to various types of stimuli and tasks.

As Begley's story reported, several studies of brain function have concentrated on gender differences. The studies usually test fairly small samples of participants and compare the average response of female and male brains. Although some of the studies have found average differences, they have also found that some brains behave more like those for the other gender—not all male brains react in ways that are typical for men, and not all female brains show the responses of the average woman. Therefore, individual variation may be as important as gender in understanding differences in brain functioning.

For example, one of the studies in Begley's report studied women and men by using functional magnetic resonance imaging as the two groups performed three tasks involving language sounds (Shaywitz et al., 1995). The results showed that men used their left cerebral hemisphere whereas women used both hemispheres in performing a rhyming task. No gender differences appeared in brain activation for the two other tasks, nor were the patterns of activation divided neatly by gender. Over 40% of the women in the study exhibited the activation pattern more typical of the men. Furthermore, the pattern of brain functioning may be of little or no practical significance because the male and female participants performed comparably. That is, the difference in patterns of brain activation made no behavioral difference.

Another structural difference that seems unrelated to brain function relates to gender differences in aging brains. Two groups of researchers (Cowell et al., 1994; Murphy et al., 1996) found that brains shrink with age, but men's brains shrink more than women's do. This difference, however, may not make any difference for mental functioning. A test of older men and women performing several types of cognitive tasks showed that the structural declines did not translate into performance differences (Larrabee & Crook, 1993). Therefore, the structural differences failed to produce performance differences.

Another study showed small gender differences by conducting PET scans measuring the brain's metabolic rate and comparing men's and women's brains at rest (Gur et al., 1995). No gender differences appeared in overall metabolic rate or in the level of activity in many areas of the brain, but there were some differences. The difference highlighted in Begley's story concerned the difference in activity level in that area of the brain related to emotion. In the majority of the men's brains, that area was more active than in the same area of the majority of the women's brains. These typical patterns were not true for all participants, as over 40% of the men and 25% of the women exhibited patterns typical of the other gender. As Ruben Gur and his colleagues (1995, p. 531) commented, "the brains of men and women are fundamentally more similar than different."

Although the research on functional differences between men's and women's brains is just beginning, the results have revealed some intriguing findings. Under some circumstances,

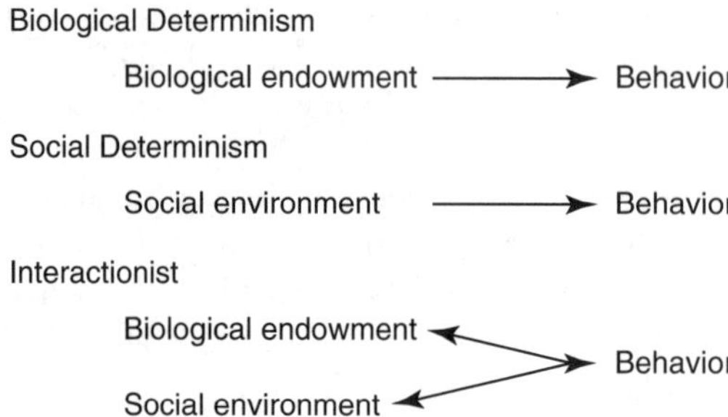

FIGURE 4.4 Three Models of Influence in Behavior

men's and women's brains (on the average) function differently. The differences, however, are not clear-cut, with cases of both female and male brains functioning in ways more typical of the other gender. Several of the studies indicate differences in function, but no difference in performance. Men's and women's brains may function differently while trying to solve verbal or mathematical problems, but if their performance is the same, then the differences have no practical importance. In addition, these studies of functional gender differences in the brain do not reveal how male and female brains come to differ, which leaves this and many other questions concerning functional gender differences in the brain yet to be answered.

What Brain Differences Might Mean

The structural differences in the brains of women and men have been interpreted as the source of "almost every imaginable behavioral difference between the sexes" (Pinel, 1997, p. 415), and "new technologies that catch the mind in the very act of thinking show how men and women use their brains differently" (Begley, 1995, p. 48). That is, reporters (and even researchers) have been eager to conclude that structural or functional gender differences in the brain underlie behavioral gender differences. In some sense, this conclusion must be correct: Behavior is related to brain structure and function.

If the brains of women and men differ in structure, function, or the ways in which neural inputs are processed, then the relative abilities and behaviors of men and women might reflect those differences. Such differences might have implications not only for educational and professional opportunities but also for many aspects of everyday behavior.

Researchers, such as Kimura (1992), believe that establishing a biological basis for gender-related behavior is possible. Kimura denied that learning and experience are the basis for gender differences and contended that these differences are "stamped into our brains before birth," resulting in a "lifelong, irreversible effect on behavior" (in Baxter, 1994, p. 52).

Kimura's argument advocates biological determinism, the one-way chain of causality from brain to behavior. Figure 4.4 depicts this view of behavior along with two alternatives. One alternative is comparably deterministic, but the cause of the gender difference is social and environmental factors. The third alternative is a more complex, interactionist view in which biology affects behavior but behavior and environment also influence biology.

Katharine Hoyenga and Kermit Hoyenga (1993) argued against the fallacy of accepting a simple biologically deterministic view of behavior. They explained how people tend to believe that biological differences are not subject to change—that labeling a difference "biological" is the same as saying it is permanent or unchangeable. They pointed out that this belief is incorrect: Factors with a biological basis are as much subject to change as psychologically based differences. Furthermore, Hoyenga and Hoyenga asserted that it is impossible to pinpoint the source of a complex behavior as biologically based because so many different biological and experiential factors interact to produce any behavior. Thus, Hoyenga and Hoyenga argued that the quest for a biological explanation for behavior cannot be successful.

Establishing a relationship between brain and behavior requires several steps. First, structural or functional differences between the brains of women and men must occur. Second, gender differences in performance on mental tasks must occur. And third, gender differences in task performance must be linked to the brain differences. This chapter has examined such evidence for sexual dimorphism in the brain, and that evidence indicates that some differences exist in the brains of women and men. Chapter 5 will examine and evaluate the research about gender differences on several types of mental tasks. If these differences exist, then the argument depends on evidence about the link between the two. Although not all researchers believe that it is possible to establish such connections, many do, and their research has influenced popular beliefs about the nature of gender differences in intelligence.

Summary

Many people believe that the differences in male and female intellectual and occupational achievement must be linked to differences in male and female brains. This chapter began with an article that reported on new technologies that allow researchers to examine the function of living brains. Some of these studies have shown that men's and women's brains function differently under some testing situations. The basic unit of the nervous system, the neuron, shows no such differences, but the uppermost part of the brain, the cerebral cortex, may.

The cerebral cortex is divided into left and right hemispheres, and the hemispheres are lateralized, with each hemisphere controlling different abilities. The left hemisphere is more capable in verbal tasks, such as speech recognition and language production. The right hemisphere is more involved in emotion and more capable of perceiving spatial relationships. Many (but not all) researchers have concluded that gender differences exist in brain lateralization, with men having more lateralized brain functions than women. However, not all experts agree on the existence of these differences.

Other brain structures show sexual dimorphism: A part of the hypothalamus called the sexually dimorphic nucleus is 2.5 times larger in men than in women. The results of these differences are not known. Some research has indicated that the corpus callosum, the brain structure that connects the two hemispheres, is larger in women than in men, but further research has failed to confirm this difference. Other possible differences are not well confirmed.

The results of studies using sophisticated imaging techniques, such as positron emission tomography (PET) and functional magnetic resonance imaging (FMRI), have shown that some differences exist in women's and men's brain functions. The implications of these results are not clear, with some men and women showing the activity patterns typical of the other gender and other studies failing to reveal advantage or disadvantage related to the differences. Therefore, the preliminary results from this new field of research are intriguing but not entirely clear.

Although history is filled with attempts to explain inferior social position with biological explanations, these explanations are invalid. Brain structure and function influence behavior, but behavior and experience also affect the brain, making separation of the two impossible. Despite the unquestioned link between the brain and behavior, the widespread acceptance of biological determinism is unwarranted.

Glossary

corpus callosum a band of nerve fibers that connects the right and left cerebral hemispheres.

functional magnetic resonance imaging (FMRI) a technique for measuring the function of a living brain.

lateralization the concept that the two cerebral hemispheres are not functionally equal but rather that the each hemisphere has different abilities.

neurons nerve cells.

positron emission tomography (PET) a technique for measuring the function of a living brain.

sexually dimorphic nucleus (SDN) a brain structure in the hypothalamus, near the optic chiasm, that is larger in male than female rats and larger in men than women.

splenium the back (posterior) part of the corpus callosum.

Suggested Readings

Hopkin, Karen. (1995). Sugar 'n spice vs. puppy-dog tails: Sex differences in the brain. *Journal of NIH Research, 7,* 39–43. This summary of brain research emphasizes gender differences, even when the differences are unclear. Not until the last page does Hopkin mention the potential for bias and the certainty that gender differences in the brain are complex and not yet well understood. Nevertheless, the article is a readable summary of a great deal of complex research.

Springer, Sally P.; & Deutsch, Georg. (1998). *Left brain, right brain* (5th ed.). New York: Freeman. This book details the history and status of the research on cerebral dominance, including a chapter titled "Sex Differences in Cognition and Asymmetry." Although Springer and Deutsch summarize a great deal of technical research, their presentation is easy to follow, and their review is critical of the sweeping generalizations that researchers and journalists have eagerly made.

Tavris, Carol. (1992). *The mismeasure of woman.* New York: Simon & Schuster. The first chapter of Tavris's excellent book contains several subsections, the last of which is titled "Brain: Dissecting the Differences." This section provides an easy-to-read (and critical) examination of the research on gender-related differences in the brain.

Chapter 5

Intelligence and Mental Abilities

HEADLINE

The Great Debate: Gender Differences

—*Current Health 2,* December 1995

> *"Need help?" Brenda asked. The woman grimaced. "I never could read maps. Where's the Emporium?"*
>
> *John tapped the map. "Turn here. Walk east four blocks, go south and— "*
>
> *Brenda cut in, pointing right. "He means to go right, at this intersection and walk four blocks to the Big Dollar Store on the corner. Go right. It's just past Tucker's Toys, on Mission Street."*
>
> *As the woman crossed the intersection, John asked, "Why did you butt in?"*
>
> *"Maps are confusing. I prefer landmarks like Tucker's Toys."*
>
> *"I'll show you how to read a map," offered John, but Brenda shook her head. (Monroe, 1995, p. 22)*

Judy Monroe (1995) reported this exchange and then wrote that some people believe that men read maps better than women. She contended that determining who is better at finding the way is not so simple because women and men tend to use different strategies. Like Brenda, many women prefer to use landmarks as a strategy to find their way. Like John, many men rely on maps. Monroe's article focused on the research that has related map reading to spatial ability and the findings that men on the average are better at these tasks than women.

The great gender debate to which Monroe's headline referred concerns differences between women's and men's mental abilities. Is the conversation between John and Brenda typical? Do women and men have different mental abilities, do they use different strategies, or both? If such differences exist, are they expressions of hormonal or brain differences between the sexes, or do these differences represent different learning and experience?

Monroe's article mentioned the controversy over mental abilities. She wrote that some researchers contend that gender differences do not exist, whereas others have argued that the differences exist and that they have a biological basis. As Monroe discussed, the research in the area of mental abilities is filled with complex findings and strongly held (but opposing) views; her article is but one of dozens that has appeared in the popular press. Monroe pointed out the conflicting findings about both the existence and source of gender differences in mental abilities, but other reports have not been so balanced.

The level of controversy reflects the strong feelings that this topic has produced. To what extent do gender differences explain mental abilities? Are differences sufficiently large to explain the distribution of men and women into different areas of coursework and different occupations, or do these findings represent insignificant differences in how women and men think? Do differences represent specific mental abilities or overall intelligence?

Mental Abilities

Other than defining intelligence as "how smart a person is" (a trivial and circular definition), an acceptable definition of this concept has been difficult to formulate. Indeed, heated debate over the nature of intelligence has occurred throughout the history of intelligence testing, a controversy not confined to psychology. The prominence of this concern highlights the importance of the issue: Understanding intelligence and the abilities that contribute to intelligence is a basic question for understanding humans.

Psychologists have been concerned with the concept of intelligence since the 1890s (Schultz & Schultz, 1992). However, the current conceptualization of intelligence was most influenced by the creation of the intelligence test in 1905. This test, formulated by Alfred Binet, Victor Henri, and Théodore Simon, measured a variety of mental abilities related to school performance, including memory, attention, comprehension, vocabulary, and imagination. A version of this test—the Stanford-Binet—appeared in the United States in 1916, and the mental testing movement became an important part of psychology, especially in the United States.

The prevailing view of intelligence during the 19th and early 20th centuries was that women's intellect was inferior to men's (Lewin, 1984a; Shields, 1975a). Lewis Terman, who adapted the Binet-Simon test into the Stanford-Binet, did not believe in the intellectual inferiority of women. He himself had no trouble accepting the results of this test, which revealed no average differences between the intelligence of men and women. Indeed, the scores on the early versions of the Stanford-Binet showed that women scored slightly higher than men, but after some of the items that showed differences were eliminated, the average scores for women and girls were equal to those of men and boys (Terman & Merrill, 1937).

With the development of the mental testing movement came increased attention to the different abilities that might be included within the tests of intelligence. The test devised by Binet and his colleagues and adapted by Terman into the Stanford-Binet included mostly items classified as verbal; that is, questions that require the understanding and use of language.

Psychologist David Wechsler created an alternative intelligence test that divided abilities into verbal and performance skills. The verbal subtests required those being tested to provide verbal answers by performing certain tasks: supplying factual knowledge (information), defining vocabulary items (vocabulary), performing basic arithmetic computation (arithmetic), repeating a series of digits (digit span), understanding similarities between objects (similarities), and properly interpreting social conventions (comprehension). The performance subtests of Wechsler's test required no verbal responses, but instead people responded by performing some action. The performance subtests included arranging pictures into a sensible story (picture arrangement), duplicating designs with blocks (block design), completing pictures that have some missing part (picture completion), assembling cut-up figures of common objects (object assembly), and learning and rapidly applying digit symbol codes (digit symbols) (Gregory, 1987). Figure 5.1 shows samples of the type of items on the Wechsler tests.

Unlike the Stanford-Binet, Wechsler's test showed differences between the scores of men and women, with women scoring higher on the verbal subtests and men scoring higher on the performance subtests. Wechsler performed no item adjustment to equate average performance of women and men on the subtests. Although the combined scores on the Wechsler tests do not show gender differences, the subtest scores always have.

Nor are the Wechsler tests the only assessments that have revealed different abilities between male and female participants. Eleanor Maccoby and Carol Jacklin's (1974) review of gender differences in intellectual performance likewise found differences in performance on verbal, mathematical, and spatial tasks. More recent research, however, has revealed that the patterns of gender differences in these mental abilities are more complex than the early reviews suggested. In addition, these differences have changed, and gender-related differences seem to be decreasing or perhaps disappearing.

Verbal Abilities

The tasks that researchers have used to study verbal ability include not only the verbal subtests of the Wechsler tests but also verbal fluency, anagram tests, reading comprehension tests, synonym and antonym tasks, sentence structure assessments, and reading readiness tests as well as the spelling, punctuation, vocabulary, and reading subtests from various achievement tests. Researchers have defined all of these tasks as verbal despite the wide variation in the tasks themselves. This variation may be one reason why research on verbal ability has not yielded entirely consistent results.

Maccoby and Jacklin (1974) reviewed dozens of studies that had compared the verbal abilities of girls and women to boys and men. Although these studies had used many different measures of verbal ability (see Table 5.1) and gender differences were not found across the board, Maccoby and Jacklin were nevertheless convinced that girls and women have a small advantage in verbal abilities.

Diane Halpern (1992, 1994, 1997) also examined the research in the area of verbal abilities, but she concluded that girls and women generally have the advantage in a variety of verbal tasks. Halpern noted that boys and men are more likely than girls and women to have language-related problems, such as stuttering and reading difficulties. Despite the preponderance of boys diagnosed with these problems, some research has suggested that the

Verbal Subtests	**Sample Items**
Information	How many wings does a bird have? Who wrote *Paradise Lost*?
Digit span	Repeat from memory a series of digits, such as 3 1 0 6 7 4 2 5, after hearing it once.
General comprehension	What is the advantage of keeping money in a bank? Why is copper often used in electrical wires?
Arithmetic	Three men divided 18 golf balls equally among themselves. How many golf balls did each man receive? If 2 apples cost 15¢, what will be the cost of a dozen apples?
Similarities	In what way are a lion and a tiger alike? In what way are a saw and a hammer alike?
Vocabulary	This test consists simply of asking, "What is a ______?" or "What does ______ mean?" The words cover a wide range of difficulty or familiarity.

Performance Subtests	**Description of Item**
Picture arrangement	Arrange a series of cartoon panels to make a meaningful story.
Picture completion	What is missing from these pictures?
Block design	Copy designs with blocks (as shown at right).
Object assembly	Put together a jigsaw puzzle.
Digit symbol	

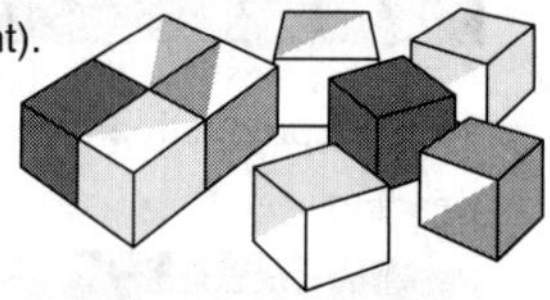

1	2	3	4
X	III	I	O

Fill in the symbols:

3	4	1	3	4	2	1	2

FIGURE 5.1 Sample Test Items Similar to Items on Wechsler's Tests of Intelligence

SOURCE: From Wood & Wood, *The World of Psychology.* Copyright © 1993 by Allyn and Bacon. Reprinted by permission.

number of boys and girls with such problems may be similar, even though boys receive referrals for these problems more often than girls (Karlen, Hagin, & Beecher, 1985; Shaywitz, Shaywitz, Fletcher, & Escobar, 1990). Halpern also pointed out that girls acquire language with greater speed and proficiency than boys and that gender-related differences in verbal abilities appear as early as children begin to talk. Girls maintain this advantage throughout elementary school. During middle and high school, the pattern becomes more complex, with girls having certain advantages in spelling and language use and boys having an advantage in verbal reasoning (Feingold, 1988).

TABLE 5.1 Examples of Different Measures of Verbal, Quantitative, and Spatial Abilities

Verbal	Quantitative	Spatial
Vocalizations during infancy	Point to a member of a set	Reproducing geometric forms
Visual-motor association	Estimating proportion	Matching geometric shapes
Talking to mother	WISC arithmetic subtest	Reading maps
Verbalization in free play	Digit-processing task	Matching photos for orientation
Parents' reports of speech problems	Digit-symbol subtest of WAIS	Distance perception
Complete sentences	Math achievement	Assembling puzzles
Anagram task	Math reasoning	Rotating shapes
Carrying out simple and complex tasks	Problem solving	Reproducing patterns
Judgment of grammatical sentences	Addition	Disembedding figures
Verbal imitation	Subtraction	Angle-matching
Verbal reproduction of story	Arithmetic computation	Maze performance
Reading speed	Number arrangement	Localization of a spatial target
Reading vocabulary	Math subtests for SAT	Discrimination of triangles and mirror-image reversals
Reading comprehension	General Aptitude Test Battery	Distinguishing right from left, east from west, and top from bottom
Errors in similes	ACT	Rod-and-frame task
Spelling		Matching pictures to objects
Punctuation		Seguin Form Board
Synonyms and antonyms		Spatial subtest from: Differential Aptitude Test; General Aptitude Battery
Verbal subtests of Peabody Picture Vocabulary; Illinois Test of Psycholinguistic Ability; Expressive Vocabulary Inventory; WISC		Piaget's water level task
		Making judgments about moving objects
		WISC Block Design

SOURCE: *The psychology of sex differences* by Eleanor Maccoby & Carol Jacklin, 1974, pp. 76–97. Stanford, CA: Stanford University Press.

Meta-analysis, a statistical technique that combines the results from many studies to estimate the size of certain effects, was not available in 1974, when Maccoby and Jacklin completed their review of gender-related similarities and differences. But Janet Hyde (1981) completed such a meta-analysis of the studies from Maccoby and Jacklin's review and concluded that the gender-related differences in verbal ability are small. About 1% of the difference in verbal ability relates to gender, leaving the other 99% of difference related to other factors.

A later meta-analysis (Hyde & Linn, 1988) examined additional studies, and their analysis indicated that women have the advantage in some verbal abilities, but men have the advantage in others. In addition, Hyde and Linn's analysis indicated that earlier studies showed gender-related differences, whereas more recent studies have not. Overall, women have a small advantage, but Hyde and Linn argued that the difference was too small to be of any practical importance. Indeed, they maintained that based on the most recent studies they summarized, gender differences in verbal abilities no longer exist.

Mathematical and Quantitative Abilities

Most studies with children as participants show either no gender differences or certain advantages for girls in mathematical abilities, defined as proficiency in arithmetic computation (Fennema, 1980; Hyde, Fennema, & Lamon, 1990). Around age 13, gender differences favoring boys begin to appear in many of the assessments of mathematical ability.

Girls who excel at arithmetic computation do not become women who are poor at such tasks. For example, the Differential Aptitude Test (DAT) numerical ability subtest shows no gender differences for students in grades 8 through 12 (Feingold, 1988). Instead, measurements for what constitutes mathematical and quantitative abilities change between the middle school and the high school years. Rather than consisting of arithmetic computation, the tests of quantitative ability begin to include tasks that are more abstract, as Table 5.1 shows. These quantitative tasks are perhaps more dependent on spatial ability, another cognitive ability for which boys and men have an advantage. (This area is explored further in the next section.) Therefore, the measurement of some mathematical abilities may not be independent of spatial ability, and the widely observed disadvantage for women in the two areas may be connected (Casey, Nuttal, Pezaris, & Benbow, 1995; Eccles, 1987; Voyer, 1996). On the other hand, the disadvantage for women may not be as large as generally believed. As Hyde's (1981) meta-analysis of quantitative abilities showed, only 1% of the difference in performance was related to gender, which indicates a very small overall gender-related difference in mathematical ability.

A later meta-analysis (Hyde, Fennema, & Lamon, 1990) revealed additional complexities concerning mathematical abilities. These researchers analyzed 100 studies and found that in the general population, women have a small advantage in quantitative ability. Although this advantage is too small to be of practical importance, this analysis suggested that the pattern of mathematical and quantitative abilities is complex and differs from the stereotype.

The meta-analysis (Hyde et al., 1990) divided quantitative abilities into different skills, and this division showed that women have a small advantage in computation and an even smaller advantage in understanding mathematical concepts. During elementary and middle school, no gender difference appears in mathematics problem solving, but boys begin to do better at solving math problems during high school, and this advantage continues during college. The gender-related differences in problem solving that begin to appear during high school show a larger discrepancy in selected groups of students than in the general population. This selection factor shows its influence in high school and college as well as in groups of gifted students.

Two tests that have consistently revealed gender-related differences in math performance are the mathematics subtests of the Preliminary Scholastic Aptitude Test (PSAT) and

GENDERED VOICES

I Was Good at Math and Science

A female chemical engineer said, "I was good at math and science, so my high school counselor suggested engineering. I looked into the various kinds of engineering. I didn't really like physics all that much, so I decided that electrical engineering would not be a good choice. I didn't consider myself very mechanical, so I ruled out mechanical engineering. I liked chemistry, so I thought chemical engineering would be a good choice, but I didn't really know what chemical engineers did. My high school had a cooperative arrangement so I could work for an engineer, but that experience didn't really let me know what the work of a chemical engineer was like. In fact, I didn't really understand the work of chemical engineers until I was a junior in college, and I learned that I didn't find the work all that interesting.

"I went to a technical college that specialized in engineering, and it was definitely male dominated; only about 25% of the students were women. But I never felt any favoritism either for or against the women. Everybody was treated fairly. The courses during the first two years were designed to weed out students, so everybody felt that the curriculum was difficult. But the women did as well as the men, and I never felt that the professors or students showed any bias.

"What was missing on campus were ethnic minorities. The campus was very White. There just weren't any Black students, and there was one Hispanic girl. The geographic area had lots of minorities, but they didn't go into engineering at this school. I noticed the absence of minority students more than the small number of women.

"I didn't feel that being a woman was a factor in school, but it sure was on the job. I didn't necessarily feel discriminated against, but the women were very visible. There were few women, and whatever a woman did stood out. If I did a great job, I got noticed more than a man who did a great job. If I screwed up, I got noticed more than a man who made a mistake. Whatever a woman did—good or bad—came to the attention of everyone."

the Scholastic Aptitude Test (SAT) (Feingold, 1988). The gender-related differences in performance on these two tests demonstrate the influence of a progressively selected group of students. The PSAT, as the name suggests, is a preliminary form of the SAT, a test often used as a college entrance examination. Students who take the SAT are typically a self-selected group taking the test as a college entrance exam, not a representative sample of the general population or even of high school students.

Performance on the PSAT reflects the scores of a more representative sample of high school juniors and seniors. Although the PSAT and the SAT are equivalent in content, the test score averages differ due to the selection of students who take each test. Both tests show advantages for boys on the mathematics subtests, but the SAT mathematics subtest shows a larger advantage than the PSAT mathematics subtest. This difference indicates that male college-bound students have a larger advantage over female college-bound students in math than male high school students have over female high school students. This comparison also suggests that the male advantage in mathematics is greater at higher levels of mathematics performance.

A large gender difference in higher-level mathematics appeared in several studies, showing that boys have a large advantage over girls (Benbow & Stanley, 1980, 1983). The differences appeared on the SAT mathematics test among intellectually gifted children under 13 years old, before these students had formally studied higher mathematics. These results are confined to mathematically gifted students, but the gender differences represent the largest in studies on mathematics. More representative samples of the population do not show these differences.

The source of these large differences has been the subject of heated debate, and the general public has often lost sight of the limitation of the study as showing advantage only to mathematically gifted children. One side of the argument (Benbow & Stanley, 1983) holds that the difference in mathematics performance is the expression of innate, biological abilities and thus reflects essential differences between boys and girls. The studies with intellectually gifted students included no biological data, which makes this conclusion unfounded (Jacklin, 1989).

Indeed, these tests do reflect several things in addition to ability (Stumpf & Stanley, 1996). Although boys and girls in the studies of mathematically gifted youth had taken an equal number of math courses, their experience with mathematics might differ according to parental attention and encouragement, computer experience, and peer acceptance. These family and community experiences in combination with school tracking for math ability contribute to a difference between the development of the math skills in gifted boys and gifted girls (Entwisle, Alexander, & Olson, 1994). That is, even before children have a choice concerning the math classes to take, girls and boys have different experiences in math.

The differential preparation of female and male students complicates assessing the underlying mathematical abilities of women and men. Starting during high school, girls take fewer math courses than boys (Fennema, 1980). Because of this difference, any assessment of ability will be inseparable from the influence of differential experience. However, this situation reflects an important and unquestionable gender-related difference: Girls make different choices than boys in their curricula. Regardless of any possible differences in ability, choices made by girls and boys can have far-reaching implications in their lives as men and women.

Beginning at age 12, girls start to feel less confident than boys about their ability to do mathematics (Eccles, 1989). As students age, the genders differ increasingly in their levels of confidence, and this trend continues into adulthood. Girls also begin to believe that math is not important to them, starting at the same age that they begin to lose confidence in their ability to do math. Boys, on the other hand, have greater confidence in their mathematical ability and evaluate math as more important to their future. Thus, different perceptions of confidence exist as the result of believing that math is a male domain (Kimball, 1995). Both children and parents share this cultural perception, resulting in the differential beliefs concerning boys' and girls' math abilities.

Girls' choice to avoid math courses may stem from their beliefs concerning the likelihood of success and the perceived lack of value of the coursework (Eccles, 1987). The combined lack of confidence and the belief that math is not important to their future form a powerful disincentive for girls during high school, when they have the option to choose elective math courses. Not coincidentally, the differences in math scores begin to appear at this time.

The choice to avoid math courses can have lifelong repercussions (Sells, 1980). The selection of high school mathematics courses can act as a filter, effectively barring female and ethnic minority students from many professions. For example, if a student has only two years of high school math, that student cannot take calculus as a freshman in college, which thereby eliminates some college majors and filters some students out of those majors and out of careers requiring those majors.

In examining the mathematics preparation of first-year university students, a large difference appeared between women and men. Only 8% of the women compared to 57% of the men had completed more than three years of high school math. These differences in preparation were reflected in their choice of majors, with the men choosing majors in physical science, life science, or mathematics more often than women.

Another intriguing finding from this study (Sells, 1980) was the strong relationship between reported social support from peers, parents, or teachers and the choice by high school girls to take advanced mathematics courses. Not only was social support associated with the likelihood of these girls' enrolling in advanced math, but social support was also significantly related to their grades. Girls who reported support for their enrollment were much more likely to earn As or Bs, whereas those who reported no social support were more likely to get Cs and Ds. These findings demonstrate the power of social support for academic choices and success and also challenge the idea of the importance of innate factors in mathematics achievement.

Support from parents and teachers might also influence feelings about math achievement. Parental attitudes influenced children's math achievement and varied according to children's gender (Yee & Eccles, 1988). Parents perceived that their daughters put more effort into math, whereas they saw their sons as having more talent for the subject. Mothers' stereotypical gender beliefs combined with their children's genders to influence the mothers' perceptions of their children's math abilities (Jacobs & Eccles, 1992). That is, mothers with stereotypical gender beliefs saw sons as more capable than daughters at math. Beliefs of both parents and teachers affected math achievement and were related to children's beliefs concerning their abilities at math (Eccles & Jacobs, 1986). Teachers' attitudes act as self-fulfilling prophecies, with teacher expectations playing a role in student achievement (Jussim & Eccles, 1992). Therefore, parent and teacher expectations influence not only children's beliefs about their own capabilities but also how children perform in mathematics.

A meta-analysis of attitudes toward mathematics showed surprisingly few gender-related differences (Hyde, Fennema, Ryan, Frost, & Hopp, 1990). Contrary to the stereotype, girls and women do not dislike and fear math, but when differences exist, women have more negative attitudes than men. Similar to the findings concerning math performance, the results concerning math attitudes showed no gender differences during elementary school, but some differences emerged during high school. The only dramatic difference revealed by this meta-analysis was in gender stereotyping, with men being most likely to perceive math as a male domain, as Kimball (1995) contended.

Gilah Leder (1990) has proposed that mathematics achievement is influenced by a combination of learner and environmental variables—her model appears in Figure 5.2. In this view, cognitive abilities are only one of the personal factors in achievement; beliefs concerning personal ability and the usefulness of math achievement also contribute to success. Environmental variables also provide a host of factors that can result in differential achievement for boys and girls, including social, home, and school factors.

Social factors in Leder's model include cultural expectations, such as the stereotyping of math as a male domain (Hyde, Fennema et al., 1990), media emphasis on differences, and peer encouragement for math-related activities. Home factors include family socioeconomic

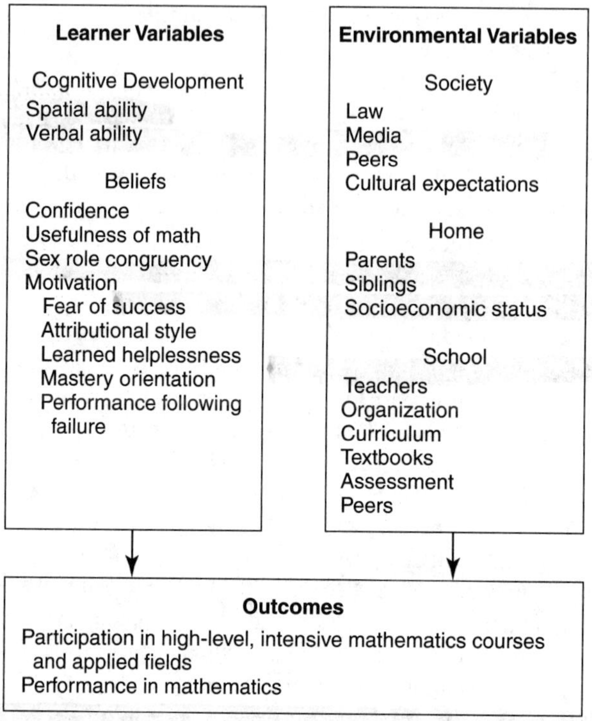

Learner Variables	Environmental Variables
Cognitive Development	**Society**
Spatial ability	Law
Verbal ability	Media
	Peers
	Cultural expectations
Beliefs	**Home**
Confidence	Parents
Usefulness of math	Siblings
Sex role congruency	Socioeconomic status
Motivation	**School**
Fear of success	Teachers
Attributional style	Organization
Learned helplessness	Curriculum
Mastery orientation	Textbooks
Performance following failure	Assessment
	Peers

Outcomes

Participation in high-level, intensive mathematics courses and applied fields
Performance in mathematics

FIGURE 5.2 Variables Studied in Relation to Gender Differences in Mathematics

SOURCE: Reprinted by permission of the publisher from Fennema, Elizabeth & Leder, Gilah, *Mathematics and Gender,* (New York: Teachers College Press, © 1990 by Teachers College, Columbia University. All rights reserved.), p. 15.

status as well as parental encouragement (or lack of such encouragement) and sibling behavior related to math. School-related factors include teachers' attitudes and behavior, organization of instruction, methods of assessment, and acceptance by peers. Although Leder constructed this model to explain mathematics achievement, the combination of factors could apply to all achievement situations.

Chapter 12 discusses the gender bias that occurs in schools and classrooms. Teachers interact with female and male students in different ways, giving boys more instruction and encouragement than they give girls. These differences are large and should produce differences in achievement:

> *When one considers that females endure remarks from teachers or texts indicating that mathematics is not a female domain, are involved in far fewer interactions with their teachers involving mathematics, are rarely asked high-cognitive-level*

> *questions in mathematics, are encouraged to be dependent rather than independent thinkers, spend more time helping their peers and not getting helped in return, and are often not placed in groups that are appropriate to their level, it is amazing that the gap [in mathematics achievement] is not considerably larger. (Koehler, 1990, p. 145)*

In summary, gender-related differences in mathematics performance do not exist in the general population, but differences do appear in selected groups. Among students, girls and boys do not differ in mathematics performance until junior high school. At this time, boys begin to show higher than average levels of math performance and confidence, and these differences persist throughout adulthood, at least for European American students in the United States. Studies of gifted children have shown that extraordinary mathematics performance is much more common among boys than girls, although this level of ability is rare even in boys. Such math talent may be the result of innate ability but may also be influenced by cultural expectations and parental encouragement.

For nongifted adolescents, differences exist in the number of math courses completed, with boys choosing to enroll in and complete more math courses than girls. Sells's research has found ethnic as well as gender differences in course enrollment, with African Americans and Hispanic Americans choosing to take fewer math courses than European Americans and Asian Americans. Such choices may limit the career options for members of these ethnic groups, just as it may for women or men who make similar choices. (See the Diversity Highlight: "Cultural and Ethnic Differences in Mathematical and Spatial Ability.")

Differences in mathematics performance and attitudes toward mathematics show small gender differences, despite the stereotype that girls and women dislike math and do poorly in the subject. This stereotype may be the underlying basis for the biased treatment of girls and women regarding mathematical ability they receive from their peer, parents, and teachers.

Spatial Abilities

Although the definition of what constitutes spatial ability has varied from study to study (Caplan & Caplan, 1994; Caplan, MacPherson, & Tobin, 1985), this variation has not hindered many people from accepting the notion that men are better at these tasks than women. Although some variation has existed in the definitions of verbal ability and quantitative ability, researchers have defined spatial ability in a wider variety of ways. Table 5.1 includes some of these definitions. These various definitions have existed because various researchers have been forced to define the concept of spatial ability in precise, specific terms in order to conduct their research. Thus, a researcher interested in studying spatial ability might choose any of these tasks as a reasonable way to measure the concept.

Once a researcher has chosen a measurement technique that resulted in a difference, the researcher might generalize these results to mean that gender differences exist in spatial ability, without considering further the validity of the connection between the concept of spatial ability and the specific task chosen to assess the concept. This process has allowed many measures of spatial ability to be developed and has created the situation in which spatial ability is not a unitary construct; thus the term should be pluralized—*spatial abilities.*

DIVERSITY HIGHLIGHT

Cultural and Ethnic Differences in Mathematical and Spatial Ability

Lucy Sells (1980) studied the effects of choices of curricula during high school on career options, with an interest not only in gender but also in ethnic background. She found that young women tend to take fewer math courses than young men during high school and that ethnic differences are even more pronounced than gender differences in high school mathematics achievement. Her examination of enrollment in California high schools indicated that only 25% of Hispanic American and 20% of African American students were enrolled in math courses that would allow them to pursue scientific and technical majors in college, compared to 79% of Asian American and 72% of European American students.

The difference in choices also appeared in college students: Asian American women chose physical science, life science, and mathematics majors not only more often than European American women but also more often than European American men. Overall, the ethnic differences were as large as the gender differences in choice of college major (Sells, 1980).

Ethnic background, gender, and mathematical ability were shown to interact when testing Hispanic American, African American, and European American adolescents enrolled in New York schools (Schratz, 1978). Unlike much previous research, the Hispanic American girls showed better mathematical performance than Hispanic American boys in this study, and African American girls showed the same trend. In contrast, the scores for European American adolescents showed much the same pattern as previous research; that is, boys scored higher than girls.

Spatial ability was also a component of this study (Schratz, 1978), in which spatial ability was measured with the embedded figures task. No difference appeared for preadolescent participants, but there was an interaction between gender and ethnic group for adolescents. These results were comparable to others found for mathematics performance. That is, for adolescent Hispanic Americans and African Americans, the girls did better than the boys, whereas the European American boys did better than the European American girls. However on this measure of spatial ability, the Hispanic American girls did better than *any other group.*

A cross-cultural analysis of verbal, mathematical, and spatial abilities failed to find the pattern of results found in U.S. samples in other cultures (Feingold, 1994). In some cultures, men score higher in math ability, but in others, women do. The same variability appeared for spatial abilities.

In summarizing the meta-analytic studies of mathematical abilities, Janet Hyde (1994) discussed analyses of different ethnic groups in the United States. The gender difference was largest for Whites, showing a small advantage for men. For African Americans, Hispanic Americans, and Asian Americans, no differences appeared. She concluded, "Perhaps the traditional belief of psychologists that men do better at math tests is a result of reliance on mostly White samples in research," (Hyde, 1994, p. 457). Therefore, the patterns discovered by U.S. researchers may be a result based on inadequate comparisons rather than universal advantage.

Researchers disagree on the number of spatial abilities that exist. One group (Linn & Petersen, 1986) placed spatial tasks into three groups, but another (Voyer, Voyer, & Bryden, 1995) contended that three categories were too few to capture the complexity of spatial abilities. Another investigator (Stumpf, 1993) argued that there are hundreds of tests of spatial ability that can be classified into 16 groups. This variety of tests illustrates the many ways that researchers have defined and measured spatial ability and substantiates the claim that spatial ability is far from unitary. The complexity of findings relates to this variety of measurement.

The three-category approach (Linn & Petersen, 1986) provides a convenient framework for summarizing (although possibly not for providing a full picture of) these spatial abilities. The three categories include spatial perception, mental rotation, and spatial visu-

Mental rotation
Which figure on the right is identical to the figure in the box?

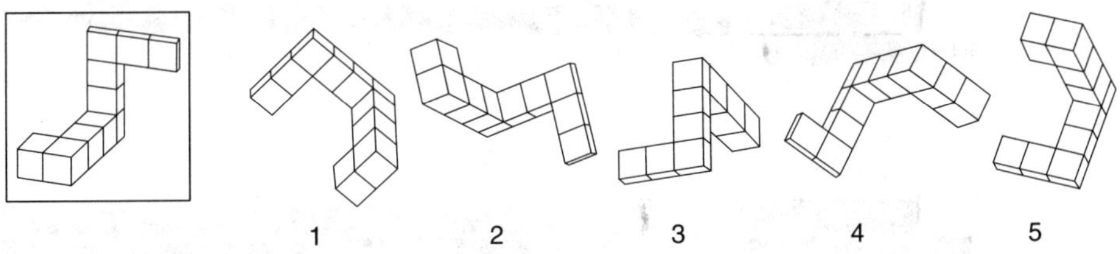

Piaget's water-level problem
This glass is half filled with water. Draw a line across the glass to indicate the top of the water line.

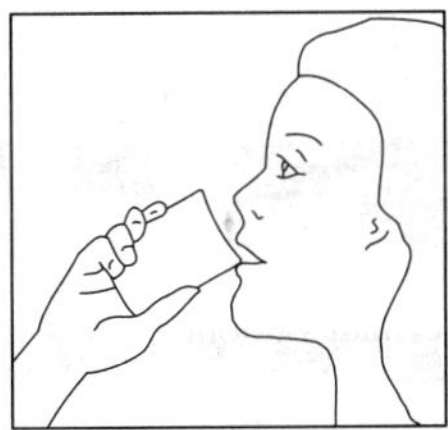

Rod-and-frame test
Ignore the orientation of the frame and adjust the position of the rod so that it is vertical.

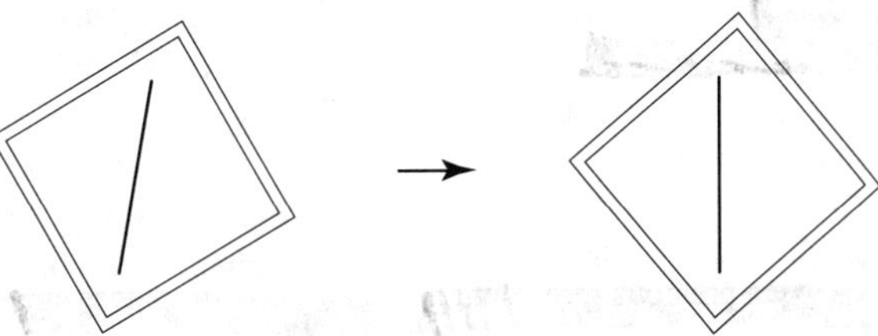

Disembedding
Find the simple figure on the left embedded in one of the four more complex figures on the right.

FIGURE 5.3 Spatial Tasks Favoring Men

alization. **Spatial perception** includes the ability to identify and locate the horizontal or vertical in the presence of distracting information. Examples of measures of spatial perception are the rod-and-frame task and Piaget's water-level task, both shown in Figure 5.3. These tasks usually show gender-related differences, with boys and men outperforming girls and women. The magnitude of this difference is small during childhood and adolescence but fairly large for adults.

Mental rotation includes the ability to visualize objects as they would appear if rotated in space. An example of a measure of this type of ability also appears in Figure 5.3. The gender-related difference for this spatial ability is large, with boys and men scoring substantially higher than girls and women on speed and accuracy of mentally rotating objects (Halpern, 1992; Voyer et al., 1995).

Spatial visualization refers to the ability to process spatial information so as to understand the relationship between objects in space, such as the ability to see a figure embedded in other figures (also shown in Figure 5.3), find hidden figures in a drawing or picture, or imagine the shape produced when a folded piece of paper is cut and then unfolded. Gender differences do not always appear on measures of these tasks. When such differences appear, they are small, and men have this small advantage.

A fourth category of spatial ability is called **spatiotemporal ability** (Halpern, 1992). This ability involves judgments about moving objects in space, such as predicting when a moving object will arrive at target. The limited research on this ability indicates that men do better than women on such tasks, but more recent research (Law, Pellegrino, & Hunt, 1993) has shown that prior experience was a factor in performance on this type of task. Feedback concerning performance improved the performance of both men and women. Thus, any advantage that boys or men show might be due to their experience with such tasks.

An additional complication in assessing gender differences in spatial ability comes from the possibility that some tasks labeled "spatial" may not constitute clear measures of spatial abilities. Instead, some of these tasks or the situations in which they are measured may include other factors. For example, the rod-and-frame task may include factors other than spatial ability (Sherman, 1978). This testing typically occurs in a darkened room, with a male experimenter testing participants. Perhaps the testing situation may contribute to the gender differences—female participants may feel uncomfortable in this situation and be less likely to persist in asking the male experimenter to continue to adjust the rod. Thus, lack of assertiveness and uneasiness with the testing situation may contribute to the gender differences that often appear on this measure of spatial ability.

The male advantage on the rod-and-frame task was eliminated by using a human figure rather than a rod and by explaining that the task was a measure of empathy (Naditch, in Caplan et al., 1985). This procedure produced a reversal in results: Women outperformed men. The task still involved the same spatial factors as the original task—namely, judging relative position in space—but the gender difference reversed.

The instructions accompanying a spatial task influenced men's and women's performance on one spatial memory and one mental rotation task (Sharps, Price, & Williams, 1994; Sharps, Welton, & Price, 1993). When instructions emphasized the spatial nature of a task, women's performance decreased compared to their performance when instructions de-emphasized the spatial nature of the tasks. Women's (but not men's) performance changed in relation to the instructions. These studies demonstrate the importance of expectation and context: Although the tasks remained the same, performance varied in stereotypical ways with different sets of instructions.

Research has also suggested that training can alter the gender differences that exist in performance on two types of spatial tasks. Two studies (Liben & Golbeck, 1984; Vasta,

Knott, & Gaze, 1996) reported on two different training procedures that erased the gender differences in performance on Piaget's water-level task. Other studies (Okagaki, & Frensch, 1994; Subrahmanyam & Greenfield, 1994) have demonstrated that video game practice is a factor in spatial performance and that practice with video games can improve mental rotation skills. Success in removing differences through training means that this gender difference changes with experience and points to socialization as the basis for the difference.

Experience is an important factor for development of both mathematical and spatial skills, and boys tend to gain more experience in these skills than girls. A meta-analysis (Baenninger & Newcombe, 1989) on the role of experience in spatial test performance confirmed the advantage of experience in such tasks. This analysis revealed that a relationship exists between participating in spatial activities and performing tests of spatial abilities, and that performance improves with training. Both findings applied to women and men, which means that both men and women are influenced by their experiences with spatial tasks, and both improve with specific practice on such tasks.

Several research findings provide evidence against a simple conclusion for a male advantage on spatial tasks. A major complication comes from the finding that women show an advantage on some spatial tasks (Kimura, 1992). Women tend to do better on tasks of perceptual speed in which people must rapidly identify matching items. Women also outperform men on tasks in which people must remember the placement of a series of objects. Examples of these tasks appear in Figure 5.4. An additional complication comes from the finding that gender differences appear in some age groups but not in others, the differences are subject to change with variations in testing procedure, and gender differences in some spatial abilities seem to be decreasing (Voyer et al., 1995). In addition, these differences do not apply to all cultures. Considering studies from nine different nations (Feingold, 1994), men showed a slight advantage overall, but in some cultures, these differences do not exist.

These various findings raise the question: Do gender differences in spatial abilities really exist? The tasks that researchers have used to measure spatial ability are varied, leading to the conclusion that it would be more accurate to think of *spatial abilities* rather than *a spatial ability factor.* Of the many spatial abilities, men show an advantage in some, and women show an advantage in others. Men in the United States produce reliably better scores than women in spatial perception, such as Piaget's water-level task, and in mental rotation, but training decreases this difference.

The embedded figures task has also yielded complex results for gender and ethnic background, suggesting that men have no clear advantage for this measure of spatial ability. Women's advantage in spatial abilities appears on measures of perceptual speed and memory for the placement of objects. Therefore, of the gender differences in spatial abilities that exist, a number favor men, a few favor women, and some vary by gender, culture, context, expectation, or some combination thereof.

Other Mental Abilities

Verbal, mathematical, and spatial abilities are important but are not the only mental abilities. These other abilities have not been investigated for gender-related differences as intensely as have verbal, mathematical, and spatial abilities. Memory, creativity, musical ability, and nonverbal communication are all abilities that have been the focus of research,

Study the objects in group **A** for one minute and cover it up. Then look at group **B** and put an X through the figures not in the original array. Score one point for each item correctly crossed out and subtract one point for each item incorrectly crossed out.

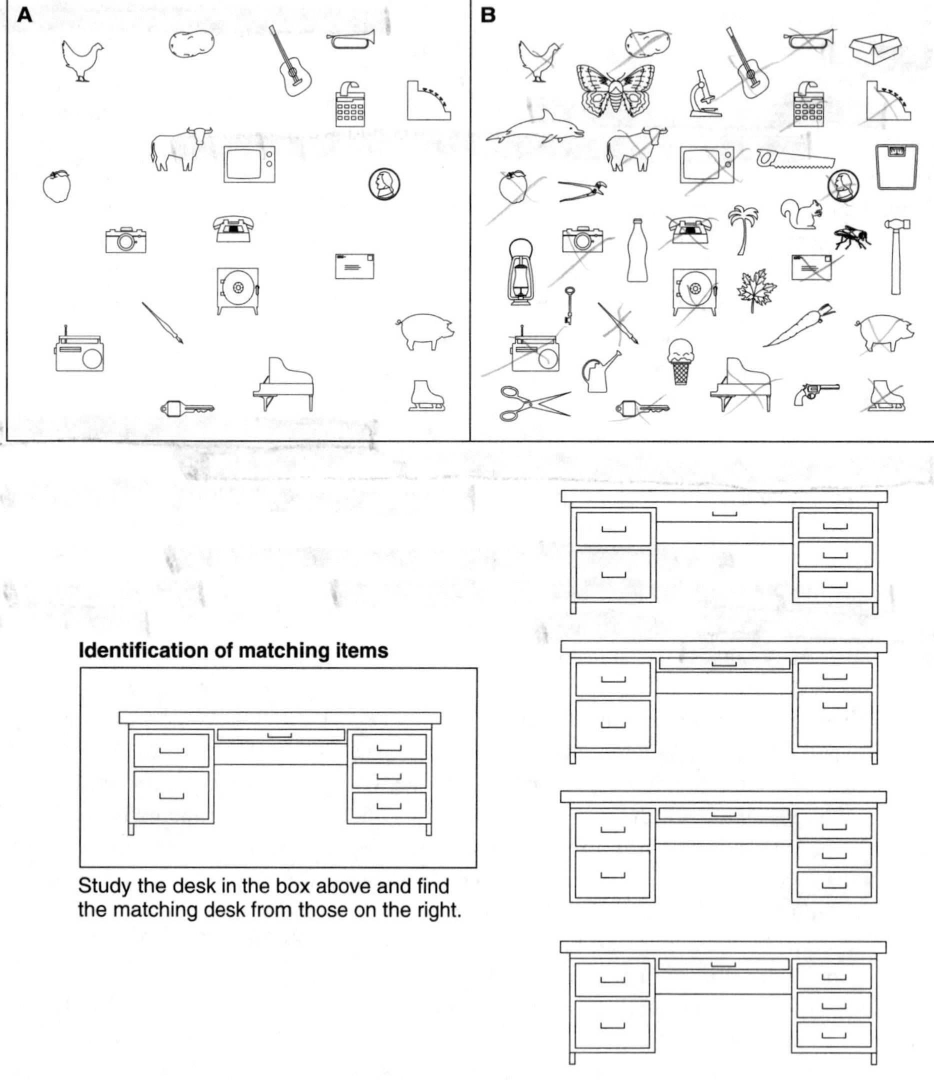

FIGURE 5.4 Spatial Tasks Favoring Women

but within this research, gender has not been the emphasis; likewise, the research has failed to show gender-related differences.

A consideration of these other mental abilities is important for putting comparisons concerning gender-related mental abilities in perspective, because these other abilities have shown that such differences are in the minority. As Diane Halpern (1992) pointed out, "It is important to note that the number of areas in which sex differences are even moderate in size is small. Males and females are overwhelmingly alike in their cognitive abilities" (p. 96).

Memory can reflect either verbal or spatial abilities, depending on the material learned and remembered. The majority of tasks that psychologists have studied fall into the category of verbal learning and memory. According to Maccoby and Jacklin's (1974) review of research in this area, few gender-related differences exist in the various types of learning and memory. When studies show differences, girls and women have a small advantage. Subsequent research has indicated similar findings: no gender-related differences (Savage & Gouvier, 1992) or only a small female advantage for learning verbal material (McGuiness, Olson, & Chapman, 1990).

Women's small advantage in verbal abilities and men's small advantage in spatial abilities lead to the prediction of differential memory performance in these areas. Do these differences hold true, as Brenda's and John's conversation (Monroe, 1995) in the chapter headline suggests? Does men's advantage in spatial orientation lead them to use maps to navigate, whereas women are more inclined to use landmarks?

Studies of route learning have offered some support for the different strategies commented on by John and Brenda. Research shows that women and men may, indeed, use different strategies to navigate (Lawton, 1994). As Brenda did, women were more likely to report that they used the strategy of learning a route; men were more likely to report that they used a spatial orientation strategy, as John did. The spatial orientation strategy may be more effective in finding the way because variations in route can diminish performance. Consistent with this finding was a study (Galea & Kimura, 1993) that showed women remembering more landmarks but men making fewer errors in learning the route.

Another study (Crook, Youngjohn, & Larrabee, 1993) also investigated route learning and also found gender differences, but the magnitude of difference was too small to be of any practical significance. That is, men's advantage in memorizing spatial information may not give them much advantage over women in getting around in the world, especially if the landmarks stay the same. Therefore, Brenda and John will both find the Emporium with comparable ease.

Some of the gender-related differences in memory seem more strongly related to the gender-stereotypical nature of the task than to the gender of the learner. For example, when women and men were asked to memorize a shopping list and directions to a particular place, the differences were in a predictable direction (Herrmann, Crawford, & Holdsworth, 1992). Women were better than men at memorizing the shopping list, and men were better than women at memorizing the directions. Furthermore, the labeling of the task influenced women's and men's memories. When people heard that the shopping list pertained to groceries, women showed an advantage, but when the same list was described as pertaining to hardware, men's memories were better. Similar results appeared in a study involving a memory test of high school students (Halpern, 1985). The procedure involved varying the name of the protagonist in the story and testing for story recall. The participants remembered more about the same-gender than the other-gender protagonist. Furthermore, participants tended to remember the other-gender protagonist as stereotypical, whereas their memory for the same-gender protagonist was more accurate. Thus, memory may depend on factors other than ability, with men and women performing according to their attention, interests, and stereotypes.

GENDERED VOICES

It's Not Something on the Y Chromosome

"I don't think that it's something on the Y chromosome," a 13-year-old girl said, referring to the ability to play percussion. "But some boys act like it is. The boys in the school band are used to me because I've played percussion all through junior high school with them, but when I go to competitions, the boys act like I shouldn't be playing percussion. Almost like it's an insult that a girl should be playing."

She explained that lots of girls play in the school band. There is generally no prejudice against girls who are musicians, but the band is gender segregated by musical instrument. The instruments toward the front of the band are more "feminine," such as violins, clarinets, and cellos. The instruments toward the back are more "masculine," such as tubas and the percussion instruments: "There are lots more girls toward the front of the band, and the boys dominate the back.

"At the all-city band competition, it was especially bad. The boys who played percussion were especially obnoxious, acting like I shouldn't be trying. They acted like it was their right as boys to be able to play drums or other percussion—like there was something on the Y chromosome that gave them the gift. Well, I guess they were really surprised when I won."

Creativity is a term that researchers have defined in a variety of ways, leading to a great diversity of findings. Studies of kindergarten and first grade children (Lewis & Houtz, 1986), children in the fourth through eighth grade (Rejskind, Rapagna, & Gold, 1992), and college students (Goldsmith & Matherly, 1988) have failed to find gender-related differences in creative thinking. In addition, a musical expert rated the compositions of female and male composers equal in possessing musical creativity (Hassler, Nieschlag, & de la Motte, 1990).

When researchers have defined creativity in terms of achievement, men have shown higher levels of creativity. This advantage, however, may not be due to greater creative ability but rather to access to training, parental and societal encouragement, and limited acceptance of women in creative fields. The greater number of prominent musicians who are men is not due to greater musical ability of boys and men: "Sex differences in most tests of musical ability are small enough to disregard" (Halpern, 1992, p. 77).

The discrepancy between the numbers of male and female visual artists and musicians may be due to encouragement rather than talent (Piirto, 1991). Creatively gifted boys and girls are very similar in personality but differ in levels of commitment to their field. The differences in creative accomplishments come from lesser commitment on the part of girls and women, and commitment comes from encouragement. Gifted girls should be encouraged to devote themselves to their talents in the same ways that boys are.

Nonverbal communication includes a variety of behaviors related to conveying and receiving information through gestures, body position, and facial expressions. According to stereotype, women are able to decipher nonverbal cues better than men. Indeed, women are believed to have "intuition"—the ability to understand social situations, people's motives, feelings, and wishes—all without being told. Sara Snodgrass (1985, 1992) has investigated this facet of gender-related behavior and has found that no gender differences exist in the ability to read such cues. Snodgrass found, instead, that people in subordinate

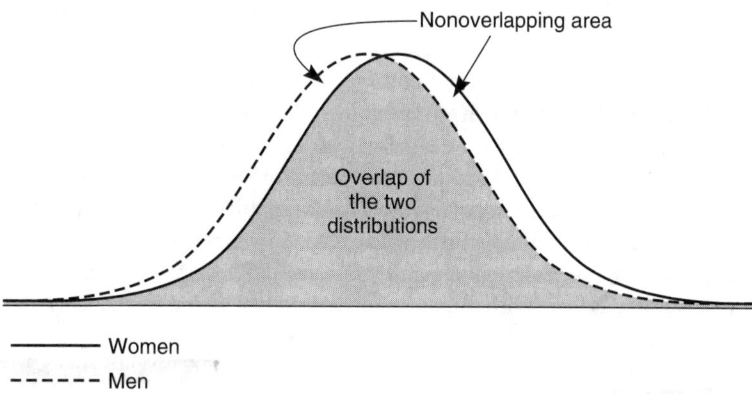

FIGURE 5.5 An Example of Two Distributions with 99% Overlap

NOTE: This distribution represents differences similar to those for verbal ability in men and women.

positions are better at reading the nonverbal behaviors of those in dominant positions. That is, women's intuition is really the intuition of subordinate status and is shared by those for whom advantage rests in understanding small nuances in the behavior of those in charge.

Although the gender differences are small in verbal, mathematical, and spatial abilities, differences do not exist in other mental abilities, such as memory, creativity, musical ability, and nonverbal communication. The studies that have revealed gender-related differences in performance in these areas have shown that the differences come from social stereotypes and expectations rather than from ability.

Implications of Gender-Related Differences

As reviewed in previous sections of this chapter, gender-related differences in mental abilities are small and may be decreasing in the areas in which they do exist. These small differences should mean equally small differences in scholastic and occupational achievement for which these abilities are required, as well as small differences in confidence in mental abilities. Instead, there are large differences in the choices that men and women make concerning careers and in their confidence in their abilities. These choices and levels of confidence may be mediated through social beliefs about the abilities of men and women. People's behavior may be more closely related to their images of what men and women can do than to what women and men actually do.

Misunderstandings of gender research have contributed to these images. Hyde (1981) has discussed the ways in which research on gender-related cognitive differences has led to erroneous beliefs about these abilities. Her meta-analyses have been important in demonstrating that the magnitude of these differences is small and possibly decreasing. These small differences mean that a factor, such as gender, that accounts for 1% of the variance in an ability leaves 99% of the difference in that ability due to other factors. Figure 5.5 presents two distributions of scores that have a 99% overlap and a 1% difference. This figure shows how similar the two distributions are. If 1% of the variance in verbal ability is due to gender, we would not know much about any specific person's verbal ability by knowing that person's gender, because too much variation in verbal ability would be due to other factors.

Assumptions about the person's verbal ability would be unfounded if they were based on the knowledge that the person was a woman, because many men have verbal abilities that equal or exceed most women's verbal abilities. Stereotypes based on gender differences in these cognitive abilities will lead to incorrect conclusions about the abilities of men and women, because women and men vary more from one person to another than from one gender to another. With only a small percentage of the variance attributable to gender, individual differences overwhelm any gender difference.

Hyde (1981) also contended that the term *well-established* should be distinguished from *large.* (At this point, using the term well-established to describe cognitive gender differences may be inaccurate, but this usage persists.) Hyde suggested that people tend to consider the two terms similar, but in this case they are not the same. When researchers conclude that a difference is well-established, that conclusion does not mean that the difference is also large, merely that it is not due to chance factors and that it has been found in several studies. Hyde criticized those psychology textbooks that include information about women's advantage in verbal abilities and men's advantage in quantitative and spatial abilities. Although many studies have found these small differences (making them well-established), such differences are by no means large. Describing the differences as well-established in texts and in the media can lead people to misunderstand their own abilities as well as the abilities of others.

Even small differences can have larger implications, as one computer simulation study (Martel, Lane, & Emrich, 1996) showed. Researchers created an organization with eight levels. A computer algorithm then simulated promotion based on ability within this hypothetical organization, with a 5% and a 1% difference in ability (with women having less ability than men). With an initially equal number of women and men in the hypothetical work force, the simulation resulted in 35% of the top-level jobs going to women (for the 1% deficit). When women were given a 5% deficit in ability, they ended up in 29% of the top-level positions.

Does this simulation mirror workplace situations? Probably not. Few specific abilities show as much as a 5% difference between women and men. Mental rotation ability shows about a 9% difference between men and women, which is enough to make a sizeable difference for any occupation that relies entirely on mental rotation. However, none does. Indeed, no occupation relies entirely on one mental ability, and social abilities also contribute to workplace success. The simulation also varied from actual employment situations in another respect: An equal number of men and women were hired, which is true of almost no occupation. The selection factors begin years prior to employment and result in a much greater gender inequality in most occupations. For example, the gender gap in engineering has been much larger than the difference in the simulation analysis showed (Martel et al., 1996). Until the 1970s, about 1% of students receiving engineering degrees were women, and that percentage rose to around 10% in the 1980s (Vetter, 1992). This magnitude of difference would not occur on the basis of the gender differences in mental abilities.

The size of the differences in gender-related cognitive ability is sufficiently small to have limited implications for men's and women's lives, yet people's beliefs allow these small differences to have a large impact. When parents, teachers, and children come to accept that boys are better at math than girls, this acceptance of a gender-related difference leads to differential expectations for math achievement. These expectations influence the level of encouragement that teachers and parents give children, thus affecting how girls and boys feel about their own abilities. These feelings affect the choices that girls and boys make concerning their elective math courses, and these choices have lifelong consequences for careers as well as attitudes toward the subject. Although the gender-related differences in cognitive abilities are small, society's acceptance of these differences creates additional divergence.

In summary, meta-analysis has shown that the magnitude of gender differences is small for verbal, quantitative, and spatial abilities. Gender differences in these three areas account for between 1% and 5% of the differences, too small a difference to explain or predict most variation from person to person. The gender stereotyping of cognitive domains has magnified small differences, thus perpetuating the belief that gender-related differences exist and that there are large differences in the abilities of women and men.

Source of the Differences

The previous chapter mentioned the controversy over the brain: Are structural or functional differences in the brains of women and men the source of gender differences in cognitive abilities? Biological determinism holds that brain structure or function determines behavior in a preprogrammed way. Biologically based theories of gender differences are very popular, as though people want to be persuaded that any observed gender difference is due to biological factors (Fausto-Sterling, 1985). Before any conclusion can be made that gender differences in mental abilities are based on differences in the brain, proponents must present several types of evidence: (1) the existence of consistent structural or functional differences in the brains of men and women, (2) the existence of gender differences in mental abilities, and (3) a link between the two. Is the evidence for sexually dimorphic brains and gender differences in cognitive abilities sufficiently strong to attempt to link the two? Except for mental rotation, the gender differences in cognitive abilities are not large and do not appear consistently in the results of research studies. This situation is problematic for a biologically determined view of cognitive gender differences.

How does the evidence for sexually dimorphic structures relate to cognitive gender differences? The strongest evidence of difference concerns the sexually dimorphic nucleus, a structure that no research to date has connected to mental abilities. Evidence for sexual dimorphism of the cerebral hemispheres, the corpus callosum, and other structures is less clear. For all of these brain structures, some research has indicated differences, but other researchers have disputed or failed to replicate these findings. Research has shown that none of the differences in these structures between women and men is large.

On first consideration, the evidence about brain lateralization might seem to fit nicely with the differences in mental abilities: The left hemisphere is specialized for verbal skills, and the right hemisphere is more expert in spatial abilities. In addition, many researchers have contended that gender differences exist in lateralization. Women have less lateralized brain functioning than men; that is, women have verbal and spatial abilities spread more evenly throughout the brain, whereas men's verbal abilities are located in the left hemisphere and their spatial abilities are located in the right hemisphere. The research on brain function confirm these gender differences.

However, the relationship is not yet clear between brain structure or function and advantage on any mental ability. The argument that lateralization improves mental abilities is not supported by the evidence: Men have an advantage in some spatial abilities but are at some disadvantage in other spatial abilities and in some verbal tasks. If strong lateralization were an advantage, then it should be an advantage for both types of abilities (Springer & Deutsch, 1998). Likewise, if less lateralization is an advantage, it should extend to spatial as well as verbal abilities. Thus, the evidence shows that differences in brain organization at the level of the cerebral hemispheres do not coincide with gender differences in mental abilities.

Neither does the characterization of the right hemisphere as "feminine" and the left hemisphere as "masculine" fit with the evidence about the function of the two hemispheres. If any gender distinction must be applied to the hemispheres, "feminine" would seem to apply to the left hemisphere, with its specialization in several of the verbal skills at which women tend to have a small advantage. Likewise, "masculine" would seem to apply to the right hemisphere, which is specialized for spatial abilities, at which men tend to have some advantage. Instead, the descriptions have been the opposite, with the right hemisphere labeled feminine and the left masculine. Only in gender-stereotypical descriptions would "feminine" be associated with the other descriptions applied to the right hemisphere—"metaphorical," "intuitive," "concrete," "impulsive," "subjective," and "holistic." The descriptions associated with the left hemisphere are equally gender stereotypical—"rational," "intellectual," "abstract," "realistic," "objective," and "analytical." Obviously, the extension of gender to the hemispheres is not warranted. This characterization arose as part of what Sally Springer and Georg Deutsch (1998) called "dichotomania," the tendency to see all contrasts everywhere reflected in the two cerebral hemispheres. Thus for every pair of oppositional adjectives, the attempt has been made to match these opposites to the left and right cerebral hemispheres. This tendency has resulted in a great deal of overinterpretation, and the masculine–feminine contrast is one such error.

Androgens and estrogens affect brain development prenatally, but do similar hormonal variations affect cognitive functioning in adults? Research on the effects of hormonal variations on women's and men's cognitive performance shows statistically significant differences. However, the magnitude of these differences is too small to have any practical significance, being "of value not so much for their practical significance as for their theoretical implications" (Hampson & Kimura, 1992, p. 397).

Developing an understanding of brain–behavior relationships is an important goal, but Doreen Kimura's research has made the front page of the *New York Times* (Blakeslee, 1988) with claims of cognitive gender differences. Although those claims were sensationalized and possibly misinterpreted (Benderly, 1989), they made an impact on the popular belief that large gender differences exist in the cognitive abilities of men and women and that these differences are based on hormones. These incorrect representations of gender research help perpetuate harmful stereotypes about women and men and about a biological basis for gender differences. The current status of both lateralization studies and research into hormonal effects on cognitive gender differences is inconclusive (McKeever, 1995).

Other problems in accepting a biological basis for cognitive gender differences come from the changes that have occurred over the past 25 years and the variations that appear across cultures and ethnic groups. If a cognitive ability has a large biological component, rapid changes or variations across cultures would not occur. Cognitive abilities vary both over time and culture.

Some research indicates that changes have occurred over time in the results of cognitive ability tests. Studying the performance of girls and boys on the Differential Aptitude Tests (DAT) administered between 1947 and 1983 revealed that the gender differences that appeared on several subtests of these tests have changed over the years (Feingold, 1988). The gender differences declined significantly from 1947 to 1980 and had disappeared completely on one verbal subtest. Boys' advantage decreased on the DAT subtests of mechanical reasoning and spatial visualization. Thus, these gender-related cognitive differences seem to be disappearing.

Studies from a variety of cultures determined that the patterns of gender difference found in the United States do not apply to men and women in other cultures (Feingold, 1994). This cross-cultural analysis indicated that women and men vary in performance on verbal ability tests, but these variations show no gender-related pattern. These findings mirror the recent research on U.S. samples, which show no gender differences in verbal ability. The analysis for mathematical and spatial abilities, however, differed from those for U.S. samples: The variability of performance did not show advantages for men. That is, the patterns of performance on these cognitive abilities differ in other cultures.

Cognitive gender differences exist for some groups at some ages. For mostly White students in the United States, women have a small advantage in some verbal abilities, men have a small advantage in some quantitative abilities, men have a large advantage in mental rotation spatial ability, and women have a small advantage in perceptual speed and accuracy. These patterns of difference do not apply to all other cultures. Women and men do not show the same patterns of mental abilities around the world as the studies from the United States have indicated: "The biology of femaleness and maleness is the same the world over, yet the gender differences that are found in cognition are not universal" (Halpern, 1995, p. 84).

Proponents of biological determinism argue that biologically based differences tend not to change over short periods of time, to vary from culture to culture, or to disappear with training. Research on gender-related cognitive differences has shown that all of these things have occurred, weakening the arguments in support of a biological basis for gender-related cognitive differences. The research on different ethnic backgrounds has supported the contention that the male advantage on mathematical and spatial tasks may be more typical of European American, middle-class U.S. students than of other social classes, countries, or age groups, and thus this pattern of abilities represents socially structured differences more than biologically determined ones.

Jacquelynne Eccles (1987) proposed an explanation of gender differences in math achievement; an extension of this model might also explain other gender differences in cognitive performance. Her model of achievement focused on choices and their link to expectancies for success and to the values individuals place on the available options. She attempted to anchor the choices an individual makes in the cultural setting by examining gender roles and different parental and social pressures on boys and girls when they decide to take a course or choose a college major. Therefore, Eccles's model emphasized the social factors that influence achievement rather than the biological factors that might influence cognitive abilities.

Eccles stressed the importance of choices for educational and vocational achievement and how women and men make different choices. She reviewed research that found that women and men have different expectancies for success, as well as different evaluations of difficulty and of the personal relevance of mathematics to future success. Eccles argued that women's lower math achievement fits into this framework. Women choose to take fewer math courses because they believe that they may not succeed in the courses, that they will have to work hard to do well, and that math achievement is not as important for them. Eccles thus presented a theory and additional evidence that could explain why men and women differ in achievement.

Eccles's model emphasizes social context, but it does not exclude the possibility that biological factors contribute to ability and performance. Not only do biological factors influence behavior, but behavior influences biology, forming a complex interaction of these factors (Halpern, 1997). No resolution of the nature–nurture controversy is possible in the case of cognitive gender differences because it is impossible to disentangle these factors. Furthermore, concentrating on the source of gender differences in cognitive abilities obscures the more important consideration: Such differences are small and may have few practical consequences, whereas the choices that women and men make differ a great deal and have enormous practical consequences.

Summary

The assessment of mental abilities has a long history in psychology, dating from the development of the intelligence test. The Stanford-Binet, an early intelligence test, showed no gender differences, but the Wechsler tests revealed advantages on verbal tasks for women and girls and advantages in performance tasks for men and boys. In addition, some types of mathematics ability tests have shown an advantage for boys and men starting at junior high school age and persisting into adulthood. These gender differences have become well-accepted, but their acceptance may be far greater than their magnitude warrants.

In addition, the verbal advantage that was once associated with women is not only small but also disappearing. Differences in some types of mathematics performance continue, but these differences are not clearly attributable to differences in innate ability and may be attributable to different experiences with math instead, especially the number of math courses completed.

Examining the gender differences in spatial ability is more complex than for either verbal or mathematical abilities because researchers have defined and measured spatial ability in many ways. Men show an advantage in performing spatial visualization and mental rotation tasks and an occasional advantage on spatial perception tasks, but women show advantages on tasks of perceptual speed and memory for placement of objects. Therefore, any conclusion about a male advantage in spatial ability is overly simplistic. Studies of other cultures and other ethnic groups have revealed that the advantage for men in mathematics and spatial ability tests may be the result of testing White college students in the United States rather than because of a universal pattern of difference.

Other cognitive abilities show no gender-related differences. These abilities include learning and memory, creativity, musical ability, and the ability to read nonverbal cues. Some studies have shown gender differences in these abilities, but these studies have fallen along gender-stereotypical lines: Women tend to have better memories for grocery lists, whereas men can better remember how to get to a particular place. The differential achievement for men and women in creative arts and music reflects variance in social support and access to these careers rather than differences in ability.

Although there is evidence for sexual dimorphism in brain structure and function, current research does not support a connection between these differences and the few cognitive gender differences that exist. Even without strong evidence, such theories continue, giving the impression that gender differences in cognitive abilities are large and important.

One biological theory for cognitive differences relies on gender differences in hemispheric lateralization to explain cognitive differences. This view is not consistent, with results showing that stronger lateralization produces an advantage on spatial tasks and a disadvantage on verbal tasks for men, even though women, who have less lateralized brains, have a slight advantage in verbal tasks and a disadvantage on spatial tasks. Hormones influence brain development, and hormonal influences may relate to brain function, but the magnitude of performance differences associated with hormonal variation is too small to be of any practical importance.

Theories that emphasize the social aspects of gender-related cognitive differences hypothesize that ethnic and cultural variations should exist in cognitive performance, and research confirms this hypothesis. Such variations should not occur if these abilities were biologically determined.

Although gender-related differences in cognitive abilities may be relatively small, the choices that men and women make in taking courses, choosing college majors, and pursuing occupations differ enormously. Differences in occupational achievement are influenced by a large number of social and personal factors, which reflect gender and ethnic differences in achievement. Biological and social factors are intertwined and impossible to separate in understanding gender-related differences in cognitive abilities, making acceptance of either the nature theory or the nurture theory unwarranted. In any case, the differences are small, and individuals vary from each other a great deal more than men differ from women.

Glossary

mental rotation a subtype of spatial ability that includes the ability to visualize objects as they would appear if rotated in space.

spatial perception a subtype of spatial ability that includes the ability to identify and locate the horizontal or vertical in the presence of distracting information.

spatial visualization a subtype of spatial ability that refers to the ability to process spatial information so as to understand the relationship between objects in space, such as the ability to see a figure embedded in other figures, find hidden figures in a drawing or picture, or imagine the shape that folding will produce on a sheet of paper.

spatiotemporal ability a subtype of spatial ability that involves judgments about moving objects in space, such as making a judgment about when a moving object will arrive at target.

Suggested Readings

Baxter, Susan. (1994, March/April). The last word on gender differences. *Psychology Today, 27,* 50–53, 85–86. Baxter's readable article takes a sarcastic and cynical look at research on gender differences in intellectual ability and the connections to hormones and brains. Baxter includes quotations from famous gender researchers that are often more revealing than their more balanced presentations in scholarly journals.

Halpern, Diane F. (1997). Sex differences in intelligence: Implications for education. *American Psychologist, 52,* 1091–1102. Halpern's review of the extensive research and theory on cognitive differences makes it impossible to view this area in overly simplistic terms. Her thorough examination of the literature includes the complications and contradictions in this work.

Hyde, Janet Shibley. (1996). Where are the gender differences? Where are the gender similarities? In David M. Buss & Neil M. Malamuth (Eds.), *Sex, power, conflict: Evolutionary and feminist perspectives* (pp. 107–118). New York: Oxford University Press. This review by one of the leading researchers in the area of gender comparisons provides a brief summary of the history of gender research, an explanation of the technique of meta-analysis, and a summary of cognitive and other gender differences and similarities.

Chapter 6

Gender Development I

The Psychoanalytic Approach

HEADLINE

Sex and Morality

—*Omni,* May 1985

> Do you think a man should steal an expensive drug to save his dying wife if he is too poor to pay for it?
>
> *Take a moment to ponder the problem. How you respond, says Harvard psychologist Carol Gilligan, may have a lot to do with your sex.*
>
> *Like other researchers interested in studying the moral development of human beings, Gilligan asked her subjects to respond to hypothetical moral dilemmas like the one above.... But unlike other researchers, including Harvard colleague Lawrence Kohlberg, who pioneered the field and formulated the above dilemma, Gilligan included women in her study.... Previous studies had either dismissed women as morally inferior beings or dropped them when their answers didn't fit the data obtained from males.*
>
> *What Gilligan found is that women differ from men in the way they approach moral decisions.... When faced with a moral conflict, men focus on a set of abstract principles, whereas women tend to weigh the impact a decision would have on the people involved. (Johmann, 1985, p. 20)*

Carol Johmann's article, "Sex and Morality," like many about Carol Gilligan's research, discussed findings of differences in moral reasoning between men and women, emphasizing the advantages of women's style of moral reasoning. Although later research showed that neither women nor men use an exclusive, gender-specific way of moral reasoning, this emphasis on women (especially the suggestion that women's moral judgments may have advantages) diverged from previous research and conceptualizations. Many theories of personality development have included different patterns of development for men and women, but the most influential of the traditional theories, Freud's psychoanalytic theory of personality, viewed the development of women's personalities as problematic. This theory postulated that the course of female personality development is likely to create individuals whose moral judgment is inferior to men's.

Do the personalities of women and men differ? Do these differences produce a different set of moral values for men and women? If so, is one set of values superior, or do the two present valid variations of ways to make judgments?

The Psychoanalytic Approach to Personality

Ironically, psychology's traditional approach to personality theory has come from outside psychology—from Sigmund Freud, a Viennese neurologist who devised a theory of personality development and a method of treatment for psychological problems. Freud developed his theory during the late 19th and early 20th centuries, a time when psychology did not include the study of personality. Only later did theories of personality development and functioning become part of psychology, and Freud's theory became the first to generate great interest.

Differences between the personality development and functioning of men and women were an essential part of Freud's theory, and those differences became a point of contention that led other theorists, including Karen Horney, to propose alternatives. The traditional approach to personality has emphasized not only gender differences but also sex and sexuality, hypothesizing that sex is a basic factor in personality. Therefore, issues of gender and sex have always been factors in traditional personality theories.

Freud's Theory of Personality

Although Freud's theory of personality has been the most influential of the traditional approaches, its popularity and acceptance in psychology have varied over the years. During the early years of Freud's theorizing, in the late 1800s and early 1900s, academic psychology did not include theories of personality, the subject matter of Freud's theory, or treatment for people with mental problems, the recipients of his treatment. Freud's background was in neurology, an area that was not well accepted either as part of medicine or of psychology (Schultz & Schultz, 1992).

As Freud's work gained prominence, his treatment became the accepted approach for dealing with people with mental problems. Also, the field of psychology underwent changes: Theories of personality came to occupy a central role, as did their practical applications, such as treatment for mental problems. The Freudian approach became associated with psychology, and many psychologists were strongly influenced by Freudian theory during the 1930s, 1940s, and 1950s.

Freud's theory dwindled in popularity among psychologists who developed other theories and therapies. The decades of interest in and association with Freud's work, however, have led to the popular belief that psychology is Freudian, when actually Freudian concepts are of greater interest in other fields, such as psychiatry and sociology. As Julia Sherman observed in 1971, "While Freud's theory is passé in some circles, psychoanalytic theory continues to be influential and important in the helping professions and in the thinking of the literate public" (p. 43). Psychoanalysis continues to play a role in intellectual debate in Europe and in the United States (Kurzweil, 1995).

Basic Concepts

Freud's theory hypothesizes the existence of the **unconscious,** a region of the mind that functions beyond conscious personal awareness. Freud was not the first to consider the existence of something like the unconscious (Ellenberger, 1970), but he was the first to place a great deal of emphasis on the influence of this region of the mind. He described the basic energy for personality development and functioning with a word that is most often translated as "instinct" but might also be translated as "drive" or "impulse" (Feist & Feist, 1998). Freud hypothesized that the life, or sexual instinct and the death, or aggressive instinct furnish the dynamic energy for personality development and functioning; that is, these **instincts** are the forces that underlie thought and action.

Freud's medical background influenced his theory in that he considered these instinctive forces to be biologically determined. The role of biology was also of essential importance in personality development, which Freud described in terms of **psychosexual stages.** These stages occurred from birth and continued through adulthood in a sequence named according to the regions of the body that were most important for sexual gratification. The early stages were the most important for personality development, emphasizing the importance of early childhood for personality development.

By hypothesizing that the first psychosexual stage began at birth, Freud described infants as sexual beings and explained many of their actions as sexually oriented. Freud termed the first psychosexual stage the *oral stage,* during which babies receive sexual gratification from putting things into their mouth. Although this interpretation can be difficult to accept, his description of infants' behavior is easy to verify: Babies have a strong tendency to put things into their mouths.

During the *anal stage,* the child receives pleasure from excretory functions. The main frustrations at this stage come from toilet training, and problems in this psychosexual stage appear in adult behavior as concerns with neatness, stubbornness, and retaining possessions.

The *phallic stage* begins in children around 3 or 4 years of age and is the first of Freud's psychosexual stages that describes a different course of personality development for boys and girls (Freud, 1933/1964). During this stage, sexual pleasure shifts from the anal region to the genitals; children begin to focus on their genitals, and they gain pleasure from masturbation. Parents are often disturbed by their children's masturbation and try to discourage or prevent this activity, furnishing one source of frustrated development during this stage.

Freud believed that the focus on genital activity resulted in a sexual attraction to the parent of the other sex and an increasing desire to have sex with this parent. These dynamics occur on an unconscious level, outside of children's awareness, and set the stage for the **Oedipus complex.** Freud used the Greek tragedy as an analogy for the interactions that occur within families during the phallic stage. According to the story, the oracle prophesied that Oedipus would kill his father and marry his mother, and this prophecy came true. Freud hypothesized that all boys feel jealousy, hatred, and aggression directed toward their fathers and sexual longing for their mothers.

GENDERED VOICES
Big Guns

"I just joined a gun club," a man told me, "and the men in the club do appear to have a relationship with their guns that seems symbolic to me. Of course, guys who own guns are pretty macho, but I have noticed two distinct styles, one of which seems more Freudian than the other.

"One style concentrates on shooting, and those men seem to like weapons that allow accuracy. Those types of guns tend to be rifles and are pretty lightweight. Maybe that's symbolic, but the other style concentrates on the size of the weapon. With some of these guns, it's just not possible to shoot accurately, but they are big guns with lots of firepower. That's all that some of these guys go for, that's all they talk about—how many guns they have and how big they are. They don't really want to shoot targets, but they want to shoot, and they seem to love their big guns. It's pretty embarrassing, in a symbolic sense."

In boys, these family interactions result in competition with their fathers for their mothers' affections and growing hostility of the fathers toward their sons. Boys in the phallic stage concentrate on their genitals and prize their penises. They notice the anatomical differences between girls and boys, which lead them to realize that everyone does not have a penis (Freud, 1925/1989). The realization that girls lack penises is shocking, disturbing, and threatening because, boys reason, penises must be removable. Indeed, boys come to fear that their fathers will remove their penises because of the boys' hostility toward their fathers and affection for their mothers. Thus, boys experience the **castration complex,** the belief that castration will be their punishment. Boys believe that girls have suffered this punishment and are thus mutilated, inferior creatures.

These feelings of anxiety, hostility, and sexual longing are all intense and produce great turmoil for boys. All possibilities seem terrible: To lose their penises, to be the recipient of their fathers' hatred, or to be denied sex with their mothers. To resolve these feelings, boys must end the competition with their fathers and deny their sexual wishes for their mothers. Both goals can be met through identification with their fathers. This identification accomplishes several goals. First, boys no longer feel castration anxiety, as they have given up the sexual competition that originated such feelings. Second, boys no longer feel hostility toward their fathers; they now strive to be like their fathers rather than competing with them. Third, boys no longer want their mothers sexually, but instead, they receive some sexual gratification from the identification with their fathers, who have a sexual relationship with the mothers. By identifying with their fathers and becoming masculine, boys develop a sexual identity that includes sexual attraction to women. Therefore, identification with fathers is the mechanism through which boys resolve the Oedipus complex and develop a masculine identity.

Freud hypothesized a slightly different resolution to the Oedipus complex in girls. During the phallic stage, girls also notice the anatomical differences between the sexes. Aware that they do not have penises, girls become envious of boys—that is, girls experience *penis envy* (Freud, 1925/1989). Freud hypothesized that penis envy is the female version of the castration complex and that girls experience feelings of inferiority concerning their genitals.

TABLE 6.1 Freud's Psychosexual Stages and Gender-Related Differences in Each Stage

Stage	Gender-Related Difference
Oral	None
Anal	None
Phallic	Boys notice that they have penises and that girls do not.
	Girls notice that boys have penises and that they do not.
	Oedipus complex
	Boys experience extreme trauma connected with the Oedipus complex, undergo stronger identification with their fathers, and develop a stronger sense of morality.
	Girls experience less Oedipal trauma, undergo weaker identification with their mothers, and develop a weaker sense of morality.
Latency	None
Genital	Women must transfer their sexual pleasure from their clitorides to their vaginas, making mature sexuality more difficult for them.
	Men's penises remain the center of their sexuality, making mature sexuality easier for them.

Their clitorides are so much smaller than penises, and they perceive their vaginas as wounds that result from their castration. Furthermore, girls hold their mothers responsible for their lack of penises and develop feelings of hostility toward them. Fathers become the object of their affection, and girls wish to have sex with their fathers and to have babies. Freud saw both the desire for sex and the wish for babies as substitutes for penises and as expressions of penis envy.

The feelings that accompany the male Oedipus complex—hostility and competition—are also present in the female version. Girls, however, cannot experience the castration complex in the same way that boys do, as girls have no penises to lose. Thus, girls do not experience the trauma of the phallic stage as strongly as boys. Girls must still surrender their sexual desires for their fathers and identify with their mothers, but the process is not as quick or as complete as it is for boys (Freud, 1933/1964).

After the resolution of the Oedipus complex, children enter the *latency stage,* during which little overt sexual activity occurs. This stage lasts until puberty, when physiological changes bring about a reawakening of sexuality and they enter the *genital stage*. During the genital stage, individuals will desire a genital relationship with people of the other sex. The regions of the body that have furnished sexual pleasure during childhood are now secondary to genital pleasure obtained through intercourse.

Table 6.1 shows Freud's psychosexual stages and the types of gender-related differences that he hypothesized for these stages. Development is similar for girls and boys in several stages but differs drastically in the phallic stage. Freud also believed that women have a more difficult time achieving a mature sexual relationship than men. He described the sexuality of the phallic stage, with its emphasis on masturbation, as immature sexuality that should be replaced in the genital stage with mature, heterosexual intercourse. For men such activity involves their penises, but women must redirect their sexual impulses away from their clitorides and toward their vaginas.

Freud believed that girls have little awareness of their vaginas until puberty and that the re-direction of their sexual energies is another difficult task for women. Freud saw masturbation as an immature form of sexuality for both men and women, and he believed that women who failed to achieve pleasure from vaginal intercourse had not achieved the mature, genital type of sexuality that signaled adequate personality development.

Moral Development

Until the resolution of the Oedipus complex, children are ruled by seeking pleasure and gratification—as controlled by a component of personality Freud called the **id.** This component is part of the unconscious and is ruled by the instincts, even to the point of irrationality. Through development of the **ego,** children learn to moderate their behavior and seek pleasure and gratification in ways that are not irrational or harmful. Nonetheless, Freud believed that the ego was practical, not moral, and that initially children, who had only an id and ego, were without morals or conscience.

Freud hypothesized that children develop a conscience by developing a third structure, the **superego,** which reflects the rules of society and is used to control sexual and aggressive impulses. Freud believed that the superego develops during the resolution phase of the Oedipus complex. But he imagined that this process happens differently in boys and girls, with unequal results (Freud, 1933/1964).

In boys, identifying with fathers prompts the development of the superego and thus of morality. Through identification with fathers, boys develop a conscience, morals, and a way to incorporate the rules of society into their behavior. Freud believed that such development is essential to maintain society and is dependent on the proper resolution of the Oedipus complex. Because the male Oedipus complex is resolved more completely and more swiftly than the female Oedipus complex, boys and men have stronger superegos than girls and women. The difficulty of resolving the female Oedipus complex results in weaker superegos and thus weaker morals in girls and women. Therefore, Freud contended that women are morally inferior to men, lacking a mature sense of justice and incapable of reaching full psychological maturity:

> *The fact that women must be regarded as having little sense of justice is no doubt related to the predominance of envy in their mental life; for the demand for justice is a modification of envy and lays down the condition subject to which one can put envy aside. . . . There are no paths open to further development; it is as though the whole process had already run its course and remains thenceforward insusceptible to influence—as though, indeed, the difficult development to femininity had exhausted the possibilities of the person concerned. (Freud, 1933/1964, pp. 134–135)*

Freud and Women

Freud knew that his theory was uncomplimentary to women, because his female associates, such as Karen Horney, told him so (Gay, 1988). He gave the matter a great deal of thought and heard many criticisms but never changed his mind about women being essentially, failed men. Although Freud may have thought women were inferior in some ways, intelligence was not among them. Freud considered that an intelligent, independent woman deserved credit and praise and might be "virtually as good as a man" (Gay, 1988, p. 507).

Freud seemed to have held contradictory attitudes about women (Feist & Feist, 1998). On the one hand, Freud was a proper Victorian gentleman who wanted women to be sweet, pleasant, and subservient. On the other hand, he admired women who were intelligent and "masculine" in their pursuit of intellectual achievement and careers. Freud acted on both beliefs. His wife, Martha, held the role of wife and mother and shared none of his professional life. Feminists were prominent among the intellectual circles of Vienna and Germany where psychoanalysis gained prominence, and many women participated in these discussions (Kurzweil, 1995). Although Freud contended that the sexes could never be equal and disparaged the efforts of feminists, who argued for the equality of men and women, he also admitted women into the ranks of psychoanalytic training at a time when women were admitted to few professions (Tavris & Wade, 1984). The person who carried on his work was his daughter, Anna, whom he encouraged to become an analyst. However, his most intimate personal friends were all men.

Therefore, Freud's attitudes about women and their personalities showed some inconsistency. Freud undoubtedly held negative attitudes about women, and he expressed his lack of understanding and lack of certainty about women in several of his papers. One of Freud's last statements about women appeared in his 1933 paper, "Femininity." He concluded with a tentative statement about women, acknowledging his awareness of the criticisms and also his own far-from-complete understanding:

> *That is all I had to say to you about femininity. It is certainly incomplete and fragmentary and does not always sound friendly. But do not forget that I have only been describing women in so far as their nature is determined by their sexual function. It is true that that influence extends very far; but we do not overlook the fact that an individual woman may be a human being in other respects as well. If you want to know more about femininity, inquire from your own experiences of life, or turn to the poets, or wait until science can give you deeper and more coherent information. (Freud, 1933/1964, p. 135)*

Other researchers and theorists have attempted the last alternative rather than the first two. In general, they have sought other information about personality and gender. One of those theorists was Karen Horney, a colleague of Freud's.

Horney's Theory of Personality

Like Freud, Horney was also a physician and psychoanalyst, but the two were a generation apart in age, and this difference contributed to their different views of the world and their different theories (Williams, 1983). Horney was one of the first German women to enter medical school, where she specialized in psychiatry. In 1910, Horney began a training analysis with one of Freud's close associates, and after her analysis was completed, she began to attend seminars on psychoanalysis (Feist & Feist, 1998). By 1917, Horney had written her first paper on psychoanalysis, which reflected the orthodox Freudian view. Her orthodoxy did not last, however, and Horney became a vocal critic of Freud's theory of personality, especially concerning gender differences in personality development. Horney reexamined Freud's concepts of penis envy, inferiority feelings in women, and the masculinity complex. In addition, Horney's interpretation of feminine masochism differed from the Freudian version.

Between 1922 and 1935, Horney wrote a series of papers in which she reexamined some of Freud's concepts and argued for a course of female personality development much different from the one Freud hypothesized (Quinn, 1987). Horney began to write about the masculine bias in psychoanalysis, and she reinterpreted psychoanalytic theory. However, Horney stayed within the framework of psychoanalysis, as shown by her acceptance of the unconscious as a motivating force in personality, her emphasis on sexual feelings and events in personality development, and her belief in the importance of early childhood experiences for personality formation. She differed from Freud in her interpretation of the significance of the events of early childhood and her growing belief in the importance of social rather than instinctual, biological forces in personality development.

Part of Horney's reinterpretation of psychoanalysis was an alternative view of the notion of penis envy, the feelings of envy that girls have when they discover that boys' penises are larger than their own clitorides. Horney argued that penis envy was a symbolic longing for the social prestige and position that men experience, rather than a literal physical desire for penises. Indeed, she hypothesized that men envy women's capability to reproduce and proposed the concept of *womb envy.* She interpreted the male strivings for achievement as overcompensation for their lack of ability to create by giving birth.

Freud argued that for women, penis envy is such a strong and threatening feeling that it must be rejected by the conscious mind and pushed into the unconscious. Horney suggested that for men, envy of women's breasts and reproductive abilities is equally strong and must also be repressed into the unconscious. Thus, both women and men have unconscious envy and fear concerning each other, and these unconscious feelings can be manifested in attempts to portray the other as inferior. Horney believed that men fear and attribute evil to women because men feel inadequate when comparing themselves to women. To feel more adequate, men must see women as inferior.

Horney postulated that men's assertion of women's inferiority exists to keep men from contending with their own feelings of inferiority. She explained that men still retain the feelings of inferiority that originated with the perception of the small size of their penises during childhood, when they initially noticed them. Therefore, men go through life needing to prove their masculinity, and they do so by having sexual intercourse. Any failure in erection will be perceived as a lack of masculinity, making men constantly vulnerable to feelings of inferiority. Women have no similar problem and do not suffer feelings of inferiority for reasons related to sexual performance. Horney (1932/1967, p. 145) summarized this conflict, by writing:

> *Now one of the exigencies of the biological differences between the sexes is this: that the man is actually obliged to go on proving his manhood to the woman. There is no analogous necessity for her. Even if she is frigid, she can engage in sexual intercourse and conceive and bear a child. She performs her part by merely* being, *without any* doing*—a fact that has always filled men with admiration and resentment.*

This resentment can lead men to attempt to diminish women, and these attempts can succeed, leaving women with feelings of inferiority. Therefore, female inferiority originates with male insecurities rather than, as Freud hypothesized, with the female perception of inferior genitals. These female feelings of inferiority are perpetuated by men's behavior toward women and by the masculine bias in society.

Horney agreed with Freud's concept of a *masculinity complex,* a manifestation of the wish to be male by choosing behavior that is achieving, active, and independent (Horney, 1926/1967). Horney saw such behavior as retreating from femininity by identifying with the father and adopting masculine behaviors. Horney believed that the masculinity complex results when girls avoid the realization of their sexual wishes for their fathers. Girls identify with their fathers because sexual attraction to their fathers is unacceptable. Identification is a more acceptable way to resolve the attraction than incest. On a more practical level, Horney also considered the social reasons for women's choosing behavior that is masculine: Men have social and professional advantages. Therefore, Horney accepted the concept but reinterpreted the reasons for the masculinity complex in women.

Horney also revised the psychoanalytic concept of **masochism**—feelings of sexual gratification from the experience of pain or humiliation. Freudian theory hypothesizes that masochism is an inevitable, biologically determined factor in the personality development of women. Thus women are *normally* masochistic, accepting and receiving pleasure from the pain of menstruation, first intercourse, and childbirth, and this masochism tends to spread to other, nonsexual areas of their lives. Masochistic men, those who show enjoyment from pain or humiliation, are exhibiting "feminine" characteristics.

Horney did not dispute the existence of masochism, but she did question its biological origin and its inevitability in women (Quinn, 1987). Her critique of the Freudian position included the method of data collection and observation. Analysts who undertook these studies had concluded that the masochism they observed in their patients was present in all women in all cultures, clearly a generalization far beyond their data. Horney called for a cross-cultural examination of women and men to determine the pervasiveness of masochism, and she described the cultural and social factors known to contribute to masochism in a society. By specifying such factors, Horney argued for the social rather than the biological determination of masochism.

Horney thus argued against several Freudian concepts that posit separate courses of personality development for women and men. She disputed the biological basis of penis envy, hypothesizing that women's envy was for men's power and social position. She also argued against the view that women see themselves as inferior because of their genitals, pointing out that men also envy women's ability to give birth and that men have feelings of inferiority about their genitals. Horney again relied on social and cultural factors to explain why women might exhibit the active, achieving behavior associated with masculinity and why both men and women might exhibit masochism.

Table 6.2 shows the points of agreement and disagreement between Freud's and Horney's psychoanalytic theories. As this table shows, both theories are psychoanalytic, in that they accept the importance of unconscious forces and early childhood experiences. However, the difference in their interpretations of the importance and cause of other events makes the two theories substantially different.

Feminine psychology was of lesser interest to Horney later in her career, but the issues that she raised and her theoretical and therapeutic endeavors contributed to her develop-

TABLE 6.2 Points of Agreement and Disagreement in Horney's and Freud's Psychoanalytic Theories

Concept	Horney's Theory	Freud's Theory
Existence of unconscious	Yes	Yes
Importance of early childhood experiences	Yes	Yes
Gender differences in personality	Yes	Yes
Source of differences	Social	Biological
Feelings of envy for other gender	Men envy women's ability to give birth.	Women envy men's penises.
Feelings of inferiority	Constant need to perform sexually leads men to feel inferior.	Lacking penises leads women to feel inferior.
Masculinity complex	Driven by girls' lack of acceptance of femininity and identification with their fathers	Driven by girls' feeling of inferiority
Masochism	Socially determined part of development that is abnormal for women as well as men	Biologically determined, inevitable part of feminine development; abnormal in men

ment of a general theory of personality that retained the emphasis on dynamic, unconscious forces in personality and the importance of early childhood experiences. Unlike Freud, she emphasized social and cultural forces rather than biological factors in shaping and maintaining personality. Her theory applied equally to men and women, but she also saw that society and culture treat women and men differently.

Women, Men, and Psychoanalytic Theory

Freud's theory of personality appeared during the late 19th and early 20th centuries in a Victorian culture that viewed women as passive, dependent, and intellectually inferior to men. This view of women was easy for Freud to accept, not only because it was the view of his culture but also because his female patients reflected these characteristics. Freud built his theory on the basis of observing his patients, many of whom were upper-class, bored, unhappy, mentally unhealthy women who lived in a repressive society that assumed women's inferiority. The extent to which their experience reflects that of contemporary women is questionable, but Freud's female patients and the culture in which they lived influenced his view of women.

During the time that Freud formulated his theory, a feminist movement was active in Europe and the United States (Kurzweil, 1995). Many of these feminists objected to Freud's theory as insulting to women, with its proposal that women experience penis envy, feelings of inferiority, and inadequate superego development. Freud (1933/1964) prefaced his remarks about personality development in women as tentative and speculative, but the majority of psychoanalysts accepted these proposals. Thus, Freud's theory was never popular among feminists, those women and men who believed in and worked for fair treatment for women, both by society and in personal relationships.

Psychoanalysis and feminism have a long tradition of interconnection because both are radical movements, and those who adhere to one are sometimes attracted to the other (Kurzweil, 1995). Early feminists argued with Freud, and some, such as Karen Horney, broke with him and formulated alternative theories. Continued interest in psychoanalysis as theory and therapy produced heated controversy within psychoanalytic circles during the 1970s and 1980s. These controversies involved an event in the history of psychoanalysis—Freud's abandonment of the seduction theory—and the appearance of an alternative psychoanalytic theory of personality development—feminist psychoanalytic theory.

Freud rejected the **seduction theory,** the view that sexual activity between children and adults is the basis for psychological problems when these children become adults, early in the history of psychoanalysis. His subsequent revision of this view had important implications for the credibility of psychiatric patients' accounts and for society's beliefs about early childhood sexuality. For many years after Freud, psychotherapists, even those who did not have a psychoanalytic orientation, often discounted women's reports of childhood sexual abuse, preferring to view such reports as mere wishful fantasies.

Feminist psychoanalytic theories provide modern alternatives to orthodox Freudian psychoanalytic theory, complete with a reinterpretation of the processes and effects of early family dynamics. These two events in psychoanalytic theory help account for its ongoing popularity and influence.

Effects of Freud's Abandonment of the Seduction Theory

Much criticism of traditional Freudian theory has appeared, ranging from the inherent difficulty in testing the theory's hypotheses in a scientific way to its male-centered point of view. However, beginning in the 1970s, several psychoanalytically trained theorists attacked Freud for rejecting the seduction theory. These attacks differed from the previous criticisms in their intensity and in their personal nature; not only Freud's theory but Freud personally was the object of these criticisms.

Although the seduction theory was part of Freud's early thinking about the source of psychological problems, he rejected this concept and postulated that attraction between the child and an other-sex parent is part of the child's *fantasy,* which has no basis in reality. Freud (1925/1959) continued to recognize that some children had experienced actual sexual abuse, but his adoption of the Oedipus complex in place of the seduction hypothesis changed the way he and many subsequent psychoanalysts viewed the psychology of women. In his final theory, Freud hypothesized that children become attracted to their other-sex parents during the phallic stage. This attraction forms the basis for the Oedipus complex, the unconscious sexual attraction to the other-sex parent combined with feelings of rivalry and hostility for the same-sex parent. Children wish to be initiated into sexual activity with their other-sex parents, but this incest never occurs except in the children's fantasies. Indeed, Freud came to believe that societies must develop strong prohibitions against actual incest, making incestuous relationships rare.

Although Freud never completely rejected the seduction theory, several of his critics have taken him to task for his emphasis on children's sexual fantasies. An early critique by Florence Rush (1977/1996) analyzed the changes in Freud's theory and the consequences of these changes. Based on clinical (and personal) experience, Rush argued that sexual abuse of children is common and, similar to Freud's early formulation, does a great deal of harm to the molested children. Rush argued that Freud's abandonment of the seduction theory was based on personal and political criteria rather than on any evidence: "When Freud arrived at the seduction theory, he did so by listening carefully and intently to his female patients; when he arrived at his Oedipal theory, he did so by listening carefully and intently to himself" (Rush, 1977/1996, p. 270).

Marie Balmary (1979/1982) concluded that Freud misinterpreted the Oedipus legend on which he based his entire hypothesis of childhood sexuality and personality development. She contended that Freud overlooked the actions of the father in the Oedipus legend as actions that set the tragedy into motion. According to Balmary, Freud's inability to see the fault of the father in the Oedipus legend came from Freud's difficulty in dealing with his relationship with his own father; he could not consciously acknowledge that his father contributed to the psychological problems exhibited by his children, including Sigmund himself. The result of this failure to acknowledge his own father's faults produced a distortion of the entire direction of psychoanalysis, including the notion that childhood seduction is a fantasy. Balmary argued that Freud incorrectly emphasized the fantasy aspect of children's seduction by a parent.

Another critic was Jeffrey Masson, who held the position of Projects Director of the Freud Archives, which allowed him access to unpublished documents. In examining letters written by Freud, Masson (1984) came to believe that the official version of how Freud rejected the seduction theory differed from what had really happened: Freud did not quickly and easily reject the notion of childhood seduction. Instead, it was the notion of parental seduction that he relinquished slowly and reluctantly. Masson concluded that Freud rejected the seduction theory because his colleagues found the notion so unacceptable. Freud believed that he would never find acceptance for his theories if he maintained that many children were molested by their parents and that these incestuous relationships produced permanent psychological damage in the children.

Masson argued that Freud had been aware of the rape and murder of children by parents, especially on the part of fathers, from the time of his early interest in "nervous disorders." This knowledge led Freud to believe his patients' stories about childhood seductions. Masson interpreted Freud's rejection of the seduction theory as an act of cowardice; Freud was not willing to endure the poor opinion of his colleagues, so he chose to disbelieve his patients and began interpreting their stories of childhood seduction as fantasy rather than reality.

Rush, Balmary, and Masson have argued that psychoanalysis might have been more useful (and closer to the truth) if Freud had kept his original notion that adult emotional problems can occur as a result of sexual abuse during childhood. By rejecting the notion of parental seduction, Freud portrayed his patients in several negative ways. First, he presented patients as unable to distinguish fantasy from reality. Although they believed the stories of their childhood seductions, these seductions were fantasies rather than reality, and therefore their stories did not need to be taken seriously. By rejecting the seduction theory, Freud cast doubt on information furnished by patients, especially information about incest, thus diminishing their credibility.

Second, by asserting that childhood seduction was a fantasy, Freud suggested that children are the ones who wish this seduction. Children want to commit incest with their parents and, during the phallic stage, may behave seductively toward the other-sex parent. Therefore, if any incest occurs, children and not parents are at fault.

Rush, Balmary, and Masson contended that Freud's influence has been great but that some of that influence has been negative. Freud established a pattern of working with people with psychological problems by attacking the credibility of these patients and by blaming the children for any sexual activity in which they had been involved. As the majority of Freud's patients were women, his rejection of the truth of their stories led to the general belief that women have fantasies about sexual abuse during childhood or rape during adulthood, but these fantasies are not based on reality. According to this view, any story that a child tells about incest is probably not true, but if evidence exists, then the incest was initiated by the child.

Those critics who accused Freud of incorrectly abandoning the seduction theory blame Freud for some contemporary problems. Freudian theory has so influenced our society that its claims about the fantasy nature of childhood sexuality and the prevalence of fantasies of rape are not only popularly accepted but have been incorporated into our legal systems. This lack of credibility of children and women who claim to have been sexually abused poses a problem for successful legal action against those who commit rape or childhood sexual abuse. If Freud had not changed his mind about the seduction theory, society might have different views about these problems.

Contemporary Psychoanalytic Theories of Personality Development

Beginning with Horney, feminist personality theorists have worked toward revising psychoanalytic theory. The urge to retain the basic tenets of psychoanalytic theory has led some theorists to either remove the objectionable elements of Freud's theory or to create revisions of his theory that are compatible with a positive view of women.

Some feminist psychoanalysts have attempted to integrate research findings about female personality development into psychoanalytic theory (Chehrazi, 1986). The resulting view is an update of psychoanalytic theory, with only minor modifications. Other theorists have departed from the Freudian tradition in more radical ways.

Sociologist Nancy Chodorow (1978, 1979, 1994) and psychologist Ellyn Kaschak (1992) have formulated psychoanalytic theories that are significant departures from Freud's view. Chodorow's theory proposes a progression of development that gives women advantages, and Kaschak's theory replaces the emphasis on male psychological development with a woman-centered view of personality. Both theories are examples of feminist psychoanalytic theory.

Chodorow's Emphasis on Mothering. Like Freud, Chodorow (1979) expressed pessimism about any potential equality between men and women. Unlike Freud (who concentrated on the perception of anatomical differences), Chodorow's reasons for believing in the continuation of inequality focused on the early experiences of children in relation to their mother. Chodorow described a psychoanalytic theory of development that concentrates on the **pre-Oedipal period** during early childhood, before the Oedipus complex, and centers on the process of being mothered by a woman.

Although Chodorow (1978) acknowledged that women are not unique in their capacity to care for infants, she also granted that most nurturing is done by mothers (or other women) and not by fathers (or other men). Thus, Chodorow explained how this early relationship between mother and infant makes a permanent imprint on personality development—an imprint that differs for boys and girls.

Chodorow (1978) described early infant development in terms similar to traditional psychoanalytic theory. Babies have no sense of self versus other people or the world; infants are one with the world, and most of their world is their mother. The early mother–daughter relationship is closer than the mother–son relationship, because mothers and daughters are of the same sex. Infants have no initial perception of their sex or gender, but mothers always know about the sex of their infants and treat girls and boys differently.

Chodorow (1978) hypothesized that when children start to develop a sense of self and to separate from their mothers, events differ for girls and boys. Girls have an easier task in developing a sense of self because they have already identified with their mothers. This identification gives them an advantage in developing a separate identity, as this identity will likely be feminine and much like their mothers. Boys, on the other hand, have a more difficult time in developing separate identities, as they have already identified with their mothers. To become masculine, boys must reject the femininity of their mothers and develop an identity that is different as well as separate. Thus, boys have a more difficult task than girls in accomplishing these developmental goals of separation and identity.

But according to Chodorow, girls never become as separate from their mothers as boys do. The gender similarity is something that both mothers and daughters know, and this similarity between the two influences each. Boys must work to accomplish their separation, even with the aid of their mothers. This effort extracts a price. Chodorow (1978) described the aftermath of boys' separation in terms of their rejection of all femininity and the development of fear and mistrust of the feminine. Chodorow thus explained the almost worldwide denigration of women by men as a by-product of boys' efforts to distinguish and separate themselves from their mothers. On the other hand, girls have no such need, and they accept their mothers and the feminine role without the turbulence that boys experience. Girls grow into women and reproduce their early relationships with their mothers in their own mothering.

Figure 6.1 shows the differences between traditional psychoanalytic theory and Chodorow's feminist psychoanalytic theory. Notice that the differences lie not only in the outcomes but also in the stage of development that each theory hypothesizes to be important in personality development and in gender-related differences.

Thus, Chodorow's psychoanalytic theory appeared as an alternative to Freud's theory, and the two theories differ in several ways. Although retaining the emphasis on early childhood, Chodorow concentrated on the pre-Oedipal period and on the early infant–mother relationship. She hypothesized a different course of personality development for boys and girls, with girls having a easier time than boys of accomplishing the goal of separation from their mothers. In their incomplete separation from their mothers, girls develop a feminine identity and the ability to mother. In the more complete separation from their mothers, boys reject femininity to develop masculinity. The difficulty of this separation leads them to reject and denigrate the feminine. In this way Chodorow explained the personality development of women and men, plus men's common tendency to believe that women are inferior.

Kaschak's Antigone Phase. Ellyn Kaschak (1992) revised psychoanalytic theory by making an analogy in personality development to Antigone, who like Oedipus is a character from the plays of Sophocles. Kaschak argued that the Oedipus legend was useful in Freud's

	Stages	Gender-Related Outcome
Chodorow's Theory	Pre-Oedipal stages	Boys work toward separation from mother, rejecting femininity. Girls retain connectedness with mother, becoming feminine.
	Oedipus conflict	Gender differences have already emerged.
Freud's Theory	Pre-Oedipal stages	No gender-related differences emerge.
	Oedipus conflict	Family dynamics and perception of differences in genitals prompt personality differences.

FIGURE 6.1 Differences between Chodorow's Feminist Psychoanalytic Theory and Traditional Freudian Theory

theory of male personality development but that the minor changes Freud made to accommodate women in his female Oedipus complex were inadequate. Instead, Kaschak casts female personality development in terms of Antigone, Oedipus's daughter (and half sister).

In Sophocles' plays, Antigone was the daughter of Oedipus and Jocasta (who was Oedipus's mother). After Oedipus learned of his incest with Jocasta, he put out his eyes, and Antigone then became her blinded father's guide and caretaker. Antigone sacrificed an independent life to care for her blind father, and he considered it his right to have this devotion. Kaschak interpreted personality development of men and women in similar terms: "As Oedipus' dilemma became a symbol for the dilemma of the son, so might that of Antigone be considered representative of the inevitable fate of the good daughter in the patriarchal family" (p. 60).

Men grow and develop in societies that allow them power in those societies and in their families, and in taking this power, men come to consider women their possessions. Men experience relationships with women that are an extension of men's needs rather than a genuinely mutual interaction. Kaschak hypothesized that mothers, wives, and daughters are all extensions of men and their needs. Women grow and develop in positions of subservience in which they are possessions of men, and women's lives and personalities reflect this status.

Kaschak hypothesized that many men and women never resolve these complexes because the social structure perpetuates differential power for women and men, encouraging both to adhere to these different roles. For men, an unresolved Oedipus complex results in treating women as extensions of themselves rather than as independent people. With this sense of entitlement, men tend to seek power and sex in self-centered ways that may be destructive to others, such as incest and rape. For example, Kaschak explained father–daughter incest in terms of fathers' feelings of owning their daughters (and, to some extent, all women) and being able to do as they wish. Consistent with Kaschak's formulation, Michael Johnson (1995) researched family violence and proposed that some men engage in systematic violence within their families because they feel that they have the right to do so. He called this form of family violence *patriarchal terrorism.*

Kaschak considered the resolution of the Oedipus complex unlikely in a patriarchal society. Those men who do resolve these feelings will relinquish their grandiosity and drive

	Not Resolved	Resolved
Men (Oedipal phase)	Patriarchical Gaining power a major goal See women as extensions of self—they have the right to have women serve them Sexually self-centered	Nonpatriarchical Gaining power not a major issue See women as independent Sexually unselfish
Women (Antigone phase)	Accept subservience Passive and dependent Accept male-defined sexuality Deny their own needs, including physical needs Cannot form friendships with other women	Reject subservient role Assertive and independent Define their own sexuality Accept and express their own needs Form friendships with other women

FIGURE 6.2 Possible Outcomes of Personality Development According to Kaschak

for power, will see women as whole persons rather than possessions, and will come to see themselves as individuals with boundaries and limits rather than as kings.

When women fail to resolve the Antigone phase, they allow themselves to be extensions of others rather than striving for independence. Girls learn that men are important and their own wishes are less so, thus limiting their lives. Among those limits are restrictions on what women may do in the world and conformity to a limited sexuality, all defined and controlled by men. In addition, women learn to deny their physicality and try to make their bodies invisible; this denial can be expressed in terms of eating disorders. These limits can lead to feelings of self-hatred and shame and the need to form relationships with others to feel self-worth.

Women who successfully resolve the Antigone phase achieve separation from their fathers and other men to become independent people. This independence allows them to form relationships with women, which Kaschak believes to be a problem for women who have not resolved the Antigone phase. In their relationships with men, women who have resolved these issues are able to stop making men central to their lives and can form interdependent, flexible relationships. Figure 6.2 shows the four possibilities in Kaschak's view of personality development—men and women who have and have not resolved major developmental issues.

Is feminist psychoanalytic theory an improvement over traditional psychoanalytic theory? Any theory that relies heavily on unconscious mental processes will rely on events that are not directly observable, which is a problem for scientific testability. All versions of psychoanalytic theory have this shortcoming. Proponents of these psychoanalytic theories tend to accept the evidence of patients and their own interpretations of what patients say, evidence that some researchers would not accept as objective. Therefore, any psychoanalytic theory shares the problem of providing adequately objective, observable research evidence.

Feminist psychoanalytic theory shares all of the drawbacks of traditional psychoanalytic theory. The feminist revisions offer a more favorable view of women, but these advantages occur at the expense of their views about men. Chodorow's theory hypothesizes that women have an easier course of personality development than men, whereas Freud's theory holds the opposite view. Kaschak's theory views men as proprietary and demanding, ignoring women except as extensions of themselves. Some women have found that these feminist theories validate their personal experiences and as such these theories are attractive. Understandably, fewer men than women consider these feminist theories relevant to them.

Therefore, both traditional and modern psychoanalytic theory emphasize the importance and inevitability of gender differences. Whereas Freud's psychoanalytic theory has a masculine bias, newer psychoanalytic theories, like the ones proposed by Chodorow and Kaschak, are part of a view of personality from a feminist standpoint, a view that emphasizes and values the unique qualities and special experiences of women.

Feminist Standpoint Theory: A Different Voice

Chodorow's (1978, 1979, 1994) and Kaschak's (1992) feminist psychoanalytic theories are only two of several theories that have concentrated on women. These theorists claim their interest in women is an attempt to remedy past exclusion; women have been secondary in theories of personality development and have been excluded as participants in many research studies. This neglect has led to theories that explain men's personality development and behavior and assume that women's will be similar. Feminist theories have attempted to consider women and their unique experiences in an attempt to enlarge personality theory to include women: "Giving voice to women's perspective means identifying the ways in which women create meaning and experience life from their particular position in the social hierarchy" (Riger, 1992, p. 734).

In their attempts to include women, feminist standpoint theorists often exclude or denigrate men. Their reasoning is that men have long been the center of existing theories and that women need special consideration or else their exclusion will continue. However, feminist standpoint theory is as exclusionary as traditional psychoanalytic personality theory, the difference lying only in who is excluded. Although both approaches can make contributions to research and theory, neither excluding men nor women will lead to a theory of personality that captures gender development; studying gender requires the inclusion of both sexes. Although feminist standpoint theory will not lead to a complete investigation of gender, this approach provides a different and valuable point of view.

When she questioned women and men about moral judgments, Carol Gilligan (1982) "began to hear a distinction in these voices, two ways of speaking about moral problems, two models of describing the relationship between other and self" (p. 1). She concluded that these two voices belonged distinctively to men and women. Her observation led to the publication of her research in the book *In a Different Voice: Psychological Theory and Women's Development,* which detailed the characteristics of the different voice Gilligan heard from women.

Gilligan's Theory of Moral Development

Gilligan began her research because of an interest in moral development and a belief about how women's moral development had been neglected and slighted by research in psychology. Two important influences on her work were Chodorow's (1978) feminist psychoanalytic personality theory and Lawrence Kohlberg's (1981) cognitive developmental theory of moral development. Chodorow's theory explained how girls develop personalities that are influenced by similarities to their mothers, thus promoting a feeling of interpersonal connection, whereas boys must work hard to separate themselves from their mothers, thereby promoting a feeling of personal separation. In Gilligan's theory, these two orientations form the psychological basis for a difference in moral reasoning.

Kohlberg's theory of moral development took a cognitive developmental rather than a psychoanalytic approach to moral development, explaining that children go through a series of stages in understanding and making moral decisions. These stages relate to cognitive capabilities, with younger children unable to make moral decisions based on abstract, rule-governed principles. Instead, young children make moral choices based first on their own needs and later on their relationships with others. Only as they mature cognitively do adolescents and adults make moral choices based on their knowledge of abstract principles of justice.

Much of Kohlberg's theory used data from a longitudinal study, a project in which he repeatedly tested a group of boys from their years in late elementary school through young adulthood. These boys answered questions about moral dilemmas, hypothetical situations involving a moral problem like the one from Johmann's (1985) story that opened this chapter—"Do you think a man should steal an expensive drug to save his dying wife if he is too poor to pay for it?" On the basis of the responses, Kohlberg formulated a theory of moral development with three levels: preconventional, conventional, and postconventional. The preconventional level involves responses based on fear of getting caught, the conventional level involves a respect for the existence of rules and laws, and the postconventional level involves an acknowledgment that moral rules should be sufficiently flexible to put human life over all other values.

Kohlberg's stages of moral development came from research on boys and men, and their answers formed the basis for his theory. But does his theory apply to girls and women? Of course, the stages can be applied to the responses of girls or women and analyzed in the same terms as responses from boys and men. Gilligan was familiar with research that indicated that, on the average, girls and women tended to fall into a lower stage than boys and men. Kohlberg's cognitive developmental theory of moral development, like the psychoanalytic theories, seems to indicate a female moral inferiority.

Gilligan (1982) maintained that girls and women develop a different moral sense from boys and men. Whereas the male moral sense is based on abstract principles of justice, the female moral sense is based on the value of human relationships. Men are oriented toward "separateness," whereas women are oriented toward "connectedness" and "care." In Kohlberg's system of classification, the emphasis on human relationships results in a score indicating a lower level of moral development than does reasoning based on abstract principles of justice. Therefore, Gilligan argued that Kohlberg's system is biased against the type of moral reasoning that girls and women tend to use, which leads to the misclassification of girls and women as morally less developed than boys and men.

Gilligan contended that women were capable of the type of abstract reasoning that would lead them to make moral judgments like men; thus, the differences were not due to cognitive deficiencies. But women value human relationships and feelings and make their moral judgments on the basis of potential damage to those relationships. Women have different priorities from men in making moral decisions, but they are not inferior in their moral reasoning.

Indeed, valuing human relationships over abstract principles might be considered superior. Women's orientation to care for others could be considered a better value system than the abstract and impersonal one that men tend to use, as Johmann's (1985) story suggested. The variation in possible approaches to moral decision making also brings up the possibility that, contrary to Kohlberg's position, no one universal set of moral principles exists. (For further discussion of this possibility, see the Diversity Highlight: "Relativism and Universality in Moral Judgments.")

Gilligan's theory qualifies as a feminist standpoint theory—it turns a traditional female "deficit" into a female "asset" by taking the position that women have a unique contribution to make and that society should acknowledge and value this contribution. Johmann's (1985) article discussed how this moral orientation might make women better suited to jobs in which personal relationships and dealing with people are an important part.

Although Gilligan's theory spurred a great deal of excitement and enthusiasm, a variety of critics have expressed misgivings. Some of those criticisms have been aimed at the methodology of Gilligan's studies, whereas other researchers have failed to find the gender differences or the orientations consistent with gender in making moral judgments that Gilligan proposed.

Criticisms have been directed at Gilligan's methodology (Colby & Damon, 1983). One claim is that Gilligan's data collection resembled clinical case studies more than objective data gathering. Gilligan's interview technique differed from Kohlberg's presentation of choices, allowing Gilligan to score the responses without a systematic evaluation of the participants' responses. Therefore, her conclusions seem to be based on some informal evaluation rather than on systematic data analysis. Furthermore, Gilligan's selective citation of illustrative examples could differ from characteristics that might appear in a more representative analysis (Davis, 1994). Gilligan's methods of data collection and analysis differ from the usual research procedures, making her conclusions more difficult for research psychologists to accept.

Gilligan's conclusions have also been contested in terms of her original contention that studies of moral development slight women (Greeno & Maccoby, 1986). The issue of gender bias in studies of moral development had been resolved before Gilligan's work appeared, and no gender differences exist in standard tests of moral reasoning. Other research (Wark & Krebs, 1996) has substantiated this claim: Women did not score lower than men on Kohlberg's moral dilemma test. Instead, the application of the care and justice orientations to real-life moral dilemmas yielded a complex pattern of findings that showed that (1) moral stages and moral orientations vary across situations and (2) both women and men used the care and justice orientations in combination in making moral judgments.

Studies by Gilligan's colleagues (Johnson, 1988; Lyons, 1988) found evidence for the justice orientation and the care orientation in moral reasoning. However, both researchers found that neither orientation was uniquely associated with men or women. Women more frequently expressed the care orientation, and men more frequently expressed the justice orientation, but both were capable of using either orientation. Studies of moral reasoning would be incomplete without considering both orientations (Gilligan & Attanucci, 1988).

DIVERSITY HIGHLIGHT

Relativism and Universality in Moral Judgments

Do people take circumstances and cultural values into account when they judge the actions of others, or do people develop toward a universally accepted set of moral principles? Lawrence Kohlberg's position was that people work toward an abstract set of moral principles that hold justice and human life as the highest moral values. As they learn to understand and accept these principles, children, adolescents, and even adults use moral reasoning that is relativistic rather than universal. The gender-related differences in moral reasoning found by Carol Gilligan and her colleagues suggest a deviation from universality in moral reasoning. Which principle governs—relativism or universality?

To determine cultural relativism or universality, researchers must test people from different cultures, asking them to make moral judgments. In one such study (Wainryb, 1993), children, adolescents, and young adults made judgments about scenarios that described several different situations. Participants first heard the scenarios, then additional information about the beliefs of people in that culture. Prior research had indicated that people are better able to vary their judgments when a different cultural belief exists about how the world works that relates to a given set of moral values.

For example, one scenario asked if it was acceptable to fail to hire a pilot because he was getting old. The information provided about the culture was that this is "a country where people believe that God helps old pilots fly their planes safely" (p. 928). Another scenario provided information about a different culture's moral beliefs involving gender bias in hiring women. The scenario included the information that this person lives "in a country where it is believed that women exist to serve men and therefore it is right to order them around and tell them where they can and cannot work" (p. 928).

The results from this study indicated that people of all ages were able to assimilate information about another culture's set of moral values in judging the actions of people in that culture, and no gender differences appeared in these judgments. In the situations in which the information concerning the moral beliefs of another culture varied from their own (like the aging pilots), two-thirds of participants took this information into account in making their judgments; they said that it was right to take such action in this context. In a culture in which people believe that God helps old pilots, U.S. residents said that it would be fine to hire them.

Participants were not so relativistic in their judgments concerning other cultures' moral values: Only 13% of judgments were relativistic, and 60% made the same judgment, with or without information about that culture's values. That is, a majority of U.S. children, adolescents, and young adults believed that it was not acceptable to discriminate against women in hiring, even in a culture that believes women are made to serve men.

These findings highlight a conflict between cultural sensitivity and moral universals: How do people accept the beliefs from other cultures when those beliefs are morally offensive to them? This dilemma is very complex (Hatfield & Rapson, 1996). One the one hand, acceptance of cultural diversity has been lacking in U.S. psychology, so inclusion of a variety of ethnic and cultural groups is a positive change. However, part of that inclusion is learning to accept these diverse cultures. On the other hand, some cultures have beliefs and practices that go against the values of many people in North America. For example, in parts of India and Southeast Asia, infant girls are killed, whereas infant boys are prized; in Thailand, very young girls are coerced into prostitution; in Africa and both the Far and Middle East, genital mutilation of girls (and, to a lesser extent, boys) is a part of the cultural heritage. These cultural differences are difficult for many people in Europe and North America to accept, despite their long traditions in these other societies. How do we accept other cultures and celebrate their diversity even though we find some of their practices morally repulsive?

This unwillingness to accept discrimination and unfair treatment may be part of a world-wide

Continued

Continued

trend toward accepting principles of equality. Perhaps a "Westernization" of values is occurring that includes an increasing value for democracy, human rights, and gender equality (Hatfield & Rapson, 1996). As these values gain wider influence, people will be increasingly likely to disagree with some cultures' practices. But also, the wider acceptance of equality will lead to a decrease in reprehensible practices and the growing acceptance of values that emphasize human rights. That is, the world may be moving toward a universal morality.

Therefore, Gilligan's original contention that women have a unique moral orientation is not a position she continued to support. Instead, Gilligan and her colleagues have provided evidence that the different voice, the moral orientation characterized by concern for people and relationships, is not unique to women. They proposed that it is more likely to be held by women than men, but other research (Davis, 1994; Wark & Krebs, 1996) has found that moral reasoning is more complex. Both the care and the justice orientations are types of reasoning that both men and women can and do use, and both are desirable for mature moral reasoning. The different voice is different but not unique to women.

Gilligan's altered position has not received the publicity that her original work did. As is often the case in media coverage of gender issues, the findings of a complex relationship between gender and morality failed to gain the media attention that the simpler, more sensational findings generated. No stories equivalent to Johmann's (1985) have appeared to publicize the advantages that both men and women derive from their ability to make moral judgments from either a care or a justice perspective. This lack of attention is a factor in perpetuating the belief that women and men are different in many essential ways, and many people want to continue to hold this position.

The Maximalist Approach and Its Implications

Gilligan's *In a Different Voice* (1982) represents an approach to gender differences that highlights the differences between men and women. This concentration on differences typifies the **maximalist** view—the view that the differences between the sexes are more important than the similarities. Although Gilligan later modified her position about women having a different voice in making moral judgments (Gilligan & Attanucci, 1988), her work inspired others and promoted the maximalist view that women and men operate on a different moral basis.

The maximalist view highlights differences, searching for the points of divergence rather than commonality. Concentrating on differences has several implications for the study of gender; these include a perpetuation of the notion that men and women are at opposite ends of a continuum, a tendency to ignore individual differences, and a concentration on one gender or the other rather than the study of both. Although some contemporary theorists take a feminist orientation to the maximalist view, this position can also reflect the opposite stance—namely, that the differences between men and women give men the advantage and put women at a disadvantage. The maximalist view, regardless of position, perpetuates polarities.

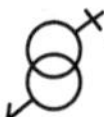

GENDERED VOICES

Carol Gilligan Should Come Visit My Home Town!

While teaching a seminar course on "Women and Justice," Carol Stack (1997) had an experience that made her think about Gilligan's contentions concerning morality and gender. One of her students, an African American man from a southern African American community expressed his disagreement with Carol Gilligan's division of the care and the justice orientations by saying

> *If Carol Gilligan is right, my brothers and I were raised to be girls as much as boys, and the opposite goes for my sisters. We were raised in a large family with a morality of care as well as injustices at an early age. Sisters, brothers, it doesn't make a difference. Carol Gilligan should come visit my home town! (Stack, 1997, p. 51)*

This opinion led Stack to investigate moral reasoning among African American working-class adolescents and adults who had migrated to the north but returned to the rural South. Her interviews with these people led her to question the validity of universal gender differences in moral judgments. She found that women and men were equal in using both care and justice reasoning. She interpreted these findings as indicating that the situation, ethnicity, and social class of the respondents influenced their choices in moral reasoning.

Feminist researchers and theorists who promote the maximalist view (Belenky, Clinchy, Goldberger, & Tarule, 1986; Brown & Gilligan, 1992, 1993; Chodorow, 1978, 1979; Gilligan, 1982) believe that emphasizing differences between women and men will allow researchers to concentrate on the strengths of the overlooked point of view and bring to it attention and acknowledgment. Chodorow (1979) wrote, "In this view, women are intrinsically better than men and their virtues are not available to men" (p. 43). For example, in researching the care orientation of moral judgments, Gilligan hoped to validate women's special perspective. Those researchers and theorists who object to the maximalist view (Crawford, 1989; Epstein, 1988; Tavris, 1992, 1994) believe that highlighting differences perpetuates stereotyping based on overgeneralization. For example, if the care orientation is unique to women, then women should be well suited to certain jobs (like elementary school teachers, who must care) and poorly suited to other jobs (like judges, who must be detached and objective).

In addition to encouraging stereotyping, the maximalist view tends to overlook individual differences. Dividing people into oppositional categories obscures the differences of individuals within these categories. Therefore, the individual differences among women and among men are of less interest to the maximalists than differences between the two groups. By ignoring individual differences, this view also minimizes the important influences of factors such as age, ethnicity, and social class. These factors have a long research history; hundreds of studies have shown that each can contribute to many facets of behavior. In overlooking these factors or assuming the influences to be small, the maximalists endanger the credibility of their research (Crawford, 1989).

Maximalists have tended to concentrate on either men or women, but not both. The traditional maximalist theories, like Freud's psychoanalytic theory of personality, have detailed the development of men but neglected women. The modern maximalist theories, put forward by feminist scholars like Gilligan, have concentrated on the unique aspects of women's experience to the neglect of men. These feminist scholars argue that women deserve special attention to compensate for the long history of neglect, but they cannot claim that their research and theories reveal anything definite about gender unless they study both men and women. Neither can these researchers rely on existing research using only male participants to furnish valid comparisons for the female subjects they have studied, as some researchers (Belenky et al., 1986; Gilligan, 1982) have done. Men who participated in research during the 1950s would not be an appropriate comparison for women who participated in research during the 1980s (Crawford, 1989). Therefore, singling out either women or men as subjects tends to endanger the scientific validity of a study.

"If masculinist values have undermined the validity of past sex difference research, do feminist values lead to more valid research or merely substitute a different set of biases?" (Crawford, 1989, p. 128). Some scholars believe that the substitution of feminist values would bring about desirable changes in research. Other scholars believe that substituting one set of biases for another offers no improvement. Both opinions have produced valuable research and have raised important questions; so this controversy shows no sign of disappearing.

Summary

Psychoanalytic theory, originated by Freud, is the traditional approach to personality theory and relies on the concepts of unconscious forces and biologically determined instincts to explain personality development and functioning. Freud's theory hypothesized a series of psychosexual stages—oral, anal, phallic, latency, and genital—to account for the influence of childhood experiences on adult personality. Gender differences appear during the phallic stage, with its Oedipus complex in which children are attracted to their other-sex parents and feel fear and hostility toward their same-sex parents. Boys experience a more traumatic and a more complete resolution of the Oedipus complex than girls, resulting in a stronger superego for boys. Freud believed that this difference in superego strength produces a stronger morality in men than in women.

Horney disputed Freud's view that women inevitably experience inferiority, penis envy, and masochism by arguing that social, not biological, forces form the basis for personality differences between the sexes. Her analysis of the differences in personality development between men and women showed that men have feelings of inferiority compared to women, especially regarding women's ability to give birth. Horney hypothesized that men try to feel more adequate by disparaging women.

Although the popularity of psychoanalytic theory within psychology and psychiatry has declined over the years, its influence has never disappeared. During the 1970s and 1980s, Freudian theory was once again brought to prominence and became controversial because of accusations that Freud acted improperly in abandoning the seduction theory. This controversy was fueled by the appearance of feminist psychoanalytic theory.

The seduction theory held that some people experience psychological problems because of childhood seductions by an adult, usually a parent. Freud formulated the seduction theory as an explanation for adult emotional problems but abandoned that explanation in favor of the view that most of these seductions were the children's fantasies rather than realities. Several psychoanalytic scholars have accused Freud of acting improperly in rejecting the seduction theory and have proposed that psychoanalysis would have been more accurate and more useful if Freud had retained this element of the theory.

Feminist psychoanalytic theory, such as the one originated by Chodorow, hypothesizes differences in the personality development of girls and boys, with girls having the advantage. Chodorow explained how gender differences begin when children strive to separate themselves from their mothers and form separate identities. This separation is easier but never as complete in girls as it is in boys, because girls are the same sex as their mothers. This similarity forms the basis for girls' identification with their mothers and causes mothers to treat daughters differently than they treat sons. This difference in treatment and the perceived difference between boys and their mothers produces a more difficult separation process, which forces boys to work harder to form separate identities. Men's success in forming a masculine identity results in a denial of all that is feminine, including a rejection of female values.

Kaschak also devised a feminist psychoanalytic theory, in which she has hypothesized that Oedipus personifies men's drives for power and feelings of entitlement, whereas Antigone, the faithful daughter, personifies women's self-sacrifice. She maintained that patriarchal culture perpetuates these roles and makes resolving these complexes difficult for men and women.

These feminist psychoanalytic theories are among feminist standpoint theories that approach personality from the point of view of women and their unique experiences. Gilligan's research on moral development is a feminist standpoint theory that originated in Gilligan's hearing a "different voice" in women's moral decisions. She studied moral development and, influenced by Chodorow's theory, decided that women are more likely to make moral decisions based on care for relationships than on abstract principles of justice. Criticisms of her method of study and conclusions resulted in additional research, indicating that the types of moral reasoning Gilligan found in women are not unique to women. Both men and women accept the care orientation and the justice orientation in their moral reasoning, and moral judgments vary according to situational factors more than by gender.

Traditional psychoanalytic theory and feminist standpoint theories both take a maximalist approach to personality, which holds that men and women show large gender differences in personal styles. Such theories tend to encourage stereotyping, obscure individual differences, and exclude one sex or the other from research. Although maximalist theories may provide interesting and valuable information about women or men, this approach does not work when applied to a study of gender, because both men and women must be included in such studies for the research to be valid.

Glossary

castration complex in Freudian theory, the unconscious fear that the father will castrate his son as a punishment for the son's sexual longings for his mother.

ego in Freudian theory, the structure of personality that is rational and practical.

id in Freudian theory, the structure of personality that is the repository for instincts and urges to seek pleasure and avoid pain at any cost.

instincts in Freudian theory, the drives or impulses that underlie action, thought, and other aspects of personality functioning, which include the sexual, or life, instinct and the death, or aggressive, instinct.

masochism feelings of pleasure as a result of painful or humiliating experiences.

maximalist a person who holds the view that many important differences exist between the sexes and that women and men are more different than similar.

Oedipus complex in Freudian theory, the situation that exists during the phallic stage in which the child feels unconscious hostility toward the same-sex parent and unconscious sexual feelings for the opposite-sex parent. Freud used the story of Oedipus as an analogy for the family dynamics that occur during the phallic stage of personality development.

pre-Oedipal period events that occur during early childhood, before the phallic stage and the Oedipus complex. Some feminist psychoanalytic theorists, including Chodorow, have emphasized the importance of this period for personality development.

psychosexual stages in Freudian theory, the series of stages ranging from birth to maturity through which the individual's personality develops. These stages include the oral, anal, phallic, latency, and genital.

seduction theory in Freudian theory, the view that sexual activity between parent and child is the basis for psychological problems when the child grows to adulthood. Freud held this view for only a short time, replacing it with the notion that the seduction was fantasized by the child rather than real.

superego in Freudian theory, the structure of the personality that incorporates the moral rules of parents and society.

unconscious in Freudian theory, a region of the mind functioning beyond a person's awareness.

Suggested Readings

Chodorow, Nancy. (1978). *The reproduction of mothering: Psychoanalysis and the sociology of gender.* Berkeley, CA: University of California Press. Chodorow's book is difficult reading, with its psychoanalytic terminology, but it offers a compelling alternative to Freud's theory and has influenced many of the scholars who take the feminist standpoint on personality.

Freud, Sigmund. (1933/1964). Femininity. In James Strachey (Ed. and Trans.), *New introductory lectures on psychoanalysis* (pp. 112–135). New York: Norton. Freud's last lengthy statement about the psychology of women is interesting to read rather than read about, because Freud seems much more tentative on some issues, but completely convinced on other issues of gender differences.

Kaschak, Ellyn. (1992). *Engendered lives.* New York: Basic Books. Kaschak's book is not easy reading, but she offers an interesting, radical alternative to traditional psychoanalytic theory. Chapter 3, "Oedipus and Antigone Revisited: The Family Drama," presents her revision of Freudian theory, but the entire book is worth reading for its different view of gender and the impact of gender on all facets of psychology and culture.

Pollitt, Katha. (1995). Marooned on Gilligan's island: Are women morally superior to men? In Katha Pollitt, *Reasonable creatures: Essays on women and feminism* (pp. 42–62). New York: Knopf. Katha Pollitt criticizes Gilligan and feminist standpoint theory in this witty essay that examines theory, research, social policy, and personal moral dilemmas.

Chapter 7

Gender Development II

Social Theories

HEADLINE

Sexist Piglets: Studies Show That Sex-Stereotyping Is Part of Childhood

—*Parents' Magazine,* December 1983

> *I'm battling with my girls all the time. At seven and nine their values are archaic. They believe that girls are dopey in math and boys should not play with dolls. Worse, one day I heard Joanne tell her younger sister that women shouldn't work! Those are the values I grew up with and it's taken me years to straighten myself out. Did I come this far just to watch my own children backslide two generations? (in Pickhardt, 1983, p. 32)*

This mother told Irene Pickhardt (1983) of her surprise and frustration at the sexism her daughters expressed. The woman was very concerned; she had tried to give her daughters positive messages about women's capabilities, beliefs that she herself had striven to demonstrate. Now her daughters seemed to be rejecting her values and accepting outdated opinions about women and men; they had become miniature "sexist pigs."

Pickhardt presented the view of sociologist Judy Corder Bolz, who specializes in gender role development. Corder Bolz suggested to Pickhardt that, no matter how liberal or egalitarian the parents, children will still show gender role inflexibility during the early elementary school years: "Starting at the age of five, children go through a fascinating stage that I call 'developmental sexism.'... For a few years they are enormously sexist in their sex-role perception and choice of play activities" (in Pickhardt, 1983, p. 34).

Between ages 5 and 10 years children have very little tolerance for exceptions to rules they have come to understand concerning gender. Children tend to conceptualize the world in terms of male or female, and variations on this dichotomy are unwelcome. This thinking leads children to have stereotypical pictures of men, women, boys, and girls. Children may even be upset by adults whose behavior goes beyond these narrow boundaries of acceptability—they may even berate their fathers for washing dishes or their mothers for fixing things around the house. Pickhardt's story contended that gender role inflexibility is an almost inevitable part of children's gender role development, but as people age, this inflexibility diminishes. Adults usually allow women and men some flexibility concerning gender roles.

A **gender role** consists of activities that men and women engage in with different frequencies. Robert Brannon (1976) discussed the origin of the concept of *role,* tracing its adoption in the field of social science back to the terminology of the theater. The word *role* was French for "roll," referring to the roll of paper on which an actor's part was printed. This usage is particularly meaningful if we consider that the role, or the part a person plays, differs from the person. Therefore, the male gender role or the female gender role is like a script that men and women follow to fulfill their appropriate parts in acting masculine or feminine. Social scientists use the term *role* to mean expected, socially encouraged patterns of behavior exhibited by individuals in specific situations. Thus, a person acts to fulfill a role by behaving in the expected way in the appropriate situation.

Chapter 6 examined the development of gender from the perspective of psychoanalytic personality theory, a view suggesting that unconscious forces and early childhood experiences form personality. The psychoanalytic view is not the only explanation for the development of personality, including gender differences. Pickhardt's story about childhood sexism concentrated on the social factors and cognitive changes that children experience as they come to understand and internalize information about gender. This orientation draws from the body of research on social learning theory, cognitive developmental theory, gender schema theory, and gender script theory.

Social Learning Theory

Social learning theory explains gender development in the same way that it explains other types of learned behaviors, by placing gender development with behaviors that are learned rather than biologically determined. This theory takes a stand on the nature–nurture controversy by describing the influence of nurture in the social environment. Biological sex differences are the basis for gender roles, but social theorists contend that a great many other characteristics and behaviors that have no relation to sex have been tied to gender roles. In this view, gender role development is the result of social factors (Bandura, 1986).

The social learning approach is a variation of traditional learning theory that includes the operant conditioning principles developed by B. F. Skinner. **Operant conditioning** is a form of learning based on applying **reinforcement** and **punishment.** To understand the relationship between social learning theory and traditional learning theory, a consideration of traditional learning theory and the concept of operant conditioning is in order.

In this traditional view, learning is defined as a change in behavior that is the result of experience or practice. Operant conditioning is one type of learning. In operant condition-

TABLE 7.1 Results of Reinforcement and Punishment for Gender-Related Behaviors

Behavior	Consequences	Result
Little girl plays with doll	*Reinforcement:* Her mother praises her toy choice	Girl plays with doll again
Little girl plays with truck	*Punishment:* Her mother scolds her for choosing a truck	Girl does not play with truck again
Little boy plays with doll	*Punishment:* His mother scolds him for choosing a doll	Boy does not play with doll again
Little boy plays with truck	*Reinforcement:* His mother praises his toy choice	Boy plays with truck again

ing, a person (or other animal) changes behavior after receiving either reinforcement or punishment. The behavior is more likely to be repeated in the future if that person (or animal) has received a reinforcer after performing the behavior in the past. That is, a reinforcer increases the probability that a behavior will recur. On the other hand, a person is less likely to repeat a behavior in the future if that person has been punished after performing the behavior in the past. That is, punishment decreases the probability that a behavior will recur. The previous consequences of a behavior thus influence the resulting behavior with reinforcers making the behavior more likely and punishments making it less likely. Patterns of reinforcement or punishment produce change in behavior, that is the definition of learning. Table 7.1 gives an example of how reinforcements and punishments can work to change gender-related behaviors.

Traditional learning theorists attempted to avoid mentalistic concepts and terminology in their explanations of behavior. They rejected all concepts of internal mental processes that might underlie learning and concentrated on objectively observable behaviors. This approach emphasized the importance of the conditions under which learning occurs and the factors that affect performance, especially reinforcements and punishments received, rather than the cognitive factors within the learner.

The experiences of reinforcement and punishment furnish each individual with a unique learning history: No other person has exactly the same experiences. The reinforcements and punishments in each individual's history contribute to present and future behavior. Thus, future behavior can be predicted from past experience.

Social learning theory also includes the concepts of reinforcement and punishment, but it also extends learning theory to include cognitive processes. This addition changes the emphasis of learning by increasing the importance of observation. Social learning theorists consider observation more important to the process of learning than reinforcement. To these theorists, learning is cognitive, whereas performance is behavioral. The social learning approach thus separates learning from performing learned behaviors and investigates factors that affect both.

According to social learning theory, learning is produced by observation rather than by directly experiencing reinforcement or punishment (Mischel, 1966, 1993). Observation provides many opportunities for learning, including the learning of gender-related behaviors among children. The social environment provides children with examples of male and female models who perform different behaviors, including gender-related ones. Those who model for children include mothers and fathers but also many others, both real people and media images of boys, girls, men, and women. In observing these many male and female models, children have abundant opportunities to learn. However, not all models have the same influence for all children, and not all behaviors are equally likely to be imitated.

The differential influence of models relates to their power or prestige as well as to the observer's attention and perception of the similarity between model and observer. Children tend to be more influenced by powerful models than by models with less power (Bussey & Bandura, 1984), but children are also more influenced by models who are similar to them. This similarity extends to gender, with children more likely to imitate same-sex models than other-sex models.

Another important factor in performing a learned behavior is observing the consequences of that behavior. If people observe a behavior that is rewarded, then they are more likely to perform that behavior than if they see the same behavior punished or unrewarded. Social learning theorists believe that reinforcement and punishment are not essential for learning, which occurs through observation. Instead, reinforcement and punishment are more important to performance; affecting the likelihood that a learned behavior will be performed in circumstances similar to those observed.

Children develop in an atmosphere in which they are exposed to models of gender-stereotypic behaviors "in the home, in schools, on playgrounds, in readers and storybooks, and in representations of society on the television screens of every household" (Bandura, 1986, p. 93). These presentations do two things. First, all children learn the gender-related behaviors associated with *both* genders; all children are exposed to both female and male models. Second, children learn which behaviors they should perform; which of a model's behaviors are specific to one gender and not the other. Children learn that certain behaviors are rewarded for girls but not for boys; for other behaviors, the rewards come to boys and not girls.

For example, children see girls rewarded for playing with dolls, whereas they see boys discouraged and ridiculed for this same behavior. Children see boys rewarded for playing with toy trucks, but they may see girls discouraged from that behavior. Both boys and girls learn how to play with dolls and trucks, but they are not equally likely to do so due to the differential rewards they have seen others receive. Their learning is not based on observation of merely a few models; the world is filled with examples of men and women who are rewarded and punished for gender-related behaviors. The portrayals of gender-related behavior are especially stereotypical in the media (Lont, 1995) and offer a multitude of sexist examples for children to model. Therefore, children may behave in ways different from their parents, including expressing sexist views that their parents do not endorse, as did the children in Pickhardt's headline story.

Not all observed consequences are consistent with each other; some people are rewarded and others punished for the same behavior. Consistency is not necessary for children to learn gender-related behaviors (Bandura, 1986). Children observe many models; they notice the consistencies among the behaviors of some models and start to overlook the exceptions. As more same-sex models exhibit a behavior, the more likely children are to connect that behavior with one or the other sex. Through this process behaviors come to be gender-related, although these behaviors may have no direct relationship to sex. Children learn to pay attention to sex and the activities associated with each, and thus they become selective in their modeling.

Children experience many sources of modeling and reinforcement, and these sources influence the development of gender-related behaviors (Beal, 1994). Beginning before birth, parents often have some preference for a boy or a girl—and more often for a boy. When their children are infants, parents interact differently with their sons and daughters. For example, children accept and show equal enthusiasm for toys typically considered girls' and boys' toys (Idle, Wood, & Desmarais, 1993), but *parents* use some gender-typical preferences in selecting activities and toys for their children. Recent research (Karraker, Vogel, & Lake, 1995) indicated that this situation may be changing—the parents in this study did not describe their newborns in the same gender-stereotypical terms that earlier studies had found.

Even if parents have stopped thinking of their infants in such stereotypical terms, they still tend to treat their male and female children in different ways. Mothers gave more instructions and directions than fathers while playing with their 18-month-old children, but fathers spent more time playing with them than mothers (Fagot & Hagan, 1991). Their different treatment of the toddlers was shown by fathers giving fewer positive responses to sons who chose playing with girls' toys and mothers giving more instructions to daughters who tried to communicate. Thus, the fathers failed to reinforce their sons for choosing feminine activities, whereas mothers reinforced their daughters for attempting verbalization, a "feminine" activity.

These forces affect gender-related thinking, social learning theory hypothesizes, through which children come to develop gender knowledge and gender standards for their own behavior. In children aged 2 to 4 years, behavior typical of their same sex was more common than cross-sex typed behavior for all ages of children (Bussey & Bandura, 1992). The younger children in the study reacted to their peers in gender-stereotypical ways but did not regulate their own behavior by these same standards, whereas the older children did both. These results indicate that these 4-year-olds had begun to develop a coherent set of cognitive strategies for controlling their gender-related behaviors.

When children start interacting with peers outside the home, these other children become a major source of both modeling and approval. Children's play groups tend to be gender segregated, especially in school settings. Children often put a great deal of effort into maintaining this segregation, and even begin to use insults and severe prohibitions aimed at those who attempt to join an other-sex group (Thorne, 1993). The formation of relationships, including the gender composition of play groups, is a topic explored in Chapter 10.

The differential treatment of boys and girls is enhanced by parents' and teachers' expectations and encouragement during the school years. Both parents and teachers are more likely to urge boys to persist in solving problems than they urge girls. By the time children reach adolescence, their models and reinforcements tend to encourage boys toward careers and sexual expression and girls toward domesticity and physical attractiveness (Lips, 1989). Therefore, children develop in environments that contain many sources of social learning that will lead to differences in the gender-related behaviors of boys and girls.

In summary, social learning theory views the development of gender-related behaviors as part of the overall development of many behaviors that children learn through observation and modeling. This theory emphasizes the contribution of the social environment to learning

GENDERED VOICES

I Wouldn't Know How to Be a Man

"I never thought of myself as very feminine, but I wouldn't begin to know how to be a man," said a woman in her 30s. "There are thousands of things about being a man or being a woman that the other doesn't know. It takes years to learn all those things. I have been struck several times by the differences in women's and men's experience, by small things.

"During college one of my roommate's boyfriends decided to paint one of his fingernails. It was an odd thing to do, but he said that it was an experience he hadn't had, and he just wanted to try it. What was interesting was that he didn't know how to go about it—didn't know how to hold the brush, which direction to apply the polish. It was interesting to watch him. That was the first time that I really thought, 'Men and women have some unique experiences that the other does not know.' I've had that thought several times since then, usually about small experiences or skills that women have and men don't.

"I'm sure that it works the other way, too. There's a world of little experiences that are part of men's lives that women don't have a clue about. For example, I wouldn't know how to go about shaving my face. In some sense, these experiences are trivial, but they made me think about the differences between the worlds of women and men."

and behavior. This view sees learning, which occurs through observation, as cognitive and separate from performance, which is behavioral. Whether a learned behavior is performed or not depends on the observed consequences of the behavior and the observers' beliefs about the appropriateness of the behavior. Thus, children have many opportunities to observe gender-related behaviors and to develop beliefs about the consequences of those behaviors. Children observe many gender-related behaviors from a wide variety of models and learn to exhibit appropriate gender-related behaviors as a result of their observation of these models.

Sandra Bem (1985) criticized social learning theory, arguing that the theory portrays children as too passive. Bem pointed out that children's behavior shows signs of more active involvement than social learning theory hypothesizes. Children do not exhibit a gradual increase in gender-related behaviors but rather seem to form cognitive categories for gender and then acquire gender-related knowledge around these categories. In addition, research evidence suggests that children may develop stronger gender stereotypes than their parents convey, which implies that children actively organize information about gender gleaned from the environment. Other social theories of gender development place a stronger emphasis on cognitive organization than does social learning theory.

Cognitive Developmental Theory

The cognitive developmental theorist Lawrence Kohlberg (1966) described this theory by saying, "Our approach to the problems of sexual development starts directly with neither biology nor culture, but with cognition" (p. 82). Cognitive developmental theory views the acquisition of gender-related behaviors as part of children's general cognitive development. This development occurs as children mature and interact with the world, forming an increasingly complex and accurate understanding of their bodies and the world.

This approach follows Jean Piaget's theory of cognitive development, which places the development of gender-related concepts into the growth of cognitive abilities and which emphasizes children's active role in organizing their thoughts (see Ginsburg & Opper, 1969). Piaget described four stages of cognitive development, beginning at birth and ending during preadolescence, throughout which children achieve cognitive maturity. During infancy, Piaget hypothesized that children have no concept of themselves as individuals separate from the world or even any idea of the permanence of objects separate from their perception of those objects. For example, children below age 6 months behave as though objects no longer exist when those objects are hidden from sight.

Even after children have developed a sense of self and a concept of object permanence during their preschool years, they still systematically misunderstand the physical world. For example, 3-year-olds are usually not able to classify objects according to any given physical characteristic such as size or color. When asked to divide objects into groups, they make choices that appear to be inconsistent. During their elementary school years, children gain in cognitive abilities but may still have difficulty in dealing with abstractions, such as the ability to imagine "what if." In addition to the limitations on children's ability to deal with abstraction, they lack the ability to solve problems in a systematic way. These phenomena result in limitations on children's thoughts, beliefs, and problem-solving abilities. For example, 6-year-old children can describe what they see, but they have great difficulty describing a scene from the point of view of anyone else, because they lack the abstract cognitive ability to visualize a scene from another's point of view.

Piaget believed that once children reach cognitive maturity, at around age 11 or 12 years, they no longer have any cognitive limitations on their understanding. (Although lack of information may be a limitation at this or any age, this problem is different from the limits on cognitive ability that appear during childhood.) Thus, Piaget explained cognitive development as a series of stages leading to an increasing ability to understand physical reality and deal with abstract, complex problems. Infants are capable of almost no abstract thought, but by preadolescence, children have fewer limitations on their cognitive abilities.

Cognitive developmental theorists see the development of gender-related behaviors as part of the task of cognitive development. Very young children, lacking a concept of self, can have no concept of their gender. Most 2½-year-olds are unable to consistently apply the words *boy* or *girl* to self or others, thus they are incompetent at **gender labeling.** Kohlberg (1966) hypothesized that children acquire some preliminary category information about gender during early childhood, but **gender constancy,** the belief that their genders will remain the same throughout life, is a cognitively more complex concept that may not appear until between ages 4 and 7 years.

By age 3 years, children are more often successful at gender self-labeling; over half of children at this age are able to correctly use the words *boy* or *girl* to describe themselves. This word usage does not signal development of **gender identity,** the process of identifying oneself as female or male. Three-year-olds apply these words incorrectly in many cases. For example, a child may label all people she likes or all members of her family as "girls" and all others as "boys."

When children can consistently apply gender labels, they may still do so on the basis of some external and irrelevant physical characteristic, such as clothing or hairstyle. In addition, children of this age do not see gender as a permanent feature; they believe that a boy can become a girl if he wishes or that a girl might become a boy if she dressed in boys' clothing (Kohlberg, 1966). Between ages 5 and 6 years, most children develop a gender identity that is based on a classification of self and others as irreversibly belonging to one gender or the other. This gender constancy is part of children's growing ability to classify objects based on physical criteria. Thus, in the development of gender identity, children below age 5 or 6 years make mistakes in understanding gender and using gender-related words, but by age 6 years, children have developed a sense of gender identity that includes correct gender labeling of self and others as well as gender constancy.

These cognitive developments in conceptualizing gender parallel other cognitive changes in children. Kohlberg observed that children below ages 5 or 6 years have an incomplete understanding of the qualities of physical objects, and he conceptualized gender identity as based on the physical characteristics differentiating the sexes. By around age 6 years, children have developed a correct, if concrete, understanding of physical reality, including gender identity. Cognitive developmental theory sees changes that occur in gender identity as part of cognitive development, and the mistakes that children make concerning gender identity are seen as part of their general cognitive limitations during the course of development.

The cognitive developmental approach is similar to the social learning approach in its emphasis on the role of cognition. However, the two approaches differ in several ways. Cognitive developmental theory hypothesizes that development moves through a series of stages, whereas social learning theory does not rely on the concept of stages in development. That is, cognitive developmental theory sees gender role development as proceeding through discrete stages. Each stage has internal consistency and a set of differences that delineate it from successive stages. Social learning theory sees development as more continuous and not bounded by stages. Figure 7.1 illustrates the difference between development as a continuous process and as a series of stages.

Cognitive developmental theory views the acquisition of gender-related behaviors as a by-product of the cognitive development of gender identity. Children begin to adopt and exhibit gender-related behaviors because they are cognizant of a gender identity and strive to be consistent with this identity. On the other hand, social learning theory hypothesizes that children come to have a gender identity because they model gender-related behaviors. Through the performance of these behaviors, children conform to either the masculine or feminine social roles of their culture. In summary, social learning theory sees gender identity as coming from performance of gender-related behaviors, whereas cognitive developmental theory sees gender-related behaviors as coming from the cognitive adoption of a gender identity.

When children develop an understanding of categories, including gender categories, they tend to concentrate on the classification rules and show a great reluctance to make exceptions. Applied to gender, this strategy would lead to classifying all women and all men by invariant physical or behavioral characteristics according to gender. That is, cognitive developmental theory predicts that children will develop gender stereotypes as part of their process of developing gender identity, just as Pickhardt's story described. A great deal of research evidence substantiates the notion that children form stereotypical gender concepts beginning early in their lives.

Children as young as 2 years exhibit stereotypical gender-related knowledge, and this level of knowledge relates to their comprehension of gender identity and gender constancy (Kuhn, Nash, & Brucken, 1978). The process of acquiring gender stereotypes, however, is complex: Chapter 8 explores this process more fully.

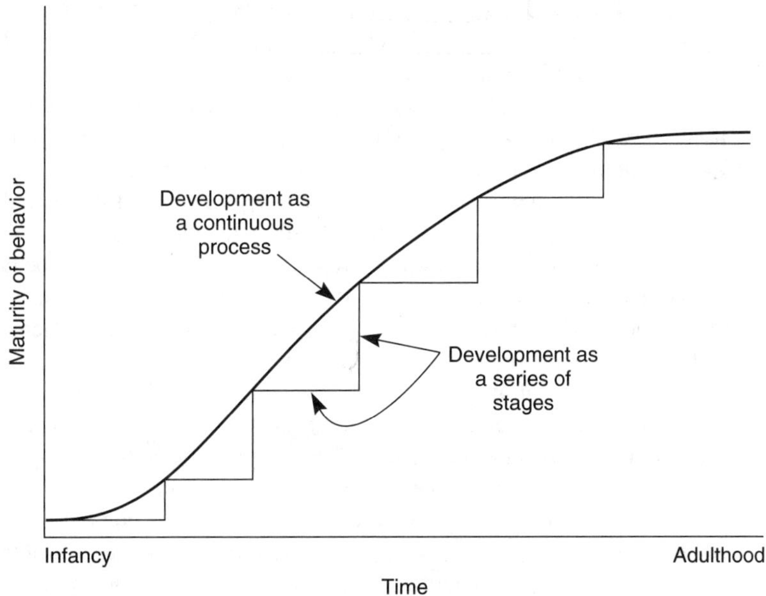

FIGURE 7.1 Two Views of Development

One problem with cognitive developmental theory comes from its emphasis on gender constancy as the primary force underlying the development of gender identity. Although Kohlberg's predictions are not completely clear on this point (Stangor & Ruble, 1987), he hypothesized that gender constancy is the most important component of cognitive developmental theory and that all other facets of gender identity stem from establishing gender constancy. Research has failed to substantiate this contention (Martin & Little, 1990), leaving a major component of this theory in doubt.

Another problem with cognitive developmental theory comes from the need to treat gender the same as any other cognitive category. As Sandra Bem (1985) put it, "The theory fails to explicate why sex has primacy over other potential categories of the self such as race, religion, or even eye color" (p. 184). This theory fails to explain why children choose gender as a primary domain around which to organize information. This problem has been addressed in gender schema theory, which extends the concepts in cognitive developmental theory of the development of gender roles.

Gender Schema Theory

Gender schema theory is an extension of the cognitive developmental theory. A **schema** is "a cognitive structure, a network of associations that organizes and guides an individual's perceptions" (Bem, 1981, p. 355). Piaget used the term *schema* (plural, *schemata* or *schemas*) to describe how cognitions are internalized around various topics: gender schema theory hypothesizes that children develop gender-related behaviors because they develop schemata that guide them to adopt such behaviors. In this view gender-related behaviors appear not only as a result of general cognitive development but also because children adopt special schemata related to gender.

According to gender schema theory, the culture also plays a role in gender development, providing the reference for the formation of gender schemata. Not only are children ready to encode and organize information about gender but they do so in a social environment that defines maleness and femaleness (Bem, 1985). As children develop, they acquire schemata that guide their cognitions related to gender. These schemata influence information processing and problem solving in memory and also regulate behavior (Martin & Halverson, 1981). Gender schema theorists believe that children use these schemata to develop a concept of self versus others and that each child's gender schema is included in that child's self-schema or self-concept. In addition, gender schemata can provide a guide for concepts of personal masculinity and femininity, including personal judgments about how people personally fit or fail to fit these schemata (Janoff-Bulman & Frieze, 1987). Thus, gender schema theory provides an explanation for the concepts of masculinity and femininity and how people apply these concepts to themselves.

Bem (1985) emphasized the process rather than the content of gender schemata. The information in the schemata is not as important as the process of forming schemata and acting in ways that are consistent with them. Gender schema theory predicts that the cognitive changes that accompany schema formation lead to the ways that children process gender-related information, which increases accuracy and memory for gender-consistent information compared to gender-inconsistent information.

A number of studies have demonstrated such memory effects in both children and adults. Gender-typed college students tended to remember words in clusters related to gender—for example, the women's proper names in a cluster and the men's names in another (Bem, 1981). Although there was no overall difference in the number of words recalled, the organization of memory differed according to participants' gender schemata. In addition, participants with strong gender schemata were faster at making gender-related judgments that were consistent with their gender schemata than judgments inconsistent with their schemata.

The types of differences found among gender schematic college students prompted further research using a similar approach, but with participants of various ages. A review (Stangor & Ruble, 1987) of the research on gender schema and information processing indicated that children with well-defined gender schemata will tend to remember gender-consistent information better than gender-inconsistent information. For example, when children see drawings, photos, or videotapes in which men and women perform activities such as cooking and sewing or driving a truck and repairing appliances, gender-schematic children remember the gender-typical pairings (women cooking and sewing and men driving trucks and repairing appliances) better than the gender-atypical pairings (women driving trucks and repairing appliances and men cooking and sewing). In addition, children tend to change their memories to fit the gender-typical activities, such as remembering a man driving a truck when he was pictured as cooking. This tendency to distort memory in ways consistent with gender schemata suggests that the development of gender schemata influences the way that people interpret information. Similar differences apply to other categories—see the Diversity Highlight: "A Schema for Race."

DIVERSITY HIGHLIGHT

A Schema for Race

Gender schema theory holds that schemata arise from the culture's differential treatment of women and men, but schemata can also be based on other dimensions. Race is one such dimension. In many ways racial and ethnic information is similar to gender in that many cultures hold differential expectancies for people from various ethnic groups and treat members of these groups differently. A category will become a schema if

> *(a) the social context makes it the nucleus of a large associative network, that is, if the ideology and/or the practices of the culture construct an association between that category and a wide range of other attributes, behaviors, concepts, and categories; and (b) the social context assigns the category broad functional significance—that is, if a broad array of social institutions, norms, and taboos distinguishes between persons, behaviors, and attributes on the basis of this category. (Bem, 1985, p. 211)*

Ethnic stereotyping has been investigated using a methodology similar to that for gender schemata (Bigler & Liben, 1993). The method involved presenting European American children with stories featuring European American and African American characters. In the course of the stories, the European American primary character encountered a secondary character who was either European American or African American. In some versions of the stories, the secondary character had a negative trait that either fit or failed to fit the cultural ethnic stereotypes. Other stories involved a European American child who encountered a social situation in which the client interacted with either people of the same ethnicity or with African Americans.

The hypothesis was that children who had formed schemata around racial and ethnic characteristics would remember the stereotypical information from the stories better than the counterstereotypical information. Similar to results from studies on gender-related information processing, this study indicated that children who have formed schemata for race and ethnicity would remember information consistent with those schemata. These results confirmed these predictions, showing that lower degrees of racial stereotyping were associated with better memory of counterstereotypical information from the stories.

Thus, schemata can be formed around characteristics that societies distinguish and emphasize. As gender schema theory predicts, other schemata are possible and lead children to make similar types of judgments, which can lead to changes and distortions in the information they encounter and process.

In developing gender schemata, children become increasingly ready to interpret information in terms of gender. A tendency to interpret information in gender schematic terms may lead to gender stereotyping—exaggerated and narrow concepts of what is appropriate and acceptable for each gender, as had the children in Pickhardt's headline story.

The formation of gender stereotypes can be understood as a natural reflection of the use of gender schemata (Martin & Halverson, 1981). Some of the effects of gender stereotyping are positive, such as increased ease in classifying behaviors and objects, which can give children the feeling that the environment is manageable and predictable. But stereotyping can also have negative effects, leading to inaccurate perceptions and failures to accept information that does not fit the stereotype. Thus, the existence of gender schemata prompt the formation of gender stereotypes, with both positive and negative consequences.

Is schematic processing and the accompanying stereotyping inevitable in children? The children in Pickhardt's headline story exhibited gender stereotyping, despite their mother's efforts to avoid perpetuating these negative attitudes. Gender stereotyping may be a typical outcome, but it is an avoidable one (Bem, 1985, 1987). Parents, however, must take measures to raise "gender-aschematic children in a gender-schematic world" (Bem, 1985, p. 213). Those measures do not include ignoring gender, because society does not. Rather, parents can attempt to eliminate gender differentiation that has nothing to do with gender, they can concentrate on the biological rather than social correlates of sex, and they can substitute some alternative schema.

Bem advised parents to eliminate the multitude of cultural messages concerning gender that have no relation with sex except by association. For example, occupations, household chores, leisure activities, and even color preferences are associated with either men or women, and none of these needs to be so. Bem advised parents to eliminate gender-related differences from their own activities and to teach their children about the culture's bias in the message. She also recommended that parents emphasize the biological rather than social correlates of sex. By teaching children about anatomy and reproduction, Bem argued that parents can limit gender-related associations to biological sex, thus minimizing the pervasive associations of gender with so many aspects of life. Bem also suggested that parents substitute alternative schemata, such as the individual differences schema rather than the gender-related differences schema that is the basis of traditional gender stereotyping.

Do Bem's suggestions help to alter the development of gender schemata and lessen the strength of gender stereotyping? Research (Fagot & Leinbach, 1995) suggests that Bem's recommendations can be effective. This study of a group of parents who had sought to establish egalitarian child care routines showed that these efforts were successful, not only in involving both parents in their children's lives, but also in altering the development of their children's gender knowledge.

Some family patterns are more likely to produce nonsexist children than others (Weisner & Wilson-Mitchell, 1990). Traditional families, of course, are likely to have children with strong gender schemata, but some nonconventional families also produce gender-schematic children. The families that followed Bem's suggestions—by using egalitarian behavior patterns combined with questioning societal norms—produced children with less gender-typed knowledge than other family patterns. Table 7.2 summarizes the factors that relate to children with and without strong gender schemata and shows the combination of factors that tends to make children sexist. Regardless of family attitudes and behavior, all children displayed gender-related information that went far beyond the knowledge that genitals determine a person's sex. That is, no family attitudes or behavior can completely counteract the influence of society's pervasive gender associations

In summary, gender schema theory extends the cognitive developmental theory by hypothesizing the existence of gender schemata, cognitive structures that internally represent gender-related information and guide perception and behavior. Children internalize their schemata for masculinity or femininity to form a self-concept, or self-schema, for gender-related behaviors. Research has indicated that gender schemata can affect the processing of gender-related information and can lead to gender stereotyping. Parents can attempt to circumvent gender-related messages by concentrating on the biological rather than the social correlates of gender, but all children come to understand their culture's messages about gender.

TABLE 7.2 Factors in the Development of Gender-Related Attitudes in Children

Children Who Exhibit Inflexible Attitudes about Gender	Children Who Exhibit More Flexible Attitudes about Gender
Have parents who exhibit traditional attitudes concerning gender-related behaviors	Have parents who question traditional attitudes concerning gender-related behaviors
(Weisner & Wilson-Mitchell, 1990)	
Have parents who concentrate on the social correlates of gender	Have parents who concentrate on the physical determinants of sex
(Bem, 1989)	
Interact more with parents	Interact less with parents
(Levy, 1989)	
Have same-gender siblings who are gender-inflexible	Have same-gender siblings who are gender-flexible
(Katz & Ksansnak, 1994)	
Have same-gender peers who are gender-inflexible	Have same-gender peers who are gender-flexible
(Katz & Ksansnak, 1994)	
Are more likely to have mothers who are homemakers	Are more likely to have mothers who work outside the home
(Levy, 1989)	

Gender Script Theory

Gender script theory is an extension of gender schema theory. It proposes that the social knowledge that children acquire concerning gender is organized in sequential form. Schemata are representations of knowledge, whereas scripts depict an organized sequence of events. That is, the concept of a script enlarges on the notion of schema by adding the component of sequential order. The script allows for the understanding of social relations and can be described as "an ordered sequence of actions appropriate to a particular spatial–temporal context, organized around a goal" (Nelson, 1981, p. 101).

Children as young as 3 years of age show evidence of the type of generalized sequential event knowledge that may be considered a script. Children can describe how to get ready to go out, how to eat lunch at day care, and many such sequences. If young children have well-organized knowledge of events, perhaps they use this organization to acquire information about gender.

Applied to gender role acquisition, gender scripts are "temporally organized event sequences. But in addition, gender scripts possess a gender-role stereotype component which defines which sex stereotypically performs a given sequence of events" (Levy & Fivush, 1993, p. 113). For scripts such as eating lunch, the gender of the actor is not important, but the script for cooking lunch is likely to be gender specific.

Researchers have investigated the existence of gender scripts in information processing and memory using tests that are similar to the ones used to test gender schema theory. Children of varying ages were given colored line drawings representing several gender scripts, such as building with tools and cooking dinner, and were asked to arrange the drawings in the order that these events would happen (Boston & Levy, 1991). The results indicated that older children were more accurate than younger children in doing so, but also that children (especially boys) were more accurate in ordering own-gender rather than other-gender sequences.

Gender scripts also influence memory. One study (Levy & Boston, 1994) presented children with two own-gender and two other-gender scripts and asked them to recall as many parts of the scripts as they could. The children were more accurate in recalling own-sex scripts, a similar memory effect to findings from research on gender schema theory. Another similarity in the cognitive difficulty with schemata is the tendency of younger children to be more strict in their adherence to the script than older children are (Levy & Fivush, 1993).

Therefore, the sequencing component of gender script theory seems to broaden the concept of gender schemata. The research on gender script theory is less complete than the other theories of gender role development, but this theory is a promising addition to the other social theories of gender development.

Social learning theory, cognitive developmental theory, gender schema theory, and gender script theory all attempt to explain how children come to exhibit gender-related behaviors and choose personal concepts of masculinity and femininity. These theories all emphasize children's surroundings in the family and in society, but each theory has a different view of how children come to understand gender. Table 7.3 compares these theories. Each of these theories hypothesizes a course of development of gender-related knowledge and behavior, but what does the research on this topic indicate? How do children come to understand gender and develop gender-typing, and how does the research fit with the theories?

Developing Gender Identity

Traditionally, a child's sex was announced at birth, but now many parents know their child's sex prenatally; this knowledge now allows for gender differentiation even before a child is born. In either event, the pinks and blues appear early in children's lives. All social theories of gender development rate this type of differential treatment as important in causing children to attend to and adopt the appropriate gender role. Thus, the process of developing gender identity might start early in infancy.

Some research indicates that infants possess the ability to begin gender typing—that they can tell the difference between male and female faces. Although studying infants' thoughts is a difficult task, one approach involves showing the infant such objects as photos of faces and measuring how long these objects hold the infant's attention. When infants see something new, they tend to gaze at the novel object; when they grow bored, they begin looking around rather than at the object. The process of attaining to an object is called habituation, and by using this procedure researchers can determine which objects or features of objects infants can distinguish and which they cannot. By noting when infants attend to objects and when they grow bored, researchers can deduce which stimuli infants can distinguish and which they cannot.

TABLE 7.3 A Comparison of Social Theories of Gender Development

	Social Learning Theory	Cognitive Developmental Theory	Gender Schema Theory	Gender Script Theory
Gender differences develop through...	reinforcement and observation of models	general cognitive development, especially gender constancy	development of gender-specific schemata	learning gender scripts
Children's participation involves...	choosing which models to imitate	organizing information about the physical world	developing schemata specific to gender	developing scripts through social interaction
Gender development begins...	as soon as the culture emphasizes it, usually during infancy	during preschool years	during preschool years	during early preschool years
Gender development proceeds...	gradually becoming more like adult knowledge	through a series of stages	through development of schemata	through learning script components
Gender development finishes...	during adulthood, if at all	during late childhood or preadolescence	during late childhood	when all scripts are learned
Girls and boys...	may develop different gender knowledge as well as different gender-related behaviors	develop similar cognitive understanding of gender	may develop different structures and schemata, depending on parents and family patterns	develop different scripts, guided through learning stereotypes

Results using such a procedure showed that infants had the ability to distinguish between women and men (Fagot & Leinbach, 1994; Leinbach & Fagot, 1993). Infants 7, 9, and 12 months old could distinguish male from female faces, mainly by using long hair as the cue. This ability gives infants some basis to begin to make gender distinctions.

Factors influential in the development of gender identity include not only the ability to distinguish between the sexes but also the ability to label each, know of gender roles, adopt gender roles, recognize gender constancy, and be flexible in applying gender roles to self and others. Research indicates that these elements of gender identity are separable and that they develop at different times.

During Childhood

The ability to make a distinction between the category of men and women is far from possessing a gender concept or identity (Fagot & Leinbach, 1993). Infants may be able to distinguish between men and women, but they use hair length to signal gender, thus they have not yet developed an understanding of gender distinctions. However, when children begin

TABLE 7.4 Stages of Developing Gender-Related Knowledge

	Gender Labeling	Gender Preferences or Knowledge	Gender Constancy
Stage 1	No	No	No
Stage 2	Yes	No	No
Stage 3	Yes	Yes	Possibly
Stage 4	Yes	Yes	Yes

SOURCE: Based on The relation of gender understanding to children's sex-typed preferences and gender stereotypes (pp. 1434–1435) by C. L. Martin & J. Little, 1990, *Child Development, 61.*

to talk, they soon start to use words that denote gender. That is, they use gender labels to refer to women (or girls) and men (or boys).

The Sequence of Development

When children begin to attach words to gender, they may not do so correctly. In one study (Fagot & Leinbach, 1989), none of the toddlers passed the gender-labeling task before age 18 months, and these children also showed no differences in gender-typed behaviors. By age 27 months, half could not apply gender labels correctly. The children who succeeded in this task, like those in another study (Fagot, Leinbach, & O'Boyle, 1992), had parents who showed more traditional gender role behavior and provided their toddlers with positive and negative feedback for playing with gender-typed toys. These studies showed not only that children start to develop the ability to label gender at around 2 years of age but also—as social learning theory predicts—that parents' attention to gender plays a role in this development.

Children's gender knowledge has several different dimensions and develops in a pattern, with older children showing more complete and complex knowledge concerning gender roles and stereotypes than younger children (Martin & Little, 1990; Ruble & Martin, 1998). Three-year-old participants were able to label the sexes, form groupings based on gender, and exhibit some knowledge of the behaviors typically associated with women and men. They did not show evidence of gender constancy at age 3, nor did they show extensive knowledge of gender-typical clothing or toy choices. Around age 4 the majority of these children could complete the tests of gender discrimination and gender stability, and their understanding of gender-typical clothes and toys was closer to the stereotypes.

The patterns of gender knowledge for the children in this study seem to fall into a sequence of development. Young children may not exhibit a great understanding of gender-related knowledge or preferences, even in the ability to label and show preferences for gender-typical toys. Those children who have succeeded in gender labeling may not have acquired gender knowledge or preferences, but children will not have a full understanding of gender knowledge or preferences without the ability to label. Those children whose gender knowledge is complete will likely be able to succeed on all the tasks. Table 7.4 shows these four stages of development. An analysis of the children's responses showed that 98% of them fell into one of these categories. Their findings revealed that, contrary to Kohlberg's

GENDERED VOICES

You Could Be a Boy One Day and a Girl the Next

"When my daughter was 2 or 3 years old, she clearly had no concept of gender or the permanence of gender," a man told me. "She would say that she was a girl or a boy pretty much randomly, as far as I could tell. One day, she would say one, and maybe even later the same day, the other—for both herself and others. You could be a boy one day and a girl the next. This lack of permanence also extended to skin color. She would say that your skin was the color of your clothes, so that changed from day to day, too. One day, you were blue, the next day, your skin was red. I thought that was very odd, even more odd than being a boy one day and a girl the next.

"She's 5 years old now, and gender is a very salient characteristic for her. She seems to realize that she is a girl, and I think she knows that she will always be a girl, but she is very concerned with gender and gender-related things—as though she is working on sorting out all this information and making sense of it."

conceptualization, gender constancy was not a critical component in the development of gender knowledge.

Gender constancy may not be an all-or-nothing development. Two components are separable: *gender stability,* the knowledge that gender is a stable personal characteristic, and *gender consistency,* the belief that people retain their gender even when they adopt behaviors or superficial physical features associated with the other gender. For example, a child who shows gender stability will say that she was a girl when she was a baby and will be a woman when she grows up. A child who shows gender consistency will say that a boy will remain a boy even if he grows long hair or puts on a dress. Some children showed gender stability without gender consistency, but never the other way around (Martin & Little, 1990). Thus, gender constancy might consist of these two separable cognitive components, which would explain why researchers have found age variation in this aspect of development.

Motivation may be an additional factor in gender role development. Children who develop gender constancy become motivated to adopt gender-role behaviors, causing them to avoid some activities and engage in others (Newman, Cooper, & Ruble, 1995). Children who are gender constant, therefore, have the motivation to adopt gender-typical behaviors.

Preschoolers, first graders, second graders, and even some fourth graders can be misled into making mistakes about gender consistency, which is the more advanced of the two components of gender constancy. Changes in appearance and name of a character can produce this confusion (Beal & Lockhart, 1989). For example, changing the appearance of a target child to make the target look more like the other sex, or changing the name and pronoun used to refer to this target child can lead children to make mistakes. Children were more likely to say that the target was the same sex, even with a changed appearance, when the target kept the same proper name throughout the transformations. This finding suggests that children whose understanding of gender constancy was not solid could be misled by changes in superficial characteristics, such as appearance or proper names. The age of the participants and their difficulties in demonstrating this facet of gender constancy are clear indications of how difficult this concept is for children and how long it takes children to develop gender constancy.

GENDERED VOICES
Yuck—I'm a Girl!

The woman knew that her young son would not like the outfit that he was to wear for the wedding, so she decided to distract him as she dressed him. She was successful, but when he looked down at the finished product, he exclaimed, "Yuck—I'm an girl!" in a surprised and disgusted tone.

When we talked about gender development in class, she said that she now understood why he was so upset. She though that he had meant that he looked like a girl, but instead, she now understood that he had not developed a concept of gender stability and he believed that, by dressing him in a frilly shirt and velvet suit, his mother had turned him from a boy into a girl.

In summary, children begin to acquire knowledge concerning gender at an early age. Although infants show some signs of being able to differentiate between women and men, this ability does not constitute cognitive knowledge about gender. Between 2 and 3 years of age, children succeed at gender labeling but usually have not developed other aspects of gender knowledge, such as gender preferences, gender stability, gender consistency, or knowledge of gender stereotypes. These aspects of gender knowledge develop between the ages of 3 and 6 for most children and do so in a regular pattern that consists of gender labeling, gender stereotype knowledge and gender preferences, and then the two components of gender constancy—gender stability and gender consistency. Even during the first few grades of elementary school, children can be misled into making mistakes of gender consistency by changes in physical appearance or proper name, which indicates how difficult this aspect of gender knowledge is for children to acquire.

Differences between Girls and Boys

The course of gender development shows some differences between boys and girls. Such a difference is reasonable, given the greater pressure placed on boys to adopt the typical and approved gender roles (Beal, 1994). Girls are allowed greater leeway in behaving in ways typical of boys than boys are allowed in acting like girls (Martin, 1995). That is, being a "tomboy" is more acceptable than being a "sissy."

Differences in attitudes toward masculine girls and feminine boys appear in college men and women (Martin, 1995) and in elementary school boys (Zucker, Wilson-Smith, Kurita, & Stern, 1995). Thus it is not surprising that boys tend to show greater stability of gender-typed preferences than girls at around age 3 (Powlishta, Serbin, & Moller, 1993).

Both gender schema and gender script theory predict that children attend to and master information about their own gender more rapidly than about the other gender (Levy & Fivush, 1993). Research has confirmed these predictions: Young children have better organized knowledge of events and behaviors stereotypically associated with their own rather than the other gender (Martin, Wood, & Little, 1990). In addition, children evaluate their own gender more positively than the other, with girls saying that "girls are better" and boys contending that "boys are better." In elementary school-aged children, these positive evaluations were not based on the value of the traits but rather on the children's association of positive characteristics with their own group (Powlishta, 1995).

Although boys receive greater pressure to adopt the traditional gender role, more boys than girls exhibit gender identity disorder. This disorder occurs when a child rejects the gender role that corresponds to biological sex and adopts cross-gender behaviors and possibly even a cross-gender identity. Most children show behaviors that represent a combination of the masculine and the feminine, which does not indicate any type of problem. A small number of children show evidence of gender identity disorder, and these children not only display cross-gender behaviors but also reject their own gender identity and behaviors associated with it and often wish to be magically transformed into the other gender.

Richard Green (1987) studied boys who showed signs of gender identity disorder in order to discover differences between these boys and others who had more typical gender role development. His study indicated that some of these "sissies" had received reinforcement and others were ignored by parents or other adults for their cross-gender behaviors. The majority of these boys continued to have gender identity disorders into adulthood, with some attempting to change their biological sex through transsexual surgery and others developing sexual attraction to men or to both men and women.

Green chose not to include girls in his study because too few girls showed symptoms of gender identity disorder. Boys were more than six times more likely than girls to be referred to a clinic for this disorder (Zucker, Bradley, & Sanikhani, 1997). Girls showed more cross-gender behaviors than boys, suggesting a greater social tolerance for such behavior from girls. Indeed, girls see advantages in being boys (Baumgartner, in Tavris & Wade, 1984). When asked what would happen if they changed sex, elementary school girls imagined advantages while boys imagined disaster. Adults make similar judgments, believing that being male offers advantages and being female presents disadvantages (Cann & Vann, 1995). Therefore, the greater frequency of gender identity disorder among boys appears inconsistent with the social advantages that men, women, boys, and girls perceive as attached to the male gender role.

During Adolescence and Adulthood

The widespread belief that gender development is complete by the end of childhood has resulted in relatively little research conducted with adolescents and adults; however, some researchers have examined continuing changes in gender identity and attitudes. Much of this research has concentrated on the development of gender role flexibility, which seems limited during childhood but becomes more apparent during adolescence and adulthood.

Some evidence suggests that gender role development continues into adolescence and adulthood. A study (Urberg, 1979) of 7th graders, 12th graders, and adults considered changes in stereotyping at various ages. The 12th graders showed the most and the adults the least gender-related stereotyping. This result indicates that stereotyping does not increase with gender knowledge in a linear fashion. Rather, the relationship between age and gender stereotyping showed a curvilinear relationship: low at early ages, before gender becomes an important factor for dealing with people; then higher, when dating and career choices become important; and finally, lower, when young adults accept greater flexibility for gender-related behavior.

Other studies have found a linear relationship between gender flexibility and age—that is, as age increases, so does gender flexibility (Katz & Ksansnak, 1994; Welch-Ross & Schmidt, 1996). When children acquire gender role knowledge, they tend to apply it inflexibly, but with increasing familiarity with stereotypes comes an increasing willingness to make exceptions, especially when applied to self.

The discrepancies among the studies of gender role flexibility may be due to the different research methods used and variations in how flexibility is measured (Bigler, 1997; Signorella, Bigler, & Liben, 1993). For example, when forced to choose whether a behavior is performed by or is an occupation held by women or men, children are likely to show increasing evidence of gender stereotyping as they get older. On the other hand, if they are allowed the option to indicate that both perform the behavior or either can have that occupation, even middle-school children show signs of gender flexibility. This difference highlights the importance of the format and wording of questions, especially in research with children.

Children and adolescents also tend to be more rigid in applying inflexible standards for gender-related behavior to others than to themselves. Therefore, researchers who ask only about others or about cases that are typical may overlook the exceptions that children and adolescents are willing to make for themselves.

Nevertheless, children, adolescents, and even adults vary in their gender role flexibility, and several researchers have explored factors that relate to flexibility versus inflexibility. In one study (Katz & Ksansnak, 1994), a complex pattern of gender role flexibility appeared, with influences from both family and peer social environment but with a general increase in tolerance for gender-atypical activities for self and others with increasing age. Another study (Welch-Ross & Schmidt, 1996) found that increases in gender role knowledge preceded increases in gender role flexibility, with flexibility beginning to develop during middle childhood. Figure 7.2 shows the course of development for gender knowledge and for application of gender-related rules over the life span, with the knowledge component increasing and the flexibility decreasing throughout childhood and then increasing in late adolescence.

Gender role flexibility increases during adolescence, but young women and men apply different standards to their own gender than to the other. One study (Urberg, 1979) found that male and female participants described themselves similarly but described the other gender in more stereotypical terms. Male and female participants had similar self-perceptions for characteristics such as affiliation, personal effectiveness, control, and impulsivity, but they tended to perceive the other gender in more stereotypical terms.

Other than age, what factors relate to gender flexibility versus inflexibility? Both family (Levy, 1989) and the combination of family and social environment (Katz & Ksansnak, 1994) have been the focus of research attention. Children who interacted more with their parents showed less gender role flexibility than children who spent less time with their parents, and children with fewer siblings showed more gender role flexibility than those with more brothers and sisters (Levy, 1989). Girls whose mothers worked outside the home and girls who expressed a preference for educational television showed more gender role flexibility than other girls. Siblings and peers are also important in developing gender flexibility; indeed, they may be more important than parents (Katz & Ksansnak, 1994). Same-sex siblings were an especially important force in the development of gender flexibility. Con-

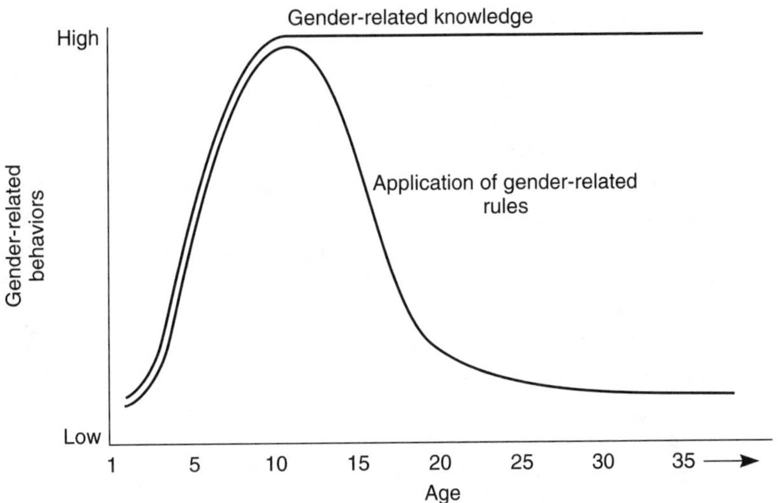

FIGURE 7.2 Course of Knowledge and Application of Gender-Related Rules for Behavior Throughout the Life Span

sistent with the findings from other studies (Signorella et al., 1993), girls were more flexible than boys in both their preferences for other-gender activities and tolerance for such activities in others.

Some related research has traced the correlates of both gender flexibility and inflexibility in men. Men who were stereotypically masculine tended to see women as stereotypically feminine; that is, men who show little gender flexibility in their own roles also show little toward women (Hudak, 1993). Some men had very different attitudes and tended to reject stereotypically masculine and feminine roles (Christian, 1994). Those who did were demographically diverse but showed several commonalties. Their early life experiences differed from those of more typical men in the study, with many of them having nurturing fathers and mothers in the work force. In addition, most of these gender flexible men had had at least one adult relationship with a feminist woman. These two themes echo the findings on the development of gender flexibility, which demonstrate that both parenting and social environment are related to gender flexibility.

It is apparent that gender identity continues to develop during adolescence and even into adulthood. When children have developed the cognitive and motivational components of gender identity, they tend to be inflexible in applying their understanding of these rules; they are intolerant of gender-atypical behavior in themselves and even more so in others. Young children appear to be tolerant of gender flexibility, but this apparent tolerance is due to a lack of understanding of gender-typed behaviors. Children are "sexist piglets" who apply rigid rules of gender-related behavior to themselves and to others, but this inflexibility begins to dissipate as early as middle childhood. Adolescents and adults tend to be more flexible in their application of gender-related rules of behavior.

Which Theory Best Explains the Data?

Each of these theories of gender development presents an orderly pattern of development, but the research shows a complex pattern with many components that do not necessarily match the theories. That is, none of the theories is able to explain all the data from research on gender development.

Social learning theory predicts a process of learning gender roles that results in a gradual matching of gender-related behaviors to the culturally prescribed pattern through modeling and reinforcement of gender-appropriate behaviors. Although the research shows that children begin learning information consistent with gender stereotypes at an early age, gender knowledge consists of several different concepts that do not appear incrementally. The finding that children learn gender labeling before gender-typical toy and clothing preferences indicates a pattern of gender knowledge development that social learning theory does not predict.

Research has substantiated the influence of parents, siblings, and peers in directing gender-related behaviors. Social learning theory predicts that family, peers, teachers, and media images of men and women affect children in their learning and performance of gender-appropriate behaviors. Modeling can be a powerful force in prompting the performance of gender-related behaviors (Bussey & Bandura, 1984, 1992), and same-sex siblings, parents, peers, and teachers are all important influences in the child's development of gender flexibility (Katz & Ksansnak, 1994). These findings are consistent with the predictions of social learning theory.

Social learning theory allows that girls and boys might differ not only in their gender-related behaviors but also in cross-gender behaviors. The male gender role carries more power, and power is one of the factors that affects children's modeling. During childhood, boys are discouraged from performing feminine behaviors, whereas girls may not be discouraged from performing behaviors typical of boys. These differences lead to the prediction that boys should be more strongly gender typed than girls, and research supports this difference. Cognitive developmental theory does not allow for a different pattern of development for boys and girls, whereas gender schema theory hypothesizes that parental attitudes and family patterns may produce variations in individual schemata. This theory does not specifically address differences in schemata between girls and boys, however.

Cognitive developmental theory hypothesizes that gender development comes about through cognitive changes that occur by way of general cognitive development. Research has indicated that gender development produces cognitive changes in accuracy and memory for gender-related information, but gender schema theory also predicts that cognitive changes come with the development of gender schema, making findings that support these cognitive changes applicable to either theory.

The prediction that gender constancy is the basis for developing all other gender knowledge has not been substantiated. Indeed, research has shown that gender constancy develops late, with many other components of gender knowledge appearing earlier. This failure is a serious problem for cognitive developmental theory. Another problem for this theory is that gender development continues during adolescence. According to this theory, children undergo no additional cognitive changes after early adolescence, but research has shown that late adolescence is a time during which individuals gain flexibility of gender beliefs.

Gender schema theory predicts that children develop a cognitive organization for gender, a schema, that forms the basis for their understanding of gender and directs their gender-related behaviors. The types of cognitive changes that this theory predicts have been found in modes of information processing, such as accuracy of judgments and memory effects. In addition, women in traditional versus nontraditional jobs have different conceptualizations of gender-appropriate behavior (Lavallee & Pelletier, 1992), a finding consistent with gender schema theory.

Gender development seems to consist of several different cognitive abilities. One team of researchers (Hort, Leinbach, & Fagot, 1991) proposed that the cognitive components of gender development do not have a great deal of coherence; they postulated that such knowledge varies among individual children of the same age and stage of cognitive development. That is, gender knowledge may not fall into a pattern sufficiently coherent to be called a schema.

Gender script theory makes many of the same predictions as gender schema theory. Differentiating scripts from schemata allows for some additional predictions, and some research has confirmed children's abilities to learn and behave according to sequentially ordered patterns like scripts. Gender script theory has not been the subject of sufficient research to make firm conclusions, but it may offer advantages over gender schema theory.

It is evident from this discussion that all of the social theories of gender development make predictions that research has supported, and all make predictions that research has failed to confirm. The picture drawn from the research shows that gender development presents a more complex process than any of the theories can fully explain. Gender development consists of separate components—gender labeling, preferences for gender-typed activities, gender stereotyping, and gender constancy. These components appear to develop in a pattern, but the pattern does not exactly conform to any of those predicted by the theories. Thus, all of the social theories of personality development have been useful and have been partially confirmed, but none is without weaknesses.

Summary

The social theories of gender development provide alternatives to psychoanalytic theory to explain how infants come to identify themselves as masculine or feminine, to understand gender, and to behave in ways that their culture deems gender-appropriate. The social learning approach is a variation on traditional learning theory that relies on the concepts of observational learning and modeling to explain how children learn and perform gender-related behaviors. Initially the family and later the broader culture provide models and reinforcements for adopting certain gender-related behaviors while discouraging others from being adopted. Research has supported the power of children's family and social surroundings to influence the development of gender-related behaviors, but the orderly pattern of gender development is not consistent with this theory.

Cognitive developmental theory holds that gender identity is a cognitive concept that children learn as part of the process of learning about the physical world and their own bodies. Children younger than 2 years of age have no concept of gender and cannot consistently label themselves or others as male or female. When children learn to classify genders, they have developed gender constancy, the understanding that gender is a permanent personal characteristic that will not change with any other physical transformation. According to cognitive developmental theory, additional facets of gender development arise from gender constancy; however, research has indicated that gender constancy is among the last types of gender knowledge to be acquired. These findings present a problem for this theory.

Gender schema theory is an extension of cognitive developmental theory that explains gender identity in terms of schemata, those cognitive structures that underlie complex concepts. When children acquire gender schemata, they change the way that they deal with information concerning gender and also change their behaviors to conform to gender roles. This theory suggests that gender stereotyping is a natural extension of the process of developing gender schemata and that children become stereotypical in their gender behavior and judgments. Parents who wish to raise nonsexist children can attempt to substitute alternative schemata that are less sexist than the ones predominant in their culture, although completely avoiding the formation of gender schemata is not possible for children.

Gender script theory is an extension of gender schema theory. Rather than holding that children develop gender schemata, this theory says that children learn about gender by acquiring scripts, ordered sequences of behavior with a gender stereotype component. These scripts allow children to organize their knowledge and to form social relationships. This theory shares many predictions with gender schema theory. Yet the body of research testing this theory is smaller than for other theories, making its assessment difficult.

The process of gender development may begin during infancy because children older than 6 months can distinguish between male and female faces. Between ages 2 and 3, most children learn to apply gender labels and to understand some behaviors and features as stereotypically associated with gender. Their understanding of gender is far from complete, however, and children may be 7 or 8 years old before they have a complete understanding of all the components of gender, including gender constancy, gender consistency, and gender stability.

When children develop an understanding of gender, they tend to be rigid and inflexible in their application of gender rules to themselves and others. Gender stereotyping is not as strong during adolescence and adulthood, indicating that additional gender development occurs after childhood.

Evaluating the social theories of gender development leads to the conclusion that although each has supporting research, this research fails to support any one theory to the exclusion of the others.

Glossary

gender constancy the knowledge that gender is a permanent characteristic and will not change with superficial alterations.

gender identity individual identification of self as female or male.

gender labeling the ability to label self and others as male or female.

gender role a set of socially significant activities associated with men or women.

operant conditioning a type of learning based on the administration of reinforcement. Receiving reinforcement links the reinforcement with the behavior that preceded it, making the behavior more likely to be repeated.

punishment any stimulus that decreases the probability that a behavior will be repeated.

reinforcement any stimulus that increases the probability that a behavior will be repeated.

schema (plural, **schemata**) an internal cognitive structure that organizes information and guides perception.

Suggested Readings

Beal, Carole R. (1994). *Boys and girls: The development of gender roles.* New York: McGraw-Hill. Chapters 3, 5 through 7, and 9 in Carole Beal's book concentrate on the social forces that pertain to gender role development. Her careful review and good examples make this book a good summary of the research in this area.

Bem, Sandra Lipsitz. (1985). Androgyny and gender schema theory: A conceptual and empirical integration. In Theo B. Sonderegger (Ed.), *Nebraska symposium on motivation, 1984: Psychology and gender* (pp. 179–226). Lincoln, NE: University of Nebraska Press. Bem evaluates other theories of gender development and presents gender schema theory, research supporting her theory, and advice about raising nonsexist children.

Ruble, Diane N. & Martin, Carol Lynn. (1998). Gender development. In Nancy Eisenberg (Ed.), *Handbook of child psychology, Vol. 3: Social, emotional, and personality development* (5th ed., pp. 933–1016). New York: Wiley. Ruble and Martin's massive review of gender development may be a bit overwhelming in length, but their discussion of the research is clear and well-organized. The article includes material other than a review of social factors in gender development. The first half of the chapter is more pertinent to this topic than the last.

Chapter 8

Gender Stereotypes

Masculinity and Femininity

HEADLINE

The Gender Trap

—*Ms. Magazine,* November/December 1994

Sherry Gorelick (1994) noticed that her daughter was the object of gender stereotyping from the first weeks of her life. An elderly neighbor made the comment that his great-grandson could be the child's boyfriend. The assumption that the baby would need (and would want) a boyfriend was only the first of many similar incidents that reflected stereotypical views of gender roles.

Male babies were also the target of gender stereotyping. The men in Gorelick's neighborhood were eager to shadowbox with any male toddler but not with the female toddlers. From infancy, the actions of boys tended to be interpreted as aggressive whereas the same actions of girls received a different interpretation. When her daughter poked another infant's eyes, Gorelick would stop her, as would the mothers of boys. Those mothers tended to explain their sons' actions by saying that boys are aggressive, but no one interpreted her daughter's same behavior in those terms.

Adults are eager to see children's actions in gender stereotypical terms. Gorelick (1994) contended, of the behaviors that signal the development of typical gender roles:

> *Better to believe—no matter how regretfully—that boys are naturally aggressive, and that every female longs for a male from when she is afloat in utero to the end of her life. So when boys act like Atilla the Hun, adults nod their heads sadly and smile. They are smiling because they are relieved. Everything is in its place, in order. Better a stereotype . . . than ambiguity. (pp. 63–64)*

In observing reactions to her infant daughter, Gorelick found a great deal of evidence that adults subject children to gender stereotypes, even while infants. She contended that adults were eager to sexualize interactions among toddlers and cast both boys and girls into gender roles that were often inappropriate for the individual child. Gorelick argued that adults enacted their culture's values by applying gender stereotypes and that they found these categorizations useful and comforting. She also contended that gender stereotypes place constraints on behavior that interfere with individual development. Therefore, stereotypes seem useful and potentially harmful.

From Gender Roles to Gender Stereotypes

role - what I do

As Chapter 7 explored, a gender role consists of activities that men and women engage in with different frequencies (see Williams & Best, 1990). For example, in the United States repairing cars and repairing clothing are associated predominantly with men and women, respectively. These gender-related behaviors thus become part of a pattern accepted as masculine or feminine, not because of any innate reason for these differences but because they are associated with women and men.

A **gender stereotype** consists of beliefs about the psychological traits and characteristics as well as the activities appropriate to men or women. Gender roles are defined by behaviors, but gender stereotypes are beliefs and attitudes about masculinity and femininity. The concepts of gender role and gender stereotype tend to be related. When people associate a pattern of behavior with either women or men, they may overlook the individual variations and exceptions and come to believe that the behavior is inevitably associated with one gender but not the other. Therefore, gender roles can become gender stereotypes.

Gender stereotypes are very influential; they affect conceptualizations of women and men and establish social categories for gender, as Gorelick noticed with her daughter. These categories represent what people think, and even when beliefs vary from reality, beliefs can be very powerful forces in judgments of self and others. Therefore, the history, structure, and function of stereotypes are important topics in understanding the impact of gender on people's lives.

Stereotypes of Women and Men

The rigid formulation of what is acceptable for women and men is not unique to children, such as the ones in Gorelick's story, or even to contemporary society. Rather, current gender stereotypes can be traced to the 19th century. Many of the elements of current stereotypes can be found in Victorian conceptualizations of masculinity and femininity.

The current gender stereotypes, especially those about women, reflect beliefs that appeared during the 19th century, the Victorian era (Lewin, 1984c). The Industrial Revolution changed the lives of a majority of people in Europe and North America by moving men outside the home to earn money and leaving women at home to manage households and children. This separation was unprecedented in history, forcing men and women to adapt by creating new behavior patterns. As men coped with the harsh business and industrial world, women were left in the relatively unvarying and sheltered environments of their homes. These changes produced two beliefs: the Doctrine of Two Spheres and the Cult of True Womanhood.

The Doctrine of Two Spheres is the belief that women's and men's interests diverge—that women and men have their separate areas of influence (Lewin, 1984a). For women, areas of the influence are home and children, whereas men's sphere includes work and the outside world. These two spheres are different, with little overlap, forming opposite ends of one dimension. Lewin contended that this conceptualization of opposition forms the basis not only for social views of gender but also for psychology's formulation of the measurement of masculinity and femininity.

The Cult of True Womanhood

The Cult of True Womanhood arose between 1820 and 1860, "The attributes of True Womanhood, by which a woman judged herself and was judged by her husband, her neighbors, and society could be divided into four cardinal virtues—piety, purity, submissiveness, and domesticity" (Welter, 1978, p. 313). Women's magazines and religious literature of the 19th century furnished evidence of that society's emphasis on these four areas. The Cult of True Womanhood held that the combination of these characteristics provided the promise of happiness and power to the Victorian woman, and without these no woman's life could have real meaning.

Religion formed the basis for the Cult of True Womanhood (Welter, 1978). During this time society saw women as more naturally religious than men. This tendency toward religion was part of women's natural moral superiority, and the belief in the moral superiority of women was stronger in the United States than in Europe and England (Lewin, 1984c). Women's natural superiority also appeared in their refinement, delicacy, and tender sensibilities. Religious studies were seen as compatible with femininity and deemed appropriate for women, whereas other types of education were thought to detract from women's femininity. Included in these other types of education were not only studying through formal means but also reading romantic novels, either of which might lead women to ignore religion, become overly romantic, and lose their virtue (that is, their virginity).

The loss of purity was a "fate worse than death." Having lost her virtue, a woman was without value or hope: "Purity was as essential as piety to a young woman, its absence as unnatural and unfeminine. Without it she was, in fact no woman at all, but a member of some lower order" (Welter, 1978, p. 315).

Men, on the other hand, were not naturally as religious and thus not naturally as virtuous as women. According to this view of True Womanhood, men were, at best, prone to sin and seduction, and at worst, brutes. True Women would withstand the advances of men, dazzling and shaming them with their virtue. Men were supposed to be both religious and pure, although not to the same extent as women, and through association with True Women, men could increase their own virtue. True Women could elevate the status of men.

The third virtue of the Cult of True Womanhood was submissiveness, a characteristic not true of and not desirable in men (Welter, 1978). Women were expected to be weak, dependent, and timid, whereas men were supposed to be strong, wise, and forceful. Dependent women wanted strong men, not sensitive ones. These couples formed families in which the husbands were unquestionably superior and the wives would not consider questioning this authority.

The last of the four virtues, domesticity, was connected to both submissiveness and to the Doctrine of the Two Spheres. True Women were wives whose concern was with domes-

TABLE 8.1 Elements of Stereotyping of Women and Men

The Cult of True Womanhood	Male Sex Role Identity
Piety: True Women were naturally religious.	*No Sissy Stuff:* A stigma is attached to feminine characteristics.
Purity: True Women were sexually uninterested.	*The Big Wheel:* Men need success and status.
Submissiveness: True Women were weak, dependent, and timid.	*The Sturdy Oak:* Men should have toughness, confidence, and self-reliance.
Domesticity: True Women's domain was the home.	*Give 'Em Hell:* Men should have an aura of aggression, daring, and violence.

SOURCES: Based on "The male sex role: Our culture's blueprint of manhood and what it's done for us lately," (p. 12). In Deborah S. David & Robert Brannon (Eds.), *The forty-nine percent majority,* 1976. Reading, MA: Addison-Wesley, and "The cult of true womanhood: 1820–1860." In Michael Gordon (Ed.), *The American family in social-historical perspective* (2nd ed.). New York: St. Martin's Press.

tic affairs—making a home and having children: "The true woman's place was unquestionably by her own fireside—as daughter, sister, but most of all as wife and mother" (Welter, 1978, p. 320). These domestic duties included cooking and nursing the sick, especially a sick husband or child. Table 8.1 summarizes the elements of the Cult of True Womanhood.

Women who personified these virtues passed the test of True Womanhood. Of course, the test was so demanding that few, if any, women met the criteria. However, beginning in the early 1800s women's magazines as well as teachings from social and religious leaders held these virtues as attainable. They urged women to work toward these qualities, and women tried to match these ideals. Although the Cult of True Womanhood was dominant during the 19th century, remnants have stayed in our present-day culture and have influenced current views of femininity.

Masculinities

The nineteenth-century idealization of women had implications for men as well. Men were seen as the opposite of women in a number of ways. Women were passive, dependent, pure, refined, and delicate; men were active, independent, coarse, and strong. These divisions between male and female domains, the Doctrine of the Two Spheres, formed the basis for the polarization of male and female interests and activities. The Cult of True Womanhood reached its height in the late Victorian period, toward the end of the 19th century. The Victorian ideal of manhood was the basis for what Joseph Pleck (1981a,b; 1984) referred to as the Male Sex Role Identity. Pleck discussed the Male Sex Role Identity as the dominant conceptualization of masculinity in our society and as a source of problems, both for society and for individual men.

Pleck (1984) and R. W. Connell (1995) explored the historical origins of attitudes toward masculinity. Connell looked back into 16th-century Europe and the changing social and religious climate to trace the development of individualism. He contended that industrialization, world exploration, and civil wars became activities associated with men and formed the basis for modern masculinity. Pleck reviewed the social climate of late 19th century, citing examples from the late 1800s of the increasing perception that men were not as manly as they once had been. Growing industrialization pressured men to seek employment in order to be good providers for their families, roles that became increasingly difficult for men to fulfill (Bernard, 1981), thus endangering their masculinity. In addition, education became a factor in employment, and men often held better jobs (and were thus better providers) when they were educated. Pleck discussed how education during early childhood became the province of women and how female elementary school teachers tried to make boys into well-behaved pupils—in other words, "sissies."

The prohibition against being a sissy and the rejection of feminine traits are strong components of modern masculinity. According to Robert Brannon (1976), No Sissy Stuff is one of the four themes of the Male Sex Role. The other three elements included The Big Wheel, which describes men's quest for success and status as well as their need to be looked up to. The Sturdy Oak component describes men's air of toughness, confidence, and self-reliance, especially in a crisis. The Give 'Em Hell aspect of the Male Sex Role reflects the acceptability of violence, aggression, and daring in men's behavior. Table 8.1 summarizes these elements.

The more closely that a man conforms to these characteristics, the closer he is to being a "real man." As Brannon pointed out, the pressure is strong to live up to this idealization of masculinity, which is equally as ideal and unrealistic as the True Woman of the Cult of True Womanhood. However, even men who are fairly successful in adopting the Male Sex Role Identity may be poorly adjusted, unhappy people—this role prohibits close personal relationships, even with wives or children, and requires competition and achievement at work.

Pleck (1981a; 1995) suggested that rather than adhering to the Male Sex Role, men have started to make significant departures from that role's requirements; they have begun to question the desirability of the Male Sex Role Identity. He proposed a new model, which he called Sex Role Strain, which departs in many ways from the Male Sex Role Identity. Pleck argued that during the 1960s and 1970s, both men and women started to make significant departures from their traditional roles as men began to behave in ways that violated the Male Sex Role. He also suggested that the features of the Male Sex Role Identity have retained a powerful influence over what both men and women believe men should be. Although many men deviate from the role and some even believe that the role is harmful to them personally and to society, the Male Sex Role Identity has retained its power to shape beliefs and to make men worry that they are not living up to this role's requirements.

Connell (1987, 1992, 1995) argued that gender has been constructed as part of each society throughout history, including sanctioned and less accepted behaviors. Thus, masculinity varies with both time and place, creating a multitude of masculinities. For each society, Connell contended that one version of masculinity is sanctioned as the one to which men should adhere, which he termed *hegemonic masculinity*. This version of masculinity attempts to subordinate femininity as well as less accepted styles of masculinity, such as male homosexuality. Like Pleck, Connell recognized many disadvantages to this narrow, dominant form of masculinity and saw many problems for society and for individual men who adhere to it.

Development of Stereotypes

In examining the research on social theories of gender development, Chapter 7 reviewed the process of developing gender knowledge and identity, including some information

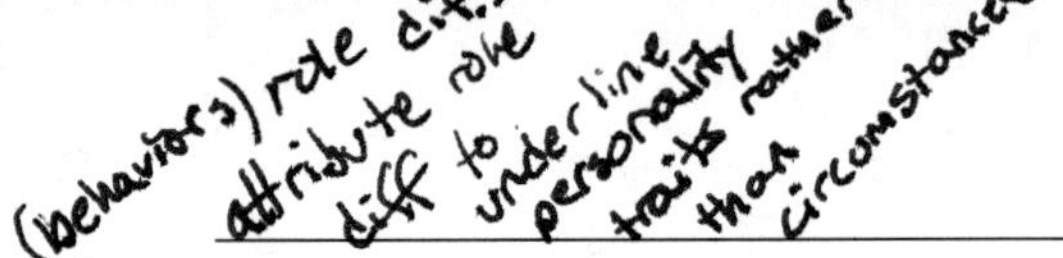

GENDERED VOICES
Raising a Sissy

"Being twins, my brother and I were closer than most brothers and sisters. We didn't look alike, but we were together a lot," a college student told me. "We had different interests. I was the one who went outside and helped my dad, while my brother stayed inside with my mother. Everybody always said I should have been the boy and he should have been the girl.

"He didn't want to play alone, so he played with me and my friends—dolls, or whatever we played with. He never got to choose. And when we played with dolls, he got the one that was left after me and my friend chose the ones we wanted. My mom said, 'Let him play with the Ken doll—you have two Ken dolls—don't make him play with a Barbie,' but we didn't. So he got the Barbie with one arm missing or something.

"I always liked the outdoor activities, and my brother didn't. I was so upset that I couldn't join the Cub Scouts. My dad was a troop leader, and I just couldn't understand why I couldn't join; I had always done outdoor things with my dad. Besides, the Brownies did wimpy things, and the Cub Scouts did neat stuff. I was so ticked off.

"When we were in about the seventh grade, I told my mother, 'Mom, you're raising a sissy,' and I told her that my brother should stop hanging around with her and start doing things more typical of boys. She was really angry with me for saying so.

"Did we change as we grew up? I don't consider myself very feminine—I don't take anything off anybody. My mom can't believe that her daughter acts like I do. I still like outdoor activities—camping, hiking, bicycling. I don't think I've changed as much as my brother has. I wouldn't consider him a sissy now. In high school he played football, and he started being more in line with what everyone would consider masculine. As an adult, he's not a sissy at all, but I'm still kind of an adult tomboy."

about forming gender stereotypes. This body of research indicates that gender learning consists of several components, which children begin to acquire around 2 years of age and may not complete until they are 7 or 8 years old. The first of the components to be learned is the ability to label the sexes, and this initial gender information may be adequate to allow children to begin to develop gender stereotypes: "Once children can accurately label the sexes, they begin to form gender stereotypes and their behavior is influenced by these gender-associated expectations" (Martin & Little, 1990, p. 1438). Thus, children as young as 3 years old start to show signs of gender stereotyping.

A pattern occurs in the course of gender stereotype development (Martin, Wood, & Little, 1990). Children between 4 and 6 years old responded to inquiries about toy interests for themselves and other children. The children demonstrated selective stereotyping, making gender-stereotypical judgments about children whose toy interests were similar to their own but failing to make stereotypical judgments for children whose interests were different from their own. This finding demonstrated not only the complexity of stereotypes but also the tendency for children to develop an understanding of their own gender before the other.

Even more gender stereotyping appeared in a second study with 6- to 10-year-olds (Martin et al., 1990). The 6-year-olds made the same stereotypical judgments as the children in the first study; that is, their judgments were stereotypical for children of their own gender but not the other. The older children, however, made stereotypical judgments for both genders, demonstrating that stereotype development is not complete until middle childhood.

TABLE 8.2 Stages of Gender Stereotype Development

Stage	Gender Knowledge	Status of Gender Stereotypes
1	Behaviors and characteristics directly associated with gender	Undeveloped
2	Beginnings of indirect associations with gender for own sex but not other	Self-stereotype but none for other sex
3	Complex, indirect gender-related associations for same and other sex	Stereotypes for self and other sex

SOURCE: Based on "The development of gender stereotype components" (pp. 1891–1904) by C. L. Martin, C. H. Wood, & J. K. Little, 1990, *Child Development, 61.*

After considering their results and reviewing research by others, Martin et al. proposed a pattern of stereotype development. This pattern is presented in Table 8.2. Children in the first stage have learned characteristics and behaviors associated directly with each gender, such as the toy preferences of each. In this stage they have not learned the many secondary associations with gender, associations that are essential for stereotypes to form. In the second stage, children have begun to develop the indirect associations for behaviors associated with their own gender but not yet for the other. In the third stage, children have learned these indirect associations for the other gender as well as their own, giving them the capability of making stereotypical judgments for both women and men.

A specific cognitive process allows children (and adults) to maintain stereotypes once they have formed (Meehan & Janik, 1990). This process is called **illusory correlation:** "the erroneous perception of covariation between two events when no correlation exists, or the perception of a correlation as stronger than it actually is" (Meehan & Janik, 1990, p. 84). These researchers maintained that people perceive that relationships exist between gender and various behaviors when no relationship exists or when the relationship is not as strong as their perception indicates.

Children in second and fourth grade saw pictures of women and men engaged in gender-stereotypical, gender-astereotypical, or gender-neutral activities and were asked to remember who did what (Meehan & Janik, 1990). Although there was actually no relationship between the pictured activities and gender for the set of pictures they saw, the children remembered more stereotypical than astereotypical or neutral activities. For example, the children were more likely to recall a male than a female carpenter and a female rather than a male librarian. The perception of correlations can be an important factor in maintaining stereotypes for both children and adults: When people believe that activities are related to one or the other gender, then they feel comfortable in thinking in terms of these categorizations.

With increased gender stereotype knowledge comes both the acceptance of such stereotypes as well as the ability to make individual exceptions to those stereotypes. This latter ability allows for gender flexibility rather than the rigid acceptance of gender stereotypes. College students showed such flexibility when they deviated from gender stereotypes in evaluating men and women; they relied more on information about the individual than on gender-stereotypical information, showing that college students can be flexible in their evaluations (Locksley, Borgida, Brekke, & Hepburn, 1980).

Studying gender stereotyping in individuals ranging from kindergarten children to college students showed that the flexible application of gender stereotypes increases with age (Biernat, 1991). Younger children relied more on gender information than on information about individuals when making judgments about people, whereas older individuals took into account information about deviations from gender stereotypes. This pattern of development indicates that the acquisition of full information concerning gender stereotypes is accompanied by greater flexibility in the use of stereotypes but that the tendency to rely on the stereotype is always present.

Therefore, the development of gender stereotypes begins early, with 3-year-olds knowing about gender-related differences in behavior. As children acquire information about gender, they become capable of forming and maintaining elaborate stereotypes for men and women, but they also become more willing to make exceptions to the gender rules they have learned. Older children and adults are more willing to allow for deviations from stereotypes when they consider people's characteristics and past behaviors. Nevertheless, gender stereotypes provide a system for classifying people that operates as a standard throughout people's lives; these influence their expectations for self and others, as well as the judgments they form about people based on their gender-related characteristics and behaviors.

Perceptions of Women and Men

How have these stereotypes influenced people's perceptions of men and women? What are the components of stereotypes for women and men? Do people measure women by the feminine stereotype of the Cult of True Womanhood? Will men experience problems if they do not adopt all of the characteristics of the Male Sex Role? Or have the changes in women's and men's behaviors produced changes in the stereotypes and broadened the boundaries of acceptable behaviors for men and women?

The content of gender stereotypes include four separate components that people use to differentiate male from female—traits, behaviors, physical characteristics, and occupations (Deaux & Lewis, 1984). All these components are relatively independent, but people associate one set of features from each of these with women and another set with men. On the basis of knowledge of one dimension, people extend judgments to the other three. Figure 8.1 shows the components of this model; the arrows indicate the associations among components. Given a gender label for a target person, people will make inferences concerning the person's appearance, traits, gender role behaviors, and occupation. Information about one component can affect the others, and people will attempt to maintain consistency among the components.

People viewed men and women as differing more in physical features than in psychological characteristics, and people relied more on physical information than on trait, behavioral, or occupational information in making gender-related judgments. As Figure 8.1 shows, physical appearance was the most influential of these components, affecting the other components more strongly than information about traits, behaviors, or occupations influenced judgments about appearance. Given information about behaviors, people make inferences about traits, and information about occupations can affect judgments about behaviors. In addition, specific personal information can outweigh gender as a factor in subsequent judgments about a person. For example, men who were described as managing

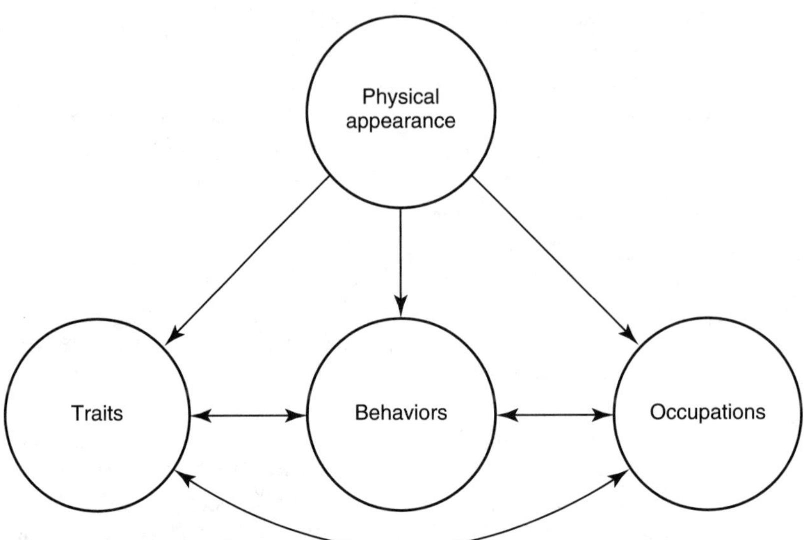

FIGURE 8.1 Components of Deaux and Lewis's Model of Gender Stereotyping

the house or taking care of children were also judged as likely to be emotional and gentle. Such astereotypical information about men also increased the likelihood that such men would be judged as likely to be homosexual.

Although the participants in this stereotyping study saw differences in the traits, behaviors, physical characteristics, and occupations of women and men, their ratings of the two categories reflected the possibility that women may have some characteristics more typical of men or men may have some characteristics more typical of women. That is, people do not view the stereotypes for women and men as separate and dichotomous but as probabilistic and overlapping categories. For example, participants judged the probability of a man and woman having certain characteristics. On a scale of 0 (no chance) to 1.00 (certainty), their participants judged the probability that a man would be strong as .66, a high probability but not a certainty. However, they also judged the chances that a woman would be strong as .44. Although these judgments reflected stereotypical views of the relative strength of men and women, being male was not perfectly associated with strength, nor was being female associated with complete lack of strength.

Therefore, people use several dimensions to categorize men and women, drawing inferences on one dimension based on information from another. What is the content of these stereotypes? Studies in the 1960s and 1970s often found evidence for beliefs that matched elements of the Male Sex Role Identity or the Cult of True Womanhood, but some more recent research has shown changes in attitudes.

Beliefs held by college students in the 1960s showed strong acceptance of gender stereotypes by both college men and women (Rosenkrantz, Vogel, Bee, Broverman, & Broverman, 1968). Table 8.3 shows the items that differentiated women and men, which describe

TABLE 8.3 Stereotypic Traits of Men and Women

Male-Valued Traits	
Aggressive	Knows the ways of the world
Independent	Feelings not easily hurt
Unemotional	Adventurous
Hides emotions	Makes decisions easily
Objective	Never cries
Easily influenced	Acts as a leader
Dominant	Self-confident
Likes math and science	Not uncomfortable about being aggressive
Not excitable in a minor crisis	Ambitious
Active	Able to separate feelings from ideas
Competitive	Not dependent
Logical	Not conceited about appearance
Worldly	Thinks men are superior to women
Skilled in business	Talks freely about sex with men
Direct	
Female-Valued Traits	
Does not use harsh language	Interested in own appearance
Talkative	Neat in habits
Tactful	Quiet
Gentle	Strong need for security
Aware of feelings of others	Expresses tender feelings
Religious	

SOURCE: From "Sex-role stereotypes and self-concepts in college students" (p. 291) by P. Rosenkrantz, S. Vogel, H. Bee, I. Broverman, and D. M. Broverman, 1968, *Journal of Consulting and Clinical Psychology, 32*. Copyright 1968 by the American Psychological Association. Reprinted with permission.

many of the characteristics of the Cult of True Womanhood and of Male Sex Role Identity. These college students applied these standards to themselves, evaluating themselves as masculine or feminine. In addition, both the women and the men in the study showed more positive ratings for masculine than feminine traits, and both the women and men showed some prejudice against stereotypically feminine and preferred stereotypically masculine characteristics. A later study (Broverman, Vogel, Broverman, Clarkson, & Rosenkrantz, 1972) confirmed the bias in favor of characteristics associated with men.

Investigating beliefs about the "typical male" showed that both children and adults described men in ways that fell into three dimensions—activity and achievement orientation, dominance, and level-headedness (Cicone & Ruble, 1978). These dimensions matched some parts of the Male Sex Role Identity. The dimension of activity and achievement orientation includes characteristics that would make a man "The Big Wheel"—ambitious, competitive, independent, and a leader. The characteristics in the dominance category described men as aggressive, powerful, assertive, and boastful; that is, "Give 'Em Hell." The characteristic called level-headedness matches the "The Sturdy Oak," a logical, self-controlled, and

GENDERED VOICES
The Problem Disappeared

"Our car was having some problem, and my wife took it to be repaired," a man said. "She called me from the auto repair place, furious with the treatment she had received. The men there were stonewalling her—failing to listen to what she was telling them and treating her as though she couldn't possibly be capable of relating problems concerning an automobile. She was steamed."

"I went down there, and the problem disappeared. I was a man and apparently privy to the innermost secrets of automobiles. They treated me as though I would understand everything perfectly. Both my wife and I thought it was really absurd."

"One of my friends was upset that it cost $3.20 to get her shirt dry cleaned," a woman told me. "She asked them why it was so much—the shirt was just a tailored, plain shirt. They told her that women's blouses cost more than men's shirts, regardless of the style, because women's clothes don't fit on the standard machine for pressing and must be hand pressed. She wondered if that was really true, and she gave the shirt to a male friend to take to the same dry cleaners. The problem apparently disappeared, because they charged him $1.25 for the very same garment. Isn't that beyond stereotyping?"

unemotional way of dealing with other people and the world. However, this last dimension was present only in studies with adults, whereas the first two appeared in both children's and adults' views of males.

"No Sissy Stuff" persists as part of contemporary masculinity. Children use gender-related information in making judgments about acceptability (Martin, 1989). Both 4- and 10-year-olds said that they disliked children who could be described as "sissies." In a later study (Martin, 1995), college students rated boys who adopt feminine behaviors—that is, sissies—as having more undesirable characteristics than traditional boys or girls and than nontraditional girls—that is, tomboys. Therefore, the prohibition against "sissy stuff" applies to boys and men, who receive negative evaluations when they exhibit behaviors that are feminine, but does not limit girls and women in the same way. Indeed, some masculine characteristics receive positive ratings when applied to either men or women (Orlofsky & O'Heron, 1987).

The social roles of men and women had begun to change during the 1960s, which might have prompted change in male and female stereotypes (Rosenkrantz et al., 1968). Despite some evidence that gender stereotypes actually got stronger during the 1980s (Lueptow, 1985), more recent research has indicated that some weakening may be in progress.

One line of research indicating changes has come from Alice Eagly and her colleagues (Eagly, Mladinic, & Otto, 1991), who have found that women as a gender class receive more favorable evaluations than men. These researchers acknowledged that women may be poorly evaluated in some situations, but their results indicated that people have positive feelings about the characteristics stereotypically associated with women: People believe that these characteristics provide fine examples of human qualities. Indeed, these participants evaluated women more favorably than men. (See the Diversity Highlight: "Do Stereotypes of Nationalities Apply to Women?" for an examination of how these positive evaluations can transcend other negative stereotyping and yet still have negative implications.)

DIVERSITY HIGHLIGHT

Do Stereotypes of Nationalities Apply to Women?

In addition to gender stereotypes, people also have stereotypes of people of different nationalities; that is, people in one nation tend to agree about the attributes they believe people of different nationalities possess. Most people do not have sufficient face-to-face interaction with people of different nationalities to supply a basis for nationality stereotypes as they can for gender stereotypes (Eagly & Kite, 1987).

One possibility for stereotypes of nationalities comes from exposure to newsworthy events involving those nationalities. For many nations this information is largely negative, being based on reports of international competition or hostilities. In addition, the people who are most visible in these international situations are most often men, so people's stereotypes of different nationalities may be based more on information associated with men than women. If so, the stereotypes of nationalities might not extend to women as they do to men, and women of different nationalities might be perceived in terms of their gender stereotype.

On the basis of U.S. college students' ratings of men and women from 28 different countries, the "stereotypes of nationalities are more similar to stereotypes of the men than of the women of these nationalities" (Eagly & Kite, 1987, p. 459). But the differences between countries was also large, with some unanticipated patterns of responses. In some positively evaluated countries, the predicted relationship—namely, that the national stereotype would match men more than women—did not occur. The participants perceived both men and women from these nations as having qualities often associated with women—being warm and concerned with the welfare of others. For the nationalities with negative ratings, participants tended to see the men as having more negative and the women as having more positive qualities. Therefore, people tend to perceive women more positively than men when the women are from negatively evaluated nationalities, but they perceive both men and women similarly when they come from positively evaluated nations.

This research demonstrated the strength of gender stereotypes and how gender and people's nationality stereotypes interact with their gender stereotypes. The gender stereotypes seemed to overrule the nationality stereotypes to form positive views of women of many nationalities. This positive view of women does not include power or competence. Women of many nationalities are seen in ways that are consistent with the feminine stereotype—as kind, caring, and nonthreatening.

Attitudes toward women have changed, according to two studies that assessed attitudes over time. Administering the Attitudes Toward Women Scale (AWS) to students at the same university over a 20-year period showed that students were least egalitarian during the 1970s and most egalitarian during the 1990s (Spence & Hahn, 1997). A meta-analysis of studies that used the AWS assessment revealed a positive relationship between the extent of feminist attitudes and the year of administration (Twenge, 1997). For women, the relationship was strong, and for men, the relationship was still positive but not as strong. Therefore, these studies show that attitudes toward women have become more feminist/egalitarian over the past 25 years, which signals some changes in the traditional stereotypes of women, but questions remain concerning attitude changes concerning men.

According to several studies, men may be the victims of more stringent stereotyping than women. College students who described their views of women and men applied more stereotypical terms to men than to women (Hort, Fagot, & Leinbach, 1990). For both physical and social characteristics, the masculine stereotype was more extreme than the feminine. The women in the study tended to describe men's physical appearance in stereotypical terms, and the men tended to stereotype men in terms of their social characteristics. This study showed that both women and men can be misrepresented through stereotyping, and men may be seen in more stereotypical terms than women—by both men and women.

Indeed, women negatively stereotype men (Edmonds & Cahoon, 1993). Women and men made judgments about the opinions of same- and other-gender individuals, and they indicated that men made more accurate judgments about women's opinions than women made concerning men's opinions. In addition, women tended to believe that men held higher degrees of bias concerning women than the men expressed. That is, women showed negative stereotyping of men. One study (Hudak, 1993) found that men who scored high in stereotypical masculinity viewed women in more stereotypical terms than men who were not so strongly stereotypical.

Therefore, some of the positive attitudes about men and negative attitudes about women found in earlier studies seems to be changing. More recent studies have shown a shift toward greater acceptance of gender role flexibility for women and an increase in positive attitudes toward women. Some studies have indicated that men have now become the object of more severe stereotyping and some negative opinions from women.

Some evidence suggests that men and women may not apply the stereotypes to themselves as strictly as they apply these stereotypes to others. U.S. college students hold stereotypical beliefs about gender, but they have also shown that they are willing to exempt themselves from these stereotypes (Williams & Best, 1990). That is, these students rated themselves as varying from the stereotype. Although people hold stereotypical views of men and women, they may make exceptions for themselves, allowing themselves a wider variety of behaviors than the stereotype would permit. By allowing such personal exceptions as routine, people decrease the power of stereotypes to control and restrict their lives.

Research has tended to confirm not only the existence of gender stereotypes but also the characteristics these share with the ideal woman from the Cult of True Womanhood and the model identified with men from the Male Sex Role Identity. Over the past 30 years of research on gender stereotypes, earlier studies found prejudice in favor of the characteristics typical of men, but more recent studies have found more favorable ratings for the feminine traits. Research also has indicated that people may be willing to make exceptions for themselves in deviating from stereotypical gender-related behaviors, thus decreasing the power of these stereotypes to control behavior. The structure of gender stereotypes is complex; they include multiple components and inferences about these components based on information about others.

Stereotypes about and across Cultures

Gender stereotypes affect how women and men think of themselves and how they evaluate their own behaviors as well as the behaviors of others. Additional categories are equally important to stereotypes. "Although every individual belongs to at least one sexual, racial, and social class category simultaneously, such categories do not have an equal social meaning" (Unger, 1995, p. 427). How do these factors interact to form the basis for stereotypical categories? Do cultures around the world and ethnic groups in North America make similar distinctions between what is considered masculine and feminine? Do other cultures stereotype gender-related behaviors, and are these stereotypes similar to those in North America?

Within the United States, stereotypes exist for various ethnic groups and for men and women within those groups. The gender stereotypes for African Americans differ from those of European Americans, and history can well explain these differences (Davenport & Yurich, 1991). Slavery and the manner in which Africans came to America have created longstanding effects of stereotypes perpetuated against slaves. Slavery disrupted the patriarchal family patterns that existed in Africa. It rendered the men powerless and caused a type of equality between women and men based on their slave status. After slavery ended, racist attitudes toward ex-slaves restricted their earning power and kept African American men from attaining the type of power usually associated with the breadwinner role in patriarchal families. Instead, women not only worked at caring for their children, but they also worked outside their homes to support their families.

The employment of African American women has led to the view that African American families are matriarchies, but this stereotype is not completely accurate (Davenport & Yurich, 1991). African American families fit several different patterns, depending on economic level and geographical location. Middle-class African American families tend to be similar to middle-class families of most other ethnicities, with the family made up of a husband, a wife, and children. Poor families are more likely to consist of a single woman and her children.

Stereotypes exist for African Americans at the various economic levels. Poor African Americans are stereotyped as lazy and dangerous; the women are perceived as being sexually promiscuous and having many children and the men are perceived as being unemployed and possibly involved in criminal activities. Media portrayals and news stories perpetuate these stereotypes despite their lack of validity for the majority of poor African Americans.

For middle-class African Americans, gender stereotypes vary from those of European Americans. African American men have trouble attaining the power associated with the White-male stereotype, but African American women, with their greater likelihood of attaining a college education, can become successful, independent professionals. These lifestyle options can put such African American women in the position of not needing men to provide for them, and the self-reliance of these women has added both to the tension between the sexes and to the stereotype of African American women as strong, resourceful women who value both motherhood and employment.

Do African American women and men differ from European Americans in their beliefs about self and others? A comparison of African American and European American students in the United States showed no differences between the two ethnic groups, but did show differences in gender (Bailey, Silver, & Oliver, 1990). Both European American and African American women held more positive attitudes toward women than men in either ethnic group. Thus, these researchers found a stronger effect for gender than for ethnic background in U.S. college students' views.

Hispanic American women have also been the topic of research on gender stereotypes related to their ethnic backgrounds. Stereotypes of Hispanic Americans include portraying the women as passive and compliant and the men as oppressive (Davenport & Yurich, 1991). Several researchers (Davenport & Yurich, 1991; Ginorio, Gutiérrez, Cauce, & Acosta, 1995; Vazquez-Nuttall, Romero-Garcia, & De Leon, 1987) have questioned the traditional concept that Hispanic culture values male dominance and female submissiveness and have conceded that the dynamics of the relationships are often more complex than the stereotypes would suggest. This complexity is especially true for the women who have come into contact with European American culture by pursuing education and professional careers. Hispanic Americans do tend to emphasize the family, and the one component of the stereotype that holds true is poverty—25% of Hispanic American families are poor, compared to less than 10% of White families, and Hispanic American women are discriminated against more often than White women in employment and salary (Ginorio et al., 1995).

Hispanic American women may hold a more feminine stereotype of the ideal woman than African American or European American women, but they may see themselves as more masculine than this ideal (Vazquez-Nuttal et al., 1987). In other words, the stereotype of Hispanic American women may be feminine, but these women feel that they do not fit these stereotypes well. This discrepancy is similar to the gap between stereotype and personal perception that appeared in European American college students (Williams & Best, 1990).

One attempt to understand the development of gender differences across many cultures led to a large cross-cultural study of the development of social behaviors (Whiting & Edwards, 1988). Children from 12 different communities in Kenya, Liberia, India, the Philippines, Okinawa, Mexico, and the United States were studied to better understand the development of gender in various regions of the world. Some differences were found in the treatment and subsequent behavior of boys and girls, but many similarities were also found in the types of interactions children experienced. The analysis showed that age was more important than gender in predicting the experiences of children in these various cultures. These differences were more apparent in the lives of older children, whose chores differed according to gender. For example, girls were more likely than boys to participate in the care of younger children, which related to greater nurturance among women. Beginning in middle childhood, especially in male-dominated cultures, boys were allowed more freedom to roam and be independent, which also related to the development of adult gender roles for men. In many of these cultures, girls experienced more pressure than boys to behave in socially acceptable ways.

Another cross-cultural investigation (Williams & Best, 1990) of gender stereotypes took place in 30 different countries in North America, South America, Europe, Asia, Africa, and Oceania. The study included children, but the emphasis was on gender stereotypes held by young adults. College students in these countries rated a list of 300 adjectives according to the extent to which each was more frequently associated with men or women. The goal was to study the associations that people in different cultures make about women and men and to look for female and male stereotypes.

The results revealed more similarities than differences in the gender stereotypes. Six adjectives were associated with males in all of the cultures—adventurous, dominant, forceful, independent, masculine, and strong—and three adjectives were identified with females in all cultures—sentimental, submissive, and superstitious. In addition, a wide list of adjectives appeared as male associated or female associated in a large majority of the cultures, and only a few adjectives were male associated in one culture and female associated in another, or vice versa. These findings furnish evidence for similarities in gender stereotypes across cultures, but the similarities were far short of being universal.

In the study of college students' stereotypes, some cultures (Williams & Best, 1990) evaluated the male stereotype more favorably than the female stereotype, but this pattern did not appear consistently. For the entire group of countries, no tendency appeared to evaluate one stereotype more favorably than the other. In addition, the young adults in some of the cultures sharply differentiated the characteristics they attributed to male and female stereotypes, whereas others made relatively few such distinctions. For example, the male stereotype was much more positive than the female stereotype in Nigeria, with views that males are much more active and much stronger than females. In Italy, the differences were reversed or minimized: The female stereotype was the more positive, and beliefs about activity and strength were not given as great a weight.

Despite similarities in many aspects of gender stereotypes, not all cultures hold the same views of what traits, characteristics, and patterns of behavior men and women should exhibit. Despite the existence of gender role differences in all cultures, a cross-cultural review (Gibbons, Hamby, & Dennis, 1997) found that no one gender distinction applied to all cultures. In many cultures, women hold more liberal views of women and the roles of women than men endorse, but even this difference is not universal. No differences in attitudes toward women appear in Malaysia or Pakistan, and men in Brazil hold more liberal views than women there. The distinction between traditional beliefs and beliefs concerning equal opportunity and equal power might apply to all cultures, but the specifics of what constitutes traditionality vary. Therefore, the only universal seems to be the division of activities and behaviors into male and female domains, without world-wide agreement about what those activities and characteristics are. Such divisions of activities, however, form the basis for gender roles and furnish the potential for gender stereotyping.

Function of Stereotyping

The term *stereotyping* has negative connotations, but some theorists have contended that stereotypes have positive as well as negative effects. They proposed that inaccuracy is not one of the inevitable consequences of the process (Jussim, McCauley, & Lee, 1995). Others have argued that stereotyping produces such a magnitude of distortions and incorrect generalizations that its disadvantages are overwhelming (Allen, 1995; Fiske, 1993).

One view (Martin & Halverson, 1981) contends that gender stereotyping is a normal cognitive process. In this view, gender stereotyping is an especially useful type of information processing that allows children to form categories based on gender and to understand this important attribute, if in a simplified and distorted way. The simplification and distortion inherent in stereotyping can have negative effects, but the positive benefits to children of forming gender stereotypes outweigh the negative effects of making some mistakes and thinking too narrowly about gender-related behaviors. Therefore, the function of gender stereotyping can be understood in developmental terms as a useful way to approach the complexities of gender.

A knowledge of gender stereotyping in children does not necessarily lead to an understanding of the factors that maintain behavior in adults (Eagly, 1987b). The existence of gender stereotypes in children does not necessitate that adults similarly maintain gender stereotypes. Research has indicated that older children, adolescents, and adults are willing to make exceptions to the dictates of their gender stereotypes, both for themselves and for others. The tendency to see gender stereotypes as inflexible prescriptions for behavior lessens with age. Then what is the point of keeping a rule with so many exceptions?

The "kernel of truth" position holds that stereotypes have some valid as well as some inaccurate points (Martin, 1987). Gender roles, the set of behaviors performed more often by men or women, form the basis for gender stereotypes. That is, the social roles that women and men fulfill allow people to perceive differences between men and women and to extend these differences to areas where none exists.

Several researchers have conducted studies to assess the accuracy of gender stereotypes, but no agreement has yet been reached. Part of the controversy is due to the difficulty in assessing gender-related behaviors (Allen, 1995). Should persons report on their own behavior, should some observer record behavior, or should researchers rely on standardized tests for their assessments? All three approaches are subject to errors that complicate assessing stereotypes accurately.

One side of the controversy proposes that gender stereotypes are accurate representations of actual differences between men's and women's reported characteristics. The inaccuracy comes from exaggeration, with stereotypes being much more inclusive than actual gender differences (Martin, 1987). A meta-analysis (Swim, 1994) of studies on the accuracy of gender stereotyping confirmed and extended this finding: Both overestimation and underestimation occur. Discrepancies between perception and actual differences may not necessarily be in a stereotypical direction, and gender perceptions are often accurate.

The other side of the controversy contends that gender stereotypes contain a great deal of inaccuracy (Allen, 1995). People make errors in which they sometimes underestimate and often overestimate gender differences. Stereotypes may not be systematic exaggerations (McCauley, 1995), but some inaccuracies are usually part of the process. Although the evidence concerning the accuracy of stereotypes is not completely clear, the findings lead to the conclusion that people are not very accurate in understanding the differences between the genders.

The process of rationalization may be an important factor in maintaining stereotypes. Observation cannot form the basis for stereotyping because many gender differences are too small to rely on personal observation as their basis (Hoffman & Hurst, 1990). Rather, people form stereotypes and perpetuate them by adjusting their attitudes. Confirmation for this view comes from two clever experiments that provided descriptions of members of two fictional categories, with the majority in each category differing in their preferred activities. These descriptions did not specify a total division of labor; one study described one group as 80% "child raisers" and 80% of another group as "city workers." The study investigated whether participants would explain the differing activities by rationalizing different personalities suited to the activity most common in its group.

The results showed strong evidence of this type of stereotyping, including differences in personality traits. When a habitual activity was specified, people deduced an underlying personality trait that explained why this difference existed. Rather than believing that circumstances are important in activities, people tend to attribute differences in behavior to underlying personality traits. Thus, the unequal distribution of activities is sufficient to form the basis for gender stereotypes, including beliefs about intrinsic personal characteristics.

People feel better, for example, about women being child-care workers or homemakers if they believe that some element of women's personalities suits them to do such work. Additionally, this view holds that if women have the personal qualities that are necessary for such jobs, then men should not hold these jobs. Such rationalizations would also extend to racial or ethnic stereotyping as well as stereotypes based on gender roles. (For an additional negative effect of ethnic and gender stereotyping, see the Diversity Highlight: "Stereotypes Can Threaten.") This view of stereotyping proposes that such cognitive processing offers rationalizations for existing situations that allow people to avoid thinking about the complexities of gender.

Power rather than cognitive processing is an additional explanation for stereotyping (Fiske, 1993). Power encourages stereotyping through differential attention of the powerless and powerful. The powerless attend carefully to the powerful to help understand their motives and predict their behaviors. This attention promotes the formation of complex perceptions of the powerful rather than stereotypes. The powerful, on the other hand, do not have the need to attend to the powerless, who do not exert control over the powerful. Their lack of close attention is conducive to stereotyping.

In addition, the powerful are often attentionally overloaded, making superficial attention common for them. They may also have a high need for dominance, making them willing to control others. Furthermore, "stereotyping and power are mutually reinforcing because stereotyping itself exerts control, maintaining and justifying the status quo" (Fiske, 1993, p. 621).

This view also highlights the negative aspects of stereotyping and points out that stereotyping has more impact simply by being convenient for cognitive processing. The function of gender (or any other type of) stereotyping may be ease of cognitive processing: Stereotypes omit some individual details. This neglect of details allows people to think in simplified ways about a class of individuals rather than considering each person on an individual basis. For children, such simplification may be a necessary part of dealing with a complex world. In contrast, adolescents and adults are capable of considering information about individuals and allowing for nonstereotypical behaviors. However, adolescents and adults still have access to strong stereotypes, and these views influence their expectations about gender-related behavior. For adults, such simplification may be a convenient rationalization for relegating women and men to stereotypical activities or the consequence of power differentials that exist between men and women in many societies.

Masculinity, Femininity, and Androgyny

The concepts of *male* and *female* are relatively easy for people to understand, as these words relate to biological differences understood by everyone except young children. But the concepts of masculine and feminine are much less closely related to biology and thus much more difficult to separate into two nonoverlapping categories: "One can be more or less feminine. One cannot be more or less female" (Maccoby, 1988, p. 762). Nonetheless, these dimensions seem important—perhaps essentially important—and psychologists have attempted to conceptualize and measure masculinity and femininity along with other important personality traits. After many years of difficulty with such measurements, the concept of **androgyny**—having the characteristics of both male and female—appeared as an addition to the conceptual framework. Several techniques now exist for measuring this attribute.

Psychologists attempts to understand and measure masculinity and femininity have a long history but not a great deal of success (Constantinople, 1973; Lewin, 1984a, b). The

DIVERSITY HIGHLIGHT

Stereotypes Can Threaten

For some ethnic minority and female students, there is "a threat in the air" (Steele, 1997, p. 614). This threat comes from the fear that "one is in a situation or doing something for which a negative stereotype about one's group applies." Claude Steele described this situation as *stereotype threat* and proposed that people feel threatened in situations in which they believe that their performance will identify them as examples of their group's negative stereotype. Even is the person does not believe the stereotype or accept that it applies, the threat of being identified with a negative stereotype can be an ever-present factor that puts a person in the spotlight and creates tension and anxiety about performance.

Although he contended that stereotype threat can apply to any group for which negative stereotypes exist, Steele has concentrated his research on African Americans and women as negatively stereotyped groups. Steele hypothesized that the threat of being identified with a negative stereotype can be an emotional factor in performance, which can hamper achievement and cause the threat to come true. He contended that identification with the area intensifies the situation: Students who are strongly identified with school feel stereotype threat whereas those less identified do not.

Steele and his colleagues have tested stereotype threat in several ways. Their basic approach has been to give information to one group of participants indicating that the test they take will demonstrate their basic ability in a specific area whereas another group is given information that the test is an ordinary one. He hypothesized that those people who are part of a negatively stereotyped group should feel threatened by the first condition but not the second. For example, women who are good math students and see themselves as such should feel stereotype threat when they hear that the test they will take is indicative of their math ability. If these women perform more poorly on such a test than a group of men with similar math ability, this outcome would demonstrate the performance effects of stereotype threat. Steele and his colleagues obtained such results, suggesting that qualified women sometimes do more poorly in math and science than their ability levels predict because of stereotype threat.

According to Steele, stereotype threat can also explain why African American students perform more poorly than European American students on standardized scholastic tests. By presenting a test as diagnostic of scholastic ability or not, Steele and his colleagues found that African American students performed more poorly than European American students only when they believed that the test reflected their underlying abilities (Steele & Aronson, 1995). Those African Americans who received no information about the test's diagnostic ability performed as well as European American students.

In addition, other negative effects result from stereotype threat. Taking a test that may confirm one's membership in a negatively stereotyped group can also motivate a person to disassociate from the group. Participants' stereotypes were activated by taking a difficult test they believed to be diagnostic of their abilities; these participants subsequently showed several signs of attempting to disassociate themselves from the stereotype of African Americans (Steele & Aronson, 1995). These actions included expressing fewer preferences for music associated with African Americans and being less likely to designate their ethnicity on the test form.

Steele (1997) argued that female and African American students feel threatened by negative stereotypes that could be applied to them. His research has demonstrated that students who identify with an area can feel threatened by the potential application of a negative stereotype. Unfortunately, this type of threat is most likely to apply to capable students who identify with school and may be among the vanguard of minority group students in the area. Therefore, stereotype threat can pose the greatest problems for those who are most able to succeed.

problems began with the first measures developed, and no measurement technique since has escaped serious criticism.

Lewis Terman, who adapted the Binet intelligence test into the Stanford-Binet, became interested in measuring masculinity and femininity (Lewin, 1984a). Terman believed that masculinity and femininity (MF) were essential components of personality, so together with his associate Catherine Cox Miles, he produced the Attitude Interest Analysis Survey, a 456-item test that appeared in 1936. This test included items that women and men answered differently, yielding scores (MF) that were increasingly positive in the masculine direction and increasingly negative in the feminine direction. Therefore, this early test conceptualized masculinity and femininity as a single dimension, with strong masculinity lying at one extreme and strong femininity at the other.

The initial conceptualization of the Attitude Interest Analysis Survey as unidimensional and the content of the test have made it the target of criticism (Constantinople, 1973; Lewin, 1984a). The test was not valid in any way other than distinguishing men from women; critics (Lewin, 1984a) thus argued that the test actually measured Victorian concepts of masculinity and femininity rather than the masculinity and femininity of individuals. This test is no longer used, but its existence influenced others to develop measurements of masculinity and femininity.

When the MF scale of the Minnesota Multiphasic Personality Inventory (MMPI) appeared in 1940, it soon became the most common measure of masculinity and femininity, largely because of its inclusion in this personality test developed to measure psychological disorders (Lewin, 1984b). This scale was also unidimensional and bipolar, with masculinity and femininity at opposite ends of the scale. The psychologists who developed the MMPI were more interested that their MF scale was able to measure homosexual tendencies in men than masculinity and femininity in heterosexual men and women. As a result of this interest, their **validation** procedure included a comparison of the MF responses of 13 homosexual men to the responses of 54 heterosexual male soldiers. They used the responses of the 13 homosexual men as a standard for femininity, thus defining femininity as the responses of these men.

The test makers knew that the scale should not be used as a valid measure of femininity, and they were initially tentative in describing its use for a nonhomosexual population. But the test was soon extended to thousands of people, and the reservations disappeared. "It is rather staggering to realize that the *femininity dimension of this popular test was "validated" on a criterion group of 13 male homosexuals!"* (Lewin, 1984b, p. 181; emphasis in original). However, the scale was not even very successful in diagnosing homosexuality in men, and this confusion of masculinity–femininity and sexual orientation posed a problem for understanding both concepts.

An alternative means of conceptualizing masculinity and femininity used the terms instrumental and expressive, with women's behaviors considered expressive and men's behaviors as instrumental (Lewin, 1984b). This distinction was based on an analysis of families around the world, with the conclusion that men occupy the role of autonomous and achievement-oriented leaders whereas women provide nurturance and support. This terminology has become important to those who have attempted to reconceptualize and measure psychological masculinity and femininity.

Despite the problems with a unidimensional measure of masculinity–femininity and the limited success with identifying homosexuals with these scales, this approach to the

GENDERED VOICE
Some Things Are Different There

"I think of femininity more in terms of what a woman wears than anything else," a young man told me. He had grown up on an island in the Mediterranean, lived in Paris for two years, and now lives in the United States. He sees some differences in what is considered feminine and masculine in the three cultures he has known. "Where I grew up, there was very little sexual activity among teenagers; it was a very conservative culture, and adolescent sexuality was strictly discouraged. The girls didn't dress in any way that was sexual, so they didn't seem very feminine to me. I guess I would consider some of them more feminine than others, probably in the same way that a person in the U.S. would: Small and dainty girls were more feminine. So I don't see any differences there.

"In Paris, nothing was hidden—things were openly sexual. The U.S. is a very sexualized culture, but there are differences. For example, kinds of clothing that people wore in Paris were different from in the U.S., and those differences related to femininity. Wearing jeans and tennis shoes would be considered very unfeminine rather than just another way to dress. I remember one girl in my student group who often wore tennis shoes, jeans, and a big sweater, and she was considered very unfeminine. Not that her way of dressing kept her from being pretty or attractive, but she didn't seem feminine. I guess I would say that Paris was less casual, and the women seemed more feminine than in the U.S. or in the Mediterranean.

"There were also some differences in what was considered masculine. At home, men tend to be small, so masculinity is not determined by size but more by behavior. Even men who are 5′4″ or 5′6″ can be macho, depending on what they do. Gangsters are very masculine, and so are those who are involved in politics, especially radical politics. The communists are considered the most masculine—lots of testosterone there. Men can demonstrate their masculinity by drinking—it has to be liquor and straight, without ice—and by smoking unfiltered cigarettes. Also, women who drink or smoke are considered masculine. So masculinity is a matter of what you do in the Mediterranean, not how you look—except the gangsters always have a three-day growth of beard.

"One of the differences in what is considered masculine involves bodybuilding and weight lifting. Men in the Mediterranean and in Paris just didn't do anything like that. They wouldn't consider bodybuilding masculine; it would be considered odd rather than a way to demonstrate masculinity. If they exercise, it's oriented more toward fitness than bodybuilding, so that seems very American to me.

"Political activism is masculine where I come from, whether men or women are involved. As I said, the communist radicals are considered very macho, and women who become involved in politics or become lawyers are considered masculine. As career opportunities increase for women, this may change, but now, women lose their femininity when they gain power through legal or political careers—even more than in the U.S.

"Also, on the island where I grew up, there was a status for women that I haven't seen anywhere else. Postmenopausal women lose their sexuality but they gain power and can become very influential in the community. They are considered almost neuter in terms of sexuality, so they are not feminine at all, but these women can have a lot of power, whereas younger women do not. As long as a woman is young and unmarried or married, she has almost no voice in the community, but these older women can make a transition to a position of respect and power.

"The only men who lose their sexuality in a similar way are artists, who are not considered feminine but almost neutral. Being an artist is well accepted and doesn't really carry any connotations of femininity, unlike homosexuality, which is strongly prohibited. It is a conservative culture, and homosexual activity is not tolerated at all—unlike Paris, where gay men and lesbians are very open about their sexuality. The U.S. seems to be the worst of both cultures in that respect; homosexuality is fairly open but poorly tolerated. That seems like a bad combination to me. As far as masculinity and femininity and homosexuality are concerned, I can't see any relationship. I know I can't tell who is homosexual by how masculine the men seem or how feminine the women seem, so sexual orientation does not seem to coincide with these characteristics to me."

measure of masculinity and femininity was the most common until the 1970s. When theorists realized that the dimensions of masculinity and femininity were separate from sexual orientation, the measurements of both changed, helping to clarify both areas.

In 1974, Sandra Bem published a different approach to the measurement of masculinity and femininity—by adding the concept of androgyny. She proposed that some people have characteristics associated with both masculinity and femininity; that is, some people are androgynous. The androgyny concept requires both masculinity and femininity in combination, so it is incompatible with a unidimensional view of MF. Instead, Bem constructed two scales to capture her concept of androgyny. Her test, the Bem Sex Role Inventory (BSRI), measured masculinity and femininity with a scale to measure each. Figure 8.2 shows the difference between the traditional unidimensional approach to personality measurement and Bem's two-dimensional approach.

People who take the BSRI respond to 60 characteristics by rating how well each of these characteristics applies to them on a 7-point scale. Of the 60 items, 20 represent cultural stereotypes of masculinity (ambitious, independent, competitive), 20 represent femininity (gentle, warm, understanding), and 20 are filler items. The 7-point scale ranges from *Always or almost always true* to *Never or almost never true.* Scores on the masculinity and femininity scales yield four different possibilities: masculine, feminine, androgynous, and undifferentiated. People who score high on the masculinity scale and low on the femininity scale would be considered *masculine,* whereas people who score high on the femininity scale and low on the masculinity scale would be considered *feminine.* These people not only accept cultural stereotypes of masculinity or femininity, they also reject the other role. Thus, such individuals fit the stereotypical notions of masculinity or femininity, classifications similar to those obtained on other MF tests.

Bem labeled those people who score high on both scales *androgynous* and those who score low on both scales *undifferentiated,* classifications that do not appear in traditional MF tests. Androgynous people evaluate themselves as having many of the characteristics

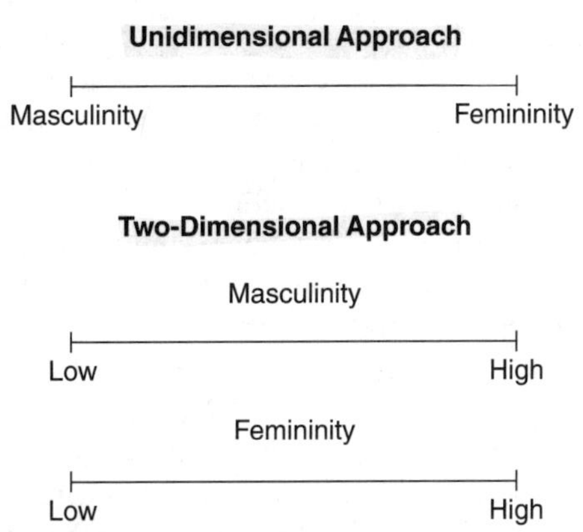

FIGURE 8.2 Two Approaches to the Measurement of Femininity and Masculinity

TABLE 8.4 Examples of Positive and Negative Femininity and Masculinity

Femininity		*Masculinity*	
Positive	Negative	Positive	Negative
Patient	Timid	Strong	Aggressive
Sensitive	Weak	Confident	Bossy
Devoted	Needs Approval	Firm	Sarcastic
Responsible	Dependent	Forceful	Rude
Appreciative	Nervous	Carefree	Feels superior

SOURCE: Lina A. Ricciardelli & Robert J. Williams, 1995, "Desirable and undesirable gender traits in three behavioral domains," *Sex Roles, 33,* 637–655.

that our culture associates with men and women, whereas those people who are undifferentiated report few traits of either gender.

The concept of androgyny grew rapidly in popularity. Another test, the Personal Attribute Questionnaire (PAQ) (Spence, Helmreich, & Stapp, 1974), soon appeared to overcome problems with the BSRI (see Spence & Helmreich, 1978). The PAQ also identified people as masculine, feminine, androgynous, and undifferentiated, and both tests have continued in use. Although the MMPI Mf scale is still widely administered as part of that personality test, researchers interested in measuring masculinity or femininity usually choose some other assessment, such as the BSRI and the PAQ.

Not all researchers accept that the concept of androgyny offers improvements. Critics contend that tests that include measures of androgyny have provided no revolutionary reconceptualization of the measurement of masculinity and femininity (Lewin, 1984b). The masculinity scales of these tests measure instrumentality, and the femininity scales measure expressiveness. Indeed, many researchers now refer to scores on these two scales in terms of instrumentality and expressiveness rather than masculinity and femininity. Janet Spence (1985), one of the developers of the PAQ, has acknowledged the weaknesses of this conceptualization of masculinity and femininity and now uses the terms *instrumental* and *expressive* to describe the traits that such tests measure. She discussed the conceptual inadequacies of measurements of masculinity and femininity in the field of psychology and proposed that these concepts are even more complex than any existent tests measure.

Some researchers have adopted David Bakan's (1966) terminology. He uses the term *agentic* to refer to the assertive, controlling tendencies that are associated with men and *communal* to refer to the concern with the welfare of others associated with women. Other research (Ricciardelli & Williams, 1995) has tested an alternative conceptualization that involves four dimensions: positive and negative masculinity plus positive and negative femininity. Table 8.4 gives examples of these four characteristics. The PAQ contains only positive aspects of masculinity and femininity, and the BSRI includes mostly positive aspects of both but has some examples of negative femininity. Although more research is necessary on this four-factor conceptualization, it seems to offers advantages over the two-factor approach.

Although the terms *masculinity* and *femininity* are meaningful to most people, psychologists have not yet managed to measure them in theoretically meaningful and valid ways. Problems exist both in the measurement of masculinity and femininity as well in with the concept of androgyny (Constantinople, 1973; Lewin, 1984b). In answering the question, "Are MF tests satisfactory?" the answer is "No. There is no evidence that the MF tests of the last sixty years provide a valid measure of the relative femininity of women or the relative masculinity of men" (Lewin, 1984b, p. 198). Instead, these tests measure our society's conceptualization of what women and men should be by using values that date from the Victorian era. The tests purport to measure masculinity and femininity but measure gender stereotypes rather than personality characteristics.

Summary

The term *gender role* refers to the activities or behaviors typically associated with women or men, whereas *gender stereotype* refers to the beliefs associated with the characteristics and personalities appropriate to men and women. Current stereotypes of women and men have been influenced by historical views of women and men. The Cult of True Womanhood that arose during Victorian times held that women should be pious, pure, submissive, and domestic. For men, several models of masculinity show gender role stereotypes. One of these is the Male Sex Role Identity, which holds that to be successful as men, males must identify with the elements of that role. These elements include the need to avoid all feminine activities and interests, have an achievement orientation, suppress emotions, and be aggressive and assertive.

Gender stereotyping begins early in development and results in children holding rigid rules for gender-related behavior. Stereotyping is maintained by the illusion that more activities and characteristics are associated with gender than actually are. Children become flexible in applying gender rules as they approach adolescence, allowing themselves more exceptions for individual variation. Research indicates that children and adults accept elements of these stereotypes and use the stereotypes in making decisions and judgments, but adults apply the rules less strictly than children do because they have the ability to make many personal exceptions.

Gender stereotypes have four different aspects—physical characteristics, traits, behaviors, and occupations. Each may vary independently, but people make judgments about one based on information about another to form an interdependent network of associations. People use this network of information in making deductions about gender-related characteristics.

Cross-cultural research on gender roles and gender stereotyping indicates that all cultures delegate different roles to men and women. The stereotypes of the gender have more similarities than differences across cultures, with the male stereotype fitting the instrumental, or agentic, model and the female stereotype fitting the expressive, or communal, model. However, not all cultures make sharp divisions between the characteristics and behaviors of men and women.

During childhood, stereotyping may serve to simplify cognitive processing and allow children to make easier decisions and judgments. During adulthood, such simplification is no longer needed but the structures still exist. The function of stereotypes has been proposed to be convenience of cognitive processing, rationalization of existing gender-related divisions, or maintenance of power differences between men and women.

The concepts of masculinity and femininity have a long history in the field of psychology as personality traits measured by various psychological tests. The Attitude Interest Analysis Survey, which appeared in 1936, conceptualized masculinity and femininity as opposite poles of one continuum. This test is no longer used, but the approach of a unidimensional scale for measuring masculinity–femininity still exists in some personality tests, most notably the Minnesota Multiphasic Personality Inventory (MMPI). In addition to its unidimensional approach to masculinity and femininity, the MMPI also attempted to measure homosexual tendencies in men. This test even went so far as to define femininity in terms of the responses of a small group of homosexual men.

A more recent approach to the measurement of masculinity and femininity includes the concept of androgyny. Several tests have adopted this strategy, and such tests include separate scales for masculinity and femininity. People who score high on one but not on the other are considered masculine or feminine, but those who score high on both scales are considered to be androgynous. However, some critics have argued that none of the personality tests that purport to measure masculinity and femininity do so; rather, these tests measure characteristics that would be better labeled as instrumental–expressive or agentic–communal dimensions of personality. At present, the underlying concepts of masculinity and femininity remain elusive.

Glossary

androgyny a blending of masculinity and femininity in which the desirable characteristics of each combine among individuals who show many socially desirable characteristics associated with both men and women.

gender stereotype the beliefs about the characteristics associated with or activities appropriate to men or women.

illusory correlation the incorrect belief that two events vary together or the perception that the relationship is strong when little or no actual relationship exists.

validation the process of demonstrating that a psychological test measures what it claims to measure; the procedure that demonstrates the accuracy of a test.

Suggested Readings

Deaux, Kay. (1987). Psychological constructions of masculinity and femininity. In June Machover Reinisch, Leonard A. Rosenblum, & Stephanie A. Sanders (Eds.), *Masculinity/Femininity: Basic perspectives* (pp. 289–303). New York: Oxford University Press. Deaux reviews not only the leading theories of gender role development but also the efforts to measure masculinity and femininity.

Lewin, Miriam. (1984a). "Rather worse than folly?" Psychology measures femininity and masculinity: 1. From Terman and Miles to the Guilfords. In Miriam Lewin (Ed.), *In the shadow of the past: Psychology portrays the sexes* (pp. 155–178).

Lewin, Miriam. (1984b). Psychology measures femininity and masculinity: 2. From "13 gay men" to the instrumental-expressive distinction. In Miriam Lewin (Ed.), *In the shadow of the past: Psychology portrays the sexes* (pp. 179–204). New York: Columbia University Press. Lewin's two articles critically review attempts in the field of psychology to measure masculinity and femininity. She points out the difficulties and the mistakes, including conceptualizing femininity as the responses of 13 gay men.

Pleck, Joseph H. (1981, September). Prisoners of manliness. *Psychology Today,* pp. 68–79. This popular article presents the elements of Pleck's concept of Male Sex Role Identity, which he sees as unrealistic and constraining for men, women, and society.

Chapter 9

Emotion

HEADLINE

Big Fat Lies about Men

—*Mademoiselle,* August 1996

Andrew Postman (1996) listed several "big fat lies about men" and offered counterarguments for each. One of the lies was that "men don't show emotion" (p. 187). Postman argued that men and women both show emotion, but sometimes the situations that elicit the emotion differ. His girlfriend cried at a romantic movie, but he couldn't stay interested. He, on the other hand, cried at the Normandy memorial to the D-Day invasion, but his girlfriend was not as moved.

There are some situations in which men and women have similar emotional reactions. Both Postman and his girlfriend watched women's basketball, and his girlfriend noticed how emotional the women were during their playoff game. The losing team sat on the bench after the game, and most were crying. When they watched the men's final, she predicted a different emotional reaction from the men than they had seen from the women. Yet "When the clock ran out, the camera focused on the losing bench. A bunch of 6′6″ men, crying furiously" (p. 187), which was not the emotional reaction that his girlfriend had expected from men.

Postman's "big fat lies about men" were stereotypes of men (and women) that turn out to be inaccurate. He pointed out how expectations concerning emotionality are incorrect for men and argued that women and men are similar in emotionality (and in many other ways). Although the situations that provoke emotion for women and men sometimes differ, the range of emotions are the same, and even the situational differences are not always present. Despite the appearance on national television of these 6′6″ crying male basketball players, the widespread perception is that women are more emotional, that they experience a wider variety of emotions and a higher level of emotional intensity than do men. On the other hand, men are restricted to a few emotions, especially anger. This chapter explores the experience and expression of emotion for women and men, then it examines two emotional reactions stereotypically associated with women and men: maternal instinct and aggression.

Physiological, Cognitive, and Behavioral Aspects

Emotion has been a subject of interest in the field of psychology since its early years as a discipline. Even before psychologists began experimental investigations of behavior, emotion was a topic of interest to philosophers. From the start, philosophers tended to conceptualize emotions as irrational and to place emotion opposite the rational thought processes (Averill, 1982). This attitude shaped the rational–emotive dichotomy that persists today.

Psychologists have devised several theories to explain the various components of emotion and their relative contribution to the experience. Early theories (McDougall, 1923) emphasized the physiology of emotional reactions and proposed their instinctual nature. Other theories attempted to bring in the contribution of cognition to explain the physiological reactions that accompany emotion (Cannon, 1927; James, 1890). All approaches held that both the physiology and the cognitive components were important to experiencing emotion.

A clever experiment by Stanley Schachter and Jerome Singer (1962) demonstrated that similar levels of physical arousal could result in different emotions, depending on the setting and the expectation of the participants. This study showed that both physiological arousal and cognitive labeling are important components in the individual's experience of emotion. Despite the results from Schachter and Singer's study, the relative contributions of physiology and cognition have been the source of continued controversy in psychology. Some theorists have asserted that the physiological component is more important (Zajonc, 1984), and others have argued that cognitions are more critical to the experience of emotion (Lazarus, 1984).

The primacy of either physiology or cognition would have important implications for understanding emotion. If cognition were the primary factor in emotion, then an emotional experience should be dependent on the setting and expectation, and the physiology of the underlying emotion should be the same, regardless of the emotion evoked. If physiology were the primary factor, then the emotional experience should vary with bodily states, and each emotion would have a characteristic pattern of physical responses.

Both theories may be correct: one for men and the other for women (Pennebaker & Roberts, 1992). In this view, women rely more on cognitive information whereas men use physical cues to signal their experience. Several types of evidence support this view. In laboratory studies, men are better than women at gauging their internal physical states such as heart rate, blood pressure, and blood glucose levels. These gender differences do not appear in studies done in more naturalistic settings, where women and men are equally adept in judging their internal physical responses. Outside the laboratory, women are better than men in gauging the emotions of others. They cannot know others' physiological responses, so this expertise must come from reading the situation. Women's reliance on situational and contextual cues in interpreting emotion may be the result of socialization that teaches them not to listen to their bodies. Women, therefore, may become skilled in interpreting cues from the environment, whereas men do not undergo this social pressure and continue to use internal bodily cues to understand their emotion. This intriguing hypothesis of a "his and

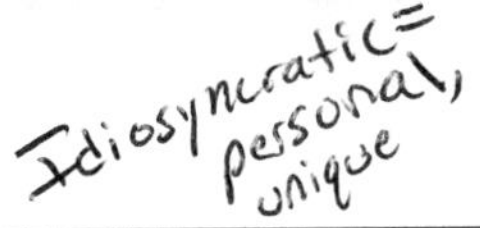

hers theory of emotion" allows that two competing theories of emotion may both be true and that both describe some gender-related differences in perception of emotion.

Paul Ekman and his colleagues (Ekman, 1984; Ekman, Levenson, & Friesen, 1983) have concentrated on similarities between genders in emotional experience. They hold that some facets of emotional experience are universal. These researchers studied the different facial movements that accompany the experience of emotion and found that facial expressions are characteristic of emotional states across societies. That is, people experience a standard set of emotions regardless of the culture of origin. Ekman argued that this consistency exists because emotions have evolved to help people deal with life tasks.

This evolutionary view can be traced to Charles Darwin (1872), who believed that both humans and animals innately experience emotions. Although Ekman's view of emotion does not exclude cognition as a factor in emotion, his evolutionary explanation emphasizes the role of physiology and the consistency of emotional experience for people in all cultures. Other investigations have tended to confirm Ekman's view, but not all investigators (Russell, 1994) accept the universal nature of emotions. When researchers use methods of investigation other than facial expressions, such as examining language for emotion-related words or investigating the social context of emotion, the results no longer support a universality of emotional experience.

Regardless of the consistency of emotional *experience,* people do not show similar consistency in emotional *expression.* That is, the behaviors associated with emotion show some consistent cultural and individual variation. (See the Diversity Highlight: "Cultural Consistency or Cultural Diversity in Emotion?") Some associations are known to exist between emotion and expression in terms of behavior, for example between anger and aggression. However, the experience of emotion requires no behavioral manifestation: People do not have to *do* anything when they feel an emotion. The emotional experience is internal, and behavior is not an inevitable consequence of that experience.

The lack of correspondence between emotion and behavior results in the ability to disguise or conceal emotion. People can experience an emotion and yet manifest no overt behavior that signals their inner experience. Ekman (1984) defined the concept of **display rules** as "overlearned habits about who can show what emotion to whom and when they can show it" (p. 320). These display rules make it possible to experience one emotion and display another, or to display no emotional reaction at all despite the internal experience of strong emotion. In addition, the learning of display rules provides an explanation for the variability of emotion from person to person and from culture to culture.

How does learning provide an explanation for the gender differences in emotion? Do men and women learn different display rules and show different emotions, or do they experience differing types and intensities of emotions?

Gender and the Experience of Emotion

"From the 19th century onwards, rationality and emotionality have largely become associated with the supposedly different natures of men and women, the former fitted for productive labor and the latter for household and emotional labor" (Fischer, 1993, p. 303). This emotional double standard holds that women are more emotional than men, but only for a

DIVERSITY HIGHLIGHT

Cultural Consistency or Cultural Diversity in the Emotions?

Researchers who have conducted cross-cultural studies of emotion and others who have reviewed the cross-cultural and anthropological evidence have concluded that emotions show both consistency and diversity across cultures. One such cross-cultural study (Scherer, Walbott, & Summerfield, 1986) surveyed students in Belgium, France, Great Britain, Israel, Italy, Spain, Switzerland, and West Germany to investigate similarities and differences of emotion. More similarities than differences appeared, one being the tendency for everyday situations to be the main source of strong emotion. Of the emotions, anger was the most commonly reported, followed by joy. Close relationships were the main source of both positive and negative emotions. This survey revealed the expected stereotypical gender differences—women reported more expressions of emotion than men—but the study also found a smaller magnitude of gender difference than the researchers had hypothesized.

This survey revealed some evidence against the emotional stereotypes associated with these countries: The English were very talkative rather than reticent; the Italians were very concerned with achievement rather than personal relationships; and the Swiss were very emotional rather than very reserved. Overall, this study showed fewer differences in emotion than the researchers had expected. Perhaps these similarities are not too surprising, considering how similar European cultures are tending to become.

Other cross-cultural studies have included a wider geographical variety of cultures, and these have found more variation in the situations that prompt emotion as well as in the emotional responses. James Russell (1991) reviewed the cross-cultural work on the categorization of emotion by using emotion words and facial expressions. He concluded that "people of different cultures and speaking different languages categorize the emotions somewhat differently" (p. 444). However, Russell also concluded that more similarities than differences exist in the categories of emotion across different cultures and languages.

Another cross-cultural study (Mesquita & Frijda, 1992) analyzed the evidence on emotion by examining the components of emotion rather than only their categorization. By doing this type of analysis, similarities and differences appeared across cultures: "There exists some evidence that, by and large, certain kinds of events elicit emotions in widely different cultures and that they tend to elicit the same emotions in these different cultures" (Mesquita & Frijda, 1992, p. 181). These similar emotions included anger, disgust, joy, fear, sadness, and surprise. For example, loss of a loved one was associated with sadness in all cultures. Interaction with strangers was a source of anger in many cultures. Within these broad similarities in emotion, specific differences were found. For example, interactions with strangers were a source of anger for 52% of Japanese, compared with 15% of Americans and 20% of Europeans—a substantial cultural difference.

The experience of shame is common to all cultures as a response to being observed doing bad things, but what constitutes "bad things" varies enormously among cultures. For example, among the Bedouins a loss of honor is cause for shame, so their culture is very sensitive to the many causes of diminished honor. Signs of dependency or weakness cause a loss of honor, and the Bedouins believe that women are at constant peril because they are weak and dependent by nature. Women in Bedouin society must be very careful when they are in the presence of men lest they do something that will dishonor them and their families. On the other hand, the Japanese are shamed by displays of emotion because their code of modesty demands that true feelings remain hidden. Not all emotions bring shame to the Utku Eskimos, but anger does; it is considered dangerous, and to display it is completely unacceptable for adults.

At an abstract level of analysis, emotions show many similarities across cultures—the types, the antecedent situations, the labels used, and the physical reactions and facial responses people exhibit. However, cultural differences exist in the specifics of each component, especially in the processes regulating emotion (Mesquita & Frijda, 1992). Cultures vary both in restricting and in prescribing the display of emotion—who should express what emotion under what circumstances. That is, although many similarities exist across cultures, the rules that govern the display of emotion and the rules that govern what emotion should be experienced vary enormously among cultures: "Although there are universal patterns of expressive behavior, there also are culture-specific behavior modes, deriving from culture-specific models and from culturally based expectations regarding behavior that is appropriate under particular circumstances" (Mesquita & Frijda, 1992, p. 199). Although people may all feel the same emotions, they do not express them in the same ways or under the same circumstances.

restricted range of emotions—happiness, sadness, disgust, fear, and surprise. Anger is notably absent from the list of emotions stereotypically associated with women. The emotions associated with boys and men are likewise restricted, with sadness and fear notably absent.

To test the stereotype of female emotionality, Stephanie Shields (1987) asked college students to think of the most emotional person they knew. She found a difference between the number of female and male students named, with significantly more women named in this category. These participants tended to think of women as displaying a negative emotion, such as sadness, depression, or anger. In analyzing the justifications for their judgments, she found that participants considered a person emotional when the reactions were extreme and exaggerated in proportion to the stimulus that provoked it. This study confirmed people's tendency to think of women in stereotypical terms—as "emotional females" who overreact.

Shields's study measured people's beliefs rather than women's emotional responses, leaving untested any possible gender differences in emotional responses. Such assessments can pose problems. Unfortunately, expectancy can bias the measurement of emotional responses, leading observers to see what they expect to see.

Two studies demonstrated people's tendency to see aggression according to gender roles. In one study (Condry & Condry, 1976), participants rated infants' emotional responses to four different situations. Half of the participants believed that they would be rating a girl and the other half thought that they would see a boy, when in fact the child was a girl dressed in such a way as to pass for either. The researchers expected that this gender information would lead participants to "see" different emotions in the infants, even when the infants and the reactions were always the same. The study revealed two gender stereotypical findings. The first was that participants tended to rate the level of emotionality according to the child's apparent gender. The second was that participants tended to interpret the "boy's" reaction as anger and the "girl's" reaction as fear in response to a surprise—the sudden appearance of a jack-in-the-box.

A second study (Condry & Ross, 1985) also manipulated participants' expectations about children's gender and asked for ratings on the level of aggressiveness for two children scuffling in the snow. When participants believed they had seen two boys, their ratings were significantly lower than for any of the other three combinations. The ratings for "boys" were lower because people expected rough play, and the scuffle met those expectations.

Seeing "girls" prompted expectations of less aggression; the scuffle contradicted that expectation, leading to a higher rating for aggression. These results demonstrated that the gender stereotypes associated with emotion tend to bias observers in their attributions of emotion, leading them to attribute to different emotions the same behaviors in boys and girls. With such expectations, raters cannot make judgments of emotional responses that would allow the unbiased evaluation of gender and emotion.

There is some evidence that women experience more intense emotions than men, but social expectations may be a factor in the difference. Women reported having a greater emotional intensity than men, resulting in women experiencing more negative but also more positive emotions (Fujita, Diener, & Sandvik, 1991). Overall, men and women reported equal happiness, suggesting that women's heightened experience of negative and positive emotion balances out for them.

Traditional gender roles may influence these stereotypical reactions. Women who endorsed stereotypical gender roles reported greater emotional intensity than men (Grossman & Wood, 1993). Manipulating the social expectation for a response eliminated gender differences in reports of emotion. This manipulation was accomplished by telling participants that previous research had shown either a positive or a negative relationship with certain emotions, and the gender-related differences in emotional reactions disappeared. Thus, women's greater emotional intensity may be attributed to expectation of such experiences.

Rather than detailing the gender differences and similarities in a list of emotions, this chapter concentrates on two types of emotional experience that have figured prominently in the stereotypes of emotion: the concepts of maternal instinct and aggression (the first a "feminine" and the second a "masculine" expression of emotion). In addition, the concept of instinct, connected with biological determinism, is often associated with both maternal behaviors in women and aggression in men. These two concepts provide a good contrast for considerations of gender and emotion. Psychologists have considered both as primary instincts basic to humans and animals (Hilgard, 1987). Those who consider these two instincts as primary believe that large gender differences exist, with nurturing and caregiving behaviors being the province of the female of many species, and anger and aggression being a male specialization.

The Myth of Maternal Instinct

The concept of maternal instinct holds that nurturing behaviors of mothers toward their children are determined by biological factors and are largely insensitive to environmental or experiential effects. The concept of maternal instinct has influenced the study of caregiving (Shields, 1984), Charles Darwin and the late 19th-century scientists who accepted the maternal instinct notion have shaped subsequent research on the topic. Notions of instinctive nurturing can be traced to assumptions belonging to the 19th century, which accepted both women's intellectual inferiority and their emotional reactions to the young. Scientific thought of that time held that women could not be as intellectually developed as men because their energies were required to go toward reproduction and caregiving. Nature had suited them to focus on immediate situations rather than abstract ones (hence their intellectual inferiority) and to be more perceptive and emotional (hence their attraction to small and helpless beings).

Instinct as an explanation of behavior fell into disfavor among psychologists with the rise of behaviorism and its emphasis on learning and certain environmental factors known to shape behavior. Furthermore, the notion of fixed behavior patterns seemed deterministic and therefore incompatible with the democratic ideal. Science takes place in a social context (Hilgard, 1987), and the United States was more receptive to the behavioral flexibility promoted by the behaviorists than the biological determinism promoted by instinct theory.

Despite the decline of instinct as a general explanation for behavior, the concept of maternal instinct did not fade from psychological explanations of behavior. Fields as different as primate biology and social policy have shown the influence of assuming that biology determines motherhood and fatherhood (Silverstein, 1993). Scientists and social policy makers have accepted the views of early primatologists, whose work emphasized a link between manhood and male aggression and sexuality, and feminine pursuits and female passivity and nurturance.

According to primatologist Sarah Blaffer Hrdy (1981), observations of a variety of primate species have changed the view of mothers as primary caregivers and fathers as only marginally involved with offspring. Observations of a variety of species showed that male primates' involvement with infants varies from being their primary caretaker to showing benign disinterest, with researchers observing only a little dangerous aggression from adult males. Individual differences appeared in the amount of male involvement with infants within their species; some males formed numerous relationships with infants and young primates, even those they had not fathered, whereas other males of the same species were less involved with the young (Silverstein, 1993). The evidence from studies of other primate species shows the behavioral flexibility of caregiving and does not support the concept of maternal instinct (and paternal disinterest). The behavior of primates offers no evidence for invariance in biological terms of nurturing among females and lack of nurturing among males.

Despite the growing unpopularity of the concept of instinct during the 1940s and 1950s, many (mostly male) scientists selected the evidence they considered appropriate, thus they continued to believe in the concept of maternal instinct. As Judith Lorber (1997, p. 13) quipped, "Believing is seeing." One of these scientists was psychologist Harry Harlow, whose research ironically provided evidence against the validity of the concept of maternal instinct.

Maternal Deprivation and Its Consequences for Nurturing

During the 1950s, Harry Harlow and his colleagues (including his wife, Margaret) conducted a series of experiments concerning affection and attachment. Harlow (1971) was concerned about the nature of attachment—of mothers for their babies, of babies for their mothers, of fathers for their babies, of children for each other, and so forth. One of Harlow's questions concerned the effects of maternal deprivation on children, but ethics prevented him from using them as human subjects. Therefore, he chose to experiment on monkeys.

Harlow's research on maternal deprivation originated from his desire to raise infant monkeys in a controlled environment. He noticed that the infant monkeys raised in isolation behaved abnormally. They stared into space for hours, circled their cages or rocked repetitively for long periods of time, and repeatedly injured themselves, especially when humans approached (Harlow & Harlow, 1962). Not only did these young monkeys behave oddly when alone, but they also exhibited abnormal behavior when placed in a social group of other monkeys. They failed to fit into the social group; they fought more and interacted less than monkeys raised normally. They were also sexually abnormal; they appeared interested in sex but unable to mate. Thus, Harlow noticed that the experience of being deprived of maternal nurturing seemed to have permanent effects on the social and sexual behavior of these monkeys.

Isolation also affected the monkeys' maternal behavior. When the isolated female monkeys became mothers themselves, they made spectacularly poor ones. These monkey mothers were negligent and abusive; refusing to allow their infants to nurse and sometimes beating them for trying to establish physical contact. Such negligent and abusive behavior did not support the concept of maternal instinct but rather suggested that the experience of isolation from their mothers affected their nurturing behavior. That is, this research suggests that caregiving is dependent on experience and not on any inherent biological factors.

Harlow (1959) initially believed that being mothered was the critical experience that would allow a monkey to become an adequate mother, but subsequently, a series of studies revealed that other social experiences could substitute for being mothered. Harlow and his associates discovered that physical contact was an important factor in learning "mothering." They constructed two types of surrogate mothers, one a wire "mother" and one a cloth-covered wire "mother." Neither type of surrogate was very much like a real monkey's mother; each did not move, hold the infants, or respond to them in any way. In some of Harlow's studies, both types of surrogates offered milk for nursing, whereas in some conditions, only the wire surrogate offered milk. Although the surrogate mothers were unresponsive, the infants were not. The infants strongly preferred the cloth-covered surrogates to the wire surrogates, even if the wire surrogate was the sole source of food. Infants nursed from the wire "mother" but clung to the cloth-covered surrogate for hours and ran to it when frightened. Harlow concluded that the cloth-covered surrogates provided some comfort that the wire surrogates could not, and he called this factor *contact comfort,* the security provided by physical contact with a soft, caring, or comforting object. However, even these monkeys did not become socially, sexually, or maternally normal, indicating that the cloth surrogate had failed to provide the experiences that are necessary for normal monkey development.

Additional research showed that the experiences that promote normal nurturing and caregiving in monkeys involve contact with other monkeys. Despite the logic of modeling and imitation, such contact does not have to include the experience of being mothered. That is, being a good mother does not require being adequately mothered. Harlow and Harlow (1962) reported on studies that indicated that same age mates can provide the social experiences necessary for normal development. The study involved separating infant monkeys from their mothers and raising them together as a group. Although these monkeys showed some abnormal behavior as infants—they clung together practically all the time they were together in their cage—these infants developed into normal adolescent monkeys. In addition, another study in which infants were raised with their mothers without peer contact showed that mothering alone would not be adequate for normal development; some contact with peers appeared to be essential.

Therefore, the studies by Harlow and his colleagues demonstrated (at least in monkeys) that maternal behavior is not instinctual. As Table 9.1 shows, nurturing and caregiving are not behaviors that appear in all females. Instead, Harlow's research showed that specific

TABLE 9.1 Types of Deprivation and Effects on Nurturing in Monkeys

Type of Deprivation	Adequacy of Nurturing
No deprivation—contact with mother and peers	Normal
Complete isolation	Inadequate and abusive
Wire or cloth "mother"	Inadequate
Contact with mother only	Inadequate
Contact with peers but not mother	Normal

social experiences are necessary for the development of adequate maternal (and other social) behavior. Without these experiences, adequate maternal behaviors fail to appear.

Attachment

Although research has demonstrated no innate, fixed pattern of caregiving, the contention that nurturing behavior has innate components has not disappeared from psychological theory. Instead, that notion has been transformed into the concept of attachment, or **bonding,** an emotional attachment that develops between infant and caregiver within a few days after birth (Shields, 1984). Bonding, however, is not restricted to mother–infant attachment but can also occur with fathers and infants, or with any others who happen to be present during the critical time period.

The concept of **critical periods** in development comes from ethnology, the study of animal behavior in natural settings, and the work of Konrad Lorenz, who discovered one type of attachment in geese (Eyer, 1992). Lorenz researched the factors that are important for baby geese as they developed an attachment to their mothers. He found a critical period in the lives of young geese, a time during which they learn to follow their mother. During this critical period, goslings learn to follow their mother after only one exposure to her walking past, showing that critical period learning is not like typical learning that requires repetition or practice.

In addition to the timing, the mother's behavior during the critical period is also important: She must walk past the goslings within two days after they hatch. If the timing and the mother's behavior coordinate, then the goslings *imprint* on their mother and follow her, which helps them to avoid danger and to learn things important to their survival. If the critical period passes without the mother walking past, then the goslings do not imprint on her, leaving them without making an attachment to a caretaker and increasing their risk for the many dangers that may befall small fowl. Although the mother's behavior is important, the attachment may occur to animals other than geese, as Lorenz himself demonstrated. By timing his behavior to the critical period, groups of goslings were imprinted to follow Lorenz as though he were their mother.

The concept of imprinting may apply to the attachment that forms between babies and their caregivers, but it does not explain how the attachment between mothers and their infants applies. That is, Lorenz's work should not resurrect the concept of maternal instinct. His work demonstrated the existence of critical periods in development, but those critical periods relate to *infant* attachment to a caregiver and not to maternal (or paternal) behavior toward a child. Of course, geese and humans are very different, and one should be hesitant about applying Lorenz's findings to humans.

The popular concept of bonding is very similar to imprinting, but bonding is a reciprocal process that applies to mother–infant as well as infant–mother attachments. This concept is a variation on maternal instinct because bonding also depends on innate components that are known to occur in the early interaction of infant and caregiver. However, bonding is not restricted to mothers, so it definitely varies on the mother's part from maternal instinct.

The concept of bonding was popularized with published research (Klaus & Kennell, 1976) contending that in the first few hours after a child's birth, their attachment to mothers is critically important. Not only do infants form a bond with their mothers, but mothers bond with their babies, forming attachments that are important for the duration of the relationship. Studies showed that mothers who were allowed to cuddle their babies felt a stronger attachment to the infants and showed more interaction with them during the children's infancy than mothers who were not allowed this physical contact. However, other researchers have failed to confirm these results and have criticized the concept of bonding (Chess & Thomas, 1982; Eyer, 1992). As a result, the concept of bonding remains more favored by the popular press than by developmental researchers. Indeed, the popularity of the concept may be connected with the desire to explain caregiving in biological terms—as another version of maternal instinct (Eyer, 1992).

Gender and Caring for Children

Although research has failed to find a biological basis that explains women's nurturing, women remain the primary caregivers for children in the great majority of cultures. The circumstances of childbearing and nursing place many women in continued contact with children. This association with caregiving is the basis for the classification of women as more nurturant than men. Two possible explanations for gender-related differences in nurturing behavior exist: responsiveness to children and pleasure in taking care of children (Shields, 1984). That is, perhaps girls and women respond more quickly and strongly to children or derive greater satisfaction from caring for children than men do, or both.

Although gender differences in responsiveness to babies increase throughout childhood, these differences may not reflect levels of nurturance (Melson & Fogel, 1988a, b). One study found that preschoolers' interest in babies is similar before age 4, but among older girls, their involvement with an infant in a play situation increased, and among older boys, their involvement decreased (Melson & Fogel, 1988a). The tendency for girls and boys to behave differently toward infants was also found in a study in which preschool children posed for photos with either a baby or a peer (Reid, Tate, & Berman, 1989). The girls stood closer to the baby than the boys, and when asked to play "mommy" or "daddy," girls stood closer than boys. Even at this age, children can exhibit gender-typical behaviors toward infants.

Boys tended to care for and nurture pets as they became less interested in babies (Melson & Fogel, 1988b). This behavior may reflect the tendency for boys to become aware of the gender role they should follow. This awareness would prompt a decrease in their responsiveness to babies, but boys would still have the capacity to be nurturant caregivers, as expressed by their feelings for and behavior toward pets. Boys may be as nurturant as girls, although this nurturance may be expressed in different ways.

GENDERED VOICES
If Men Mothered

"I think that men could do as good as women at taking care of children," two college students told me. Both the young man and the young woman said that they believed that women have no instinctive advantage in nurturing children. Both of them said that the differences were due to experience rather than inherent biological factors. Indeed, both said that they believed there were few differences in ability to care for children.

"Well, men can't breast-feed," the young man said, "but I think that is about the only advantage women have except for experience. They have a lot more experience in caring for children. Girls babysit, and boys don't." He knew how difficult it was for men to get experience caring for young children because he had attempted to get such experience. He had volunteered to care for the young children in his church while their parents attended the service and had answered advertisements for babysitters. Neither of these efforts had met with enthusiasm from others; he had gotten the impression that wanting to care for children was considered odd for a man. He considered the possibility that people might think he was a pedophile, when all he really wanted was to learn to be more nurturant.

"I think if men were responsible for caring for children, there would be more changes in men than in children. If men had to learn to care for children, then they would. It wouldn't be automatic, because they don't have the experience, but they could learn. I don't believe in maternal instinct—that women have some innate advantage over men in caring. But women do have more experience, and men would have to learn the skills they lack.

"Men would learn to care for children if they had to, and they would become more nurturant in other aspects of their lives, maybe even in their careers. They might not care so much about competition and high-status careers."

The young woman had a slightly different view: "I think that the children would be different. This opinion is based on my own family and the differences between my mother and my father. My father was more willing to let us be on our own, but my mother was more involved. My mother took care of us, but my father let us make our own decisions. Maybe that wouldn't be good for young children, but I think I would have learned to be more self-reliant with my father's style of caretaking. Maybe if he had been the one who had to look out for us, he would have been as protective as my mother was."

A review (Berman, 1980) of studies that had investigated gender differences in responsiveness to infants showed that researchers have used many different representations of infants, such as real babies, photographs of infants, and the young of nonhuman animals, to investigate responsiveness to infants. In addition, the measurements of responsiveness have included self-reports, such as ratings of liking; behavioral measures, such as speed of response to crying; and physiological measures, such as changes in heart rate or respiratory rate. These different measures have revealed different results.

According to this review, the strongest gender differences have come from studies using self-report measures of responsiveness to children. Girls and women are more likely than boys and men to report that they find infants more appealing and attractive and to respond more positively to pictures of infants. As many of these studies have not used real babies, the self-reports of liking or attraction could be responses to the situation rather than to infants. That is, the girls and women who participated in such studies may have responded to the situation of being asked about their feelings about babies, and in these cases, they may have been more willing to say that they would find babies appealing. Girls and women may have been more willing to express (or believe that they should express) positive feelings about babies than boys and men. Such behavior would conform to the stereotype of what these female participants believed they should say. Girls and women are supposed to like babies, and boys and men are supposed to be more restrained in their enthusiasm for infants. Therefore, the significant gender differences found in girls' and women's self-reports of responsiveness to infants may reflect their conformity to social roles.

In examining the studies that have used physiological measurements of responsiveness, the review found little evidence for gender differences. The studies that have used behavioral measurements of responsiveness have revealed complex findings; many show no simple gender-related differences but rather interactions between gender and situational factors. For example, the gender of the experimenter and the gender of the participant might interact, producing different behaviors in male experimenter–male participant interactions than in male experimenter–female participant interactions or some other combination of testing situations. The lack of clear gender-related differences in behavioral and physiological measures of responsiveness confirms the view that social roles may be the most important factor in the gender-related differences in responsiveness to infants.

The differences in patterns of child care—namely, that women perform the vast majority of child care—complicate comparisons of the pleasure that women and men derive from these activities. Although some fathers are involved in all aspects of child care, the accepted role for fathers is helper, and the role for mothers is primary caregiver. "Mothers provide the 'continuous coverage' that babies require" and "fathers are novel, unpredictable, physical, exciting, engaging, and preferred playmates for young children," according to one study (Thompson & Walker, 1989, p. 861). Therefore, any comparison of the pleasure of nurturing is not based on a direct comparison of the satisfaction each derives from specific caregiving activities but rather on a comparison of their roles as mothers or fathers and the types of caregiving each provides.

The time and effort mothers spend in child care lead to feelings of both satisfaction and dissatisfaction (Thompson & Walker, 1989). The experience of involvement in parenting, coupled with their feelings of the social value of nurturing children produce satisfaction, but the loss of freedom and the irritation of attending to the demands of small children lead mothers to feel dissatisfaction. Indeed, many mothers feel disappointment over mothering because they had expected the experience to be both easier and more fulfilling.

Mothers tend to find more pleasure in taking care of their children than do fathers, unless the fathers are as involved with child care as are mothers. Fewer fathers have become the primary caregivers of young children, although several researchers have managed to investigate situations in which men are equally as involved as women in child care.

One such situation occurs in families in which the fathers are gay. The majority of gay fathers are men who have fathered children in heterosexual relationships. These men do not often get custody of their children, but an increasing number of gay couples are adopting or choosing surrogacy in order to become fathers (Patterson & Chan, 1997). These men are highly motivated to become fathers, and they place a high value on relationships with their children. Without gender roles to attach to themselves, gay fathers tend to divide child care more evenly than heterosexual couples and to be more satisfied with this division of labor.

Heterosexual fathers who participated in the care of their children experienced feelings and behavior toward their young children similar to those of women who provided similar levels of care (Risman, 1989). Therefore, the greater pleasure that women derive from caring for children seems to be a function of their greater involvement with their children, and men who have similar levels of involvement experience similar feelings.

If no instinctive force compels women toward and men away from nurturing, why, then, have men been involved so little in caring for children? Powerful forces operate to prevent fathers from becoming more intimately involved with their children, but those forces are social and not biological. In industrialized societies, fathers hold the role of breadwinner, which usually takes them outside the home and away from their children's lives. Social pressures toward achievement and monetary success have convinced men that they can best contribute to their families by devoting themselves to their jobs, and this devotion results in many hours at work.

The traditional pattern of the male breadwinner who is a distant, uninvolved father has undergone changes over the past 40 years (Pleck & Pleck, 1997), but the well-publicized image of the "new" father who is involved with children's upbringing may be an overstatement (Silverstein, 1996). Nevertheless, fathers are more involved with their children than in past decades, and an increasing number of fathers feel motivated to be more intimately involved in their children's lives (Pleck, 1997). Few institutional supports exist for increased paternal nurturance (Silverstein, 1996), and the fathers who have created such relationships have deviated from traditional expectations. The limited research on these fathers indicates that the children, mothers, and fathers all can benefit from positive involvement by fathers in their children's lives (Pleck, 1997).

Prominence of Male Aggression

Aggression has also been the primary focus of gender role studies of instinct, again with explanations of men's evolutionary advantage (Cairns, 1986). The standard version says that during human prehistory, while the women were at home caring for the children, the men were out hunting and defending the group against various threats. In both the hunting and the defending, aggressive actions could be adaptive and even essential. Thus, women became passive homebodies and men became aggressive conquerors.

This view of human prehistory may be fictionalized and based more on the theorists' personal views than on prehistoric human behavior. There have been questions about both the idea of female passivity and whether men had an adaptive advantage from aggression (Benderly, 1987; Hrdy, 1981; Weisstein, 1982). Women in the hunter-gatherer societies of prehistory probably not only gathered plants for food but participated in small game hunting, thus making them essential contributors to their groups' food supply and far from passive. As for aggression, it can offer advantages if directed at the proper targets outside the group, but it can also be disruptive and dangerous within a group. The men in these societies must have needed to become selectively rather than pervasively aggressive; therefore, natural selection would not favor those who were aggressive in all situations.

Despite the widespread acceptance of an instinct for aggression, a definition has been difficult to formulate. Although most people would agree that aggression is active and behavioral and that the result (or at least the intent) is harm to another, not all people would easily agree on which behaviors should be included and what consequences of these behaviors constitute harm. Actions like hitting, kicking, biting, and even yelling seem obviously aggressive, but sulking might also be considered aggressive by some (Tavris, 1982). Aggression can cause not only physical but also psychological harm. An additional problem in defining aggression arises when determining what counts as aggression; intent as well as action both are important considerations. For instance, would doing harm to someone accidentally count as aggression?

Psychologist Leonard Eron (1987) discussed how he had solved the dilemma of defining aggression after 30 years of aggression research. He decided on a behavioral, objective definition of aggression, which he defined as "an act that injures or irritates another person" (p. 435). Eron contended that intentionality is very difficult to measure, especially in children; his definition avoided this problem by ignoring aggressive intent and sticking to harm or irritation as the outcome. He acknowledged that some accidents would be included in his definition, but he argued that assertive acts would largely—and in his opinion correctly—be excluded. His approach avoided not only the issue of intent but also the complex relationship between anger and aggression.

Anger and Aggression

Anger and aggression seem intimately related—anger is the internal emotion and aggression is its behavioral reaction (Plutchik, 1984). However, the two are not inevitably connected: A person can experience anger and take no action, aggressive or otherwise, but a person can also act aggressively without feeling anger, such as the violence shown by a hired killer.

Psychological and popular explanations of aggression have accepted that aggression is the outcome of some prior circumstance, either in the emotions or in the environment. Psychologist William McDougall and psychoanalyst Sigmund Freud believed that aggression was the result of instinctive expressions of frustrated wishes. This contention gave rise to the frustration–aggression hypothesis (Dollard, Doob, Miller, Mowrer, & Sears, 1939), which holds that aggression is the inevitable result of frustration and frustration is the inevitable consequence of aggression. In this formulation, anger is not an important concept (Averill, 1982). The volume of research testing the frustration–aggression hypothesis has been conducted primarily in laboratory settings with a limited set of frustrating stimuli and measures of aggression. These experiments have yielded information about one facet of aggression but have failed to explore aggression prompted by everyday events in more natural settings.

Several investigations have surveyed people about their experiences of anger and subsequent aggression. Although these surveys rely on self-reports and do not directly measure either anger or aggression, the survey method provides a way to investigate a wider range of topics than is possible through laboratory experiments. In a survey of university students in eight European countries, Klaus Scherer and his associates (Scherer, Wallbott, & Summerfield, 1986) found that anger occurred more often than other emotions, with about 75% of participants reporting anger within the four weeks prior to the survey.

What is the relationship among the three factors involved: the angry person's experience of emotion, the consequences of anger, and gender? By surveying community residents and college students in the United States about their experiences of anger and subsequent aggression, James Averill (1982) sought to answer these questions. He found that anger was very common—85% of those surveyed reported at least one experience of anger within the week. However, Averill also found that physical aggression was rare during anger and that even the impulse to use physical aggression is not all that common. Although aggression may be a visible manifestation of anger, Averill concluded that anger could be expressed in a great variety of ways.

This survey yielded surprisingly few gender differences in the experience of anger, but gender differences appeared in the targets of anger, with men being somewhat more frequent targets of anger than women. However, the relationship between the two people was also an important factor. Among people who were not well-known to each other, men were more likely than women to be the targets of anger. Among loved ones, men and women were equal targets. Among friends, anger toward same-gender friends was the most common pattern. Averill also found that women reported more intense experiences of anger than did men, and women's responses were more varied, especially in their tendency to cry when they were angry.

The tendency for women to cry when they feel angry was a circumstance that June Crawford and her colleagues (Crawford, Kippax, Onxy, Gault, & Benton, 1992) discovered. Crawford and her group conducted their study by exploring their own memories of emotional experiences, including those involving anger. They found a common experience of crying in response to anger. They explained this experience as an acceptable means for girls and women to express anger, whereas physical aggression is less acceptable. However, crying is often misinterpreted as sadness or grief, especially by men. If the situation is one in which anger is appropriate, then women would appear to behave differently from men by exhibiting an inappropriate response of sadness.

Few gender differences appear in the experience of anger: Both men and women feel angry in response to the same types of provocations. These include actions that lead to violations of their plans or expectations, personal insults, and persons breaking social rules (Tavris, 1982). However, what counts as a personal insult may differ for women and men, which produces some apparent differences in the circumstances that prompt anger. In addition, the expression of anger has many negative social consequences and limited effectiveness in bringing about change. Therefore, expressions of anger tend be construed as more destructive than constructive.

Gender role—not gender—may have a consistent relationship to anger and the expression of anger (Kopper & Epperson, 1991, 1996). In one study (Kopper & Epperson, 1996), masculinity (rather than being male) was related to the expression of anger and aggression, and femininity (rather than being female) was related to the suppression of anger. These studies show that the stereotypical association of men and anger is incorrect, although men are more likely than women to respond to anger with physical aggression.

In summary, the relationship between anger and aggression is far from automatic, with feelings of anger occurring far more often than acts of aggression. Of the studies that have explored gender differences in the experience of anger, few have found differences between men and women. Instead, these studies have shown that men and women both experience anger from being similarly provoked. Other studies have indicated that gender role—not gender—shows a relationship between the expression of anger as physical aggression.

Developmental Gender Differences in Aggression

Observing gender differences in aggression during the early months and even early years of life is very difficult, because what counts as aggression in an infant is virtually impossible to define. Rather than attempting to assess aggression in young children, researchers have used other behaviors, beginning with children's activity level during infancy. Some studies have failed to find a gender difference in activity level, but Maccoby and Jacklin's (1974) review concluded that boys showed higher activity levels than girls.

The existence of gender differences in aggression among preschool children is controversial, but for elementary school children, differences are clear: Boys are more aggressive than girls. One meta-analysis (Hyde, 1984) evaluated the developmental nature of these differences and their magnitude. This analysis indicated that gender differences decrease with age; that is, boys and girls show greater differences in aggression during elementary school than during college. In addition, a decrease in the magnitude of aggression occurs over the course of development, with both boys and girls becoming less aggressive as they develop into adults.

Another way to approach the question of the stability of aggression over the course of development is through longitudinal research—in studies that test the same group of people over many years. Eron and his colleagues (Eron, 1987; Huesmann, Eron, Lefkowitz, & Walder, 1984; Lefkowitz, Eron, Walder, & Huesmann, 1977) conducted one such longitudinal study of aggression that tested 600 children, beginning when the children were in the third grade (approximately 8 years old) and continuing for 22 years. By using this longitudinal approach, the researchers hoped to determine the stability of aggressive behavior from middle childhood into adolescence and adulthood.

When the children were in third grade, they were asked questions about who acts aggressively. One such question was "Who in the class pushes other children?" The children could name as many of their peers as they wanted, providing a score representing peer-defined aggression for each child. As the initial phase of their study, the researchers compared this aggression score to parenting styles and found that parents who were less nurturant and acceptant at home tended to have children who behaved more aggressively at school than the children brought up by more nurturant and acceptant parents.

In the second phase of the study, the children were located 10 years later to determine if their aggression had changed: It had not. Both the girls and boys rated as aggressive at age 8 received similar ratings from their peers 10 years later. In addition, those who received ratings as aggressive tended to see themselves as aggressive, rate others as such, and see the world as an aggressive place. These results show the persistence of aggression as a way of relating to people and viewing the world.

This longitudinal study also investigated the influence of watching violent television programs. It found that the violence on television acted as an effective model for aggressive children. Indeed, the preference for violent television programs at age 8 was a good predictor of how aggressive the male adolescents would be at age 19. However, this study failed to find a similar relationship between viewing habits and aggression in girls. Another longitudinal study (Eron, Huesmann, Brice, Fischer, & Mermelstein, 1983) found that violent television viewing was significantly related to aggression in both boys and girls. In addition, the relationship between viewing violence on television and aggression increased until children were 10 to 11 years of age. These findings indicate a cumulative effect of observing violence on television, and showed a developmental period during which children are especially sensitive to the effects of televised violence. Although the girls were not as aggressive as the boys at any grade level, the patterns were similar, showing an increase in aggression through the fifth grade.

TABLE 9.2 Aggression over the Life Span

Children identified at 8 years of age by their peers as aggressive toward other children.

At Age 8	At Age 18	At Age 30
Had less nurturant and acceptant parents	Were still rated by peers as aggressive	Were more likely to have a criminal record
also	*also*	*also*
Preferred violent TV programs	Rated themselves as aggressive	Were more likely to abuse spouse
	also	*also*
	Rated others as aggressive	Were more likely to have DWI (DUI) conviction
	also	*also*
	Saw the world as a dangerous place	Were more likely to have traffic violations
		also
		Were more likely to use severe punishment with children

In the third phase of this 22-year longitudinal study (Eron, 1987; Huesmann et al., 1984), researchers again contacted these participants, who were by then around 30 years old. Table 9.2 shows the stability of aggression among the participants in these studies. Aggression during elementary school predicted a number of aggressive behaviors during adulthood, including criminal behavior, traffic violations, convictions for driving while intoxicated, aggressiveness toward spouses, and severity of punishment of children. The stability of aggression over this 22-year time span was higher for the men than for the women and, as had been the case when they were boys, the men showed more aggressive behavior than the women.

The results of this longitudinal study demonstrated that adult aggression can be predicted to some degree from childhood aggression, indicating that the two are related on a conceptual level. However, the specific behaviors that constitute adolescent and adult aggression will differ substantially from the behaviors measured in studies of children. Although children may fight and provoke trouble at home and at school, physical maturity and access to weapons makes adolescents and adults much more capable of doing serious harm.

Another longitudinal study (Cairns, Cairns, Neckerman, Ferguson, & Gariépy, 1989) explored the development of aggression by concentrating on the developmental differences in aggression between boys and girls. In this study, a group of children was tested annually, beginning from middle childhood when they were in the fourth grade and continuing for the next six years to early adolescence.

The researchers found that the fourth grade boys were much more likely to have confrontations that involved physical aggression with other boys than with other girls, and this pattern became stronger over the 6-year time span. As adolescents, boys were much more likely to engage in physical confrontation than were girls, and the chance of physical confrontations between boys and girls was unlikely. Indeed, these researchers found an age-related trend in which boys and girls did not like cross-sex aggression. Expressions of aggression among girls in this age group tended to be social, involving attempts to alienate or ostracize another girl from the social group or to defame her character. This type of social aggression increased from fourth grade, when about 10% of the girls reported it, to over 33% by seventh grade. Boys very rarely reported this type of conflict.

Social standards for the expression of anger in the form of physical aggression may differ for men and women, but both boys and girls are discouraged from being physically aggressive by their parents and teachers. However, by middle childhood both boys and girls have developed different expectations about expressing aggression. Boys expected less parental disapproval for their aggression, and both expected less parental disapproval for aggression against a boy than against a girl (Perry, Perry, & Weiss, 1989). Even with general parental disapproval for aggression, children learn about circumstances under which their aggression is at least somewhat acceptable, and boys learn different rules for displaying aggression than girls.

In this study (Cairns et al., 1986), teacher and counselor ratings of aggression showed a gender difference: Boys were rated in the most serious categories of aggression far more often than girls. Despite the mean difference in aggression between boys and girls, teachers and counselors rated some girls and boys at the high extreme in their ratings of aggression. When considering these most aggressive participants, no gender differences appeared. This finding suggests that on the average, girls may exhibit less aggressive behavior than boys but that very aggressive children are similar to each other, regardless of gender.

Some gender differences exist among the most violent of adolescents, according to a study of girls and boys in gangs (Campbell, 1993). Male and female violence has been shown to serve different purposes, not only in gangs but in other contexts as well. Men use aggression to exert control over others, whereas women's aggression usually represents a loss of emotional self-control. The violence in male gangs is consistent with this interpretation: Boys in gangs use aggression and violence to gain social recognition and to get money. Girls in gangs also use violence to create recognition, but unlike boys, they do not seek money as much as they seek to avoid becoming victims by creating a reputation for being tough. These gang girls represent an extreme, but their use of violence to achieve their goals is similar to their male counterparts, even though their goals differ.

Therefore, two longitudinal studies and a meta-analysis of aggression have confirmed the prevalence of a developmental trend toward a decrease in aggression from middle childhood to young adulthood. These studies also confirm a gender-related difference in aggression. Although the difference is not large, it exists, with boys and girls using different strategies and behaviors in their displays of aggression. Adolescent aggression, however, is much more dangerous than childhood aggression, especially from the physical confrontations that are more typical of adolescent boys. With their size, strength, and greater likelihood of owning a weapon, adolescent boys become more likely to use aggression that causes serious damage and violates the law than are adolescent girls.

Gender Differences in Aggression during Adulthood

If gender-related differences in aggression decrease during development as children age, then few differences should exist between adult men and women, although differences

TABLE 9.3 Situations that Provoke Aggression in Women and Men

Type of Provocation	Tendency toward Aggression
No provocation	Men respond with much more aggression in everyday contacts
Physical attack	Men respond with slightly more aggression Men consider attacks more serious
Insults— Insensitive behavior Condescending behavior Impolite treatment Rude comments	Women respond with more aggression Women consider insults more serious
Frustrations— Not able to succeed Not able to finish task Recognize own inability Traffic congestion	Men respond with more aggression
Negative feedback concerning intelligence	Men respond with much more aggression Women are not angered by this type of provocation

SOURCE: B. Ann Bettencourt & Norman Miller. (1996). "Gender differences in aggression as a function of provo cation: A meta-analysis," *Psychological Bulletin, 119,* 422–447.

might exist in the styles of expression. Reviews of the experimental research on aggression have confirmed these predictions, finding that the differences between levels of aggression in men and women are not large but that significant differences in circumstances and styles do exist.

Both literature reviews and meta-analyses have been used to explore gender differences in aggression. One such review (Frodi, Macaulay, & Thome, 1977) evaluated experimental studies in psychology but omitted surveys and crime statistics and concentrated on laboratory studies. These situations are artificial but controlled. Several meta-analyses have since evaluated research on gender differences in aggression (Bettencourt & Miller, 1996; Eagly & Steffen, 1986).

The earlier analyses (Eagly & Steffen, 1986; Frodi et al., 1977) found that men were more aggressive than women under neutral and unprovoked situations. When women were provoked or felt justified, however, they became as aggressive as men. The later meta-analysis (Bettencourt & Miller, 1996) was directed toward understanding the factor of provocation, and this analysis showed that gender differences decreased or disappeared with some types of provocation. Not all provocations affected women and men similarly. Some of the gender differences found in experimental research are due to the various provocations researchers have used. For example, women do not as readily respond aggressively to insults to their intelligence as men do, but both respond similarly to the frustration of someone blocking their path through an intersection. Table 9.3 summarizes some of these gender-related differences in tendencies to respond with aggression.

Aggression can be a very effective way of exerting power and forcing others to behave according to one's wishes (Cairns, 1986; Campbell, 1993). When considering aggression as a method of exerting power, women may be reasonably concerned about the potential for reprisal; the size and strength differential between men and women makes women more vulnerable to the effects of aggression. Women's reluctance to use aggression is related to their fear of retaliation. Even when women and men hear the same description of a situation, women's fear of retaliation is greater than men's, and this factor decreases their likelihood of responding with physical aggression (Bettencourt & Miller, 1996).

When the action inflicts psychological or social harm, however, women are likely to become as aggressive as men. These situations are more common among adults than other situations involving physical aggression (Bjorkqvist, 1994). Adults engage in a variety of aggression strategies that include not only verbal statements but also *indirect aggression,* which causes harm through indirect means, such as arranging for someone to be blamed for a serious mistake at work or mocking someone's actions. Although not without the danger of retaliation, verbal and indirect aggression are less risky than physical confrontation, and women in several cultures are more likely to use this strategy than men.

One of the limitations of laboratory research is that it is unable to provide a context to determine when people choose aggression and how. Lab studies typically offer a limited range of choices in carefully controlled (and contrived) situations. Such situations are unlikely to reveal female aggression because women are generally not aggressive in public, though they may be in private (Ben-David, 1993). Women have been shown to be as likely as men to initiate domestic partner violence and more likely to hit and mistreat children (U.S. Department of Health and Human Services, 1997). Domestic violence is less likely than public violence to result in arrest, so women and men do not have similar levels of involvement with the criminal justice system. These statistics apply to North America and Europe, but not necessarily to all societies, as discussed in the Diversity Highlight: "Aggression in an Egalitarian Society."

Gender and Crime. Given the relatively small gender difference in aggression found in laboratory studies, the statistics on societal aggression reveal large gender differences. Men commit many more criminal acts than do women, and their arrest and incarceration rates are much higher. According to the U.S. Department of Justice (1996b), men are about four times more likely than women to be arrested for various types of offenses, such as murder, robbery, vandalism, fraud, drunkenness, and so forth. Although not all of these violations involve violence, many do; as Table 9.4 shows, such offenses are more likely to be committed by men than women.

Not all crimes result in arrest, and the possibility exists that the ratio of crimes committed by men and women is more equal than the arrest rates suggest. Surveys have indicated that although the reported rates of crime exceed the arrest rates, men still outnumber women in committing crimes (Feyerherm, 1981; Osgood, O'Malley, Bachman, & Johnston, 1989).

Crime was so strongly associated with men before the 1970s that most criminologists and officials in the criminal justice system assumed that crime was an almost exclusively male problem (Warren, 1981). During the 1970s, research interests turned to female offenders, prompted by the increase of criminal activity among women. Although one hypothesis about this increase is that it resulted from the women's movement—equal opportunity

DIVERSITY HIGHLIGHT

Aggression in an Egalitarian Society

If the social roles that women and men occupy were equal, would men still be more aggressive? Finding such a society is not easy, but the Vanatinai people of a small island society in the south Pacific near New Guinea, are an example of an egalitarian society (Lepowsky, 1994). This society values assertiveness and independence for both women and men. No adult has the right to tell another what to do, and no system exists that allows one adult greater authority than another.

Like any group, these people experience conflicts, but they rarely exhibit physical aggression. Indeed, cases of physical aggression are considered shameful, and adults who commit such acts are thought to be out of control and embarrassing to their family members. Fighting is even rare among children. In the 10 years of the study, only five cases of physical aggression occurred between adults. In four of the five, women were the aggressors.

Although the Vanatinai do not believe in resolving conflict through physical violence, they do believe in witchcraft and sorcery. Instead of physical confrontation, they believe that someone who is wronged will cast a spell to do another person harm. Most illness and injury is attributed to the power of magic, so the Vanatinai fear magical power. They cast spells to do harm, a practice which matches researchers' description of indirect aggression (Bjorkqvist, 1994).

What occurs in this remote island community is not a simple reversal of gender roles from those seen in North America or Europe. The men of Vanatinai are neither passive nor peaceful; they are fierce warriors. Nor are the women aggressive; they do not participate in warfare and are even forbidden to hunt with spears. Vanatinai society includes gendered behaviors, but some of the behaviors that our societies consider gender-related, such as physical aggression within the family and social group, are not gendered in Vanatinai culture.

applied to crime—research has indicated that female offenders tended to be traditional rather than feminist in their beliefs. Even considering the increase in crime rates among female offenders, the rate of offenses remained lower and the offenses were less serious for women than for men (Tjaden & Tjaden, 1981). That is, the increase in crimes committed by women was due more to nonviolent rather than violent crimes. Therefore, the gender difference in violent crime persists, with men being several times more likely than women to commit and be arrested for such crimes.

Men are not only more likely to commit acts of violence, they are also more likely to be the victims of crime than are women (U.S. Department of Justice, 1996a). This pattern of male–male violence substantiates research on aggression during childhood and adolescence (Cairns et al., 1989), which has indicated that boys were much more likely than girls to use confrontation and aggression as a strategy for managing conflict and that physical aggression between boys and girls decreased during adolescence. Despite decreases in physical violence among male adolescents, their size, strength, and likelihood of owning weapons made young men more likely to become both perpetrators and victims of physical aggression.

Despite their lower rate of victimization, women are more likely than men to fear being the victims of crime. Women's perceived risk of crime victimization follows two principles: perceived severity of the crime and feelings of personal vulnerability (Warr, 1985). In general,

TABLE 9.4 Percent of Male and Female Offenders Arrested for Various Offenses

Offense	Men	Women
All violent crimes	85.1%	14.9%
All property crimes	72.7	27.3
Murder	90.5	9.5
Rape	98.8	1.2
Robbery	90.7	9.3
Aggravated Assault	82.3	17.7
Burglary	88.9	11.1
Larceny/theft	66.7	33.3
Arson	84.3	15.7
Forgery	64.1	35.9
Fraud	59.0	41.0
Embezzlement	56.4	43.6
Vandalism	86.4	13.6
Prostitution	38.9	61.1
Domestic violence	79.8	20.2
Drunkenness	88.2	11.8
Disorderly conduct	78.3	21.7
Curfew violation/loitering	70.4	29.6
Runaway	42.6	57.4

Source: Based on information from "Uniform Crime Report for the United States, 1995," 1996, U.S. Department of Justice, Washington, DC: U.S. Government Printing Office.

the more severe the crime, the less at risk women feel, with one exception—rape. Women of all ages reported a fear of rape, and among women aged 35 and younger, it was the most feared crime—more than assault, robbery, or murder.

Sexual Violence. Women's fears of sexual violence are not misplaced—rape is a common crime. In addition, rape often goes unreported, making the official estimates lower than actual occurrences (Koss, 1992). The U.S. Department of Justice (1996b) reported that rape—defined as some form of forced sexual intercourse (vaginal, oral, or anal) by the use of force or threats of force—occurs at a rate of 3.7 per 1,000 people. This estimate is restricted to women as the only victims and is based on the number of rape reports. Men's exclusion and women's reluctance to report rape has led to the belief that the actual rate may be several times larger.

A study (Koss, Gidycz, & Wisniewski, 1987) of U.S. college students clarified the rate of sexual violence. Asking both men and women about their sexual behaviors revealed that

15.4% of the women reported being raped since the age of 14 years, and another 12.1% reported experiences that met the legal criteria for attempted rape. Yet only 7.7% of the men reported behaviors that met the legal definition of committing rape, including attempted rape. These rates yielded estimates for rape that were 10 to 15 times greater than the arrest rates for this crime as well as perpetration rates that were 2 to 3 times higher than official estimates for the risk of rape. These results suggest that many rapes go unreported.

Not only does rape go unreported to legal authorities, many women are reluctant to tell anyone about being raped. Although this reluctance is common, African American women are significantly less likely to tell anyone about being raped than European American women (Wyatt, 1992). However, no significant differences exist in the numbers of attempted or completed rapes for the women in the two ethnic groups, and women from both ethnic groups had equal difficulty in identifying attacks by their acquaintances as "real" rape. Rape is similar for all women, yet African American women have a unique history of rape, and that history has had an impact on attitudes toward rape among women of this ethnic group.

Asian Americans hold more negative attitudes toward women as rape victims than European Americans (Mori, Selle, Zarate, & Bernat, 1994). Both Asian American men and women were more likely than European Americans to endorse rape myths, such as the myth that rape is the woman's fault or that women secretly enjoy rape. Asian American men had more negative attitudes about women than any other group, so Asian American women's acceptance of blame for rape may make them particularly unlikely to report this crime.

The stigma of rape involves the sexual nature of the crime and the tendency to blame the victim. Blaming and stigmatization are particularly common in rape cases, but the stigma is even more severe when men are the victims (Dreyfus, 1994). Men as the victims of rape or other types of sexual coercion have been accorded much less attention than female victims, partly because they are not as often victimized and partly because of the difficulty of accepting that men can be raped (Struckman-Johnson, 1988).

Despite these obstacles, a growing body of research indicates that men are sexually coerced and victimized by women as well as by men in ways similar to women's experience of coercion: through bribery, threats of withdrawal of affection, intoxication, physical intimidation, physical restraint, and physical harm (Struckman-Johnson & Struckman-Johnson, 1994). Both men and women are victims of sexual coercion, and both are censured for being victimized. The problem of female victimization is much more urgent because of its frequency and because women are more traumatized by coercive sexual experiences than are men (Struckman-Johnson & Struckman-Johnson, 1993). Therefore, a great deal of research has concentrated on understanding the characteristics of men who rape and coerce women into sex.

Rape was once considered a rare form of deviation, but research has shown that rapists do not differ from many other men in terms of their attitudes. Diana Scully (1990) studied convicted rapists by conducting extensive interviews. Her results revealed that in many ways the rapists were ordinary. They had not experienced an unusually high level of treatment for psychopathology or an unusually high rate of childhood physical or sexual abuse. Their family histories were filled with instability and violence, but so were the backgrounds of other felons in Scully's study. The rapists were able to form relationships with women, and most had wives or girlfriends at the time they committed rape. Their attitudes toward women showed a rare combination of beliefs: that women belong "on a pedestal" and that men have the right to treat women with violence.

Some of the rapists in Scully's study conformed to the classic pattern of attacking a stranger and using force or weapons to accomplish the rape. Many of these rapists told Scully that they planned their actions because they were angry with their wives or girlfriends and wanted to do violence to some woman. These men reported that the common characteristic of these women was their vulnerability: They were in the right place at the wrong time—usually alone somewhere at night. Their physical appearance made no difference—many of the rapists had trouble describing their victims. This disregard for appearance highlights the violence of the act and argues against having a sexual motive for rape.

Scully's sample was skewed because the proportion of rapists who were acquainted with their victims was underrepresented; acquaintance rape is less likely to result in complaint, prosecution, or conviction than stranger rapes. Yet the violent attack by a stranger is the vision of rape that women fear, even though the most common experience of rape is an attack by an acquaintance, now termed *date rape* or *acquaintance rape.* One survey (Koss et al., 1987) of rape and attempted rape included questions that allowed participants to estimate their involvement in various types of sexual coercion. A total of 54% of the women in the survey reported that they had been sexually victimized in some way, but only 25% of the men in the survey admitted to some level of sexual aggression. The discrepancy in the rates for men and women is not due to a few sexually predatory men but rather to some degree of denial or failure by many men to recognize their own sexual aggression. This failure to recognize sexual aggression also occurred among the convicted rapists in Scully's study and in a study with a representative sample of U.S. residents (Laumann, Gagnon, Michael, & Michaels, 1994). All of these researchers have found that men may have trouble recognizing their own behavior as sexually coercive.

Rather than conceptualizing rape as the action of pathological men, recent views of sexual violence have shifted; current research holds that these are the actions of men behaving in ways that their culture allows and perhaps even encourages under some circumstances (Brownmiller, 1975; Herman, 1989). A relationship exists between acceptance of traditional social beliefs and sexual aggression in men (Walker, Rowe, & Quinsey, 1993). Acceptance of rape myths, acceptance of interpersonal violence, desire for dominance, and hostility toward women are all factors known to be related to the appeal of sexual aggression. Although all men who find sexual aggression appealing may not act, this factor is a predictor of sexually aggressive behavior.

Neil Malamuth and his colleagues (in Malamuth, 1996) have worked toward developing a model to predict sexual aggression. Drawing from the fields of evolutionary psychology and feminist scholarship, Malamuth proposed that the convergence of two factors relate to rape: (1) high levels of uncommitted, impersonal sex, and (2) hostile masculinity—hostility toward and desire to dominate women. When combined, these two factors relate to men's use of sexual coercion. Figure 9.1 presents this model and the paths leading toward coercive sexuality. Malamuth's research team has conducted several studies that validate the model and its ability to predict coercive tactics to obtain sex.

Women commit sexual violence but at very low rates, making sexual violence men's problem and women's fear. This fear is not without some basis: The arrest records indicate that about 8% of women will be victims of rape. Other methods have estimated rape at

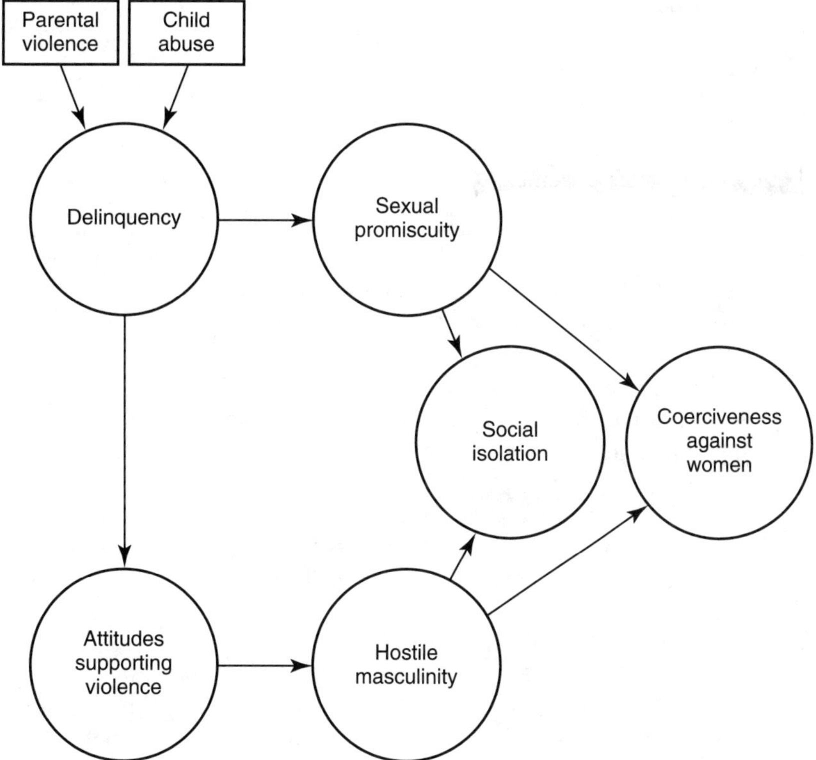

FIGURE 9.1 Model of Characteristics of Men Who Are Coercive against Women

Adapted from: N. Malamuth, R. Sockloskie, M. P. Koss, & J. Tanaka, 1991, "The characteristics of aggression against women: Testing a model using a national sample of college students," *Journal of Consulting and Clinical Psychology, 52,* p. 676. Adapted by permission of Neil Malamuth and the American Psychological Association.

much higher rates—15.4% of women have reported being raped and 54% have reported some type of sexual victimization. Convicted rapists differ surprisingly little from other men, but their attitudes toward women are extreme: they believe that "good" women should be placed on a pedestal but that men have the right to use violence with women. Malamuth's concept of hostile masculinity is one component in his model. Combined with uncommitted, impersonal sex, hostile masculinity seems to have some validity in predicting sexual aggression.

In summary, male aggression is not a myth, but the notion that men are aggressive and women are passive is not true. Both genders experience similar levels of anger, but men are more likely to express their anger as physical aggression. This likelihood can be traced to differing social expectations and reinforcements for aggression from boys or girls. As adults, men are more likely to be violent in public, to use aggression to gain power over others, and to experience legal problems associated with their aggression. Women are more likely to be violent in private, to use indirect or social aggression, and to respond violently if they feel justified in doing so and protected from retaliation. These patterns of aggression show gender-related differences, but they do not suggest that aggression is a male instinct.

Expressivity and Emotion

The similarities in the feelings that men and women experience and the differences in their behavior suggest that the gender difference in emotion may be in the way emotions are expressed. Indeed, women have been described as the expressive gender, whereas men fail to express their emotions (Fischer, 1993). This interpretation is only possible using a selective definition of what counts as emotion (Shields, 1994). Only by concentrating on the emotions of fear and sadness in women and by overlooking aggression in men could women be considered more expressive than men. Such evidence agrees with Postman's view from the headline for this chapter—it's a big, fat lie to believe that men are not emotional. As Postman proposed, both women and men feel similar emotions under similar circumstances, but women are more likely to express the emotions of sadness, anxiety, and fear than men, who are more likely to express their anger than women. This difference in expressivity can be explained by differences in display rules: Men and women are supposed to restrain displays of certain emotions yet are free to show others.

In his discussion of compliance with the Male Sex Role Identity, Robert Brannon (1976) listed four criteria, two of which relate to these gender differences in emotionality: (1) No Sissy Stuff, meaning men must avoid anything vaguely feminine, and (2) Give 'Em Hell, meaning men are proud to display anger and aggression. (See Chapter 8 for a discussion of all four components.) The stereotype holds that because women are emotional, anything feminine that is prohibited would include displays of most emotions. Anger is acceptable, however, because it is the essence of "giving 'em hell." These two components are essential elements of the display rules for men, which allows women to express more of what they feel, with the exception of anger.

The discrepancies among the three types of measures of emotionality (self-reports, observed behavior, and physical arousal) support these gender differences in display rules. When researchers have used participants' self-reports to measure emotion, they often find that women are more emotional than men. For example, one review of self-reports of emotionality (Maccoby & Jacklin, 1974) showed that girls and women were more likely than boys and men to admit to feelings of fear and anxiety. When researchers have used observations of participants' behavior in public, they have measured the enactment of display rules and the potential bias of observers, who may be influenced by the stereotypes governing emotion. Such studies tend to find gender differences (Eagly & Steffen, 1986), although the differences are not large, on the average. When researchers unobtrusively measure behavior in private, participants are more likely to display their emotions, and such studies often fail to find gender differences (Eisenberg & Lennon, 1983).

Measuring the physiological component of emotion provides a method of comparing the emotional responses of women and men, and some studies have used physiological measures of emotionality, often in combination with self-report or behavioral measures. One

GENDERED VOICES

They Put a Lot of Effort into Showing Nothing

I talked to a psychologist who had been employed as a therapist in a prison, and he told me that the prisoners exhibited what he considered to be an inappropriate level of emotion—none. He said, "I thought they put a lot of effort into showing no emotion. Their goal seemed to be to show no sign of any emotion. For example, even if they were hurt, their faces didn't change expression. Every once in a while, I would see a slip, and a prisoner would show some sign of pain when he got hurt. I assume that they had feelings that were similar to anyone's, but their expression of emotion was very abnormal.

"Showing no emotion didn't mean that they let things go. They would retaliate against another prisoner who had hurt them, even if it was mostly an accident and he hadn't meant to hurt anyone. But they didn't show any emotion when they were hurt or when they hurt the other guy. It was part of the prison society to keep their faces like masks, showing nothing about what they felt, closing themselves off from the others."

such study (Frodi & Lamb, 1978) measured behavioral and physiological responses of children who were interacting with babies. A behavioral difference appeared between girls and boys—the girls responded to and interacted with the babies more than their counterparts—but no difference appeared in the physiological measures.

Women learn a slightly different set of display rules for emotion than men do, and the behavior of both men and women tends to conform to the display rules they have learned. According to these display rules, women should be more nurturant than men, and in self-reports and in public behavior, they are. Boys and men should not be interested in babies or responsive to them, and under some circumstances, they are not. However, boys tend to nurture pets, and men who care for children are as nurturant and responsive as women who perform these tasks. According to these display rules, men should be more physically aggressive than women, and in self-reports and in public behavior (including criminal violence), they are. However, women experience anger as strongly as men, and when they feel justified (and anonymous), women are as likely to show as much physical aggression as men. Women also use indirect aggression, which involves doing harm indirectly. Therefore, the gender differences in emotion are more a function of circumstances and social learning of display rules than biologically determined differences due to instinct.

Summary

The stereotype of gender and emotion presents women as emotional and men as rational, but research on the different components of emotion has revealed that there may be few gender differences in the inner experience of emotion yet substantial gender differences in how and when emotion is displayed. Included in the components of emotion are the physiological dimension and the cognitive dimension. A classic experiment by Schachter and Singer demonstrated that expectations and setting can exert dramatic effects on the experience of emotion. Although psychologists continue to debate the relative contributions of physiology and cognition to the experience of emotion, most psychologists acknowledge that both are important.

The notion that some emotions are the result of instincts can be traced to Charles Darwin's theory of evolution. In psychology the explanation that emotion is instinctive has faded, with the exception of beliefs about a maternal instinct and an instinct toward aggression. Scientists have continued to believe in a maternal instinct, although research by Harlow and his colleagues has demonstrated that monkeys deprived of contact with other monkeys during the first six months of their lives failed to show adequate nurturing and caregiving. Another version of maternal instinct supports the concept of bonding—the attachment formed between adult and infant during the first hours of the infant's life—although this concept has not found as much research support.

Research on gender differences in responsiveness to babies has shown differences in self-reported behaviors but not in behavioral observations of young children or in physiological measures of older children and adults while responding to babies. These findings indicate that girls and women show more responsiveness to babies because they believe they should and that boys and men show less responsiveness for the same reason. Women still have a great deal more involvement in child care than men. Self-reports indicate that the greater pleasure of women in caring for children is coupled with their greater irritation in caring for them; however, men who are very involved in child care tend to report similar feelings. Although fathering has not included the type of intimate caregiving that mothering has, research indicates that fathers have increased their involvement with their children, demonstrating their interest and ability in nurturing. Therefore, the concept of maternal instinct has no support as a biologically based explanation for caregiving, and both men and women have similar emotions related to nurturing.

Aggression has also been nominated as an instinct, with the belief that men have more innate tendencies toward showing aggressive behavior than women. When considering the link between anger and aggression—that is, between emotion and behavior—few gender differences appear. Women and men experience anger similarly, but there are gender differences in how emotions are expressed. Boys and men tend to be more likely to use direct, physical confrontation when they are angry, whereas girls and women are more likely to avoid physical confrontation. There is no difference in the use of verbal aggression; however, girls and women are more likely to cry when angry, an expression that men often misunderstand.

Developmental gender differences in aggression exist, with boys more likely than girls to use physical aggression at all ages. Longitudinal studies have revealed that aggression is moderately stable over time, and aggressive children are more likely than less aggressive children to become violent adults. However, both boys and girls tend to become less aggressive as they develop, and by adulthood, the gender difference in aggression has diminished.

Despite small gender differences in aggression shown in laboratory studies and others indicating the overall decrease in aggression during adolescence and adulthood, very large gender differences exist in crime rate—men are about four times more likely than women to commit a violent crime. The victims of these violent crimes are more likely to be other men. However, women fear crime victimization more than men, especially sexual violence. Nor is their fear unfounded: Official reports indicate that about 8% of women will be raped during their lifetime, and surveys indicate the rate of rape might be as high as 15%. Explanations of rape have changed historically from the view that a few pathological men commit sexual violence to the current view that cultural factors support violence against women. One study of convicted rapists indicated that they are like other men in many ways; however, their attitudes differ markedly in the extent to which they want to put women "on a pedestal" and in the extent to which they find violence against women acceptable.

Although men have more experience with violence and less with nurturance than women, these differences may relate to how emotion is expressed rather than to women's or men's subjective experiences of emotion. The cultural display rules that govern the behaviors associated with emotion differ for men and women, and these allow women more expression and restrain men from expressing many emotions. Therefore, the gender differences in emotion may more accurately reflect differences in expressivity.

Glossary

bonding an emotional attachment that develops between mother or primary caregiver and infant within a few days after birth.

critical period a time period in development during which animals are capable of rapid learning when presented with the necessary stimulus. Once the critical period has passed, no amount of exposure will produce the learning.

display rules the learned social rules that govern who may display which emotion and in what situation each emotion may be displayed.

Suggested Readings

Eyer, Diane E. (1992). *Mother–infant bonding: A scientific fiction.* New Haven, CT: Yale University Press. Eyer critically reviews not only the concept of bonding but other versions of biological determinism in caregiving. Her book also offers a criticism of science in the media and how medical practice can be influenced more by popular beliefs than by valid research.

Fischer, Agneta H. (1993). Sex differences in emotionality: Fact or stereotype? *Feminism & Psychology, 3,* 303–318. This article from Fischer is a good place to begin considering the issue of gender and emotion. She critically reviews the stereotypes, the research, and simplistic thinking concerning emotionality.

Risman, Barbara J. (1989). Can men "mother"? Life as a single father. In Barbara J. Risman & Pepper Schwartz (Eds.), *Gender in intimate relationships: A microstructural approach* (pp. 155–164). Belmont, CA: Wadsworth. Risman explores the responses of men who are called upon to nurture children and how they respond to the situational demands by "mothering."

Tavris, Carol. (1982). *Anger: The misunderstood emotion.* New York: Simon & Schuster. This popular book is not recent, but Tavris provides a readable review of research on the subject. She contends that the benefits of getting in touch with and expressing anger have been overrated, and she argues that the benefits of control outweigh the advantages of expression.

Chapter 10

Relationships

HEADLINE

Why Are His Feelings My Responsibility?

—*Woman's Day,* July 18, 1995

"Like many women, I've always considered myself the 'emotional manager' of my household. The man I love doesn't share his feelings easily, so I regard it as my job to coax him into opening up—about himself, me, us," Susan Jacoby (1995, p. 160) wrote. In writing about her relationship, Jacoby described a specialization in feelings that Francesca Cancian (1986) called the "feminization" of love. That is, women's style of relating has become the standard for intimacy, with sharing of feelings and disclosure of personal information. Women have become the experts in relationships, as Jacoby was.

This designation of women as the relationship experts gives women both power and pressure in their relationships, and Jacoby discussed both facets of this role. The power comes from being in charge of this important area of the relationship. In drawing out his feelings and getting him to discuss them, Jacoby felt useful and powerful—like she was performing an essential function. She also felt drained by the energy that she was devoting to emotional management for herself, her loved one, and the relationship. She felt that caring had become caretaking, which was more of a burden than she wanted.

She fantasized about how much easier her relationship would be if her partner were more emotionally open in his dealings with her. She wanted him to adopt the "feminine" style of disclosing personal information, but she was also aware of the problems that can arise when men are more open in discussing their feelings with their partners. Jacoby recounted a friend's experience and how unhappy her friend had been when her husband began to tell about his fears and insecurities. Revealing such feelings is inconsistent with the male gender role, and the friend, who had urged her husband to be more emotionally open, also wanted him to be strong and dependable. Even realizing the inconsistency didn't

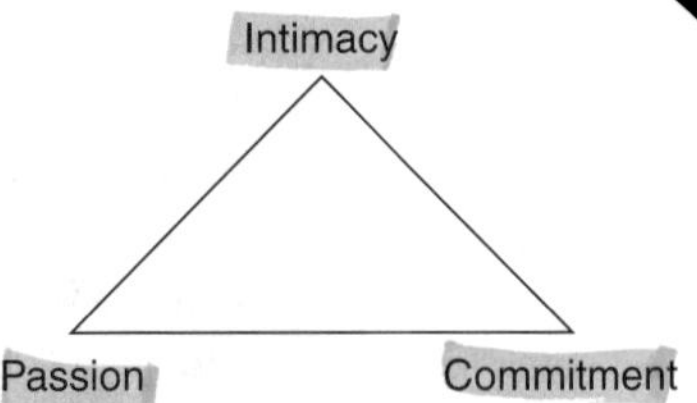

Liking = Intimacy without Passion or Commitment
Companionate love = Intimacy + Commitment without Passion
Romantic love = Intimacy + Passion without Commitment
Empty love = Commitment without Passion or Intimacy
Fatuous love = Passion + Commitment without Intimacy
Infatuated love = Passion without Commitment or Intimacy
Consummate love = Passion + Commitment + Intimacy

FIGURE 10.1 Sternberg's Triangular Theory of Love

SOURCE: Adapted from "A triangular theory of love," (pp. 123, 128) by R. J. Sternberg, 1986, *Psychological Review, 93.* Adapted by permission of Robert Sternberg and the American Psychological Association.

stop these women from wanting both strength and openness from their partners, no matter how difficult the combination.

Jacoby's story highlights some of the issues in contemporary love relationships. First, women and men often use different styles of relating that they enact in both friendships and love relationships. As Jacoby's story indicated, women are often in charge of the emotional work in relationships, managing the feelings for both partners and maintaining the relationship. Second, many women find this role difficult and would like their partners to be more open about feelings.

Women's and men's different styles in relationships have implications for friendships and love relationships, both with same-sex and other-sex individuals. Robert Sternberg (1986) proposed a model for understanding all relationships, including friendship and romantic love. He called this model the triangular theory of love because it hypothesizes love's three points: intimacy, passion, and commitment. His conception of intimacy encompasses feelings of closeness, passion includes romantic and sexual attraction, and commitment involves the decision that love exists and the relationship should continue. Figure 10.1 shows Sternberg's model and the different types of relationships that result from the combinations of these elements.

Sternberg argued that if none of these components exists, there is no relationship. His model distinguishes between two types of friendships—liking and companionate love. Liking occurs when people share intimacy but not passion or commitment. Sternberg (1987) included both sharing feelings and sharing activities as intimacy. The combination of intimacy and commitment without passion results in **companionate love,** a definition that comes close to what most people regard as close but platonic friendship.

ar theory of love makes no distinction between intimacy lings or through sharing activities, these two styles tend to be men, respectively. These gender differences in relationship feel that their friendships are deficient because they do not way that women do (Nordheimer, 1991). The view that men as not always existed, nor do all cultures discourage intimate, en men (Nardi, 1992a). The Greeks believed that true friend-n free and equal individuals, which omitted all women, slaves, nding from the experience.

The natu[illegible] iendships has changed over the past 100 years (Nardi, 1992a). During the 19th century, intimate friendships were common for both men and women. Courage and loyalty were seen as the basis for a special type of friendship that men could share, and men were considered capable of experiencing closeness and feelings for other men that women could not feel for other women, nor that women and men could feel for each other. Currently, women are seen as more capable of intimate friendship, and women's style of friendship is viewed as more intimate than men's relationships.

Development of Styles

Children tend to segregate themselves according to gender starting at preschool age and continuing throughout elementary and middle school (Maccoby, 1988). This segregation is noticeable during preschool, and it becomes much more pronounced during the elementary school years, perhaps by being imposed by parents or teachers. When the two are put into situations in which they must interact, they do, but the tendency to group into same-gender associations is a persistent pattern for children. Furthermore, the interaction patterns of boys and girls differ, beginning very early in development.

Interactions between pairs of 33-month-old children showed their reactions to each other (Jacklin & Maccoby, 1978). The pairs consisted of all possible combinations—boys with boys, girls with girls, and boys with girls. These children interacted more with children of the same than with the other gender, for both positive and negative behaviors. Children in boy–boy or girl–girl pairs were more likely to offer toys to their partners or try to take toys from their partners than the children in girl–boy pairs. Indeed, children in mixed-gender pairs behaved differently from those in same-gender pairs, with the girls being more passive and the boys more unresponsive when each interacted with the other. Girls in such pairs tended to stand by and watch the boys play or to withdraw and seek their mothers. The boys in such pairs tended to ignore what the girls said to them, but they paid attention to other boys.

The appearance of these behaviors seemed to be part of the situation rather than characteristic of the children. Girls and boys behaved similarly when they interacted with children of the same gender: The girls were active in their exchanges, and the boys were responsive to their partners' messages. However, in mixed-gender pairs, these children's behaviors changed. Even before age 3, children seemed to understand that there are differences between the genders, and their reactions fell along stereotypical lines. Furthermore, the unequal interactions in mixed-gender pairs may have related to the gender segregation that is typical of children's play and friendships. Playing would not be that much fun if your partner failed to react and listen. Therefore, the types of interactions exhibited by boys and girls would tend to make each more eager to seek the company of others of the same gender.

Children as young as second grade have a concept of friendship and expect friends to behave differently toward them than toward other children who are only acquaintances (Furman & Bierman, 1984). At this age their notion of friendship centers mostly around what friends should do for each other, such as helping each other and sharing secrets. As they develop, children add to their notion of friendship so that personal characteristics such as loyalty become important. Children also begin to rely on friends for emotional and tangible support during the elementary and junior high school years, and they consider these types of support important to friendship (Berndt & Perry, 1986). During preadolescence, children become increasingly able to integrate the notion that conflict is an acceptable part of friendship, forming a more complex concept of friendship during the years of middle childhood and preadolescence. This concept includes the types of things that friends should do for each other and the type of characteristics that friends should share: Children start to acknowledge that friends may disagree.

During elementary school, children begin to rely on peers for companionship and intimacy, shifting from a complete reliance on siblings and parents (Buhrmester & Furman, 1987). These relationships reflect the closeness or intimacy component of Sternberg's triangular model of relationships. The research on elementary school children demonstrated that same-gender friends were important sources of companionship for the second, fifth, and eighth graders who participated in the study. The study also revealed gender differences in the development of intimate friendship, with girls both seeking and valuing intimacy at younger ages than boys. Like other investigations, this study showed that children exhibit a resistance to cross-gender friendships; only the eighth graders valued the company of the other gender.

One possible basis for the gender differences in friendships during middle childhood comes from the different activities that girls and boys enjoy during these years. For example, boys are more fond of rough-and-tumble play than girls. Such play involves play-fighting, and chasing and is very common among preschool children, especially boys (Humphreys & Smith, 1987). The persistence of rough-and-tumble play throughout middle childhood and into preadolescence might seem to escalate into aggression, but such play is actually done in a spirit of fun. Boys also tend to play in somewhat larger groups, to spend more time outside (Maccoby, 1990), and to be more fond of activities that involve **gross motor skills,** such as running, jumping, and throwing a ball.

Activity preferences may also be a reason for gender segregation during childhood (Bukowski, Gauze, Hoza, & Newcomb, 1993). Boys who preferred high levels of motor activity preferred the company of other boys, and girls who disliked such activities preferred the company of other girls. However, the conception of girls playing quietly with their dolls is stereotypical rather than typical: Girls engage in active and even athletic play, but their preferred partners are other girls rather than boys.

A large part of children's play time is occupied by gender-neutral activities, but the decision to play with children of the same gender persists (Maccoby, 1990). The more active, assertive girls—the "tomboys"—tended to have the strongest preference for the companionship of other girls (Maccoby, 1988). Also, the play groupings of girls tended to be smaller than those of boys, with girls forming more intimate but fewer relationships.

Evidence also indicates that girls tend to evolve a different style of group interaction than boys (Maccoby, 1988, 1990). Girls make more polite requests and use persuasion to get their way, whereas boys make more direct demands and attempt to get their way through dominance within their group. Girls try to involve other girls in the ongoing activities of the group, whereas boys tell other boys what to do. Girls do not lack assertiveness, but their style of assertion and influence differs from that of boys. Furthermore, during middle childhood the style of persuasion typical of girls begins to be less effective with boys than with other girls, providing an additional basis for restricted association.

Gender segregation is common during the elementary school years, but girls and boys do interact with one another. Observations in elementary schools showed that gender segregation is a strong force, with few children voluntarily crossing the boundary (Thorne, 1993). Children imposed this division on themselves, but the organization of the schools and the teachers contributed to this gender segregation. For example, teachers often organized classroom competitions in which the girls formed one team and the boys the other, and school staff considered one section of the playground to be the girls' and another to be the boys' area. Thus, schools and adults may be perpetuating the tendency for girls and boys to form separate work and play groups.

This investigation of the areas and conditions of cross-gender interactions revealed the animosity that often accompanies such interactions. "It's like girls and boys are on different sides," an 11-year-old girl said (Thorne, 1993, p. 63). The animosity took the form of name-calling, invading another's space, pollution games and rituals ("cooties"), and occasional fights. Some of the hostile interactions contained the hint of heterosexual awareness and future romantic relationships, but sexuality was more commonly used as a way to taunt.

Situations of comfortable interaction did appear between girls and boys. These situations tended to be either very absorbing activities, such as group projects or interesting games, or activities organized by an adult so as to include both girls and boys, such as games involving assigned rather than chosen teams. Few children traveled easily between the social worlds of girls and boys.

Gender segregation poses a dilemma for preadolescents: They must avoid members of the other gender except under certain sanctioned circumstances, yet each gender must have sufficient contact to learn about the other. Gender segregation is important in preadolescent social groups (Sroufe, Bennett, Englund, & Urban, 1993). Preadolescents who maintained gender segregation were both more popular with their peers and rated as more socially competent by adults than children who violated the boundaries between the genders. Same-gender friendships during childhood may allow individuals to learn how to form relationships without the pressure of sexual contact. Referring back to Sternberg's model of relationships, these relationships allow children and preadolescents to develop intimacy and commitment without passion. Childhood friendships, then, might be regarded as a type of practice for adolescent and adult romantic relationships. (See the Diversity Highlight: "Friendship in a Desegregated School.")

Although preadolescent children avoid friendships with children of the other gender, they are acutely aware of their future roles as romantic partners. Gender segregation seems forced during preadolescence (Maccoby, 1988), and children of both genders use threats of contact and proposed romantic feelings—threats to kiss, teasing about who "likes" whom,

DIVERSITY HIGHLIGHT
Friendships in a Desegregated School

Gender is not the only basis for self-segregation during the early school years. Ethnic and racial background are also characteristics that children notice and use as a basis for forming groups. A study (Schofield, 1981) of adolescents in a desegregated junior high school (containing grades 6 through 8) examined the influence of both gender and race on children's interactions. The school was located in a large, industrial northeastern city in the United States, and the racial composition was approximate 50% African American and 50% European American. The staff of the school was also biracial and dedicated to operating a racially desegregated school. Teachers did not view race as an appropriate characteristic for grouping and tried to encourage children of both ethnic groups to work together and to get along with each other.

The teachers' efforts to promote equal and harmonious interactions were not entirely successful. Although the teachers did not group the children according to race, the children still tended to group themselves. Even when the arrangements of classes ensured an equal balance of African Americans and Whites as well as boys and girls, the students "often resegregate themselves along racial and gender lines to a remarkable extent, avoiding even surface contact when possible" (Schofield, p. 62). In classrooms the children divided themselves into four groups according to race and gender and seated themselves accordingly, unless the teachers arranged them into a different pattern.

Seating patterns in the school's cafeteria, where children could sit where they wished, showed individual preferences. On a typical day, fewer than 10 of 200 students chose cross-race seating arrangements, and even fewer chose cross-gender seating. When children had to choose whether to interact with someone of their own gender or someone of their own ethnic group, they chose the child of the same gender, crossing ethnic lines. The reluctance to cross gender lines was so strong that children accepted a punishment rather than interact with a child of the other gender.

A similar study (DuBois & Hirsch, 1990) obtained similar results. These junior high school students were reluctant to cross ethnic lines to form friendships, but more evidence of interracial friendships appeared. These friendships tended to be restricted to school and did not carry over to activities outside the school environment. The African American and European American students who were most likely to be friends were those who lived in integrated neighborhoods and attended integrated schools.

Thus, children in integrated schools behaved like other children in avoiding the opposite gender, but in addition, they also tended to avoid peers from other ethnic groups. The two studies showed a tendency toward more interracial friendships over time, but these friendships tended to be limited to school rather than extending to the full range of preadolescents' friendship activities. Even with these restrictions, friendships between children of different ethnic groups were more common than cross-gender friendships, revealing the most salient type of segregation for children.

and avoidance of physical contact for fear of catching "cooties"—as ways to harass each other (Thorne, 1993). This active avoidance changes to active interest during adolescence; contact between girls and boys becomes more common, but friendships between girls and boys remain uncommon.

Friendship over the Life Span

Friendships during adolescence are similar to those of preadolescence, but adolescents intensify the intimacy in their relationships with a greater degree of personal sharing and self-disclosure than those of younger children. The gender differences in the value and attainment of intimacy persist, with girls more likely to be interested in forming emotionally intimate friendships with a smaller set of girls and boys more likely to form activity-based friendships with a more extensive set of boys. This pattern results in boys being alone less often than girls but girls talking with each other more often than boys (Smith, 1997).

Adolescent girls use talk as a way to develop intimacy, to reveal and learn intimate knowledge about each other (Berndt, 1982). A meta-analytic review (Collins & Miller, 1994) showed that self-disclosure is an important factor in friendship, increasing liking in those who hear disclosures. Self-disclosure is not as characteristic of boys' as of girls' friendships, and this difference may relate to different conceptualizations of friendship for boys and girls (Berndt, 1982). Boys are less likely than girls to say that they would treat friends differently than other classmates, so perhaps boys value self-disclosure less than girls.

Fear of homosexuality is a factor that discourages boys from forming the same type of intimate friendships that girls experience (Berndt, 1982). The current prohibitions against same-gender sexual activity make men hesitant about emotional closeness in friendships, and the activity-based relationships of adolescent boys and adult men illustrate one strategy for avoiding the emotional intimacy that could suggest homosexuality (Nardi, 1992a).

Some gender asymmetry may exist in adolescent friendship. Not only do adolescent girls form more intimate relationships with other girls, but they increase their intimacy with boys more rapidly than boys do with girls (Sharabany, Gershoni, & Hofman, 1981). Another type of asymmetry exists in the emotional fulfillment people derive from relationships (Wheeler, Reis, & Nezlek, 1983). Spending time with other men did not decrease men's feelings of loneliness, but meaningful interactions with men did. Spending time with women, however, decreased loneliness, regardless of the meaningfulness of the interaction. Indeed, for both women and men, spending time with women seemed to protect against feeling lonely, possibly because women are better at providing these qualities to both their male and female friends.

A study of friendship among college students (Caldwell & Peplau, 1982) confirmed findings from previous studies—namely, that gender differences exist in what each considers the basis for friendship and that young men and women differ in their conceptualizations of friendship. College students were questioned about their friendships as well as observed in a role-playing exercise: No differences appeared in the number of friends or the amount of time spent with friends for young men and young women, but men were more likely than women to choose an activity to do with a friend rather than "just talk" and to choose their friends on the basis of shared activities rather than shared attitudes. These differences did not lead to differential evaluations of intimacy: Women and men were equally likely to consider their friendships intimate.

Unmarried, childless college students may have the most time to devote to friends, making this often-studied group different from others. In addition, the demands of friendship for men and women may be most similar among college students (Caldwell & Peplau, 1982). As individuals become involved with romantic relationships, families, and careers, existing friendships often change, occupying less time and possibly becoming less intimate.

Marriage or other committed love relationships introduce a different pattern of friendship, when relationships with other couples are added to relationships with individual friends. Interviews with married couples were used to explore the factors that relate to the formation and maintenance of these people's social networks (Wellman, 1992). Traditionally, men have formed friendships as a result of their work and public lives, whereas women have formed networks of friends and family relationships centered around the home. The home had become the base for friendships for both the male and female working-class participants in this study. Furthermore, the women were the monitors of social activity, arranging most social gatherings as well as get-togethers with other couples. These associations with other couples did not require both members of a couple to be equally close friends; the most typical pattern was for either the husbands or the wives to be friends and for their counterparts to be tolerant of these friends. This pattern of friendship tends to promote fairly superficial friendships, at least for one member of the couple.

The men in this interview study also had buddies whom they saw separately from couple-oriented activities. These buddies were likely to be companions for activities such as going to ball games, but these buddies also helped with small services (fixing a car) or large services (roofing a house). The men in this sample got less emotional support from their friends than their wives received from their friends, but then the men did not necessarily feel that their friends should provide emotional support. As Jacoby's (1995) headline story indicated, husbands tend to rely on their wives for emotional support rather than their male friends, and the husbands in this study behaved similarly.

During the early years of marriage, both spouses may relinquish other relationships to develop their marriage, seeking emotional intimacy and support from each other. In addition, when couples have children, the children take up time that might have been devoted to friends or to spouses. Thus, young marrieds, especially those with children, tend to devote less time to other friendships than people who are unmarried or childless. The men in one study (T. Cohen, 1992) had restricted their friendships both when they were married and again after the births of their first children. Some of these restrictions were due to time limitations and the obligation to fulfill the husband and father role, but some withdrawal from friendship was due to friends' perception of the married friends' roles. That is, unmarried men perceived that married men were not supposed to spend as much time with their friends, so they restricted their attempts to stay in contact when a friend married. Married men reported that they felt they should restrict their other relationships so as to maintain greater intimacy with their wives rather than with other male or female friends. This process may also apply to women. Thus, each member of a married couple may restrict their outside friendships.

When children become adults, their family members may become their friends. Due to the wide difference in power and authority between parents and children, this possibility is not likely during childhood or adolescence, but adult children and their parents can form relationships that have the emotional sharing and self-disclosure that characterize other friendships. These relationships also show gender differences consistent with other findings: Women (daughters and mothers) are closer than other combinations of family members (Lye, 1996). Indeed, the closeness of families with adult children often depends on mothers' efforts to maintain contact. In addition to parent–adult child relationships, siblings are often close after they become adults, maintaining relationships that are as close as friends (Floyd, 1995).

Aging produces changes in friendships, with the elderly needing more practical support while the number of friends decreases due to death. Children often become the source of this caregiving and practical support, but the elderly attempt to maintain social networks (Akiyama, Elliott, & Antonucci, 1996). Women become more numerous in the social networks of the elderly because men die at younger ages, leaving more women. Thus, same-gender friendships tend to be replaced with relationships with women for both women and men. Therefore, friendship becomes more female-based among the elderly.

Flexibility of Styles

Men may find emotional intimacy easier with women than with other men. As Cancian (1987) proposed, love has come to be defined in feminine terms, as the expression of feelings and as self-disclosure. These characteristics are commonly associated with women and are actually more common in women's than men's friendships. Some evidence exists that men can also use this style of relationship and tend to do so when they relate to women. That is, men may be able to use different styles of relating to different friends. This flexibility appeared in a study (Reid & Fine, 1992) that focused on self-disclosure in same-gender and cross-gender friendships. One of the important factors in self-disclosure was the type of relationship between the two people. For instance, lovers and spouses reported more intimate self-disclosure than close platonic friends.

Both men and women were hypothesized to conform to a role in maintaining different types of relationships, and the rules of relating were hypothesized to differ both for the type of relationship and for the gender of the target person in the relationship. Women's emphasis on talking and sharing feelings is part of the pattern people generally accept for women's friendships, but a different pattern exists for friendship among men. Contrary to expectation, one study (Leaper, Carson, Baker, Holliday, & Myers, 1995) showed that men were more likely to disclose information about themselves. Women, however, showed a pattern of active listening and understanding with their female friends that did not appear in any other gender combination.

As this research implies, cross-gender friendships may face even more constraining rules than same-gender friendships. Cross-gender friendships are a recent development that did not exist 100 years ago when Western societies were strongly gender-segregated, when women governed the home and men occupied the world of work, politics, and business (Swain, 1992). Although gender segregation still exists in many situations, school and work offer opportunities for cross-gender relationships, and women and men have formed such friendships. Such friendships may experience difficulties in a society that emphasizes same-gender friendships and cross-gender sexual relationships, but some research (Monsour, Harris, Kurzweil, & Beard, 1994) found that these problems affect only a small percentage of cross-gender friendships. For most cross-gender friends, these special challenges and problems were "much ado about nothing" (Monsour et al., p. 55).

The ability to adapt to the situation by using a more "feminine" or "masculine" style of interaction indicates that styles of friendship are indeed roles that men and women learn. Although not all men may learn the intimate sharing and self-disclosure that are typical of women's friendships, some do, and these men use this style when they form friendships with women. More likely, men learn the behaviors but feel uncomfortable in enacting this friendship style. As several researchers have pointed out, **homophobia**—the unreasonable fear and hatred of homosexuality—restrains men from seeking emotional intimacy with other men. Even when men know the style, they may be reluctant to use it. When they use it, they may feel more comfortable in this type of relationship with women rather than other men.

The constraints on women's behavior are not as strong; their typical style of emotional intimacy with other women carries no homosexual connotations. However, emotional intimacy between women and men often has an element of a sexual relationship, so women who seek friendships with men also must be vigilant in maintaining these as nonsexual friendships. Women who adopt an activity-based style of relationship with men, being "one of the boys," can participate in the same activities that men enjoy with each other—playing baseball, poker, or other recreational activities. This choice creates a style of relationship typical of men and not necessarily one infused with emotional intimacy. Some men and women have chosen to break the boundaries established during preschool and form friendships with members of the other gender. The research indicates that men and women know about both friendship styles, suggesting that any limitations in creating cross-gender friendships come from reluctance to apply these styles.

The restriction of one style of relationship to women and the other to men has forced each into a way of relating that fails to allow the development of full potential for either (Cancian, 1987). As Jacoby's headline story illustrated, women have become the designated experts in relationships, and many men feel incompetent at relationships because they may have problems with the emotional, intimate style of relating. These restrictions have affected love relationships even more strongly than friendships. Both styles have benefits, and the equation of emotional intimacy with romantic love has negative consequences. The history of love relationships suggests the possibility that the male and female roles restrict the development of both men and women.

Love Relationships

As Jacoby's (1995) headline story described, women and men fulfill different roles in modern love relationships. Women's role encourages them to specialize in emotional bonding and building intimacy between the partners whereas men's role encourages them to concentrate on their careers and being good providers. These roles for women and men differ over the world and over time. Elaine Hatfield and Richard Rapson (1996) contended that romantic, passionate love is universal, but this type of love has not been the basis for permanent relationships in industrialized Western countries until recently.

Historically, passionate romantic love has posed a threat to the existing social structure and has rarely been the basis for permanent relationships (Hatfield & Rapson, 1996). Many cultures have literature or legends about lovers who have died tragically as the result of their passion and the unsuitability of any permanent relationship. The story of Romeo and Juliet is an example familiar to English-speaking cultures, but Hatfield and Rapson have described similar stories from ancient and modern societies around the world. Passionate love has been seen as madness rather than a good basis for marriage. The more common pattern for forming permanent relationships has been (and in many cultures remains) arranged marriages in which families choose mates for children. In such arranged marriages, financial considerations rather than love or passion have been the motivations for the match.

Several different patterns of love relationships have existed over the past several centuries in Western cultures (Cancian, 1987). Before the 1800s, few differences existed between masculine and feminine love. Agriculture was the basis for most people's livelihood, and both men and women worked together on family farms, making the family the center of both men's and women's lives. Although men were the head of households, both men and women believed that marriage gave them the duty to love and help one another. Despite sharply divided gender roles in the home and community, love was not differentiated according to gender.

In Sternberg's (1986) triangular model of love, this Family Duty blueprint ensured an equal relationship between the partners. Such marriages were formed around commitment, and the sharing of home life made intimacy very likely, but the component of passion might have been missing from such duty-bound relationships. In arranged marriages, this component might never be part of the relationship of a married couple.

By the end of the 1700s, the Industrial Revolution had changed the pattern of many people's lives, including marriage and family. Work and family had been separated, with men working in jobs in factories and offices rather than around the home. Women, too, might work in factories, but the ideal pattern of family relationship was for men to fulfill the Good Provider role (Bernard, 1981) and for women to be mothers and wives. This division led to the Doctrine of the Two Spheres (Welter, 1978), the division that resulted in women's preeminence in family life and men's dominance in the outside world.

Women became responsible for the maintenance of the home and family, a sanctuary from the hostility of the outside world of business and factory. This responsibility made women the experts in love: They were the ones who had the tender feelings and experienced the emotions; they were the ones who needed love and depended on men and children for it; they were the ones most capable of providing love to others.

Through this family arrangement, women became dependent on men for financial security, so maintaining the love of a husband was essential to women's financial security. During the 1920s, women started to invade the male world of work, taking paid jobs outside the home. With increasing economic power, women were less dependent on men for financial security, which changed the blueprint for marriage to the Companionship model (Cancian, 1987). Cancian credited the Companionship blueprint for love relationships with the feminization of love. This model focused on affection and support for each other, but women were still the experts on love and held the responsibility for the relationship: "Marriage was to be all of a woman's life but only part of a man's" (Cancian, 1987, p. 34).

The Companionship model for marriage emphasized the similarity of the partners, and personal characteristics in the selection of marriage partners became important as this model of marriage became better accepted. Spouses were supposed to love each other before they married and to choose their partners rather than relying on partners chosen by family. Using Sternberg's model to analyze these relationships, consummate love was the ideal, with an equal mixture of intimacy, passion, and commitment. However, romantic love was also a possibility, with its combination of passion and intimacy but lack of commitment. As evidence for the rising lack of commitment under the Companionship blueprint, the divorce rate increased (Cancian, 1987).

The emphasis on personal compatibility and romance in marriage prompted a different method of selecting marriage partners. Rather than relying on the family to choose their partners or making decisions on an economic basis, individuals started to choose their own mates. Dating arose as a way of finding suitable marriage partners for Companionship-style marriages.

Dating

Although dating began during the 1920s as a form of courtship, it has expanded to fulfill other functions—recreation, status and achievement, socialization, learning about intimacy, sexual exploration, companionship, and identity formation (Santrock, 1993). Since the 1940s, dating has become less formal and structured (Miller & Gordon, 1986). Rather than following the traditional pattern in which boys ask, plan, and pay for dates, current dating patterns include girls taking the initiative in asking, planning, and paying for dates in addition to a pattern of mixed-gender group dating.

Dating has become an important part of adolescent life, and most young people in the United States have their first date between the ages of 12 and 16 years, with girls dating slightly earlier than boys. By age 16 years, more than 90% of adolescents have had a date (Santrock, 1993). Dating becomes more frequent for older teenagers, with about 50% of adolescents in high school having at least one date per week.

Changes in the reasons for dating occur throughout adolescence. Younger adolescents (6th graders) said that they dated as a recreational activity or as a way to achieve status (Roscoe, Diana, & Brooks, 1987). These adolescents were self-focused in their dating patterns, showing concern for status, acceptance, and physical appearance rather than concern for their dating partner or for developing a relationship. Older teenagers showed more concern for the social and companionship aspects of dating and less concern for superficial characteristics, such as a fashionably dressed date. Personal characteristics, such as kindness and confidence, were more important to adolescents of all ages than prestige factors, such as money or ethnic group membership.

Boys and girls in this study showed some differences in the characteristics they valued in a date, with boys being more concerned with physical appearance and more interested in dating a sexually active partner than were girls. Adolescent boys who hold traditional attitudes toward masculinity reported more sexual partners, less intimacy with their sexual partners, and a greater belief that relationships with girls are adversarial than have adolescent boys who have less traditional views of masculinity (Pleck, Sonenstein, & Ku, 1993).

For girls, confidence, kindness, dependability, parental approval, and abstinence from alcohol were more important characteristics in a date than they were for boys (Roscoe et al., 1987). In general, younger adolescents used self-centered reasons and looked for superficial characteristics in choosing dating partners, perhaps indicating unrealistic standards for dating choices. Older adolescents, on the other hand, showed that they had developed more flexible and personal standards for dating.

Traditional gender role behavior is evident in the dating behavior of both genders. Young men's and women's behavior on dates follows a script, a model that people use to guide their behavior (Rose & Frieze, 1993). College students adhere to this script in describing an actual and a hypothetical first heterosexual date, with a great deal of agreement between the two scripts. A difference in behavior appeared for the two gender roles: Following the script would lead men to act and women to react. The man's active role

GENDERED VOICES

I Was Terrible at Being a Girl

"I was fairly bad at being a girl when I was a child," a middle-aged woman told me. "I did tomboy-type things. But I was really terrible at it when I was a teenager and trying to date and attract boys. Dating seemed like a game, and the rules were so silly. And I was bad at the game. Flirting was a disaster—I felt so silly and incompetent.

"My mother practically despaired of my ever behaving in ways that would lead to dates. She would give me advice, such as 'Hide how smart you are, because boys don't like to date girls who are smarter than they are' and 'Wait for him to open the door for you.' I thought both those things were pretty pointless. Why should I hide how smart I was? I had gone to school with most of the guys in my high school since we were all in elementary school, so they knew how smart I was. Besides, if I could have fooled one, I didn't think that I could have kept up the charade. I wasn't smart enough to play dumb for all that long. Also, why would I want to date a guy who wanted a dumb girl? Sounded like a poor prospect to me.

"I know that opening doors became an issue in the 1970s feminist movement, but my objections were about 10 years earlier. It just seemed silly to me that a perfectly capable person, me, should inconvenience a guy to open a door. I was more than capable of doing so, and I never saw why I shouldn't—still don't for that matter. I now see having doors opened as a courtesy, which is O.K. I open doors for both men and women. There's probably too much made of that particular issue, but when I was a teenager, it was something my mother warned me about on numerous occasions. I just had a hard time getting the rules of the game—I was terrible at the girl stuff. I am much better at being a women than I was at being a girl."

includes initiating the date, controlling the activities, and initiating sexual activity. The woman's reactive role includes being concerned about her appearance, participating in the activities her partner planned, and reacting to his sexual advances. Both the hypothetical and actual dates reflected this script, which follows traditional gender stereotypes.

Although dating is the method through which most people now choose mates, only around 7% of the college students, and even fewer of the younger adolescents said that mate selection was the reason for dating (Roscoe et al., 1987). Interestingly, the characteristics preferred by late adolescents in dating partners and the list of characteristics that young married adults find desirable in mates were very similar (Buss & Barnes, 1986). People seek both dates and mates who are kind, intelligent, physically attractive, and socially exciting. In this study of mate selection as in the selection of dating partners, men valued physical attractiveness more than women.

Evolutionary psychology is an area of psychology that examines the factors that have influenced success in producing offspring. This view emphasizes gender differences, hypothesizing that women and men share many factors but also have some differences in selecting what is desirable in a mate (Buss, 1994). Preference for physical attractiveness is one of the factors that evolutionary psychology sees as a gender difference, with men valuing attractive partners because attractiveness is a sign of health and reproductive fitness. Men do emphasize attractiveness more than women, but attractiveness is not perfectly related to health; people can be ill and still be nice looking. In addition, a more reliable sign of reproductive capability is having borne children; however, the evolutionary psychologists do not hypothesize that women with young children are the most attractive potential mates, despite their demonstrated reproductive success.

The value of attractiveness in reproductive success is questionable, not only as it indicates the ability to reproduce successfully but also in its relation to reproduction. Few differences in partner preference appeared in the descriptions of desirable partner characteristics in male–male, female–female as well as male–female couples (Howard, Blumstein, & Schwartz, 1987). All said they wanted romantic partners who were kind, considerate, and physically attractive. The partners in same-gender couples expressed a preference for partners who were more athletic and expressive about their feelings than the mates described by partners in male–female couples, but these differences were small. Regardless of sexual orientation, people seek similar qualities in romantic partners. The results of this study raise questions about the belief that reproductive fitness is the primary factor in mate selection.

Other characteristics that attract people to romantic partners include similarities of personal values. Mate selection is more a matter of "birds of a feather flock together" than "opposites attract" (Antill, 1983). That is, people are romantically attracted to others who are more like them than different from them. These similarities include not only personal values but also social class, religion, and gender role acceptance. The notion that opposites attract may relate to the concepts of masculinity and femininity and the belief that the two lie on opposite ends of a continuum. (See Chapter 8 for a discussion of the inaccuracy of this conceptualization.) According to this view, masculine men should be attracted to their "opposite"—feminine women—and vice versa.

An alternative interpretation of compatibility and gender roles holds that men and women who have traditional beliefs about gender roles are not opposite but similar to each other: Both accept stereotypical gender roles. This match might make people more compatible, because similarity is important in close relationships (Aubé & Koestner, 1995).

In studying gender roles and relationship stability, a longitudinal study (Peplau, Hill, & Rubin, 1993) followed dating couples beginning in the 1970s and continuing over 15 years. A great deal of variability in gender role attitudes existed during the 1970s; some couples held traditional attitudes and some believed in egalitarian relationships. Both members of a couple tended to be similar in their beliefs, but the men were more conservative than the women. No relationship emerged between satisfaction and gender role attitudes, with both traditional and egalitarian couples forming equally satisfactory relationships. Gender role traditionalism was more strongly related to relationship stability for the women than for the men. College women with traditional gender role attitudes were more likely to marry their boyfriends and to be married to them 15 years later than more liberal women.

Despite the opinion of adolescents that their dating is not oriented toward mate selection, dating is the process through which most men and women find partners. The patterns of relating to each other established during dating carry over into marriage, but marriage is a major life transition. When people marry, they assume the new roles of husband and wife.

Marriage and Committed Relationships

Marriage is not the only form of a committed romantic relationship. Both heterosexual as well as gay and lesbian couples cohabit without marrying. Gay and lesbian couples cannot legally marry in most places, and heterosexual couples sometimes choose to live together without marrying. For some heterosexual couples, cohabitation can be a type of trial for marriage, whereas others cohabit as a form of very steady dating. The number of cohabiting heterosexual couples has dramatically increased since the 1960s. Between 1965 and 1974, cohabitation preceded about 11% of marriages, whereas between 1980 and 1984, 44% of heterosexual couples lived together before they married (Brown & Booth, 1996). In the United States in the 1990s, around 4 million couples cohabit. However, the number of marriages far outnumber other types of committed heterosexual love relationships, and the majority of research on gender and committed relationships has focused on marriage.

Several styles of marriage now exist, following the patterns Cancian (1987) called the Companionship, the Independence, and the Interdependence blueprints. The Companionship blueprint discussed earlier was the model for most marriages in the United States from the 1920s until the 1960s. Partners who follow this pattern tend to have well-defined and separate gender roles, and women are responsible for maintaining the love relationship. This type of marriage is now considered traditional, because its adherents oppose self-development for women, a major tenet of the Independence blueprint.

The Independence blueprint arose during the 1960s, a period of personal freedom and change. Increases in paid employment for women and the women's movement led to an examination of the ground rules for relationships, and both men and women started to believe that marriage should be a partnership of equals. This model emphasizes self-development over commitment and obligations, holding that relationships are the meeting of two independent individuals. The emphasis on self-development resulted in less well-defined gender roles, and the concept of androgynous marriage arose. Cancian criticized this blueprint for encouraging empty relationships without sufficient commitment.

Interdependence is an alternative to the Independence blueprint. The Interdependence model also includes flexible gender roles but calls for commitment based on mutual dependence. Cancian argued that self-development and interdependence were compatible goals for relationships and that partners are always dependent on each other in marriage. Both the Companionship and Independence blueprints ignore this inevitable interdependence. Table 10.1 shows the three blueprints and the important characteristics of each. The Companionship blueprint proposed that women depend on men but ignores men's dependence on women, whereas the Independence blueprint discourages dependence: "Interdependent couples try to strike a balance between opposing forces—to have a relationship of equality

TABLE 10.1 Cancian's Blueprints for Love Relationships

	Companionship (devotion to each other)	*Independence* (self-development)	*Interdependence* (mutual dependence)
Are traditional gender roles maintained?	Yes	No	No
Is the relationship stable?	Yes	No	Yes
Who is responsible for maintaining the relationship?	Women	Neither partner	Both partners
Who develops personal interests?	Men	Both partners	Both partners

unconstrained by traditional gender roles and still depend on each other for emotional and material support" (Cancian, 1987, p. 131).

Sternberg's (1986) triangular model of love explains these different blueprints for marriage as differing in the three components of intimacy, passion, and commitment. Companionship-style marriages would have all three components but not in equal proportion for men and women. Under this blueprint women seek more intimacy than men, producing an unequal balance between such partners. As Cancian contended, the Independent blueprint lacks the component of commitment, but Interdependent marriages should fit what Sternberg called consummate love, the equal balance of all three components.

Marriages and other committed relationships may follow any of the blueprints, and contemporary couples may build any of these various types of relationships. Researchers interested in love have investigated gender and relationships, including men's and women's concepts of romantic love and marriage, communication between partners, division of labor in households, power and conflict in marriage, and the stability of love relationships.

Concepts of Love and Marriage

Contrary to popular expectation, men have more traditional concepts of love and marriage and are more romantic than women. Although men and women tend to choose partners who have similarly traditional or nontraditional beliefs about gender roles, the man of any given couple is likely to be more traditional than the woman and more likely than women to endorse statements like "Women's activities should be confined to the home" (Peplau & Gordon, 1985). This tendency for men to be more traditional concerning gender roles appears in many cultures (Hatfield & Rapson, 1996), but some research (Mirowsky & Ross, 1987) has indicated that these discrepancies become smaller through the years of marriage. The continued association of marriage partners does not produce identical beliefs, and the majority of the differences remain. Thus, even after years of marriage, husbands are more likely than wives to hold traditional, conservative beliefs about gender roles.

Despite the stereotypical view that women are the romantics, a review of the research (Peplau & Gordon, 1985) has indicated that men are more romantic than women. Men report that they fall in love earlier in relationships than women. Also, while women say that they would be more likely to marry someone they did not love, a majority of men say they would not marry without love. Men are also more likely to have romantic beliefs such as "Love lasts forever" and "There is one perfect love in the world for everyone." Women, however, are more likely to report physical symptoms of being in love, such as feeling like they are "floating on a cloud." This willingness to report on physical symptoms of love is the only sign of romanticism in which women exceed men. In most ways, men are more romantic than women.

Romanticism does not necessarily make men feel more favorably toward marriage. Men are supposed to elude marriage, considering it a "trap," whereas women plan and scheme to "land a husband." Jessie Bernard (1972) pointed out that this characterization is unfair, as men tend to profit from marriage more than women. Bernard contended that in any marriage there are actually two marriages—his and hers. She further argued that "his" marriage is more of an advantage to him than "hers" is to her. That is, marriage offers benefits to men that do not accrue to women. Married men are physically and mentally healthier than unmarried men, but married women are less healthy than their unmarried counterparts.

Married men report higher levels of life satisfaction and happiness than unmarried men, and studies have found few gender-related differences in marital satisfaction (Peplau & Gordon, 1985). Most of the studies of marital satisfaction have questioned only European American participants, and this choice has limited the conclusions about attitudes toward marriage (Ball & Robbins, 1986). Investigating marital satisfaction among African Americans showed that married African American women were more satisfied with their lives than single women. However, this difference in satisfaction disappeared when these researchers controlled for demographic factors such as age and health. That is, the positive attitudes about marriage may be attributable to factors associated with marriage, such as having a stable life and financial security, rather than to positive feelings about marriage itself. The life satisfaction of African American men, on the other hand, was lower among married than single men, and these differences did not disappear when controlling for demographic factors. These results suggest that African American men may differ from African American women and European American couples in their feelings of satisfaction in marriage.

Communication between Partners

The issue of communication in marriage has also been a topic for gender researchers. Indeed, it has become an industry—John Gray's (1992) *Men Are from Mars, Women Are from Venus* topped the bestseller list for years, prompting sequels, and allowing Gray to hold seminars and to train other counselors. His concept of men and women from different planets originated from his advise to women to communicate with their husbands as if they were beings from another planet. Gray's characterization of men and women from different planets is an overstatement of gender differences in communication, but differences do exist.

The same gender differences that researchers have found in friendship styles also influence communication in marriage: Women create emotional intimacy through talk and self-disclosure, whereas men do so through activity. In marriage, sex is often the activity that men use to create intimacy. Cancian (1987) argued that in most contemporary couples, wives do not count sex as communication or as a method for establishing intimacy. This difference can produce a discrepancy in what each thinks is the level of communication in their relationship. Her survey of couples revealed that wives value talking about feelings more than husbands, but husbands may feel threatened when their wives want to talk: "Talking about the relationship as she wants to do will feel to him like taking a test that she has made up and he will fail" (Cancian, 1987, p. 93).

Communication is a major task for couples, and the differences between men's and women's typical styles of communication provide one potential source of conflict in marriage. Deborah Tannen (1990) examined the barriers to communication for men and women, citing different strategies for men and women even when the goals are similar. Tannen argued that men and women see communication as "a continual balancing act, juggling the conflicting needs for intimacy and independence" (p. 27). She contended that women's communication is oriented toward intimacy, focusing on forming communal connections with others, whereas men's communication is oriented toward hierarchy, focusing on attaining and demonstrating status.

The differences in communication styles make it difficult for women and men to talk to each other. Both interpret the underlying messages as well as the words, and the differences in styles may lead men and women to understand messages that their partners did not intend to send. For example, Tannen cited an example of a husband who had failed to tell his wife about a pain he had been feeling in his arm. When his wife found out, she was very upset with him for withholding information, which was important to her. She felt excluded from his life. He had not intended to exclude her from anything important, but instead had wanted to protect her from worrying about his health. Tannen contended that such miscommunication is common for women and men and constitutes a persistent problem for couples.

According to Tannen, learning the conversational style of the other is not the answer to all communication problems. She described sensitivity training as an attempt to teach the conversational style of women to men and assertiveness training as a method for teaching the conversational style of men to women. Although flexibility of styles has benefits, Tannen expressed pessimism concerning changes in communication that would blend these divergent styles—both women and men like their way of communicating.

In addition to differences in styles of communication, influenceability is another factor in communication in intimate relationships. Research has indicated that men and women differ in ability to be influenced and styles of influence. Gender differences in influenceability can be understood in terms of power (Eagly & Wood, 1985). In laboratory experiments, few gender differences appear in people's ability to influence or be influenced, but outside the lab, women are more easily influenced than men. These differences may be a reflection of the subordinate role that women typically occupy in relationships with men. Subordinates are supposed to be easily influenced; it is part of the role. Their subordinate role is also a factor in patterns of communication in love relationships.

Thus, men and women emphasize different activities to establish intimate communication—self-disclosure for women and sex for men. These different strategies for establishing intimacy are not the only gender differences in communication. Women and men tend to use different verbal styles, with women adopting a communal, empathic style and men adopting a competitive, hierarchical style. These differences can cause misunderstanding rather than foster communication. No influence strategy is associated uniquely with men or women, but rather, the association occurs relative to the power in a relationship. As women are more likely to have the subordinate role in marriage, their subordinate status has an impact on their communication and influence strategies.

Division of Household Labor

The division of household labor has become an area of interest to gender researchers, and their results have revealed another potential source of conflict for couples. Traditional gender roles involve a division of labor in households, with men working outside the home for wages and women working in the home providing housekeeping and child care. This division arose during the Industrial Revolution, when men started working for wages rather than working in agricultural or home-based trades, and the association of household chores with women began. The separation of labor occurred when women did not work for wages outside the home, but throughout the 20th century, an increasing number of women have joined the paid workforce. Now, a majority of women, even those with young children, work for wages outside the home.

The changes in paid labor for women might have prompted a concomitant change in the division of housework, but instead, few changes have occurred in the division of household work. Sociologist Arlie Hochschild (1989) called this arrangement the Second Shift, an arrangement in which women work for wages outside the home plus perform the majority of housework and child-care chores at home. This arrangement can result in a situation in which women work the equivalent number of hours of two full-time jobs. According to one extensive review (Thompson & Walker, 1989), wives have two to three times more housework and child care work than husbands. Looking at the division of labor in a different way, only 10% of husbands do as much work at home as their wives.

One factor that changes the balance of labor around the house is the status of wives' careers (Bernardo, Shehan, & Leslie, 1987). Wives who hold professional or managerial jobs spend less time on household chores than women in less prestigious careers or wives who do not hold paying jobs outside their homes. Husbands whose spouses also work spend proportionally more time on household chores than other husbands, but they do not spend more hours than their wives doing housework. This situation possibly occurs because the wives in dual-career families spend less time doing housework than other wives, making the husbands' contribution proportionally more but not more in terms of absolute time. This finding suggests that wives who have professional or managerial careers do less housework. Because their husbands do not compensate by doing more chores, the housework either does not get done or is done by hired workers.

The types of household chores that men and women perform tend to be divided along gender-stereotypical lines: Women clean, cook, shop, care for children, do laundry, and straighten; men take out the trash, mow the lawn, garden, work in the yard, and make household repairs. This division is not only stereotypical but also allots women repetitive, routine, time-locked tasks while allowing men irregular chores that they can arrange to their convenience (Thompson & Walker, 1989). In addition, the timing of these chores differs during the day, with women's chores occurring both in the morning and during the early and late evening, whereas men often have leisure time during the evening. Men can often arrange their chores so that they can do them on the weekend, but women have daily housework as well as larger chores they do on weekends.

One measurement of the division of household labor confirmed the gender segregation of housework and the stereotypical nature of the division (Blair & Lichter, 1991). This analysis indicated that employment was not a significant factor in bringing about a more equitable division of household labor but that earning power was. Employment and earnings alter the power structure within marriages and thus alter the balance of housework—as women's wages increase, they perform less housework and their husbands perform more. Gender role stereotypes are important in perpetuating the division of labor in housework, but the power balance within a marriage is a factor in who does the dishes.

Gender role attitudes are also important in who does the dishes. Men are unlikely to do much household work unless both they and their wives hold egalitarian attitudes (Greenstein, 1996). That is, the interaction of husbands' and wives' attitudes determined whether or not husbands performed housework. When husbands or wives held traditional gender role attitudes, men did little work around the house. Even when men held egalitarian beliefs but their wives did not, men still avoided chores. Only the combination of both husbands and wives with egalitarian attitudes resulted in men performing a nearly equal share of household work—25% of the men performed 40% of the household work. Egalitarian attitudes are increasing, which may predict an increasingly equitable sharing of chores.

Married couples allot tasks primarily on the basis of gender, but gay and lesbian couples cannot use this strategy and use different methods to determine who does what chores (Kurdek, 1993). Both gay and lesbian couples tended to share household work more equitably than heterosexual married couples, but the patterns of sharing differed. Gay couples were more likely to split tasks, with each partner performing a set of chores. Lesbian couples were more likely to share tasks, taking turns in performing the same chores.

The division of household chores may be a source of conflict in marriage (Thompson & Walker, 1989). Between 25% and 33% of wives believe that their husbands are not doing a fair share of housework and want them to do more. These figures do not equal the discrepant contributions of husbands and wives, indicating that some wives are satisfied with the housework their husbands do even if the division is not equal. If wives do a disproportionate share of chores, husbands tend to be happier with their marriages. Perhaps some wives find the extra housework an acceptable price to pay for happier husbands.

On the other hand, some wives resent the disproportionate amount of housework they do. Wives who hold views of equal participation in housework for men and women and yet do more chores than their husbands might feel overburdened and perhaps have marriages at risk (McHale & Crouter, 1992). Husbands who hold traditional beliefs about segregation of household chores yet who are doing an equal share should also feel overburdened, and their relationships would also be at risk. Such wives and husbands rated their marriages less favorably than other spouses who felt less burdened, and for the wives, the feelings persisted over the time span of a year. The persistence of resentment may be a factor in the stability of marital relationships.

Division of chores can be a major source of marital conflict (Benin & Angostinelli, 1988). The greatest satisfaction occurred when the division of chores was almost equal (with wives doing more than husbands); both husbands and wives were dissatisfied with inequitable divisions of household labor. However, husbands wanted both an equitable division and a low number or hours spent doing housework, whereas wives wanted an equitable division and their husbands' help. These shared goals of equitable sharing of chores may not be compatible with the secondary goals for husbands and wives. Therefore, even a mutual desire to share household work may not allow husbands and wives to negotiate this problem.

The division of household labor may fall into traditional "masculine" and "feminine" tasks, or the division may be one of necessity dictated by the time constraints of women's work schedules. For example, women who work the evening shift may have to go to work immediately after an early dinner, leaving their husbands and families with the night-time chores. Shift work is more common in working-class than middle-class or upper-middle-class families, making working-class couples somewhat more likely to share equally in housework than more affluent couples (Thompson & Walker, 1989). Although working-class men do not have more egalitarian attitudes than other men, their family situations may result in a greater sharing of household work. Therefore, social class is an important indicator in family patterns of work.

The differences in division of household labor by social class and gender role attitudes may relate to the differences of power in these couples. Working-class wives' economic contributions are more essential to their families' subsistence than middle-class wives' salaries. By making essential contributions, these women may gain power in their marriages, and their husbands may respond to the more equal balance of power by sharing housework.

More equal contributions to family income related to shared household chores (Coltrane & Valdez, 1993). For middle-class Hispanic American couples, wives whose income made them coproviders were more likely to get their husbands' help than women who contributed less to family income. Husbands' assistance was not easy to get: Even the husbands who acknowledged the importance of their wives' income were often reluctant to do household chores and child care, using their own job demands as an excuse for not contributing to household work.

Wives who have high-status, highly paid employment (such as professional or managerial jobs), may also experience increased power in their marriages, and this increased power may give these wives the freedom to do less housework (Bernardo et al., 1987). When husbands and wives experience discrepancies in their attitudes about household labor, conflict may arise in the marriage. Therefore, the issue of household work may be related to both power and conflict within marriages.

Power and Conflict

Most dating couples believe that marriages should be an equal sharing of power and decision making, but the members of these couples acknowledged that their own relationships have failed to show an equal balance of power (Felmlee, 1994; Peplau & Campbell, 1989). Although a large majority of both women and men said that they believed each partner should have an equal voice in the relationship, just less than half reported equal power in their relationships. This finding suggests that, even before couples marry, the balance of power is unequal.

For those couples whose relationships are not equal in power, either the men or the women could have more power, but traditional gender roles dictate that the man will be the leader and head of the household. These traditional gender roles shape current relationships, and men are likely to have more power in marriages than women. According to an extensive survey of couples by Philip Blumstein and Pepper Schwartz (1983), almost 64% reported an equal balance of power. The remaining couples reported an unequal balance of power in their marriages—28% of husbands and 9% of wives said they had more power. Thus, for couples who do not share power equally, husbands are likely to say they have more power in the family than wives. Table 10.2 shows the ideal and actual power structure in couples.

One drawback of Blumstein and Schwartz's survey was the educational and ethnic composition of their sample: Many couples were college-educated and most were White. The

TABLE 10.2 Ideal and Actual Power Structure in Couples

	Peplau and Campbell Study (1989)		Blumstein and Schwartz Study (1983)
	Men	Women	Couples
Believe in equal power	87%	95%	
Have equal power	42	49	64%
Husband has more power			28
Wife has more power			9

concepts of **matriarchy** and **machismo** are associated with African American and Hispanic American families, respectively. A review of research on families, however, found that both patterns of unequal power were more myths than descriptions of the balance of power in these families (Peplau & Campbell, 1989). Although African American families are more likely to be headed by women than White families, Black couples do not have significantly different power relationships in the family than White couples. An equal sharing of power, the most common pattern in Blumstein and Schwartz's study, was also the most common pattern in African American couples. For couples with an unequal balance of power, male dominance was more common than female dominance. The same patterns appeared in Mexican American families, with the most common pattern being one of shared power. Therefore, some equal balance of power seems to be the rule for most couples.

Saying that couples exhibit an equal balance of power does not mean that both partners have an equal say in all decisions. Decision-making power may be divided along traditional lines, with men making financial decisions and women making household decisions (see Peplau & Gordon, 1985). What couples report as an equal balance of power may actually be a division of decision making into husbands' or wives' domains. This division may reflect wives' lack of real power; wives may be put into the position of making decisions that their husbands consider too trivial for their own attention. For example, wives may decide what to have for dinner and what brand of cleaning products to use, and husbands may decide which house to buy and where to live.

Paid employment is a factor in the balance of power in marriage. Women who do not have paid employment tend to have less power in their marriages than women who earn money (Blumstein & Schwartz, 1983; Peplau & Campbell, 1989; Peplau & Gordon, 1985; Steil, 1989). The amount earned is also a factor: Husbands who earn more money have more power, but wives' earnings show a complex relationship to their power. In working-class couples, wives who earn more money have more power, but middle-class wives may not gain power by making money (Thompson & Walker, 1989). These differences may have to do with the necessity of wives' earning income in the two social classes. Working-class wives' salaries are more likely to provide essential incomes, whereas middle-class wives' salaries may not be as necessary to their families. When husbands know the importance of their wives' salaries, this knowledge may give wives more or less power. In the rare families in which wives earn more than their husbands, however, the balance of power does not tip in the wife's favor. These couples tend to follow the male dominant tradition in their gender roles (Thompson & Walker, 1989), perhaps because wives abdicate the power that their incomes could give them. Therefore, wives' income has a curvilinear relationship to power in marriage; that is, wives who earn no income have low power, wives who earn more money have increased power to the point of equal incomes, but wives who earn more than their husbands exercise less power than their spouses.

Consistent with the income and power interpretation, Blumstein and Schwartz (1983) found that money was an important factor in the power equation for couples other than married couples. Blumstein and Schwartz studied not only married couples but also cohabiting couples—heterosexual as well as gay and lesbian. They found that money was an important factor in determining which partner had more power for all except the lesbian couples, who tried to maintain an equal monetary contribution in their relationship so as to avoid unequal power. The failure to do so was a source of problems for these women.

GENDERED VOICES
When I Got Sober

"The balance of power in my marriage didn't change when I went to work but when I got sober," a woman in her 40s told me. She had been a homemaker for a number of years before she started a career, and she said that earning money didn't make much of a change in her marriage. By the time she began her job, she had already started drinking heavily, and she continued to do so.

"Everybody took care of me, so I could drink and take drugs and get away with it. So I did. My daughter took care of me for most of her childhood. My husband also let me get away with being drunk most of the time. I was dependent on them, but then I got sober, and things changed.

"When I got sober, I started being able to take care of myself, and my family wasn't used to it. The balance of power changed in my marriage, and we eventually split up. I was sober and involved in AA, and my husband was still drinking, but that wasn't the main problem. I started to become independent, and he couldn't adjust. I realize that it was quite an adjustment: I had never taken care of myself—never in my life—and then I started.

"I remember one incident in particular. I was trying to change the batteries in my small tape recorder, and my husband came over and took the recorder out of my hands and did it for me. I thought, 'I can do that for myself.' I started thinking that about a lot of things. As I started to become more independent, our marriage changed. In fact, our entire family changed, and most of those changes were good. The kids could come to me rather than go to their father for everything. I became a responsible person. With that responsibility came a growing desire to be independent, and now I am. The marriage became an emotional power struggle, with my growing self-reliance and my husband still trying to be in control."

Some evidence suggests that men and women experience some differences in the sources of conflict and use different tactics to resolve conflict. Among recently married couples in one such study, the wives' most frequent complaint was that their husbands were inconsiderate, and the husbands' most frequent complaint was of their wives' moodiness (Buss, 1991). Not surprisingly, both husbands and wives who were low in emotional warmth, high in selfishness, low in security, and high in temper behaved in many ways that angered their spouses and caused conflict in the relationship.

Conflict management in couples shows gender differences in the ways that wives and husbands seek to understand their own and each other's behavior (Lavin, 1987). The husbands tended to take personal credit for both their positive and negative behavior, attributing them to stable internal traits, but husbands saw their wives' behavior as determined by unstable internal forces. Wives did not explain their husbands' behavior in different terms than they described their own. In this light, husbands would be likely to resist their wives' requests to change because as men their behavior reflects unchanging personality traits, whereas they believed wives should change in response to their requests because as women the wives' behavior is not only changeable but also under personal control. Lavin argued that the husbands' beliefs about conflict management gave them more power in the relationship; they could rightfully demand changes but could not reasonably be asked to change.

Women may be more eager than men to avoid conflict and preserve their relationships (Cancian, 1987), but women are more likely to bring up problems (Blumstein & Schwartz, 1983), perhaps in an attempt to correct them. Women's tendency to use emotional appeals to influence and win arguments can be seen as the same style of conflict management used by other subordinates (Thompson & Walker, 1989). That is, gender differences in resolving conflicts may be a reflection of the differential power within marriage relationships.

Wife battering illustrates both power and conflict in marriage. Historically, domestic violence has often been considered appropriate, with women as targets of marital (and even premarital) violence in many societies and throughout many time periods (Gelles & Cornell, 1990). Even though physical abuse is not the most common method of resolving conflicts in contemporary relationships, violence is not unusual between married or cohabiting partners. Both men and women use violence toward each other, but women are at a disadvantage in physical conflicts with men (Gelles, 1979). The rate of violence may be close to equal, but injury is not: Women are much more likely to sustain serious injury as a result of domestic violence.

Based on a national survey (Straus & Gelles, 1986), 16% of homes reported some kind of violence between spouses within the previous year. This figure represented a decrease from a similar survey in 1975 and includes minor violence, but 1 in 22 women in the United States were victims of abusive violence within the year preceding the survey. Discounting the acts of minor violence in domestic conflict is not wise; even minor violence is predictive of more serious violence between spouses (Feld & Straus, 1989). Furthermore, women who fight back are likely to escalate rather than halt the violence directed toward them.

Unfortunately, many people find violence between partners acceptable. About 25% of wives and over 30% of husbands found violence toward each other acceptable under some circumstances (Straus, Gelles, & Steinmetz, 1980). With these attitudes, the escalation of minor violence to abuse is not surprising, nor is it likely to change.

Marriages in which the partners have an equal balance of power are less likely to involve physical violence than marriages in which one partner is dominant (Thompson & Walker, 1989). Regardless of which partner has more power, both partners are more likely to be the targets of violence in couples with a dominant and a subordinate partner (Gelles & Cornell, 1990). That is, women are more likely to be battered in both female-dominant and male-dominant marriages, and men are more likely to be the targets of violence in not only female-dominant but also male-dominant relationships. Inequalities of power promote violent conflict in couples, putting both partners at increased risk.

Therefore, a connection exists between the issues of power and conflict in committed relationships. The majority of couples endorse equal power within their love relationships, but most also acknowledge that their relationships have not attained an equal balance of power. Men are more likely to be dominant than women, as they traditionally occupy the provider role and typically earn more money. Both gender roles and money affect the balance of power in relationships. Power also affects conflict and conflict management. Women tend to either avoid conflict or use emotional appeals to resolve conflict—tactics associated with subordinate status. When conflict results in violence, women are more likely than men to be injured in the confrontation. Both women and men find physical violence acceptable as a conflict resolution strategy under some circumstances, an attitude that perpetuates domestic violence. (See the Diversity Highlight: "Too Cool for Relationships.")

Stability of Relationships

Relationships that involve physical violence are less stable than those with no violence, but some of these violent relationships endure. Many people find it difficult to imagine why a

DIVERSITY HIGHLIGHT
Too Cool for Relationships

Coolness is a desirable trait in many modern social groups, but its origins can be traced back to ancient African civilizations (Majors, Tyler, Peden, & Hall, 1994). Coolness was associated with peace, but the contemporary meaning has changed, and now coolness is represented by a set of behaviors (Langley, 1994). This set has been labeled *cool pose* by Richard Majors and his colleagues (Majors & Billson, 1992; Majors et al., 1994). Cool pose is a way to present oneself, used as a compensation and coping strategy by African American men. The poses, postures, humor, readiness to use violence, and suppression of emotional displays are intended to create visibility for those who have been made invisible by a society that fails to grant African American men the status of European American men. The violence and suppression of emotion are elements of the masculine gender role, and cool pose uses an exaggeration of this role. This exaggeration allows African American men to feel a sense of masculinity.

Cool pose magnifies some of the destructive elements of the masculine gender role, creating problems for those who take this pose. The readiness to use violence as a means to deal with interpersonal conflict results in high rates of injury and death from violence. Indeed, homicide is the leading cause of death for young African American men (U.S. Bureau of the Census, 1996). Violence also intrudes into personal relationships, creating a higher rate of abuse of female partners by African American men than European American men (Majors et al., 1994). One of the situations that can precipitate a violent exchange is a perceived threat to masculinity.

The emotional remoteness that is essential to the cool pose also inhibits the development of intimacy, both with women and with other men. Although relationships with other men are important, these relationships are not close because they are governed by rules that keep men from sharing. This style of relating prevents genuine sharing of emotion and the creation of intimacy. Therefore, the cool pose with its exaggerated elements of violence and emotional isolation produces men who are even less willing to become involved in close relationships than men who do not take such a cool pose.

woman would stay with a man who repeatedly abuses her, though some women do. Abusive men often work to isolate their wives from family and friends, depriving them of social support and alternative residences (Gelles & Cornell, 1990). Abused women who are unemployed, with few marketable skills, and young children in need of the financial support may feel as though they have no options except to stay in the relationship, no matter how abusive. With the rise of shelters for women to escape abusive homes, abused women have an option, and thousands take this option each year.

Abusive relationships are an extreme case of conflict in love relationships, but all couples experience some level of conflict. These conflicts tend to decrease the stability of a relationships and increase the chances of the relationship ending. Blumstein and Schwartz (1983) found that couples who experienced conflicts over money, wives' employment, power, division of household labor, or sex were more likely to split up than couples who experienced fewer of these conflicts. They found that couples who were married were less likely to break up than cohabiting heterosexual, gay, or lesbian couples, but married couples also tended to have a lower level of conflict except in the early years of marriage. The institution of marriage holds couples together when they might otherwise dissolve their relationships. Couples who do not have the support of the institution behind them are thus more likely to part.

Similarity is not only a factor in attraction, it is also a factor in the stability of relationships. Dating couples are more likely to stay together if their attitudes match rather than conflict (Felmlee, 1994; Hendrick, Hendrick, & Adler, 1988). Members of a couple are not the only ones whose opinions should match; parents of dating couples can also contribute to the stability and progress of a dating relationship (Leslie, Huston, & Johnson, 1986). Mothers' opinions are most important, and young adults try to influence their mothers to think well of their partners. The more serious the relationship, the more frequent the attempt to convince parents of the partner's merits.

Congruence of partners' attitudes and values is also important in marriage (Blumstein & Schwartz, 1983). The similarity also extends to gender roles; married couples are happier if both partners have expressive ("feminine") rather than instrumental ("masculine") characteristics. That is, partners who are cheerful, warm, gentle, and understanding have happier marriages than those who are assertive, dominant, decisive, individualistic, and ambitious.

Conflict, even heated conflict, is not necessarily threatening to the stability of marriages. Indeed, some elements of conflict have been shown to strengthen relationships over the long run, whereas other factors are known to be destructive and predictive of separation or divorce. John Gottman and Robert Levenson (in Gottman, 1991; Levenson, Carstensen, & Gottman, 1994) have investigated the stability of marriages and found factors that predicted separation for young, middle-aged, and older couples. Surprisingly, their research indicated that marital satisfaction was not a strong predictor of separation, but the level of physical arousal during conflict was. That is, couples whose heart rates, blood pressure, sweating, and physical movement during an argument were elevated were more likely to separate within the next three years than couples with lower levels of arousal. Couples whose physiological reactions were calmer tended to have marriages that improved over a three-year span.

Behavioral factors also predicted divorce, including wives' tendency to be overly agreeable and compliant and husbands' tendency to "stonewall" by withdrawing emotionally, avoiding eye contact, holding the neck rigid, and being unresponsive to their wives during an argument. In their conversations, both members of couples who were likely to separate were more defensive; additionally, the wives complained and criticized more and the husbands disagreed more than did couples who remained together. The couples who were headed toward separation also showed different facial expressions during their conversations, the most important of which was wives' expressions of disgust. Husbands' fear also related to later separation, as did a facial expression Gottman called the "miserable smile," a smile that affected only the mouth, as when people try to "put on a happy face." Gottman concluded that the couples who would later separate were in the process of dissolving their relationship emotionally, and their physiological reactions, conflict tactics, and facial expressions signaled their impending separation. Table 10.3 summarizes these factors.

According to Sternberg's (1986, 1987) triangular theory of love, relationships that have only one of the components will lack stability. Two-component relationships will be less stable than those that have all three. Friendships will be less enduring if only intimacy is present, rather than intimacy plus commitment. Furthermore, love relationships that have

TABLE 10.3 Factors Relating to Marital Separation

Factor	Prediction
Marital satisfaction	No strong relationship to separation
Physical arousal during conflict—heart rate, blood pressure, sweating, moving	Higher levels predict increased likelihood of separation; calmer reactions predict strengthening of relationship
Wives being overly agreeable	Increased likelihood of separation
Husbands participate in housework	Increased satisfaction for husbands and wives; increased health in husbands
Husbands "stonewall"	Increased likelihood of separation
Wives criticize and complain	Increased likelihood of separation
Husbands disagree with wives	Increased likelihood of separation
Couples are defensive	Increased likelihood of separation
Facial expressions during conflict—"miserable smile," wives' disgust, husbands' fear	Increased likelihood of separation

two components will be more stable than those with only one. For example, romances that have only the passion component would not last as long as those with both passion and commitment. Indeed, passion alone is the classic "one night stand," whereas passion plus commitment is a "whirlwind courtship." A combination of all three components in equal proportion would offer the most stability, but maintaining all three components is difficult.

The commitment component of Sternberg's model is the most important for relationship stability. Commitment "can be essential for getting through hard times and for returning to better ones. In ignoring it or separating it from love, one may be missing exactly that component of loving relationships that enables one to get through the hard times as well as the easy ones" (Sternberg, 1986, p. 123).

Dissolving Relationships

Relationships go through phases of attraction, development, and sometimes dissolution (Duck, 1991). All relationships are subject to these stages, but people expect the dissolution of casual relationships and believe that such breakups pose no problems for the people involved. Unfortunately, even relationships with commitment sometimes fail to endure. When close friendships or love relationships dissolve, the end of such relationships poses problems for both people involved as well as for their social network of friends and family, who must make adjustments in their relationships with the members of the separated couple.

Love relationships without institutional support, such as cohabitation, are more likely to break up than are marriages. Only about 10% of heterosexual cohabiting couples live together long-term without marrying (Brown & Booth, 1996). In their study of couples, Blumstein and Schwartz (1983) found that married couples were more likely to remain together than cohabiting couples. In follow-up interviews 18 months after the initial interviews, they found that lesbian couples were most likely to have broken up and that married couples were least likely to have done so. Figure 10.2 shows the separation rates for the four types of couples in Blumstein and Schwartz's survey.

The institutional support for marriage is no guarantee of stability for such relationships. Although marriages have never been permanent, divorce has increased over the past 80 years (Hendrick & Hendrick, 1992). The rising divorce rate has resulted in approximately 50% of marriages ending in divorce. This divorce rate is not necessarily a condemnation of marriage as much as the failure of women and men to fulfill their vision of what they believe marriage should be.

In her extensive interviews with divorced men and women, Catherine Riessman (1990) found that both held an ideal of marriage as the fulfillment of three components: emotional intimacy, companionship and primacy (the belief that the relationship with the spouse constitutes the primary relationship), and sexuality. That is, these people's vision of marriage matches what Cancian called the Companionship blueprint for marriage. When they separated and divorced, women and men did not question the blueprint. Rather, they found fault in their own marriages, blaming either their former spouses or themselves for failing to fulfill some component of their marital ideal. Riessman's interviews showed the ways in which men and women found fault in their marriages and how they coped with separation and divorce.

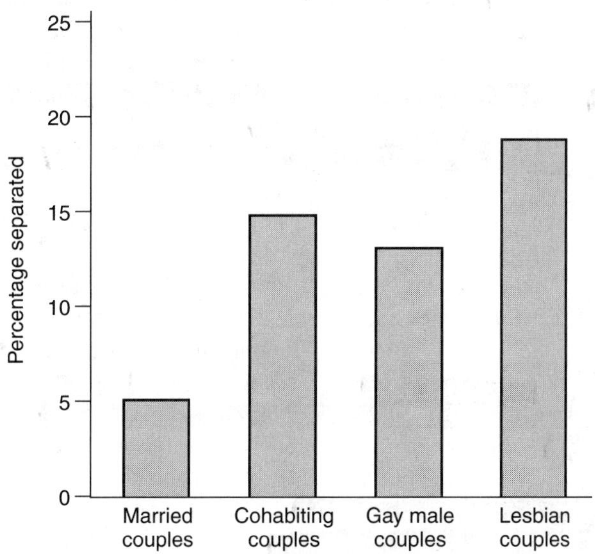

FIGURE 10.2 Separation Rates for Couples over an 18-Month Period

SOURCE: Based on *American couples* by Philip Blumstein & Pepper Schwartz, 1983, New York: Pocket Books.

GENDERED VOICES
I Wasn't Any of His Business Anymore

A woman, talking with her friend about her ex-husband, said, "I saw Ed at a country western club last Friday night. He was there with some of his friends, drinking. I went there because I wanted to get out and have some fun. He didn't see me at first, and then he kept looking in my direction, trying to make sure he was seeing right.

"Finally, he came over to me and said, 'What are you doing in a place like this? You shouldn't be here.' I told him that what I did wasn't any of his business anymore. We were divorced, and I could do what I wanted. I didn't need his permission to go to a bar, and he didn't have any right to say anything to me. He said some pretty ugly things, calling me a bitch and a whore, and I just walked away from him. I had enough of his ordering me around when we were married."

Although divorced men and women both described failures to live up to their ideals, their descriptions showed some variation according to gender and social class. Both women and men saw failures in achieving emotional intimacy, but each attributed the failures to different reasons. Two thirds of the women said that they did not get the emotional intimacy they expected from their husbands, which they defined as talking and sharing feelings. They claimed their husbands just didn't communicate with them.

Divorced men largely agreed with this assessment, blaming themselves for not communicating with their former wives and maintaining that they had difficulties in talking about their feelings and sharing the important elements of their work. One-third of the divorced men also believed that their wives had failed to give them emotional support, which they tended to define as physical affection. The working-class men repeatedly said that their wives were not waiting "with their arms open and a kiss" when the men came home from work. Such physical manifestations of intimacy were lacking, resulting in their feelings that their marriages lacked emotional intimacy. These gender-related differences reflected the talk-based versus action-based styles of showing support that are typical of women and men and highlighted the importance of these differences in the dissolution of relationships.

The divorced men and women also believed that their marriages had fallen short of the ideal in the second component of companionate marriage—companionship and primacy. Both the women and men in Riessman's study described differences in interests that prevented each from being primary companions for the other, and both reported that they felt slighted by this lack of shared interests. The discrepancy of leisure interests was a factor in this problem, especially for working-class women whose husbands' involvement with sports was a common complaint. The men reported that their wives' devotion to friends, family, and children was a problem; these other relationships made the husbands feel that they did not come first. The women did not resent such other relationships of their husbands, but some described their husbands' work as an intrusion, especially middle-class women whose husbands had prestigious, time-consuming careers.

Sex is the third component of the companionship model of marriage, and the divorced people in Riessman's study mentioned problems with sex in connection with their divorce.

GENDERED VOICES

My Ex-Wife Acts Like We're Still Married

"Although we were divorced three years ago, my ex-wife acts like we're still married," a man in his mid-30s said. "I understand why she calls me when something involves the kids, but she calls me when she needs things done to the house." He considered these requests inappropriate because he and his ex-wife had both remarried. "I can't help it if she married a wuss who can't fix the toilet. I don't think she should be calling me to do the chores. We're not married anymore, and taking care of her house is not part of my job now."

The men mentioned dissatisfaction with the frequency of sex and resentment over their wives' refusal to have sex as often as husbands had wanted. Sexual affairs were a factor in 34% of the divorced people in this study, and both women and men believed that affairs had been the impetus for the dissolution of their marriage. The women took their own as well as their husbands' affairs as a sign of emotional betrayal, signaling that their marriage was over. The men did not necessarily share that attitude, but they also acknowledged that affairs had been a factor in their divorces. Wives found it difficult to forgive husbands' affairs, and wives who had affairs tended to leave their husbands for their lovers.

These feelings suggest that women might be the ones to initiate breakups; research (Duck, 1991) has confirmed this finding, stating that women initiate 80% of the breakups of heterosexual couples. This gender difference may be due to women's tendency to be more vigilant about monitoring their relationships so that they know when something is going wrong more quickly than men. This finding highlights a substantial asymmetry in love relationships: Women fall out of love more quickly and fall in love more slowly than men.

Women and men both experience different lives after the dissolution of a love relationship. For couples who have been married or have cohabited, the dissolution of the relationship is usually financially as well as emotionally difficult. Women's lower earning power, coupled with their custody of children, tends to create financial hardship, whereas men's financial position tends to improve after divorce. Studies show that divorced women experience a 73% decline, whereas men experience a 42% increase in their standard of living a year after their divorces (Weitzman, 1985).

Both men and women find positive as well as negative consequences as a result of the divorce experience (Riessman, 1990). Both women and men said they enjoyed the freedom that came with divorce, but their feelings had different sources: Women liked being free from their husbands' dominance, whereas the men liked being free of their wives' expectations. The women in Riessman's study experienced more positive as well as more negative emotions in connection with their divorces than the men. All of the women found something positive in the experience, whereas 15% of the men found nothing positive about their divorces. The women experienced more symptoms of depression, but they also discovered heightened self-esteem and feelings of competence through performing activities their husbands had done when they were married.

Dissolution of marriage often deprives men not only of companionship and emotional support from their wives but also of their children and of their network of friends and family (a network typically maintained by women). Women tend to use these support networks after divorce, but men do not. The men in Riessman's study were surprised at the difficulties of being alone, but they also described feelings of satisfaction from their developing competencies in domestic chores.

Divorced men and women are likely to feel displeased with their ex-spouses rather than with marriage itself, and most showed their endorsement of marriage by remarrying. With the growing acceptability of cohabitation, some divorced people choose to live with a new partner rather than marry; cohabitation is also a form of trial marriage for some of these couples, who married after living together for one or two years (Blumstein & Schwartz, 1983). Some evidence exists that the second marriage is less traditional than the first, with a more equal balance of power and a more equal sharing of decision making and household chores (Furstenberg & Spanier, 1984). Second marriages are even more likely to end in divorce than first marriages, which Riessman interpreted as an increased unwillingness to endure an unhappy relationship combined with the knowledge that divorce offered positive as well as negative experiences.

Summary

Women are often put into the role of emotionally managing the relationship they have with men because women tend to have a style of relating that emphasizes emotional sharing and intimacy. Women's friendships are more likely to be based on emotional intimacy and sharing, whereas men are likely to develop a style of friendships based on activities. These gender differences in friendship styles appear early in development. Children voluntarily segregate themselves according to gender and resist attempts at interaction before age 5, possibly because girls are fond of talking and sharing secrets and boys tend to enjoy active games. Even the girls and boys who do not like their gender-typical activities are not welcome in cross-gender groups.

Adolescents are more concerned with developing emotional intimacy in their relationships, but girls emphasize this aspect of relationships more than boys. Although young men say that they value intimacy in relationships, they often find it difficult to develop such relationships, especially with other men. Some men develop emotionally intimate love relationships with women, and such relationships often decrease the amount of time and emotional energy men have to devote to male friends. Friendships tend to be tied to developmental stages of life, and marriage and the birth of children tend to restrict friendships.

Cancian has argued that love has become feminized. The current concept of love is emotional intimacy—a pattern closer to the typical relationship for women than for men. This definition slights the styles of intimacy men tend to adopt—the activities of providing help and doing things together. Some research has indicated that both men and women have a flexibility of friendship styles and that they use different styles to relate to male and female friends. Cross-gender nonsexual friendships are a recent phenomenon, and both men and women acknowledge that such relationships require special rules.

Love relationships currently form through dating, an activity that first arose during the 1920s as a response to changing patterns of mate selection. Dating has now become not only a method of courting but also a forum for recreation, socialization, and sexual exploration. Adolescents tend to choose dates similar to future mates, preferring dates who are kind, considerate, socially exciting, intelligent, and physically attractive. People with either heterosexual or homosexual orientation describe their preferred partners in similar ways, but men emphasize the importance of physical attractiveness more than women.

Currently, marriage and other committed relationships can follow several different blueprints—Companionship, Independence, and Interdependence. The Companionship blueprint involves separate gender roles and emphasizes the woman's role in maintaining a love relationship. Both the Independence and

Interdependence blueprints emphasize self-development for both men and women, but they differ in the importance of commitment.

Gender researchers have explored several issues in love relationships, including beliefs about love, communication, division of household labor, power and conflict, and relationship stability. Men are more romantic in their conceptualization of love than women, and marriage tends to benefit them more, but they are not necessarily happier with their marriages. Men and women may have trouble communicating in love relationships, partly because their styles and goals of communication differ, with men trying to establish independence and dominance and women trying to share feelings and make connections.

The division of household labor is usually unequal in marriages: Women perform far more of this work than men, even when women have paid employment outside the home. The ideal pattern of household work for both partners is closer to an equal distribution than exists in most marriages, but both women and men feel satisfied with women performing a disproportionate share. When women do most household work and hold outside jobs, their disproportionate work load may be a source of conflict. Although paid employment is a source of power, both partners do not usually have equal power in a marriage. Couples experience conflict from many sources, but some marital conflict results in violence. Over 25% of women and men find violence acceptable in their personal relationships under some circumstances, but women are more likely to be injured as a result of relationship violence.

Violence decreases the stability of relationships but does not necessarily end them. Stable love relationships tend to occur in couples with similar attitudes and values, and the commitment factor in marriage produces greater stability than in other love relationships. Even marriages dissolve, and divorce has increased in the past several decades. People who have divorced tend to see the fault in their ex-spouses rather than in the institution of marriage. Although divorce brings financial and emotional problems, most women and men also find positive factors in divorce. Most remarry, and some evidence suggests that both women and men form more equitable second marriages.

Glossary

companionate love a combination of commitment and intimacy without passion.

gross motor skills skills involving use of large muscles of the body, producing large movements, such as throwing, kicking, running, and jumping.

homophobia the unreasonable fear and hatred of homosexuality.

machismo a Spanish word meaning strong and assertive masculinity and implying complete male authority.

matriarchy a family pattern in which women are dominant or a pattern in which women are the head of the household due to the father's absence.

Suggested Readings

Blumstein, Philip; & Schwartz, Pepper. (1983). *American couples.* New York: Pocket Books. Although not recent, this book examines the relationships of all types of couples—married and cohabiting heterosexual partners as well as gay and lesbian couples. Through interviews with couples, Blumstein and Schwartz explore attitudes toward power, money, and sex, and their impact on individual happiness and relationship stability.

Gottman, John, with Nan Silver. (1994). *Why marriages succeed or fail.* New York: Simon and Schuster. Gottman's popular book summarizes his research on factors related to success and failure in marriage. In addition, he includes self-quizzes so that couples can assess their relationship.

Hatfield, Elaine; & Rapson, Richard L. (1996). *Love and sex: Cross-cultural perspectives.* Boston: Allyn and Bacon. Hatfield and Rapson's book examines love and sex across contemporary cultures as well as delving into history for additional examples. They consider attraction, the difficulties of forming relationships, and the problems involved in ending romantic relationships. Their cross-cultural and historical review adds a valuable (and fascinating) point of view to the understanding of passionate love.

Maccoby, Eleanor. (1990). Gender and relationships: A developmental account. *American Psychologist, 45,* 513–520. Maccoby summarizes and reviews the research on gender differences and similarities in social interactions and relationships. Her developmental approach includes children, adolescents, and adults, and this brief review is easy to read.

Chapter 11

Sexuality

HEADLINE

In the Dark

—*Men's Health,* December 1995

Michael Lafavore (1995, p. 71), editor of *Men's Health* magazine, contended that men are often "in the dark" when it comes to sex: "In the Dark Ages, men got their health information from barbers.... Nowadays we live in the Information Age. But when it comes to information about our sexual health, we're still getting our advice at the barbershop, so to speak. Most of what we know about sex we learned as teens, most likely from other teens who knew as little as we did."

Lafavore discussed the problems of men's sex education, saying that men face several barriers in knowing about sex. Despite the pervasiveness of sexual themes in the media, very little of this coverage is oriented toward dispersing useful information, especially about sexual problems. Also, men receive so many negative messages about their sexuality: "At every turn, male sexuality is portrayed as something bad: something dark and dangerous and in need of containment" (p. 71).

Men's Health conducted a survey (Bechtel & Stains, 1995) of its readers, and those results revealed men who differ from the popular conception. These men reported that women's personality was more important than beauty in attractiveness; sense of humor was more important than breasts. Over half the men thought sex was very important to a long-term relationship, but fewer than 20% thought sex was essential to such a relationship. The majority said that their sex lives were good or excellent. Do these results provide a more accurate picture of male sexuality than other depictions? How does this survey compare to other surveys? Does male and female sexuality differ in ways that are similar to the popular conceptions?

The Study of Sexuality

Researchers who want to know about sexual behaviors and attitudes have several options in choosing a method of investigation. They may question people about their sexual behavior, as *Men's Health* did, or they may directly observe people's sexual behavior. Both of these approaches present scientific, practical, and ethical problems.

Those researchers who choose to question people about their sexual behaviors or attitudes are using a method called the survey method. Chapter 2 described surveys, along with their advantages and disadvantages. One limitation is especially relevant to sexuality research: Some people feel that sex is a private, personal issue and do not want to share this information with researchers. These people refuse to participate in sex surveys, and they very likely differ from people who are willing to answer questions about their sexual attitudes and behavior. Potential participants who refuse to cooperate can bias results because their opinions are systematically excluded.

Another possibility for investigating sexual behavior is through direct observation of sexual activity. Most people are even less willing to participate in this type of research than in a survey, but nonhuman animals have (or at least have voiced) no such objections. The problems with generalizing results from these studies to humans are even more serious than with generalizing from one group of humans to another. Nevertheless, this strategy has been useful, adding breadth to the study of sexual behavior. A prominent example of this type of research appears in *Patterns of Sexual Behavior* (1951) by anthropologist Clellan Ford and psychologist Frank Beach. These two researchers presented not only a cross-cultural study of human sexual behavior but cross-species comparisons as well.

Only a small percentage of people have been willing to have sex in a research laboratory. Such participants allowed William Masters and Virginia Johnson (1966) to study human sexual behavior in ways that no other researchers had managed. Not only were Masters and Johnson's participants willing to answer questions about sex, they were willing to have sex in the lab and to have their physical responses measured during the activity. Although the results of Masters and Johnson's research have become widely accepted, their participants were less typical of the general population than those of any of the major surveys, a situation that Masters and Johnson considered unimportant but that others have criticized.

Thus, although researchers who want to study sexual attitudes and behavior have several options; most researchers have surveyed people about their attitudes or behavior or both by asking questions and recording the responses. The problems with survey research include finding a **representative sample**—a group of people that reflects the characteristics of the general population—as well as securing truthful and accurate responses. Despite the problems connected with surveying people about sex, this approach has been the most common one. Several magazines other than *Men's Health* have undertaken sex surveys. All of these surveys suffer from the problem of **self-selection of participants.** When participants rather than researchers choose who is to complete the survey, then the sample is not representative. Such surveys can still reveal interesting and important information, but self-selected participants prohibit researchers from generalizing the results to the general population.

Sex Surveys

Before Alfred Kinsey's ground breaking survey of men's and women's sexual behavior in the 1930s and 1940s, several other investigators had compiled reports on sexuality (Brecher, 1969). Henry Havelock Ellis, a British physician, wrote a series of books between 1896 and 1928 in which he detailed the differences in sexual customs of various cultures and collected sexual case studies of women and men. These studies led him to the conclusion that the Victorian social norms of repression and denial of sexuality that he saw around him were not reflected in people's sexual behavior. Ellis came to believe that sexual behavior was varied and complex: "Everybody is not like you and your friends and neighbors," and even, "Your friends and neighbors may not be as much like you as you suppose" (in Brecher, 1969, p. 39). Ellis was one of several sex researchers in the 1800s who was important in making sex an acceptable topic for scientific research, and this research helped to end the sexual repression that was the standard of that time.

Historian Carl Degler (1974) discovered an unpublished sex survey conducted by Dr. Clelia Duel Mosher, a physician who began questioning women in the United States about their sexual behavior and enjoyment in 1892. Although Mosher's sample size was small—only 45 women—and far from representative—all were college students—the responses indicated that sexual repression might not have been as common as Victorian standards held. About half of the women reported that they had no knowledge of sex before their marriages, but 35 of the 45 women reported sexual desires, and 34 of the 45 said they experienced orgasm. This small, unrepresentative sample might not reveal the average woman's attitudes for that time, but the existence of women who enjoyed sex seems to contradict the prevalent view of the Victorian period. The marriage manuals of the day portrayed women as lacking in sexual feelings, but after examining Mosher's data, Degler warned against relying on the marriage manuals of the Victorian era to understand female sexuality during that time.

Several other researchers completed small-scale sex surveys during the early 1900s. The most famous of the surveys on sexual behavior were those completed by Kinsey and his colleagues.

The Kinsey Surveys

In 1920, biologist Alfred Kinsey took a position as instructor at Indiana University. In 1937, he began to teach a newly created course in sex education, which at that time was a controversial topic. Kinsey found that little systematic research existed on sexuality, and this gap prompted him to begin such research. He started collecting data in 1938 with a preliminary interview that he later expanded to include extensive information about nine areas: social and economic background, marital history, sex education, physical characteristics and physiology, nocturnal sex dreams, masturbation, heterosexual history, history of same-gender sexual activity, and sexual contact with animals. Each of these areas included subdivisions, making the interview extensive and time consuming. Amazingly, Kinsey completed more than 7,000 such interviews himself. His associates, Wardell Pomeroy, Clyde Martin, and Paul Gebhard, conducted other interviews, for a total sample of 17,500 (Brecher, 1969).

Although the interviews were extensive and large numbers were conducted, the sampling procedure did not yield a representative sample of people in the United States. Kinsey's sample was drawn primarily from the university and the surrounding community. He did not necessarily strive to obtain a representative sample—his goal was to test as great a variety of people as possible. He accomplished that goal, but his sample did not allow generalizations to all U.S. residents. Kinsey questioned African Americans, but he excluded their data from his analysis because he knew that the individuals he had questioned were not a representative group. This choice further biased his results. His final groups of 5,300 men and 5,940 women were therefore White, well-educated, mostly from Indiana, and largely Protestant.

Kinsey was skilled at getting a wide variety of people to talk with him candidly about their sexual histories (Brecher, 1969; Hyde, 1990). His technique included asking questions that required participants to deny rather than admit a practice, such as "At what age did you first experience full intercourse?" This approach assumed that everyone had done everything. Perhaps this strategy helped to make people more comfortable and encouraged them to tell the truth. Reinterviewing some participants 18 months after their first interview revealed that people supplied consistent information about their sexual behavior, which indicated to Kinsey that they were telling the truth. Some inconsistencies appeared, but of the type primarily due to memory lapses rather than intentional deception. Thus, Kinsey's surveys managed to overcome some problems associated with survey research.

The results from Kinsey's surveys appeared in two parts, *Sexual Behavior in the Human Male* (Kinsey, Pomeroy, & Martin, 1948) and *Sexual Behavior in the Human Female* (Kinsey, Pomeroy, Martin, & Gebhard, 1953). The results surprised (and even shocked) many people, because the participants reported such a wide variety of sexual behaviors, including some that were socially unacceptable and even illegal. Kinsey's reports appeared during a time when sex was not a topic of polite conversation; when women were supposed to be reluctant to have sex; and when same-gender, premarital, and extramarital sexual activities were illegal in many areas.

Kinsey's results indicated that women enjoyed sex; that many men had participated in male–male sexual behavior; that children experienced sexual excitement and activity; and that masturbation, premarital, and extramarital sex were common for both women and men. Around 90% of the women in the study had experienced orgasm by age 35 years. Of the 10% who had not, another 8% reported experiencing sexual arousal, leaving only 2% of women who had failed to enjoy sexual activity, a figure much lower than most people imagined.

Some of Kinsey's most controversial findings concerned same-gender sex. People with sexual partners of their own gender have objected to the term *homosexual,* a term that Kinsey used to describe male–male and female–female sexual behavior. The term has become stigmatized because it highlights the sexual aspect of these individuals' lifestyle. A relationship with a same-gender partner is much more than sexual (Blumstein & Schwartz, 1983), and other terms have replaced *homosexual.* The term **gay** is an alternative that many find preferable and which may apply to both men and women, but it is more often used for men. The term **lesbian** refers to women who have sexual relationships with other women.

A total of 37% of the men in Kinsey's survey reported at least one sexual experience with another man; that is, an experience with another man that led to orgasm. This figure included men who had sexual experiences with other men only as young adolescents and men who had only one such experience. Some of these men reported that they no longer felt sexual attraction toward other men or had no subsequent sexual experiences with other men. When considering the men who had sexual experiences only with other men (4%), only with men for a period of three years or longer (4%), and predominantly with men (5%), the total reached 13%. Both the percentage of men who had some type of sexual experience with other men (37%) and the percentage of men who primarily or exclusively had sex with other men (13%) were higher than previous estimates (Brecher, 1969). Kinsey's figures on female sexual activity with other women were similar to the figures for men, but the percentages were smaller. That is, few women reported exclusively lesbian (3%) or primarily lesbian (4%) sexuality, but a larger number (28%) had at least some sexual experience with other women. Table 11.1 shows these figures.

TABLE 11.1 Percentage of Participants Reporting Sexual Activities in Three Sex Surveys

	Kinsey Surveys (1948, 1953)		*Playboy Foundation Survey (1974)*		*National Opinion Research Council (1994)*	
Sexual Activity	Men	Women	Men	Women	Men	Women
Masturbation to orgasm	92.0%	58.0%	94.0%	63.0%	—	—
Masturbation before age 13	45.0	14.0	63.0	33.0	—	—
Masturbation during marriage	40.0	30.0	72.0	68.0	57.0%	37.0%
At least one homosexual experience	37.0	28.0	—	—	7.1	3.8
Primarily homosexual orientation	13.0	7.0	2.0	1.0	4.1	2.2
Premarital intercourse	71.0	33.0	97.0	67.0	93.0	79.0
Extramarital sex	50.0	26.0	41.0	18.0	< 25.0	< 10.0
Sexual abuse during childhood	10.0	25.0	—	—	12.0	17.0

These figures for the frequency of same-gender sexual attraction and activity are at the center of a continuing controversy. Kinsey's figures for the number of men who primarily or exclusively have sex with other men are not only higher than previous estimates, they are also higher than later estimates (Hunt, 1974). A recent biography of Kinsey (Jones, 1998) contended that Kinsey's figures were biased by his personal interest and participation in sexual activity with men and his desire to portray these sexual activities as common. He, therefore, chose to question a disproportionate number of gay men, inflating the figures for this type of sexual activity.

Many participants in the Kinsey survey reported that as children they had sexual feelings and sometimes acted on those feelings. The most common type of childhood sexuality was **masturbation,** manipulation of the genitals to produce sexual pleasure. Infants and young children masturbate, some to orgasm. A total of 14% of the women and 45% of the men in Kinsey's survey said that they had masturbated before the age of 13 years. They also remembered other-gender and same-gender exploratory play with peers as well as sexual contact with adults. Men recalled preadolescent intercourse more frequently than women. Almost one fourth of the women recalled incidents during which adult men had shown their genitals, touched them, or attempted intercourse. Over half of these incidents involved acquaintances or family members. The recollections of adults of their childhood sexual activities are most likely not completely accurate, but Kinsey's results suggested that children experience sexual curiosity and exploration as well as sexual abuse by adults.

Kinsey's survey revealed that masturbation was a common sexual activity. Although the percentages of people who reported preadolescent masturbation were not large, the activity increased during adolescence, and by the time they were adults, almost all of the men and about two thirds of the women had reached orgasm by masturbating. Married women and men told Kinsey that they continued to masturbate, although they also had sex with their spouses. Around 30% of married women and 40% of married men reported that they masturbated. These figures contradicted the popular notion that masturbation was primarily a practice of adolescence and that people with a sexual partner no longer masturbated.

Kinsey surveyed people who lived in a society that accepted different sexual standards for men and women. Although both were supposed to be sexually inexperienced before marriage and to have sex only with their spouses, men were not held to this standard but women were. This **double standard for sexual behavior** has a history that stretches back at least a century, and Kinsey found evidence for it in the different rates for both premarital and extramarital sex. By 25 years of age, 83% of unmarried men but only 33% of unmarried women said that they had participated in intercourse. A similar discrepancy occurred in the reports of extramarital affairs—that is, about half the men but only 26% of the women admitted extramarital affairs.

In summary, Kinsey and his associates interviewed thousands of men and women during the 1930s and 1940s to determine the sexual behavior of people in the United States. They questioned a variety of people but not a representative sample, so the results have limitations. Kinsey's results suggested that people engage in a wide variety of sexual activities, beginning during childhood. He found that most women experience orgasm and that masturbation and extramarital sex are common. In addition, Kinsey's results showed that more than one third of men have had some type of sexual experience with another man but that few were exclusively gay. The reports of female–female sexual activities were less common but with parallel findings: Few women were exclusively lesbian, but more had past or occasional sexual experiences with other women. After the Kinsey reports, many other sex researchers have chosen the survey method of investigation.

Hunt's Playboy Foundation Survey

In the 1970s, the Playboy Foundation commissioned a survey of sexual behavior in the United States, and in 1974 Morton Hunt reported the results in his book *Sexual Behavior in the 1970s*. The researchers involved in this survey wanted to update the Kinsey findings, and they attempted to obtain a more representative sample than Kinsey had managed.

The survey began with a sample of people randomly drawn from the telephone books of 24 U.S. cities, which is not a representative sample. In addition, 80% of those contacted declined to participate, which further biased the sample. Despite the problems with the sampling procedure, Hunt contended that the sample matched characteristics of the U.S. population in terms of ethnic background, education, age, and marital status. The 2,026 participants filled out a lengthy questionnaire about their backgrounds (including sex education), attitudes toward sex, and sexual histories. A total of 200 also participated in an even more lengthy interview that was similar to the Kinsey interviews.

As Table 11.1 shows, this survey confirmed the prevalence of masturbation found by Kinsey but found a higher rate of preadolescent masturbation, and rates of masturbation similar to those Kinsey reported by the time people reached adulthood. Hunt found a lower percentage and a different pattern of same-gender sexual activity than Kinsey. He concluded that most such activity occurs as a form of adolescent experimentation, with most of the women and men who had same-gender sexual experiences discontinuing this form of sexuality by age 16 years. Hunt estimated that 2% of men and 1% of women were exclusively gay or lesbian in their sexual orientation.

Hunt found some evidence for a sexual revolution in the form of increases in certain sexual activities. More unmarried people had engaged in intercourse than the Kinsey surveys reported. A total of 97% of the unmarried men and 67% of the unmarried women reported having intercourse by age 25 years, representing an increase in intercourse and a decrease in the double standard. According to Hunt, by the 1970s extramarital sex was more common, especially among younger women.

The Playboy Foundation survey also found evidence that more people were engaging in a wider variety of sexual activities than Kinsey reported. For example, a higher percentage of respondents in the Playboy Foundation survey reported oral–genital sexuality than in Kinsey's surveys. **Fellatio** is oral stimulation of the male genitals, and **cunnilingus** is oral stimulation of the female genitals. Kinsey found a difference in popularity of oral–genital sexuality according to educational background, with such activity more likely among college-educated people (60%) as compared to those with a high school education (20%) or a grade school education (10%). Hunt reported that 90% of the young married couples in his survey said they had engaged in oral–genital stimulation, revealing a dramatic increase in prevalence and a leveling of social class differences.

In summary, Hunt's Playboy Foundation survey attempted to obtain a representative sample of U.S. residents and question them about their sexual attitudes and behavior. One of the goals was to complete an interview similar to Kinsey's technique so as to furnish updated comparisons. This survey showed that Kinsey was correct in concluding that people's sexual behavior is more varied than the social norms suggest, and it confirmed the prevalence of masturbation and childhood sexuality. Hunt's estimates for same-gender sexuality were much lower than Kinsey's figures, but Hunt found evidence for an increase in premarital, extramarital, and oral–genital sexual activity.

The National Opinion Research Center Survey

Two major sex surveys appeared during the 1990s, one conducted by Samuel and Cynthia Janus (1993) and the other by a team headed by Edward Laumann, John Gagnon, Robert Michael, and Stuart Michaels (1994) for the National Opinion Research Center (NORC). Although both groups claimed that theirs was the first survey to obtain a representative sample of adults in the United States, the NORC survey relied on a random sampling technique rather than on volunteers. After collecting their information, Laumann and his colleagues compared their sample to information known about U.S. adults and concluded their group was representative.

The NORC survey revealed a slightly different picture of sex in the United States than either the Kinsey or Hunt surveys had shown. One difference manifested itself in the continuation of the trend toward more liberal sexual standards, with sex serving as an important factor in love relationships (regardless of marital status) or as a recreational activity (without any necessity for a committed relationship). Only around 30% of respondents expressed the traditional, conservative view that sex outside marriage is always wrong and that procreation is the main reason for having sex.

The other difference expressed in the NORC survey indicated some degree of conservatism concerning sex. For example, a low percentage of participants reported attraction to and practice of a variety of sexual behaviors. Indeed, the NORC survey found that vaginal intercourse was not only the most frequent form of sexual activity with a partner but also the most appealing to both men and women. Giving and receiving oral sex and watching a partner undress were at least somewhat appealing to a majority of participants, but group sex, anal intercourse, sex with strangers, and forcing or being forced to do something sexual were not appealing to the majority of participants.

This survey also found gender differences in sexuality, just as the other surveys had done. One large gender difference related to the experience of first intercourse: 28% of women but only 8% of men said that they did not want to have intercourse at the time but went along out of affection for their partners or were forced. Men also reported more varied sexual interests and behavior, including more lifetime sex partners and a slightly higher interest in group sex, anal intercourse, watching others do sexual things, visiting sex clubs, viewing sexually explicit books or videos, and giving and receiving oral sex. Men were more likely to masturbate, but women were more likely to report feeling guilty about masturbating. Table 11.1 presents information from this survey.

"The general picture of sex with a partner in America shows that Americans do not have a secret life of abundant sex (Michael, Gagnon, Laumann, & Kolata, 1994, p. 122). The most common category for frequency of intercourse was *a few times a month,* and only about 7% reported having sex four or more times a week. In addition, about two thirds of both men and women said that they had only one sex partner within the past year, with reports showing only small variations across different ethnic groups, religious affiliations, or educational levels. The NORC survey reflected a less sexually varied United States than the media or people's imaginations often present.

Gender Differences (and Similarities) in Sexual Attitudes and Behavior

The three major sex surveys have shown gender differences in several sexual behaviors and in some attitudes toward sexuality. Although the more recent surveys have indicated a smaller difference in sexuality of men and women, even the NORC report indicated that men are more sexually active at a younger age than women. A meta-analysis (Oliver & Hyde, 1993) revealed that gender differences exist in some aspects of sexuality but not in others.

Two large gender-related differences emerged from this meta-analysis: incidence of masturbation and attitudes toward casual premarital sex. Studies of male adolescents and adults have indicated a higher rate of masturbation and a greater acceptance of casual premarital sex than for female adolescents and adults. These researchers pointed out that the magnitude of the differences for these comparisons surpasses other gender-related differences, such as those in mathematics or verbal abilities. (See Chapter 5 for a discussion of these cognitive differences.) The greater acceptance of casual premarital sex applies to men in a variety of cultures, including Canada, Africa, Hong Kong, Sweden, and all ethnic groups in the United States (Hatfield & Rapson, 1996).

Gender-related differences in other aspects of sexuality were smaller, and some of the meta-analysis (Oliver & Hyde, 1993) comparisons failed to show gender differences. Of the differences that appeared, men reported being, and actually were, more acceptant of sexual behaviors than women. Small differences also appeared in the acceptance of premarital and extramarital intercourse, sexual permissiveness, number of sexual partners, and frequency of intercourse. In addition, men reported feeling less sexual guilt or anxiety than women. Analysis of acceptance of the double standard for sexual behavior indicated, ironically, that women believed in the double standard more than men. No gender differences appeared in attitudes toward same-gender sexuality, rights for gays or lesbians, attitudes toward masturbation, incidence of oral sex, or sexual satisfaction. Table 11.2 shows some of the behaviors and attitudes from this meta-analysis, along with the magnitude of gender-related differences.

TABLE 11.2 Sexual Attitudes and Behaviors Showing and Failing to Show Gender-Related Differences

Sexual Behaviors/Attitudes	Direction of Difference
Large Differences	
Incidence of masturbation	Higher for men
Acceptability of casual sex	Higher for men
Moderate to Small Differences	
Acceptability of sexual permissiveness	Higher for men
Incidence of sex in committed relationships	Higher for men
Incidence of intercourse by engaged couples	Higher for men
Acceptability of premarital sex	Higher for men
Age at first intercourse	Lower for men
Frequency of intercourse	Higher for men
Incidence of same-gender sexual experiences	Higher for men
Anxiety, fear, and guilt associated with sex	Higher for women
Acceptability of double standard of sexual behavior	Higher for women
Acceptability of extramarital sex	Higher for men
Number of sexual partners	Higher for men
No Differences	
Incidence of oral sex	
Incidence of kissing	
Incidence of petting	
Acceptability of masturbation	
Acceptability of same-gender sexuality	
Belief that gays and lesbians should be given civil rights	
Sexual satisfaction	

Changes over time were also among the results of the meta-analysis (Oliver & Hyde, 1993): All gender differences showed signs of becoming smaller over time. Thus, this analysis confirms the trends that appeared in the comparison of the three major surveys, as shown in Table 11.1—that is, a decrease of differences between men's and women's sexual attitudes and behavior, along with some persistent differences.

Masters and Johnson's Approach

As noted earlier, researchers who want to observe sexual behavior directly can conduct their studies on nonhuman animals, or they can enlist the cooperation of people who are willing to engage in sex in a research laboratory. Although such participants are far from average, they might furnish important information about the physiology of sex. Other researchers have taken this approach, but the most famous of these have been William Masters and Virginia Johnson.

Masters began his study of the physiology of the sexual response in the 1950s by interviewing prostitutes (Brecher, 1969). However, he was interested in taking measurements during sexual activity and considered prostitutes unsuitable participants because of their atypical sexual behaviors. He sought volunteers from the medical community in St. Louis and found people who were willing to masturbate or have intercourse while being observed in the laboratory. During the time Masters was recruiting participants for the laboratory studies, he also recruited Virginia Johnson to assist him with the interviewing, and she became an essential part of the research.

Masters and Johnson chose a total of 694 people to serve as research participants, including 276 married couples as well as 106 single women and 36 single men. These participants not only had to be willing to have sex in the lab, but the researchers selected women who regularly experienced orgasm, a criterion that restricted the sample of participants. All participants received payment for their participation, resulting in an overrepresentation of medical school students who were interested in contributing to scientific research and who also needed the money. These criteria and procedures were reasonable but resulted in a sample that was far from representative. Masters and Johnson were not as concerned with drawing a representative sample as other sex researchers. They believed that the physiological sexual responses they were studying varied little from person to person; thus, any sample should include the characteristics of interest to them. Lenore Tiefer (1995) argued that Masters and Johnson's selection of participants biased their results. In addition, she contended that they knew what they wanted to find and interpreted their data according to their preconceived notions, forcing the sexual experience into stages that are not necessarily appropriate for everyone.

In these laboratory studies, the married couples had intercourse, masturbated each other, or engaged in oral–genital stimulation. The unmarried participants did not have sex with a partner; the men masturbated and the women either masturbated or were stimulated by an artificial penis designed to measure vaginal responses during sexual arousal and orgasm. In addition to collecting information by measuring genital activity during sex, Masters and Johnson gathered physiological measurements such as heart rate, muscle contraction, and dilation of the blood vessels from both women and men.

Masters and Johnson measured physiological responses during more than 10,000 orgasms and presented their findings in *Human Sexual Response* (1966). Their findings suggested that four phases of sexual excitement exist—excitement, plateau, orgasm, and resolution. The two researchers contended that these four phases describe the sequence and experience of sexual arousal and orgasm for both women and men. Figures 11.1 and 11.2 show the four phases and how the organs are affected in both women and men.

The *excitement phase* refers to the initial physiological responses for sexual excitement—erection of the penis in men and the clitoris in women. The responses of both men and women are produced by vasocongestion, the swelling of tissues due to engorgement of the area with blood. The penis and clitoris are not the only areas affected; the testes, nipples, vaginal opening, and labia also swell, and the skin may become flushed. The vaginal walls secrete lubrication, and the heart rate, blood pressure, and muscle tension increase.

A leveling off of sexual arousal occurs during the *plateau phase,* with fewer dramatic changes than those experienced during the excitement phase. In women, the outer third of the vagina swells while the inner part expands. The clitoris withdraws beneath its hood, becoming shorter, and secretions from Bartholin's gland appear. The labia minora deepen in color. In men, the penis may enlarge slightly more than in the excitement phase, and it turns a deep purple color. The testes elevate further, and the Cowper's gland secretes a small amount of fluid that appears at the tip of the penis. Heart rate, blood pressure, and muscle tension increase slightly. Flushing of the skin is even more likely to occur in this phase than in the excitement phase.

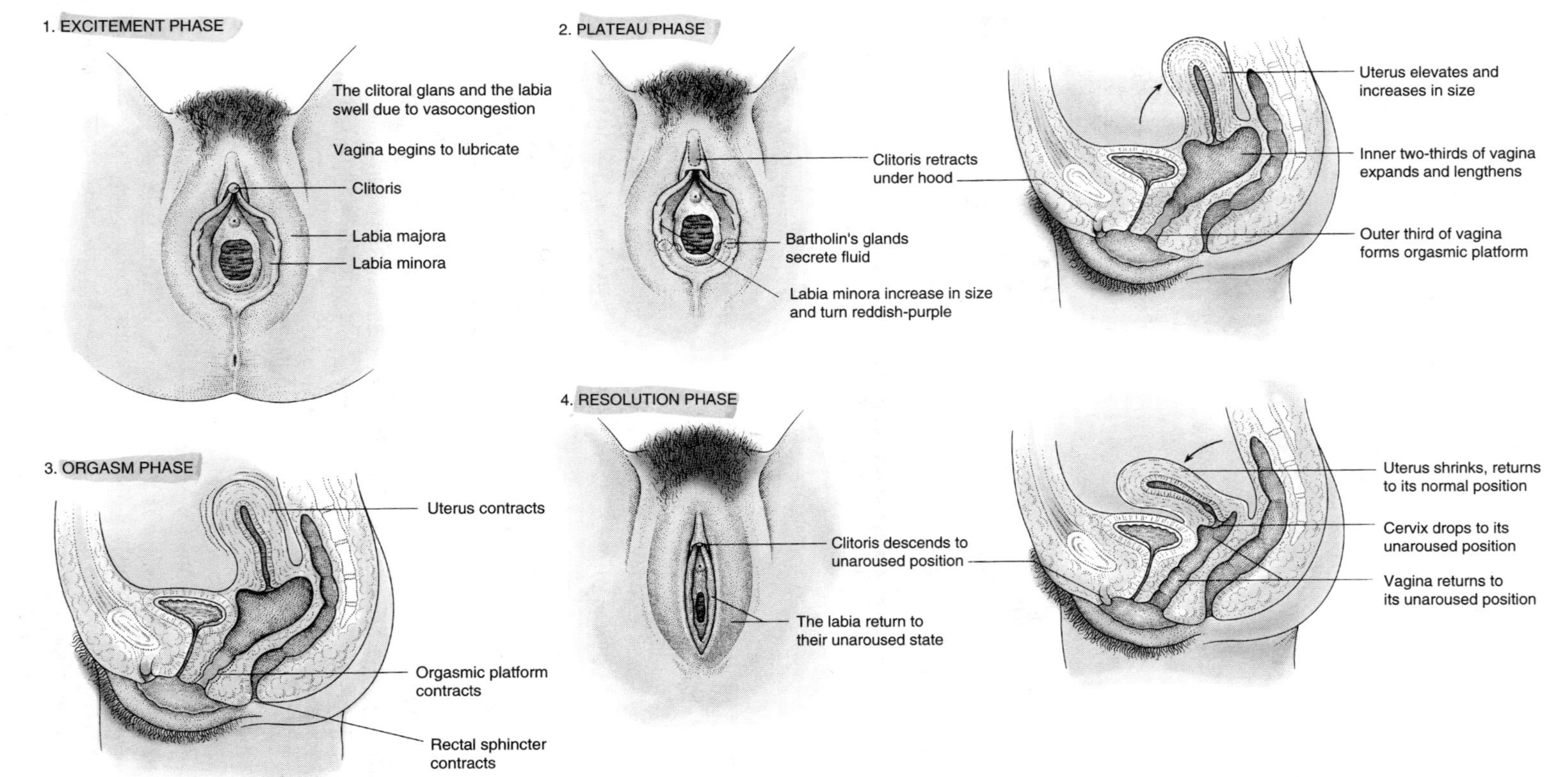

FIGURE 11.1 Female Genitals during the Phases of the Sexual Response Cycle

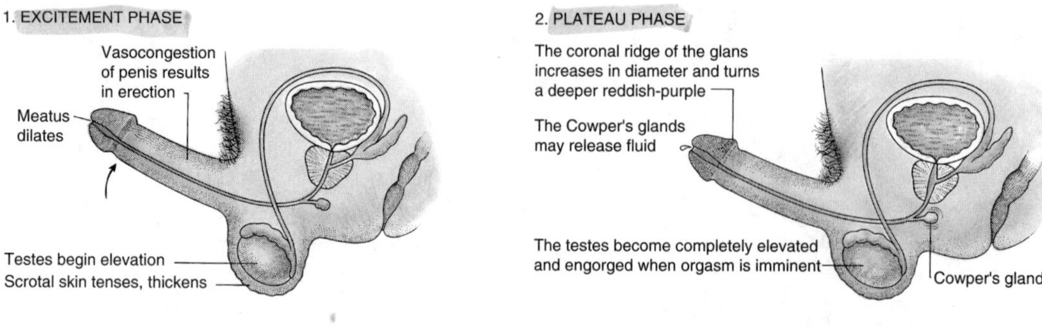

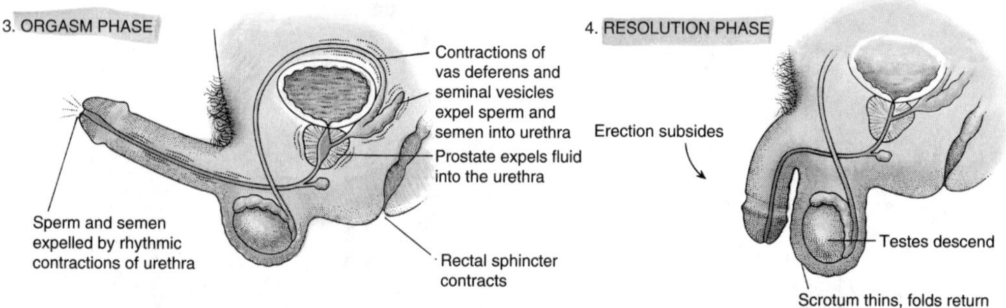

FIGURE 11.2 Male Genitals during the Phases of the Sexual Response Cycle

The *orgasm phase* for both women and men consists of muscle contractions at 0.8-second intervals, releasing the tension that has built up during the first two phases. In women, between 3 and 15 contractions occur in the muscles that surround the vagina, and an additional three to six contractions may also occur, although these are weaker and slower. In men, orgasm occurs in two stages. In the first stage, seminal fluid collects in the urethral bulb due to muscle contractions of the vas deferens, seminal vesicles, and ejaculatory duct. In the second stage, semen is ejaculated from the body through the urethra due to a series of three or four muscle contractions at 0.8-second intervals, possibly followed by several additional slower contractions. For both women and men, other spasmodic muscle movements occur for muscles in the abdominal region and throughout the body. Heart rate and blood pressure also peak in this phase.

In the *resolution phase,* the body returns to its normal prearousal level. In women, the clitoris, vagina, labia, nipples, and uterus all return to their normal sizes. In men, the penis loses its erection over a period of about a minute, and the testes and scrotum return to normal size. Both women's and men's skin returns to its normal, low level of flush. All of these responses are part of the decreased vasocongestion that occurs in this phase. The muscle tension has been dissipated during the orgasmic phase, and the decrease of vasocongestion returns to prearousal levels. This process may take as long as five minutes after experiencing orgasm, but for those who do not experience orgasm, return to prearousal functioning may take as long as an hour.

Not only did Masters and Johnson's research suggest that both women and men are similar in experiencing four stages of sexual response, it also showed that women experience one type of orgasm. Freud hypothesized that women experience two types—clitoral and vaginal orgasm. He believed that girls experience clitoral orgasm during masturbation, beginning during early childhood, and that women are immature if they continue to require clitoral stimulation for orgasm. Freudian theory described women who experience orgasm through intercourse as healthier and more mature than women who have only clitoral orgasms. Masters and Johnson's results showed that women experience only one type of orgasm—a clitoral orgasm. Their data provided no evidence for different types of orgasms, thus refuting Freud's contention that two types of orgasm exist. Some women have clitoral orgasms during intercourse and some do not; intercourse may not provide sufficient clitoral stimulation to produce orgasm in some women.

Masters and Johnson's research has been both controversial and influential. As with other physiological processes, individual variations exist in whether stages are experienced, which Masters and Johnson ignored (Tiefer, 1995). Their conceptualization has become so well-accepted that people who do not conform to these stages are open to diagnoses as having sexual dysfunctions. According to their findings, all people experience four phases of sexual response—excitement, plateau, orgasm, and resolution. Their research proclaimed similarities in sexual response for women and men but failed to address issues of individual differences. Their findings about the physiology of sexual response showed that women have one type of orgasm produced by clitoral stimulation, but they failed to test women who did not easily experience orgasm. The Masters and Johnson research has been valuable in measuring sexual physiology, but their research findings may not be as universal as they have contended.

Childhood Sexuality: Exploration and Abuse

As the Kinsey, Playboy Foundation, and NORC surveys have shown, sexuality begins before puberty. Even as infants, children take part in sexual exploration, and they are sometimes the victims of sexual abuse. Before birth, male fetuses have erections; infant boys have erections and infant girls experience erections of the clitorides as well as vaginal lubrication (Masters, Johnson, & Kolodny, 1992). Infants touch their genitals as they explore their bodies, and this exploration teaches children that their bodies can produce pleasurable sensations. Preschool-aged children masturbate, sometimes several times a day.

Parents who notice their children's masturbation may accept it, or they may be surprised or shocked. Their attitude and their method of dealing with their children's masturbation can convey positive or negative messages about sexuality, and these messages can have a permanent impact (Masters et al., 1992). Parents who say, "That's not nice" or "Nice boys and girls don't do that" or who move their children's hands away from their genitals send negative messages about sexuality.

Another aspect of childhood sexuality that may make parents uncomfortable revolves around their children's questions about sexuality, pregnancy, and birth as well as their children's sexual exploration with other children. By age 4, most children have begun to form a concept of gender and the roles that women and men occupy. Part of this knowledge is that women have babies and men do not, and pregnancy and birth are topics that stimulate curiosity and questions. Parents may feel embarrassed about giving straightforward descriptions and resort to analogies such as "Daddy plants a seed inside Mommy." Due to their concrete thought processes, children have the tendency to misinterpret these fanciful descriptions and analogies (Masters et al., 1992). For example, children may interpret the seed analogy literally, believing that women have small plots of dirt inside their bodies in which men plant seeds that one or the other must water and weed so that the seeds will grow into babies.

The entire story of reproduction may be too complex for preschool children to assimilate, so simple, correct explanations usually satisfy children and avoid confusion. Due to children's tendency to invent and fill in the details of stories they do not fully understand, concealing information will not keep children from "knowing" about sex. But what they "know" may be incorrect. Therefore, formulating appropriate answers to young children's questions about sex and birth requires a delicate balance of providing the correct amount of information without excessive details. Parents' discomfort with the topic of sex complicates these discussions.

"I would love for him to grow up to be a doctor, but I sure wish he'd wait another twenty years to specialize in gynecology," the mother of a 5-year-old said (Segal & Segal, 1993, p. 131). This mother humorously expressed her concern over her son and the neighbor's daughter who were exploring each other's genitals. The Segals explained to the mother that her son's explorations were more curiosity than sexuality and that his behavior was normal. They advised this mother to set limits on her son's explorations and urged her not to be concerned about her son's curiosity about female genitals.

Punishing children for exploring their sexuality can convey the message that something is wrong with the genitals, giving negative messages about sexuality. Masters et al. (1992) contended that sexual explorations during preschool or elementary school are rarely harmful but warned that parental punishment can be, and can leave a permanent impression that something is wrong with such activities. They also argued that the double standard for sexual behavior starts during this age range, with girls being warned about sexual explorations and sex play and boys being allowed more freedom in their sexuality.

Parents may be unaware that sexual explorations during childhood include same-gender as well as other-gender sexual play (Masters et al., 1992). In addition, parents are not aware of most sexual contact between siblings. The majority of such contact consists of examining the genitals and touching, and a low percentage of sibling sexual activity includes attempted or successful intercourse. Nonetheless, sexual activity between siblings qualifies as **incest**—sexual activity between family members. David Finkelhor (1980) reported that 15% of college women and 10% of college men recalled sexual experiences with their siblings. The majority of these college students did not believe that the experience had harmed them, but an important factor in this evaluation was the age difference between the two siblings; a large age difference was associated with a greater perception of harm.

Age has been a critical factor in defining sexual exploitation of children (Finkelhor, 1984). When sexual contact occurs between children who are close to the same age, this activity falls into the category of *exploration.* When a child has sexual contact with an adult or an adolescent at least five years older than the child, that activity falls into the category of *exploitation* or *sexual abuse.* Also included as abusive are sexual relationships between adolescents and adults whose age exceeds the adolescents' age by at least 10 years.

GENDERED VOICES

My Parents Never Said Anything until...

"My parents never said anything to us about sexual abuse until my brother was molested," a teenager said. "Then our whole family talked sexual abuse. My brother had to tell us what happened, tell us what the person had done very explicitly. Maybe that wasn't a good thing for him to have to do, because he had to talk about it a lot, but we learned about what to be careful about. And they never said anything before he was molested.

"It was tough on the family, because the person who molested him was a cousin. He was about 4 or 5 years older than my brother, and our families don't speak to each other anymore. It was hard to know what to do, because the cousin had been molested when he was younger, so he was just repeating what happened to him. Should he be punished for doing what he had learned? My brother was still hurt, but it was difficult not to feel sorry for my teenage cousin.

"We went for counseling as a family, and I think it helped. I hear that it can be much worse to ignore it, because it won't go away if you don't talk about it. We talked about it afterward, but not before something happened."

Incest is one form of sexually abusive relationship, but children can also be sexually abused by nonrelatives, including strangers and adults in positions of authority, such as neighbors, day-care workers, priests, and teachers. Kinsey's (1948, 1953) surveys included questions about childhood sexual experiences with adults, and his results revealed that 25% of girls and 10% of boys reported such contact. In over 50% of the cases, the activity consisted of an adult man exhibiting his genitals to the child. Kinsey also found that over half of the incidents involved adults whom the children did not know. Later research on the sexual abuse of children has confirmed the high percentage of abuse and the gender difference in rates of sexual abuse, but it has failed to confirm that most abusers are strangers.

Beginning in the 1970s, several groups of researchers attempted to determine the rate of sexual abuse of children. This research is even more difficult than other types of sex surveys. The honesty and memory problems that affect all surveys are more serious when adults are asked about sexual abuse during childhood; honesty is a major problem when questioning adults about abuse they may have committed. Those who sexually abuse children are capable of convincing themselves that the relationships are "special" and have not harmed the child (Gilgun, 1995), which can led them to distort their reports of the events.

Assessment of childhood sexual abuse has been conducted with a wide variety of people in different geographic locations using varying definitions of sexual abuse and several differing research methods (Bagley & King, 1990). These variations resulted in differing percentages of people who reported being sexually abused as children, with percentages ranging from 11% to 40% for women and from 3% to 8.6% for men. Due to the sampling techniques in the various studies, these percentages might be underestimates, as at least 15% of girls and 5% of boys are sexually abused during childhood or adolescence.

Despite the differences, the studies reviewed (Bagley & King, 1990) showed some commonalties: Girls were sexually abused more often than boys, and men were the instigators of abuse far more frequently than women. Both girls and boys are at risk during their entire childhoods and adolescence from family members, family friends, adult authority figures, and strangers, but the risk is not equal for all ages or from all adults. Table 11.3 shows the range of estimates and the characteristics of sexual abusers and victims.

Girls are not only more likely to be sexually abused, but they are more likely to be abused at younger ages than boys. The preadolescence years are the riskiest age period for both, with girls between ages 10 and 11 years and boys between ages 11 and 12 years at the highest risk. These ages represent the time during which the first victimization is most likely to occur. For many children sexual abuse continues for years, often for as long as they remain in contact with their abusers.

Between 94% and 100% of those who abused girls were men, and around 84% of those who abused boys were men. Although abusers are sometimes strangers, more often these men are known to their victims as family members, family acquaintances, or adult authority figures such as teachers, scout leaders, or priests. Ethnic differences exist in sexual abuse

TABLE 11.3 Summary of Offender and Victim Characteristics for Childhood Sexual Abuse

	Range of Estimated Occurrence	
Characteristic	Lowest	Highest
Girls abused while under age 16 (average age 10.2–10.7 years)	11.0%	40.0%
Girls who rated the experience negatively	66.0	
Girls whose abuser was male	94.0	100.0
Boys abused while under age 16 (Average age 11.2–12 years)	3.0	8.6
Boys who rated the experience negatively	38.0	
Boys whose abuser was male	83.0	84.0
Children whose offender was a stranger	11.0	51.0
Children whose offender was a friend or an acquaintance	33.0	49.0
Children whose offender was a relative	14.0	50.0
Girls whose offender was a sibling	15.0	
Boys whose offender was a sibling	10.0	
Children whose offender was a biological parent	1.0	6.8
Girls whose offender was a stepfather	7.6	17.0
Children who had force or threats used against them	55.0	
Children whose abuse consisted of exhibition	26.0	28.0
Children whose abuse consisted of being fondled	26.0	40.0
Children whose abuse consisted of forced fondling of offender	10.0	14.0
Children whose abuse consisted of intercourse	15.0	18.0

SOURCE: Based on *Child sexual abuse: The search for healing* by C. Bagley & K. King, 1990, London: Tavistock.

for African American and European American women, and abusers tend to choose victims within their own ethnic group—in 81% of the cases ethnic backgrounds of victim and abuser matched (Wyatt, 1985).

Both female and male abusers exist, but the emphasis in research and therapy has been on boys and men as perpetrators and girls and women as victims. This emphasis is not entirely inappropriate because most sexual abuse follows this pattern. The pattern of female–male abuse differs from the male–female pattern. Whereas male strangers represent approximately one third of the cases of male abusers, almost all of female abusers are acquaintances of those whom they molest. A common pattern among female perpetrators consists of babysitters molesting the children in their care (Johnson, 1989). In addition, female perpetrators are very likely to have themselves been the victims of abuse, most commonly by a family member.

The scant research on female perpetrators and male victims has demonstrated that many of the instances of such abuse occur in the pattern Toni Johnson (1988, 1989) found—abused girls who molest younger children when in positions of authority over them. But some women victimize boys in the guise of initiating them into sexuality, and these cases are rarely reported to authorities (Sleek, 1994), making the proportion of male abusers seem higher than it actually is. Another type of female abuser includes those who are coerced by men into committing the abuse, and yet another type includes adolescent girls who commit sexual abuse as part of their initiation into gangs. The overwhelming focus on female victims and male perpetrators has left sexually abused men and sexually abusive women neglected in both research and treatment. However, this situation is beginning to change.

Incest involving biological fathers and their daughters is not the most common type of sexual abuse: stepfathers are much more likely to force this type of relationship. Diana Russell (1986) found that 17% of stepdaughters were molested by their stepfathers, whereas only 2% of daughters were victims of sexual abuse by their biological fathers. Indeed, living with a stepfather is a major risk factor for sexual abuse. Other research (Finkelhor & Baron, 1986) came to similar conclusions. Living with a stepparent increased the risk for abuse, and this risk was proportionate for all ethnic and social class groupings. In addition, living apart from biological parents or having a mother who was unavailable due to illness, handicap, or employment increased the risk for abuse. Children whose parents had relationships filled with conflict and whose parents used harsh punishment as discipline were also at elevated risk for sexual abuse.

Cases of father–daughter incest have serious, long-term consequences for the daughters, who often have difficulties in school and in their personal relationships, sometimes throughout adulthood (Herman, 1981). Some evidence exists for both the short-term and long-term effects of sexual abuse (Browne & Finkelhor, 1986; Finkelhor, 1990). The short-term effects include fear, anxiety, depression, anger, and sexually inappropriate behavior, and the long-term effects include anxiety and depression and also poor self-concept, sexual adjustment problems, and substance abuse disorders. A review of sexually abused boys (Finkelhor, 1990) found that few gender differences exist between boys and girls who have been the victims of sexual abuse; both suffer similar negative effects from their victimization.

In one study (Herman, 1981) the fathers who committed incest tended to be traditional men who held unquestioned authority in their families and considered sexual activity with their daughters to be part of their right as the head of the family. Although this pattern of sexual abuse is not the most common, it suggests the underlying commonalty in child sexual abuse—power. Adults have social power and power in the family, and this power allows them to abuse children. The family structure usually grants more power to men than women, and this power differential may be an important reason for the gender difference in perpetrators.

In summary, childhood sexuality is more active than most parents imagine; it begins during infancy when children explore and manipulate their own genitals and then progresses to curiosity about and exploration of others' genitals. Although parents may find these signals of sexuality distressing, they are normal. Sexual explorations during childhood are confined to activities with peers; when older adolescents or adults initiate sexual activity with children, this is abuse. Various surveys have asked adults about their experiences of being molested as children, with the results indicating that at least 15% of women and 5% of men have been sexually abused as children. Girls are much more likely to be abused than boys, and men are much more likely than women to be abusers. There are few gender differences in short-term and long-term effects of childhood sexual abuse, which include anxiety, depression, and anger, as well as adult sexual and substance abuse problems.

Heterosexuality

Most people develop erotic or sexual interests that result in attraction to people of the other sex rather than people of the same sex. That is, most people develop a heterosexual rather than a same-gender **sexual orientation.** Signs of heterosexual erotic interest may begin during childhood, but childhood sexuality is difficult to characterize. Sexual activity during childhood mainly takes the form of masturbation and exploratory play, which can be directed toward same- or other-gender children. Thus, children's sexuality often is not clearly heterosexual.

During late childhood and preadolescence, children seek the company of same-gender peers and avoid associating with other-gender peers (see Chapter 10). This gender segregation restricts the opportunities for heterosexual activity but does not signal children's lack of interest in the other gender. Indeed, children often tease each other by announcing who "likes" whom and by threatening to kiss others who are unwilling (Thorne, 1993). Such games demonstrate an awareness of heterosexuality and an early knowledge of gender roles in heterosexual interactions.

During Adolescence

Although a distressing number of children are introduced to sexuality through force or coercion, adolescence is the period during which most people explore sexuality. These explorations consist of formal and, as Lafavore (1995) pointed out, far more informal educational programs. The traditional view in the United States and many other societies has situated sexuality within marriage, which discourages adolescent sexual activity. These cultures also send many messages about sex and its pleasures, which pose problems for adolescents who see the promised joys of sex but who are forbidden to participate. These messages are not equal for girls and boys: Girls receive many more messages to beware of sex than do boys.

GENDERED VOICES
Sex De-Education

"A shiver goes up my spine remembering my 'sex education' experience in the sixth grade. Now, I don't know if the teacher had some problems with sexuality in general, or if perhaps it was part of her job, but I'll never forget the fear of sex and sexual contact she put into about 95%, if not all, of the young girls in that class.

"The majority of the information was in reference to reproduction and sexually transmitted diseases. My teacher brought in this old, old medical book and proceeded to show these pictures of people with severe stage STDs. These pictures showed people with ulcerated sores all over their bodies; parts of their flesh were falling and she said, 'This is what happens to people who have sex when they're not married.' It was disgusting, not to mention terrifying.

"As if that wasn't bad enough, when she taught the section on the male genitalia, she brought another visual aid. She brought in a rubber replica of a male penis and testicles, and the thing was HUGE and she represented it as actual size. I've never heard so many young girls gasp in terror at the same time in my life. She was very quick to relay how painful sex with a man was. I never understood her motivation. She was married with three kids. Maybe her husband was that big, but it seems unlikely.

"To this day, I still wonder how many of these young girls were traumatized by their 'sex education' and how that affected their first sexual encounter with a man. I've also wondered what techniques were used to teach the boys in our school."

Although a double standard of sexual behavior is sharply apparent in adolescent sexuality, according to Lafavore (1995), boys also experience less than adequate sexuality education. His headline article contended that, although men figure out how to have sex, they have no resources to help them develop their sexuality. Other critics (Fine, 1988; McCormick, 1994; Whatley, 1990) have made similar accusations regarding sex education for girls. Publicity about teen pregnancy, date rape, and sexual exploitation conveys the impression that sexuality is dangerous, especially for young women, and this danger has been the focus of most sex education. Rather than emphasizing the pleasures of sex and how to develop successful sexual relationships, most sex education for teenagers focuses on abstinence as the best choice and pregnancy, sexually transmitted diseases, and vulnerability to rape as the alternatives.

This emphasis would appear to be successful in conveying a sense of sexual vulnerability in young women, because research (Burt & Estep, 1981) has indicated that feelings of sexual vulnerability develop during adolescence. The men in this study expressed few feelings of sexual vulnerability compared to the women, suggesting that boys get different messages than girls about their sexuality. Boys get negative images of male sexuality, however, and this portrayal was one of Lafavore's criticisms of sex education.

Although adolescents are exposed to sex education that does not help them develop healthy sexuality, they begin sexual exploration through several avenues, one of which is dating. When adolescents start dating, opportunities for sexual activity increase. A small percentage (2 to 17%) of adolescents in one study (Roscoe, Diana, & Brooks, 1987) listed sex as the motivation for dating. For the 6th graders, 11th graders, and college students in the study, boys listed sex as a more important reason for dating than did girls, reflecting differential interests or the double standard.

First intercourse has been a developmental milestone that traditionally has been associated with marriage. Kinsey's surveys during the 1930s and 1940s revealed that a majority of young men had intercourse before marriage. The substantially smaller percentage of young women who had intercourse before marriage reflected the double standard, but this discrepancy has decreased. Changes in adolescent sexual behavior have occurred over the past 50 years (Brooks-Gunn & Furstenberg, 1989). In 1938 approximately 7% of European American girls had intercourse by age 16, but by the 1980s the percentage had risen to 44%. Information does not exist to make comparisons for boys, but estimates suggest that boys were more sexually active than girls from the 1940s to the 1960s, with between one-third and two-thirds of boys having intercourse as teenagers. The difference diminished during the 1970s and 1980s. By age 18, 60% of young men had intercourse, and by age 19, the percentage was similar for young women. The National Opinion Research Council (Laumann et al., 1994) survey's age comparison for first intercourse has confirmed these diminished gender differences in sexual activity. When comparing adolescents who are currently sexually active, the differences are even smaller—42.5% of boys and 36.4% of girls have had intercourse (Centers for Disease Control, 1992).

The small gender differences hold across ethnic backgrounds, but age of first intercourse varies with ethnic background. First intercourse occurs at a lower age for boys than girls among Chicano (Mexican ethnic background), Latino (Cuban or Puerto Rican ethnic background), African American, and European American teens (Day, 1992). Black adolescents had first intercourse at a younger age (16.8 years for girls and 14.3 years for boys) than any of the other groups, the rest of which did not differ from each other (over age 17 for girls and around age 16 for boys).

Despite the small age differences in girls' and boys' initiation into intercourse, each gender decides to have intercourse for different reasons (Day, 1992). The factors controlling young women's sexual behavior included religion, career goals, and self-esteem, whereas young men were more likely to be controlled by factors in the family and community. For both, having a biological father (but not a stepfather) present in the home raised the age for first intercourse.

Level of acculturation may be a factor in the similarity of Hispanic Americans' and European Americans' sexual attitudes and behavior. Traditional Hispanic cultures prescribe a set of conservative sexual values and behaviors, especially for women, but U.S. culture has become more sexually liberal. In a study of Hispanic American high school students' sexual behavior (Ulibarri, Wilson, Grijalva, Hunt, & Seligman, 1994), participants' level of acculturation related to their sexual behavior. Those students who were more acculturated to U.S. cultural values in general were more likely to engage in a variety of sexual behaviors than the less acculturated students. The factor of acculturation also played a role in the sexual attitudes of Mexican American college women. Mexican American college women, an acculturated group, did not differ significantly from European American college women in their sexual attitudes (Valdez, 1994).

Female and male adolescents show a great deal of agreement over what constitutes intimacy in relationships, except on one point: Young men associated intimacy with sex, whereas young women associated intimacy with openness (Roscoe, Kennedy, & Pope, 1987). These different expectancies for intimacy point to the different meanings of sex for young men and women and may contribute to conflict in adolescent couples. "For teenage boys, their first sexual experience may be the primary symbol of manhood—a rite of passage" (Stark, 1989, p. 12). Girls are also subject to peer pressure to have sex, but additional pressure comes from boys, who may feel compelled to have sex with them to prove a point.

On the other hand, young women may need to *refuse* sex to prove a point because women who readily consent to sex may be considered promiscuous. This refusal may be social rather than personal; women feel desire, but openly acknowledging that desire may lead to many unkind labels. Being labeled "easy" was one reason that women showed token resistance to sexual activity (Muehlenhard & Hollabaugh, 1988). That is, women sometimes said no when they were willing to have intercourse and had every intention of later saying yes. Almost 40% of women sometimes showed this type of token resistance. The double standard encourages women to deny their sexuality, and women's refusals provide them with a way to appear to resist and also a way to exert power in their relationships by withholding sex. This result means that the majority of women who say no mean what they say, but the large minority of women reporting insincere resistance indicates that communication about sex is not always honest.

Such dishonesty might relate to the high incidence of **date rape** or **acquaintance rape,** the forced sexual activity between people who are acquainted. If no is not the final answer, what level of persuasion is permissible? Chapter 9 discussed rape as an aggressive crime disproportionately committed by men. Most people picture rape as an attack by a stranger, but the majority of rapes and other acts involving forced or coerced sex occur between acquaintances. Mary Koss and her colleagues (1987) surveyed college students about sexual activities and found that 54% of the young women in the survey claimed to have been the victims of some type of coerced or forced sexual activity at some time during their lives, and over 15% had been raped. Questioning a more representative group of women, the NORC survey (Laumann et al., 1994) found that 22% of women said that they had been forced to do something sexually by a man. Of these women, 46% said that they were in love with the man and another 22% said that they knew the man well who forced them. As this study shows, women are less likely to report sexual assaults if they know (and especially if they are in love with) the perpetrator, leading to an underrepresentation in the crime statistics of the incidence of rape by acquaintances.

Miscommunication may be a factor in acquaintance rape. The dynamics of sexual negotiation are complex, but the acceptability of forced sex is an important factor in the prevalence of acquaintance rape. Some men consider forced sex acceptable, at least under some conditions (Muehlenhard, Friedman, & Thomas, 1985). Men with more traditional attitudes toward women rated date rape as acceptable under a wider variety of conditions than men with nontraditional attitudes. If the woman asked the man out, the man paid the expenses of the date, and the woman agreed to go to his apartment, men found rape more justifiable than if the date followed another script. Women, however, may be unaware of these conditions and may not feel that they owe sex to their partners. Thus, dating partners follow complex, often unexpressed, and possibly unshared rules about sexual activities on dates. Their assumptions about the right to have sex may make men more likely to force women into the sex they believe they deserve—that is, to commit date rape. When women offer insincere refusals, they are contributing to men's reluctance to believe that the answer is really no.

Concerns about pregnancy play a role in the restraint of sexual behavior, especially in teenage girls. Although some pregnancy education is aimed at teenage boys, most is directed at girls, and emphasizes the danger of sex. The concern is not without reason; approximately one million teenage girls become pregnant each year in the United States (WIN News, 1997). Teenage boys are also involved in these pregnancies, but a substantial number of the fathers are at least 5 years older than their teenage partners (Lindberg, Sonenstein, Ku, & Martinez, 1997). Specifically, 27% of pregnancies in 15- to 17-year-old girls are fathered by older men. Therefore, some teen pregnancies appear to involve sexual relationships that fit into the category of exploitation or abuse.

The recent emphasis on condom use as a method of contraception and as a method for controlling sexually transmitted diseases would predict a change in the balance of responsibility for birth control, stressing male responsibility, but merely emphasizing condom use may not have prompted any change in responsibility. Gail Wyatt (1994) described a number of interventions for risky sexual behaviors in which women were the targets for change but men's behaviors were the risk. These programs have often targeted African American and Hispanic American women to encourage them to avoid pregnancy or decrease their risk of sexually transmitted diseases. For example, some programs have encouraged women to be responsible for condom use to prevent HIV infection from male partners, and these programs tend to have disappointing success rates. Wyatt pointed out that Black women's resistance to these programs is reasonable: Why should they be the targets of these programs when men's behavior is the problem?

In summary, as adolescent sexuality becomes increasingly oriented toward heterosexual encounters, some gender differences appear. Sex education may not meet the needs of either girls or boys. Girls receive messages of danger and vulnerability rather than pleasure, and boys receive messages about how pleasurable sex is but also hear negative information about the damage their sexuality can produce. Greater numbers of adolescent boys tend to have intercourse and have it at earlier ages than adolescent girls. These gender differences have diminished over the past 50 years, and now the differences in the percentage of adolescent girls and boys having intercourse at each age are similar, as is the average age of first intercourse. Although these changes signal a decline of the double standard, sex may have a different meaning for boys and girls. Although peer pressure is a factor for both, boys use sex as proof of their masculinity, whereas validation of their femininity is not a common reason for girls to have sex.

During Adulthood

Traditionally, marriage has not only been a major transition but also the primary context within which adult sexuality appears, often in the form of vaginal intercourse. The more recent studies of college students and surveys with more representative samples have indicated that the standards for sexual behavior have changed. Lower ages of first intercourse, increases in sexual activity among female adolescents, and increases in the acceptability of a variety of sexual activities suggest that more frequent and more varied sexual behaviors are now accepted for both women and men.

One specialized survey of Canadian college students (Netting, 1992) found evidence of three styles of sexuality among these young adults—celibacy, monogamy, and free experimentation. Although these styles can apply to same-gender sexuality, this survey concentrated on heterosexual college students. These styles represent very different choices, but students who had chosen one style were acceptant of those who had made different choices: "The only value shared almost universally was the right to choose" (Netting, p. 970).

Celibacy, refraining from sexual activity, was a fairly popular choice; about one-third of the students were in this category. This group included students who had never had intercourse plus those who had had no sexual partners for the previous year. A similar percentage of men and women were celibate, but for different reasons. For the women, celibacy was most often a choice; their most common reason for remaining celibate was that they were waiting for love. For the men, celibacy was often not a matter of choice—their most common reason was that they were waiting for an opportunity to have sex. A similar but smaller percentage of both men and women said that they remained celibate because of moral or religious reasons, but few students said that they were waiting for marriage to have sex.

Monogamy means having only one sexual partner in a committed love relationship. This style of relationship was the most popular alternative, being the choice for 61% of the women and 37% of the men. These percentages included students who were in monogamous relationships at the time of the survey and those who were celibate but waiting for such relationships. A lower percentage of both women and men reported monogamy as their current choice. In addition, many of the students who chose this category described their current behavior rather than their lifetime sexual behavior, and more than half of those who had chosen this style had had more than one sex partner during their lifetimes. Others who were in supposedly monogamous relationships had sex with other partners but considered this behavior to violate their commitment (although they still classified themselves as monogamous). Thus, many of these students subscribed to the ideal of monogamy without adhering to the practice of having one sexual partner for life. The percentage of men who had or wanted this type of relationship was lower than the percentage of women.

The students who chose the free experimentation style valued sexual freedom and wanted to participate in a variety of sexual relationships. Counting those who had more than one partner during their lives, about half the students were in this category. Some of these young adults were in committed relationships with one partner at the time of the study but believed in having different partners on the way to a monogamous relationship. More students believed in than practiced free sexual expression, but some in this group had many sexual partners and fit the description of experimenting freely with their sexuality. More men than women fit this pattern—28% of men but only 5% of women said that they were sexually active but not monogamous. Table 11.4 summarizes the styles of sexuality among the college students in this study.

All of the styles that appeared in this Canadian study are reflective of adult sexuality in Canada, the United States, and other Western countries. Indeed, the Western concepts of love and sex are spreading to other parts of the world (Hatfield & Rapson, 1996), making these patterns of sexual behavior more similar throughout the world than in the past. Some adults are celibate, some are monogamous, and others have many sexual partners and freely experiment with sexuality. In addition, the gender differences that appeared in the survey of Canadian students also are reflective of adult heterosexuality, and these gender differences relate to some of the problems in heterosexual couples.

Any specific individual can fit into one of these categories—celibacy, monogamy, or free experimentation—at different times in life. A person may be a celibate adult while waiting for an opportunity to have sex or for a relationship in which sex would be desirable.

TABLE 11.4 Styles of Sexuality among College Students

	Percentage		
Style Chosen	Women	Men	Reason for Choice
Celibacy	36%	32%	Women were waiting for love; men were waiting for an opportunity
Monogamy	61	37	Considered monogamy the ideal type of sexuality
	48	34	Were currently monogamous
	25	19	Had had only one partner during their lives
Free Expression	14	33	Valued freedom of expression, including expression of sexuality
	5	28	Sexually active but not currently monogamous

While in that relationship, the person may be monogamous, but the relationship may not last, and the person may then form another relationship. This pattern of **serial monogamy** has become a common pattern in the United States and other Western countries. Serial monogamy results in a person having several sex partners consecutively, which may occur over a series of dating relationships, marriages, or a combination of these. Some people who hold monogamy as the ideal do not live up to their own standards, and they engage in sex while involved in a relationship, whereas others do not believe in monogamy and engage in a variety of sexual relationships. Therefore, adult heterosexuality includes a number of choices, though gender differences in attitudes and behavior can provide obstacles in forming and maintaining sexual relationships.

According to the NORC survey (Laumann et al., 1994), about 9.8% of men and 13.6% of women did not have sex in the year prior to the survey. Lifelong celibacy is, however, unusual—only 2.9% said they never had a sex partner. Those who are ill or whose partners have died are especially likely to be celibate, and both circumstances are associated with increasing age. Thus, celibacy increases sharply after age 60. Older women are far more likely to be celibate than men of the same age, due to the combination of their longer life expectancy and the cultural acceptability of men choosing younger women as partners.

Monogamy is most common for married couples. Indeed, 93.7% of married couples in the NORC survey were monogamous in the year prior to the study (Laumann et al., 1994). Unmarried cohabiting heterosexual partners (76.7%), those who had never been married and were not cohabiting (38%), and those who were divorced or separated (40.5%) were less likely to be monogamous.

The sexual attitudes and behaviors of women and men show few differences, but those few differences may have larger implications for heterosexuality, including the choice of monogamy or free experimentation. One way to understand these gender differences is through the framework of script theory (Simon & Gagnon, 1986). This view proposes that sexual behavior follows a sequentially organized set of steps and that men and women learn and internalize somewhat different scripts. The sequence of events occurring during a couple's first intercourse are so tightly scripted that college students can arrange the sequence from a set of randomly organized statements (Geer & Broussard, 1990), demonstrating that young adults know the scripts very well. The differences between male and female scripts can throw couples into conflict.

One of the large gender differences in sexuality is in the acceptability of casual sex, with men being more acceptant than women (Oliver & Hyde, 1993). The script approach helps in understanding this gender difference and its implications. Women are encouraged to associate sex with love, and they come to believe that sex should occur in the context of a committed relationship whereas the script for men is not so relationship centered (McCormick, 1994). Thus, sex may have a different meaning for women and men.

The implications of this difference can be large, forming areas of conflict for couples. For women, the association between commitment and sex leads them to believe that commitment should exist before having sex, but men may not share these requirements or expectations. These differing beliefs lead to differences in expectations about the timing of intercourse in a relationship (Cohen & Shotland, 1996). As predicted, men expect sex after significantly fewer dates (9 to 11) than women (15 to 18). These differing expectations could be a source of conflict if men begin to pressure women to have sex and the women do not feel ready.

The difference in acceptability of casual sex can also have an impact on sex outside the primary relationship. With less acceptant attitudes, women are more likely to be monogamous than men, and they are more likely to consider sex outside the relationship as violations of trust or as betrayals by their partners. Therefore, this gender difference can be a major source of conflict in couples and would account for the discrepancy of men and women who fit into the category of free experimentation.

The other large gender difference in sexuality is the frequency of masturbation (Oliver & Hyde, 1993), with men masturbating more often than women. At first, any relationship between masturbation and partnered sex may not seem apparent, but Janet Hyde (1996) has explained such a connection. She proposed that women's lower frequency and greater guilt concerning masturbation results in less familiarity with their bodies and less certain knowledge of how to reach orgasm. Women are less likely to experience orgasm during intercourse than are men, and this difference causes distress in many couples. Hyde pointed out that many sex therapists direct women who are having orgasmic difficulties to masturbate, thus demonstrating to them the importance of masturbation. She hypothesized that women's lower frequency of masturbation may lay the foundation for women to have difficulties in reaching orgasm during heterosexual sex.

Other gender differences in sexuality are not as great as frequency of masturbation or acceptance of casual sex, but those differences may also have some relationship to the problems that heterosexual couples face. One gender difference in sexuality appears in the desire for and frequency of intercourse. The double standard proposes that women will be less interested in sex because they are less sexual creatures than men, and evolutionary psychology (Buss, 1994, 1996) holds that women must be more sexually selective than men in order to choose mates who will be able to provide for offspring. These two views agree that women are less sexual but disagree over the reason. Determining a social or biological explanation is very difficult because society influences everyone, and because many societies control women's sexuality, any interpretation of "natural" sexuality is impossible.

Sarah Blaffer Hrdy (1981, 1986) criticized the view that women are less sexual than men, which she called the Myth of the Coy Female, by reporting on females unaffected by cultural expectations and the double standard—nonhuman primates. She argued that male scientists who have seen females reluctant to engage in sex have been influenced by the double standard and have projected these human differences onto nonhuman primates.

According to Hrdy, the sexual behavior of nonhuman animals varies from species to species. The females of some species, such as baboons and chimpanzees, initiate multiple, brief sexual relationships and show no coy reluctance to engage in sex, whereas the females of other species, such as blue monkeys and redtail monkeys, are very selective about their mating habits and might appear to be coy in their selectivity. Hrdy argued that any tendency to see patterns similar to human sexual behavior in the behavior of other species tells more about the human observer than about the observed species.

Women's lower interest in sex may be related to accepting the double standard for themselves, another difference revealed by meta-analysis (Oliver & Hyde, 1993). An alternative explanation comes from script theory, which suggests that women have internalized the cultural view that their sexuality is weaker. If women believe that they are or should be less sexual, they may behave accordingly and become less sexual. A meta-analysis of attitudes toward sexuality (Oliver & Hyde, 1993) showed that women accepted the double standard more strongly and felt more guilt over sex than men, which is consistent with this interpretation. Masters and Johnson (1966) argued that women could be just as or even more sexual than men if women were free to express their sexuality and to participate in the activities that gave them sexual pleasure. Rather than loosening the constraints on female sexuality, Masters and Johnson's research may have added to these restrictions by prescribing that women should be as sexual as men and that the sexuality of the two genders should be similar (Tavris, 1992).

Is sexuality very different for women and men? Were the Victorians correct about men's sexual nature and women's disinterest in sex? Sex surveys as far in the past as Kinsey's have shown that women are indeed interested in sex and also experience pleasure from a variety of sexual activities. More recent research (Laumann et al., 1994; Oliver & Hyde, 1993) has shown that some gender differences persist: Women have higher average ages of first sexual intercourse than men, men are more acceptant of casual sex, fewer women than men masturbate, women are less likely than men to experience orgasm during intercourse, women experience more fear and guilt associated with sex, and women are slightly less accepting of oral sex than are men.

Gender differences in sexual behavior have decreased over the time since the older studies, suggesting that both female and male sexuality are subject to change and are influenced by social standards. During the Victorian era women were presumed to be less sexual than men, and so they became. In our sexualized modern culture, women are portrayed as being more sexual than in the past but still less so than men, and so they have become. Sexuality is created by each culture and shows enormous differences in those cultures. Thus, women and men exhibit a wide variety of sexual behaviors depending on their physiologies, cultures, personal backgrounds, and personal expectations. (See the Diveristy Highlight: "The Sexual Buffet.")

Carol Tavris (1992, p. 245) summarized heterosexuality by saying, "The question is not whether women are more or less sexual than men. (The answer to that is yes, no, both, and sometimes.) The questions are: What are the conditions that allow women and men to enjoy sex in safety, with self-confidence, and in a spirit of delight? And how do we get there?"

DIVERSITY HIGHLIGHT
The Sexual Buffet

Cultures around the world have chosen a variety of sexual activities for acceptance as "normal" and have designated other choices as abnormal, sinful, or repulsive. Cultures shape sexuality by "choosing some sexual acts (by praise, encouragement, or reward) and rejecting others (by scorn, ridicule, or condemnation), as if selecting from a sexual buffet" (Vance, 1984, p. 8). This selection from the array of available choices has resulted in virtually no universally accepted and no universally rejected set of sexual behaviors: What some cultures have found disgusting, others have found essential.

Forced fellatio performed on adult men by adolescent boys would be the basis for criminal prosecution in many cultures, but the Sambia in New Guinea find this practice not only acceptable but also required (Herdt, 1981). According to their beliefs, a preadolescent boy must leave his mother and live with men in order to become a man himself. Part of the process involves swallowing semen, and the Sambia encourage boys to engage in fellatio with unmarried adolescent and adult men. The men must restrict their same-gender sexual activities to these boys, and fellatio with men their own age is strictly forbidden. When these adolescents and young men marry, they are supposed to make the transition to heterosexuality and to end all same-gender sexual activities.

In their examination of dozens of cultures, Clellan Ford and Frank Beach (1951) found that kissing was a common activity, but not all cultures had invented kissing. The Balinese do not kiss but bring their faces close together and inhale each other's scent. On the other hand, the Thonga of Africa found the practice of kissing odd and slightly disgusting.

Heterosexual intercourse has been a common form of sexual expression in most cultures, but it rarely has been the only form of sexual expression for any culture (Ford & Beach, 1951). The Lepchas of India engage in only limited sexual activity; they have intercourse, but kissing, breast stimulation, or genital stimulation is almost completely absent. The Trobriand Islanders of the South Pacific include a variety of other types of stimulation with intercourse—kissing, stimulating the breasts, rubbing the skin, biting, pulling hair, as well as manual and oral stimulation of male and female genitals.

Children in some societies are allowed and even expected to experiment with sex, whereas other societies restrict sexuality during childhood (Ford & Beach, 1951). For the societies that allow children to express their sexuality, genital touching and simulated intercourse are more likely to be allowed between peers than between a child and someone older. The Sambia, with their institutionalized adult–adolescent fellatio are an exception, and so are the Lepcha, who believe that girls will not mature unless they engage in early intercourse.

Societies that restrict childhood sexuality tend to do so through restricting not only intercourse but also limiting information about sex, prohibiting masturbation, and enforcing different standards of sexual behavior for men and women. That is, sexually restrictive societies tend to have a double standard and put more restrictions on the sexuality of girls and women than on boys and men.

The variety of selected and rejected options are not equal across cultures. Some activities (kissing, heterosexual intercourse) are a common choice in many societies; other activities are less common but still appear in many societies (intercourse for unmarried adolescents, oral–genital stimulation); still other activities are very uncommon in the world but standard in one society, such as biting off one's partner's eyebrows during intercourse. Although not common, this activity is also one of the choices from the buffet.

Homosexuality

Some people develop erotic attraction toward people of the same gender and choose to engage in same-gender sexual activities. For years, psychologists failed to make a distinction between *gender role*, the social behaviors associated with one or the other gender, and *sexual orientation,* the erotic attraction to members of one or the other gender (or to both). Psychologists confused gender role and sexual orientation, constructing tests that measured masculinity and femininity, which are aspects of gender role. Men who expressed sexual attraction for other men were assumed to be feminine, and women who were attracted to women were assumed to be masculine, a reversal or inversion of the typical gender role (Constantinople, 1973; Lewin, 1984a, b).

The conceptualization of same-gender sexual orientation as an inversion of gender role was not productive, and these tests generally failed to correctly identify individuals with same-gender sexual orientations (Lewin, 1984a). A separation of gender role and sexual orientation has clarified the process of measuring masculinity and femininity and demonstrated that same-gender sexual orientation has a far from perfect relationship to these traits. That is, men who are erotically attracted to other men are not necessarily feminine in appearance or behavior, and women who find other women sexually attractive are not necessarily more masculine than other women.

The number of people with same-gender sexual interests, behavior patterns, and identities constitute a minority, but estimates vary on how small a minority this is. Most of the variation in estimates can be explained according to the definition that the researchers have used. Is sexual attraction to those of the same gender sufficient? Are persons lesbian or gay if they have engaged in sexual activity with persons of the same gender at any time during their lives? Does having sex primarily or exclusively with members of one's own gender define homosexuality? Or must persons identify themselves as gay or lesbian? These varying criteria produce different estimates.

Kinsey and his colleagues (1948) found that 37% of the men said that they had engaged in male–male sexual activity at some time during their lives. When asked the equivalent question, 28% of women reported at least one female–female sexual experience during their lifetimes (Kinsey et al., 1953). Therefore, a substantial number of both men and women who participated in the Kinsey surveys had sexual experiences with members of their own gender, but most did not choose such relationships as the primary form of sexuality throughout their lives. About 13% of the men and about 7% of the women in Kinsey's surveys said that their sexuality had been primarily gay or lesbian, but this estimate has been controversial (Jones, 1998).

Other surveys have yielded lower estimates. The NORC survey (Laumann et al., 1994) found that 3.8% of women and 7.1% of men reported same-gender sex partners at some time since puberty, but these researchers also measured other aspects of same-gender sexuality. In addition to behavior, they asked about attraction and identity, which differ from behavior. About 2.4% of the men and 1.4% of the women in this survey reported all three components—same-gender desire, behavior, and identity—whereas 8.6% of the women and 10.1% of the men reported only one component, the most common of which was desire. An international study (Sell, Wells, & Wypij, 1995) also found that many people have same-gender attractions but do not act on these desires.

Table 11.5 presents a comparison of the various measures of homosexuality for several studies, one of which questioned people in three countries. As this table reveals, the different measures (and cultures) show variations in the percentage of people who might be classified as gay or lesbian. Thus, same-gender sexual orientation is complex, and estimates

TABLE 11.5 Differing Estimates of Same-Gender Attraction and Behavior

Study	Percent	
	Men	Women
Kinsey et al. (1948, 1953)		
At least one same-gender sexual experience	37.0%	28.0%
Primarily or exclusively same-gender sex	13.0	7.0
Janus and Janus (1993)		
At least one same-gender sexual experience	22.0	17.0
Primarily same-gender sex	4.0	2.0
Laumann et al. (1994—NORC survey)		
Same-gender desires or experiences	10.1	8.6
Done anything sexual with same-gender partner	9.1	4.3
Same-gender sex partner since puberty	7.1	3.8
Same-gender sex partner in past year	2.7	1.3
Attracted to same-gender individuals	7.7	7.5
Self-identified as gay or lesbian	2.8	1.4
Sell, Wells, and Wypij (1995)		
United States		
Same-gender attraction but no activity	8.7	11.1
Same-gender sexual activity since age 15	6.2	3.6
United Kingdom		
Same-gender attraction but no activity	7.9	8.6
Same-gender sexual activity since age 15	4.5	2.1
France		
Same-gender attraction but no activity	8.5	11.7
Same-gender sexual activity since age 15	10.7	3.3

depend on whether researchers ask about attraction or behavior as well as the frequency of behavior and the age of respondents.

Attitudes toward same-gender sexuality vary from culture to culture, and some cultures have positive, acceptant attitudes. Among tribal societies in Africa, 64% accept same-gender sex, at least for some members of the tribe (Hatfield & Rapson, 1996). In ancient Greece, men (but not women) were free to engage in same-sex love affairs. European and North American societies came to disapprove of same-gender sexuality and to impose harsh social and legal penalties for such activities. During the 20th century, experts began to use the term *homosexuals,* which made sexuality the defining characteristic of the person.

The identification of persons with their sexuality allowed for a coalescing of negative attitudes:

> *According to many church leaders, homosexuals are sinners; according to the law, they are criminals. Mental health professionals until recently have viewed homosexuality as pathological. . . . Although these perspectives differ and are at points*

> *mutually exclusive, the underlying message is clear: Homosexuality is bad and shameful, to be feared and suppressed.* (de Monteflores & Schultz, 1978, p. 59)

This statement represents not only the current view in many (but not all) places in the world but also the attitudes from recent history. Homosexual activity has been condemned and suppressed, making the choice to express sexual feelings toward members of one's own sex difficult.

The social stigma associated with acquired immune deficiency syndrome (AIDS) has been an additional difficulty for gay men. During the early years of the epidemic, the vast majority of those in North America infected with the human immunodeficiency virus (HIV) were gay men and intravenous drug users. A common perception developed that gay men carried AIDS and that any type of association with them was dangerous. This perception was and is, of course, incorrect. Most of the people in the world who are infected with HIV are heterosexual. Most gay men are not infected with HIV, and being associated with infected persons will not transmit the virus. Transmission of the HIV infection requires close contact with bodily fluids, such as blood or semen; casual contact will not transmit this infection.

Although many people already disliked and even feared gays, associating gay men with the HIV infection fueled a growing homophobia, which has led to job and housing discrimination and even physical attacks. The widespread prejudice against gay men and lesbians has implications for many aspects of the lives of those who identify themselves as either. In addition, gays and lesbians must contend with identity issues concerning their sexual orientation. Many feel the pressure to be heterosexual, and many people consider sexual orientation a choice, putting gays and lesbians into the position to defend their stigmatized "choice." The changeability of sexual orientation has not been established. Indeed, the basis for the development of sexual orientation—either homosexual or heterosexual—remains elusive. This question is the center of a heated controversy: Is sexual orientation the result of biological, environmental, or some mixture of factors?

Early biological theories of sexual orientation focused on genetics and hormones, but research failed to confirm any simple relationship between sexual orientation and either genetic background or hormonal levels. Both genetics and hormone levels may exert an influence, but in complex ways that involve prenatal hormone levels and their influence on the developing brain (Breedlove, 1994; Money, 1987b). The brains of women and men show some differences (see Chapter 4), including a difference in size of the third interstitial nuclei of the anterior hypothalamus. This structure is larger in men than in women, and in 1991, Simon LeVay proposed that this structure was smaller in gay men than in heterosexual men.

LeVay studied the brains of three groups: gay men (all of whom had died of AIDS), heterosexual men (fewer than half of whom had died of AIDS), and heterosexual women (only one of whom had died of AIDS). He found that the third interstitial nucleus of the anterior hypothalamus was, on the average, twice as large in the heterosexual men as in the gay men. LeVay claimed that he had found a biological basis for male–male sexual interest, but the differences in cause of death for the three groups may have biased the results. That is, the people in LeVay's three groups died of different causes, making them different in a way other than their sexual orientation. This bias weakens the study and casts doubt on his conclusions. In addition, these results have not yet been replicated (Bohan, 1996).

LeVay's evidence produced a great deal of controversy. The notion that sexual orientation might be traced to some biological difference fits into an essentialist view of sexual behavior, and essentialists hold that a biological basis places behavior beyond personal choice. Many people who want to restrict same-gender sexual activity need to believe that such behavior is a choice so that those who have made this choice can change their sexual behavior to a heterosexual orientation. Members of the gay community have viewed LeVay's research with ambivalence (LeVay, 1996), with many agreeing that they feel as though their sexual orientation is innate but disputing that their sexuality is a problem that should be changed. Rather, they see their sexuality as a difference to be accepted. Accepting that difference is a major issue for those adolescents who feel attracted to members of their own gender.

During Adolescence

Adolescence is a time of sexual exploration, and adolescent sexual activity has become more common and more accepted over the past 40 years—for heterosexual couples. Despite the increased opportunities for same-gender sex offered by the gender segregation during childhood and adolescence, the great majority of these contacts have no sexual connotations. These opportunities, however, may account for the larger number of people who have engaged in same-gender sexuality as adolescents but not adults. Indeed, most of the people who have same-gender sexual experiences do so as part of adolescent experimentation and not as the beginning of gay or lesbian sexual identities. However, some adolescents who are attracted to persons of the same gender do not act on these desires during adolescence (Savin-Williams, 1995). Therefore, sexual orientation and sexual activity during adolescence do not correspond completely to sexual identity or to sexual activity during adulthood.

Some gays and lesbians say they knew that they were different even before adolescence, but many of them have tried to develop heterosexual interests and fit into this accepted pattern of sexuality (Zera, 1992). Some may succeed, but it is more common for someone identified as heterosexual during adolescence and young adulthood to adopt a gay or lesbian identity than for a gay or lesbian to adopt a heterosexual orientation (LeVay, 1996). Rather than reflecting a change in sexual orientation, this trend probably occurs as part of developing a gay or lesbian identity.

The acceptance of same-gender attraction is a major challenge for gay adolescents. They often struggle with feelings that something is wrong with them, and self-esteem may be a problem. Self-acceptance is different (and often comes more easily) than revealing one's same-gender sexual orientation or behavior to family and friends. **Coming out** is the process of personally recognizing and acknowledging a gay or lesbian orientation to others (Bohan, 1996). The term originated with the phrase "coming out of the closet," referring to the hidden (closeted) nature of sexuality for many gays and lesbians. Thus, coming out is a positive affirmation of sexuality. This process may be part of adolescent development, or it may occur at any time during adulthood.

Coming out may include a public acknowledgment of sexual orientation, or the revelation may be limited to only friends and family. Parents may be acceptant and supportive, or they may be angry and have trouble accommodating the sexual orientation of this child (Bohan, 1996; Zera, 1992). In addition, friends may react negatively to coming out, and peer verbal or physical attacks are not unusual (Savin-Williams, 1995). Thus, gay and lesbian adolescents may be estranged from family and peers, and they are at increased risk for home- and school-related problems.

For adults, coming out often includes acceptance into the gay community. For adolescents, such acceptance is not as easy, because activities in the gay community are oriented toward adults. Charges of seducing adolescents or of promoting same-gender sexual activities present situations that make gay adults sensitive about including adolescents in the gay community.

Coming out can be a positive statement of sexuality for adolescents as well as for adults, but adolescents face many challenges in establishing a gay or lesbian identity: "Despite the pain and confusion in this process of development, it is important to bear in mind that most gay people do successfully resolve these issues and are able to be happy with themselves and participate in healthy relationships" (Zera, 1992, p. 854).

During Adulthood

Women and men who engage in same-gender sexual activities are often in danger of being arrested if they make their sexual activities public because such activities are often illegal. This lack of legal sanctions reflects the lack of social acceptability for gays and lesbians as well as for same-gender sexual activities (Kite & Whitley, 1996). Men have more negative attitudes than women toward homosexuality, especially regarding gay men. This lack of acceptance is one reason for the formation of self-contained gay communities. In many large cities, such communities form the context for the lives of many gay people, who may rarely interact with the outside world of heterosexuals. This life is not typical of gays, however, and the vast majority must deal with disapproval and lack of acceptance from the larger society in which they live. This lack of societal approval means that the need to form friendships and social networks is an essential part of gays' and lesbians' social lives. (See the Diversity Highlight: "The Berdache in Native American Culture.")

The development of friendships and sexual relationships differs in gay men and lesbian women (Nardi, 1992b). Gay men were much more likely than lesbians to have had sex with both casual and close friends. Indeed, among gay men sexual activity can form the basis for later friendships, which may represent conformity to the traditional masculine gender role in which men use sexual activity as a means to establish intimacy.

Women's romantic friendships have a long history, but until recently these relationships have been presumed to be nonsexual (Faderman, 1989). Perhaps the passionate friendships that were common among women in the 18th and 19th centuries included no sexual activity, but in other respects, these love relationships were similar to today's lesbian relationships, having an emphasis on feelings of closeness and emotional expression (Peplau, Cochran, Rook, & Padesky, 1978).

Lesbians and gay men form love relationships that have the elements of intimacy, passion, and commitment in them, just as are found in heterosexual couples' relationships. Philip Blumstein and Pepper Schwartz (1983) surveyed gay male and lesbian couples as well as heterosexual couples, and their survey revealed similarities as well as differences among these various configurations of couples. The survey included questions about sexual activities and satisfaction with these activities.

GENDERED VOICES

I Never Imagined the Pain

"Lesbians have been telling me about their problems in coming out," a female graduate student in counseling said. "For some reason, two women have confided in me about the problems with staying in the closet and coming out. They are women I knew and they came to trust me, but I'm not their counselor. I never imagined the pain and the problems. I guess I have led a sheltered life. I have known gays and lesbians, but I had never known or imagined the difficulties in essentially leading two lives—one for the public and the real, private one.

"One woman has been in a relationship for 17 years. During those years she and her lover have had to pretend to be 'just roommates' who share a house. She felt that she could never let the people at work know she was lesbian; she thought she would lose her job.

"She said that she felt pressured and tried to be heterosexual. She was even engaged to be married when she was in her early 20s, but her mother sensed something was wrong and told her that she didn't have to get married if she didn't want to. She broke the engagement and stopped trying to be something she wasn't, but she kept her sexual orientation secret for another 20 years.

"This woman has started to come out selectively to people she trusts. Her family still doesn't know—or at least she hasn't told them. She has found coming out a great relief and would like to be able to be completely out but does not feel comfortable enough to do so.

"The other woman has not yet come out. I guess you would say she is bisexual rather than lesbian; I'm not sure about these classifications. She is married and has a child, but she is attracted to women and has had a number of lesbian affairs, but they upset her. She says that she was 'good' when she went on a shopping trip to a large city and did not pursue a lesbian relationship but 'bad' when she did. She is very unhappy and troubled over whether she should leave her husband and come out as a lesbian. I am really very concerned for her, because she is suicidal, and I am afraid that she might harm herself. This conflict is really a problem for her.

"In listening to these women, I was struck by their pain in essentially living a charade, pretending to be something they know they are not. That must be so difficult and so stressful. Coming out has been like removing a huge burden for the women who has, but I see the problems in that choice, too. Talking to these two women has really been an education for me."

Lesbian couples reported a lower level of sexual activity than any other type of couple and had some reluctance to perform cunnilingus. Blumstein and Schwartz speculated that lesbians' socialization as women might have had an influence on their sexuality, making both partners hesitant about initiating sex. The result was a lower frequency of sexual activity than in couples formed with men, who are socialized to initiate sex. Lesbians who had frequent oral sex were happier with their sex lives and with their relationships than those who had less oral sex. Nevertheless, only 39% of the lesbian couples in the survey reported having oral sex very frequently, and mutual masturbation was the most common sexual activity among these couples. Lesbians also valued nongenital physical contact, such as hugging and cuddling, activities that promoted intimacy but not orgasm.

The validity of Blumstein and Schwartz's analysis has been questioned (Frye, 1997), and the study has been accused of harboring a heterosexual bias that did not allow for an understanding of lesbian sex. "Having sex" was defined as genital contact and intercourse,

DIVERSITY HIGHLIGHT
The Berdache in Native American Culture

When Europeans arrived in North America, they began to impose their religions and values on the Native American tribes, including their sexual values. In many of these societies, gender roles were less fixed than in European societies (Roscoe, 1993). More than 130 Native American societies accepted *berdaches*—men or women who adopted the gender-related behaviors of the other gender, and often established sexual relationships with those of their own gender.

The male berdache tradition was the more common, and male berdaches were not only well accepted but also achieved high spiritual status in their societies. Lakota, Navajo, Crow, and Zuni societies all included berdaches who were not thought of as homosexual but as a merging of feminine and masculine spirits, which they attained through a blessing from the spirits (Roscoe, 1993). These departures from the ordinary gender roles, therefore, were not viewed as deviations because they were chosen as special, and there was no connotation of deficiency or pathology. Their cross-gender behaviors represented a blending of male and female that may have constituted a third gender rather than an adoption of the gender role of the "opposite" gender.

The European missionaries and colonists held different views of berdaches, considering them homosexual and thus depraved (Wieringa, 1994). Along with attempting to replace Native American religions, missionaries tried to enforce heterosexual monogamy and sharply different gender roles, which put the berdache tradition in peril. These changes lowered the status of women and berdaches in Native American societies, and in contemporary Native American societies, attitudes toward homosexuality are usually as negative as those of the larger society. Gays and lesbian activists within Native American cultures are attempting to recover the berdache tradition, along with the respect that their cultures have traditionally accorded the berdache.

and lesbian sex may not conform to these boundaries. What body parts must be touched for sex to occur? Did a couple "have sex" if neither experienced orgasm? "What violence did the lesbians do their experience by answering the same question the heterosexuals answered, as though it had the same meaning for them?" (Frye, 1997, p. 206). Therefore, simple comparisons of heterosexuality and homosexuality may not be valid.

Sex is a very important part of life for gay men, and their relationships typically include a lot of sexual activity, especially early in the relationship (Blumstein & Schwartz, 1983). Fellatio is an important activity for gay men, but their sex lives are varied, and mutual masturbation is also a common activity. Anal intercourse was never as common an activity as either oral sex or manual stimulation, and its dangers for spreading HIV infection have made it less common than before the appearance of AIDS. Gay men engage in a variety of sexual activities, and their frequency of sexual contact is higher than for any other configuration of couples during the early years of their relationships. The frequency of activity with their partners falls sharply after approximately the first two years of the relationship, but this decrease in frequency may only be a decrease in sex with their long-time partners and not in total sexual activity.

Gay men are more acceptant of casual sex than lesbians, and even gay men who are involved in long-term relationships often have sex with men other than their partners. Indeed, gay men often work out relationships in which they may have sex with men other than their companions and yet keep their long-term relationships. Affairs can present a problem for any couple, but sex outside the relationship is not as likely to be a factor in the dissolution of gay men's relationships as it is for other couples.

Marriage is not a socially accepted context for sexual activity for gay men and lesbians, which gives their love relationships less official sanction than those of heterosexual couples. Perhaps this lack of official acceptance is one factor in the lower level of stability for these couples' relationships than for married couples. Blumstein and Schwartz found that gay men and lesbians were more likely to end their relationships than married couples and that lesbians were even more likely to break up than gay men.

Many similarities appeared among the couples that Blumstein and Schwartz studied. For example, sex was important to heterosexual, lesbian, and gay couples, and couples who had sex less than once a week were not as happy as couples who had sex more often. Sex formed a physical bond for all the types of couples and helped them maintain their relationships, but it was also a common source of problems. Those couples who fought about sex were less stable than those who were happy with their sexual relationships. For all of the couples, their sexual relationships reflected the problems that happened in other aspects of their relationships: Sex went well when the relationships went well, and unhappiness with the sexual activity in the relationships tended to be associated with unhappiness in the quality of affection in the relationships.

Bisexuality

In Kinsey's survey of sexual behavior, a relatively high percentage of men and women reported some same-gender experiences but did not have an exclusive same-gender orientation. This situation suggested to Kinsey that sexuality should not be considered in terms of independent categories. He created a continuum for classifying people's sexual experience and attraction to members of their own and the other gender. This 7-point scale ranged from strongly heterosexual to strongly homosexual, with gradations in between representing people who have both types of sexual relationships in varying proportions. These gradations reflected people who are attracted to individuals of both genders, who are referred to as **bisexual.**

The status and even the existence of bisexuality remain controversial (Fox, 1996). In psychoanalytic theory, attraction to both sexes was part of sexual development but one that was abandoned in normal gender development. In this view, bisexuality is not an acceptable form of sexuality. Those who find homosexuality unacceptable will object to the same-gender sexual element of bisexuality. For gays and lesbians, bisexuality is seen as an unwillingness to acknowledge a gay or lesbian identity by clinging to heterosexuality. Therefore, bisexuality has been condemned by several discrepant groups.

Although one view of bisexuality holds that this sexual orientation represents conflict, another view sees it as flexible (Zinik, 1985). Both views may be correct. For some individuals, bisexuality represents a developmental step on the way to forming a gay or lesbian sexual orientation. These individuals experience conflict over their sexuality, and bisexuality is a way to postpone accepting their sexual identity. For others, bisexuality is a successful integration of same- and other-gender sexuality and represents flexibility.

The frequency of bisexuality is difficult to assess. With a behavioral criterion, the vast majority of gays and lesbians would be considered bisexual. That is, most gay men and lesbians have had heterosexual experiences at some time during their lives. In addition, some individuals whose primary sexual orientation is heterosexual have had same-gender sexual experiences. A behavioral criterion would count these groups of individuals as bisexual, making a substantial percentage.

Heterosexual activity may represent a type of adolescent sexual exploration among gay and lesbian adolescents (Herdt & Boxer, 1995). Just as many adolescents who go on to have a heterosexual sexual orientation experience some same-gender sex, many adolescents who develop a gay or lesbian sexual orientation experiment with heterosexuality. Indeed, they do so in greater proportions than heterosexual adolescents experiment with same-gender sex because heterosexuality is socially sanctioned, and many gay and lesbian adolescents want to "test" their unconventional sexual orientation.

Those who identify themselves as bisexual and who maintain romantic and sexual relationships with both women and men are found in much lower numbers than those who identify themselves as gay or lesbian. According to the NORC survey (Laumann et al., 1994), 0.8% of men and 0.5% of women identified themselves as bisexual. So few people are bisexual that no community exists to offer support, and most bisexuals are not integrated into the existing gay and lesbian communities, leaving many bisexuals isolated (Bohan, 1996). This situation is beginning to change, and many gay and lesbian community centers and agencies include services oriented to bisexuals. Despite this increased acceptance, bisexuality remains the least-researched and understood sexual orientation.

Summary

Gender differences in sexual attitudes and behavior have been the object of speculation and research. Most sex research has used the survey technique, questioning people about their sexual attitudes or behavior. Several problems arise in using this technique, including the accuracy of self-reports. In addition, people who are willing to answer questions about sex may not be a representative sample of the general population. These drawbacks of sex surveys create doubts about how accurately such surveys reflect people's attitudes and behaviors, but the survey technique has been the most common approach to the study of sexuality.

Although not the first sex surveys, Kinsey and his colleagues conducted the most famous sex surveys of male (1948) and female (1953) sexual behavior. The results showed the prevalence of same-gender sexual activity, female orgasm, masturbation during childhood and during marriage, and premarital and extramarital sex diverged from the social norms and shocked many people. Kinsey's results have been disputed, but the importance of his work has not. He made the study of sexuality a legitimate part of scientific research.

Many other sex surveys have been completed, including the Playboy Foundation survey during the 1970s and the National Opinion Research Council survey in the 1990s. Both of these surveys attempted to obtain a representative sample of U.S. residents and succeeded to a greater degree than Kinsey had. These surveys indicated some changes in sexuality over the intervening years—especially a decrease in the double standard of sexual behavior for men and women—but all of the surveys have shown that people engage in a wide variety of sexual behavior.

Masters and Johnson measured sexual responses directly during masturbation and intercourse in an attempt to understand the physiology of sexual response. Their 1966 book detailed four stages of the sexual response—excitation, plateau, orgasm, and resolution. Although the people who are willing to have sex for the sake of science are not representative of the general population, Masters and Johnson believed that sexual response is similar in all people.

Childhood sexuality includes both exploration and the potential for abuse. Exploration begins very early, with infants manipulating their genitals, young children masturbating to orgasm, and kindergarten children exploring each other's genitals. Parents may find these explorations disturbing, and condemning these behaviors may convey the impression that sexual feelings and activities are unacceptable.

The unequal power between children and adults can create situations for sexual abuse. Sex surveys have revealed that at least 15% of women and 5% of men were sexually abused as children. The large majority of the perpetrators of sexual abuse of children are men, often family members or those in positions of authority, but older girls and women are also perpetrators of abuse. Living with a stepfather dramatically increases a girl's chances of being abused. Abuse has both short-term and long-term negative effects for male and female victims.

Sex education tends to emphasize the dangers rather than the pleasures of sexuality, leaving boys with information about the damage that their male sexuality can do and leaving girls with a sense of vulnerability. Although children's sexual explorations involve same- and other-gender children, most adolescents show increasing heterosexual interest. Sexual activity is one of the reasons for dating, although boys emphasize sex as a reason for dating more often than girls do. Boys also tend to begin intercourse at a younger age than girls, and this difference appears in many ethnic groups. Gender differences in premarital intercourse as well as in other sexual activities have decreased over the past 50 years.

Marriage is no longer the only acceptable context for sexual activity; a majority of both young men and young women now have intercourse before age 25. Celibacy is a choice made by about one-third of college men and women, but more women than men choose monogamy as an ideal style of sexual relationship (61% versus 37%), whereas more men than women choose free sexual experimentation (28% versus 5%). This difference may relate to men's greater acceptance of casual sex, which is one of the largest gender differences in sexuality. Another large difference is frequency of masturbation, which may lead to women being less likely to experience orgasm during partnered sex.

Another difference that influences sexuality is the existence of a double standard for sexual behavior, which holds that girls and women are less sexual than boys and men. Comparisons of the data from the Kinsey surveys and more recent analyses show that acceptance of the double standard has declined, but its continuation is a factor influencing the sexuality of women and men and contributing to conflicts in couples.

Same-gender sexual activity is not uncommon among children and adolescents, but a minority of people experience erotic attraction to only members of the same gender. Estimates vary according to the definition, but a small percentage of men and an even smaller percentage of women have primarily or exclusively gay or lesbian sexual orientations. The underlying reasons for a gay or lesbian sexual orientation are not understood, but recent research has concentrated on biological factors that may relate to sexual orientation. The third interstitial nucleus of the hypothalamus seems to be larger in heterosexual men than in homosexual men and heterosexual women, but these conclusions are in question due to bias in the study.

Lesbian and gay lifestyles are not well accepted, and adolescents who are attracted to members of their same gender have trouble accepting themselves and their sexual orientation. The process of coming out, of revealing gay or lesbian interests and behavior, can be a process of positive self-acceptance but can also create family conflict due to parents' difficulty in accepting a child's sexual orientation.

The sexuality of gay men and lesbian women differs, and these couples have both similarities with and differences from heterosexual couples. For instance, both gay men and lesbians value oral sex, but lesbians are more reluctant to perform cunnilingus than gay men are to perform fellatio. One survey indicated that lesbian couples have sex less often than other couples, but the definition of what constitutes sex is typically intercourse, which does not fit within lesbian sexuality. Gay men value and have sex often, especially in the first several years of their relationships. For all types of heterosexual, gay, and lesbian couples, sex provides both a bond of pleasure and a potential for conflict in their relationships.

When individuals form romantic and sexual relationships with both men and women, they are bisexual. This sexual orientation is controversial and difficult to define because many individuals experiment with sexuality, having both male and female partners. Few, however, have a true bisexual sexual orientation, so this sexual orientation remains the least researched and most poorly understood of the sexual orientations.

Glossary

bisexual a person who is sexually attracted to individuals of the same as well as the other gender.

celibacy refraining from sexual activity.

coming out the process of recognizing and publicly acknowledging one's gay or lesbian sexual orientation.

cunnilingus oral stimulation of the female genitals.

date rape or **acquaintance rape** forced sexual activity occurring between people who are acquainted.

double standard for sexual behavior the social standard that allows men greater freedom of sexual expression than women.

fellatio oral stimulation of the male genitals.

gay an alternative for the term *homosexual,* emphasizing the entire lifestyle instead of only the sexual aspects of it; sometimes used to refer to both men and women but more often to men.

incest sexual activity between family members.

lesbian a woman who feels sexual attraction for and chooses sexual activity with other women.

masturbation manipulation of the genitals to produce sexual pleasure.

monogamy having only one sexual partner.

representative sample a sample (subset) of the population that reflects the characteristics of the population from which the sample was drawn.

self-selection of participants when participants rather than researchers choose who will take part in the research. This problem biases the results and prevents generalization to a wider population.

serial monogamy the practice of having a series of monogamous sexual relationships.

sexual orientation the erotic attraction to members of the same or the other gender (or to both).

Suggested Readings

Blumstein, Philip; & Schwartz, Pepper. (1983). *American couples.* New York: Pocket Books. This book examines married, cohabiting, gay, and lesbian couples, interviewing them about money and work as well as sex. The chapter about sex is a fascinating examination of what couples do and enjoy as well as what role sex plays in conflict and maintenance of the relationship.

McCormick, Naomi B. (1994). *Sexual salvation: Affirming women's sexual rights and pleasures.* Westport, CT: Praeger. Although McCormick concentrates on women's sexuality, she addresses a range of topics for women's sexuality in an outspoken way. She believes that women can construct a sexuality that will give them salvation—freedom and pleasure.

Netting, Nancy S. (1992). Sexuality in youth culture: Identity and change. *Adolescence, 27,* 961–976. This study reports on sexual attitudes of college students in 1980 versus 1990 and analyzes the styles of sexuality in young heterosexual adults. The categories of celibacy, monogamy, and free experimentation correspond to choices for other adults.

Oliver, Mary Beth; & Hyde, Janet Shibley. (1993). Gender differences in sexuality: A meta-analysis. *Psychological Bulletin, 114,* 29–51. This meta-analysis concentrates on sexual attitudes and reports of sexual behaviors. The authors have determined the size of gender differences, finding large differences for a few aspects of sexuality, smaller differences for some attitudes, and no difference for others. Their interpretation is tied to the various theories of sexuality and makes an interesting summary of gender differences in sexuality.

Chapter 12

School

HEADLINE

A Room of Their Own

—*Newsweek,* June 24, 1996

"Eighth-grade girls say they prefer doing physics experiments without boys around to hog the equipment. Boys say they'd rather recite Shakespeare without girls around to make them feel 'like geeks,'" LynNell Hancock and Claudia Kalb (1996, p. 76) wrote. Would girls and boys benefit from gender-segregated classrooms, as these eighth-graders told Hancock and Kalb? These reporters examined the trend to establish gender-segregated classes in public schools and asked whether it represents an opportunity for girls and boys to help when they approach problematic subjects or whether it sends education back about 100 years. Gender-segregation was common in the schools of 100 years ago; boys and girls entered the school through separate doors and attended gender-segregated classes.

During the last half of the 20th century, few schools continued this practice. Some school administrations opened their institutions to both women and men, and others admitted the other gender only under the force of legal mandates. Coeducational classrooms became the norm. A 1992 report from the American Association of University Women (AAUW) questioned how equitable education has been for women, pointing out many problems in the process and outcome of schooling for women. One problem was the disproportionate attention and access to equipment received by boys. One response was the creation of single-gender classrooms.

This answer, however, is controversial. With gender, as with race, separate is usually not equal, and federal law permits few reasons for segregation by gender in public schools. Contact sports, singing groups, and human sexuality classes are among those exceptions, but science and literature are not, making gender-segregated classes legally questionable. A growing number of public schools have instituted such classes, usually for girls in science or math but sometimes for boys in language and literature. Teachers who use this approach see the benefits of letting students "think with something besides their hormones" (Hancock & Kalb, 1996, p. 76).

Others have questioned the long-term benefits of gender-segregated public school classes. After all, the world is coed, and girls and boys must learn to deal with each others' presence at some point. Single-gender schools can offer girls some advantages in terms of higher confidence (AAUW, 1992), but little research exists on advantages, especially in the long term, of single-gender classes in coed schools. Single-gender classes were not associated with decreases in gender stereotyping in one longitudinal study (Signorella, Frieze, & Hershey, 1996), which found the advantages of such classrooms questionable for most students. The feelings on the issue are strong, with both enthusiasts and skeptics looking for ways to remedy gender inequities in schooling. What are those inequities? When do they start? And what are the long-term consequences for women's and men's lives?

The School Experience

Even before children begin school, their parents and the society in which they live treat boys and girls differently. Chapter 8 included examples of the process of gender stereotyping: dolls for girls but trucks for boys, quiet games for girls but noisy games for boys, frilly dresses for girls but grubby jeans for boys, staying close to home for girls but venturing out for boys.

Not all girls or all boys conform to these stereotypes, but by age 4 or 5, children have developed a concept of gender and know what behaviors are expected and approved for each. (See Chapter 7 for a more complete discussion of the development of gender identity.) Thus, when children start kindergarten, they hold beliefs about what clothes, games, and behaviors are appropriate for boys and girls, and they bring these beliefs to the school experience. Schools often reinforce these stereotypical beliefs, producing differences in attitudes and expectations about careers that result in differences in preparation to pursue careers.

Title IX of the Education Amendments of 1972 prohibits gender discrimination in school programs that receive federal funds. Although gender discrimination is now prohibited by law, a study by the American Association of University Women (AAUW, 1992) presented a great deal of evidence illustrating a continuing lack of gender equity. Problems included unequal attention and access to education materials, promotion of stereotypical gender roles, unequal expectations concerning careers, and increased sexual harassment in school by classmates and teachers.

Attitudes of teachers and counselors allow the continuation of gender bias in schools, and several studies have indicated that educators exhibit both gender and ethnic biases. One study of gender (Avery & Walker, 1993) asked prospective teachers to explain differences in educational accomplishments between girls and boys and between Whites and ethnic minorities. The future teachers' explanations for gender-related differences in accomplishments tended to revolve around social expectations—that is, prospective teachers explained the greater educational attainment of boys as due to expectations for boys' achievement, discrimination against girls, and lack of encouragement for girls' achievement. Another common attribution given was family encouragement and expectations, and a very small percentage of the explanations were in terms of innate differences in ability.

These future teachers exhibited few signs of gender bias, but the attributions of ethnic differences in achievement revealed some bias against ethnic groups that diverged from mainstream culture. Although discrimination was listed as a reason why students from different ethnic backgrounds differed in their educational accomplishments, the most common explanation was that the students' ethnic cultures influenced their values, producing differences in attainment. These results indicate that these prospective teachers were more sensitive to gender bias than to ethnic bias.

Has the recent emphasis on education reform and the increased sensitivity to gender equity in the classroom produced teachers who are more gender fair? If so, differences in teacher–student interaction should exist between recently trained teachers and those who received their training at earlier times. A study testing this hypothesis (Jones, 1989) failed to find such differences; instead it showed that both experienced and new teachers gave boys more attention, feedback, praise, and warnings than they gave girls. Regardless of teaching experience or gender of the teacher, interactions with female students were different and less helpful than were teacher interactions with male students.

Gender equity is not a large part of the curriculum for prospective teachers; neither is it a frequent topic of inservice training for teachers (AAUW, 1992; Sadker & Sadker, 1985). A 1980 examination of textbooks used for teacher training found that these texts devoted very little space to gender equity issues (Sadker & Sadker, 1980). This study concluded that teachers could not be trained to be gender fair when their training minimized these issues. In 1993, a similar study produced similar results (Titus, 1993). Thus, teachers are known to enter their profession with gender stereotypes that their training as teachers failed to address, leaving them with a tendency to treat their students in gender-stereotypical ways.

Early School Experience

The problem of teachers promoting stereotypical gender roles can begin very early in the school experience. Teachers channel children into gender-stereotypical activities, beginning during preschool; they encourage different play activities with boys than with girls and spend the majority of their time—60%—with boys (Jones, 1989). In addition, children have the experience of being taught by an overwhelming majority of female kindergarten and elementary school teachers. Several factors discourage men from teaching young children, including the poor salary, low prestige, and poor image of elementary school teachers (D. Cohen, 1992). The women who choose to become elementary teachers also differ from men who have made the same choice (Montecinos & Nielsen, 1997). Women reported that they had decided to become elementary teachers when they were in elementary school more often than men, and more women than men expected to teach in elementary school for the duration of their careers. Thus, the men and women who choose to teach young children were shown to have different expectations from their careers.

Male elementary school teachers are still rare, but their behavior is similar to female elementary school teachers: Both tend to reward children for being compliant (Cohen, 1992). Children benefit by having male elementary teachers by their decrease in students' gender stereotyping: Those with male teachers make significantly fewer stereotypical explanations for the behavior of men and women than students who have had only female teachers during the elementary grades (Mancus, 1992). Both boys and girls benefit from

GENDERED VOICES
Treated Like a King

"I'm not sure why I wanted to work with kids," a young male elementary school teacher told me. "I started as a camp counselor, and that job was attractive because of the other counselors—lots of girls. They thought it was cool that I was a counselor and was good with kids. They seemed to think that getting along with children meant I was sensitive. I can get a line of my ex-girlfriends who will testify that I am not any more sensitive than most guys, but I do like working with kids, so I became a teacher.

"The principal and coach are both men, but there is only one other male teacher in my school, so I get a lot of attention from the students and from the female teachers. The kids love me; I'm treated like a king. When I walk down the hall, they want to be near me, and my attention is something special. Some of them live in single-parent families with their mothers, but even the ones who live with fathers seem starved for male attention. I believe that their fathers may not be too emotionally accessible and I am, so they are drawn to me. I try to have good relationships with them, and it is work that I enjoy, but the administration keeps hinting that I should get a degree so that I can become an administrator. I don't want to; I'm satisfied doing what I'm doing."

seeing men perform the job of teacher during their early years of schooling, but there is no clear evidence that girls benefit and boys are damaged by the gender imbalance shown by elementary school teachers.

The preponderance of female elementary school teachers has led to the "myth that early-education environments meet the needs of girls better than boys" (AAUW, 1992, p. 18). The AAUW report argued that the opposite is true: Early schooling consists of activities in which girls have more proficiency than boys, giving boys more training in the skills they lack, such as reading, while ignoring those that girls lack, such as science investigation. Girls need practice with gross-motor activities, investigatory activities, and experimental activities, but these activities tend to be considered part of "play" rather than part of their education. Furthermore, these activities are more likely to result from boys' play than the play preferred by girls. Thus, the activities of the early elementary classroom may strengthen the skills boys lack while failing to provide the same benefits for girls.

Physical education during elementary school is likely to perpetuate rather than remedy these inequities (Ignico, 1989). Physical education teachers often label activities according to gender and funnel children into the activities they consider gender appropriate. Team games are usually labeled as appropriate for boys and not girls, whereas most expressive movements and less vigorous activities are considered appropriate for girls and not boys. When physical education teachers choose activities for children based on their gender biases, they are perpetuating gender inequalities. These differences in physical activity leave girls with less experience in playing on teams and with limited vigorous physical exercise and boys with less cooperative experience in playing and with limited opportunities to develop sensitivity to others.

The gender stereotyping in children's books and textbooks has been the subject of extensive research, indicating that portrayals of women and girls have changed over the past

30 years. Portrayals of characters and historical figures in texts reflect the current social expectations for each gender (Hoffman, 1982). The early research on this topic indicated that children's readers tend to ignore women and girls, containing more boy-centered than girl-centered stories, more adult male than female characters, more biographies of men than women, and even more stories of male than female animals. Even the illustrations in children's books show more boys and men and portray them in more active, powerful ways (Sadker, Sadker, & Steindam, 1989).

An examination of the contents of the stories before the 1980s (Hoffman, 1982) showed that male characters were more likely than female characters to show creativity, bravery, curiosity, and achievement, and female characters were often portrayed as passive, fearful, and incompetent. Adult characters fit the gender stereotypes of female domesticity and male achievement. All these character portrayals gave children the message that girls and women have contributed less and do less interesting things than boys and men. When the main characters of stories were women doing nontraditional things, both girls and boys widened their views of what girls could do, indicating a potential for unbiased treatment of genders through altering story characters.

Later examinations of gender role stereotyping in children's books have found changes in the ways that female and male characters are portrayed. The frequency of male and female characters has become more evenly distributed (Kortenhaus & Demarest, 1993; Turner-Bowker, 1996). Unfortunately, male and female characters continue to be portrayed in ways that reflect stereotypical roles. That is, female characters are still not as active and powerful as male characters in children's picture books. The portrayal of girls as active has increased, but such portrayals of boys have not decreased, leaving a continuing imbalance in the characterizations of girls and boys in children's stories.

Beginning in the 1980s, the gender bias in books has become more subtle, with an equal representation of male and female characters as central in the stories but with male characters appearing more often in titles and in illustrations for these books (Turner-Bowker, 1996). Girls are described in more positive terms than boys, possibly because they behave in ways that are consistent with traditional gender roles. Both girls and boys are disadvantaged by these portrayals—girls are not given sufficient models for activity and competition and boys lack models for nurturance and tenderness.

Few gender differences exist in school achievement during the early years of school. Some standardized, national tests have shown that girls outscore boys on some types of verbal ability, but other similar tests have shown boys to have a small advantage (AAUW, 1992; Maccoby & Jacklin, 1974). Whatever the direction, the magnitude of the difference is small. Socioeconomic status is a much stronger predictor of elementary school achievement than is gender, with children from the lower socioeconomic levels having consistently poorer school records than children from wealthier families. Even controlling for socioeconomic status, girls tend to make better grades in school, beginning during the elementary grades and persisting through college.

Several social factors combine to predict academic success and to explain gender differences during elementary school (Serbin, Zelkowitz, Doyle, Gold, & Wheaton, 1990). Girls' advantage relates to their tendency to respond to social cues and to comply with adults' requests. That is, the training that girls receive in complying with the female gender role is a factor in their early school success. The academic ability most strongly related to school success was visual–spatial competence, and because boys performed better in this realm, it partially compensated for their lesser responsiveness and compliance to adults.

High scores on the visual–spatial factor were an advantage for all children. Visual–spatial ability related to access to stereotypically masculine toys at home, such as Legos or science kits. Of course, boys were more likely to have such access, but playing with such toys allows the difference between female engineers and scientists and women in more traditional fields to diminish (Schiff, 1997). Fathers' educational level and mothers' occupational status related to the availability of such toys (Serbin et al., 1990). Therefore, experience seems to be an important factor in developing spatial ability, as some studies have indicated (Baenninger & Newcombe, 1989). Indeed, the differential experiences of boys and girls during the elementary years may lay the foundation for the larger differences in spatial abilities that appear during junior high school and thereafter.

Considering both social and intellectual ability in predicting academic success led to a complex model that included both types of variables (Serbin et al., 1990). As previous research had indicated, socioeconomic variables predicted academic success, including mothers' occupational and fathers' educational levels. These variables also indirectly influenced the single cognitive factor most strongly related to academic success: visual–spatial ability. This study suggested that conformity to gender-typical behaviors plays a role in girls' academic success and in boys' poor performance. Thus, a complex picture emerges to describe academic success during elementary school, with socioeconomic factors, gender role socialization, and cognitive abilities all contributing. Figure 12.1 shows the relationships among these factors.

Like the differences in academic success, the gender differences in self-perception are small during elementary school. These differences, however, reflect the beginnings of gender

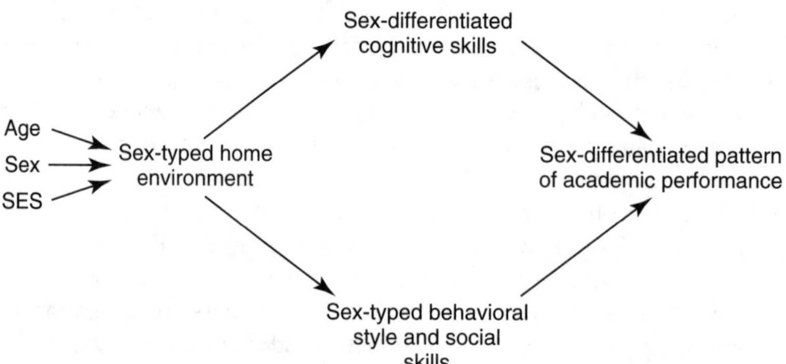

FIGURE 12.1 Model of Social and Cognitive Abilities Predicting Academic Performance

Source: From L. A. Serbin, P. Zelkowitz, A. Doyle, D. Gold, & B. Wheaton, 1990, "The socialization of sex-differentiated skills and academic performance: A mediational model," p. 616, *Sex Roles,* vol. 23. Reprinted by permission of Plenum Publishing and Lisa Serbin.

stereotypes (Eccles, Wigfield, Harold, & Blumenfeld, 1993). As early as first grade, children show differential beliefs in their abilities at various activities. Girls express more positive beliefs about their competence in reading and music, whereas boys are more positive about their mathematics and sports abilities. No gender differences exist for these skills at this age, so these differences reflect children's beliefs rather than their abilities. As children grow older, the gender associations of male and female begin to show greater differences.

Changes during Junior High

Gender differences in achievement start to appear during the junior high school years. Girls experience a decreased interest in math and science and a change in career orientation, with an increased interest in marriage and children and a narrowing of career interests to those careers most commonly occupied by women (Bush & Simmons, 1987). Adolescent girls believe that they will combine a family with paid employment, reflecting the current reality of contemporary family life, but the image of this combination may not correspond to the difficulty of balancing these different roles. Adolescent boys experience a widening of career interests and give less attention to their future family plans, assuming that they are preparing for a career that will be a primary focus of their lives.

During elementary school, girls and boys exhibit few differences in academic abilities, but girls make better grades. During junior high school, boys' achievement in math and science begins to exceed that of girls, although the differences are small and vary within different areas of math and science (AAUW, 1992). For example, the male advantage in math problem solving is minimal throughout junior high school but becomes larger during the high school years. The gender difference in science achievement begins during these years but does not affect all sciences equally. Girls do as well or better than boys in life sciences, and boys perform better in physical sciences (Lee & Burkam, 1996).

Achievement differences mirror girls' and boys' science experiences during junior high school (AAUW, 1992). There are no differences in *interest* in participating in science activities, but boys are more likely to participate in using equipment and performing science activities, as the eighth-grade girl in the headline story complained. Boys are more likely to use science equipment, such as microscopes and electricity meters, and these different experiences with science activities both in and outside of the classroom are a factor in girls' lower achievement and interest in science (Lee & Burkam, 1996). These differences in experience contribute to confidence and possibly to the choice to enroll in advanced courses.

Girls start to experience a decline in confidence in their academic abilities during junior high school, whereas boys start to feel more confident (Bush & Simmons, 1987). The AAUW report (1992) hypothesized that girls' diminished confidence might be a reason for their tendency to discontinue studying math and science, whereas boys who stop studying math and science might do so due to their difficulties in mastering the material. Girls tend to view their mastery problems in math as lack of ability, whereas boys explain their decisions to discontinue math courses as lack of interest.

The decrease in academic confidence for girls and the increase for boys may be part of the developmental changes that accompany puberty, forming a complex interaction between school experience and social structures (Bush & Simmons, 1987). One possibility is that gender-related role expectations intensify during puberty for both boys and girls, with each becoming more stereotypical in their interests and achievement-related behavior (Hill & Lynch, 1983). A review of the research in this area (Eccles & Bryan, 1994) indicated that development of more stereotypical interests may be more typical of boys than girls, with boys developing more gender stereotypical views for themselves and for girls. Girls become more stereotypical in their views of academic subjects, developing the opinion that their math abilities are lower and their language abilities are higher than for boys, even when standardized tests reveal similar abilities.

The timing of puberty affects girls and boys differently (Tobin-Richards, Boxer, & Petersen, 1983). For girls, early puberty presents problems: They must deal with bodies that are more developed than those of their peers, and they must cope with people's reactions to their physical maturity. These reactions often include comments on or interest in their developing sexuality, which many girls find embarrassing. For boys, early onset of puberty is an advantage: As they increase in size and strength relative to their peers, they have advantages in social dominance and athletic performance, making for welcomed changes.

Athletic performance becomes more gender segregated during late childhood and early adolescence. "That's a game for girls" is an insult to boys, and girls are unlikely to be competent at boys' sports. The preferred activities of girls and boys continue to differ along paths that appeared during early childhood: Boys more often engage in physical activities requiring gross motor skills that use the large muscles of the body. Games that include running, jumping, throwing, and kicking—namely baseball, football, soccer, and basketball—are preferred by boys more than by girls.

Girls are not necessarily more sedentary than boys, but their leisure activities are less likely to involve gross motor skills. Indeed, both boys and girls watch television and play video and computer games, resulting in a more sedentary lifestyle and decreased levels of physical fitness. The intensification of gender roles during junior high school pushes girls away from and boys toward athletics, producing gender differences in physical activity and in confidence in physical abilities.

Therefore, the junior high school years mark the beginning of differences in academic accomplishment for girls and boys. Girls continue to make better grades than boys, but girls become less assertive about classroom activities, such as science demonstrations and equipment use. Their decreased participation may be one reason for their decreased interest in science, but the continued lack of encouragement by their teachers and parents may also contribute to girls' falling interest in science and math during junior high school. Boys also experience a decline of interest in science during this time, but their interest remains higher than that of girls.

High School

The differences in academic achievement that begin during junior high school become more pronounced during the high school years, as do differences in confidence and attitudes toward various subjects. These changes in academic achievement, attitudes, and confidence relate to an even more important gender difference: in choices. During secondary schooling, students begin to have choices in their coursework, and girls and boys make different choices that can have life-long consequences for each. For example, girls' choice not to take advanced math and science courses can affect their access to certain college majors and careers.

Both girls and boys feel more confident in their abilities at age 9 than at 17 (Freiberg, 1991). During elementary school 60% of girls and 67% of boys have positive feelings about themselves and their abilities, whereas by high school only 29% of the girls and 46% of the boys still hold these beliefs (see Figure 12.2). Although both experience a decrease, girls report less self-confidence than boys. These feelings extend to physical appearance and abilities as well as academic subjects.

Physical appearance and athletic ability are important to high school students because both are ways to gain prestige in the school social structure (Suitor & Reavis, 1995). Both female and male high school students have other ways to gain social stature, but in comparing students from the late 1970s to those from the late 1980s, physical appearance remained a primary way for girls to attain social prominence in their schools, and athletics continued as important for boys. The 10-year comparison showed that sports had become more and cheerleading less important ways for girls to gain prestige. For boys, having fast cars became less important but having sex remained a way to gain prestige in the high school environment. For both girls and boys, getting good grades and being considered intelligent conferred equally high levels of prestige.

The increased emphasis on sports for young women has resulted in the current acceptance of sports as a way for young women to gain positive recognition. Their increased sports participation has been dramatic. In 1971, girls constituted only 7% of athletic participants in high schools, but in 1991, the percentage had grown to 36% (Mansnerus, 1992). Not only has the number of female athletes grown but the variety of sports in which they participate has also increased. High schools have added women's teams in cross country, gymnastics, soccer, field hockey, softball, swimming, track, volleyball, and other sports. These additions have expanded opportunities for high school girls to develop their physical abilities and talents in ways that were reserved for boys.

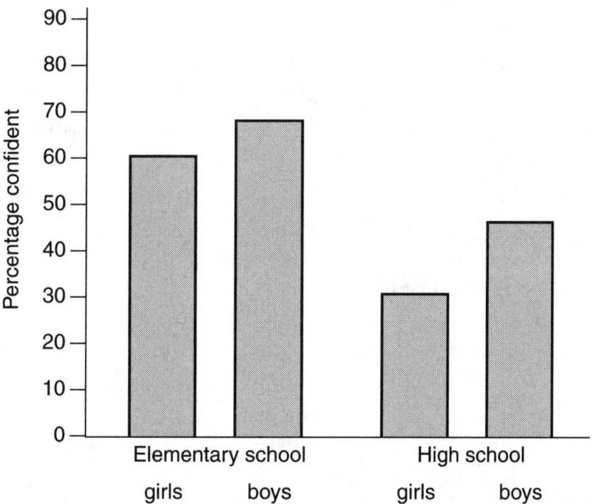

FIGURE 12.2 Self-Confidence of Girls and Boys during Elementary and High School

From junior high to high school, girls experience more of a decrease than boys in interest and confidence concerning math and science. A meta-analysis (Weinburgh, 1995) indicated that boys had more positive attitudes toward science than girls and that the relationship between attitudes and achievement were positive. Furthermore, the relationships was stronger for girls than for boys indicating that their attitudes may have a stronger influence on their performance.

High levels of ability do not guarantee that students will have positive attitudes or high achievement. The lack of confidence in math and science extends to intellectually gifted young women, who have the ability to succeed at the highest levels but fail to believe that they are academically gifted (Walker, Reis, & Leonard, 1992). Mathematically talented girls have lower aspirations than comparable boys, and girls do not use their abilities as much as boys do (Benbow, 1992). High-achieving girls, however, have positive attitudes toward science (Weinburgh, 1995), highlighting the importance of attitudes in achievement.

The lack of personal and academic confidence is a factor in the choice of coursework for both boys and girls during high school. The overall gender differences in mathematics course participation are small and decreasing (U.S. Department of Education [USDE], 1995). Until the 1990s boys and girls completed an average of three math courses during high school, but boys were more likely to enroll in more advanced courses (AAUW, 1992). These differences have disappeared, and in 1992 girls and boys were equally likely to take advanced math classes (USDE, 1995). The differences in test scores on standardized tests remain: Boys score higher on tests such as the Scholastic Aptitude Test.

Male and female high school students who pursue science are not equally represented in all types of science courses (AAUW, 1992). Female students are more likely to enroll in advanced biology and social sciences classes, whereas boys are more likely to take chemistry, physics, and physical sciences. In addition, students enrolled in the same course may have different views of how the course fits into career plans. For example, young men who enroll in calculus and advanced science in high school are very likely to take these courses in preparation for careers in engineering, whereas very few young women enrolled in the same courses even consider engineering careers. Therefore, young women not only choose to take fewer advanced math and science courses than boys, but they also fail to develop an interest in science careers, even when they have the ability and preparation to do so.

The differential enrollment of young men and women in advanced math and science courses has been considered a problem for women because they miss these educational experiences and the career preparation the courses offer. When they judge the enrollment of women as low, education experts are using men and their enrollment statistics as the standard (Noddings, 1991). The implication is that women's enrollment is deficient and something to be remedied. Nel Noddings suggested that educators have given too little consideration both to what women are doing and to the reasons behind their choices. She pointed out that stereotypical thinking has imposed limitations on both young women and young men, restricting both from a full range of choices in coursework and careers. Most of the criticisms and research have centered on girls and how they are diverted from math and science. Fewer considerations have been directed toward boys and how they might be steered toward subjects and careers for which they may not have the highest interest or aptitude.

A major criticism from the AAUW report was that boys get more attention in the classroom than girls. Myra Sadker, David Sadker, and their colleagues (Sadker & Sadker, 1985;

Sadker, Sadker, & Klein, 1986; Sadker, Sadker, & Steindam, 1989) have studied teacher–student interactions in the classroom and these findings contributed to the AAUW's conclusions. They described the classroom situation:

> *Girls and minorities are short-changed in the critical currency of classroom interaction. Teachers from grade school to graduate school ask males more questions, give them more precise feedback, criticize them more, and give them more time to respond. Whether the attention is positive, negative, or neutral, the golden rule of the American classroom is that boys get more. (Sadker, Sadker, & Steindam, 1989, p. 47)*

Counselors' stereotyping of gender-appropriate careers is a factor in the courses that boys and girls take in school as well as in the careers each chooses. Gender bias in counseling may be either overt or covert (Hoffman, 1982). Overt bias includes sexist statements, such as telling girls that they are not expected to be good at math or discouraging boys from enrolling in cooking classes. Covert bias includes encouraging girls and boys to behave in stereotypical ways, such as providing information concerning traditional but not nontraditional careers or failing to take nontraditional career interests seriously. Research on career education materials indicates that these materials are largely oriented toward boys, leaving girls unrepresented or portrayed in stereotypical ways (Hoffman, 1982). Only 3% of the materials contained clear references to both women and men, and 60% made reference to only one gender. These tests and materials used by counselors present barriers to career development, especially for girls.

Counselors tend to steer adolescents toward traditional careers (Hoffman, 1982). They may counsel girls about careers that require education and ability but not careers that lead to high status and prestige. That is, counselors are more likely to recommend that girls become science teachers than chemists and that boys become chemists rather than science teachers. Furthermore, girls are discriminated against at increasing levels as they get older and closer to career choices.

Vocational education is another area in which girls and boys have received unequal attention: "Vocational education was originally designed to give work skills to high school boys who were not planning to attend college. But research indicates that it may not serve either males or females very well in the current environment" (AAUW, 1992, p. 42). This pessimistic assessment comes from the finding that men who complete vocational educational courses in high school earn less money than those who have not taken these courses. Vocational education also does young women a disservice, routing them into office and business occupations that are low-paying and often dead-end jobs. Only around 4% of the students enrolled in construction, mechanics, and machine repair are young women (Burge & Culver, 1990), and the choice to take nontraditional vocational courses places young women at risk for harassment from male classmates and from some teachers.

Sexual harassment, unwanted sexual attention, from male students and teachers becomes a source of stress for young women at school. Although young men can also experience sexual harassment, few mention being troubled by unwanted sexual attention by their female peers or teachers (AAUW, 1992). This reticence may be part of the gender role young men are attempting to fulfill rather than because their is no sexual harassment.

GENDERED VOICES
I Might Have Been an Engineer

"I probably would have been an engineer if I had been given the opportunity. Well, maybe *opportunity* isn't exactly the right word, because nothing really prevented me, but nobody encouraged me, either," a high school science teacher in her early 40s said. "I always liked science and did well in it, but none of my counselors mentioned engineering or being a chemist or any science career except teaching. I think they mentioned those careers to the boys who were good at science but not to the girls. They steered us toward teaching. That's just the way it was, and I'm not sure how much it has changed.

"They just didn't expect girls to be good at science and math, and when we were, they didn't consider science careers, so they didn't tell us about being a scientist. Teaching science, yes, but not being a scientist. If a boy was interested in science, they wouldn't have mentioned teaching, even if that was what he would have been best at. I wonder how many women would have been better scientists and engineers than science teachers and how many men would have been better science teachers."

This harassment may be sexually oriented or not; it consists of unwanted sexual remarks, statements about the unsuitability of women for various types of jobs, or derogatory remarks about women and their abilities. As the AAUW (1992) report pointed out, harassment is about power and authority, and the vast majority of incidents involve boys harassing girls. Although sexual and other harassment that affects the educational process is prohibited by Title IX of the Education Amendments of 1972, those who harass are often allowed to continue. The attitude is often "boys will be boys," with harassment not considered a serious offense. Thus, fear of harassment may make girls reluctant to enroll in courses with a majority of boys or to enroll in nontraditional vocational courses.

A survey of 8th to 11th grade students in public schools in the United States (American Association of University Women, 1993) revealed that sexual harassment was a common experience. Four out of five students said they had been the target of unwelcome sexual behavior while at school or a school function. Adult school employees were the perpetrators in 25% of incidents when girls were targets and 10% when boys were targets, showing that the majority of harassment incidents are perpetrated by other students. Girls were more common targets than boys, but both girls and boys admitted perpetrating sexual harassment. The student perpetrators tended to consider harassment part of school life and "no big deal" (Bryant, 1995, p. 41). The targets felt differently. Harassment made school more difficult; victims were less interested and involved in school, made lower grades, and expressed more doubt about graduating. Although sexual harassment may be part of high school life, it is a major problem with serious consequences. (See the Diversity Highlight: "Lesbians and Gays in School.")

In summary, both overt and subtle forces affect adolescents during high school, with both girls and boys making more traditional and stereotypical choices. Although girls' skills in math and science classes equal those of boys, girls enroll in fewer of these classes than boys. Those girls who complete advanced math and science courses tend not to view these courses as part of their career preparation, resulting in a gender imbalance in math and science careers. High school counselors are a major source of gender bias, steering

DIVERSITY HIGHLIGHT

Lesbians and Gays in School

School is a major factor in adolescents' lives, and school can be a major problem for gay and lesbian adolescents. Those who disclose their sexual orientations are at increased risk of harassment, especially from peers. Indeed, the majority of sexual harassment in school comes from other students. Accusation of homosexuality are frequent instances and may even be aimed at students who are heterosexual (AAUW, 1993). The harassment sometimes goes beyond name calling and into physical attacks, with gay young men in particular peril.

These incidents of harassment and violence take their toll, making school unpleasant and dangerous for gay and lesbian students. These students are more likely to drop out of school and attempt suicide than other students (Uribe & Harbeck, 1992). To combat these problems, several schools have programs that offer various remedies.

One program is Project 10 in Los Angeles (Uribe & Harbeck, 1992), a support group and counseling service for gay, lesbian, and bisexual adolescents. The service attracted a group of students and had a positive influence on the school climate. Other schools have approached the problems in similar ways, by beginning counseling programs and by appointing personnel to coordinate services for gay, lesbian, and bisexual students (Livingston, 1994).

The Triangle Program in Toronto is another approach that offers services to gay and lesbian adolescents (Dwyer, 1997). This program is a community service rather than a school program, but it offers gay and lesbian adolescents help in getting back into school. Students who have left may attend classes that emphasize the positive contributions to society of gays and lesbians. Despite the alternative program, its goals include integrating gay and lesbian adolescents back into schools.

Yet another approach is to open schools for gay and lesbian students. Three such schools have opened in the United States: the EAGLES Center (Emphasizing Adolescent Gay Lesbian Education Services) in Los Angeles, the Harvey Milk School at the Hetrick-Martin Institute in New York (Van Gelder, 1996), and the Walt Whitman Community School in Dallas, Texas (*Jet,* 1997). These school are dedicated to providing a supportive environment where gay, lesbian, and bisexual adolescents can learn without the sexual harassment that is common in the schools.

All of these solutions to the problems faced by lesbian and gay students are controversial (Dwyer, 1997). Schools have looked for remedies for racial and gender inequities, but all of the programs offering school support for gay and lesbian students have met with opposition. Homophobia is not only widespread in schools, but some people want schools to remain hostile places for gays and lesbians.

more boys than girls toward prestigious careers. In vocational education, boys are more likely to be guided toward higher-paying skilled craft jobs and girls into lower-paying business jobs. However, vocational education may not serve boys well, as those who have and have not completed this coursework earn comparable salaries. Girls who enroll in nontraditional courses face the possibility of sexual or other harassment, and although illegal, this behavior is often not considered a serious infraction of the school's rules.

College and Professional School

The effects of stereotyping and gender bias influence young women and men before they enter college, creating differences in expectations and choices. Young men receive messages from their high school counselors and from society that they should prepare for careers that will support a family. Young women get a different message: Their careers will be less important than their husbands' employment, so their college majors need not lead to specific job-related skills.

These differing expectations are consistent with the history of women's roles but not necessarily with contemporary employment patterns. College education for women developed gradually during the 19th century but never approached equal education for men and women, either in numbers or in type of training (Fox, 1989). Instead, women went to college to find husbands and to prepare for careers that would last only until they married. Thus, higher education for women confined them to careers that would be flexible, but with little chance for advancement. One of the early careers available to women was teaching, and beginning in the 1800s women were in demand as teachers in the growing public school system. One of the reasons female teachers were in demand was their willingness to work for low salaries.

Throughout most of the 20th century, men attended college in greater numbers than women, but the number of female college students in the United States and Canada has grown to the point that women now receive more undergraduate degrees than men (Jacobs, 1996). This pattern applies to few other countries. Especially in countries that are less industrialized, women do not participate in higher education nearly as often as men. Table 12.1 presents the percentage of women of the entire college enrollment in various countries. This table shows the percentage of students who are women but does not reveal what percentage of students who are eligible to attend college actually do so. The United States has a higher percentage of high school graduates enrolling in college than most other countries, even among industrialized countries. That high percentage combined with the proportion of female U.S. college students results in U.S. women being better educated than their counterparts in most other countries (U.S. Department of Education, 1995).

TABLE 12.1 Percentage of Female College and University Students in Various Countries

Country	Percentage of Women	Country	Percentage of Women
Argentina	47%	Japan	29
Australia	53	Kenya	28
Brazil	53	Mexico	45
Canada	55	Nigeria	27
China	20	Peru	34
France	55	Russian Federation	50
Germany	41	Saudi Arabia	42
India	32	South Africa	48
Iran	31	Switzerland	40
Israel	51	United States	53

SOURCE: Adapted from "United Nations International Conference on Population and Development," 1995, New York: United Nations.

The college enrollment rate is not equal among all ethnic groups in the United States, with more Asian American and European American high school graduates enrolling in college than comparable Hispanic Americans or African Americans. A higher proportion of African American and Hispanic American women attend college than men from those ethnic groups (U.S. Department of Education, 1995).

The changes have resulted in male and female high school students taking an equal number of math courses and a more equal number of science courses than in the recent past, but these patterns do not continue in college where choice of majors remains gender segregated. This gender segregation has changed somewhat, but women and men still show different patterns in choice of college majors. For example, women are much more likely to major in education or nursing than men, and men are still more likely to major in engineering, computer science, or physical science than women.

Men have historically received the overwhelming majority of advanced and professional degrees (such as medical, dental, law, veterinary), but that pattern also has changed (Fox, 1989). In the 1960s, women earned only about 3% of professional degrees, but by the 1980s, the percentage had grown to 33%, and in 1993, women received 54% of all master's and 38% of all doctoral degrees granted in the United States (U.S. Bureau of the Census, 1996). This growing number of women in professional fields has changed the composition of most professions, but past differences will take many years to equalize. Like undergraduate and professional degrees, doctoral degrees also show patterns of gender segregation: A greater proportion of doctoral degrees in physical sciences and engineering still go to men, whereas a greater proportion of doctoral degrees in education and psychology go to women.

Table 12.2 shows the percentage of degrees awarded to women in 1971 compared to 1993 for different majors. Most professions now have a larger proportion of women as a result of the changes in degrees awarded during the past 20 years. Some areas, however, have become even more strongly dominated by women, and a few changes have occurred in other areas. In addition, the concentration of doctoral recipients in some areas, such as in education and ethnic studies, is even more pronounced for African American and Hispanic women. Over half of the doctoral degrees earned by these women are in the field of education (Fox, 1989).

Gender disparities also exist on college athletic fields, and the attempts to remedy these inequities have become the center of continuing controversy. Title IX of the Educational Amendments of 1972 prohibited discrimination in educational programs that receive federal funding, including college athletic programs. Funding has been far from equal in athletics, as men's sports receive far more scholarships, equipment, facilities, staff, and publicity. Colleges have struggled (and sometimes mounted legal challenges) against increased funding for women's athletics (Tarkan, 1995).

Critics of Title IX argue that women and men do not show the same interest in sports participation, making equal funding unfair to men who want to participate. Supporters contend that a low level of interest in college reflects the bias against women in sports that begins even before girls go to school (Tarkan, 1995). Increased opportunities for women to participate in competitive athletics have increased the number of women who compete. In the 1970s, only 7% of college women participated in organized athletics, but that percentage has grown to about 35%. The increase has not resulted in equal participation, equal funding, or equal acceptance for women in athletics. Enforcement of Title IX has not yet

TABLE 12.2 Percentage of Women Earning Degrees in Various Fields, 1971 versus 1993

	Bachelor's Degree		*Master's Degree*		*Doctoral Degree*	
Field	1971	1993	1971	1993	1971	1993
Agriculture	4.2%	34.0%	5.9%	37.5%	2.9%	25.1%
Architecture	11.9	35.2	13.8	37.6	8.3	29.1
Ethnic studies	52.4	63.9	38.3	51.9	16.7	49.4
Biology	29.1	51.4	33.6	50.7	16.3	39.9
Business and management	9.1	47.2	3.9	35.7	2.8	28.0
Communications	35.3	59.7	34.6	62.0	13.1	51.5
Computer and information science	13.6	28.1	10.3	27.1	2.3	14.4
Education	74.5	78.4	56.2	76.9	21.0	59.2
Engineering	0.8	14.4	1.1	14.9	0.6	9.6
Foreign language	74.0	71.1	64.2	66.8	34.6	57.2
Health science	77.1	83.1	55.3	79.7	16.5	57.4
Home economics	97.3	89.2	93.9	83.0	61.0	71.9
Law	5.0	67.6	4.8	32.6	—	24.4
Liberal studies	33.6	60.3	44.6	65.2	31.3	53.1
Library science	92.0	89.2	81.3	80.3	28.2	66.2
Math	37.9	47.2	27.1	39.6	7.6	23.8
Military technologies	0.3	<.01	—	7.4	—	—
Philosophy and religion	25.5	31.1	27.1	38.0	5.8	17.3
Physical Science	13.8	32.6	13.3	29.0	5.6	21.9
Psychology	44.4	73.2	40.6	72.4	24.0	61.2
Protective services	9.2	37.7	10.3	38.3	—	28.1
Public affairs	68.4	77.3	50.0	70.4	24.1	53.2
Social sciences	36.8	45.8	28.5	43.1	13.9	36.3
Visual/performing arts	59.7	61.0	47.4	56.6	22.2	45.8

Source: From *Statistical abstract of the United States, 1996* (116th ed.) (pp. 192–193), U.S. Bureau of the Census, 1996, Washington, DC: U.S. Government Printing Office.

resulted in equal opportunities for training, use of locker rooms, medical services, or scholarships (Dubbert & Martin, 1988).

Women compete in a growing variety of sports and athletic activities, which allows them to begin to break down some of the stereotypes about female athletes. The stereotype of masculine-looking, unattractive (and possibly lesbian) female athletes has begun to diminish (Theberge, 1991). Increased media coverage of a variety of athletics has allowed people to see a wider variety of female athletes, including many who meet most people's definition of beauty.

The growing number of women who compete in college athletics receive support in the form of scholarships from their colleges and universities, but they have also received encouragement to develop their athletic abilities before they reach college. Mothers, older siblings, friends, and coaches in high school and junior high were all forms of social support to women who were college athletes (Weiss & Barber, 1995). Furthermore, these sources of support have improved over the past 15 years. Therefore, today's female athletes have benefited not only from the laws that mandate access to sports but also from the changes in attitudes that have made athletic competition more acceptable and admired for women.

Athletic departments have struggled to provide funding for women's athletics in times of dwindling budgets. Indeed, much of the controversy over women's athletics concerns money rather than a desire to prohibit women from participating in sports (Sandomir, 1997). After a 1988 U.S. congressional affirmation that campuses cannot discriminate in funding for sports and athletics and a 1997 U.S. Supreme Court ruling that leaves Title IX intact, college athletic departments must become reconciled to following this law.

In many ways, college amplifies the gender inequities that occur in high school, making the college experience different for women and men in the classroom as well as in the locker room. The choice of coursework results in some majors and classes that are dominated by one gender or the other. Men dominate college classroom discussions and ask questions more frequently than women (Pearson & West, 1991). In addition, college instructors are more likely to be men, and this factor influences classroom interactions. Students ask male instructors more questions than female instructors, but male instructors are also more likely to sexually harass female students.

Although both women and men report a generally positive campus climate (Fischer & Good, 1994), women experience more feelings of gender bias than men, and these feelings relate to the number of male instructors and classmates. Men report feelings of indifference

GENDERED VOICES

I Didn't Get to Play

"When I was a teenager, I was interested in sports, and I was good, especially at baseball," a woman in her 40s told me. "That was before Title IX, and there was no effort at all to allow women access to athletics, so I didn't get to play. It was partly social censure. Girls weren't supposed to be athletic, except for acceptable athletics. Dancing and cheerleading were acceptable for girls, but not baseball, which was the sport I liked.

"My mother didn't like my athletic inclinations and tried to urge me away from baseball and volleyball. I think I could have made the boys' baseball team, but of course, that was out of the question. No more. The changes are amazing. Girls play on boys' teams in baseball and even football in junior high and high school. Of course I regret not being able to play the sports I liked, but the changes in access to sports for women and even in attitudes toward athletic women are substantial.

"Rather than being discouraged from pursuing sports, my cousin got a volleyball scholarship that paid for her college education. I saw a news story about a girl who played linebacker on her junior high school football team. Those changes have not come easily, but I can remember when things were much different for athletic women. There has definitely been improvement."

and lack of recognition from their instructors. Both men and women agree that women were not as well represented in the curricula as men, but reports of overt sexual harassment were uncommon among these university students.

Women and men also have different preferences for classroom interactions with teachers and peers (Kramarae & Treichler, 1990). Women feel more comfortable in discussions in which teachers and students collaborate than in situations in which teachers try to impose their views on students. Men feel more comfortable in classrooms with a clear hierarchy and an emphasis on specified goals. Thus, women and men carry their conversational preferences (see Chapter 10) to classroom interactions, and the preferences of each gender may make the other uncomfortable.

Fox (1989, p. 225) summarized the college classroom situation:

> *Faculty promote and reinforce the invisibility of women students by subtle practices such as calling directly on men but not on women, addressing men by name more often than they do women, giving men more time to answer a question before going on to another student, interrupting women more frequently or allowing them to be interrupted, and crediting the contributions of men but not those of women.*

These subtle differences in interactions extend to professional and doctoral training, at which point women feel less encouraged and supported than their male colleagues (Fox, 1989). The majority of professors are men, and they tend to support, encourage, and assist their male students. The lower percentage of female faculty cause female undergraduates to be less likely to attain advanced degrees (Rothstein, 1995). Role models and mentoring relationships can be very important to career advancement, not only in academia but also in business (Wilbur, 1987) where young professionals benefit from the guidance and aid of older, more experienced professionals. Mentors tend to choose protégés who reflect themselves, so there is a tendency for men to choose men and women to choose women. With fewer women in high positions in academia and business, young women are thus at a disadvantage in finding mentors.

The close working relationships of mentoring provide situations that can lead to sexual attraction and action. With the imbalance of power between students and faculty, sexual relationships are almost inevitably exploitative. When those in positions of power exert pressure for sex on those in subordinate positions, sexual harassment occurs. The imbalance of power in the university is an arena in which instructors, professors, and administrators addicted to power may sexually harass students, staff, and instructors without much in the way of official objections (Carr, 1991). A review of sexual harassment on college campuses noted the lack of concern on the part of university officials as well as the ambiguities involved in identifying sexual harassment and the problems in estimating its prevalence (Hotelling, 1991).

Despite a 1980 court interpretation of Title IX of the Education Amendments of 1972, unwanted sexual remarks and advances continue on campus. Surveys have revealed that students report behaviors that meet the definition of sexual harassment, although the students may not label them as such (Barak, Fisher, & Houston, 1992). Confirmation of this reluctance to report such incidents came from a study in which college students read scenarios of situations that met the legal definition of sexual harassment (Olson, 1994). When

students evaluated whether they thought the scenarios constituted harassment, both women and men had difficulty in defining these situations as harassment. These college students tended to see these situations as free speech issues and hesitated to label even offensive remarks as harassment. In addition, these students tended to see women as responsible for letting men know that their remarks were offensive and to see men as blameless unless they had received a warning about the offensiveness of their behavior.

Perhaps due to the difficulty in defining or identifying the experience of sexual harassment, surveys have obtained different estimates of its prevalence. One survey (Cammaert, 1985) found that 20% of female students in a Canadian university reported inappropriate sexual behavior by someone in a position of authority over them, and another survey (McKinney, Olson, & Satterfield, 1988) found that 9% of men and 35% of women reported that they had been harassed at the university they were attending. Yet another survey (Schneider, 1987) found that 60% of the women who responded to the questionnaire had been exposed to some form of harassment, including being asked on dates or pressured by male faculty to socialize.

When including the behavior of peers, over 80% of both female and male students in a small Canadian university reported at least one incident of sexual harassment, the majority of which occurred in a classroom or with peers (Mazer & Percival, 1989). According to a review of sexual harassment on campus (Rubin & Borgers, 1990), the majority of harassers are men in positions of authority who harass younger women in subordinate positions. A survey of male faculty (Fitzgerald, Weitzman, Gold, & Ormerod, 1988) found that 26% admitted sexual involvement with female students.

Sexual harassment is a more common experience for women than for men; between 20% and 30% of college women are sexually harassed (Hotelling, 1991). This estimate means that over one million college students in the United States will experience sexual harassment each year. Due to the close working relationships that form between professors and graduate students, female graduate students are at greatest risk. Students most often cope with harassment by trying to avoid the harassing faculty member and the situation—evading professors, changing majors, and altering examining committees (Hotelling, 1991). Although harassment produces stress for the one targeted, these incidents usually go unreported, because the reporting process causes additional stress. Whether reported or unreported, students' careers are affected by harassment from those in positions of power.

Therefore, like high school, college is another school situation in which women and men receive different treatment, which is a factor in making different choices, including their majors and careers. Women and men choose a similar range of majors and careers, but not in equal numbers. Women choose education and social science majors more often than men, who choose engineering and physical science majors more often than women. Although women now receive more undergraduate degrees than men, they do not receive equal numbers of professional and doctoral degrees. The number of women in professional programs has increased in the past 25 years, and these women have had to contend with less attention and support than their male peers. Sexual harassment is not an uncommon experience on college campuses despite legal prohibition, and women are more likely than men to be harassed by those in positions of authority as well as by their male peers. The problem is more common for female graduate than undergraduate students, providing an additional barrier to women in professional training.

Achievement

Achievement can have many meanings, including success in school. As the previous section showed, girls and women are successful in school, as measured by grades, but men are more successful when the criteria include prominence in prestigious careers and high salaries. How achievement is defined determines the extent to which women and men are high or low achievers.

Achievement Motivation

Traditionally, researchers have defined job success and recognition as achievement and have not considered personal or family relationships as comparable achievements. Therefore, neither women's nor men's roles in homemaking and family care have gained the same type of recognition as business, scientific, and political accomplishments. Indeed, women did not have a prominent part in psychology's early studies on achievement.

David McClelland and his colleagues (McClelland, Atkinson, Clark, & Lowell, 1953) studied the motivation to achieve, formulating the concept of *need for achievement.* These researchers looked at the expression of this need by asking people to interpret ambiguous drawings; that is, to tell a story about a picture that had many possible interpretations. The rationale behind this technique is that people reveal inner wishes and motivations in interpreting ambiguous situations by projecting their personal thoughts and feelings into unclear situations.

McClelland and his colleagues used this type of projective technique, reasoning that people would reveal their need for achievement by including achievement-related imagery in their stories about the pictures. Their results confirmed this prediction, revealing that people varied in the amount of achievement-related imagery in their stories. The need for achievement not only varied among people but was stronger in people who had chosen achievement-oriented careers and in college students who had chosen careers with high risk and high responsibility.

This definition of achievement may be too restrictive (Mook, 1987) and ignore forms of achievement other than business careers. In addition, the need for achievement construct was formulated by examining only men, even though McClelland et al. found some overlap in the achievement needs of some men and women. However, another achievement-related concept has been applied specifically to women—fear of success.

Fear of Success

As David McClelland and his colleagues had done, Martina Horner (1969) investigated the imagery associated with achievement and success. When she presented women and men with a description of a successful medical student, the women sometimes imagined negative consequences for the successful female medical student, but the men usually described the successful male medical student in positive terms.

Horner interpreted the women's descriptions of negative consequences accompanying success as a **fear of success,** or a *motive to avoid success.* She reasoned that women equate success with loss of femininity and feel anxious about success, especially when it involves competing with men. Her investigations showed that women often do better when working alone or when in competition with other women than when they must compete against men. Men, on the other hand, often perform better when they are in competition than when they work alone. Horner concluded that competition is a negative factor in women's achievement and that women see achievement situations differently than men do.

Although Horner used the terms *fear of success* and *motive to avoid success,* these labels might be somewhat misleading, as they imply that women do not wish to succeed. What she called fear of success may have been women's acknowledgment that success in male-dominated professions is not socially well accepted for women and that success will have negative as well as positive consequences. What Horner found was that competition may pose problems for women. She did not demonstrate that women try to avoid success but that they anticipate and attempt to manage some of the negative consequences they believe will accompany success in male-dominated fields. Rather than finding that women fear success, Horner may have demonstrated that women understand the social consequences of competing with men in school and careers.

The social consequences of success in nontraditional careers may be negative for both men and women. An early study (Cherry & Deaux, 1978) found that men showed fear of success when describing a man in nursing school compared to a man in medical school, and women indicated awareness of negative consequences of success for a woman in medical school but not for a woman in nursing school. That is, perceptions of the negative aspects of success were related to the perceived gender appropriateness of the occupation rather than the gender of the person making the evaluation. Both women and men showed misgivings about violating gender stereotypes related to occupations.

A review during the 1980s (Paludi, 1984) showed that both men and women were motivated to avoid success at similar rates. In 64 studies on the topic, a median of 49% of women and 45% of men exhibited the fear of success. These figures represent a considerable acknowledgment of the negative aspects of success but show few gender differences.

A more recent study (Yoder & Schleicher, 1996) has indicated changes in these negative evaluations, possibly related to changes in the gender composition of occupations. When an occupation is no longer dominated by one gender, then it is not "gendered," and neither women nor men in the occupation should receive negative evaluations for pursuing that career. Such a change seems to have occurred in medicine; women no longer receive negative evaluations when they are described as being at the top of their medical school classes. Indeed, both men and women in nontraditional occupations received positive evaluations concerning their competence and success. Women, however, were seen as less socially competent and less attractive when they were successful in nontraditional occupations. Therefore, women are no longer judged to fear success, but their success is seen as having personal costs.

Examining the dilemma of achievement from both a gender and an ethnic point of view (Gonzalez, 1988), achievement for Mexican American women can be seen as a double-bind situation. This dilemma occurs as a result of the desire to form relationships with men from the same ethnic background plus the tendency of Mexican American men to feel threatened by women's achievements. The men in the survey reported that they were not threatened by women's accomplishments but that the women believed otherwise. This situation creates stress in the women from what they see as conflicting demands for achievement and relationships. Wanting to preserve their ethnicity, these Mexican American women may be caught more severely in the dilemma of all women who strive for high achievement because they "experience conflict as their behavior is changing more rapidly than their sex role attitudes and the attitudes of their male counterparts" (Gonzalez, 1988, p. 378).

Self-Esteem and Self-Confidence

Although men and women have comparable concerns about success in nontraditional fields, their self-esteem and confidence in their own abilities show some differences. The AAUW report (1992) contended that girls experience a sharp drop in self-esteem during junior high school, which negatively influences their education and careers. Self-esteem is conceptualized as a global evaluation of self that can range from positive to negative (Kling & Hyde, 1996). Two recent meta-analyses have failed to find evidence of a dramatic decrease in self-esteem for girls during adolescence.

Both meta-analyses compared women's and men's self-esteem, but one (O'Brien et al., 1996) concentrated on adolescence and the other (Kling & Hyde, 1996) included adolescence through later adulthood. Both studies found that boys and men have higher levels of self-esteem than girls and women. These differences were small, however, even during adolescence. Within the United States, European Americans showed a small advantage for men, but for African Americans, no gender differences appeared in self-esteem (Kling & Hyde, 1996). Table 12.3 summarizes findings from several countries, showing that not all have the pattern that appears in the United States. Therefore, gender differences in self-esteem may be of little practical importance.

Self-esteem may be a factor in confidence, but other factors seem more important and more specific. Situational factors are important to one's confidence in achievement (Lenny, 1977). That is, no global concept of confidence applies to all situations. Similar to fear of

TABLE 12.3 Differences in Self-Esteem for Males and Females

Age Group	Sample Population	Size of Effect	Higher In
Children	U.S. resident	Small	Males
Young adolescents	Norwegian	Small	Males
Adolescents	English-speaking	Small	Males
Adolescents	Chinese	Small	Females
Adolescents	Finnish	None	—
Young adults	Japanese	Small	Males
Young adults	Canadian	Small	Males
Adolescents to adults	U.S. European American	Small	Males
Adolescents to adults	U.S. African American	None	—
Adolescents and adults	Australian	Moderate	Males
Adults	U.S. resident	Small to moderate	Males
Elderly	U.S. resident	Moderate	Males

success, confidence in one's ability to succeed varies with the gender typing of the activity. Men express more confidence in their abilities than women when they perceive a task as "masculine," but this advantage disappears when the task is perceived as "feminine."

In addition, ability for specific tasks is an individual factor differentiating the self-confidence of men and women. When such information is available, the ability estimates of men and women are similar, but when this information is absent, men estimate their ability more highly than women. The same is true for situations in which people expect their performance to be compared to others; that is, women make lower estimates of their performance than men but similar estimates when expecting comparisons on social rather than performance factors. Thus, situational factors are important in self-confidence and women experience no overall deficit in self-confidence.

Other peoples' evaluations also influence men's and women's self-assessments of their performance in achievement situations, with women tending to be more responsive to others' evaluations than men (Roberts, 1991). That is, women are more likely than men to revise estimates of their performance based on the evaluations they receive from others. This responsiveness might be due to women's greater social responsiveness or lower confidence, but it may also be due to women's tendency to accept the feedback from others as more informative than men would.

A later study (Roberts & Nolen-Hoeksema, 1994) confirmed this interpretation while demonstrating that differences in self-confidence were not the source of women's more ready acceptance of evaluative feedback. Girls' and boys' experiences with evaluative feedback may lead to a difference; girls receive less feedback about their classroom performance, so they take what feedback they get quite seriously. Boys, on the other hand, tend to receive not only information about their performance but also about their (mis)behavior. Indeed, a great deal of the attention that classroom teachers give to boys is to correct misbehavior. This situation could lead them to discount evaluative feedback, which sets up a gender difference. Women tend to consider the evaluations of others important, whereas men tend to reject these evaluations. Either strategy has advantages and disadvantages (Roberts, 1991; Roberts & Nolen-Hoeksema, 1994). Women may be overly responsive and rely too little on their own evaluations, but men may be overly resistant to advice from others and fail to change their behavior when changes would improve their performance.

Confidence and ability are not the same; one may be inappropriately confident or inappropriately unsure of one's abilities. Low self-confidence does not seem to be the source of willingness to accept evaluative feedback, and those with high ability and high achievement can still be uncertain about their future accomplishments (Dweck, 1986). Indeed, unduly low expectancies are more characteristic of girls and women than of boys and men. The low expectancies of success among girls and women may represent underestimates of their abilities, but the high estimates by men and boys may represent overestimates, indicating that both females and males are somewhat inaccurate in predicting their abilities.

Attributions for Success and Failure

Research has also indicated that gender differences exist in explanations for success and failure. People can attribute success or failure to either internal factors, such as ability and effort, or external factors, such as luck and the difficulty of the task. Although both ability and effort are factors that come from within each person, ability is a stable factor, whereas effort can vary from situation to situation. Persons who believe that they succeeded because they worked hard have no assurance that they will succeed again without additional, similar effort. On the other hand, those who attribute their successes to intelligence should believe that similar success will continue—that is, they will still be intelligent next week and next year. Likewise, the external reasons for success and failure differ in their stability. People who believe they failed because of bad luck would believe that their luck can change, leading to success on another attempt at the same task. People who attribute their failure to the difficulty of the task should believe that the task will always be difficult and that they will fail on each attempt. Therefore, people can explain success or failure in terms of either internal or external factors, and they can see each as either stable or unstable. Figure 12.3 shows the possibilities in combining these two dimensions. These explanations, or attributions, for success and failure can affect the amount of effort and time a person is willing to expend in order to succeed.

Although some research (Deaux, White, & Farris, 1975) showed that women were more likely than men to prefer activities in which luck determined the outcome and to explain success and failure in terms of luck, other research (Karabenick, Sweeney, & Penrose, 1983; Rosenfield & Stephan, 1978) has revealed the gender typing of the activity to be a factor in preferences and attributions for success. One study (Karabenick et al., 1983) demonstrated that men preferred tasks with high skill components when the tasks were "masculine," and women showed the same preference pattern on "feminine" tasks. Rather than varying by gender, the preference for a skill- versus a chance-determined task was related to the participants' expectancy of success on the tasks, which was influenced by the gender typing of the tasks.

Gender typing can also be studied by varying the description of an activity. A study using this method (Rosenfield & Stephen, 1978) presented the same task to everyone. Half the participants believed the task to be a masculine design coordination task involving geometric shapes and mathematical abstraction, and half believed it to be a feminine design coordination task involving delicate design and sensitivity to subtle cues. The men tended to explain success on the "masculine" task as due to internal factors and failure as due to

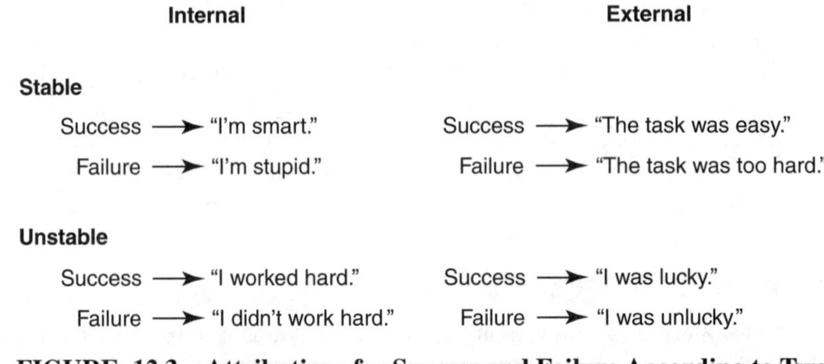

FIGURE 12.3 Attributions for Success and Failure According to Two Dimensions

external factors. That is, if they succeeded, they took personal credit, but if they failed, bad luck was to blame. The women showed a similar pattern for the "feminine" task, taking personal credit for success and attributing failure to external factors. Both men and women tended to use different attributions for their performance on the cross-gender task, explaining success or failure in less personal terms and attributing the outcome, either positive or negative, more to external factors, such as luck or task difficulty.

In summary, achievement may consist of a variety of attainments, but studies of achievement have concentrated on career success rather than success in relationships or families. This emphasis has led to the portrayal of men as having higher achievement motivation than women. In considering women and achievement, the fear of success or their motivation to avoid success became popular as a way to explain women's lower levels of achievement. Under this definition, women who exhibited fear of success acknowledged that negative as well as positive consequences accompany success. Further studies have indicated that negative evaluations of people and predictions about the future may be related to the gender appropriateness of the achievement situation. Men as well as women exhibit misgivings about achievements in gender-inappropriate occupations, but women continue to use pessimistic predictions about their personal characteristics and future lives when they succeed in nontraditional occupations. The social consequences of achievement are a double bind for all women, but for women from minority ethnic groups, these problems are compounded by the desire to retain their ethnicity.

Studies have shown that women exhibit less confidence in their ability to achieve than do men, but these gender differences in confidence depend on the situation rather than on a general trait of men or women. Again, the gender typing of the situation plays a role in the confidence of both men and women, with each having more confidence in gender-appropriate compared to gender-inappropriate situations. The gender typing of the task also influences the attributions that women and men use to explain their performance, with both men and women attributing success to internal, personal sources on gender-typed tasks and resorting to external, situational explanations for failure. Thus, gender role stereotypes are important factors in achievement, with both men and women being influenced by the perceived characteristics of the achievement situation.

Summary

Men and women have different experiences in education, and thus their employment differs. Although Title IX of the Education Amendments of 1972 prohibits discrimination based on gender in schools that receive federal funds, girls and boys do not receive the same treatment in schools. Teachers treat boys and girls differently, beginning during the earliest school years and continuing throughout college and professional training. Boys receive more attention and feedback about their performance in classroom work than girls. The number of stereotypical images in textbooks has decreased, but male characters are more prominent and active than female characters and reinforce gender-typical behavior. Despite the different treatment, girls and boys have similar levels of achievement during elementary school. During junior high school, however, girls become less confident of their academic and physical abilities, and their achievement in math and science begins to lag.

During high school, girls' and boys' choices of coursework differ. Until recently, girls seldom pursued advanced courses in math and science. The difference in number of math courses completed has disappeared, but girls are still less likely to take advanced physical science courses. Counselors convey higher career expectations to boys and fail to present the full range of career options to girls. Boys who enter vocational education programs are more likely to be steered toward lucrative skilled trades, whereas women in vocational education learn low-paying clerical skills. Athletics continues to be a way for boys to gain prestige, but the increase in sports participation among girls has led to greater acceptance of female athletes. Sexual harassment, especially from peers, becomes a problem for both girls and boys during high school. Perpetrators tend to consider their behavior harmless, but after harassment incidents the victims experience school-related problems more often than students who have not been harassed.

Although women have not historically attended college in numbers comparable to men, that pattern has changed. Women now receive more undergraduate degrees than men, but gender differences in choices of major persist, with a small percentage of the science and engineering degrees and a large percentage of the education and liberal arts degrees going to women. An increasing number of women are receiving advanced and professional degrees, but the choices remain disproportionately stereotypical.

The college experience is not the same for men and women in several respects. Women receive less support for achievement from faculty and are more likely to experience sexual harassment from both faculty and peers. Although Title IX of the Educational Amendments of 1972 also applies to athletics, women are less likely than men to be involved in college athletics, and equitable funding for women's athletics has become a source of controversy. Despite legal challenges, support for women's athletics is part of the law mandating equal opportunities in education, and this situation has resulted in a large increase in the number of women involved in sports.

Although achievement consists of a variety of attainments, studies of achievement have focused on career success rather than success in relationships or families. This emphasis has led to the portrayal of men as having a higher motivation for achievement than women. In considering women and achievement, the fear of success or the motivation to avoid success have become popular as a way to explain women's lower levels of achievement. Under this definition, women who exhibited fear of success acknowledged that negative as well as positive consequences will accompany success. Further studies have indicated that negative evaluations of people and predictions about the future may be related to the gender appropriateness of achievement situations. Men as well as women exhibit misgivings about achievements in gender-inappropriate occupations, but women continue to make pessimistic predictions about their personal characteristics and future lives when they succeed in nontraditional occupations. The social consequences of achievement are a double bind for all women, but for women from ethnic minority groups, these problems are compounded by the desire to retain their ethnicity.

Contrary to widely publicized reports, girls do not experience a sharp decrease in confidence during adolescence, but boys and men show slightly greater self-esteem than girls and women from adolescence thorough middle adulthood. Women also exhibit less confidence in their ability to achieve than do men, but these gender differences in confidence depend on the situation rather than on a general trait. Again, the gender typing of the situation plays a role in the confidence of both men and women, with each having more confidence in gender-appropriate compared to gender-inappropriate situations. The gender typing of the task also influences the attributions that women and men use to explain their performance, with both attributing success to internal, personal sources on gender-typed tasks and resorting to external, situational explanations for failure. Thus, gender role stereotypes are an important factor in achievement, with both men and women being influenced by their perceptions of the characteristics of the achievement situation.

Glossary

fear of success the term applied to negative consequences associated with success.

sexual harassment unwanted sexual attention.

Title IX of the Education Amendments of 1972 the federal act that prohibited educational institutions that receive federal funds from discriminating against women.

Suggested Readings

Bryant, Anne. (1995, March). Sexual harassment in school takes it toll. *USA Today Magazine, 123,* 40–41. This article in a popular magazine provides a readable review of a survey on the frequency, motivations, and results of sexual harassment for public school students.

Jacobs, Jerry A. (1996). Gender inequality in higher education. *Annual Review of Sociology, 22,* 153–182. This review provides an evaluation of access to higher education, along with a historical and cross-national comparison. The experience of attending college is also critically reviewed, as well as the gender differential in majors and students' likelihood to be the target of sexual harassment.

Serbin, Lisa A.; Zelkowitz, Phyllis; Doyle, Anna-Beth; Gold, Dolores; & Wheaton, Blair. (1990). The socialization of sex-differentiated skills and academic performance: A mediational model. *Sex Roles, 23,* 613–628. This article is neither easy reading nor recent, but the presentation and integration of information concerning gender differences in academic achievement into a model are good.

Chapter 13

Careers and Work

HEADLINE

Trouble at the Top: A U.S. Survey Says a "Glass Ceiling" Blocks Women from Corporate Heights

—*U.S. News & World Report,* June 17, 1991

The trouble at the top that Amy Saltzman (1991) reported was the lack of women in high-level corporate jobs. Despite their education and experience, few women or members of ethnic minorities pass from middle-level to upper-level management or government jobs; instead, the vast majority of these positions are occupied by White men. Saltzman reported that only 3 of every 100 top executives are women, with little increase in this statistic in the past decade.

The story also discussed a government report that surveyed nine major companies and concluded that "women's routes to the top are blocked by a 'glass ceiling' of subtle discrimination that limits their opportunities to participate in everything from overseas assignments to company sponsored training programs" (p. 41). The **glass ceiling** to which she refers is the description for the invisible barrier that seems to prevent women and ethnic minorities from advancing to the highest levels of their professions.

Although the glass ceiling describes a barrier to the highest levels of corporate and government jobs, most women do not even hold the mid-level management jobs that would give them access to such positions—60% of women in the work force have lower-level clerical and sales jobs rather than management or professional positions. She noted, "The pay gap between men and women is still yawning. Overall, women now earn just 72 cents for every dollar a man takes home, compared with 64 cents 10 years ago" (p. 42).

The difference in wages extends not only to the overall average but also applies field by field. In the fields in which women occupy most positions, such as nursing and secretarial work, the gap in wages is small, but the relatively few men in these fields still average more money than women in those same jobs. In careers in which men occupy most positions, such as law and college professorships, the gap in wages is much wider.

Part of the reason for the wage gap between men and women is the concentration of women in low-paying jobs; that is, gender segregation in the workplace. Millions of women work in jobs where they have few male coworkers, and millions of men have few female coworkers as colleagues (although women may be subordinates). The jobs dominated by men, such as machinist and computer programmer, tend to be better paying than those dominated by women, such as elementary school teacher and nursing aide. Even in jobs in which men and women have comparable training and do the same work, the differences in wages favor men.

Saltzman's story also examined the changes in composition of the work force in the United States; she noted the shrinking pool of skilled White male workers and the growing ethnic diversity of the work force. Ethnic minorities and women have faced similar discrimination at work and in education. Although the patterns of discrimination based on gender and ethnic background have not been identical, the glass ceiling applies to all workers except White men, who occupy over 90% of the highest-paid and the most prestigious jobs. The basis for this pattern can be found in history, and the foundation for gender and ethnic differences in work can be found in school.

Careers

"Career, in its broadest sense, means 'life path' and thus includes all the roles a person plays throughout life," (Farmer & Sidney, 1985, p. 338). This definition places careers in a developmental framework and emphasizes the lifelong nature of career development and the many choices and roles that contribute to career development. Ideally, all people should choose careers on the basis of their interests, abilities, and potential contributions to society, but widespread gender stereotyping provides obstacles to the full development of both men's and women's potentials.

Despite the encompassing social definition of career as the role people play throughout their lives, the study of career development has been limited to the choices and patterns that men have taken, with little study or attention given to women's career development. Barbara Gutek and Laurie Larwood (1989) wrote, "There was little reason to study the career development of women. It was easily summarized: There was none. Men had careers; women had temporary employment or jobs that took second place to family interest and obligations" (p. 8). This view led to research and theory on men's career development, the neglect of women's career development, and the assumption that the existing research and theories about men would extend to the women who pursued careers.

Women's careers, however, do not easily fit into the same framework as those of men, and men and women are likely to continue to have different career paths in the near future (Gutek & Larwood, 1989). One reason for this difference relates to the expectations about the types of careers each gender will occupy. Although both men and women are now violating these expectations by making gender-atypical choices at higher rates than in the past, most continue to choose gender-traditional occupations. Another expectation is that wives' careers will be secondary to those of their husbands. If someone must stay home with a sick child or if one person must relocate due to job demands, the husband's career nearly always takes precedence and the wife must accommodate her schedule and employment. These expectations tend to result in interruptions in the careers of women, who may take years away from employment to care for children or to support a husband's career before rejoining the work force.

Women are more likely to hold part-time employment than men—68% of part-time workers are women (U.S. Department of Labor, 1996). Part-time employment not only means lower salaries for women but also problems for them in career advancement. Men's careers are more likely to follow a smooth line of development, meaning clear career choices during schooling, uninterrupted employment, and continuing career advancement throughout adulthood (Larwood & Gutek, 1989).

Indeed, homemaking is considered a legitimate career for women, one that excludes them from the paid workforce. Homemaking is not directly comparable to paid work in a number of ways: It has no training requirements, no wages, no retirement benefits, no job security, and no opportunity for advancement (Betz, 1993). For most women, homemaking does not allow them to use and develop their abilities and talents: "This is not to discount the importance of childrearing, but only its insufficiency as a lifelong answer to the issue of self-realization" (Betz, 1993, p. 629).

Helen Astin (1984) formulated a model showing gender similarities and differences to explain career development for both women and men. Astin's model includes four components—motivation, expectations, gender role socialization, and opportunity. She assumed that motivation was the same for men and women but that their expectations differed due to differing gender role socialization patterns. Both the differences in gender role socialization and in opportunities create different outcomes in the work force for men and women. Men have had the opportunity to participate in more highly paid and more prestigious work and a wider variety of work than women. Astin contended that changes have occurred, which give women greater freedom to choose careers dominated by men and which equalizes the opportunities in those careers. Yet Lucia Gilbert (1984) questioned the adequacy of Astin's model, especially her optimism about women's greater freedom in career choices and success. Does research on motivation, expectations, gender role socialization, and opportunity support Astin's model? Do women have strong career motivations?

An exploration of college women's career orientations (Baber & Monaghan, 1988) indicated that some women were planning careers in areas traditional for women, whereas others were not. Some young women were innovators who planned nontraditional careers (as engineers, regional planners, or military officers), whereas others fit into the traditional category (teachers, day-care workers, social workers), but all of the young women in their study were planning a working life that fit more closely into the category of career than job. Although this study did not compare women and men, it did demonstrate that young women have strong career motivations, substantiating this factor in Astin's model.

This strong motivation also applies to older women who have chosen and are pursuing careers. A survey of adults in New Jersey (Sigel, 1996) included women of varying ages and educational levels ranging from high school dropout to advanced professional degrees. The women in this study valued meaningful, rewarding work and showed ambition and dedication to their various careers.

Career Expectations and Gender Role Socialization

Young women still have family- and child-related expectations, but the career expectations of college women have changed between the 1940s and the 1970s (Phillips & Imhoff, 1997;

Komarovsky, 1982). In the 1940s, few college women planned to continue their careers after they married, but beginning in the 1970s, the opposite was true—very few planned to discontinue their careers after marriage. However, most women, regardless of their career plans, also anticipated marriage and raising children as part of their life goals. The requirements of combining family duties and paid work could account for women's lower career aspirations (Phillips & Imhoff, 1997).

College women have begun to anticipate combining marriage, motherhood, and careers (Baber & Monaghan, 1988). Young women have expanded their career choices to include some areas traditionally dominated by men, but the young women in this study still anticipated few difficulties in meshing career and family demands. The choices to remain single or to have no children were infrequent, with less than 2% of the young women planning to remain single and less than 3% anticipating lives without children.

These expectations about marriage and motherhood suggest that traditional gender role socialization has affected even college women who plan nontraditional careers. In a study of female and male students from other countries who were pursuing graduate studies in the United States (Stromquist, 1991), women in nontraditional fields anticipated having more conflict over their marriages and careers than men in nontraditional fields. Few anticipated serious conflicts with future spouses, but women were more likely to see such possibilities than men. These women indicated that should conflicts arise, their families would take precedence. It seems surprising that women who had made unconventional choices about their careers would anticipate such traditional choices of sacrificing their careers for their families.

What factors lead women and men to make nontraditional choices? For women, acceptance of traditional roles relates to the likelihood of being in more traditional occupations for women (Schutte, Malouff, Curtis, Lowry, & Luis, 1996). Choosing a nontraditional career is related to similar nontraditional aspects of personality and behavior. That is, women who exhibit more instrumental ("masculine") traits combined with more expressive ("feminine") traits are more likely to pursue nontraditional careers than women who are more traditional in their gender roles (Phillips & Imhoff, 1997).

In addition, beliefs concerning egalitarianism contribute to nontraditional choices for both women and men. The belief that they and other women should be allowed the opportunity to develop their individual abilities makes women more likely to act on these beliefs by pursuing nontraditional careers (Phillips & Imhoff, 1997). Having employed mothers, supportive fathers, highly educated parents, and positive female models also contribute to women's likelihood of pursuing nontraditional careers. Family and personal beliefs also influence men (Christian, 1994). Those men with employed mothers, nontraditional fathers, and experience in personal relationships with nontraditional women are more likely to be egalitarian and to pursue nontraditional careers.

Ethnicity also plays a role in career expectations. Compared with European American women, African American women are more likely to expect that they will be employed throughout their adult lives (Betz, 1993). Those expectations are consistent with history: African American women have been more likely than European American women to be the heads and sole supporters of their households. The proportion of African American women who enter professional occupations is higher than for European American women, but African American women are even more concentrated in traditionally female occupations, which influences their incomes.

In comparing Mexican American and European American high school students, both gender and ethnic differences appear (McWhirter, 1994). Female students perceived more barriers to careers than male students, and Mexican American students saw more barriers and had less confidence in their abilities to overcome these barriers than European American students. For the young women, family-related problems were more common reasons for their lack of confidence than were their abilities, and the Mexican American students were more likely than the European American students to expect negative attitudes from their families should they attend college. The average ratings for the perception of barriers indicated uncertainty rather than pessimism, but the Mexican American students and the young women perceived more barriers than the European American students and the young men.

Gender role expectations also influence the occupations men and women choose. Gender segregation of occupations is so prominent that choosing certain occupations often places persons within gender roles strongly identified with these occupations, whereas other careers do not have similar role demands. The percentage of women in the U.S. work force has risen to 46%, with projections for additional increases (U.S. Department of Labor, 1996), yet during the 1980s over two thirds of employed women were concentrated in occupations that were more than 70% female (Jacobs, 1989). These occupations include a narrow range of clerical, service, or professional positions, such as clerical workers, secretaries, child-care workers, teachers, and nurses.

Furthermore, women are moving into male-dominated occupations at a higher rate than men are moving into female-dominated jobs (Gutek, 1985). These choices have perpetuated a gender-segregated work force, with the majority of employed women and men working in jobs occupied by others of the same gender. This gender segregation promotes traditional gender role identification and hinders the career development of both women and men, especially those who have an interest in gender-atypical careers.

Career Opportunities

Different education and training create different employment patterns. Table 13.1 shows the gender differences in career choices and presents the number of men and women in the various occupational categories. Within each category are many different jobs, some of which reflect different levels of prestige and compensation as well as different proportions of men and women. For example, the "professional" category includes jobs such as nursing, teaching, and social work as well as accounting, law, and medicine. That is, this category includes professions that are dominated by women as well as those dominated by men. Therefore, an equal balance of men and women in professions does not imply that any given profession has an equal number of women and men.

Table 13.2 shows the gender gap in wages. For every occupational category, women earned less than men. For two of the categories, too few people held these occupations to allow good estimates—that is, too few women were employed in construction and too few men were employed in household service (maids, cooks, child care) for comparisons. Note that for these two categories, the salaries favor men; construction is more lucrative than household service.

Both gender differences in career choices and gender discrimination in hiring create differences in career opportunities (Gupta, 1993). Discrimination in hiring restricts

TABLE 13.1 Percentage of Women and Men in Occupations, 1997

Occupation	Women	Men
Executive and managerial	47%	53%
Professional	52	48
Technical	48	52
Clerical	76	24
Sales	45	55
Mechanics	5	95
Production and skilled crafts	21	79
Construction	2	98
Labor	18	82
Household service	94	6
Protective service (firefighters, police, guards)	16	84
Other service (food, healthcare, cleaning, and personal services)	56	44
Machine operation	36	64
Farming, forestry, and fishing	11	89

SOURCE: From *Bureau of Labor Statistics, United States Department of Labor News,* July 22, 1997, Table 3, Washington, DC: U.S. Government Printing Office.

women's more than men's opportunities for access to careers. Therefore, schooling and gender role expectations create differences in career opportunities for men and women.

Discrimination in Hiring

Discrimination in hiring may be the primary factor in the wage differential between men and women (Gerhart, 1990). An examination of the wage differential between men and women who worked in a large private firm showed that the women's salaries were 88% of the men's salaries, even after controlling for background, training, length of service with the company, and job title. This difference was attributable to inequitable initial salaries, and when this factor was taken into account, the salary advancements were comparable. The initial salary differences, however, prevented women's salaries from ever equaling the men's salaries.

Gender stereotypes are one source of discrimination in hiring, with both men and women subject to positive and negative discrimination on the basis of gender stereotypes (Martinko & Gardner, 1983). The gender role of job positions is a major factor in discrimination: Men have the advantage in applying for "masculine" jobs, and women have a disadvantage. On the other hand, men can face negative discrimination when they apply for "feminine" jobs, whereas women can have the advantage. Specific, job-related information about applicants can overcome some gender stereotypes and can thus eliminate some discrimination, but the tendency toward gender stereotyping is a factor in hiring decisions.

TABLE 13.2 Weekly Earnings of Men and Women in Various Occupations, 1997

Occupation	Women's Earnings	Men's Earnings
Executive and managerial	$599	$850
Professional	653	878
Technical	484	680
Clerical	397	530
Sales	348	592
Mechanics	504	571
Production and skilled crafts	352	582
Construction	*	541
Labor	301	357
Household service	212	*
Protective service (firefighters, police, guards)	428	527
Other service (food, healthcare, cleaning, and personal services)	281	314
Machine operation	315	437
Farming, forestry, and fishing	256	296

SOURCE: *From Bureau of Labor Statistics, United States Department of Labor News,* July 22, 1997, Table 3, Washington, DC: U.S. Government Printing Office.

*Too few people in these categories for good estimates.

Additional evidence of gender discrimination in hiring came from a study of gender stereotypes in hiring decisions (Glick, Zion, & Nelson, 1988). Fabricated résumés went to business professionals for evaluation in one hiring decision. Some résumés contained information giving the female or male applicants some characteristics more typical of the other gender, some résumés had information magnifying the stereotypical characteristics of the applicant's gender, and some résumés had neutral personal information. These researchers hypothesized that both men and women would be affected by gender discrimination based on stereotypes but that specific, personal information in the résumés could overcome this bias.

The information in the résumés affected the business professionals' ratings of the applicants' personalities and suitability for the job but not exactly in the ways the researchers had predicted. Those applicants with "masculine" characteristics were more likely to be rated as worthy of interviews for employment, even when the job's characteristics were "feminine." When the personal information was neutral rather than gender stereotypical, the business professionals were more likely to choose the male rather than the female applicants for interviews, demonstrating the existence of gender discrimination in hiring decisions. Business professionals appear to have strong gender stereotypes for occupations, and these stereotypes promote gender discrimination in the hiring process.

Therefore, discrimination based on gender, and especially on the match between gender and gender stereotypes associated with the job, presents problems in making fair hiring

GENDERED VOICES

How Can I Do That to the Women?

Toni had been the auditor for the bank in the small town where she grew up, and she was the first woman to be promoted to vice president of the bank. After three years as vice president, she had a talk with the president of the bank.

She knew that she had made some big mistakes, and she was afraid that she might lose her job. He assured her that she was in no danger of losing her job, but he agreed that she had made some pretty serious mistakes and couldn't expect the bonuses she had gotten last year.

In their conversation, Toni told the president of the bank that she didn't really like being a vice president as much as she had liked her auditing job, and he mentioned that it might be possible for her to have that job again, if she wanted. She said, "Oh no, I couldn't do that to the women." She felt that her promotion was so visible and her performance so crucial to other women in business in the town that she couldn't leave the job she disliked—it would be an admission of failure not only on a personal level but for all women. She couldn't consider the possibility.

decisions. Such discrimination is an important factor in the wage gap between men and women. Providing specific information that shows that applicants have some characteristics of the other gender can diminish stereotypical perceptions of these applicants and influence hiring. Unfortunately, gender stereotyping is resistant to change, and women experience more disadvantages than men because of such discrimination.

Barriers to Career Advancement

The barriers to career advancement can come from situational and organizational as well as individual sources. One of the organizational sources is the glass ceiling—the subject of this chapter's headline story. Only 5% of senior-level managers in major corporations are women, and these women tend to be concentrated in jobs traditionally associated with women, such as humans relations or communications (Chartrand, 1996). Women in corporate jobs often believe that they have hit the glass ceiling.

A total of 52% of female executives blamed male stereotyping for their lack of advancement, whereas 82% of male chief executives said that women did not have sufficient experience to be promoted (Chartrand, 1996). Half of the women believed that they were excluded from informal networks at work—the "old boy's" networks—whereas only 15% of men believed that women were excluded. To succeed, female vice presidents reported the necessity of working harder and taking more risks than men in similar positions. Thus, women in corporate life see the glass ceiling as real and a barrier to their advancement, whereas male executives do not see the situation in the same way.

Although the concept of the glass ceiling was created to describe corporate careers, barriers also exist in other prestigious careers. Science and engineering have long been inhospitable to women and ethnic minorities (Long & Fox, 1995). The low participation rates can be attributed to a "filtering" of women and minorities out of science and engineering through choices not to pursue the required education (see Chapter 12 for a discussion of this process). Differential advancement in scientific careers is similar to business: Female and ethnic minority scientists and engineers are more likely to be employed in less prestigious academic settings and at lower rank than White men. Their academic situations and ranks limit their opportunities to participate in research, and these limitations affect their likelihood of receiving recognition. The specific factors that limit career success in the field of science differ from business, but the barriers are similar—a "glass ceiling" exists in science careers.

Ironically, women have no advantages in attaining higher positions, even in traditionally female-dominated fields. Indeed, men seem to have advantages in all types of jobs. The advantages that men have in female-dominated fields has been referred to as the *glass escalator* (Williams, 1992). This term conveys the image that some invisible force produces an easy ascent to higher positions, in contrast with the glass ceiling, the invisible barrier that prevents women and minorities from reaching the highest levels of career achievement. Men who choose careers traditionally dominated by women face some discrimination from society in general, but these men have career advantages in terms of rapid promotion. These advantages may come as a result of the perception that men should not be in jobs that women usually perform, and thus men receive promotions to administrative or supervisory positions within that occupation.

For example, a male librarian described how happy and confident he had felt in his abilities as a children's librarian. Reading stories to children and helping them find books were part of his job, but many people mentioned to him that this was inappropriate for a man to do, and he was transferred to another library and given the position of research librarian. When asked why he did not consider a discrimination lawsuit, the man reported that his new job was really a promotion to a more prestigious position, so he felt benefited rather than being harmed from these clearly discriminatory actions. Gender role discrimination and occupational stereotypes provide the basis for both the glass ceiling and the glass escalator.

Gender stereotyping and discrimination in promotion contribute to the phenomena of the glass ceiling and the glass escalator, but the *sticky floor* is also a factor in women's lower wages and problems in career advancement. The concept of a sticky floor also contrasts with the glass ceiling as a means to describe low-status occupations with little opportunity for advancement. That is, occupations in which employees get stuck at the lowest levels. Many of the occupations dominated by women fit this description, including clerical and secretarial jobs, beauticians, garment workers, and household service workers. Greater numbers of ethnic minority women tend to be concentrated in these low-level jobs, with both African American and Hispanic American women more likely to occupy blue-collar jobs than White women (Green & Russo, 1993). Ethnic differences exist within blue-collar occupations, with Black women more likely to work in health service jobs and Hispanic women more likely to be employed in manufacturing. All of these jobs have lower wages than jobs typically occupied by White women or by Black and Hispanic men.

Factors other than gender stereotyping and discrimination contribute to the gender gap in wages—different career choices, career schedules, and workplace climate. Women occupy jobs and pursue careers that are less prestigious and not as well paid as those that men choose. For example, only 27% of lawyers and judges are women compared to 90% of nursing aides, orderlies, and attendants; only 31% of managers in marketing, advertising, and public relations are women compared with 98% of secretaries and stenographers (Saltzman, 1991). In addition, women in science, engineering, and management tend to

GENDERED VOICES

I Never Felt Discriminated Against

A man who had gone to nursing school almost 30 years ago told me, "I decided to be a nurse when I was in the 10th grade, after I had surgery. The woman who lived across the street told me about the salaries of nurse–anesthetists, and the work interested me and the money sounded good. I don't remember my parents saying anything, my school counselor got information about nursing, and I didn't discuss it with my friends, so I don't recall any negative comments.

"During a career day at school, we had to choose the areas to attend, and I wrote down that I wanted to be a nurse. Much to my surprise, so did one of my friends, and neither of us knew that the other had thought about becoming nurses. One other guy wanted to be a surgeon, and we were the only three who had signed up for the health care option. The guy who wanted to be a surgeon was really mad at us, because he thought we were kidding about being nurses and were making fun of him.

"There were only two men in our nursing class. Now many men go into nursing, but then it was uncommon. There had been another guy about 10 years earlier and the two of us. That's it. I never felt discriminated against by either the teachers or the female students. Everybody was supportive and more than fair. My fraternity brothers were another story—they gave me a lot of static about majoring in nursing. The jokes were pretty good-natured, but there were a lot of jokes. I joke around a lot too, so it wasn't really a problem, but it was something that came up a lot.

"The women I have worked with were great. If anything, I think that being a man has been an advantage to me in my career. Rather than being discriminated against, I think that I was at some advantage. Maybe I got promotions and advancement faster than women, but those who chose me and recommended me were almost always women. I think I was competent and deserved the promotions, so I would have a hard time saying that I advanced in my career because I was a man, but I certainly never felt that it held me back."

I told him about the frequency of sexual harassment in jobs in which the gender ratio is far from equal and asked him if his female-dominated work situation had led to harassment. He replied, "Did I ever feel sexually harassed? That's hard to say. I never was put in the position of 'You do this or it's your job.' Never. But I've had my butt grabbed, and I've gotten a lot of offers. If that's harassment, then I guess I've been harassed, but I can't say that it really bothered me."

choose public institutions rather than private industry. This choice may be due to the different climates that these work settings offer to men and women, but the consequences are lower salaries for women (Melamed, 1996).

The gender wage gap decreased during the 1980s, mostly due to the increased frequency that women began to train for and to enter fields that paid better (Loury, 1997). Therefore, the choices are not as different as they once were, and wages have changed as a result. Even within each occupation, women's wages lag behind men's in every field (see Table 13.2). As research on the glass escalator shows, men in female-dominated occupations tend to reach higher-level positions more easily than women in these professions, boosting men's salaries in these occupations.

The differences in women's and men's career development schedules also differentiate the genders in promotions and wages. Women are more likely than men to take time off from their careers to attend to family affairs, such as staying home with young children.

These employment gaps take women out of the work force and pull them off the track to advancement, slowing their progress. Although employment gaps are even more damaging to men's career advancement plans (Schneer & Reitman, 1990), the fact that women are more likely to interrupt their careers than men means that the overall impact of interrupted employment decreases women's wages and limits their opportunities for advancement more than it does for men.

What about those women who place a high priority on their careers? Does equal emphasis on work create equal rewards for women? One study of the career progress of corporate men and women led to the conclusion that the same behavior did not result in the same success: "Although the women had done 'all the right stuff'—getting a similar education as the men, working in similar industries, not moving in and out of the work force, not removing their names from consideration for a transfer more often—it was still not enough" (Stroh, Brett, & Reilly, 1992, p. 251). When women followed the traditionally male pattern of career advancement, they still did not advance at comparable rates. However, both women and men who did not do "all the right stuff" fared more poorly in terms of career progress than women who did. If deviating from the pattern does not work and following the pattern does not work, then perhaps the route has not been a map to career success and salary equality for women.

Another factor in career advancement comes from the work climate and the informal social structure at work. The work climate and informal work structure can help or hinder the advancement of new employees, and women perceive their work environments as more hostile in terms of the informal social structure, standards they must meet for advancement, sexist attitudes, and the possibility for solving problems that arise at work (Stokes, Riger, & Sullivan, 1995). Women see barriers to making effective adaptations to work, including exclusion from informal social networks.

Achievement-oriented women who pursue careers in male-dominated fields are in the minority, and minority status can handicap career advancement through isolation from the informal structures (Kanter, 1977). When a minority member (either a woman or a member of an ethnic minority) enters the corporate world, the person becomes a **token** of the minority group. The token stands out, becoming more visible than other employees, and feels pressure to succeed and to reflect well on the ability of everyone in that minority group.

As tokens try to fit into the existing corporate and social structure, the dominant group may work toward keeping them on the periphery. The process of excluding women and minorities may function either overtly or in a subtle manner (Lorber, 1989). New workers either become part of the "inner circle" or not, and those who are not accepted never fit into the organization. As a result of this failure to fit in, these employees never gain the trust and confidence of coworkers. Such mistrust can isolate tokens and prevent them from joining interaction with the dominant work group. (See the Diversity Highlight: "Working Twice as Hard.")

Tokens are also handicapped in forming mentoring relationships, these relationships between younger and more experienced workers offer younger workers valuable support in the form of friendship, advice, or even direct intervention in the organization. Mentor–protégé relationships tend to form within gender and ethnic lines. Neither women nor ethnic minorities are common in the upper echelons of organizations, and this situation places barriers on finding mentors (Leong, Snodgrass, & Gardner, 1992). Access to mentors can be

DIVERSITY HIGHLIGHT
Working Twice as Hard

"In a society less marked by racist history, the intellectual achievements of people of color might be accepted as a matter of course. In this society, however, they are either ignored or applauded, but never accepted as a matter of course," wrote Stephen Carter (1991, p. 62). This special status, Carter argued, puts African Americans in the spotlight, where they and their accomplishments can never be accepted without qualification. Carter, who was always an excellent student, had many such experiences. Despite his accomplishments, he was not seen as the best but rather as the best Black student. Even when his accomplishments were outstanding, his skin color was what everyone noticed.

Through affirmative action, Carter and thousands of other ethnic minority students were admitted to elite schools and entered legal, medical, academic, or corporate careers. Affirmative action made their entry possible, and their skin color, Carter argued, eased their entry into these professions. The criteria for entry were lower for ethnic minorities than others. The chances for advancement, however, were slimmer: "Once hired, people who are not White face difficulties in finding mentors, powerful institutional figures to smooth their paths, then they will naturally advance more slowly" (Carter, 1991, p. 64).

Later research (Biernat & Kobrynowicz, 1997) confirmed Carter's beliefs: Stereotypes influence judgments and evaluations of ability and performance in much the same way that Carter had experienced. When judging African Americans and women, participants set lower competency standards. Thus, it may be easier for ethnic minorities and women to stand out in a job interview or application process. The standards for judging ability were higher for African Americans and women, putting them in positions of having to be twice as good to be considered half as good.

an advantage for those who find them and an impediment to advancement in the careers of those who do not (Wilbur, 1987).

For example, women and ethnic minority graduates from one master of business administration (MBA) program were less likely to have mentors than White men who had completed the same program (Dreher & Cox, 1996). Establishing a mentor relationship with a White man was advantageous. Those MBAs who did form such relationships earned over $16,000 more per year compared with those without mentors and those whose mentors were women or ethnic minorities. Therefore, women and minority employees encounter barriers within the organization when they fail to find mentors or when those mentors are female or ethnic minority members, whereas White men are more likely to find other White men who will mentor them and will help advance their careers.

The workplace environment and interactions in it affect performance and influence both colleagues' and supervisors' ratings of female workers. Management is a category that has been associated with men and has thus traditionally been considered male (Kanter, 1975). Despite a growing number of women who have entered management, the managers' perception of management as a male position continues. A group of researchers (Heilman, Black, Martell, & Simon, 1989) studied the perceptions of male managers concerning the following characteristics of management: perceptions of men and women (in general), male and female managers, successful male and female managers, and middle managers (whose gender was not specified). They asked the managers to complete extensive ratings of each of these seven categories; they found that men as a general category were rated as more similar to the category of successful managers than the category of women in general. These negative stereotypes of women's abilities are important to the perceptions of who is competent and suitable for managerial positions. When women were described as "managers" and "successful managers," some of the negative stereotyping disappeared, indicating that specific information about particular women can decrease the extent to which the stereotype applies to them. However, this study demonstrated the persistence of gender stereotypes and their general application to women in management positions.

Unfortunately, these stereotypes are also resistant to change (Owen & Todor, 1993). When undergraduate business students and human resources professionals responded to questions about the suitability of women for management positions, evidence of stereotypical perceptions of female manager's abilities appeared. The negative evaluations were especially strong among the business students, providing a pessimistic note about the future of women in business. However, a more recent study of business managers provided a more optimistic outlook: Managers' evaluations and explanations of their subordinates' performance showed no gender bias (Rosenthal, 1996).

This finding of no gender bias in a field study is particularly optimistic because research participants were managers rather than students and research took place in organizations rather than in labs. Therefore, the existence of persistent stereotypes may be more of a factor for laboratory research than for ratings that appear as part of work settings with real people. Indeed, the opportunity to know persons allows managers to make ratings that are individual and specific rather than relying on stereotypes, as participants in laboratory research often must. This single finding does not overrule the possibility of gender bias operating in organizations, but it does suggest that knowing persons can allow some people to overcome the stereotype bias.

Some researchers have found that there are situations in which gender stereotypes produce more favorable views of women than men. Alice Eagly and her colleagues (Eagly, Mladinic, & Otto, 1991) found that college students rated the social category of women more favorably than the social category of men, but Eagly (1994) contended that this positive evaluation depended on women adhering to the traditional gender role. When women diverge from this role, they no longer receive such positive evaluations.

Women can also receive more positive ratings by overcoming perceived discrimination (Abramson, Goldberg, Greenberg, & Abramson, 1977). When college students evaluated the competence of a male or female attorney or a male or female paralegal worker, they rated the female attorney as the most vocationally competent due to the barriers to achievement for women. Unusual success magnified the individual's achievement.

These studies demonstrate that women can be perceived as competent and capable of high levels of achievement, but the stereotype holds women as less competent. Therefore, to break through the gender stereotype, some evidence must exist to the contrary. That evidence can come from specific information about a person or from information about that person's competence. Without information that women are exceptions, men receive higher ratings of competence than do women.

Therefore, women and ethnic minorities encounter several barriers to their career advancement. Many of those barriers relate to negative stereotypes of women and minorities involving questions of their abilities, competence, and dedication to work. Even with similar qualifications and performance, few women and ethnic minorities attain the highest levels of career advancement, which suggests that discrimination is a deciding factor in the difference.

Balancing Career and Family

Family demands can influence career paths in several ways for both men and women. Although most people marry and have children, the historic association of women with household work and child care has made family concerns more of an issue for women's than men's careers. However, men also face problems of balancing career and family.

For women, family demands can take them out of the work force, decrease the amount of time they spend on their careers, or place physical and emotional strains on their abilities to fulfill the multiple roles of employee, wife, and mother. Research indicates that women outside the work force are not as psychologically or physically healthy as those who are employed (Betz, 1993), suggesting the benefits of needing to fulfill multiple roles. On the other hand, women who postpone marriage and have no or few children have advantages in pursuing careers.

A large majority of women still choose to marry and to have children, placing them in the situation of balancing work and family demands. Society, employers, and many husbands assume that women will perform most household chores and become the primary caregivers for children. Women who choose to concentrate on their careers are perceived as neglecting their families. On the other hand, men's gender role is compatible with career development. This difference in gender roles puts women at a disadvantage in pursuing careers.

For men, family demands can take them away from their families while they devote time to careers, but that choice has been (and remains) more socially approved for men than for women (Steil, 1995). Changes have occurred and continue to occur as men want to participate more fully in their children's lives (Adler, 1996). These desires to become active fathers as well as good providers can conflict. The most lucrative careers tend to be the ones that take the most time. When men work 80 hours a week, they have little time to attend Little League games.

When men want to provide for their families but work hard at their jobs, they spend time away from their families and leave the wives (who are often employed) to take up the slack in child care and household chores. This situation, therefore, decreases the time (and energy) that the wives have to devote to their careers and the time and energy that men have to devote to their families. These societal factors form barriers to women's career advancement and to men's family lives.

What does it take to balance these demands? Pepper Schwartz (1994) studied marital relationships to understand how some couples manage to find an equitable balance of family and career for each spouse. Couples with children had a much more difficult balancing act than those without children. One reason was the added demand of raising children, but another came from the expectation that women will be the primary caregivers for children. The expectation was often equally true for husbands and wives, and couples with such expectations did not form equitable relationships.

Partners can see such an inequitable relationship as accommodating to the demands of society and their current situations. Most husbands make more money than their wives, so if some sacrifice needs to be made for the family, wives' careers are the best financial choice. Working fewer hours per week and emphasizing husbands' careers both undermine women's career advancement. Schwartz found that couples who had formed equal partnerships often had chosen to sacrifice high-prestige careers. For many such couples, the decision was a deliberate acknowledgment that current corporate, scientific, and academic careers require more than full-time devotion to the job.

The social structure of work and family make it difficult for women to fulfill both career and family demands. "In our society, both families and professional careers are 'greedy' institutions. Until changes occur, women who want both can expect to face conflicting and overwhelming demands" (Kaufman, 1995, p. 302). With men wanting (and often expected to) be involved in family life, men as well as women feel the demands from career and family life to be "greedy."

Gender Issues at Work

The gender gap in wages reflects the barriers that women face when entering and advancing in careers. Although women have entered male-dominated professions in greater numbers in the past decades than at any previous time, women remain underrepresented in the highest levels of their professions. Even when factors such as education, age, position, job tenure, and type of job are equated, women earn less money than men (Landau & Arthur, 1992). About 25% of the wage gap between men and women is the result of gender segregation of occupations (Jacobs, 1989).

Gender Segregation on the Job

The gender-typical choices that most men and women make in careers have resulted in gender segregation in most jobs. That is, in most work situations the large majority of jobs are held by either men or women but not by an equal (or nearly equal) mix of both. These associations have created the perception that the jobs are gendered. That is, regardless of the job demands, some jobs have become so associated with either men or women as to be considered male occupations or female occupations.

According to Barbara Gutek (1985), women have a less diversified range of occupations than men. Consequently, women are concentrated in a few occupations, whereas men are employed in a wider variety of jobs. Over two thirds of women have jobs in clerical or professional fields, but the professional fields are those traditionally dominated by women—nursing and teaching. Gutek pointed out that women are most underrepresented in skilled blue-collar jobs, such as electricians and plumbers. (Refer to Table 13.1 for the percentages in the "construction" and "production and skilled crafts" categories.) (See the Diversity Highlight: "At the Bottom of the Work Heap.")

In Gutek's study of employment in the Los Angeles area, over 60% of men worked in occupations that were dominated by men (defined as 80% representation by men for that job category). Women were also employed in gender-segregated occupations, but not to the same extent as men. Using the same criterion, Gutek found that over 40% of women worked in jobs that were female dominated. That is, more men work in male-dominated fields than women work in female-dominated fields. Furthermore, women have entered traditionally male-dominated fields, but men have not usually entered traditionally female-dominated

DIVERSITY HIGHLIGHT

At the Bottom of the Work Heap

Women who are disabled have all of the employment problems that women face plus all of the problems that people with disabilities face, putting them at the bottom of the work heap (McLain & Perkins, 1990). The problems of women with disabilities include overcoming the prejudice that their disabilities bring as well as gender bias. These two factors result in these women's *unemployment* and *underemployment.*

Both men and women with disabilities face harsh workplace environments that include barriers to their career success and a lack of acceptance from their coworkers. This lack of acceptance can create a chilly climate in the workplace, or a more serious situation described as *disability harassment* (Holzbauer & Berven, 1996). People with disabilities are subjected to a variety of taunts and ridicule, some of which are subtle and others of which are blatant. Disability harassment is not restricted to the workplace but also occurs in school and in public, and this type of harassment can endanger the employment and success of these people.

The unemployment rate among women with disabilities is 50% to 90%. This high unemployment results in poverty, with their disabilities more likely to bring a living standard below the poverty level. Women with disabilities have disadvantages compared not only to able-bodied women but also to men who are disabled. Such women have the lowest percentage of employment compared to able-bodied women and to men with and without disabilities (Altman, 1985). Those women who are employed tend to have jobs that rank low in both prestige and salary.

Women with disabilities earn 64 cents for each dollar able-bodied women earn. All women's wages are lower than men's wages, with women earning an average of about 72 cents for each dollar men earn (McLain & Perkins, 1990). Around 67% of able-bodied women are part-time workers, whereas 89% of women with disabilities work on a part-time basis. These rates compare unfavorably with the part-time employment of men. Men with disabilities are also restricted to part-time employment more often than are able-bodied men, with 26% of able-bodied men employed part-time versus 70% of such men.

Men with disabilities are also at a disadvantage when compared to employed able-bodied men. Such men earn 85% of the wages of able-bodied men, a higher percentage than that of women with or without disabilities, which puts these women at a greater disadvantage than the men. Thus, as McLain and Perkins contended, women who have disabilities have poor work prospects, and the result is disadvantages in income, standard of living, and low feelings of accomplishment.

Such women are also at a disadvantage when compared to the men in their access to rehabilitation services. Compared to men, women with several types of disabling conditions were less likely to receive rehabilitation services, including job counseling and financial assistance (Altman, 1985). In summary:

> *The experience of disability in our social structure is defined differently for men and women. In both rehabilitation and financial assistance areas the disabled male role is associated in one way or another with an active, work related non-stigmatizing philosophy. Rehabilitation for men includes job counseling and job placement.... Women's disabled role on the other hand is a compounding of the dependent identity already associated with the female role.... The financial assistance received by women is primarily in the form of welfare payments, once again a very dependent model without even the redeeming quality of 'having been earned' that the male model provides. Thus disabled women experience more stigma (Altman, 1985, pp. 74–75).*

occupations, leaving more women in male-dominated occupations than men in female-dominated jobs.

Few people work in gender-integrated fields. Even with the gains for women in traditionally male-dominated occupations, gender segregation at work remains. During the early 1980s, over 60% of employed men and women would have needed to exchange jobs to end gender segregation (McCann & McGinn, 1992). As of 1990, an end to gender segregation would have required a change in jobs for more than half of the men and women in the work force.

Gender integration at work poses strategic problems, especially during the early stages of the process. Men in mixed-gender work settings reported less satisfaction and more depression about their jobs than men in either male-dominated or female-dominated work settings (Wharton & Baron, 1987, 1991). Men were significantly less satisfied with gender-integrated compared to gender-segregated work situations. Not surprisingly, women were most dissatisfied in work situations in which women were in the majority and the few men received preferential treatment. Women in both male- and female-dominated workplaces reported more job-related demands than men in the same jobs (Hochwarter, Perrewe, & Dawkins, 1995). Therefore, gender integration presents problems for both men and women.

The dissatisfaction may be greatest at the beginning of the integration process (Allmendinger & Hackman, 1995), when either men or women dominate the workplace. When women held between 10% and 40% of positions within an organization, both genders were dissatisfied, and the organization did not function as effectively as it had previously. As the proportion of women increased toward 50%, many of the problems and conflicts diminished. When the workplace was integrated, no gender differences appeared in the perception of work-related demands (Hochwarter et al., 1995). Although the integration process may create problems, those problems diminish when gender integration progresses.

Gender segregation may be more extreme in specific work situations than in any occupation as a whole. For example, both men and women wait on tables, but some restaurants hire only waiters, whereas others hire only waitresses. Research supports this pattern: Within jobs in establishments, gender segregation is greater than in occupations (Groshen, 1991). Even people who choose occupations that are not dominated by one gender may work in companies or offices in which that occupation is gender segregated and will spend their time with same-gender colleagues. Gender segregation tends to raise men's and lower women's salaries. At least 11% and as much as 26% of the gender wage gap is attributable to gender segregation, with the variation depending on the industry.

Gender segregation declined between 1970 and 1980, which may be related to a decreasing wage gap (Fields & Wolff, 1991). Not all occupations showed decreasing gender segregation, and occupations that experienced rapid growth during this time period showed the greatest decline in gender segregation. Rapid growth is associated with lowered barriers for women entering the field as well as diminished practices of wage discrimination.

Although jobs are gender segregated for most workers, the workplace is likely to include both men and women, who, though they may hold different jobs, must work together under one roof. For example, most secretaries are women, most managers are men, and most managers have secretaries. Thus, men and women often work together but not at the same job. Indeed, the work situations that allow for interaction between men and women often involve a power differential, with men having the more powerful positions and women the more subordinate.

Gender, Communication, and Power in the Workplace

Communication style is one possible explanation for the gender differences in career advancement. Robin Lakoff (1975) contended that "women's language" differs from "men's language," with women adopting a more tentative and deferential style of communication than men. She hypothesized that this style of speaking fails to convey the assertive, commanding qualities necessary for leadership, which makes the women's speech style a handicap in their careers.

Would women be more successful at work if they talked like men? This question was tested by asking participants to evaluate applicants who presented one of two versions of a job interview (Wiley & Eskilson, 1985). The two versions varied only in speech style, with one version having many pauses, hedges, and questions and the other none of these characteristics. Each style was used by a female and male applicant, for a total of four conditions. The results indicated a complex pattern of relationships for speech style, gender of applicant, and gender of rater. A significant effect appeared for speech style, with raters judging applicants with the hesitant style as less likely to be successful. Neither the applicant's nor rater's gender produced an effect, but a complex pattern of interactions for the three variables occurred. For instance, speech style made less difference to male raters than to female raters; in addition, male raters liked women who used the hesitant speech style and disliked women whose speech style was more assertive, but women rated women higher when they used assertive speech styles. These results indicated that no simple relationship exists between speech style and ratings of ability.

Elizabeth Aries's (1987, 1996) reviews on gender and communication confirmed these results: No distinctive patterns of communication are uniquely associated with success or even with women or men. That is, the hesitant speech style that Lakoff characterized as "women's language" and the assertive style that she identified as "men's language" are not specific to either. Although women and men may have different goals in speaking, the notion of a male versus a female way of talking is not supported by research. Furthermore, the emphasis on group differences obscures more important individual differences. Gender-related differences in communication are complex, and both the setting and situation in which communication takes place are critical factors in men's and women's speech patterns.

Conversational style also reflects power, and power is one of the situational differences that affects speech. Speakers with more power speak differently than speakers with less power (Aries, 1987, 1996). Those in positions of power tend to use more assertive language. In the workplace, power and gender are related, and this power differential reflects the power differential in society. Thus, work roles mirror social roles just as social stereotypes of gender affect behavior and expectations in the workplace. Aspects of the female role carry over into the workplace to produce **sex role spillover** (Nieva & Gutek, 1981). Gutek (1985) expanded the concept, emphasizing that sex role spillover focuses on gender role behavior that is irrelevant (or even an impediment) to the work role. Sex role spillover can take several different forms, including the expectation that women will be more nurturant or loyal than men, that women will occupy subordinate positions, and that women will be sexual at work.

When men and women are together in the workplace, they may rely on their habitual patterns of interaction, and gender stereotypes may be prominent. As Gutek pointed out, most men have experience with women as mothers, girlfriends, wives, daughters, and secretaries but possibly not as their professional colleagues. When a man is faced with a women in the same job, he may rely on one of the other role relationships to guide his interaction with his female colleague. Although treating the new female executive like his mother or his secretary may not be appropriate, these relationships are familiar and may be the chosen patterns. His stereotypes of women will thus inevitably affect his behavior, because he has no experience forming an equal relationship with a female colleague.

The new female executive may also fall back on habitual patterns of interacting with men on the job, perpetuating inappropriate work behavior for everyone involved. On the other hand, her behavior may be shaped by the account executives she has known, most of whom were men, as well as her beliefs about how an executive should act. Thus she may act like a male executive, enacting a version of the role with which she is most familiar. Some evidence exists that women who occupy jobs most commonly filled by men adopt a male style of work-related behavior, and this behavior demonstrates how powerful situational demands in the workplace can be. A review of the research on gender and leadership roles (Eagly & Johnson, 1990) showed that both women and men who have attained managerial status in organizations tend to be similar in leadership styles. Job requirements and the selection of people for the job make the managers more alike than different, regardless of gender.

When women adopt the same power styles as men, they may not be evaluated equally positively. Men are not more effective leaders than women (Eagly, Karau, & Makhijani, 1995), but their styles of leadership can be perceived as differing in effectiveness, depending on the extent to which the styles match the gender stereotype. Authoritative and even autocratic styles of management are common for men, but women are expected to be more "people oriented" and interpersonally sensitive. When managers exhibit different styles, the choice of autocratic versus democratic often corresponds to the male versus the female style (Eagly & Johnson, 1990). The choice of a democratic style is a wise one on the part of female leaders (Eagly et al., 1995; Eagly, Makhijani, & Klonsky, 1992), and women who use the directive male power style of leading are devalued by their associates, in contrast to the men who choose this style.

The story of Ann Hopkins provides a dramatic example of what can happen when women violate gender stereotypical expectations on the job (Fiske, Bersoff, Borgida, Deaux, & Heilman, 1991). Ann Hopkins was an employee of Price Waterhouse, and she was so successful that she was nominated for partner in that company, the only woman nominated that year. She was not chosen as a partner, and she became the object of criticism for being too aggressive and "macho" as well as for not being sufficiently feminine in her behavior and appearance. Hopkins sued the company for applying different criteria to its male and female employees, contending that gender stereotyping was a factor in their decision. Eventually, the U.S. Supreme Court agreed with these arguments by condemning the double bind that women face—they are penalized for using an aggressive, powerful style when only this style can lead to success.

If women are penalized for using the same methods to gain power that men use, how do women achieve power at work? Women have many obstacles that inhibit them from accumulating power in organizations (Ragins & Sundstrom, 1989). The social system and most organizational systems work to prevent women from gaining power. Different career expectations, entry-level jobs, assignments within the company, and promotion rates all favor the accumulation of power by men rather than women. One method open to women is the use of expert power—that is, using their specific expertise to accomplish tasks. Studies of successful female executives have shown that these women tended to accumulate power by being expert in performing their jobs and that such power was especially important early in their careers. After they had a power base, these women were more likely to turn their attention to gaining power through interpersonal skills and influence.

Expert power can be very effective in determining social dominance. One study (Dovidio, Ellyston, Keating, Heltman, & Brown, 1988) manipulated who had expert power and observed the effects on the nature of the social interaction. The results revealed an interaction between gender and expert power: When women had expert power, they behaved in dominant ways, and their male partners acknowledged this dominance by their reactions. When the women gained no power in the situation, the nature of the male–female interactions fell into more gender-stereotypical patterns: The men showed signs of social dominance and the women of social submission. Thus, expert power can change the power dynamics away from gender-stereotypical patterns, giving women ways to assert and accumulate power at work.

In summary, although research has failed to support the notion of different communication styles that are unique to women or men, it has shown that communication styles relate to the power of the speaker and the communication situation. The issues of gender, communication, and power also relate to adherence to stereotypical gender roles in the workplace, which give power to men and place obstacles in the way of women's career advancement. Using habitual patterns of interaction between men and women in the work place produces a power differential, with men having the advantage. When women use the same behaviors as men to exert power, they are often perceived as behaving inappropriately and are penalized. Women have the option of relying on expert power to gain a power base and working from it to attain power at work, but the spillover of gender roles to work situations gives men an advantage in the accumulation and use of power.

The power difference between men's and women's positions offers not only the opportunity for men to be more successful at work but also the opportunity for men to sexually exploit the women who work for them. Although sexuality at work can also be interpreted as a power issue, the term **sexual harassment** is now used as the label for sexual exploitation in the work place.

Sexual Harassment at Work

According to Gutek (1985), "sex role spillover facilitates the expression of sexuality at work to the extent that the sex object aspect of the female sex role and the sexual aggressor aspect of the male sex role carry over into the work setting" (p. 18); that is, sexual harassment is a function of sex role spillover. Men and women also choose to enter sexual relationships in the workplace, making it difficult to distinguish between this type of sexuality and harassment.

In 1976 sexual harassment became illegal as a form of gender discrimination in the United States through a court interpretation of Title VII of the 1964 Civil Rights Acts (Fitzgerald, Swan, & Magley, 1997). The first form of sexual harassment recognized was the **quid pro quo form** in which employers or supervisors demand sexual favors as a condition of employment or as a condition for promotion. This form of harassment involves a supervisor using threats or pressure toward a subordinate, making it a clear abuse of power. Men are more often supervisors and women more often subordinates, resulting in women as the common targets of this form of harassment.

TABLE 13.3 Examples of the Three Types of Sexual Harassment

Quid Pro Quo Type
Demands for sex in exchange for hiring
Demands for sex in exchange for promotion or favorable job evaluation
Demands for sex to keep a job
Demands for sex to avoid being put into an undesirable job

Hostile Environment Type
Sexual touching
Sexual comments and jokes
Displays of sexual material, such as drawings or photographs
Nonverbal sexual posturing, including sexual gestures
Personal remarks about sexuality
Sexually oriented comments about appearance
Discussions about a person in sexual terms in the person's presence but phrased as though the person was not present

Gender Harassment Type
Degrading comments about the ability of women (or men)
Hostile comments about women's (or men's) behavior as a group, not confined to sexual comments
Insults directed toward women or men because of their gender rather than any actions or characteristics of individuals

Another form of sexual harassment was legally recognized in the United States in 1986 and involves **hostile environment sexual harassment.** This concept of harassment is based on the notion that unwanted sexual attention or offensive or hostile behavior directed toward persons because of their gender can produce psychological harm or threaten the effectiveness of the work environment (Fitzgerald et al., 1997). Unwanted sexual attention is one type of behavior that can cause a hostile environment, but a third classification of sexual harassment is **gender harassment,** which occurs when people are subjected to offensive or hostile behavior because of their gender. This type of harassment is distinctive because it does not involve sexuality; rather, it involves hostile or disparaging remarks directed toward a person because of that person's gender. Table 13.3 gives examples of each type of harassment.

In addition, the standards for what constitutes a harassing environment have changed. Prior to 1991, what a "reasonable man" would consider objectionable was the criterion, but now the **"reasonable woman" standard** applies. This change in the standard may have contributed to the increased number of lawsuits over inappropriate sexuality in the workplace because "What may not seem offensive to a man can traumatize a woman" (McCann & McGinn, 1992, p. 3). Although women are more likely to judge ambiguous situations as sexual harassment, using women as the standard may not enlarge the definition of sexual harassment (Gutek & O'Connor, 1995). Women vary from one another more than they differ from men in their judgments, so pinpointing gender discrimination using the standard will continue to be imprecise.

Many countries also have laws and regulations that have been used to prohibit sexual harassment, and some countries have laws that specifically apply to sexual harassment (Barak, 1997). The United Kingdom, Canada, Australia, Israel, Austria, Ireland, and New Zealand have laws that prohibit sex discrimination or sexual harassment, and the establishment of the European Community led to additional laws. The cities of Berlin and Tokyo enacted regulations of their own rather than wait for Germany and Japan to pass legislation. Yet sexual harassment is a common experience throughout the world. For countries where surveys have been done, the prevalence of the crime falls between 30 and 50%.

The forms of sexual harassment are not equal in frequency or in perceived severity; the hostile environment form is more common, but the quid pro quo form is perceived as more serious (Riger, 1991). Despite the perceived lack of severity of hostile environment sexual harassment, Louise Fitzgerald (1994) found that workplaces that spawn this type of harassment tend to also have the quid pro quo type. Indeed, Fitzgerald contended that all of the types of sexual harassment are interrelated, as Figure 13.1 shows. Fitzgerald emphasized environmental rather than personal factors in sexual harassment and reported that environments that allow insulting remarks and unwanted sexual attention also tend to be permissive of sexual coercion. Despite the separate legal standards for the types of sexual harassment and the differences in frequency and their perceived severity, they often coexist.

Women are more frequently the targets of all sexual harassment, when defined in terms of *unwanted* sexual attention. In Gutek's (1985) study, men reported a comparable number of sexual overtures as women and as many instances of sexual touching, but men were less likely than women to find sexual attention unwanted and thus to label their experience as harassment. These different standards may contribute to miscommunication and exacerbate harassment.

Gender differences appear in what are perceived as sexual signals (Saal, Johnson, & Weber, 1989). When people observed social interactions between men and women, the

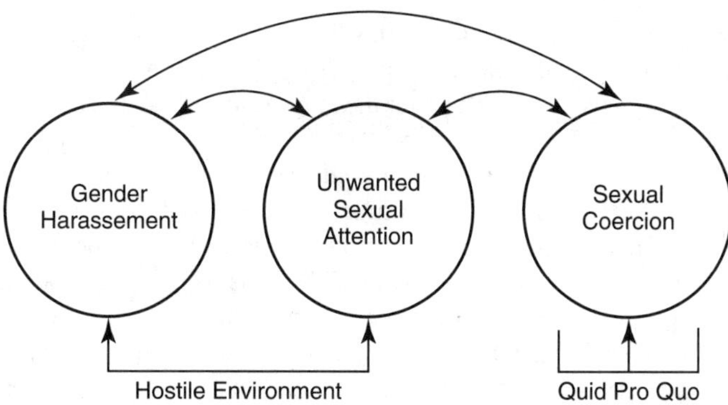

FIGURE 13.1 A Model of Sexually Harassing Behaviors

SOURCE: From Louise F. Fitzgerald, Suzanne Swan, & Vicki J. Magley, 1997, "But was it really sexual harassment? Legal, behavioral, and psychological definitions of the workplace victimization of women." In William O'Donohue (Ed.), *Sexual harassment: Theory, research, and treatment,* (p. 11). Copyright © 1997 by Allyn and Bacon. Reprinted by permission.

GENDERED VOICES
Hardly a Day Went By

In two stories I heard about sexual harassment, the behaviors of the perpetrators and the targets were amazingly similar. One story was about a woman and the other about a man who harassed a coworker.

A man told me, "I worked in a car dealership selling cars after I graduated, and one of the other salespeople was a woman—the only woman who was in sales. She sexually harassed the finance manager. It was blatant. She propositioned him in front of everybody, saying things like 'Let's go in the back room now,' and things much more vulgar.

"He seemed embarrassed and usually didn't reply; he tried to ignore her. He was married, and he never gave her any encouragement at all. She would go over and stand very close to him, never touching him but standing close and making him uncomfortable. And she would proposition him; rarely a day went by when she didn't. The guy was clearly uncomfortable, but nobody ever did anything."

A young woman said, "I worked as a cashier in a discount store, and one of the department managers sexually harassed me. He would come over to the cash register where I was working, and he would proposition me. He made reasons to be close to me, and he kept saying what a good idea it would be for us to have sex. I didn't think it was such a good idea. I always said no, and I asked him to stop asking. His offers embarrassed me. Hardly a day went by without some sexual offer from him or some remark with sexual connotations. He never touched me or fondled me, but he made my job harder, and he embarrassed me.

"I complained to my supervisor, but she told me to just ignore him. He wasn't my boss, and he never made any threats or attacked me or anything. But I think that he shouldn't have been allowed to harass me the way he did. Nobody did one thing to stop him. I don't think that the store manager ever said a word."

male participants saw less friendliness and more sexiness in the women's behavior than the female observers saw. These findings suggested that men and women may not have the same interpretations of sexual intention, even when they observe the same behavior. These differences may lead to misunderstandings about sexual intentions, with men believing that women are *sending* signals of interest when men *perceive* such signals.

Gender-related differences in perceptions of sexuality are also problematic when defining sexual harassment. Gutek (1985) found that the biggest gender difference concerning sexuality at work had to do with attitudes about sexual propositions. She found that two thirds of the men in her study said that they felt flattered by such propositions, but only 17% of women felt the same way. Indeed, over 60% of the women said that they would feel insulted by sexual propositions at work. The main problem, however, comes from the perceptions of both; neither the men nor the women in Gutek's study were aware of the perceptions of the other gender. The men believed that the women felt flattered by sexual attention when in actuality the women felt insulted or angered.

If the sexual attention that men receive at work is welcome, are men exempt from being the targets of sexual harassment? The legal definition does not specify the gender of the target, so either women or men could be the targets of unwanted sexual attention at work. The vast majority of the complaints are brought by women against men, but men are sometimes the targets of sexual harassment. A survey of employed men and women (Berdahl, Magley, & Waldo, 1996) revealed that sexual harassment of men was rare in this employment setting, but some incidents had occurred. No men reported sexual coercion (the quid pro quo form of sexual harassment), but a few said that they had been targets of unwanted sexual attention (the hostile environment form). Gender harassment violations also occurred, with women using such such comments as "You men are all alike" and "Men have only one thing on their minds" (Berdahl et al., 1996, p. 540). In addition, several men mentioned a type of gender harassment that women did not. This type of harassment came from other men and harassment involved comments about the target man not living up to the standards of manliness by showing too much concern or sympathy with women. For example, a man who failed to share a joke that is derogatory toward women might be censured by other men who enjoyed the joke.

Although women often feel insulted and angered by sexual comments and propositions from supervisors and coworkers, they may have problems in labeling these behaviors as harassment (Gutek, 1985). Therefore, the estimates about rates for harassment may be low if the figures are based on personal reports. Gutek estimated that 21% of women in the United States had definitely been the targets of sexual harassment at some time during their work lives and that up to 53% were probable victims. For men, at least 9% and up to 37% had experienced sexual harassment. Thus, sexuality at work is common, but women are more likely than men to label sexual experiences at work as harassment.

Men who sexually harass women do not differ from employed men in general (Gutek, 1985), but an analysis of the situational as well as personal factors has been more useful in understanding those who harass (Pryor & Whalen, 1997). Men who are likely to sexually harass tend to view sex and power as linked, making them more likely to use their power at work to sexually exploit women who are their subordinates. Women who are targets of harassment differ in some ways from typical women in the workforce; they are more likely to be unmarried, younger than the average employed woman, and attractive. Women who initiate sexual relationships at work are much less likely to be perceived as harassing men than vice versa, and like the women who are the targets of harassment, they are younger and more likely to be unmarried than the average employed woman. In cases of men who reported they were sexually harassed, their harassers were similar to the women who initiated sex at work—young, unmarried, and attractive.

Another difference between male and female perpetrators of harassment is their status. Men who harass are likely to be in supervisory positions and thus have power over the women whom they harass, but women who initiate harassment are not, giving them no power to demand or coerce sexual favors from men with whom they work. Gutek hypothesized that the small percentage of men (as few as 9%) who describe incidents of being sexually harassed may feel harassed by the seductive behavior of their coworkers or subordinates, but the men's careers are not at risk from the sexual behavior of women at work.

Women's careers, on the other hand, are often endangered by sexual harassment. Over 30% of employed women had experienced some negative job consequences as a result of sexual harassment, compared to around 10% of men (Gutek, 1985). These problems included quitting their jobs, asking for transfers, or losing their jobs for refusing to have sex with employers or supervisors.

Perhaps these differences in consequences of sexuality at work explain the differences in perceptions of harassment: Why should men feel harassed by sex at work when they are very unlikely to experience negative consequences? Why should women welcome sexual attention at work when their careers are so much more likely to be harmed? Given an equal interest in sexual relationships with people at work, the unequal consequences of sexual behavior on careers suggests that men and women should have different views of sexuality at work—and they do.

Summary

Theories of career development have concentrated on men, because women's careers have traditionally revolved around their families rather than their employment. Although career motivation is similar for men and women, social expectations still hold that family rather than career will be women's priority. Research indicates that college women expect to combine both, but employment statistics indicate that women have fewer career opportunities than men.

The limitations on women's careers come from their career choices, interruptions in employment, and discrimination in hiring and promotion. Career choices and preparation lead men into a wider variety of occupations than women, and men's jobs typically pay better. Interruptions in employment affect both men's and women's careers negatively, but women more often interrupt their careers to devote time to families. Discrimination in hiring is a major factor in the wage gap between men and women. Specific, personal information about job applicants can partially overcome the gender stereotyping that affects hiring decisions, because employers have a tendency to try to match the gender of the applicant to the gender stereotype of the job, discriminating against both women and men who apply for gender-atypical jobs.

Women occupy a very small percentage of executive positions, often being blocked in their career progress by an invisible barrier called the glass ceiling. Many factors have contributed to the formation of barriers to the advancement of women and ethnic minorities. The informal social structure in corporations excludes newcomers who differ from the majority. Thus, token women or minorities have difficulty being trusted and have trouble forming important mentoring relationships. Gender stereotypes influence perceptions of female managers' performance, by making their competence difficult to acknowledge. Gender stereotypes can boost men in gender-typical careers, providing them with easier access to promotions. Even women who have comparable training, personal backgrounds, and performance do not advance in their careers as rapidly as men, which shows evidence of discrimination in career advancement.

Gender-based interactions at work obstruct women from gaining power and from demonstrating their competence, as these characteristics are not part of the feminine stereotype. Women who fail to adhere to traditional standards of femininity can be penalized, but by following these standards women cannot succeed in the corporate world. Women can gain power through using their expertise, but women also have to overcome many barriers to gain power at work.

Balancing work and family is a task for both men and women, but the gender role for women holds that they rather than men should devote themselves to family concerns. These social expectations lead men toward and women away from career success by placing the burdens of household chores and child care on women. Ironically, being the primary breadwinner for a family may take a man away from that family. Work and family both require time and effort, and currently, prestigious careers require support at home over responsibilities and chores, so these careers are unlikely for partners who have equitable relationships.

The work force is gender segregated: Most men and women work with colleagues of the same gender, and few occupations have an equal proportion of men and women. Even in occupations that are not gender segregated, jobs situations may be. This segregation is more pronounced for men than women, as women have moved into traditionally male-dominated fields more rapidly than men have moved into female-dominated jobs. Gender segregation on the job has resulted in certain jobs being associated with gender, and this has resulted in a spillover of male and female characteristics into the work environment. This gender role spillover tends to produce patterns of interaction between men and women rather than between coworkers, bringing sexuality into the workplace.

Another consequence of sexuality at work is sexual harassment. Although illegal, both women and men are pressured for sexual favors from employees and supervisors and are subjected to unwanted sexual attention or hostile comments concerning characteristics and behaviors of their gender. Women are more likely to find sexual attention unwanted than men, possibly because they are more likely to be harmed by sexual relationships with coworkers. Men are likely to find sexual attention flattering that women find insulting. Although there is little difference in the amount of sexual attention men and women receive at work, women are more likely to label their experiences as sexual harassment than are men.

Glossary

gender harassment a type of sexual harassment that occurs when people are subjected to offensive or hostile behavior because of their gender.

glass ceiling the invisible barrier that seems to prevent women and ethnic minorities from reaching the highest levels of business success.

hostile environment sexual harassment the type of sexual harassment that occurs when employers allow offensive elements in the work environment.

quid pro quo form sexual harassment in the form of demands for sexual favors in exchange for employment or promotion.

"reasonable woman" standard the standard that defines a sexually harassing environment in terms of what a reasonable woman would find offensive.

sexual harassment unwanted sexual attention.

sex role spillover the hypothesis that gender role characteristics spill over into the workplace, creating stereotyping and a sexualized atmosphere.

token a symbol or example, in this case, of a minority group.

Suggested Readings

Fitzgerald, Louise F.; Swan, Suzanne; & Magley, Vicki J. (1997). But was it really sexual harassment? Legal, behavioral, and psychological definitions of the workplace victimization of women. In William O'Donohue (Ed.), *Sexual harassment: Theory, research, and treatment* (pp. 5–28), Boston: Allyn and Bacon. Fitzgerald is one of the leading researchers and theorists in the field of sexual harassment, and this article provides a review of both. In addition, the brief legal history and examination of the psychological definitions of harassment add clarity to a confusing issue.

Lopata, Helena Znaniecka. (1993). The interweave of public and private: Women's challenge to American society. *Journal of Marriage and the Family, 55,* 176–190. Lopata examines the history of women's work and employment, using the Doctrine of the Two Spheres as her theoretical basis. She contends that the increase in women's employment has posed challenges not only to women but to society.

Phillips, Susan D.; & Imhoff, Anne R. (1997). Women and career development: A decade of research. *Annual Review of Psychology, 48,* 31–59. This lengthy review covers only women's career development, but it provides a comprehensive examination of careers and topics related to career choices.

Sigel, Roberta S. (1996). *Ambition and accommodation: How women view gender relations.* Chicago: University of Chicago Press. Sigel reports on a survey and an interview study she conducted with working women and men to find out their views concerning the changing work world. Her respondents told her about the uncertainties and confusion that accompany these changes as well as how they feel about gender relations at home and at work.

Chapter 14

Health and Fitness

HEADLINE

Is the Longer Life the Healthier One?

—*New York Times,* June 22, 1997

"The male–female mortality gap starts in the womb, holds into very old age and has widened in recent decades. It is now about seven years in the United States, compared with two to three years early in this century. As longevity improves for both men and women, it is uncertain whether the gap will grow," wrote Lawrence Altman (1997, p. 18). Despite the advantage in years, women are not necessarily healthier. The phrase "Women are sicker; men die quicker" (in Altman, 1997, p. 18) expresses this apparent contradiction. As Altman's (1997) story discussed, the evidence for women's poorer health is not clear and the reason for their longer lives is likewise unknown.

Women's poorer health is widely accepted, possibly because women make more doctor and hospital visits than men. This situation leads to the acceptance of women's higher **morbidity,** that is, higher rate of illness. Altman interviewed an epidemiologist who contended that the health care system may be part of the reason why women are considered less healthy. Women receive more health care than men due to birth control and childbearing. During health care visits, providers may routinely ask about other problems, prompting patients to become vigilant concerning problems and to report problems that might otherwise be too minor to prompt doctor visits. Mentioning a problem leads to more health care. With more routine health care visits, women have more opportunities to experience such situations of expanding treatment.

The reasons for women's lower death rate, that is **mortality,** are also poorly understood. Women and men have different explanations for their varying life expectancies (Wallace, 1996). Men attributed their shorter life spans to their greater physical labor and more stressful lives than women, whereas women report that they live longer because they take better care of themselves. These opinions came from college students and not health experts, but health habits may play a role in longevity.

Do women's longer life spans offer only years of poorer health? Those who live longer certainly have more time to develop health problems, but the extra seven years of life that women have beyond men in the United States are not filled with greater illness and disability than men's later years. Indeed, women and men experience comparable proportions of their later years with disability. Barring any disabilities, life expectancies beyond age 65 are about 8 years for men and 10 years for women, and the overall pattern of their life expectancies is 14 and 19 years, respectively (Robine & Ritchie, 1991). Therefore, both women and men experience health problems during their later years, but women live longer.

Mortality: No Equal Opportunity

As the headline story related, women's advantage in life expectancy is not a recent development; this discrepancy has existed for over 100 years throughout the world. (See the Diversity Highlight: "Life Expectancy around the World.") Figure 14.1 highlights the longer life expectancy for women in the United States over the past 90 years. Notice the increasing discrepancy between men and women in the first half of the 20th century and the recent narrowing of figures for women's survival. Also notice the difference between life expectancies for Whites and nonwhites, including the small discrepancy between men and women in the early 1900s, the advantage for Whites, and the increasing discrepancy in life expectancies for nonwhite women and men after the 1910s.

In addition, these gender differences are predominant in economically developed countries for the leading causes of death—cardiovascular disease, cancer, and accidents. These three causes of death account for about 70% of all deaths in the United States. For cardiovascular disease and cancer, men tend to die at younger ages than women, resulting in not only an excess of overall deaths of men but death at younger ages.

Cardiovascular Disease

Cardiovascular disease (CVD) includes a group of disorders involving the heart and circulatory system, some of which are life threatening and some of which are not. For example, angina pectoris is one of the disorders in this category; this disease causes shortness of breath, difficulty in performing physical activities, and chest pain, but it poses no immediate threat to life. On the other hand, myocardial infarction (heart attack) and stroke can be immediately fatal. Heart disease and stroke account for 39% of deaths in the United States (U.S. Bureau of the Census [USBC], 1996). Deaths from heart disease and stroke have decreased over the past 20 years, with deaths from stroke decreasing more rapidly than from heart disease.

As Table 14.1 shows, heart disease mortality for women and men does not differ greatly over the life span. Women have more fatal strokes than men, but men die from CVD at younger ages than women. The discrepancy in heart disease deaths for men and women between ages 35 and 74 is especially dramatic, showing how much men are affected by premature death from this cause.

Cardiovascular disease is one of the **chronic diseases**—those health problems that develop over a period of time, often without noticeable symptoms, and persist over time

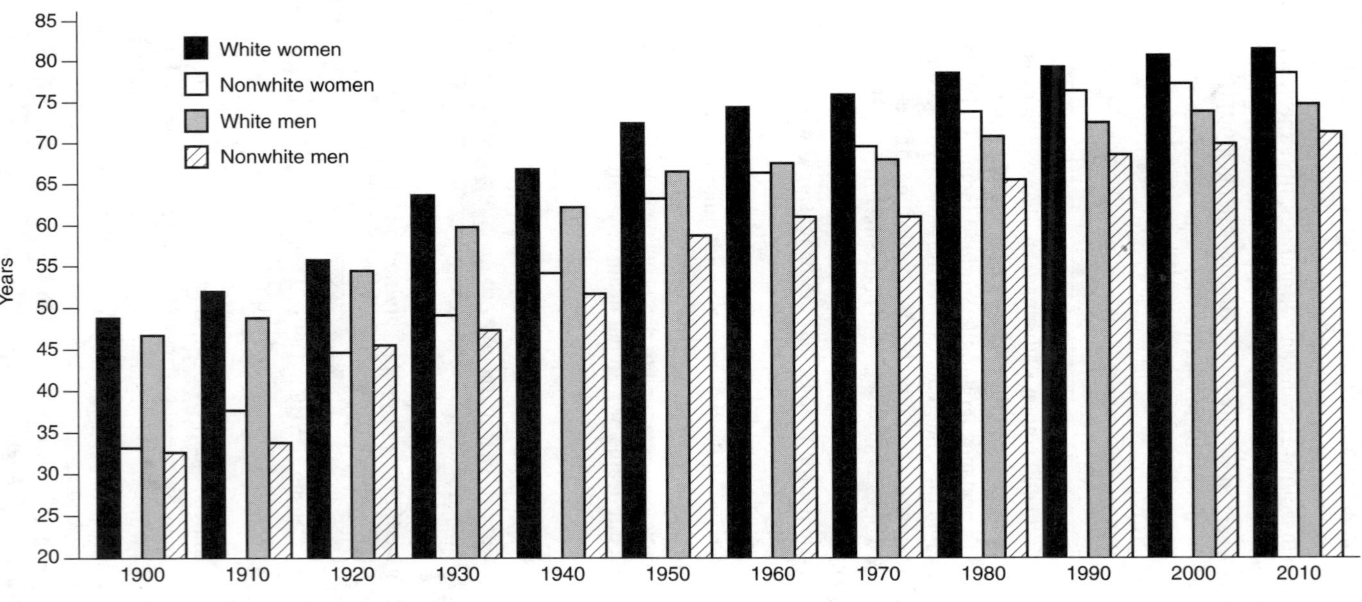

FIGURE 14.1 Life Expectancy Increases for U.S. Women and Men from 1900 to 2010

SOURCE: From *Historical statistics of the United States, Colonial times to 1970,* (p. 55), U.S. Bureau of the Census, 1975. Washington, DC: U.S. Government Printing Office; and *Statistical abstract of the United States, 1992* (112th ed.), (p. 76), U.S. Bureau of the Census, 1992, Washington, DC: U.S. Government Printing Office.

DIVERSITY HIGHLIGHT:
Life Expectancy around the World

The pattern of mortality rates in the United States also appears in other developed, industrialized countries. Cardiovascular disease and cancers are also the leading causes of death in other countries, including Australia, Canada, Finland, Israel, Italy, Japan, the Netherlands, Norway, Sweden, Switzerland, and the United Kingdom, but violent death is not as common in many of these countries as in the United States (Britannica Book of the Year, 1992). A different pattern appears in developing countries, and a third pattern occurs in undeveloped countries.

These three patterns can be seen in the table below. Notice the high rates of cardiovascular disease and cancer deaths in the developed countries compared with the developing countries. Countries such as Brazil and Egypt have lower death rates for cardiovascular disease and cancer but higher rates for infectious diseases. Infectious diseases tend to be

Average Life Expectancies, Death Rates, and Causes of Death for Developed, Developing, and Undeveloped Countries

	Life Expectancy			Causes (per 100,000 population)			
Country	Men	Women	Death Rate (per 1,000)	CVD	Cancer	Accident	Infectious Disease
Developed Countries							
Australia	74.0	80.0	7.0	337.6	179.1	48.5	
Canada	74.0	81.0	7.0	302.4	195.8	52.6	
Germany	73.0	79.0	11.4	571.9	258.9		21.0+
Japan	77.0	81.9	6.7	224.9	172.5	24.8	52.0+
Sweden	75.0	81.0	11.1	531.8	233.6		
United Kingdom	73.0	79.0	11.2	529.8	282.9	36.7	61.0+
United States	72.0	79.0	9.0	359.0	203.0	55.3	30.0+
Average	73.3	80.0	9.0	396.6	203.9	50.2	37.0+
Developing Countries							
Brazil	62.3	69.0	7.0	156.2	52.8	39.9	37.2
Iran	64.0	66.0	8.0	298.8	77.5	175.3	58.0+
Mexico	69.0	76.0	5.3	68.5		76.4	32.3
Thailand	67.0	71.0	6.0	155.2	113.5	101.2	50.0+
Undeveloped Countries							
Angola	42.9	47.0	20.2	19.2	6.5	89.0	73.2
Haiti	53.0	55.0	15.0	11.9			46.0
Laos	49.0	52.0	16.0	Bronchitis, influenza, malaria			
Mozambique	46.0	49.0	18.5	Tuberculosis:55.9 Measles:227.4			

SOURCES: Causes of death from *Britannica book of the year, 1992* (pp. 538–741), 1992. Chicago: Encyclopedia Britannica. Life expectancies from *The world factbook 1992,* Central Intelligence Agency, 1992, Washington, DC: U.S. Government Printing Office.

Continued

Continued

fatal for infants and children more often than for adults, so the life expectancies in these countries are lower than that in developed countries.

Undeveloped countries such as Angola, Chad, Bangladesh, and Laos have lower life expectancies than developing countries and higher rates of death due to infectious diseases. Undeveloped countries also have poorer reporting standards concerning causes of death, so the figures from these countries may not be as accurate as in more developed countries, which keep better health records (Kane, 1991). The picture, however, is clear: A higher incidence of infectious illness decreases life expectancy, and countries with longer life expectancies show higher death rates for cardiovascular disease and cancer.

Cardiovascular disease and cancer are diseases that occur much more frequently in old age than in childhood or young adulthood, and countries with high rates of death from these causes tend to have longer life expectancies than countries with lower CVD and cancer rates. Some developed countries, however, have much higher CVD and cancer rates than others, contributing to their relatively higher death rates.

The survival advantage for women is larger in developed than in developing and undeveloped countries, and this difference is mainly attributable to the higher death rates due to complications from pregnancy and childbirth (Kane, 1991). Poor health care services for pregnant women increase the chances of maternal mortality as well as infant mortality due to complications during delivery. In some countries, complications during pregnancy and childbirth are the leading causes of death for women during their reproductive years.

Another practice that can decrease the survival advantage for girls and women is *son preference*—that is, the preference for sons over daughters (Kane, 1991). Son preference can lead to the murder of infant girls, but more often it is expressed through preferential treatment for sons—better feeding and medical attention. These advantages increase male chances for survival. Son preference is common in South Asia and, combined with these countries' high rates of death during pregnancy and childbirth, results in the close to equal life expectancies for men and women. In countries where girls and boys receive more equal treatment during infancy and childhood, girls have a survival advantage over boys, as women do when compared to men. Thus, the female survival advantage holds across many cultures. Furthermore, women can benefit more from the better health services that accompany economic prosperity and thus remain at a survival advantage in developed countries.

without a complete recovery. Such diseases differ from acute conditions such as infectious diseases or accidents. Acute conditions have rapid onsets accompanied by specific symptoms, and people can recover completely. CVD develops over years but exhibits few symptoms until the condition is serious. For many people, heart attack is the first symptom of cardiovascular disease, and almost half of those who have heart attacks die as a result (Ellestad, 1986). Thus, for many people, death is the first sign of CVD.

About half of the people who have heart attacks survive, and that percentage has grown since the 1960s (Cohn, Kaplan, & Cohen, 1988). Improved hospital treatment and greater availability of paramedic care have contributed to the improvement in survival rates, and several options now exist for diagnosis and treatment. Women who develop CVD have several disadvantages (Knox & Czajkowski, 1997). Physicians refer men who report symptoms of CVD for further testing and treatment more often than they refer women with similar symptoms (Ayanian & Epstein, 1991; Steingart et al., 1991). Men are also twice as likely to be recommended for extensive cardiac testing or for coronary bypass surgery than

TABLE 14.1 U.S. Death Rates for Cardiovascular Disease in Men and Women, 1993 (rates per 100,000 population)

	Women		Men	
Age Range	Stroke	Heart Disease	Stroke	Heart Disease
< 15	—	2.6	—	2.8
15–24	0.6	2.0	0.5	3.4
25–34	1.8	5.6	2.0	11.3
35–44	5.6	17.2	6.8	47.0
45–54	15.8	57.9	19.6	172.8
55–64	40.1	204.5	52.2	499.2
65–74	118.7	589.3	157.4	1175.3
75–84	451.6	1808.2	523.7	2788.7
85 +	1623.9	6414.6	1541.9	7331.9
Average	69.0	284.9	46.9	292.1

Source: From *Statistical abstracts of the United States, 1996* (116th ed.) (pp. 96–97) by U.S. Bureau of the Census, 1996, Washington, DC: U.S. Government Printing Office.

women (Steingart et al., 1991). These delays in diagnosis result in women receiving treatment for CVD when their diseases are more advanced, and their poorer outcomes may be related to the later times of diagnosis (Knox & Czajkowski, 1997).

These differences in treatment indicate either overt or covert bias on the part of health care professionals, who may choose to minimize women's complaints, dismissing their reports of symptoms as inaccurate or overstated. Alternatively, these professionals may be influenced by the stereotypical belief that women do not experience CVD as frequently as men and thus discount the likelihood that women's symptoms indicate CVD. Either or both of these two approaches in dealing with women's reports of symptoms might account for the less aggressive treatment of CVD among women.

As with other chronic diseases, the causes of cardiovascular disease are not well understood. No infection or other specific agent appears to be responsible; instead, several physical conditions and behaviors are risk factors in the development of CVD. A **risk factor** refers to a condition associated with the increased probability that a condition will develop. For example, high blood pressure is a risk factor for CVD in that people with elevated blood pressure have an increased risk of heart attack and stroke.

Gender is a risk factor for CVD, with men at elevated risk compared to women. Karen Matthews (1989) hypothesized that biological sex might not be as much of a risk factor in disease as gender role assumptions and the behaviors related to these roles. Male physiology might not be the primary risk factor, but risky behaviors that are more typical of men might be. For example, smoking and eating a high-fat diet are risk factors for cardiovascular disease, and more men than women smoke and eat diets high in fat. Thus, behaviors that increase risk are part of gender roles, leading to the possibility that the male gender role may carry health hazards (Harrison, 1978; Messner, 1997).

Some aspects of the male role are known predictors of heart attack severity (Helgeson, 1990). Both gender roles contain positive and negative aspects. For example, aggression, hostility, and not needing others are negative aspects of the masculine gender role—that is, characteristics associated with men that are not positive attributes—whereas decisiveness is also stereotypically masculine but is a positive characteristic. On a questionnaire that separated the positive from negative aspects of masculinity and femininity, differences appeared for men and women who had experienced heart attacks. Men were more likely to have high scores on negative masculine traits than women, and high scores on this index of negative masculinity were related to heart attack severity for both men and women. This research demonstrated that the association between sex and health risks may be mediated by gender role factors.

A link between stress and the physical responses to stress might be a clue in the development of cardiovascular disease. Physiological responses to stress also show gender differences, including differences in the release of epinephrine in response to stress (Frankenhaeuser, 1991). Boys and men reacted more strongly and their bodies released more epinephrine than girls and women under conditions of performance stress. These gender-related differences were greatest when the stress was less severe and decreased under conditions of more severe stress, although even under extreme performance stress, men showed higher levels of epinephrine release than women. Because epinephrine elevates heart rate and blood pressure, increases in its release could relate to cardiovascular problems.

However, women and men who held similar management positions and experienced similar stresses showed similar levels of epinephrine release, highlighting the role of situation rather than biological sex. That is, this gender-related difference in reactivity to stressful situations may relate to the positions that men and women typically occupy. Nonetheless, these differences may account for some of the gender differences in the development of CVD.

In summary, cardiovascular disease, including heart disease and stroke, is the leading cause of death in the United States (and other industrialized nations), accounting for about 39% of deaths. Men die of heart disease at younger ages than women, but the overall death rates are similar. Stroke is a more common cause of death in women than men, but women die of stroke at older ages. The death rates from both heart disease and stroke have fallen in the past 25 years, with strokes decreasing at more rapid rates than heart disease. These gender differences in risk may be related to physiological differences between the two genders, but they may also reflect gender-related behaviors. Research has indicated that negative aspects of the masculine role are related to heart attack severity, demonstrating that the masculine role identification may be a factor in this leading cause of death.

Cancer

Cancer is the term applied to a variety of malignant neoplasms—tissues that have sustained uncontrolled growth that may form a tumor, as well as spread to other areas of the body. Most types of tissue can develop cancers. These growths are not restricted to human or even to animal tissues: Plants and all types of animals develop malignancies. Such uncontrolled tissue growth can become life threatening; cancer is the second leading cause of death in the United States, accounting for about 23% of deaths.

Men have higher overall death rates from cancer for most types of cancer and at most ages than women. Table 14.2 presents the mortality rates for women and men for various types of cancer at various ages. As the table shows, some gender differences exist. For example, women are much more likely to develop breast cancer than are men (although men do get breast cancer), and women have earlier mortality rates for cancer of the genital and reproductive organs than men. Lung cancer is the leading type of fatal cancer for both men and women, but more men die of lung cancer than women.

Cigarette smoking is a major factor in lung cancer death rates. The gender rates also differ for men and women. Until recently, men smoked at a much higher rate than women. Smoking takes time to cause health problems, so differences among men and women in past

TABLE 14.2 U.S. Death Rates for Cancer in Women and Men by Age, 1993 (rates per 100,000 population)

Women							
Age Range	Lung	Breast	Digestive System	Genital	Lymphatic (excluding leukemia)	Leukemia	Urinary
35–44	5.0	15.2	5.5	6.8	2.0	2.0	0.7
45–54	31.6	42.0	21.5	17.9	6.0	3.9	3.0
55–64	107.3	72.2	67.9	38.1	18.4	8.7	8.4
65–74	199.2	105.7	151.8	67.0	42.5	19.1	19.5
75–84	226.3	146.4	287.7	97.4	78.4	37.7	38.0
85+	173.9	206.0	487.0	114.4	95.5	68.2	64.5

Average: 189.8 per 100,000*

Men							
Age Range	Lung	Breast	Digestive System	Genital	Lymphatic (excluding leukemia)	Leukemia	Urinary
35–44	8.3	—	9.1	0.6	4.7	2.5	1.5
45–54	54.6	0.3	37.6	2.7	10.3	5.2	7.4
55–64	216.0	0.7	122.0	27.0	26.1	14.7	22.3
65–74	441.2	1.2	259.6	117.9	59.0	36.7	53.3
75–84	384.8	2.3	441.7	356.6	107.8	71.4	103.4
85+	559.7	5.1	668.5	842.2	145.6	115.6	190.3

Average: 222.1 per 100,000*

Source: From *Statistical abstracts of the United States, 1996* (116th ed.) (p. 100), U.S. Bureau of the Census, 1996. Washington, DC: U.S. Government Printing Office.

*For all ages, including individuals under age 35 and cancers of other sites.

GENDERED VOICES
I Have Breast Cancer

An announcement of breast cancer is shocking but not unusual—unless the person is a man. That unusual situation happened to Robert Riter (1997), who noticed a lump in his breast. Like many people, Riter thought it was a cyst and that it would go away. When he started bleeding from his nipple, he sought medical advise and treatment. His treatment included a biopsy, which revealed a malignancy. Although breast cancer is rare among men, the disease affects over a thousand men per year in the United States.

Riter's experience was both similar to and different from women's experience of breast cancer. Like many women, he had a mastectomy and chemotherapy. Unlike many women, losing the breast was not as traumatic an event for him. His greatest distress came from examining the survival statistics, which are virtually identical for men and women. Riter learned that his chances of surviving for 5 years were about 80%, but his likelihood of living 10 years was only about 60%.

Riter was the first man to join his area's support group for breast cancer survivors. "I'm probably not the only male in this area with the disease, but . . . men find it hard to discuss their prostate cancer, let alone a 'female' disease," he said (Riter, 1997, p. 14). He also encountered some surprised reactions, like the lab technician who questioned the referral slip with the diagnosis of breast cancer. He felt odd going to a "women's imaging center" to get a mammogram and, he said, "My follow-up letter from the center was addressed to Ms. Robert Riter. The radiology tech did note that I had the hairiest chest she's ever seen in a mammogram room" (p. 14).

Riter noted that his experience with breast cancer had taught him more about women's health issues that he would otherwise have known, but having a life-threatening "female disease" was a difficult way for him to gain knowledge and empathy.

smoking behaviors continue to appear in health statistics (USDHHS, 1989). However, the increase in women's rates of smoking and the decrease in men's rates of smoking have begun to show changes in this pattern: Women have begun to develop lung cancer at increased rates, whereas men's rates have leveled off. In 1986 lung cancer surpassed breast cancer as the leading cause of cancer deaths among women.

Use of tobacco products accounts for about 30% of cancers and diet for another 35% (Doll & Peto, 1981). In addition to foods that contain known or suspected carcinogens, dietary components have been implicated in the development of cancer, especially a high-fat diet. A substantial amount of evidence indicates that people who eat a high-fat diet are at increased risk for cancers of the digestive tract. In addition, a high-fat diet for women can increase their chances of breast cancer (Travis, 1988a). On the average, women eat lower-fat diets than men, so this behavioral difference may explain part of the discrepancy in cancer death rates.

Another dietary difference that may relate to cancer comes from intake of foods high in beta carotene, vitamins C and E, and selenium. Mounting evidence indicates that these nutrients may offer some protection against cancer. This choice puts "meat and potatoes" men at an increased risk of cancer because such nutrients are more abundant in green vegetables and fruits. In addition, the fiber in fruits and vegetables provides dietary benefits that may include protection against some cancers.

Occupational exposure accounts for another 4% of cancer deaths (Doll & Peto, 1981). Men are at increased risk for cancer due to their exposure to workplace hazards (Waldron, 1991). Men are more likely than women to hold jobs that bring them into contact with carcinogens such as asbestos, benzene, and various petroleum products. Exposure to such substances may also be a factor in the difference in cancer deaths between women and men.

Sexual behavior and reproduction also contribute to the development of cancer, and about 7% of cancers are attributable to these factors (Doll & Peto, 1981). Women who have sexual intercourse at an early age and have many sexual partners are at elevated risk for cancer of the reproductive tract (Levy, 1985). Such cancers constitute less of a risk than breast cancer. Furthermore, women who complete pregnancies before age 20 are at decreased risk for breast cancer compared to women with later pregnancies and to women who do not bear children. Thus, early intercourse presents a risk and early pregnancy a protection against cancer.

Men's sexual behavior can place them at risk for cancer, but their behavior can also be a risk for their female sex partners (Levy, 1985). In addition, men who are the receptive partner in unprotected anal intercourse are at increased risk for anal cancer as well as for infection with the human immunodeficiency virus (HIV), which is related to the development of acquired immune deficiency syndrome (AIDS). One of the diseases associated with AIDS is a form of cancer, Kaposi's sarcoma. Thus, receptive anal intercourse is a direct risk for anal cancer and an indirect risk for Kaposi's sarcoma. Men who have many sexual partners, especially those who have sex with prostitutes, endanger their partners by elevating the women's risk for cervical cancer. In addition, poor genital hygiene in men is associated with increased risk of cervical cancer in their female sexual partners.

As Table 14.2 shows, women experience higher mortality rates from cancer of the genitals than men until after age 65 years. Cancer of the genitals and reproductive tract plus breast cancer deaths account for the large proportion of women's cancer deaths during their early and middle adult years. Indeed, cancer is responsible for a greater proportion of women's deaths than cardiovascular disease until after age 65. The opposite pattern occurs for cardiovascular deaths among men, who are more vulnerable to premature death from CVD.

Violent Deaths

Violent deaths (accidents, suicides, homicides) account for about 6.5% of deaths in the United States (USBC, 1996), reflecting a relatively high rate of violence compared to other industrialized, economically developed countries. Violent death rates are lower in Australia, Canada, Japan, most of the countries in Western Europe, Scandinavia, and other countries scattered throughout the world (Britannica Book of the Year, 1992). Men are about three times more likely than women to die from violent deaths. This discrepancy holds for all ages, from birth until old age, and the differences are most pronounced early in life. Violent death is the leading cause of death for adolescents and had been the leading cause of death for young adults until 1993, when AIDS took that place (CDC: News. . . , 1995). Men are at least three times more likely to be victims of violence than are women (Waldron, 1991).

People from different ethnic backgrounds are not equally likely to die of violence. As Table 14.3 shows, African Americans in the United States are much more likely than European Americans to die from accidents and homicides, but European Americans are more likely to die from motor vehicle accidents and suicide. The ethnic and age differences in violent deaths are reflected in Table 14.3, revealing that young men are at much greater risk than young women and that African American men are disproportionately vulnerable, especially to deaths from homicide.

The gender differences in risky behaviors account for the differences in violent deaths. Men tend to behave in ways that increase their risks, such as heavy alcohol use, low seat belt use, occupational risks, and illegal activities. Alcohol use increases the chances of accidents, suicide, and homicide (Eckhardt et al., 1981). By slowing responses and altering judgment, alcohol contributes to traffic crashes. People who have been drinking (even those who are not legally intoxicated) are more likely to be involved in fatal traffic accidents; about half of all traffic fatalities are related to alcohol. Seat belt use is an important factor in reducing traffic fatalities, and women are more likely to use seat belts than men (Tipton, Camp, & Hsu, 1990). For the same reasons that alcohol use increases the chances of traffic accidents, alcohol use is also related to deaths from falls, fires, and drownings as well as from boating, airplane, and industrial accidents. Others' intoxication also increases the

TABLE 14.3 U.S. Death Rates from Accidents and Violence, 1993 (rates per 100,000 population)

	European American		African American	
Cause	Women	Men	Women	Men
Motor vehicle	10.3	22.7	8.7	24.6
Other accidents	13.2	24.3	13.8	33.7
Suicide	5.0	21.4	2.1	12.5
Homicide	3.0	8.6	13.6	69.7

All Accidents and Violent Deaths

	European American		African American	
Ages	Women	Men	Women	Men
15–24	28.2	99.1	39.9	242.2
25–34	24.8	92.0	46.2	197.3
35–44	24.9	82.9	40.1	169.9
45–54	24.3	70.5	28.7	137.2
55–64	26.7	71.7	31.9	112.1
65–74	39.0	91.1	47.1	136.3
75–84	87.1	187.3	94.9	185.9
85+	236.2	449.1	190.3	399.2
Average (including persons under 15 years old)	31.5	77.0	38.2	140.6

SOURCE: From *Statistical abstracts of the United States, 1996* (116th ed.) (p. 101), U.S. Bureau of the Census, 1996. Washington, DC: U.S. Government Printing Office.

chances of becoming a pedestrian victim of an auto accident (U.S. Department of Health and Human Services [USDHHS], 1990).

About 60% of adults in the United States drink alcohol, but only about 6% are heavy drinkers (National Center for Health Statistics, 1995). This 6% of the population accounts for almost half of all alcohol consumed. Any amount of alcohol consumption can increase the risk of accidents, but heavy drinking is especially risky. Men are more than three times more likely to be heavy drinkers than women (Travis, 1988a). In addition, drinking varies by age group, with younger adults being heavier drinkers. These gender and age differences in drinking patterns correspond to the differential risks of violent death. The gender differences in alcohol consumption may be decreasing, because more women have begun drinking at light and moderate levels, and a corresponding significant increase in problem drinking has taken place among women (Rodin & Ickovics, 1990). These changes have the potential to decrease the current female advantage in avoiding violent death.

Men are also more likely to hold risky jobs than women (Waldron, 1991). In addition to exposure to hazardous materials, which increases the chances of cancer, men are more likely than women to have jobs that involve working around or operating dangerous machinery. Around 95% of the fatal accidents at work involve men, and gender differences in workplace accidents account for between 2% and 3% of the overall gender difference in mortality in the United States (Waldron, 1991). Therefore, occupational hazards and violence are substantial factors contributing to the gender difference in accidental deaths.

Men are more likely to commit suicide, but women are more likely to attempt suicide (Kessler & McRae, 1983). This difference in suicide rates for men and women began to appear during the 1950s, increased during the 1960s, and began to decrease during the 1970s. The ratio of attempted to completed suicides is about 10 to 1 (Travis, 1988a). The main reason for the higher rates among men of suicides completed is that they tend to choose more lethal methods, such as guns and jumping from high places, whereas women more often attempt suicide by taking drugs. (No method is certain to be nonlethal, so any suicide attempt is serious.) The lethality of the methods chosen produces higher suicide rates among men, despite women's more frequent suicide attempts.

Chapter 9 described a gender difference in crime rate, explaining that men are more likely than women to commit crimes. This discrepancy is even greater for crimes involving violence, with men more likely to both perpetrate crimes and be victims of crime (U.S. Bureau of the Census, 1996). The increase in lawbreaking among women in the past decades has not changed these figures, because increases in the number of women reflect primarily nonviolent crimes. Thus, homicide affects men to a larger degree than women, and has an especially disproportional impact on young African American men.

In summary, men die in accidents, by suicide, and by homicide at a higher rate than women. Men are also more likely to be heavy users of alcohol than women, and alcohol use contributes to all of these causes of violent death. In addition, women are more likely to use automobile seat belts, which protect them in crashes. Men are more likely to have jobs that place them at greater risk of workplace accidents than women. Although women make more attempts, men complete suicide more often. Men are more likely to be involved in violent illegal activities and are the more frequent perpetrators and victims of homicide. This difference is especially prominent for African American men. All of these causes of violent death put men at a survival disadvantage and account for some of the survival advantage of women. Women, however, do not experience the same advantage when seeking health care; women experience greater morbidity than men and have more difficulty receiving treatment for serious conditions than men.

The Health Care System

As the headline story for this chapter discussed, women live longer than men, but they are sick more often. Defining what constitutes being sick is not simple, but doctor visits, hospital admissions, restriction of activities, or reports of distress are some of the indicators, with women meeting any of these definitions of illness more often than men (Travis, 1988a). The combination of greater morbidity with lower mortality seems a contradiction, but gender roles as well as physiology contribute to the situation. The possibility mentioned in the headline story is that women's reproduction and its medicalized treatment account for the increased use of medical services among women—pregnancy and childbirth are functions that now receive medical attention, require medical appointments, and are cared for by hospitalization. Another explanation involves the difference in gender roles related to seeking and receiving health care. A third possibility is that women are not as healthy as men but that their health problems are less often life threatening, producing the combination of poorer health but longer lives.

Gender Roles and Health Care

People seek and receive health care from a variety of formal and informal sources, and gender roles contribute to receiving help from each source. Traditional male and female gender roles differ in the amounts of vulnerability each is allowed and the permissibility of seeking help. One facet of the masculine role, the Sturdy Oak, holds that men are strong and invulnerable; this aspect of the role causes men to restrain from showing signs of physical illness or seeking medical care (Brannon, 1976). The traditional feminine role, on the other hand, allows and even encourages weakness and vulnerability for emotional and physical problems (Lorber, 1975).

The female gender role also relates to patterns of reporting symptoms of illness (Klonoff & Landrine, 1992). Unemployment was a significant factor in symptom reporting in this study, and women were more likely than men to have no employment outside their homes. Lack of paid employment was named as a factor in women's reports of poorer health in a nationwide sample of U.S. adults (Ross & Bird, 1994). Adherence to traditional gender roles may, therefore, hinder men from seeking help for their symptoms, but elements of the traditional feminine gender role relate to greater distress for women as well as to their increased readiness to seek medical care. After women and men enter the health care system, they also receive different care.

Gender and Seeking Health Care

The decision to seek medical care is influenced by many factors, including the perception of symptoms and beliefs about the consequences of seeking or failing to seek treatment.

People who feel healthy may enter the medical care system to receive routine exams, but many skip such screening procedures, finding it easy to ignore their health as long as they feel well. Men are more likely to avoid regular health care than women (Muller, 1990). Men are less likely than women to have regular physicians, sometimes avoiding checkups for years. Men explain these omissions in terms consistent with the masculine gender role, saying that they feel fine and thus do not need to consult physicians. This belief can be fatal, as cardiovascular disease often develops with few symptoms, and the first sign of heart disease can be a fatal heart attack. Nonetheless, the belief that a lack of symptoms equals good health can lead men to avoid regular contacts with the health care system.

Women, on the other hand, find it more difficult to avoid the health care system, regardless of how well they may feel. Young women must seek medical advice to obtain many forms of contraception, especially birth control pills (Kane, 1991). These young women count in the statistics as having consulted physicians, although no illness is involved in their medical care. As Altman's (1997) headline story suggested, such medical consultations often include physical examinations that may reveal health problems that require additional treatment. For example, blood tests may reveal anemia, and blood pressure readings may show hypertension. Each of these conditions merits further treatment, which leads these women into additional physician visits and medication. Young men receive no comparable medical attention during young adulthood that might reveal physical problems, and these differences in treatment for healthy young men and women contribute to the statistics concerning gender differences in seeking health care.

The personal perception of symptoms is an important factor in seeking medical care. People who sense that their bodies are not working correctly are more likely to seek medical advice than those who sense no problems. Perceiving symptoms, however, is not sufficient to lead people to make appointments with their physicians. Although some people readily seek professional medical advice and care, most people experience some reluctance to become part of the health care system.

This reluctance has many origins, including financial resources, convenience and accessibility of medical care, and personal considerations. Health care costs have risen faster than personal incomes, creating problems for many people in paying for health care. Scheduling appointments and changing daily routines to keep these medical appointments are additional problems that contribute to personal reluctance to seek medical treatment. Anxiety about the diagnosis or treatment may keep people from seeking professional care; the diagnosis may be threatening, or the treatment may be painful or expensive, or both.

These factors that influence reluctance to seek medical care may not affect men and women equally. Women are more likely than men to be outside the paid work force and to be employed on a part-time basis, whereas men are more likely to have the types of jobs that offer health insurance benefits. Employment situations can put women at a disadvantage in seeking health care, which leaves them with less money to pay for health care and to be without the health insurance that might cover their expenses (Muller, 1990).

Unemployed women can receive these benefits if they are married to men who have good insurance plans. For both men and women in these situations, continued health insurance depends on the continued employment of the spouse and the continuation of the marriage. Not only can women lose their health insurance through divorce, but children can also lose insurance coverage due to their parents' divorce. Mothers are most often granted custody, and the children may lose their coverage unless their mothers have employment that includes these benefits. Thus, women and children are less likely to have health insurance than men, making health care less accessible for them.

The male gender role, with its emphasis on physical invulnerability, influences men by making them less willing to seek medical care (Verbrugge, 1986). Men and women might have similar experiences of recurring health symptoms, but women are more likely to seek medical care for these symptoms. The reasons for this readiness may lie in two circumstances. Women are more sensitive to their body's signals than men, making women more capable of reporting these physical symptoms (Pennebaker, 1982). In addition, their traditional gender role allows them to do so more readily than men.

Men and women also seek health care from different types of providers (Kane, 1991). Both women and men are more likely to consult pharmacists than any other category of health care professional, and women make more inquiries than men. Women may ask pharmacists for advice about over-the-counter remedies for their entire families, so the number of consultations may not reflect any gender difference in personal need. Men experience more injuries due to accidents and sports participation, so they are more likely to seek the services of physiotherapists than are women. Women, on the other hand, are more likely to seek the services of chiropractors or nutritionists. Women are also more likely to use alternative health care services, such as herbal medicine and acupuncture. None of these differences is large, thus, the types of health care professionals that men and women seek vary only to a small extent.

The different preferences in seeking medical care may be partly attributable to access to medical care, with women at a disadvantage due to their financial resources and poorer insurance coverage. Another difference may lie in women's greater sensitivity to symptoms, but a difference also exists in the willingness to report symptoms. These differences are consistent with the gender roles, with men denying and women accepting help.

Gender and Receiving Health Care

After a person has contacted a health care professional and become part of the health care system, gender becomes a factor in treatment. Again, gender roles influence the behavior of both patient and practitioner. Although some patients and practitioners are coming to view their relationship as a collaboration, the traditional conceptualization of the patient–practitioner relationship has included the subordinate patient and the controlling practitioner. The patient role is thus more compatible with the stereotypically feminine than the stereotypically masculine role, whereas the practitioner role is more consistent with traditional masculinity. The combination of gender roles and patient–provider roles puts women at a disadvantage in receiving equitable medical care.

Men may have more trouble adopting the patient role than women. Being a patient requires a person to relinquish control and follow the advice or orders of the practitioner. Gender is not a reliable predictor of patient compliance (Brannon & Feist, 1997), but the combination of the demographic factors of gender, age, ethnic background, cultural norms, religion, and educational level relates to patients' compliance with physicians' treatment advice. For example, people who are part of a culture that trusts physicians and accepts their advice as the best way to get well are more likely to follow physicians' advice than people from cultures that accept herbalists as the preferred health care professionals. Therefore, gender is only one factor from among a configuration of variables that relate to compliance with medical advice. Indeed, the interaction between patient and practitioner is more important to the patient's willingness to follow health advice than a patient's personal characteristics, and gender often plays a role in that interaction.

The medical profession has been criticized for its treatment of female patients, and this criticism has taken several forms. The most radical form of criticism holds that women were healers throughout history but have been replaced by technological, male-dominated forms of healing, examples of which are female nurses and male physicians (Ehrenreich & English, 1973). Other criticisms (Travis (1988a) have claimed that negative stereotypes of female patients have led to poorer levels of medical care for them than for men. Yet other criticisms (Tavris, 1992) have been brought against the use of men as the medical standard to which women are compared, claiming that omitting women from medical training and research leaves physicians ill-prepared to treat women.

Physicians often have stereotypical views of women, and these views influence their treatment of female patients (Travis, 1988a). Medical school educational standards have promoted the view that women are emotional and incapable of providing accurate information about their bodies. This view leads physicians to discount the information provided by female patients and to believe that women cannot participate in decisions concerning their own health and treatment. Such physicians may reveal too little information to female patients to allow them to make informed choices or to know about options concerning their care. An increasing percentage of physicians are women, but gender bias still exists in medical education, with few provisions to remedy these problems (Bickel, 1997). At present, the majority of practicing physicians are men who were trained in medical schools during a time when negative attitudes toward women prevailed, and their stereotyping helps to perpetuate this biased treatment of women.

The treatment that women receive when they have heart disease supports the view that physicians view women as incapable of participating in their own health care. Women are less likely than men to receive additional testing and treatment when they report symptoms of heart disease (Steingart et al., 1991). Instead, women are more likely to be referred for psychiatric treatment. This failure to take symptom reports that indicate heart disease seriously and the tendency to refer women instead for psychiatric services demonstrate that women do not have the credibility that men have when they report symptoms of heart disease. Only after women have experienced heart attacks is their treatment comparable to men's treatment.

Another criticism is aimed at a more subtle type of discrimination in medicine (Tavris, 1992). This view contends that medical training presents men as the standard by which to measure all health concerns. Physicians receive instruction in how to dissect and prescribe drugs for the standard patient, a 154-pound man. With men as the standard, women become the exception. Thus, any condition that men do not develop comes to be considered as deviant, including even the normal conditions associated with women's physiology—menstruation, pregnancy, and childbirth.

In addition to holding men as the standard in medicine, a great deal of medical research has omitted women entirely; that is, many studies have failed to include women as research subjects. The rationale for omitting women is that women bias the research because of their low rates of certain diseases and their hormonal variations. For example, women develop cardiovascular disease at a rate lower than men of comparable ages, so studies that follow healthy people until they show signs of cardiovascular disease would have to include many more women than men to obtain a group of women with this disorder. Using only male participants results in studies that are easier to complete, but these studies reveal nothing about cardiovascular disease in women. For researchers to assume that women are similar to men in their development of CVD is unwarranted, because women are excluded from these studies precisely because of their physical differences.

Medical researchers have also excluded women from studies that test the safety and effectiveness of new drugs, as women would bias results because they experience cyclic variations in their hormonal levels. The researchers have feared that hormonal variations may interact with variations due to medication, making the task of assessing the effects of a test drug more difficult. Omitting women from such studies may be convenient for research but dangerous for women. If women have not participated in the testing, then the drug's safety and effectiveness have not been clearly established for them.

During the 1980s, the practice of excluding women from medical research was increasingly criticized, and pressure mounted to give women's health additional emphasis. That pressure resulted in the creation of the Office of Research on Women's Health, a part of the National Institutes of Health (Kirschstein, 1991). This office's mission is to improve the prevention and treatment of diseases in women, and one of its first steps was to attempt to end the exclusion of women from medical research studies with the help of U.S. government sponsorship.

This Office has sponsored research on women's health, including the Women's Health Initiative (Blumenthal & Wood, 1997; Matthews et al., 1997). This study is designed to investigate factors involved with health problems experienced by older women, including cardiovascular disease, cancer of the breast and digestive tract, and osteoporosis. The plan includes a 16-year longitudinal study with over 150,000 women, with both medication and psychosocial components of assessment and treatment. Additional areas of interest include improving the accessibility and quality of mammograms and research on infertility and contraception. The focus is on coordinating research efforts and including women in research and treatment priorities.

Although medicine remains male dominated, men are not the focus of comparable health initiatives. Indeed, men may not receive optimum or even adequate care. During childhood, parents are somewhat more likely to take their sons to the doctor than their daughters (Kane, 1991), but once men are responsible for seeking their own medical care, they tend to avoid regular medical care. Men seek care for their injuries but not for regular exams and screening tests. In a survey on recent health status (in Kane, 1991), men were more likely than women to say that they had been ill within the past two weeks but had failed to seek medical care. This study showed that men are less likely to have regular physicians than women, so getting an appointment to see a physician is a greater inconvenience for a man in that he must first find a physician. Prostate cancer kills almost as many men as breast cancer kills women, yet many times more funds go toward breast cancer research than for prostate cancer (Stipp, 1996). Men have not mobilized to exert political pressure that spurs funding in the same way that women have, leaving men's health issues with fewer vocal advocates. However, when men become involved in the health care system, they are more likely to be taken seriously in their reports of symptoms and are more likely to receive aggressive treatment, as in the case of heart disease.

In summary, the Sturdy Oak component of the male gender role may be a factor in men's avoiding health care; feelings of invulnerability and the belief that illness represents weakness lead men to ignore their health. Such avoidance can result in serious health problems that might be prevented or detected through routine physical exams. Men can avoid regular physical exams more easily than women, as they typically do not have the same contacts with the health care system connected with reproduction or contraception that women of reproductive age have. Thus, men seldom use the health care system until they become ill, perhaps to the detriment of their health. Not only do reproduction and contraception concerns prompt women but not men to seek medical care during the reproductive years, but the differences in their reproductive systems also account for a large proportion of the gender difference in seeking and receiving health care.

Reproductive Health

Many of women's encounters with the health care system do not involve illness but occur as a result of contraception, pregnancy, childbirth, and menopause. Although these functions were completed throughout history with little medical assistance, they became increasingly "medicalized" during the 19th and 20th centuries (Ehrenreich & English, 1973). Knowledge of physiology increased dramatically during the 19th century, with resulting changes in medicine; developments in the field increased educational requirements for medical practice. During this time, college education was largely restricted to men, and they came to dominate the growing profession of medicine.

This expansion of medicine included attending women during childbirth, a role that had been performed by midwives. Childbirth was not the only function to gain medical attention; pregnancy came to be considered an appropriate area for regular medical care. The increasing number of contraceptive technologies during the 20th century depended almost exclusively on controlling women's rather than men's fertility, and physicians assumed control over access to contraception techniques such as birth control pills. During the middle of the 20th century, even menopause became a "disease" that could be "cured" by hormone replacement (Wilson, 1966). Thus, medical technologies came to be involved in all facets of women's reproductive health, from contraception during adolescence to hormone replacement after menopause.

Some critics have argued that access to the medical field has burdened women by forcing them to give birth in sterile, impersonal surroundings and subjecting them to increasingly large hospital bills for these services. According to this argument, birth is a natural process requiring no medical intervention. However, comparing statistics from undeveloped countries and from times in the United States before routine medical care during pregnancy and delivery, death could also be seen as a natural process. There is no question that technological medicine has dramatically cut both maternal and infant mortality (Kane, 1991). Nonetheless, women may receive treatment that is inappropriate. They may be overtreated in some ways (as in too many hysterectomies or Cesarean section deliveries) and undertreated in other respects (as in too little testing for symptoms of heart disease or too few surgeries for CVD).

Women's more numerous consultations with health care professionals are due largely to their complex reproductive systems (Kane, 1991). Not only do women get pregnant and bear children, but their reproductive organs are subject to a greater variety of problems than are male organs. Figure 14.2 shows the female and Figure 14.3 the male reproductive systems. Except for children under age 15 years, girls and women receive more treatment for problems related to their reproductive systems than boys and men.

Both systems can develop problems in utero, producing congenital conditions that are more common in boys than girls. During infancy and early childhood, boys have more problems with their genitourinary system than girls, requiring more hospital stays and physician consultations for these problems (Kane, 1991). Beginning at age 15 years, girls make more visits to health care professionals regarding their reproductive systems and require more hospitalizations.

The majority of the physician visits and hospitalizations for women during their reproductive years involve contraception, pregnancy, and childbirth; most of these contacts with the health care system are not due to illness or health problems but because women's reproductive functions have come under medical supervision. Although a large percentage of pregnancies and deliveries proceeds without any problem, most women in industrialized countries receive medical care during their pregnancies, and the majority of deliveries take place in hospitals. In addition, about one-fourth of the deliveries in the United States are Cesarean section (C-section) surgeries (DiMatteo & Kahn, 1997). C-section deliveries can save mothers' and children's lives, but the surgery carries morbidity and mortality risks. This system of medical treatment for childbirth has unquestionably decreased mortality for women during pregnancy and delivery, but these visits and hospitalizations count as statistics showing (and often put women into the situation of receiving) more health care.

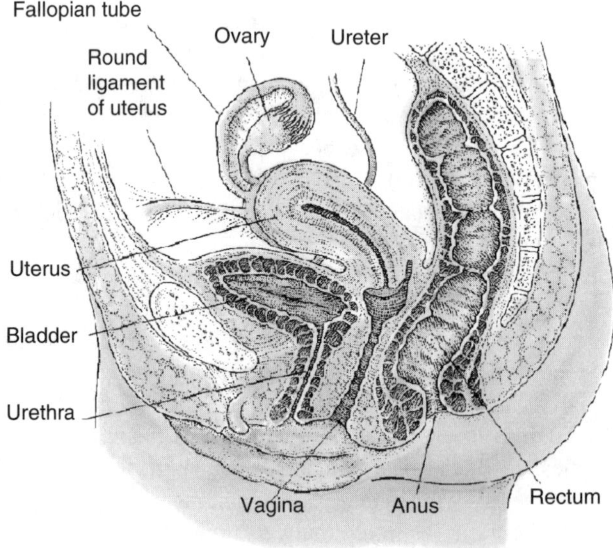

FIGLURE 14.2 Female Reproductive System

Many of the methods of contraception for women—birth control pills, implants, intrauterine devices (IUDs), diaphragms, sterilization, abortion—not only require medical supervision but also increase health risks. For example, birth control pills provide very effective contraception, but women over age 35 years who take contraceptive pills have significantly increased risks of stroke, and smoking multiplies this risk (Rodin & Ickovics, 1990). Therefore, contraception is not only more often a woman's responsibility but also more of a health threat to women.

Both men and women are subject to **sexually transmitted diseases (STDs),** infectious diseases that are spread through sexual contact. The infectious agents can be bacterial, viral, fungal, or parasitic, and many can be transmitted by vaginal, oral, or anal sexual activity. These bacterial infections include gonorrhea, syphilis, and chlamydia, and do not always produce symptoms; women are especially likely to be symptom free until advanced stages of the diseases. Although bacterial infections can be cured by antibiotics, people without symptoms may not receive treatment until their diseases are serious. Furthermore, delays in treatment allow infected persons to transmit the disease to others.

Delays in treatment are also likely to escalate the growth of the fungal and parasitic STDs. *Candidiasis albicans,* a yeast-like fungus, produces itching and swelling of the genitals. It can be transmitted through sexual intercourse, but this infection is not always an STD because it is more common in women who take contraceptive pills or who are pregnant or diabetic. These conditions alter the chemistry of the vagina, allowing this fungus to

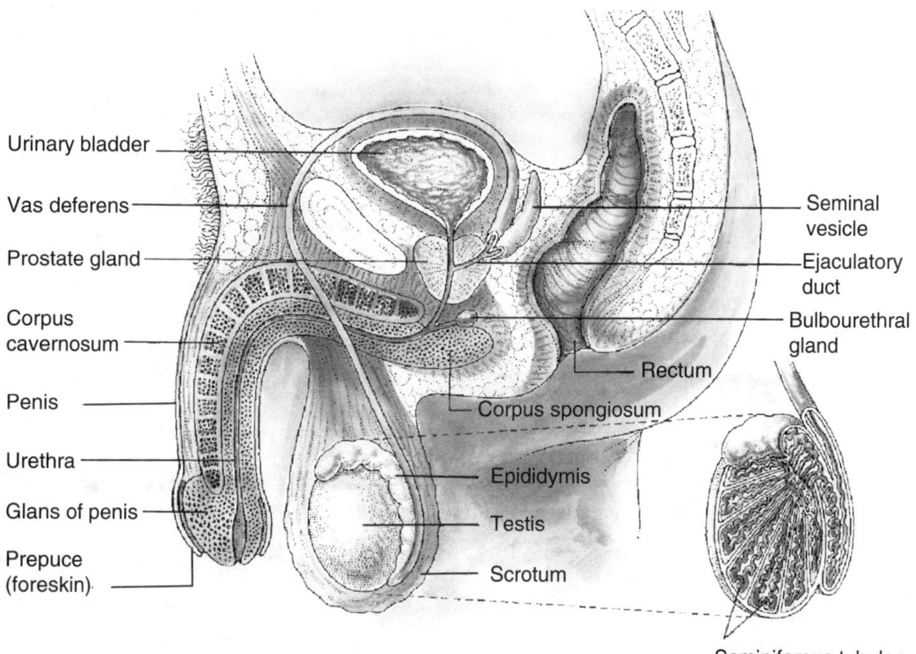

FIGURE 14.3 Male Reproductive System

grow at a rapid rate to produce annoying and painful symptoms. Chemical treatments exist to control this type of infection. Trichomoniasis is a one-celled animal that can infect the vagina in women and the urethra in men. It is almost always sexually transmitted, and an effective drug treatment exists.

No drugs exist to cure viral diseases, thus the viral STDs pose an even more serious problem than other types of STDs. The human immunodeficiency virus (HIV) is the virus that produces acquired immune deficiency syndrome (AIDS), a virus that can be sexually transmitted. The virus damages the immune system, leaving the body open to a variety of opportunistic diseases. Years may pass between time of infection and the development of symptoms, allowing infected persons to be unaware of the presence of the condition and able to unknowingly transmit the infection to others.

Genital herpes, viral hepatitis, and genital warts are also viral STDs. Genital warts can sometimes be surgically removed, and several medications exist to manage the symptoms of herpes infections. Like other viral infections, these STDs are difficult to manage and are presently without a cure. Herpes infections are especially problematic, producing chronic problems with painful blisters on the genitals.

Not all medical problems of the reproductive organs are related to reproduction; that is, these organs can be the site of disease and cancer. Again, women are more likely than men to seek health care concerning problems with their reproductive organs. Although women are at greater risk for cancer of organs in the reproductive system than men throughout young and middle adulthood, men are most likely to develop testicular cancer between ages 15 and 34 years (Parker, 1997). This form of cancer is quite rare, but rates are increasing; men are most likely to develop this form of cancer during the years when they tend to avoid regular physical checkups. A man may have no regular physician to tell about the lump he has detected on a testicle, and the tumor may go untreated for a dangerously long period. This form of cancer is rarely fatal if treated early, but fatality rates rise sharply with delays in treatment, going from a 90% survival rate to only a 25% survival rate. Thus, this rare form of cancer that affects men in their 20s and 30s may be fatal more often than it would be if men gave more attention to their health.

Prostate cancer is much more common than testicular cancer and tends to develop in older men. This form of cancer is not common until after age 75 years, when it increases sharply (USBC, 1996). Even without malignancy, as the prostate enlarges, which begins during puberty, it can cause problems, such as difficulty during urination, that require surgery. Malignant tumors of the prostate typically are small and grow slowly, and many elderly men die *with* rather than *from* prostate cancer (Stipp, 1996). The development and use of a diagnostic test, the prostate specific antigen test, has allowed earlier diagnosis, and men are beginning to mobilize as advocates for improved treatment.

Endometrial cancer affects the uterine lining and is the most common form of cancer of the genitals (Paskette & Michielutte, 1997). Women can also develop cancer of the cervix, ovaries, vulva, vagina, and Fallopian tubes. None of these sites is the most common for cancer—the breast is. About one in nine women will develop breast cancer. (Even so, lung cancer is the leading cause of cancer death for both men and women due to its high fatality rate.) From ages 15 until 45, cancer in the reproductive system is a major cause of mortality for women but not for men.

During menopause women lose their fertility; they cease ovulation and menstruation, and their production of estrogen and progesterone declines. Some women experience uncomfortable symptoms associated with menopause; the most common of these is the "hot flash," a sudden feeling of heat and skin flushing. These feelings may be uncomfortable and embarrassing but are not health threatening. Only 10% of menopausal women experience serious problems with hot flashes (Hyde, 1990). Estrogen replacement therapy can alleviate the symptoms, but this medical intervention remains controversial (Derry, Gallant, & Woods, 1997). Critics contend that hormone replacement is an example of overtreatment of women because menopause is not a disease. In addition, this treatment can increase the risk for breast cancer (Steinberg et al., 1991). Proponents cite the continued protection from heart disease and lowered risk of osteoporosis as benefits of hormone replacement therapy. Proponents and critics agree that hormone replacement therapy should be an individual decision made after considering both benefits and risks.

Men's hormone production also drops with aging, but they undergo no symptoms as visible as those of women during menopause. The decrease in hormone production in men results in the decline but not the end of their fertility. Men who lose the ability to get erections may receive hormone replacements, but far fewer men than women receive analogous hormone replacement therapy.

Thus, treatment for malignancies of the reproductive system accounts for a small portion of the reproductive health care received by women but a larger portion for men. Women not only get pregnant and bear children, but they also have the majority of responsibility for contraception. In addition, menstruation is often painful, and some women experience pain sufficiently serious to prompt them to consult health care professionals. The decline in hormone production associated with menopause also causes some women to seek medical treatment. Therefore, a great deal of the added health care received by women is due to their reproductive system needs, but this is only part of the reason for women's greater number of contacts with the health care system.

Gender, Lifestyle, and Health

Men have shorter average life spans than women in all developed and most undeveloped countries, now and in the past, yet women are more likely to use health care. Both men's shorter lives and women's poorer health may, as women believe (Wallace, 1996), be related to their lifestyles. That is, men may lose years from their life span by their behaviors, and factors in women's lives may increase their morbidity. Karen Matthews (1989) hypothesized that women's healthier lifestyles are a factor in their longer lives and that men's lifestyle choices and occupational health risks place men in greater danger than women for life-threatening diseases and accidents. These risky behaviors are associated with adopting the male gender role, which may be dangerous to men's health (Harrison, 1978).

Adopting the female gender role may likewise endanger health (Gove & Hughes, 1979). The nurturant role that many women fulfill places them in the position of taking care of everyone except themselves. Women are in the position of providing social support and nurturant care for their families and friends, but these demands can be emotionally and physically draining. In addition, women may not receive the same quality of care that they give, leaving them without the support they offer to others. Women reported that they were too busy to take care of themselves when they felt unwell, that chores still needed to be done when they were sick, and that family members interrupted their rest when they were unwell.

Research has confirmed that the female role may offer risks for morbidity. Women are more vulnerable to stress and feel more vulnerable to illness than men (Verbrugge, 1989). Additional evidence of the dangers of the female gender role came from a study (Helson & Picano, 1990) that related gender roles during young adulthood to women's health 20 years later. The results indicated that the young women who fulfilled the traditional female gender role were well-adjusted, but during middle age, traditionally feminine women were more poorly adjusted and less healthy than more nontraditional women.

Therefore, both traditional gender roles carry health risks. Women's morbidity is a factor that significantly decreases the quality of their lives (Kaplan, Anderson, & Wingard, 1991), but their more frequent illnesses are usually not ones that threaten their lives. Men, on the other hand, tend to experience health problems that are more likely to be life threatening. In other words, "One sex is 'sicker' in the short run, and the other in the long run" (Verbrugge, 1985, p. 163). The causes of death, however, are similar, although men die earlier from these causes than women.

Two behaviors that relate to health and longevity are eating and exercising, and these behaviors show gender-related differences.

Eating

Everyone eats, but not everyone shares the same eating pattern, and eating does not have the same meaning to everyone (Belasco, 1989). Women show more concern with eating to control weight and are more likely to diet than men. This concern with weight and their attempts to restrict food intake lead women to hold different attitudes toward eating than men do.

Gender differences in eating patterns start during adolescence (Rolls, Fedoroff, & Guthrie, 1991). Adolescent boys, on the average, eat enough food to obtain the required calories, but adolescent girls do not. This food restriction puts adolescent girls at risk for nutritional inadequacies. Adult women also eat less than adult men, but the discrepancy is not as great as during adolescence. Nonetheless, women may eat too little to receive adequate nutrition.

Not only do men eat more than women, but they have somewhat different patterns of food consumption. Observing the eating patterns of men and women for over six hours in a laboratory setting allowed one researcher to compare the two patterns (J. Green, 1987). Although both genders showed similar patterns of food consumption, men ate more calories because they took bigger bites. Eating less and taking smaller bites may relate to efforts to appear feminine (Mori, Chaiken, & Pliner, 1987). Male and female participants snacked and talked with same-gender or other-gender partners while researchers observed what they ate and what they said. The female participants ate less when they were paired with attractive male partners than with unattractive men or with other women. The men in this study did not alter their eating patterns in response to the characteristics of their partners as much as women did, but the men showed a tendency to eat less when paired with female partners.

A later study (Pliner & Chaiken, 1990) demonstrated that men too are affected by the desire to present themselves in a socially desirable way by eating less. Both the men and women in this study ate less when paired with attractive other-gender partners. This study also revealed that women's eating is motivated by the desire to appear feminine as well as the desire to give a good social impression. Thus, women have two constraints on their social eating, whereas men have only one. Additional research (Chaiken & Pliner, 1987) demonstrated that eating style can affect social perception; people form an impression of others based on how much they see them eating. Participants in this study described women who ate small meals as more feminine, more concerned about appearance, and better looking than women who ate larger meals. Therefore, women and men eat somewhat differently, partly due to men's greater caloric requirements and partly due to the impression that women may wish to convey through their eating style.

Differences in eating styles may be more than a way to make an impression; the thinner ideal body image for women mandates a difference in eating from men. Women have more body fat than men, but the ideal body image for women demands thinness. Thus, women may believe that they must diet to achieve the desired weight. Extreme concerns with weight and dieting can produce abnormal eating habits and severe eating disorders. A growing consensus holds that body image and eating disorders are linked; an unattainably thin body image can prompt these unhealthy eating patterns.

Body Image

The image of what constitutes an attractive female or male body currently emphasizes thinness for women and muscularity for men. The contemporary ideal body image for women has developed over the past 100 years (Chernin, 1978; Wooley, 1994). In the past plumpness was the ideal for women, signifying their health and wealth, but that ideal has faded. The thin image arose during the early part of the 20th century, signifying a departure from the plump image of traditional femininity. The thin ideal has a social class basis (Polivy & Thomsen, 1988). When rich women began to have a preference for thinness, this preference began to spread throughout all social classes. This image now affects African American (Hsu, 1990), Hispanic American (Hsu, 1990), Asian American (Bradshaw, 1994), and Native American women (LaFromboise, Berman, & Sohi, 1994).

The ideal body image for men does not emphasize thinness as much as muscularity, and men are also under pressure to conform to their own ideal body image (Mishkind, Rodin, Silberstein, & Striegel-Moore, 1986). Men who are overweight are not as socially censured as overweight women (Stake & Lauer, 1987), but being overweight has become a stigma for both.

Although images of body build and weight affect men as well as women, men and women are not equally affected by the changed standards for weight. The changes in ideal body image have been more extreme for women than for men. The degree of change in the ideal body for women is reflected in a comparison of two images—*Playboy* centerfolds and Miss America contestants (Garner, Garfinkel, Schwartz, & Thompson, 1980). Women in both categories became thinner over the 20-year period from 1959 until 1978. An extension of that research through 1988 (Wiseman, Gray, Mosimann, & Ahrens, 1992) showed that Miss America contestants became significantly thinner, and both images were significantly thinner than average women of comparable ages. The actual average weight for women did not decrease over the time period of these two studies, but the image of the ideal weight did. What women saw as their ideal became thinner and thus more difficult to attain.

Women experience pressures to be thin, and these social forces affect how women feel about their bodies (Rodin, Silberstein, & Striegel-Moore, 1985). Women develop images of both their own bodies and the ideal body, and a comparison of the two leads almost all women to be discontent. No matter how attractive, every person's body has flaws: "The ideal female weight, represented by actresses, models, and Miss Americas, has progressively decreased to that of the thinnest 5 to 10% of American women. Consequently, 90 to 95% of American women feel that they don't 'measure up'" (Seid, 1994, p. 8). The vast majority of women do not (and cannot) meet the standards presented as ideal, resulting in discontent as the norm.

This discontent is not limited to adults or even adolescents. Body image discontentment appears even in preadolescent children (Collins, 1991). As young as age 6 or 7, both girls and boys chose an ideal body thinner than their own, but boys' choices were less extreme than girls' choices. The girls also chose ideal adult bodies that were significantly thinner than the boys' choices. The thin ideal affects girls more than boys, but both experience self-criticism concerning weight, and this tendency begins before adolescence. The concern with weight and appearance not only starts early but persists throughout life. Individuals as young as 10 and as old as 79 exhibit concerns with eating, body weight, and physical appearance (Pliner, Chaiken, & Flett, 1990). The concern with weight and appearance among women was apparent at all ages, but a similar degree of concern did not appear for the men in this study.

Dissatisfaction with weight also occurs among college men (Drewnowski & Yee, 1987). Indeed, comparable rates but different patterns of dissatisfaction with weight and body image appeared among college men and women. The 85% of women who were dissatisfied with their weight reported that they wanted to lose weight, expressing discontentment similar to that found in other studies. A comparable percentage of men expressed dissatisfaction with their weight, but 40% of the men wanted to lose and 45% wanted to gain weight. The men and women who felt overweight had similar negative feelings about their bodies, but the men were more likely to use exercise as a way to control weight, whereas the women were more likely to diet. These results suggest that discontentment with weight and body image is widespread among both men and women, but the behavioral strategies for dealing with these dissatisfactions might show gender differences.

Ironically, both women and men are erroneous in their estimates of what body type the other finds most attractive. Asking male and female college students to indicate their current body sizes, their ideal bodies, and the body that would be most attractive to the other gender yielded interesting contrasts (Fallon & Rozin, 1985). For men, the differences among these three body images were small, but for women, the three differed greatly. Women rated their current bodies as heavier than the one most attractive to men, which was heavier than the women's ideal bodies. In addition, women believed that men would like bodies that were thinner than the men actually rated as most attractive, and men believed that women would like heavier bodies than women rated as most attractive. These findings suggest that both women and men are striving for ideal bodies that are not ideal to the other gender, but men tend to see their bodies as closer to the ideal than do women.

Media portrayals of beauty influence the images of what women and men want. An examination of magazines popular with young adults (Andersen & DiDomenico, 1992) found that women's magazines contained over 10 times as many advertisements and articles oriented toward weight loss than men's magazines. The magazines for men contained messages to change body shape rather than to lose weight. Therefore, both women and men are subjected to pressures to change their bodies, but the methods for achieving these changes differ. If these messages are effective, men and women would be likely to take different strategies to achieve their ideal bodies: Women would be more likely to experience eating disorders, whereas men would be more likely to encounter exercise-related problems.

Eating Disorders

Anorexia nervosa and bulimia are two eating disorders that have received a great deal of publicity, but dieting has reached such proportions, and in some cases such severity, that it may also be considered an eating disorder (Polivy & Thomsen, 1988). Indeed, dieting is related to the development of the more serious eating disorders of anorexia and bulimia. **Anorexia nervosa** is a disorder caused by self-starvation in pursuit of thinness, and **bulimia** consists of binge eating followed by some method of purging (induced vomiting or excessive laxative use).

Dieting, anorexia, and bulimia are all more common among women than men. Beginning during the early years of adolescence, girls express greater dissatisfaction with their bodies and diet to lose weight more frequently than boys. This dissatisfaction continues into late adolescence and adulthood, and the gender differences persist. In surveying high school students and adult women and men (Serdula et al., 1993), dieting was found to be more common among women. About two-thirds of the girls and women were either trying to lose or trying not to gain weight, compared to about one-third of the boys in high school and one-half of the men. When considering lifetime dieting, 72% of the women and 44% of the men said they had dieted.

More women than men near ideal weight will diet—30% of women versus 10% of men (Jeffery, Adlis, & Forster, 1991). For these normal-weight dieters, perceptions of overweight are body image problems rather than body fat problems. The percentages are even more divergent for eating disorders, with around 90% of people who are treated for eating disorders being women (Rolls et al., 1991). Being female, therefore, is a predictor for dieting and for developing eating disorders. Feminine gender role orientation, however, is related to dieting but not to developing eating disorders (Lancelot & Kaslow, 1994).

Dieting itself produces physical and psychological effects, including fatigue, low blood pressure, anemia, headaches, cardiac problems, and other physical problems (Polivy & Thompson, 1988). The psychological problems associated with dieting include irritability, anxiety, poor concentration, and depression. The relationship between dieting and depression is common in both women and men, but the relationship is stronger for men (Zimmer-Schur & Newcomb, 1994). Furthermore, the evidence is not entirely optimistic concerning the effectiveness of dieting as a way to control weight (Brownell & Rodin, 1994). Thus, dieting may not be the only answer to the problem of being overweight. For some people, the risks of dieting outweigh the benefits.

Dieting is very common, but anorexia and bulimia are much less frequent. Anorexia is most common among young women, but only around 1% of adolescent girls have this disorder, and its appearance in the general population is even lower (Dolan, 1994). Bulimia is more common, occurring in about 2% of women. Again, young women are most likely to be bulimic; on college campuses some estimates of the frequency of bulimia run as high as 4%. Although these percentages are low, these disorders affect hundreds of thousands of people, so the problem is not a minor one.

Several factors relate to the development of eating disorders. As the rates of anorexia and bulimia suggest, both gender and age are factors, with women at a higher risk than men

GENDERED VOICES

I'm Afraid Some of Them Are Not Going to Be Around

"I'm afraid some of them are not going to be around," a 14-year-old dancer told her mother concerning other dancers who showed symptoms of anorexia. The dancers in her classes were encouraged to be thin, and the girl believed that several were in danger; they were so thin that she considered them in danger of dying. Her mother was angry because she believed that the instructor was encouraging unhealthy eating in students by telling her normal-weight daughter that she needed to lose weight. The girl knew that she was heavier than many of the other dancers, but she believed that they had the problem, not her.

She had begun to hear criticisms about her weight when she was 12, and she started to become self-conscious about it; but she had resisted dieting, partly because she thought the other girls were too thin and partly because she didn't want to change her eating habits. She had also received conflicting messages about her weight, with her mother and others telling her that she wasn't too heavy, her dance teacher telling her that she needed to be thinner, and her classmates dieting to the point of anorexia.

Another girl's story confirmed the prevalence of weight consciousness among early adolescents. This 12-year-old came home from school one day and told her mother that when they had gone swimming for gym class, most of the girls had gone into the pool with their T-shirts over their bathing suits. She didn't understand why they had done so; a wet T-shirt made swimming more difficult. When she asked one why she had kept her shirt on, the other girl said, "Because I'm so fat. I don't want anyone to see me in a bathing suit." The 12-year-old told her mother, "But they're not fat." She considered her classmates' perceptions of their bodies very odd. Judging from the number of girls who had been reluctant to be seen in their bathing suits, her classmates' distorted perception was more common than her accurate assessment of what was normal and overweight.

and young women more subject to eating problems than older women (Hsu, 1990). Social class has been a factor in the past, but pressures for thinness now occur in all social classes, so this factor no longer differentiates risk for eating disorders. Occupation is also a factor, with young women who are in modeling or dance school more likely to have eating disorders than comparable young women whose careers do not demand thinness (Garner & Garfinkel, 1980).

Feminine gender role orientation does not relate to the development of eating disorders (Lancelot & Kaslow, 1994), but conflict over how the gender role is enacted may. Brett Silverstein and his colleagues (Perlick & Silverstein, 1994; Silverstein, Carpman, Perlick, & Perdue, 1990; Silverstein, Perdue, Wolk, & Pizzolo, 1988; Silverstein & Perlick, 1995) have found evidence that a syndrome of problems exists in women who experience ambivalence over the gender role. This ambivalence arises as a result of the rewards associated with achievement and the need to associate achievement with the masculine rather than feminine gender role. This conflict applies to young women who are achievement oriented and have opportunities to succeed. In addition to eating disorders, Silverstein and his colleagues have presented evidence that this conflict is associated with depression, anxiety, and headaches. According to this view, eating disorders are associated with other psychological and physical problems, and young women are more likely than others to experience the inner conflicts that lead to this combination of problems.

About 10% of people with eating disorders are male (Rolls et al., 1991). Some of these men have occupations that require thinness, such as jockeys, dancers, or models. The demands of their careers make them subject to pressures for slimness in the same way as women who are dancer or models. Athletes also develop weight concerns so serious as to change their eating to a pathological pattern. Wrestlers and runners are at specific risk, and intensity of training is a factor. High-mileage runners have a greater chance of showing symptoms of eating disorders than those who run less (Kiernan, Rodin, Brownell, Wilmore, & Crandall, 1992).

Sexual orientation may also relate to disordered eating in men. In a study of body preferences (Herzog, Newman, & Warshaw, 1991), gay men chose a thinner ideal body than heterosexual men. This body preference puts such men at risk for eating disorders, and about a fourth of men who are anorexic are gay (Seligmann, 1994). Therefore, the majority of anorexic men are heterosexual, but among men, gay men are at an increased risk for eating disorders. The men who develop anorexic or bulimic eating patterns share the abnormal eating patterns and body concerns exhibited by women with such disorders, but men generally do not express their body concerns through disordered eating as frequently as women.

Both anorexia and bulimia are serious disorders, but anorexia is more likely to be life threatening. Between 5% and 15% of anorexics starve themselves to death (Hsu, 1990). Furthermore, treatment for anorexia is difficult. Anorexics do not cooperate with their treatment and persist in their desire to lose weight—even at the risk of their lives. Bulimia is more easily treated because bulimics typically feel guilty about their binge eating and purging and desire to change their behavior. Therapy can fail with both disorders, resulting in persistent eating problems that can lead to permanent damage to health.

Eating disorders, then, may be the result of concerns with body image and exaggerated attempts to attain thinness. Because their ideal body images are thin, women are more likely than men to develop eating disorders. Over the past several decades, both men and women have begun to feel increased pressure to attain and maintain attractive bodies, and women tend to try to achieve this goal through dieting and exercise, whereas men use exercise as a primary means and dieting as a secondary means of shaping their bodies.

Exercising and Fitness

Exercise is a factor in the weight maintenance equation. To maintain a steady body weight, the energy (calories) from food consumed must equal body energy expenditures. Such expenditures come from the energy required to maintain basal metabolism and from the energy required for physical activity. Increases in physical activity require more calories, or weight loss occurs. Thus, increases in physical activity can produce weight loss.

As noted earlier, men are more likely to exercise and women are more likely to diet as their main strategies to lose weight. When dieters eat less, their basal metabolism slows, and their bodies require fewer calories, which protects against starvation but makes weight loss difficult (Polivy & Herman, 1983). To overcome this problem, the dieter must eat even less, increasing the chances of nutritional deficits and difficulties in maintaining the diet. Thus, dieting is not only difficult, it also is not as effective for weight control as dieting plus exercise.

Increased concern with body image and the growing evidence that dieting may not be a good weight control strategy has led to an increased emphasis on exercise. Weight control, however, is a minor factor in considering the benefits of exercise; physical activity is a basic part of life. The amount of physical activity varies from person to person and from time to time, but people are physically active creatures.

Some people enjoy exercise and participate in various types of activities that require a great deal of physical effort, whereas others prefer more sedentary lives. Some people have jobs that require high levels of physical effort, but most jobs in technological societies are sedentary. The choice of leisure activities is another factor that influences exercise, with some people preferring active sports and others choosing television or other sedentary activities as a way to spend their leisure time.

Even during the preschool years, gender differences appear in levels of physical activity, with boys being more active than girls. Family attitudes toward exercise influences young children's activity levels (Poest, Williams, Witt, & Atwood, 1989). That is, the social environment can encourage or discourage physical activity, and gender stereotypes hold that boys are more active than girls. Not only parents but also nursery school and day-care workers can influence the activity levels of their pupils, either promoting more active or a more sedentary orientations.

Throughout childhood boys are more likely to engage in physical activities requiring gross motor skills that use the large muscles of the body. Boys' preferences for baseball, football, soccer, and basketball put them into more active situations than many girls' games require. Girls and boys do not play together often during childhood, decreasing the chances that girls will participate in many games and sports involving vigorous activity. (See Chapter 10 for a discussion of gender segregation and friendships during childhood and Chapter 12 for a consideration of athletics in schools.)

Watching television and playing computer games have become popular recreational activities for children. Until recently, the computer game market has been dominated by games aimed at boys, with few oriented toward girls' interests. This situation has changed, and computer games with traditional feminine themes have appeared (Rothstein, 1997). Regardless of the content, computer games can take the place of more active games and decrease the physical activity of both boys and girls.

Although children with athletic talent are encouraged to participate in sports, the emphasis on sports may leave the majority of children without adequate encouragement to be active. Many children of both genders avoid physical activity. Not having the ability to excel, they shun exercise, resulting in poor fitness and an increased probability of obesity.

Gender differences in exercising increase during adolescence, with girls decreasing and boys increasing their participation in athletics. The traditional gender roles hold that women should look slender and dainty and should feel reluctant to compete. Men, on the other hand, should look muscular and strong and should feel eager to compete. Athletic participation, with its emphasis on size, strength, and competition, is more compatible with the male than the female gender role. Adolescents feel the pressures to adopt these gender roles, thus, boys are urged to "try out" for sports whereas girls may not receive similar encouragement.

Title IX of the Education Amendments of 1972 prohibited sex discrimination in education, which included support for school athletics. The subsequent development of athletic programs for high school girls and college women has changed opportunities and attitudes toward women's athletics. More women now participate in athletics, establishing a pattern of physical activity that, like men's, can carry over into adulthood and provide long-term health benefits.

A growing body of research evidence indicates that exercise provides physical and psychological benefits to both men and women (King & Kiernan, 1997). A review of research on exercise and cardiovascular disease showed benefits, especially for men (Dubbert & Martin, 1988). Most of the studies on cardiovascular disease have excluded women, resulting in less conclusive evidence for the benefits of exercise for women. The role of exercise is better established in connection with **osteoporosis,** the process of bone demineralization. This disorder affects older individuals and is more common among women than men. Orthopedic problems such as fractures are common and can lead to decreased mobility, which is a major factor in decreased quality of life for the elderly (Robine & Ritchie, 1991). Exercise slows and may reverse this process.

In addition to the physical benefits, exercise promotes psychological benefits (Dubbert & Martin, 1988; Plante & Rodin, 1990). Exercise is related to improvements in mood and to feelings of psychological well-being and self-esteem. The efficacy of exercise to counter depression is particularly noteworthy. Thus, people who exercise show improvements in psychological and physical health, but relatively few people accrue these benefits; most children and adults lead sedentary lives (Dubbert, 1992).

Men's greater sports participation during adolescence makes them more likely than women to continue this athletic activity throughout their lives, but this background is no guarantee of an active lifestyle (Verbrugge, 1989). After they leave school, men become less likely to continue with physical activity, becoming adult men who lead sedentary lives, with desk jobs and sedentary hobbies.

Recent pressures on women to be thin have extended to fitness, with an increasing number of articles in women's magazines urging women to achieve thinness not only through diet but also exercise (Weisman, Gray, Mosimann, & Ahrens, 1992). Although they may or may not have histories of participation in activities that promote physical fitness, women are subject to increasing pressures to exercise. Women feel the pressure to pursue physical fitness as a way to achieve their weight goals rather than as fitness goals. An investigation of physically active men and women (McDonald & Thompson, 1992) looked at their exercise motivations, eating habits, and body satisfaction. Women were more likely than men to exercise to achieve good body tone and weight loss rather than fitness. In this study, both the women and men who exercised for reasons of health and fitness were less likely to show symptoms of eating disorders than those who exercised for weight control and to improve appearance.

As the studies have shown, people who exercise may not have fitness as a goal, and their exercise may be symptomatic of problems with eating and body image rather than healthy lifestyles. Exercise may allow both women and men to achieve fitness, but exercise may also provide a format for enacting body image dissatisfaction and unrealistic weight concerns. Research has indicated that exercise can be pathological and that those who are addicted to exercise are more likely than others who engage in more moderate exercise to have psychological problems and eating disorders (Ashel, 1991; Davis, Elliott, Dionne, & Mitchell, 1991; Pasman & Thompson, 1988). People addicted to exercise seem similar to anorexics; they share an obsession with a thin body image and a fanatical pursuit of the ideal body. Therefore, despite the benefits of exercise, commitment to exercise is not always healthy.

In summary, exercise can be a healthy habit that provides a number of physical and psychological benefits. Although men are more likely to have backgrounds in sports, both women and men may pursue exercise for a variety of reasons. Men are more likely to use exercise as a way to shape their bodies, and women are more likely to use exercise as an adjunct to dieting to lose weight. Both of these goals may be the basis for pathological exercising, but moderate exercise is a factor in a healthy lifestyle, with men more likely to be physically active than women.

Summary

Women live longer than men. This gender difference has existed in most countries and in most time periods. In economically developed countries, such as the United States, Canada, Australia, and the countries of Scandinavia and Western Europe, deaths from cardiovascular disease, cancer, and violence account for the majority of deaths. These causes of death do not affect men and women equally; women have lower rates of mortality from all these causes.

Cardiovascular disease (CVD) refers to diseases of the heart and circulatory system. Although not all CVD is life-threatening, the categories of heart attack and stroke account for almost half of the deaths in the United States, with men more likely to die of CVD than women, especially before the age of 65 years. Women do develop CVD; however, their reports of symptoms are not taken as seriously or treated as aggressively as the same symptoms reported by men. This differential treatment suggests bias on the part of physicians.

Cancer is the second most common cause of death, and men are more likely than women to die from this cause. Lung cancer, the deadliest form of cancer for both men and women, is strongly related to cigarette smoking. Until recently, men have smoked at a higher rate than women, and this habit is reflected in their higher incidence of lung cancer. With the rise in women's smoking, their lung cancer rates have and will continue to increase. Both women and men develop cancer of the reproductive organs, but women are more likely to die of such cancers, especially before age 65.

The gender difference in violent deaths is large, with men dying of accidents, suicides, and homicides at higher rates than women. The male gender role, which holds that men are supposed to be reckless and aggressive, may play a part in the high death rates from these causes. Men's greater prevalence of heavy alcohol use increases their chances of dying of any of these violent causes. Violent deaths also vary from country to country, with the United States having one of the higher rates of violent deaths. Within the United States, different ethnic groups are not equally affected by violence—African Americans are especially vulnerable to violent death.

Although women live longer than men, women seek health care more often. Gender and gender roles influence who seeks health care. The female gender role allows and even encourages vulnerability to illness, but the male gender role discourages the acceptance of any weakness, including illness. Although women may be more sensitive to symptoms, they may be less financially able to seek health care. Their lower rates of employment, lower salaries, and lower insurance coverage affect their access to medical care.

The interaction of gender roles of the patient and health care provider has an impact on the type of health care patients receive. Physicians have been the target of criticism concerning their treatment of female patients; three of these include being reluctant to believe female patients, using men as a standard against which all patients are judged, and omitting women from medical research. These biases in medicine against women do not necessarily mean that men receive the best health care, but they do result in women's treatment being less than optimal. Concern over these problems has prompted procedures in medical research to be revised to include women.

Reproductive health is a major reason for the gender difference in receiving health care. Women not only become involved in the health care system due to pregnancy and childbirth, but see contraception and menopause as reasons for consulting physicians. Both women and men are affected by sexually transmitted diseases and disorders of the reproductive organs. Both develop cancer of the genitals, and among women, breast cancer is the most frequent cancer.

Lifestyle differences may account for some of the gender differences in morbidity and mortality. The thin body has become such a widespread ideal among women that dieting is now a way of life for millions of women. Because they cannot be as thin as the ideal, women develop body image problems and are more prone to eating disorders such as anorexia nervosa and bulimia. Men also experience body image dissatisfaction, but they are more likely to attempt to alter their bodies through exercise rather than through dieting.

Exercise can be a positive factor for fitness and weight control, and men are more likely to participate in sports and physical activity than women. The passage of Title IX of the Education Amendments of 1972 removed some barriers that prevented women from participating in athletics, but the negative image of female athletes continues to be a factor in preventing women from sports participation. In an increasingly technological and sedentary society, most men and women must use their leisure time to pursue fitness. Athletic activities can build fitness and contribute to health, but excessive exercise can also be symptomat' of body image problems.

Glossary

anorexia nervosa an eating disorder consisting of self-starvation in pursuit of thinness.

bulimia an eating disorder consisting of binge eating, followed by some method of purging, either by induced vomiting or excessive laxative use.

cardiovascular disease a group of diseases involving the heart and circulatory system, with heart attack and stroke the most common.

chronic diseases health problems that persist over time without complete cures.

morbidity illness.

mortality death.

osteoporosis the process of bone demineralization, resulting in greater likelihood of orthopedic problems and injuries.

risk factor any condition or factor that increases the probability that an illness will develop.

sexually transmitted diseases (STDs) infectious diseases that are spread through sexual contact, including bacterial infections, viral infections, fungal infections, and parasitic infections.

Suggested Readings

Kane, Penny. (1991). *Women's health: From womb to tomb.* New York: St. Martin's Press. This book offers an interesting look at gender differences in health from a cross-cultural and developmental perspective. Kane draws on information from cultures throughout the world, offering not only information on these various cultures but also an opportunity to see the differences among economically developed, developing, and undeveloped countries.

Brownell, Kelly D., & Rodin, Judith. (1994). The dieting maelstrom: Is it possible and advisable to lose weight? *American Psychologist, 49,* 781–791. In this evaluation of the dieting controversy, Brownell and Rodin discuss healthy and unhealthy variations on dieting and seek to evaluate some of the myths and misinformation connected with dieting.

Strickland, Bonnie R. (1988). Sex-related differences in health and illness. *Psychology of Women Quarterly, 12,* 381–399. Strickland's article concentrates on data from the United States, but this review of gender differences in health provides a brief summary of the physical and behavioral differences that may relate to these gender differences.

Verbrugge, Lois M. (1989). The twain meet: Empirical explanations of sex differences in health and mortality. *Journal of Health and Social Behavior, 30,* 282–304. Verbrugge explains the apparent contradiction between women's lower mortality and higher morbidity by relying on behavioral and social factors for the differences.

Chapter 15

Stress, Coping, and Psychopathology

HEADLINE

Is It Sadness or Madness?

—*Newsweek,* March 15, 1993

The subtitle of Jean Seligmann and David Gelman's (1993) *Newsweek* story was "Psychiatrists Clash Over How to Classify PMS." The classification of a behavioral syndrome related to the menstrual cycle is one of the controversies raised in connection with the *Diagnostic and Statistical Manual of Mental Disorders* (DSM), the system constructed by the American Psychiatric Association and used by most professions involved in the diagnosis of behavior problems. As Chapter 3 detailed, premenstrual syndrome (PMS) is well accepted, despite sparse research support, and its classification as a mental disorder by the American Psychiatric Association (ApA) has sparked great controversy.

The American Psychiatric Association and its manual is at the center of this controversy, which began in 1987. At this time, **late luteal phase dysphoric disorder (LLPDD)** was included as a classification in the appendix of the revised third edition of the *Diagnostic and Statistical Manual of Mental Disorders* (DSM-III-R). Although its placement in the appendix among "disorders needing further study" should have placed limits on the use of this diagnostic category, LLPDD came to be used much as any of the other diagnostic classifications. This misuse prompted an outpouring of criticism from those (both inside and outside the psychiatric community) who believed that the classification put millions of women at increased risk for psychiatric diagnosis.

The controversy over the LLPDD diagnosis, together with the vote to include a similar diagnosis of **premenstrual dysphoric disorder (PMDD)** in the fourth edition of the DSM (DSM-IV), has continued the controversy. The headline article reported that the ApA's task force on the topic recommended that PMDD should be included in the main text of the

DSM-IV as a mood disorder, in the same category as depression. The proponents argued that including PMDD would allow women with this diagnosis more credibility when reporting their symptoms and increase their chances for insurance reimbursement for treatment. The critics claimed that a psychiatric diagnosis only for women would stigmatize the entire gender and open millions of women to diagnosis and labeling under this heading.

Paula Caplan (1993), a vocal critic of the diagnosis, argued, "There is a danger that real causes of women's depression or other problems will be ignored. Attributing symptoms to hormones also increases the risk of overlooking serious medical problems" (p. 4). Caplan also cited a lack of research support for this diagnosis as well as a lack of evidence showing that such a diagnosis would be helpful to women who present these symptoms. Those who oppose this diagnosis "are saying that the physical premenstrual symptoms some women experience are not signs of mental illness" (p. 13) and thus do not belong in a system to diagnose mental disorders.

Despite her public objections, Caplan was involved as an advisor and consultant to the subcommittees on late luteal phase dysphoric disorder, which became premenstrual dysphoric disorder in the DSM-IV. Caplan (1991) reported on her experiences with the DSM development and revision, and leveled charges of political expediency and gender bias in the organization's acceptance of DSM categories.

Premenstrual dysphoric disorder was not included as a mood disorder in DSM-IV. When the new edition of the *Diagnostic and Statistical Manual of Mental Disorders* appeared in 1994, PMDD was in an appendix rather than in the main text of the manual itself, still among the disorders requiring further study. This continued controversy highlights the political nature of the process of diagnosing problem behavior and suggests that women and men may receive different diagnoses based not only on their behavior but also on the characteristics of the diagnostic system.

These controversies continue because the discrepancy in diagnosis of mental disorders for women and men still exists—women have a higher rate of diagnosis and treatment for psychological problems than men. Does this higher rate of diagnosis for psychopathology mean that women are at a disadvantage in the diagnosis process? Is their disproportionate representation among psychiatric patients a reflection of differences in stress patterns, differences in coping resources or strategies, biases in the diagnostic criteria, biases in the diagnostic process, or some combination of these factors?

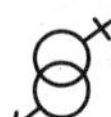

GENDERED VOICES

I Think I Have It

Male psychologist: "Have you read the new description of PMS that will appear in the fourth edition of the DSM? I'm really very concerned."

Female psychologist: "Yes, I have. Premenstrual dysphoric disorder will replace late luteal phase dysphoric disorder. I'm concerned, too. It's supposed to appear in the main body of the classification under mood disorders, and I understand that the treatment will be antidepressant drugs. It's been very controversial, and I think that this move will keep it that way. What bothers you?"

Male psychologist: "According to my reading of the diagnostic criteria, I think I have it."

Stress and Coping

The explanations for psychological problems have ranged from possession by demons to genetic vulnerability. The belief that madness results from demonic possession has faded, but many authorities accept that some mental disorders, including depression and schizophrenia, have a genetic component. The gender differences in diagnoses, however, are too large to be accounted for by genetics (Cleary, 1987). Therefore, the search for risk factors for mental disorders has focused on life circumstances and stresses.

Stress is an inevitable part of life, so searching for the stresses that relate to the development of mental disorders becomes a complex task. Researchers cannot simply identify sources of stress but must investigate how people perceive various stressors and how they cope with the resulting stress in their lives.

Sources of Stress for Men and Women

The stresses that relate to the development of behavioral problems show some differences for women and men. As Chapters 10 and 13 explored, the many combinations of marriage, parenthood, and employment provide women with complex roles. Men have traditionally occupied the breadwinner role and have not been involved with providing much in the way of housekeeping or child care, making their roles more straightforward and their stress related to occupation. Both women's and men's roles may be stressful, but the research emphasis has been on women's multiple roles. Fulfilling these roles may be stressful and thus related to the development of some mental disorders.

An additional reason for gender differences in life experience concerns violence. As Chapter 9 presented, men are more likely to commit violence as well as to become the victims of violence. However, women are much more likely to be the targets of sexual abuse and violence in families, which places them at risk for the aftermath of such violence. Poverty is yet another possibility for prompting stress and producing mental problems; sexism and gender discrimination are also significant potential sources of stress. How do these life experiences relate to the development of mental disorders—and are the gender differences in mental disorders related to these differences in life experience?

Family Roles

No inherent gender differences exist in life events and psychological distress (Wethington, McLeod, & Kessler, 1987), but the roles women occupy have associated stresses that men's roles do not. One source of stress is that women's roles include supplying nurturance to other family members (Gove, 1980, 1984). The process of tending to others' needs can be draining for the women who provide emotional and physical care to husbands, children, and sometimes aging parents as well. Women's roles obligate them to respond to others, and these demands are an important cause for women's problems in mental health. In addition, women usually perform the majority of family work but their duties have more flexibility and thus less structure, which may add to rather than reduce their stress. The duties must be done, and finding time to do them adds to the stress. On the other hand, men's roles tend to be structured, with many fixed components typically furnished by occupations but including a limited amount of family work.

The gender differences in family roles revolve around marriage, parenthood, and employment. Marriage roles may be analyzed into "his" and "hers," and "his" tends to be more beneficial than "hers" (Bernard, 1972). Applied to mental health concerns, married men also show better mental health than married women (Fowers, 1991; Hughes & Galinsky, 1994). Indeed, the differences in mental health are greatest among married people (Rosenfield, 1989). For married people, the greatest difference is between employed men and women who are homemakers (Cleary & Mechanic, 1983). Thus, both marriage and employment are factors in the mental health of men and women, with men having fewer mental health problems when they are married and employed.

In support of the notion that family roles are associated with depression, married women with children and single parents show higher rates of depression than married men and unmarried women (Aneshensel, Frerichs, & Clark, 1981). One explanation for these differences involves lifestyles that lead to depression and anxiety through a combination of low power and role overload (Rosenfield, 1989). The occupation of housewife is an example of a position with low power, and full-time employment plus caring for children constitutes role overload. Research has confirmed that housewives and those who are responsible for the care of young children are especially vulnerable to depression (Cleary & Mechanic, 1983).

Women do not need to fulfill the role of wife and mother to be psychologically healthy (Barnett & Baruch, 1987). Women who are mothers may benefit from that role, depending on their other roles and the assistance they receive in fulfilling their family and workplace obligations. Unmarried mothers with many young children are at a disadvantage in maintaining both physical and mental health, and married women's advantage disappears when their husbands do not help with family work. (See Chapter 10 for more information about gender-related divisions of labor in marriage relationships and how likely it is that women perform a disproportionate amount of household work.) One study suggested that parents with children living in the household were more likely to be depressed than people without children or whose children lived elsewhere (Aneshensel et al., 1981). This effect was stronger for women than men, and single mothers and married women with children at home showed the highest rates of depression. Similar findings appeared in a study (Hughes & Galinsky, 1994) that compared employed women and men. Women showed higher levels of psychological distress, and these were related to child care inequity and child care difficulties at home. Therefore, work and family can interfere with each other, and what causes stress for women is not the same for men.

Multiple roles do not inevitably lead to stress and stress-related problems, and the amount of strain from each role is important (Aneshensel & Pearlin, 1987). When employed mothers experience little strain in either role, they are at a low risk for depression. When married, employed mothers experience strain in each role, they are at a high risk for depression—a level of risk comparable to that of housewives. When family demands are equal for employed men and women, they have comparable rates of depression and anxiety disorders. But when the burdens of family care fall disproportionately on women, these women's social circumstances pose risks for the development of depression.

Women have fewer mental health problems when they are employed, but their husbands may not. The shift in power that accompanies wives' employment may be a problem for their husbands (Rosenfield, 1992). When the wife's employment decreases the husband's relative contribution to family income and increases his share of domestic duties, the husband's mental health suffers. Thus, men are also subject to role overload and the negative effects of loss of power and diminished personal control.

The research on stresses in men's lives has concentrated on job-related stress and its effects, but some investigators have explored men's multiple roles in the workplace and family. Family roles are important to men's psychological health (Barnett, Marshall, & Pleck, 1992). Work roles and family roles contribute equally to men's feelings of distress and well-being. Research has shown that the quality of men's marital relationships and the quality of their parental relationships are important factors in their lives, but little is known about family roles for men. Satisfaction with family roles can buffer men against the stresses of the workplace: "Men operate in two areas—home and work—and the quality of their experiences in each area contribute equally to their psychological health" (Barnett et al., 1992, p. 366).

High commitment to the breadwinner role can be a source of strain for men, especially those who do not perceive their wives as supportive in their attempts to fulfill work and parenting roles (Greenberger & O'Neil, 1993). Women also experience strain when husbands spend many hours on their jobs and when they feel their husbands and neighbors are not supportive of their employment and parenting efforts. Thus, both husbands and wives can experience role strain when they believe that their efforts are not supported by their partners, but men tend to feel more strain and anxiety over their work roles than do women.

Both men and women experience distress or satisfaction with the roles that come with marriage, parenthood, and employment. Whether these roles result in satisfaction or distress depends on the combination and quality of each. Women and men with good marriage relationships are less likely to experience psychological problems than those with marital problems. Indeed, divorced men and women are at heightened risk for psychological problems.

Parenthood is more likely to be a risk for distress in women than in men. For men, pleasure in parenting can buffer against other stresses, but women who care for small children are more likely to experience psychological problems than women without child care responsibilities. This stress is ameliorated by sharing the responsibility for child care. Employment is related to positive mental health for both women and men, but women may experience stress and psychological problems from the overload of family and work responsibilities.

Violence

As discussed earlier, men are more likely than women to be both the perpetrators and the victims of violence, but women's victimization may be especially traumatic, because women are more likely to be the victims of violence by family and friends than by strangers (Russo, 1990; Walker, 1989). Further, women are more likely to be injured in violent encounters by persons they know (Dutton, Haywood, & El-Bayoumi, 1997). A growing body of research has implicated violence as a risk to mental as well as physical health, and this research has concentrated on intimate violence in families, namely childhood sexual abuse, rape, and marital violence.

Mary Koss wrote, "Experiencing violence transforms people into victims and changes their lives forever. Once victimized one can never feel quite as invulnerable" (Koss, 1990, p. 374). A history of violence is related to the development of a wide variety of psychological problems, including posttraumatic stress disorders, depression, substance abuse, obsessive–compulsive disorders, eating disorders, and suicide attempts (Koss, 1993). Psychology has largely overlooked the role of violence in explaining the development of mental disorders.

The American Psychological Association established a Task Force on Male Violence Against Women in 1991 (Goodman, Koss, Fitzgerald, Russo, & Keita, 1993). This task force estimated that between 21% and 34% of women in the United States are physically assaulted by men who have close relationships with them, and between 14% and 25% of adult women will be raped at some time during their lives. These figures demonstrate the prevalence of male violence toward women.

Despite thc widespread publicity of male violence toward women, Clifton Flynn (1990) contended that the attention to domestic violence has been selective and that the rate of female violence toward men is nearly as high as male violence toward women. He examined evidence from many studies and concluded that the rates of violence toward intimate partners are similar for women and men, yet the patterns differ. Women are most likely to be violent in protecting themselves from and in retaliation for violent attacks by men, whereas men are more likely to initiate such attacks. Therefore, the rates of violence may be similar, but the repercussions may not be. A growing body of research indicates that the aftermath of victimization has implications, especially for the mental health of women.

Being at risk for depression and anxiety disorders rises in rape victims. Boyfriends and husbands are more likely to be the rapists than strangers (Kilpatrick, Best, Saunders, & Veronen, 1988), and the aftermath of women's rape experiences are costly in terms of their mental health. Compared to the women who had not been raped, the victimized women were 11 times more likely to be clinically depressed and 6 times more likely to be fearful in social situations.

Violence may be a significant contributor to the prevalence of depression among women and might be one main factor that accounts for the gender difference in this disorder (Cutler & Nolen-Hoeksema, 1991). Childhood sexual abuse is more common for girls than boys, and evidence links childhood sexual abuse with anxiety, depression, and low self-esteem. Support for this relationship has come from a study of women who were sexually abused as children (Yama, Tovey, & Fogas, 1993). A comparison of these women to those with no history of sexual abuse demonstrated that this type of childhood abuse has lasting effects for the development of anxiety and depression.

Other research has shown that sexual abuse at any age increases the risk for a variety of mental disorders in both men and women (Burnam et al., 1988). This research revealed that being a victim of sexual abuse increases the chances of depression, substance abuse or dependence, phobic disorder, panic disorder, and obsessive–compulsive disorder, with the magnitude of increase reaching between two and four times that of men or women who have not been abused. The effects were especially dramatic for those who had been abused during childhood. Women are much more likely to be the victims of sexual abuse than men, but this study found no gender difference in likelihood of developing psychological problems following abuse. The form of subsequent problems differed somewhat for men and women, with men more likely to experience drug and alcohol problems than women, but sexual victimization clearly increased the risk for a variety of problems for both genders.

Violence in the form of criminal victimization also relates to the development of psychological disorders, especially posttraumatic stress disorder (PTSD) (Resnick, Kilpatrick, Best, & Kramer, 1992). Those women who were victims of crimes involving violence or the threat of extreme violence were much more likely to develop symptoms of PTSD than women who were the victims of less violent crimes. However, all crime victims had elevated risks of PTSD, demonstrating the psychological risks of criminal victimization.

The evidence concerning family roles and mental health concerns are complex, with many different configurations and effects. Table 15.1 presents some of the influences of various roles on psychological health. The evidence for the relationship between violence and mental disorders is much more straightforward. Violence increases the risk for several mental disorders, and childhood victimization is especially harmful. Women are more likely to be the targets of childhood sexual abuse and rape, two types of violence that research has related to psychological disorders, but men who are victimized are also at elevated risk of such problems.

Poverty

Poverty also presents a risk for mental disorders for women, men, and children (Attar, Guerra, & Tolan, 1994; Neugebauer, Dohrenwend, & Dohrenwend, 1980). Those who live in poverty are at least two and a half times as likely to receive diagnoses of mental disorders compared to those who are not poor. Not only are poor people more likely to receive diagnoses of mental disorders, but a community study (Holzer et al., 1986) indicated that mental disorders are almost three times more common among those who are in the lowest as compared to those in the highest socioeconomic class.

Life circumstances associated with poverty are also associated with poor mental health (Belle, 1990). That is, not only is low income itself a problem, creating many stresses, but unemployment or underemployment, divorce, and single parenthood are all sources of stress that are associated with poverty. In addition, low income can lead to poor housing in high-crime neighborhoods, subjecting poor people to greater risks of violence and its psychological effects. Poverty may be an independent risk factor for mental disorders, but it is associated with other risks that increase the likelihood for problems.

Poverty affects women and ethnic minority families more than other groups (Belle, 1990). Single mothers are more likely to be poor than any other demographic group, affecting not only their mental and physical health but also placing their children at risk for the stress associated with poverty. The National Institute of Mental Health has recognized the

TABLE 15.1 Influences of Various Roles on Psychological Health

Role	Affects	Consequences
Caregiving	Women more than men	Stress; emotional and physical exhaustion
Marriage	Both genders	Positive
Parenthood	Both genders	Depends on other roles occupied and the support available
Child care	Women more than men	At risk for mental and physical health problems
Employment	Both genders	Positive
Homemaker role	Women	At risk for depression
Breadwinner role	Men more than women	At risk for mental health problems
Employed wife	Men	At risk for mental health problems

negative impact of poverty on women's mental health and has made the topic a priority for the Women's Research Agenda; however, poverty is also a risk to men's mental health.

Poverty has a negative impact on the ability to cope. Financial limitations deprive people of the ability to deal with other problems that can produce stress. Lack of money limits opportunities and choices, putting people in positions of dependency on government bureaucracy for housing, health care, food, and other essentials. The economically advantaged may be able to extricate themselves from problem situations and relationships that poor people cannot avoid. Both situations and any lack of control over them can produce stress.

Discrimination

In a community study of mental health functioning (Hendryx & Ahern, 1997), poverty was one of the community problems reported that related to lower levels of mental health functioning. Violence was another factor, and so was racism. Using the Schedule of Racist Events as a discrimination reporting measure (Landrine & Klonoff, 1996), a sample of African Americans reported a high incidence of racist discrimination within the past year, and 100% reported having experienced racist discrimination during their lives. The study also examined the stressful effects of the experience of racist discrimination and found that a positive relationship existed between experiences of racist discrimination and psychiatric symptoms.

Sexist discrimination is also known to be a source of stress. The large traumas like childhood sexual abuse or criminal victimization can produce problems; however, so can being subject to frequent discrimination and harassment, such as having to listen to sexist jokes. These sexist experiences are often a source of stress in women's lives. In one study (Landrine, Klonoff, Gibbs, Manning, & Lund, 1995), the experience of sexist discrimination related to psychological distress in women and predicted some symptoms better than more general measures of stress. Adding this factor to other sources of stress may help in explaining why women experience greater levels of distress than men. Also, sexist discrimination is a more common experience for ethnic minority women than for other women, placing them at increased risk of stress due to discrimination.

Coping Resources and Strategies

The number and intensity of stressors are important factors in predicting any resulting problems, but resources and strategies for coping are even more important. Those who have resources to cope with the stress in their lives may not perceive the situations as stressful. One theory of stress (Lazarus & Folkman, 1984) proposed that each person's appraisal of a potentially stressful situation varies according to his or her perception of the personal importance of the situation plus personal resources to deal with the situation. Those who do not have or believe that they do not have the resources to cope with events in their lives are vulnerable to stress, whereas others who experience the same events but have the resources to cope do not experience stress from the events. Thus, stress varies according to perception, and that perception depends on the evaluation of resources for coping.

The resources for coping may differ for women and men, as men often have more power and greater financial resources than women. Power and money offer advantages for avoiding many of life's problems and for dealing with others. For example, the loss of a job may be more stressful for a single mother of two with only a high school education and skilled as a sales clerk than for a married male engineer with an employed wife and a sizable savings account. Neither of these jobless people will avoid stress; losing a job is stressful for almost everyone. However, the engineer has resources for dealing with his situation that the sales clerk lacks.

One of the most important differences between the male engineer and the female sales clerk is the social support the engineer has in the form of his family. The sales clerk may receive support from her children, but she must also offer them care and support. Women's roles generally carry obligations for providing support for others, whereas men's roles more often offer them the provision of emotional support (Gove, 1980, 1984). Providing care for others can be stressful, whereas receiving social support is more likely to relieve stress. On the other hand, the possibility exists that involvement in social relationships offers more advantages than costs in coping with stress.

Social Support

Social support is more than a matter of social relationships or social contacts; support implies providing emotional and material resources. Therefore, the number of acquaintances persons have or the number of people with which they associate are not good measures of social support. Four different elements of social support include emotional concern, instrumental aid (such as money or other assistance), information and advice, and feedback (House, 1984). If a person has few contacts with other people, then that person is more likely to be socially isolated than the person with many contacts. Social support requires more than contact or acquaintanceship, and friends and family are the usual sources of social support. People who have a high amount of social support have a wide network of people on whom they can count for emotional and material support.

As discussed in the Friendships section of Chapter 10, women are more likely than men to form friendships that include emotional intimacy, which may give them the advantage in creating networks that provide them with social support. Men's friendships tend to be activity oriented, which may offer them the material support but may lack the emotional intimacy that is important for social support. Men's advantage in social support probably comes from their relationships with women, on whom men tend to rely for emotional support as well as many aspects of physical care.

Women's roles obligate them to provide support for their families and friends, and husbands are major recipients of this support (Wethington et al., 1987). Thus women often provide more support than they receive in marriage placing them at a disadvantage and their husbands at an advantage. This difference may contribute to the gender difference in mental health between married men and women.

Single, childless women have less risk of developing mental health problems compared to married women or single women with children, especially women who have no employment outside their homes. Employment can enhance social support by increasing the number of friends. Single and divorced men are at greater risk than married men, again indicating that social support is a factor in men's mental health. Those at greater risk typically have less social support, and those at lesser risk typically have more sources of social support.

The breadth and strength of social networks vary with ethnicity as well as with gender (Renzetti & Curran, 1992). Some ethnic groups maintain close family relationships, whereas in other ethnic groups increased mobility and small families decrease the chances of having close friends. Also, these family patterns complicate family contact. The isolated

TABLE 15.2 Examples of Coping Strategies

Coping Strategy	Behaviors That Exemplify This Strategy
Seeking social support	Talk to someone who could help Talk to someone who has experienced similar problems Talk to friends or family who will sympathize
Problem-focused	Analyze the situation Plan a strategy to solve the problem Take action to get rid of the problem Concentrate on the problem
Emotion-focused	Become upset Express negative feelings
Denial	Refuse to accept the reality of the problem Try to ignore the problem
Turn to religion	Seek God's help Pray
Disengagement	Work on other activities Sleep more than usual Engage in distracting activities Consume alcohol or other drugs

nuclear family consisting of father, mother, and children has become the image of family life in the Western world, but many people live in extended families in close contact with other relatives.

Hispanic, African, and Asian American families tend to form extended family groupings, meaning grandparents, parents, children, and other relatives live in close proximity. This pattern differs from the isolated nuclear family typical of many (but by no means all) European Americans, with resulting advantages and disadvantages. The advantages of an extended family include a wider range of people who offer their emotional and material support and advice. The disadvantages may include many demands for emotional and material support. If these other family members are poor (and members of ethnic minorities are more likely to be poor than members of the dominant ethnic group), then being part of a support network can lead to many demands and obligations to fulfill those demands. Thus, being part of an extended family network can not only provide social support but can also impose social costs, and these networks are more common among some ethnic groups than among others.

Coping Strategies

How people deal with the events in their lives makes a critical difference in the amount of stress they experience, so having coping strategies is an essential factor in relieving stress. Coping is the process of changing thoughts and behaviors to manage situations that involve potential stressors (Lazarus & Folkman, 1984). These management strategies vary among people and situations, and these differences may distinguish among people who feel more or less stress. Table 15.2 lists coping strategies and gives examples of each.

Researchers have considered several gender-related factors involved in coping with stress. Two views of gender and coping exist (Ptacek, Smith, & Zanas, 1992). One view of gender differences in coping strategies concerns the way men and women are socialized. The *socialization view* holds that the expectations for women and men differ, with women being expected to react to stress emotionally and men being expected to react with active, problem-solving strategies. This view predicts that men and women will react differently in similar situations, whereas the *structural view* holds that the major differences between men and women come from the different stressful situations they encounter.

More evidence exists for gender differences in the experience of stress than for differences in coping strategies (Folkman & Lazarus, 1980). A survey of a community sample of adults showed that women were more likely to report stress from health-related concerns, and men were more likely to report stressful situations at work. More men than women in this study were employed, so the results may have reflected situational rather than strategy differences.

The men in this study were likely to use problem-focused coping strategies to deal with their workplace stress; they were more likely to use cognitive strategies or to take action to solve the problem that produced the stress. This tendency for men to use action-oriented techniques is consistent with the stereotypical view of men as taking action to solve problems. But no difference appeared in the frequency of emotion-focused coping efforts—the cognitive and behavioral efforts that are directed toward managing or reducing emotional distress. The stereotypical view that holds that women will be more likely than men to use this type of strategy was not confirmed in this study. Indeed, both men and women tended to use both types of strategies to manage the various stresses. The gender difference in this study might not reflect a difference in strategies but a difference in situations; the women and men in this study did not have comparable lives.

Several studies have attempted to assess coping strategies for men and women in comparable situations. One, a longitudinal study (Hamilton & Fagot, 1988), involved interviewing male and female college students over a two-month period to test for frequency and perception of stressors and their use of coping strategies. Women reported more stressors, but few other gender differences emerged. Both women and men reported the same types of events as stressful or not stressful and used the same strategies for dealing with each. Interestingly, the situations each judged as not stressful may have been rendered so by the use of direct, problem-focused coping techniques, which both women and men said they used in such situations. Both reported that negative interpersonal interactions were sources of stress, and both said that they did not often approach these situations with problem-solving strategies. This study showed few gender differences but did demonstrate that both men and women use similar coping strategies in similar situations.

Matching women and men for job experience and pay in one investigation allowed researchers to examine stress and coping mechanisms that controlled for job-related situational factors (Fontenot & Brannon, 1991). Few gender differences but significant situational differences emerged. Both women and men said that personal conflict situations were more likely to prompt emotion-focused coping and that task-related stress situations were more likely to elicit problem-focused coping strategies. This study also demonstrated that specific situations were more likely than gender to be the source of differences in coping efforts.

Some studies found gender differences in coping strategies, but other studies have cast doubt on these interpretations. College women reported that they found more events stressful than did men, but women and men both tended to use a variety of coping methods and to use problem-focused coping more often than other strategies (Ptacek et al., 1992). Women, however, made greater use of social support networks as aids to coping than did men, but only for relationship stresses. Both men and women were similar in their approaches to coping with school-related stresses. They were also similar in evaluating problem-focused coping strategies as most effective and emotion-focused coping strategies as least effective, with use of social support ranked between the other two strategies in perceived effectiveness.

Equating the type of stressful event failed to equate the coping strategies that women and men reported (Ptacek, Smith, & Dodge, 1994). Women reported seeking social support as their first strategy choice, and they used more emotion-focused coping strategies than men. However, a later study (Ptacek & Millman, 1996) cast doubt on these gender differences and on the results from other studies that relied on self-reports of coping strategies. That study investigated the social desirability of reporting various coping strategies in men and women and found differences. As gender stereotypes suggest, women were seen as more likely to report emotion-focused coping and seeking social support whereas men were seen as more likely to report strategies that disengaged them from the stress. Therefore, various coping strategies may have been subject to a reporting bias, which casts doubt on many previous studies that have shown gender differences.

Thus, gender differences in coping mechanisms do not reflect other gender differences in stress; those differences seem to be more easily attributable to lifestyle and social circumstances. The magnitude of the gender differences in stress and coping do not account for the preponderance of women in treatment for behavior problems. Possibilities for the source of these differences lie in the criteria used and in the process of diagnosis.

Diagnoses of Mental Disorders

Before a sick person can receive appropriate treatment, the person must receive a **diagnosis,** a statement of the classification of the problem. Without a diagnosis, treatment would be haphazard and not connected with the problem. Thus, classification of both physical and mental problems is an essential step in offering proper care. A good clinical classification system has several characteristics (Sarason & Sarason, 1993). Specifically, such a system should provide information about the cause of the condition, enable clinicians to make predictions about the course of the disorder, and suggest a course of treatment as well as methods of prevention. In addition, a system of classification should provide a set of common terminology for professionals to communicate among themselves. No system of diagnosis meets these goals perfectly, but the goals are common to the diagnosis of physical and mental problems.

Diagnosis is not a simple task; it consists of matching information about what constitutes a disorder against a description of symptoms. Because any person's symptoms will not match the textbook description of a disorder, the clinician must use personal judgment in the diagnostic process. This judgment provides for the possibility that personal bias and subjective attitudes can enter the diagnostic process.

Although diagnosis by a system of classification is a necessary part of treatment, diagnosis can offer a patient disadvantages as well as advantages (Sarason & Sarason, 1993). The advantages include providing an accepted standard that allows reliable diagnosis of the same problem by different clinicians. One of the problems involves labeling—the need to apply a label to the diagnosis. With mental disorders, many labels carry a stigma, and people who have been labeled with diagnoses of mental disorders may be the targets of discrimination. Furthermore, labeling also puts people into categories, and grouping people tends to magnify the similarities and obscure the individual differences of those within a category.

The diagnosis of mental disorders dates back to the time of Hippocrates, who used a simple four-category classification—mania, epilepsy, melancholia, and paranoia (Lerman, 1996). During the late 19th century, interest in mental disorders increased, and in 1917 the National Committee for Mental Hygiene in the United States published a manual to aid in diagnosis. Currently, two systems exist for the classification of mental disorders—the International Classification of Diseases (ICD) of the World Health Organization and the *Diagnostic and Statistical Manual of Mental Disorders* (DSM) of the American Psychiatric Association, the controversial system that was the subject of this chapter's headline story.

These systems are not entirely separate, and the two organizations have cooperated in the development of their respective systems. The American Psychiatric Association, however, wanted a system specifically suited to psychiatric diagnoses in the United States. Until the fourth edition of the DSM, the two systems coexisted but were not very compatible, but greater compatibility with the ICD has been one of the goals for the latest edition.

The DSM Classification System

The *Diagnostic and Statistical Manual of Mental Disorders* (DSM) of the American Psychiatric Association (ApA) has become the standard for professionals who provide mental health care, especially in North America. The first version of the manual appeared in 1952, with a second edition in 1968 (Sarason & Sarason, 1993). These two editions were relatively brief, both were strongly influenced by psychoanalytic theory, and both were heavily weighted with psychoanalytic terminology. To make a diagnosis using the system of classification described in the DSM-I or -II, the clinician needed to understand the patient's internal, unobservable psychological processes. Understandably, these schemes of classification led to a great deal of variation in diagnoses.

The third edition of the DSM appeared in 1980 and represented a substantial revision. The goal was to create a description-based system of classification for mental disorders—a set of unambiguous descriptions of mental disorders that would lead clinicians to make reliable judgments. A revision of the DSM-III appeared in 1987 and consisted of relatively minor changes in the existent system. The DSM-IV, which appeared in 1994, contained no major changes but allowed for greater compatibility with the ICD.

The system of the DSM consists of five dimensions or *axes,* which allow for comprehensive physical, psychological, and social diagnoses. The first three axes provide the diagnosis, and the two other axes provide an evaluation of stressors and overall functioning. The manual contains over 240 different diagnoses along with descriptions of the symptoms that characterize the disorders. Information also appears concerning typical age of onset, course of the disorder, and the gender ratio of the disorder; that is, how common the problem appears in men compared to women. In addition, the manual also contains information concerning the similarities among each diagnosis and other similar disorders so that clinicians can distinguish among disorders that have similar symptoms.

Axis I describes the major clinical disorders, such as schizophrenia, depression, and anxiety disorders, among others. Axis II includes mental retardation and personality disorders, such as antisocial personality, histrionic personality, and dependent personality disorders. Axis III contains a classification of physical disorders and is compatible with the ICD diagnosis system. Axis IV allows for reporting of psychosocial and environmental problems related to the diagnosis of psychopathology, including events such as death of a loved one, problems in school, homelessness, or loss of a job. Axis V allows for an overall rating of functioning on the Global Assessment of Functioning Scale, which takes psychological, social, and occupational functioning into account. Diagnosis includes a rating on each of the five axes.

For example, a diagnosis on Axis I might be **posttraumatic stress disorder (PTSD),** a subclassification within the category of anxiety disorders. The DSM-IV describes the diagnosis for this disorder as composed of several criteria. To be diagnosed with posttraumatic stress disorder, the person must meet five criteria: (a) "the person experienced, witnessed, or was confronted with an event or events that involved actual or threatened death or serious injury, or a threat to the physical integrity of self or others" and "the person's response involved intense fear, helplessness, or horror" (ApA, 1994, pp. 427–428), (b) reexperience of the event in some form, (c) avoidance of stimuli associated with the traumatic event or numbing of responsiveness, (d) increased arousal, such as irritability, difficulty concentrating, or hypervigilance, and (e) duration of at least one month.

The combination of these criteria must be present and must produce "clinically significant distress or impairment in social, occupational, or other important areas of functioning" (ApA, 1994, p. 429) before a diagnosis of PTSD can be made. The DSM-IV offers guidelines to the clinician for the different forms of reexperiencing the event, the types of avoidance and numbing that might occur, and the symptoms of increased arousal that accompany PTSD.

In addition, the manual includes examples of the unusual events that might precipitate PTSD, examples of the behaviors of affected individuals, and descriptions of disorders that often accompany PTSD. Depression and substance-related disorders often coincide with PTSD, sometimes preceding and sometimes developing after the traumatic stress. If evidence of these disorders exists, the clinician should diagnose all of the conditions. Although the DSM provides the gender ratio for many diagnoses, no such information appears for PTSD.

For a person with a diagnosis of PTSD on Axis I, the Axis II diagnosis might or might not indicate pathology. That is, an Axis I diagnosis of a certain clinical disorder does not directly coincide with a problem in the developmental and personality disorders described on Axis II. Nor does one prohibit the other. The clinical disorders on Axis I and the personality disorders on Axis II can be related, but the diagnoses are made according to separate criteria. Thus many people who receive a diagnosis of PTSD have no other conditions that predispose them to the disorder and might receive diagnoses of "no problem" on Axis II (Sarason & Sarason, 1993). Alternatively, people with PTSD might have other separate developmental or personality disorder, and these problems might relate to the PTSD. Some personality disorders, such as paranoid personality disorder, would tend to worsen PTSD.

If the person with a diagnosis of PTSD has developed the disorder as a result of a combat experience or rape, then the person may also have physical injuries that stem from the same situation. Indeed, some evidence exists to indicate a much greater likelihood of PTSD in soldiers (Helzer, Robins, & McEvoy, 1987) and in crime victims (Resnick et al., 1992) who have been injured. The Axis III diagnosis would note these or other physical conditions that could affect the person's psychological functioning.

Axis IV includes an opportunity for the clinician to note the social and environmental problems that might affect the development, recurrence, or exacerbation of mental disorders. The DSM-IV instructs clinicians to note as many of these problems as are relevant and the ones that have occurred within the prior year. PTSD is an exception; these events may have occurred more than a year before diagnosis and still be relevant to the problem.

Axis V allows a rating of the global functioning of the person on the Global Assessment of Functioning Scale based on the person's overall psychological, social, and occupational functioning (excluding physical and environmental limitations). This scale ranges from 1 to 100, with low numbers indicating a low level of functioning and high numbers indicating fewer impairments. A person with PTSD resulting from combat experiences might also show alcohol abuse, sleep problems, sensitivity to loud noises, and outbursts of violence with little provocation. Such a person would probably receive a global assessment between 50 and 60, indicating moderate difficulty in social and occupational functioning, but PTSD can produce more symptoms that result in impairments in either direction.

The DSM-III, DSM-III-R, and DSM-IV represent improvements over the earlier versions of the *Diagnostic and Statistical Manual.* The extensive descriptions of problem behavior allow clinicians to match patients' symptoms to the descriptions without relying on unobservable, internal psychological processes. The descriptive nature of the DSM makes diagnosis more reliable, but as the headline story for this chapter suggested, the system has sparked controversy. Criticisms include a lack of research support and adding diagnoses that may not be abnormal. The lists of behaviors that serve as criteria for each diagnostic category gives the impression of objectivity, but little research supports these criteria (Lerman, 1996). Therefore, the impression of objectivity is an illusion.

Criticism has also arisen concerning the DSM's inclusiveness; some of the diagnostic categories describe behaviors that are arguably within the normal range. For example, nicotine dependence and nicotine withdrawal are diagnoses applied to smokers and smokers who have quit, respectively. Applying diagnoses in such cases implies that these behaviors represent mental disorders and should be labeled. Many people, including mental health care professionals, disagree with the extension of diagnostic classifications to behaviors that fall within the range of normal for many people.

Gender Inequity in the Diagnosis of Mental Disorders

Criticisms of the multiaxial system of the DSM appeared immediately following its release in 1980. Some of these criticisms concerned gender bias in this diagnostic system. Some critics (Kaplan, 1983a, b; Lerman, 1996; Tavris, 1992) have asserted that the DSM system includes descriptions of disorders that make women likely to be diagnosed with problem behavior, even when the behavior is not due to any pathology. Indeed, the assumption that men provide a standard makes it likely that any behavior found more commonly in women will be viewed as pathological. The process of diagnosis is influenced by social values, and generally "professionals have used male-based norms to define healthy versus pathological behavior" (Cook, Warnke, & Dupuy, 1993, pp. 312–313). This bias has resulted in behaviors such as independence and assertiveness to be considered important for healthy mental functioning whereas emotional expressiveness may be considered the sign of a problem.

The DSM system has also received criticism for its failure to consider the life circumstances of those receiving diagnoses (Cook et al., 1993; Lerman, 1996). The DSM system focuses on personal behavior, assuming that disorders are personal problems and not attributable to the circumstances or situational contexts of behaviors. A DSM diagnosis implies that the person creates the mental disorder and that the person's circumstances, although possibly relevant, are not the source of the problem. Thus, if a battered woman experiences distress or depression, she will still be diagnosed by her symptoms as having depression or one of the anxiety disorders. The violence of her home life may be taken into account; however, even though the symptoms warrant a diagnosis of mental disorder, that diagnosis is given to her, not her batterer or her home circumstances. Thus, people may receive diagnoses and then treatment for depression or substance abuse disorders without the social context of the problem being addressed and without the clinician considering it appropriate to do so. A survey of clinical psychology interns (Middaugh, 1994) showed that 19% of male (but only 5% of female) interns believed that female clients must learn to adjust to their circumstances. Although these percentages indicate that a minority of clinicians hold such attitudes, the criticism against these attitudes is that such attitudes make women responsible for the behavior of others. One example is an abused woman who could receive a psychiatric diagnosis and treatment for her abusive husband's problems (Stephenson & Walker, 1979).

As noted in Chapter 14, normal female functions of reproduction and childbearing have become "medicalized." The accusation of "medicalized" normal female behavior also extends to other problems that should fall within the range of normal. This criticism applies to premenstrual dysphoric disorder (PMDD), the diagnosis given to symptoms very similar to premenstrual syndrome (PMS), the topic of the headline story for this chapter. As this headline story (Seligmann & Gelman, 1993) suggested, a diagnostic category limited only to women is destined to provoke controversy; such controversy has continued with the publication of the DSM-IV and its inclusion of PMDD as a diagnostic category.

The Axis II personality disorders have also been the target of criticism and a source of controversy. The diagnostic categories on this axis have much poorer research support than are necessary for their acceptance, so they allow for gender, ethnic, and social class biases. "The claims to a scientific basis for these diagnoses hang upon an extremely slender thread" (Brown, 1992, p. 215). The DSM-IV warned clinicians that they "must be cautious not to overdiagnose or underdiagnose certain Personality Disorders in females or in males because of social stereotypes about typical gender roles and behaviors" (ApA, 1994, p. 632), but research has suggested that such bias occurs and affects diagnoses. (See the Diversity Highlight: "Ethnic Diversity and Psychiatric Diagnosis.")

Gender biases are not limited to stereotypes of the feminine role. Some of the DSM diagnostic categories seem to draw heavily from elements of the traditional female gender role, but other categories seem to be exaggerations of the traditional male gender role (Williams & Spitzer, 1983). For example, **schizoid personality disorder** is characterized by "detachment from social relationships and a restricted range of expression of emotions in interpersonal settings" (ApA, 1994, p. 638). **Antisocial personality disorder** appears as a "pervasive pattern of disregard for, and violation of, the rights of others" (p. 645) including

DIVERSITY HIGHLIGHT
Ethnic Diversity and Psychiatric Diagnosis

Gender stereotypes are not the only possibility for biased diagnosis with the DSM system; ethnic stereotypes can also influence the labeling of mental disorders. The DSM system represents the summary of the American Psychiatric Association's evaluation of mental disorders, and the psychiatrists who compose this organization are mostly male and mostly White. The descriptions of categories within the DSM system may themselves include gender and ethnically based components. The DSM system has been criticized for containing a Western bias, and this bias may be a problem for people from different cultures who live in a Western country (Solomon, 1992). People may be judged by standards that they do not understand or accept. Alternatively, the application of the system may be biased by practitioners' ethnic stereotypes (Landrine, 1987). Or both biases may occur in the process of psychiatric diagnosis.

In a study of clinician bias, psychiatrists received case descriptions for diagnosis with the gender and ethnic backgrounds of the cases varied to determine the effect on diagnosis (Loring & Powell, 1988). Even with clear-cut diagnostic criteria, the psychiatrists were influenced in the stereotypical direction by gender and ethnic information.

In one mental health agency, the expected differences among ethnic groups did not appear in psychiatric diagnoses and treatment for African American, Mexican American, Vietnamese American, Philippino American, and European American clients (Flaskerud, 1986). In this study of over 26,000 clients of a county mental health system, the relationship between ethnic background and psychiatric diagnosis showed differences for ethnic background in certain categories of diagnosis (Flaskerud & Hu, 1992). These categories included a greater proportion of African American and Asian American clients who received diagnoses of serious mental disorders compared with European American clients, who in turn, received more of these diagnoses than Latino clients. Asian American clients were less likely than any other ethnic group to receive diagnoses involving substance abuse. Surprisingly, these researchers failed to find any differences in diagnoses relating to social class.

Other researchers have found that both ethnicity and social class relate to psychiatric disorders. An inverse relationship exists between socioeconomic status (SES) and psychiatric disorders; that is, as SES decreases, psychiatric disorders increase (Holzer et al., 1986). Diagnosis and social class have an inverse relationship for both African Americans and European Americans (Williams, Takeuchi, & Adair, 1992). The strongest relationship was for alcohol abuse, but other disorders showed similar relationships. For European Americans, depression increased as SES decreased; for African Americans, no relationship appeared. White men with lower SES had a higher rate of mental disorders than their African American counterparts. Gender differences also appeared, forming complex interaction patterns of gender, ethnicity, and socioeconomic class.

These findings suggest that to eliminate diagnostic bias, the criteria and the clinicians using them should be sensitive to the cultural background of the individual who is being diagnosed, and that diagnosis should relate to the individual rather than be an expression of the dominant culture. Behaviors that may seem dysfunctional to members of the dominant culture may not be in minority cultures (Solomon, 1992). The fourth edition of the DSM addressed these problems by including information about various ethnic and cultural groups in each diagnosis to allow clinicians to take this information into account. Perhaps the professionals who use the DSM will be able to include this information to attain the cultural sensitivity in their diagnoses that has been lacking, but the listing of symptoms as shown in the multiaxial DSM system does not easily lend itself to the type of flexibility that will be necessary for culturally sensitive diagnoses.

TABLE 15.3 Prevalence and Gender-Related Differences in Personality Disorders

Disorder	Estimated Rate in General Population	Gender Difference
Paranoid	0.5–2.5%	More common among men in clinical populations
Antisocial	3.0% men, 1.0% women	More common among men in both general and clinical populations
Borderline	2.0%	More common in women–75.0% of those diagnosed are women
Histrionic	2.0–3.0%	More commonly diagnosed in women
Narcissistic	<1.0%	More common among men
Dependent	Most common of personality disorders	More commonly diagnosed in women
Schizoid	Uncommon	More common among men

SOURCE: Based on *Diagnostic and statistical manual of mental disorders* (4th ed.), American Psychiatric Association, 1994, Washington, DC: Author.

lying, fighting, stealing, and physical cruelty. Both these personality disorders include exaggerations of the traditional male gender role (Brannon, 1976). Indifference to social relationships resembles the Sturdy Oak facet of the role, with its emphasis on self-reliance and lack of emotion. Elements of antisocial personality disorder resemble the Give 'Em Hell facet, with its emphasis on dominance and aggression. Not surprisingly, men receive these two diagnoses more often than women (ApA, 1994; Kass, Spitzer, & Wiliams, 1983). Table 15.3 shows some of the personality disorders, along with their prevalence and the gender-related differences in their diagnosis.

If some DSM diagnostic categories are biased against men, then why is there no protest from men against this categorization? The charges of gender bias in the DSM have come mostly from women who have contended that the system is unfair to them. Although some diagnostic categories are exaggerations of the male gender role and men receive these diagnoses more often than women, no analogous criticisms have come from men about gender bias in the DSM. Perhaps this silence is related to the overall lower rate of psychiatric diagnosis for men. The protests of gender bias coming from women apply not only to the DSM but also to diagnoses of mental disorders according to any system. That is, some critics have expressed concern that women will be considered less psychologically healthy than men because men constitute the standard for what is mentally healthy (Bem, 1993b).

An early study that laid the foundation for the concerns over gender bias in the clinical diagnosis of mental disorders was the influential work by Inge Broverman and her colleagues (Broverman, Broverman, Clarkson, Rosenkrantz, & Vogel, 1970). These researchers investigated what constitutes a well-adjusted, healthy adult and found that the description significantly differed from what constitutes a well-adjusted, healthy woman. The gender role for socially desirable behavior in women was not consistent with the psychological standards for a well-adjusted adult. For example, such stereotypically feminine traits as dependence and emotionality are not part of the concept for adult mental health.

These researchers contended that the discrepancy between the ideal of mental health for a woman and for an adult reflects a double standard.

Clinically trained psychologists, psychiatrists, and social workers exhibited a double standard for mental health in rating a normal adult, a normal adult man, and a normal adult woman (Broverman et al., 1970). These professionals' ratings showed that their concept of a healthy adult and a healthy man were similar, whereas their views of a healthy adult and a healthy woman differed. These results pointed out that the standard for mental health is male whereas feminine traits were viewed as detracting from health.

This study has been influential and widely cited, but the choice of questions may have biased the results (Widiger & Settle, 1987). Alternatively, mental health professionals may have changed views, showing less bias now than when Broverman et al. performed their study over 25 years ago. A later study with a comparable method (Phillips & Gilroy, 1985) showed no significant gender-related differences for standards of mental health. However, these nonsexist attitudes concerning standards for mental health may not be translated into the practice of diagnosis.

Some research has suggested that gender bias does exist in the diagnosis of behavior problems. In one study (Adler, Drake, & Teague, 1990), clinicians received descriptions of patients that met the criteria for several different personality disorders. Two versions of these descriptions differed only in the gender of the patients; findings indicated that the patients' gender affected the clinicians' views in stereotypical directions.

In 1972, Phyllis Chesler proposed that diagnosis of mental disorders is fundamentally gender biased. Chesler contended that women who overconform or underconform to the traditional feminine gender role are subject to diagnosis; if they are either too aggressive or too submissive, they are deviant. Although Chesler's argument centered on the diagnosis of women's problems, the rationale can also extend to men. Those men who fail to conform to the male gender role may be at increased risk for diagnosis. This early critique of the diagnosis of psychological disorders created interest in gender bias, and subsequent research has confirmed Chesler's contention that adherence to and deviation from traditional gender roles are factors in the diagnosis of mental disorders.

Clinicians exhibit some bias in diagnosing personality disorders. Personality disorders are diagnosed on Axis II, which has less research support and is more controversial than diagnoses on Axis I. One study (Hamilton, Rothbart, & Dawes, 1986) included descriptions of histrionic personality disorder and antisocial personality disorder. Histrionic personality disorder is characterized by excessive emotionality and attention-seeking in a variety of situations, whereas antisocial personality disorder is characterized by a persistent disregard for and violations of the rights of others. The former is more often diagnosed in women and the latter more often diagnosed in men. When the case studies were equated for severity of pathology, case descriptions of women were found to receive more extreme ratings for histrionic personality disorder than case descriptions portraying men, even when the symptoms were identical. No comparable bias appeared for antisocial personality disorder, demonstrating a tendency to maximize female but not male pathology.

The differential diagnosis for mental disorders can be conceptualized by viewing personality disorders as extensions of gender role stereotypes (Landrine, 1987, 1989). Many of the characteristics of personality disorders are very close to stereotypes of male and female gender roles. Even without prejudice on the part of clinicians, differential rates of diagnoses seem likely. Indeed, not only clinical psychologists and psychiatrists (Landrine, 1987) but also college students (Landrine, 1989) were able to match descriptions of stereotypical cases to the various personality disorders. For example, participants assigned the description of a lower-class man a diagnosis of antisocial personality disorder, the single middle-class woman was histrionic, and the married middle-class woman received a diagnosis of dependent personality disorder. Only the married upper-class man was without pathology. Given descriptions of the personality disorders, college students supplied demographic information that was similarly stereotypical. Thus, both professionals and university students perceive consistent gender and social class patterns associated with the personality disorders, which typify the frequency of such diagnoses.

Gender differences also appear in several diagnoses for Axis I, such as anxiety disorders, depression, and substance abuse disorders. Gender role stereotyping relates to these categories of psychiatric diagnosis (Rosenfield, 1982). Women and men who showed signs of psychopathology more typical of the other gender were more likely to be judged as candidates for hospitalization than those who showed gender-typical disorders. Men with depression or anxiety disorders and women with personality disorders or substance abuse problems—patients displaying "deviant" deviance—were judged more likely to be candidates for hospitalization than were men who showed substance abuse disorders or women who showed depression—the more "normal" disorders.

These research studies have confirmed and extended Chesler's understanding of the relationship between deviance and gender role behaviors by showing not only that gender differences exist in diagnoses but also that gender roles and stereotyping play a part in the process of arriving at the diagnoses of mental disorders.

According to Steven Regreser López (1989), the process of diagnosis can include two types of judgment errors: overdiagnosis and underdiagnosis. The most commonly studied form of diagnostic bias has been *overdiagnosis,* identifying people as having disorders when they do not. *Underdiagnosis* is the mistake of failing to identify problems by overlooking symptoms. López conceptualized the clinical diagnostic process as a complex decision making skill, complete with the strategies and mistakes that occur in such situations. Rather than presenting the clinician as a biased individual, López pointed out the problems in diagnosis and contended that bias in clinical diagnosis is not a matter of the clinician reacting to one single patient characteristic, such as gender or ethnic background. Rather, López asserted that gender and ethnic background are pieces of information that a clinician considers in making a diagnosis and that prejudice is rarely a part of the process.

Research on under- and overdiagnosis has confirmed their existence but has also found a pattern of gender bias (Redman, Webb, Hennrikus, Gordon, & Sanson-Fisher, 1991). Overdiagnosis was more common for female patients, and underdiagnosis was more common for male patients. These gender differences appeared when contrasting the diagnoses on a questionnaire measuring psychological disturbance with physicians' ratings of the degree of disturbance. The questionnaire assessed a similar number of men and women as psychologically disturbed, but the physicians did not. Instead they showed a tendency to underrate the psychological disturbances of men and to overrate those of women. Furthermore, no differences appeared between interns and practicing physicians, indicating that no recent changes in medical training have altered the gender stereotyping in physicians' diagnoses of psychological problems.

If López is correct concerning bias in clinical diagnosis, then the overdiagnosing and underdiagnosing of behavior problems is not part of overt prejudice on the part of clinicians. His explanation, however, does not reduce the bias in diagnosis or change the outcome of the biased decisions. Even without simple prejudice or malice, problems arise for patients in under- or overdiagnosis both by identifying problems in people who have no pathology and by failing to diagnose problems in others who have mental disorders. With the evidence that overdiagnosis is more common in female patients and underdiagnosis is more common in male patients, the picture is one of systematic gender bias.

Gender Comparisons in Psychopathology

Chapter 14 presented information about gender differences in seeking health care, showing that women are more likely to seek health care than men. This tendency also applies to psychological problems. Data from four large-scale surveys of mental health problems showed that women have a greater tendency than men to interpret nonspecific problems and distress as related to their mental health and thus to seek mental health care (Kessler, Brown, & Broman, 1981). All gender differences in mental health treatment are not due to women's greater tendency to seek help, but between 10% and 28% of the difference in treatment of women for mental health problems is due to their greater tendency to seek such care.

Women, however, are not more likely to be patients under all circumstances. Women are more likely than men to consult general physicians about mental health problems, but no gender difference appears in the use of mental health specialty services (Leaf & Bruce, 1987). This situation can occur because the context of general health visits can open the possibility for mental health consultations (Travis, 1988b). Men do not make as many physician visits as women (see Chapter 14), so a comparable number of opportunities do not arise for them. Thus, men who seek mental health consultations are likely to seek that service directly, whereas women are more likely to receive such care in the context of regular health visits. The overall rate of hospitalization for mental disorders is somewhat higher for women (Kane, 1991), but the difference is limited to the elderly. For men and women in other age groups, men have higher hospitalization rates than women, suggesting that men's mental health problems may be more severe or that men's symptom reports may be taken more seriously.

Not all disorders show gender differences, but several do. Anxiety disorders, depression, and substance abuse disorders are among those problems that show marked gender differences, whereas other diagnoses are evenly distributed between women and men.

Depression

Use of the term depression has varied from the popular conception of minor, temporary low mood to the extreme of a severe, debilitating disorder that requires treatment (Miller, Norman, & Dow, 1988). Although depression is a common experience, the disabling problems of severe depression lie outside the range of normal experience. In the DSM system, depression is classified as a type of mood disorder and appears as a diagnosis on Axis I. Two subclassifications of depressive disorders exist—**major depression** and **dysthymia.** Table 15.4 shows the prevalence and gender-related differences for mood disorders.

Symptoms of major depression include dissatisfaction and anxiety, loss of interest and loss of pleasure, feelings of helplessness and hopelessness, changes in sleep or eating habits, and difficulty in concentrating. These symptoms must persist for at least two weeks to warrant a diagnosis of major depression. Dysthymia is milder than major depression and tends to be a chronic condition that may last for years. This diagnosis applies to people who chronically experience depressed mood, loss of interest, or other symptoms of depression, much as they would a personality trait. Major depression and dysthymia can co-occur or exist separately.

The ratio of depression in women compared with men is about 2 to 1, considering either the figures obtained from treatment or those from community surveys (ApA, 1994; Culbertson, 1997). These numbers apply to many (but not all) societies around the world, and the explanations for these figures have included biological as well as social and cognitive theories. The biological theories rely on the differences in reproductive hormones to account for gender differences in depression, but these theories have very little clear support (Nolen-Hoeksema, 1987). Studies have failed to consistently demonstrate a link between hormonal fluctuations and mood, and in addition, the differences in depression are not found in all cultures.

The exceptions to the greater prevalence of depression among women provide evidence that gender differences are not biologically based. If reproductive hormones were responsible for the greater prevalence of depression in women, then these differences would appear in all cultures. Although most societies show a ratio of female to male depression similar to that of the United States, several rural nonmodern cultures have similar rates of depression in women and men. Among these cultures are the old order Amish, a rural farming society in the United States. In addition, university students, the elderly, and the bereaved show no gender differences in rates of depression. These exceptions suggest that the gender differences in depression have a social basis, and a number of researchers have pinpointed social and family roles as the source of this difference. (See the Family Roles section earlier in this chapter for a review of the stresses that are common for women.)

Alternative explanations for gender differences in depression come from differences in the use of cognitive strategies for dealing with distressing events. One formulation (Nolen-Hoeksema, 1987) proposes that women tend to ruminate on their feelings, whereas men tend to deal with negative feelings by taking action. Dwelling on problems and negative feelings tends to amplify the feelings, which can lead to depression. Although action may not solve problems, activity is at least a distraction, preventing people from focusing on their problems. The tendency to ruminate on problems magnifies negative feelings, and if more women than men use this strategy, then this difference in cognitive coping styles

TABLE 15.4 Prevalence and Gender-Related Differences in Mood Disorders

Disorder	Estimated Rate in General Population	Gender Difference
Major depression	2.0–9.0%	More common in women, with a ratio of 2:1
Dysthymic disorder	3.0%	More common in women, with a ratio of 2–3:1
Bipolar disorder	0.4–1.6%	No difference

SOURCE: Based on *Diagnostic and statistical manual of mental disorders* (4th ed.), American Psychiatric Association, 1994, Washington, DC: Author.

might account for the differential rates of depression in women and men. A program of laboratory experimental research and naturalistic studies on depression demonstrated that the rumination style of dealing with negative events magnifies depression, whereas the action-oriented style minimizes negative emotions (Nolen-Hoeksema, 1994).

Another cognitive explanation for women's higher rates of depression is that their genuine emotion, goals, and desires are suppressed (Jack, 1991). According to this view, women are more prone to depression because society devalues women and the feminine, placing women in a position in which they must deny who they really are to get along in the world and to maintain their relationships; when women lose their sense of self, they become depressed. Research support for this view is mixed. Several studies have confirmed that scores on Silencing the Self Scale relate to depression (Carr, Gilroy, & Sherman, 1996; Gratch, Bassett, Attra, 1995; Page, Stevens, & Galvin, 1996), but not for everyone. This relationship was true for European American women but not for African American women (Carr et al., 1996). In studies that included men (Gratch et al., 1995; Page et al., 1996), the relationship between self-silencing and depression was significant, but men showed higher self-silencing scores than women. Finding that men's scores are higher than women's complicates this conceptualization of depression and leaves women's higher rate of depression unexplained.

Although gender differences exist in the diagnosis of depression, perhaps no differences occur in the frequency of negative mood (Nolen-Hoeksema, 1987; Tavris, 1992). That is, women and men experience the negative feelings that underlie depression at similar rates, but they express their feelings differently. Women tend to turn their negative feelings inward, whereas men tend to express their negative feelings in action. In women, the feelings produce symptoms consistent with the female gender role and hence with the DSM diagnostic criteria for depression. In men, the feelings produce symptoms such as substance abuse, risk taking, and violence.

Support for this conception comes from a study that examined symptoms among high school seniors (Casper, Belanoff, & Offer, 1996). The young men reported anger as their most common problem whereas the young women listed sadness as their most common problem. Therefore, the symptoms of depression may be seen as an expression of gender role socialization for women, but men exhibit different symptoms that receive other diagnoses.

In summary, two types of depression appear in the DSM classification—major depression and dysthymia. Women from many cultures are more likely than men to report symptoms of and receive treatment for depressive disorders at an approximately 2 to 1 ratio. The exceptions to this pattern suggest that gender differences in depression are not biologically based. Several socially based explanations for the gender differences in depression exist, including family role differences, personal control differences, and cognitive differences in coping with negative events. Another view holds that the gender differences in depression are a product of the ways in which women and men deal with distress. Women become passive, expressing symptoms of depression, and men become active, expressing symptoms of risk-taking, violence, drug use, or some combination of these three behaviors.

Substance-Related Disorders

Substance-related disorders involve the use of **psychoactive substances,** drugs that affect thoughts, emotions, and behavior. Examples include alcohol, amphetamines, marijuana (cannabis), cocaine, hallucinogens, opiates, sedatives, and hypnotics. In order to be diagnosed as having one of the types of substance-related disorders, the person must not only use the drug but must also exhibit a strong desire to use the substance and experience problems in social or occupational functioning due to drug use.

Alcohol is the most frequently used and abused substance, and men drink more than women in all categories of drinking (Biener, 1987). That is, more men than women fall into the categories of light, moderate, and heavy drinking. Drinking and drunkenness are associated with the male, and not the female, gender role (Landrine, Bardwell, & Dean, 1988). People expect men to drink beer and to get drunk, but the same expectation does not apply to women. Indeed, women (and especially feminine women) are not expected to drink beer (but are expected to drink wine) and should *not* get drunk.

Alcohol is not equally intoxicating for men and women. Women tend to weigh less than men, and body weight affects intoxication, meaning that each drink has a greater effect the smaller the person. In addition, some research has indicated that women's metabolism of alcohol produces a higher alcohol concentration in the blood compared to men, even with the body weight factor taken into account (Frezza et al., 1990). Both these factors result in greater risks to women who drink heavily. Because fewer women than men are heavy drinkers, men are more likely to experience the problems associated with heavy drinking, including the health risks and social problems associated with alcohol abuse.

A variety of evidence suggests that drinking is related to depression, both in men and in women. Alcohol consumption shows a relationship to depression and mood (Berger & Adesso, 1991). Among depressed and nondepressed men and women who were nonproblem drinkers, men expected more positive effects from drinking and drank more than women. The depressed men consumed more alcohol than any other group, and drinking decreased these men's perception of depression. This study demonstrated the relationship between negative mood and drinking, especially for men. Perhaps these men are at risk for developing problem drinking, but their strategy of drinking to manage depression showed some signs of being effective.

Research has confirmed the relationship between depression and problem drinking. Among alcoholic men and women in treatment for their drinking problems, those problem drinkers with a history of depression reported that they drank to relieve their depressive symptoms (Hesselbrock, Hesselbrock, & Workman-Daniels, 1986). Another study tested the relationship between depression and problem alcohol use over a 3-year time span (Horowitz & White, 1991). A significant relationship existed between depression at age 21 years and alcohol problems at age 24 for men, but no such relationship appeared for women. Thus, men who use the strategy of drinking to manage negative emotions are at increased risk for problem drinking.

Illegal drug use is also higher among men than women, with men more likely to use and abuse drugs such as heroin, amphetamines, cocaine, and marijuana—a pattern that parallels their alcohol use (Biener, 1987). On the other hand, women are more likely to use prescription tranquilizers and sedatives. That is, women are more likely to describe symptoms to physicians that lead to their diagnoses of having mental disorders treatable by drugs. The higher rate of prescription drug use by women and the greater use of illegal drugs by men result in similar rates but different patterns of substance use. Table 15.5 summarizes the prevalence and gender-related differences in substance use.

Men's drug use is more apt to be illegal, making them more likely to receive diagnoses because of their drug use. This difference in diagnosis may not reflect much of a differential

TABLE 15.5 Prevalence and Gender-Related Differences in Substance-Related Disorders

Disorder	Estimated Rate in General Population	Gender Difference
Alcohol	5.0–8.0%	More common in men, with a ratio as high as 5:1, varying with age and cultural backgrounds
Amphetamines	Possibly as high as 2.0%	More common in men, with a 3:1 ratio
Cannabis	4.0%	More common in men
Cocaine	0.2%	No difference
Hallucinogens	0.3%	More common in men, with a 3:1 ratio
Opiates	0.7%	More common in men, with a ratio of 3–4:1
Sedatives, hypnotics or anxiolytics	1.1%	Women are at higher risk

SOURCE: Based on *Diagnostic and statistical manual of mental disorders* (4th ed.), American Psychiatric Association, 1994, Washington, DC: Author.

tendency in substance use. Perhaps women too might resort to illegal drug use if physicians were less willing to prescribe drugs for them: "The sex differences in the use of alcohol and prescription psychotropics are not inconsistent with the hypothesis that men and women are equally likely to resort to substance use for coping, and that the sex difference is merely in the choice of substances" (Biener, 1987, p. 336).

In summary, the research indicates that a relationship exists between depression and drinking; depressed people drink more than the nondepressed and even attribute their drinking to depression. The tendency to drink more heavily when depressed is stronger among men but not exclusive to them. Perhaps men choose this strategy for dealing with negative feelings more often than women (Nolen-Hoeksema, 1987; Tavris, 1992), so this difference in dealing with negative feelings may account for some of the gender differences in depression and substance abuse disorders. The overall pattern of drug use for men and women probably differs little, but women tend to use legal prescription drugs, whereas men's drug use is more likely to come in the form of alcohol and illegal drugs.

Anxiety Disorders

The group of disorders labeled anxiety disorders includes panic attack, phobias, obsessive–compulsive disorder, and posttraumatic stress disorder, all involving features of anxiety and avoidance of problem situations. A survey of over 18,000 people indicated that anxiety disorders affect more than 7% of adults in the United States (Regier, Narrow, & Rae, 1990). No gender differences exist for some types of anxiety disorders, but other types appear much more often in women than in men.

Panic attack is characterized by periods of intense fear that occur without any fear-provoking situation. These attacks are typically accompanied by physical symptoms of distress, such as sweating, dizziness, and shortness of breath. This disorder is about equally common in women and men, but panic disorder with **agoraphobia** is about twice as common in women: "The essential feature of Agoraphobia is anxiety about being in places or situations from which escape might be difficult (or embarrassing) or in which help may not be available in the event of having a Panic Attack... or panic-like symptoms" (ApA, 1994, p. 396). These feelings of anxiety lead people to avoid the situations that might provoke such feelings.

Agoraphobia can also occur without panic disorder, and women are also more likely to have this disorder (ApA, 1994; Cameron & Hill, 1989). Other phobias, meaning unreasonable fears concerning some object or situation, constitute a second category of anxiety disorder. *Social phobias* appear as persistent fears of certain social situations, such as speaking in public, in which the person is judged by others or in which the person may do something embarrassing. The American Psychiatric Association (1994) stated that women in the general population are more likely to have social phobias, but in clinical populations, the gender ratio is closer to equal or men predominate. *Specific phobias,* fears of some object or situation besides anticipating a panic attack or being in a certain social situation, are more common among women.

Obsessive–compulsive disorder is the combination of obsession, which refers to recurrent, intrusive thoughts about something the person would prefer to ignore, and compulsion, which refers to repetitive behaviors intended to prevent anxiety. To receive this diagnosis, a person must be distressed by the obsessive thoughts and must spend over an hour per day on the compulsive behaviors. According to the DSM-IV (ApA, 1994) and other research (Cameron & Hill, 1989), this pattern of behavior is equally common in women and men, but other research (Cleary, 1987) has found it more common among women.

Posttraumatic stress disorder (PTSD), defined and discussed earlier, was originally applied to men who experienced lasting effects from their war experiences. As research accumulated on PTSD, its wider application became evident. Now the diagnosis is given to people experiencing the prolonged aftereffects of many different types of trauma, including natural disasters, accidents, and violent crime as well as military combat. There is no information about gender differences for PTSD, but a random sample of women revealed that over 12% met the criteria for PTSD, a much higher percentage than previous estimates (Resnick, Kilpatrick, Dansky, Saunders, & Best, 1993).

Although gender differences may exist for anxiety disorders, no coherent pattern has appeared. Table 15.6 summarizes the prevalence figures presented in DSM-IV and the differences associated with gender for these disorders. Research has shown a consistent pattern of the higher prevalence for agoraphobia (with and without panic disorder) and for specific phobias among women. Contradictory findings exist concerning gender differences for social phobia and obsessive–compulsive disorder. Overall, more women than men receive the diagnosis of some type of anxiety disorder, indicating that agoraphobia and specific phobias are sufficiently common to cause women to dominate this diagnosis.

Women with anxiety disorders experience more severe symptoms than men with anxiety disorders, and in one study (Scheibe & Albus, 1992) stress within marriage was the most frequent event that preceded the development of the disorder. Anxiety and fear are more characteristic of the feminine stereotype than of the stereotypical male role. The match between gender role traits and mental disorders that appears in personality disorders (Landrine, 1987, 1989) may also apply to anxiety disorders and may constitute an explanation for the higher overall rate of anxiety disorders among women. The gender differences among the different anxiety disorders suggest varying gender-related ways of expressing anxiety.

Other Disorders

Several important classifications of mental disorders show few or no gender differences in prevalence, but men and women with these disorders may not exhibit identical symptoms or the same time course of the disorder. For example, **schizophrenia**—a serious and complex disorder involving thought disturbances, problems in personal relationships, and possibly hallucinations—has been diagnosed equally in women and men.

This equal prevalence does not require that men and women have identical experiences with the disorder, and they do not. One study (Chu, Abi-Dargham, Ackerman, Cetingök, & Klein, 1989) found that male schizophrenics were younger than female schizophrenics at the time of their diagnosis and that the men were less likely to be married than the women. In terms of symptoms, female schizophrenics tended to be talkative, agitated, irrelevant, and silly, whereas male schizophrenics were less active than normal, grandiose, withdrawn, and more likely to have auditory hallucinations.

Other research (Lewis, 1992) showed similar patterns, but male schizophrenics tended to have poorer functioning before the onset of their disorders and were more likely than female schizophrenics to be involved in substance abuse. In addition, women were more likely to respond favorably to treatment. Despite these differences, male and female schizophrenics exhibited more similarities than differences.

Bipolar disorder is one of the mood disorders, along with major depression and dysthymia (see Table 15.4). Bipolar disorder is characterized by periods of mania, high activity, and elevated mood alternating with periods of depression. These drastically different

TABLE 15.6 Prevalence of and Gender-Related Differences in Anxiety Disorders

Disorder	Estimated Rate in General Population	Gender Differences
Panic attack with and without agoraphobia	1.5–3.5%	More common in women, at a ratio of 2–3:1
Agoraphobia	More common than with panic attack	Much more common in women
Specific phobias	9.0–11.3%	Women have 55 to 95% of specific phobias
Social phobias	2.0–13.0%	More common in women in general population; more common in men in clinical settings
Obsessive–compulsive disorder	1.5–2.1%	No difference
Posttraumatic stress disorder	1.0–14.0%	Not specified in DSM-IV

SOURCE: Based on *Diagnostic and statistical manual of mental disorders* (4th ed.), American Psychiatric Association, 1994, Washington, DC: Author.

mood states change in a cyclic fashion such that the affected person experiences both mania and depression over a period of weeks or months, interspersed with periods of normal moods. Unlike the other two mood disorders, bipolar disorder shows no gender differences in prevalence (ApA, 1987; Cleary, 1987).

An examination of individuals with bipolar disorder in the United Kingdom (Sibisi, 1990) revealed that the time course of the disorder was somewhat different for men and women. No overall gender differences in prevalence appeared, but women were more likely than men to receive a diagnosis during their middle years. As with schizophrenia, men are more likely than women to be diagnosed with bipolar disorder at younger ages.

The **somatoform disorders** show some gender differences. This classification of disorders includes problems with physical symptoms but no physical basis for disease. As a group, women are more likely to receive the diagnosis, of somatoform disorder, but some of these disorders show no gender differences. *Conversion disorder,* the loss of physical function without any physical basis for the disability, was originally called *hysteria.* In the late 1800s, this disorder was so strongly associated with women that the extension of the label to men was controversial. The DSM-IV (ApA, 1994) states that this disorder occurs rarely in men, and another study (Tomasson, Kent, & Coryell, 1991) found that the diagnosis of conversion disorder was three times more common in women than men.

Another of the somatoform disorders is *somatization disorder,* the recurrence of physical complaints and the seeking of medical attention without receiving any diagnosis of a physical problem. These complaints are often dramatic or exaggerated, and the affected person seeks care from many medical professionals. Women account for 95% of somatization disorder patients (Tomasson, Kent, & Coryell, 1991). The diagnosis is so rare for men that some have questioned its existence in men. However, one investigation (Golding, Smith, & Kashner, 1991) found that this disorder does occur in men. In addition, the symptoms and the course of the disorder are similar for men and women.

The DSM-IV cautions that physical disorders that involve many variable symptoms can erroneously lead to the diagnosis of somatization disorder. Given physicians' tendency to dismiss the physical complaints of women and attribute those complaints to emotional problems (see Chapter 13), this diagnosis may be erroneously applied to women with physical rather than mental problems. Indeed, physical and psychiatric disorders share many symptoms, and diagnostic bias can cause women to receive psychiatric diagnoses for physical disorders (Klonoff & Landrine, 1997).

Sexual disorders consist of two groups of disorders, paraphilias and sexual dysfunctions. **Paraphilias** are characterized by intense sexual feelings in response to objects or situations such as nonhuman objects, children, nonconsenting persons, and may even involve suffering for the person or others. These nonhuman objects include items of clothing or animals, and the situations include exposing one's genitals to strangers, fondling strangers in public places, observing sexual activities, or dressing in gender-inappropriate clothing. Sexual masochism—experiencing pleasure from pain or humiliation—and sexual sadism—experiencing pleasure from hurting one's sexual partner—are also among the paraphilias. About 20% of the sexual masochists are women, and this disorder is the most common paraphilia among women, which indicates that women are rarely diagnosed as having any of the paraphilias.

Sexual dysfunctions, the other subcategory of sexual disorders, consist of low levels of sexual desire or difficulty in arousal or orgasm. Women are more likely to receive diagnoses indicating abnormally low levels of sexual desire or inhibited orgasm, but men also experience these sexual problems. A summary of the prevalence and gender-related differences in schizophrenia, somatoform, and sexual disorders appears in Table 15.7.

When people receive diagnoses of abnormally low (or high) sexual interest or activity, these diagnoses require a standard of comparison, which may be their previous behavior as compared with their currently lowered (or raised) interest. The standard can also be the clinician's judgment about what is normal, and this standard may be biased or arbitrary. Despite warnings in the DSM concerning other physical or behavioral problems that can produce sexual dysfunctions, the possibility exists that patients may be held to some arbitrary standard of what constitutes normal levels of sexual activity and diagnosed on the basis of behavior that is simply deviant by definition.

In summary, several mental disorders show patterns of gender differences, and some disorders that have no overall discrepancy in prevalence show gender differences in onset or experience. The most dramatic gender differences occur for anxiety and somatoform disorders, diagnoses overwhelmingly given to women, and sexual paraphilias, diagnoses overwhelmingly given to men. Schizophrenia and bipolar disorder show no gender difference in prevalence, but male schizophrenics show some behavioral differences compared to female schizophrenics. The gender differences in bipolar disorder relate to age of onset, with women receiving more diagnoses in middle age than men, who tend to be diagnosed at younger ages.

Although psychopathology constitutes more than exaggerated gender role behavior, all gender differences in mental disorders lend themselves to interpretations relating to gender roles. People tend to exhibit pathology related to their gender roles; that is, women show signs of weakness and physical complaints, whereas men show violence and unusual sexuality. Male schizophrenics are more violent and socially withdrawn, whereas female schizophrenics are more talkative and silly; both behaviors are consistent with traditional gender roles.

The patterns in rates of mental disorders for men and women reflect the power accorded to male and female gender roles. The most common patterns of disorder for both

TABLE 15.7 Prevalence of and Gender-Related Differences in Rate of Selected Axis I Disorders

Disorder	Estimated Rate in General Population	Gender Differences
Schizophrenia	0.2–2.0%	No difference in prevalence
Somatoform disorders		
Conversion disorders	11–300 per 100,000	More common in women, with a ratio of 2–10: 1
Somatization disorders	0.2–2.0% in women, less than 0.2% in men	Rarely diagnosed in men
Sexual disorders		
Paraphilias	No estimate	Rarely diagnosed in women, with the ratio of men to women at 20:1
Sexual dysfunctions	No estimate	More common in women

Source: Based on *Diagnostic and statistical manual of mental disorders* (4th ed.), American Psychiatric Association, 1994, Washington, DC: Author.

GENDERED VOICES
The Doctor Wouldn't Listen

The case of a young women who was in one of my classes is a good example of a woman whose physician failed to take her complaints seriously. This young woman felt unwell, experiencing a variety of symptoms including chest pain, abdominal pain, and lack of energy. She consulted her physician, who had been her family's doctor since she was a child. He asked her about her symptoms and about her life. She described how she felt and where it hurt, along with the stresses and problems she had recently experienced: Her parents were getting divorced, and she felt so tired that school was difficult to manage. The physician said that she was experiencing stress and told her to relax, assuring her that she would feel better.

She tried but felt no better. After several visits, the woman was convinced that she had a problem that the physician was missing, and he was equally convinced that she had a mental problem that she failed to acknowledge. She consulted another physician, who might have behaved much as the first did, but instead, the physician did a series of tests that revealed a kidney tumor, which required immediate surgery. Her many symptoms and the stresses in her life were consistent with a number of diagnoses, but her family physician failed to take her physical complaints seriously, insisting that she was experiencing psychological distress rather than organically based physical problems. This woman's experience is by no means unique. Men may also be erroneously diagnosed in a medical examination, but the overwhelming majority of horror stories of physical problems diagnosed as psychological disorders come from women who have experienced biased diagnosis and treatment. Therefore, biased diagnosis may be the source of some of the gender differences in somatization disorder.

men and women show consistencies with what are considered to be appropriate gender-related behaviors. When violations of gender roles occur, clinicians are likely to perceive that these patients have more severe problems than patients who exhibit psychopathology consistent with their gender roles.

Summary

Gender differences in patterns of psychopathology have been the source of accusations of gender bias in the way these are diagnosed. The patterns of gender difference in mental disorders may also relate to differences in stress and coping strategies. Research indicates that women experience more stress than men, and women's roles are the most probable sources of these differences. Women's roles often obligate them to provide physical and emotional care for their families, but they may not receive as much social support as they give. The stress of women's role obligations and their more extensive involvement with social support networks indicate differences from men in the way perceived stresses are managed.

Although men are the more common targets of violence, women are more commonly the victims of intimate violence, including childhood sexual abuse, rape, and spouse battering. Both women and men become the victims of violent crime, and both are subject to the resulting effects. An increasing body of evidence has implicated violence as a factor contributing to a variety of mental disorders. Poverty is also a source of stress that disproportionately affects women and ethnic minorities, both of whom have higher rates of mental disorders than White men. Discrimination is a pervasive experience that increases stress in the lives of both ethnic minorities and women.

Comparisons of women's and men's coping strategies have been complicated by the need to examine differences in stressful situations in their lives. Studies that fail to control for these factors tend to support the stereotypical view that women use emotion-focused techniques more often and men use problem-focused coping. Not only do situational factors affect coping, but women and men seem ready to report the use of gender-stereotypical coping strategies, which suggests that self-report studies are biased.

Accusations of gender bias in psychiatric diagnosis have centered around the *Diagnostic and Statistical Manual of Mental Disorders* (DSM) of the American Psychiatric Association (ApA). This publication contains a system for assigning diagnoses to people's behavioral problems; the third edition of this volume (ApA, 1980) proposes a descriptive, multiaxial system of classification. Revisions appeared in 1987 (DSM-III-R) and 1994 (DSM-IV), and these revisions have refined but have not made basic changes in the system of classification.

Using the DSM system, clinicians match each patient's symptoms against a description and make diagnoses on each of five axes. Axis I contains descriptions of the major clinical disorders, Axis II describes mental retardation and personality disorders, and Axis III provides a diagnosis of physical conditions. Axis IV contains a listing for the stressors in the patient's life, and Axis V allows for an overall rating of level of functioning.

Women's higher rate of treatment and the gender differences in some categories of disorders have led some researchers to argue that there is gender bias in the DSM, especially in the personality disorder diagnoses that appear on Axis II. Some personality disorder diagnoses are more common in women, whereas others are much more common in men. Indeed, the descriptions of these disorders appear to exaggerate traits of the female and male gender roles.

The clinicians who apply the criteria may also be biased, holding men as the standard for both women's and men's mental health. Early research indicated that clinicians value masculine traits above feminine ones, but later research has indicated that these biases may be weakening. However, physicians are known to be more likely to overdiagnose women's and underdiagnose men's mental disorders. Although clinicians may not be personally prejudiced, their limited attention to gender and ethnic information can lead them to use this information in biased ways in their diagnoses, creating differences in the numbers of women and men who are given various diagnoses.

In addition to the personality disorders that show gender differences, the statistics concerning some Axis I diagnoses reflect different rates for women and men. Many categories of mental disorders show few gender differences, but major depression and substance-related disorders show marked gender differences, with women being more often diagnosed with depression and men with substance abuse problems. Various explanations for these differences exist, including biological, social role, and cognitive theories. An alternative explanation holds that the gender differences in these two behavior problems reflect differences in expressing similar underlying negative feelings: Women express their negative feelings in the form of depression, and men express their negative feelings in the form of alcohol and drug abuse.

Other mental disorders show some differences in women and men. Some anxiety disorders, such as phobias, are more common among women, but others, such as obsessive–compulsive disorders, show little gender difference in prevalence. Likewise, bipolar disorder and schizophrenia are about equally common in men and women, but the paraphilias are very rare in women. Therefore, the pattern of mental disorders seems to reflect the gender roles appropriate to men and women; that is, the patterns of abnormal behavior reflect aspects of the gender role of each. Research indicates that when people deviate from gender-typical patterns in displaying disordered behavior, their problems are judged to be more severe than those who conform to the pattern of disorders typical of their gender.

Glossary

agoraphobia a phobic disorder characterized by anxiety about being in places or situations in which escape would be difficult or embarrassing.

antisocial personality disorder a personality disorder that is characterized by irresponsible and antisocial behavior such as lying, fighting, stealing, and physical cruelty.

bipolar disorder one of the mood disorders characterized by periods of mania, high activity and elevated mood, alternating with depression.

diagnosis classification of a physical or psychological problem.

dysthymia diagnosis within the category of mood disorders that is applied to those who experience depressed mood, loss of interest and pleasure, or other symptoms over an extended period, often for months or years.

late luteal phase dysphoric disorder (LLPDD) a diagnosis with symptoms that resemble premenstrual syndrome. This controversial category appeared in the appendix rather than the body of DSM-III-R, along with other personality disorders that require more study.

major depression diagnosis within the category of mood disorders that is applied to severe symptoms of depression, such as loss of interest and pleasure, feelings of helpless and hopelessness, and changes in eating and sleep habits.

panic attack one of the anxiety disorders, characterized by periods of intense fear that occur without any fear-provoking situation and accompanied by physical signals of distress.

paraphilias a type of sexual disorder characterized by intense sexual feelings in response to objects or situations that are unusual.

posttraumatic stress disorder (PTSD) one type of anxiety disorder that involves the experience of some distressing event outside the range of normal human experience, the reexperience of the event, avoidance of stimuli associated with the event, and increased sensitivity to associated experiences. These symptoms must persist for at least one month.

premenstrual dysphoric disorder (PMDD) a controversial diagnostic category that appears in an appendix of DSM-IV. Its symptoms are those of premenstrual syndrome, and the broad description of these symptoms presents the possibility that vast numbers of women could be diagnosed as mentally ill.

psychoactive substances drugs that affect thoughts, emotions, and behavior.

schizoid personality disorder a personality disorder that is characterized by lack of concern about personal and social relationships as well as a restricted range of emotional experience and expression.

schizophrenia a serious and complex disorder involving thought disturbances, problems in personal relationships, and possibly hallucinations.

sexual dysfunctions a subcategory of the sexual disorders that includes problems with low level of sexual desire or difficulty in arousal or orgasm.

social support receipt of emotional and material resources from friends and family members.

somatoform disorders a classification of disorders that includes problems with physical symptoms of disease but with no physical basis for these symptoms.

Suggested Readings

Culbertson, Frances M. (1997). Depression and gender: An international review. *American Psychologist, 52,* 25–31. Culbertson's review provides a concise summary of the evidence on gender differences from a cross-cultural perspective. In addition, she considers explanations for depression with the goal of understanding how to approach its treatment.

Landrine, Hope. (1989). The politics of personality disorder. *Psychology of Women Quarterly, 13,* 325–339. Landrine demonstrated the congruence between social stereotypes and various descriptions of personality disorders. She argues that by incorporating these ethnic and gender stereotypes, the diagnosis of personality disorders becomes politicized.

Lerman, Hannah. (1996). *Pigeonholing women's misery: A history and critical analysis of the psychodiagnosis of women in the twentieth century.* New York: BasicBooks. Lerman's provocative book includes a historical review of the diagnostic process and many varieties of criticism of the ways that women's distress has been categorized.

Wethington, Elaine; McLeod, Jane D.; & Kessler, Ronald C. (1987). The importance of life events for explaining sex differences in psychological distress. In Rosalind C. Barnett, Lois Biener, & Grace K. Baruch (Eds.), *Gender and stress* (pp. 144–156). New York: Free Press. These authors take a social role point of view in examining the gender differences in stress that relate to mental distress. They propose that women's roles carry obligations for care and support that men's roles do not and that these differences are important for mental health.

Chapter 16

Treatment for Mental Disorders

HEADLINE

Sex and Psychotherapy

—*Newsweek,* April 13, 1992

Psychotherapy creates an intimate relationship between a client and therapist. From the early years of psychotherapy, that intimacy has sometimes been expressed in a sexual relationship between client and therapist (Beck, Springen, & Foote, 1992). One element of the Freudian approach to therapy was that patients develop strong positive feelings for their therapists, and these feelings often included sexual attraction. Therapists might also develop similar feelings, but they were supposed to refrain from allowing the therapeutic relationship to become personally intimate.

The majority of patients treated by early psychotherapists were women, providing many opportunities for sexual feelings to develop and to be expressed. Despite the warnings not to become sexually involved with patients, several early psychoanalysts, including Carl Jung and Otto Rank, established sexual relationships with their patients. Although these relationships were not sanctioned, no regulations existed to prevent them. In addition, patients had no one to whom to complain, and no mechanism existed to restrain therapists. Sexual relationships with patients were considered personal indiscretions rather than professional problems, and therapists have been reluctant to report colleagues who have sexually exploited patients.

"The conspiracy of silence is fast breaking. A spate of widely publicized cases, a series of tell-all books and Hollywood's growing infatuation with the topic are forcing the profession to take stronger action" (Beck et al., 1992, p. 54). These actions include passing regulations to prohibit sexual contact between client and therapist; all helping professions now have such regulations. Clients are taking action in the forms of lawsuits and revealing books, but these actions have not necessarily been effective in restraining therapists. One therapist was expelled from the American Psychiatric Association, but her license was not revoked, and she continues to practice. She summarized the results of her censure: "All that happens is that I don't have to pay my dues" (in Beck et al., 1992, p. 57).

The results for the clients are often more severe, with clients experiencing negative effects as a result of sexual relationships with therapists (Beck et al., 1992). Sixty-five percent of psychiatrists reported that they had treated clients who had been involved in sexual relationships with other therapists, but only 8% said that they had reported their colleagues. Therefore, though these erotic relationships are not unusual, they are harmful and largely go unreported. The situation exists partly because the majority of clients are women and the majority of therapists are men and partly because the nature of many types of psychotherapy is quite intimate.

Approaches to Therapy

Formal psychological treatment for mental disorders or behavior problems has a relatively short history, and throughout that history, the approach to treatment has been related to conceptualizing the source of these problems. Until the middle of the 19th century, few treatment procedures existed for people with mental disorders, and the dominant belief was that abnormal and socially unacceptable behavior was a moral or spiritual problem (Russell, 1995). Several changes brought about improved methods of treatment for psychological problems, including a changed perspective on the source of mental disorders and a large growth in medical knowledge. The reconceptualization of mental disorders from possession by demons or moral deficiencies to being problems in mental functioning came about during the 19th and early 20th centuries, and medicine became the model for understanding these problems. With the growing acceptance of mental illness as analogous to physical illness, medical researchers began to seek methods of treatment for abnormal behavior.

Therapies for the treatment of mental disorders arose and became part of psychiatry and psychology. The earliest modern therapy was **psychoanalysis,** Freud's version of treatment for psychological problems, although other therapists who were dissatisfied with psychoanalysis as the preferred method of treatment devised new talk-based therapies. In addition, psychological research on operant conditioning was applied to changing undesirable behavior, resulting in the therapy called **behavior modification.** Also, psychiatrists use psychoactive drugs in the treatment of behavior problems—sometimes instead of, and sometimes in addition to psychotherapy. Therefore, these professionals now provide a variety of treatments for people with mental disorders.

Psychoanalysis

Sigmund Freud was among the early researchers who investigated causes of and sought cures for mental disorders. He developed a system of therapy that has influenced treatment as well as contemporary thinking about mental disorders. Freud's system of therapy is psychoanalysis, a talk-based approach geared toward understanding and alleviating psychological problems. Psychoanalysis was part of Freud's comprehensive theory of personality development and functioning. (Chapter 6 presented the Freudian approach to personality development.) Freud believed that psychological problems develop when people are incapable of dealing with problems and use **repression** to push problematic material into the region of the unconscious. The unconscious does not function rationally, so repressed material has the potential to remain in the unconscious throughout childhood and adulthood and can produce problems at any time.

Problems typically result from conflict during childhood, when the ego is not sufficiently well developed to deal with the many difficulties of early childhood. Adult problems often reflect childhood traumas that have been repressed and that leave the troubled person with mental conflict, distress, or problems in functioning. Psychoanalysts attempt to help patients resolve their problems by bringing unconscious material to consciousness so that patients may deal with these problems rationally. Once patients gain insight into the source of their conflicts, Freud believed that their conscious minds could deal with the problems, thus alleviating the source of conflict. Therefore, bringing repressed material to consciousness was a goal of psychoanalysis. Table 16.1 summarizes the elements of psychoanalytic therapy.

Although Freud and his colleagues were physicians, psychoanalysis developed as a psychological treatment for mental disorders. That is, the source of mental disorders was psychological, and the treatment was accomplished through talking about the source of the problem. This approach influenced popular thought and prompted the development of other talk-based treatments. Although medically based treatments for mental disorders also developed, talked-based psychotherapy remains a prominent approach to the treatment of problem behavior.

Some talk-based therapies arose in a direct opposition to the Freudian system. Karen Horney (1939) was one of the psychoanalysts who protested the Freudian view of women and offered alternative approaches to dealing with psychological problems. Her theory and therapeutic interventions are the basis for contemporary talk-based therapy (Westkott, 1997). (See Chapter 6 for more about Freud's theory and Horney's alternatives to Freudian theory.) Other alternative therapies originated with Carl Rogers (1951), who developed a humanistic approach to therapy called client-centered therapy, and Albert Ellis (1962), who developed a cognitive therapy called rational–emotive therapy. These therapists objected to the emphasis on the unconscious in psychoanalysis and offered therapies that emphasized coping with current life problems rather than exploring developmental trauma from childhood.

TABLE 16.1 Elements of Psychoanalytic Therapy

Category	Description
Underlying source of problems	Childhood trauma and insufficient ego to deal with trauma
Cause of problems	Repression of unconscious conflict
Immediate cause of problems	Repressed material escapes from unconscious
Goal of therapy	To bring repressed material to consciousness
Techniques	Talking, free association, dream analysis
Practitioners	Psychoanalysts (who are usually psychiatrists)

Humanistic Therapies

The psychoanalytic view of human nature is rather pessimistic, holding that psychological development is filled with potentially debilitating problems and that few people develop into healthy adults, even those who have undergone psychoanalytic treatment. Psychoanalysis can help people resolve the problems that result from unconscious conflict and trauma, but helping them to maintain a healthy, functioning personality is always a delicate balancing act. The humanistic theories of personality, in contrast to psychoanalysis, hold the more optimistic view that people are innately drawn toward fulfilling their human potential. If they fail, the reasons lie in their circumstances and in their environments, which somehow prevent the complete development of their full potentials. This context-sensitive, optimistic view of humanity is reflected in humanistic psychotherapy, as for example in Carl Rogers's client-centered therapy and Frederick (Fritz) Perls's Gestalt therapy.

Rogers (1951, 1961, 1980) proposed that human development follows a natural course toward health unless some event impedes this development. Rogers believed that problems originate from distortions in self-concept, and these distortions arise from a lack of acceptance of true feelings. When children get messages that the feelings they experience are unacceptable, they begin to deny these feelings. Lack of acceptance of feelings leads to inaccuracies in self-concept and interferes with many facets of development.

Client-centered therapy seeks to help people develop their full potential by providing a safe therapeutic environment (Kaplan & Yasinski, 1980). To form a relationship with an empathic, acceptant, and genuine counselor is of primary importance. Thus, client-centered counselors offer three nurturing conditions—unconditional acceptance, empathy, and congruence to their clients. The most important of these is congruence: "To be congruent means to be real or genuine, to be whole or integrated, to be what one truly is" (Feist & Feist, 1998, p. 468). These three conditions are essential for clients to experience growth, and all three arise from clients' relationship with the counselor. Given these three conditions, the process of therapy occurs.

A major goal of client-centered therapy is to eliminate discrepancies between clients' actual feelings and the feelings they recognize. By coming to recognize their true feelings—including negative feelings—clients can accept themselves. That is, clients develop congruence during the course of successful client-centered therapy. In addition, they become open to change and new experiences, develop a freshness of attitude, and come to trust in themselves.

The counselor does not work directly on changing clients, who must do that for themselves. The counselor's job is to provide clients with therapeutic relationships so that clients can reclaim their abilities to move toward personal growth and development. This approach focuses on allowing clients to think in undistorted ways, assuming that behavior changes in them will follow.

Gestalt therapy is another humanistic therapy, and it has similarities to client-centered therapy. The word *gestalt* means "whole" in German, and Perls (1969), the originator of this therapy, believed that the basis of psychological problems comes from feelings of not being whole. The failure to acknowledge their emotions leads people to this feeling of not being whole; they have a sense that parts of themselves have been psychologically disowned. Gestalt therapy seeks to help clients become whole again by allowing them to recognize and express their emotions, and Gestalt therapists use a variety of techniques oriented around understanding and integrating emotions to further this goal.

The humanistic therapies all share the view that fulfillment is a natural goal that people can reach, but barriers exist that block psychological growth. Humanistic therapists attempt to provide an atmosphere that permits clients to move in the natural direction of self-enhancement. Table 16.2 summarizes the elements of humanistic therapy.

Cognitive Therapy

Clients' thoughts are important in humanistic therapy, but these thought processes are the major focus in cognitive therapy. Cognitive therapists believe that thought processes are the basis of feelings and behavior; they create psychological problems and also provide the potential for alleviating those problems. Behavior and emotions follow from cognition, so changes in cognition provide the foundation for changes in behavior.

Ellis (1962) developed rational–emotive therapy, one of the earliest cognitive therapies, in response to what he saw as the failure of psychoanalysis to solve people's problems. Ellis objected to both the length and nondirective nature of psychoanalysis, insisting instead that therapists should set goals and that therapy should be brief and problem oriented.

Rational–emotive therapy views psychological problems as a result of people's irrational beliefs. Such beliefs lead people to unrealistic views of themselves and the world, and when these expectations go unmet, people make themselves miserable. Rational–emotive therapy attempts to change these irrational thoughts and assumes that a change in cognition will produce changes in emotions and behavior. Correcting these irrational beliefs is the basic goal of rational–emotive therapy.

Aaron Beck (1985) developed a cognitive therapy specifically for depression, which concentrates on the distorted, self-defeating thoughts that accompany depression. Beck contended that depressed people overgeneralize personal failures into the belief that they are worthless and explain positive occurrences as exceptions to the general rule of failure. Depressed people also magnify the enormity of negative events, seeing these events as catastrophic and unchangeable. Selective perception is another cognition that adds to depres-

TABLE 16.2 Elements of Humanistic Therapy

Category	Description
Underlying source of problems	Discrepancy between genuine feelings and acknowledged emotions; feelings of not being whole
Cause of problems	Blockage of development toward full potential
Immediate source of problems	The problem that prompts a client to seek therapy
Goal of therapy	To provide an atmosphere that allows clients to move toward personal growth
Techniques	Empathic listening, providing unconditional positive regard, showing congruence
Practitioners	Psychologists, social workers, counselors

sion, causing depressed people to notice the negative elements of their surroundings and ignore the positive ones. These distortions of thinking magnify and maintain negative cognitions and thus perpetuate depression.

Beck's cognitive therapy attempts to help clients change their negative thinking patterns by testing the beliefs to evaluate their validity. Rational–emotive therapy attempts to confront irrational beliefs with logic, but Beck's cognitive therapy is less directive and more experiential. Rather than arguing against such cognitions, Beck might formulate ways for clients to evaluate their thought processes and test their accuracy. Lack of pleasure is often a prominent component of depression, and Beck's cognitive therapy urges depressed people to introduce pleasurable experiences into their lives.

Table 16.3 summarizes cognitive therapies. These therapies, such as rational–emotive therapy and Beck's cognitive therapy, assume that cognitions underlie psychological problems and that changing cognitions will change behavior. Rather than concentrating on behavior itself, these therapies concentrate on thoughts. Another therapeutic orientation takes an alternative approach—behavior modification emphasizes behavior rather than cognitions.

Behavior Modification

Behavior modification arose from laboratory research in psychology on the process of learning (Kantrowitz & Ballou, 1992). In exploring learning principles, researchers discovered that the principles of operant conditioning—reinforcement and punishment—are powerful forces in determining behavior. Not only do these principles apply to the nonhuman animals commonly used in laboratories but also to humans and their complex behaviors. As applied to problematic behavior, behavior modification theory holds that such behaviors are learned and maintained by reinforcement and punishment, and application of these two principles can change unacceptable behavior.

Behavior modification strives to replace inappropriate or deviant behaviors with other, healthier behavior patterns through operant conditioning. Although both have been used in behavior modification programs, reinforcement for desirable behavior is more common than punishment for undesirable behavior.

Behavior modification is more specific and task-oriented than talk-based psychotherapies. For example, behavior modification is often used for various skills training, such as

TABLE 16.3 Elements of Cognitive Therapy

Category	Description
Underlying source of problems	Irrational beliefs
Cause of problems	Application of irrational beliefs to personal circumstances
Immediate source of problems	The problem that brings a person to therapy
Goal of therapy	To change irrational to more rational beliefs
Techniques	Confronting and disputing irrational beliefs, testing the validity of negative cognition
Practitioners	Psychologists, social workers, counselors

developing assertiveness, dealing with phobias, or changing eating patterns. In such programs, a client "learns a repertoire of behavior likely to produce desirable consequences in specific situations" (Blechman, 1980, p. 225). Women are the major category of clients using behavior modification, as they most often seek treatment for assertiveness problems, eating disorders, depression, and phobias.

Cognitive behavior therapy is a variation that incorporates the concept that cognition is an important factor in behavior, and the application of principles of reinforcement is used to bring about behavioral changes (Fodor, 1988). As with behavior modification, this therapeutic approach assumes that problems are the result of learned patterns of maladaptive behavior.

The process of cognitive behavior therapy typically differs from behavior modification in several ways. Rather than concentrating on behavior and ignoring internal cognitive processes, cognitive behavior therapy attempts to change thought patterns and thereby change behavior. This therapy tends to be more collaborative than behavior modification, with the client playing an active role. Client and therapist cooperate to establish goals, and the client rather than the therapist may monitor and reward the desired behavior. Table 16.4 summarizes behavior modification and cognitive behavior therapy.

Behavior modification and cognitive behavior therapy have been used as alternatives to more traditional therapies and differ from the psychoanalytic and humanistic approaches. The behavior modification approach emphasizes specific problems and the need to analyze the behavior that contributes to the problem. This behavior-oriented emphasis is also important in knowing when and how to apply reinforcement to change maladaptive to more adaptive behaviors. Therefore, behavior modification and cognitive behavior therapy represent different approaches to understanding and treating problem behavior.

Some therapists use behavior modification and cognitive behavior therapy with all clients and for all problems. Many therapists, however, take a more eclectic approach, using a variety of techniques rather than adhering to a single therapy orientation. These therapists argue that an eclectic approach offers them the opportunity to choose from a variety of approaches, fitting the problem and the client to the approach.

TABLE 16.4 Elements of Behavior Modification and Cognitive Behavior Modification Therapy

Category	Description
Underlying source of problems	None
Cause of problems	Behavior that is not adaptive or successful in specific situations
Immediate source of problems	The problem that brings a person to therapy
Goal of therapy	To change behavior (or cognitions that underlie behavior) to more acceptable alternative behaviors
Techniques	Reinforcement for acceptable behaviors, desensitization for phobias, assertiveness training
Practitioners	Psychologists, social workers, counselors

Medical Therapies

Talk-based psychotherapies and behavior modification are practiced by psychologists, social workers, counselors, and psychiatrists, but psychiatrists and other physicians can also use medical therapies for behavior problems. Psychoactive drugs are the most common of the medical therapies, but **electroconvulsive therapy** is also a medical approach to behavior problems. These medical therapies take the approach of altering brain functioning in order to change thoughts and behavior, but the exact mechanisms of the therapeutic benefits for both psychoactive drugs and electroconvulsive therapy are not completely understood. Nonetheless, physicians may use these therapies in conjunction with psychotherapy or alone.

Since the 1950s, both the use of and the number of psychoactive drugs has increased. Psychiatrists now use psychoactive drugs to treat schizophrenia, depression, and anxiety disorders. Women receive more drug prescriptions than men, and this difference is higher for both psychoactive as well as other types of drugs. Nearly 30 years ago, a review of the patterns of prescription psychoactive drug use in Canada, the United States, and the United Kingdom showed a consistently higher rate of use for women (Cooperstock, 1970). In addition, this review revealed evidence for both differences and similarities in patterns of drug use for men and women. The similarities included a higher rate of use for women not in the work force. The differences included a greater use of tranquilizers by women during early adulthood and middle age, compared to men's use, which peaked at older ages.

Since that review, the prescription of psychoactive drugs has increased for both men and women, but the pattern remains similar (Ashton, 1991). Since new drugs have appeared for the treatment of schizophrenia, anxiety disorders, and depression, women in North America and Europe have been prescribed psychoactive drugs twice as often as men. The trend in psychiatry is toward a greater use of drug therapy and a decline in talk-based therapy.

Advertising of pharmaceuticals is one possible reason for overprescription of drugs. Drug company representatives and advertisements are major sources of information for physicians about drugs (Russell, 1995). An analysis of drug advertising (Nikelly, 1994) showed that the advertisements for drugs for depression tended to depict women far more often than men, to show women in stereotypical ways, to present depression as a medical problem, and to ignore the social contexts of depression. For example, one advertisement showed a color photograph of a well-ordered kitchen superimposed over a black-and-white photograph of a disorderly kitchen, with the message that the drug allowed patients to get back to their normal kitchen activities. Such drug advertisements convey not only the impression that female patients should receive such drugs but also that these drugs are the best approach to treating depression, despite the evidence that occupational, marital, economic, and social factors contribute to the problem (see Chapter 15).

The use of electrical shock to alter behavior became common during the 1940s and remains in use today. This therapy involves delivering electric shocks to the brain, and the resulting convulsions have a therapeutic effect. Although the reasons for the beneficial effects remain unclear and serious side effects can occur, electroconvulsive therapy is now used almost exclusively for depression in patients who have failed to respond to antidepressant drugs (Sarason & Sarason, 1993). Because a majority of the cases of depression occur in women, they are the most frequent recipients of this therapy.

Table 16.5 summarizes medical therapies. Despite the growth of medically based treatments for behavior problems, this approach is controversial. Drugs and electroconvulsive shock alter behavior and sometimes bring about substantial improvements, but both carry risks for serious side effects. In addition, these therapies do not cure mental disorders but rather decrease or diminish the severity of symptoms. These effects can be beneficial but are not permanent; the symptoms may reappear when patients stop taking the drugs, and the therapeutic effects of electroconvulsive therapy rarely last for more than a few months (Sarason & Sarason, 1993). Psychoactive drugs, like other drugs, can cause serious side effects, and electroconvulsive therapy typically produces some memory loss. The benefits of medical treatments can outweigh the risks for some people, but the risks exist.

Accusations of Gender Bias in Therapy

Freudian therapy and psychoanalytic theory on which it is based, have come under heavy criticism for their sexism (as Chapter 6 presented). Traditional therapy was designed primarily by men to treat women (Levant, 1990). The cultural views of gender roles accepted during the late 1800s came to be incorporated into psychoanalysis, so the cases treated by Freud and his colleagues reflect men's views of women and their problems in that era. Freud's behavior in treating Dora, one of his most famous case studies, exemplified his mistreatment of female patients and the sexism of his system (Hare-Mustin, 1983). He refused to listen to or believe her and treated her as a child. Critics have long argued that psychotherapy in general and psychoanalysis in particular have failed to meet the needs of female patients.

The American Psychological Association's Task Force on Sex Bias and Sex-Role Stereotyping in Psychotherapeutic Practice (Brodsky & Holroyd, 1975) listed the sexist use of psychoanalytic concepts as one of the four main causes of gender bias in therapy. The gender bias in psychoanalysis comes from the notion that female development is a variation of male development and that girls' perceptions of their gender inadequacy is a critical element in personality development. Freud and his followers accepted men as the standard and women as deviating from normal psychological development—deviations that could never meet the male standard. Thus, critics have argued that psychoanalysis is inherently gender biased. This bias extends not only to psychoanalytic therapy but also to all of the other therapies that have accepted Freudian concepts, which includes some (but not all) of the other talk-based psychotherapies.

TABLE 16.5 Elements of Medical Therapy

Category	Description
Underlying source of problems	Biological or biochemical abnormalities
Cause of problems	Chemical or biological malfunctioning in the brain
Immediate source of problems	The problem that brings a person to therapy
Goal of therapy	To change biological functioning
Techniques	Psychoactive drugs, surgery, electroconvulsive therapy
Practitioners	Psychiatrists and other physicians

Neither humanistic nor cognitive therapy is inherently gender biased in the way that psychoanalysis is, but both emphasize personal rather than social and environmental factors in functioning (Lerman, 1992). Such neglect makes client-centered counseling inadequate for women due to its emphasis on the individual and its failure to take the social and political aspects of personal problems into account (Waterhouse, 1993). By stressing the individual and orienting counseling toward the "here and now," women can be made to accept responsibility for the problem behavior of others, thus intensifying rather than diminishing their problems.

The practices of humanistic and cognitive therapy can become gender biased if therapists apply their own personal values to therapy situations. Although not part of the therapy process, therapists might impose their personal values when they encourage their clients to adhere to traditional gender roles as a way to handle their problems. Such therapists may encourage clients to adopt more traditional gender roles, and such perscriptions make their practice sexist.

Behavior modification is value free and has no theoretical component related to gender. Any behavior can be the target for modification, however, and the choice of which behaviors to encourage or discourage can reflect traditional or nontraditional values. Although behavior modification is not inherently gender biased, its practice can also be sexist (Blechman, 1980). Normative standards enforce traditional gender roles, and critics (Kantrowitz & Ballou, 1992) fear that behavior modification can and has been used to enforce women's compliance rather than their personal development.

Medical therapies have also been the target of criticisms of sexist bias. As Chapter 14 detailed, women and men receive different levels of treatment in the health care system. Physicians tend to take men's symptom reports more seriously than similar reports from women and to attribute women's complaints to psychological rather than physical causes. This tendency toward overdiagnosis of women and underdiagnosis of men results in inappropriate psychological treatment for women and a lack of appropriate psychological treatment for men.

Women are more likely to receive prescriptions for psychoactive drugs than men, a pattern that has persisted since the 1960s (Ashton, 1991; Cooperstock, 1970). Some of these prescriptions are unnecessary, and both women and men may be overmedicated with psychoactive drugs (Ashton, 1991). Table 16.6 summarizes the potential sources of bias in the various types of therapy.

In an early and vehement indictment of gender bias in diagnosis and therapy, Phyllis Chesler (1972) argued that diagnosis has been used to identify women who deviate from their traditional gender roles and that therapy has been used to restore women to those roles. Chesler contended that women experience problems when they either conform too little or too much to traditional gender roles and that therapy is a process used to reimpose the traditional feminine role. Women may behave in many deviant ways, but when they fail to be subservient and domestic, they are labeled as needing therapy.

This therapy may be of any variety, but according to Chesler, all therapies seek to restore women to the traditional feminine gender role. One of the respondents to a survey by the American Psychological Association (APA Task Force on Sex Bias, 1978) confirmed Chesler's views by saying, "I have had women report to me that they could not continue in therapy because the objective seemed to be for them to learn to adjust better to their

TABLE 16.6 Sources of Gender Bias in Therapies for Behavior Problems

Type of Therapy	Source of Potential Gender Bias
Psychoanalysis	Psychoanalytic theory assumes that women are inferior.
Humanistic	Therapists may apply personal standards that are sexist; therapy focuses on the individual and ignores the social context of personal problems.
Cognitive	Therapists may apply personal standards that are sexist; therapy fails to address the social context of personal problems.
Behavior modification	Therapists may choose to reinforce traditional, gender-related behaviors.
Medical	Women and men are diagnosed and treated according to stereotypical and traditional values.

roles as wives, mothers, daughters (underlings of one kind or another), and they needed to become free persons" (p. 1122).

By surveying female psychologists, the APA Task Force (Brodsky & Holroyd, 1975) determined that sexist bias exists in four main areas of the practice of psychotherapy. As mentioned previously, sexist use of psychoanalytic concepts was one of the four. The other areas included fostering traditional sex roles, having biased expectations concerning women, devaluing women's potential, and responding to women as sex objects, including therapists' sexual exploitation of clients.

Men are also subject to gender bias in therapy. Therapist bias against men is similar to one type of bias against women: practitioners who urge the adoption of gender-typical behaviors. When a male patient in one study described a lifestyle that included providing housework and child care, therapists tended to concentrate on these atypical behaviors, emphasizing the gender role as a potential source of problems (Robertson & Fitzgerald, 1990). A second male patient who described his role as more typical of a breadwinner received no comments on his gender role behavior as a potential source of problems.

Therapists are also less likely to encourage men than women to develop their expressiveness (Fowers, Applegate, Tredinnick, & Slusher, 1996). In both work-related and relationship situations, therapists took an instrumental view concerning men's problems, but their orientation to women's problems was a more situation-specific mixture of instrumental and expressive. Therefore, evidence exists that the practice of therapy is not value free and that therapy tends to work toward preserving traditional values, especially for men.

Gender Issues in Therapy

Besides therapist bias, treatment presents several other gender issues. One issue is a gender preferences for counselors, with the assumption that clients prefer male counselors. In one study, however, the most common preference was no preference (Bernstein, Hofmann, &

Wade, 1987). Between 30 and 50% of college students expressed no preference for either a male or a female counselor. Of those who had a preference, male counselors were more commonly preferred, especially for vocational–educational or social–personal concerns. For sexual concerns or problems, people showed some tendency to prefer same-gender counselors. Those people who expressed a preference for a male counselor tended to be traditional in their gender roles, with both traditional men and women preferring the male counselor. People with less traditional gender role attitudes showed no preference concerning counselor gender.

Gender role rather than gender may be the source of the gender preference for counselors (Blier, Atkinson, & Greer, 1987). Variation in descriptions of counselors produced no difference for counselor gender, but gender role produced a significant difference. Prospective clients were more willing to see a feminine rather than a masculine counselor for personal concerns but preferred a masculine counselor for assertiveness and academic concerns. These results demonstrated the power of gender role stereotyping in influencing expectations about the counselor's behavior and thus on clients' preferences of counselor gender. These preferences, however, do not supersede the desire for an effective counselor (DeHeer, Wampold, & Freund, 1992). Competence, not gender, was a factor for all types of participants. Therefore, under some circumstances, some people prefer male or female counselors, because the effectiveness of the counselor is more important than gender in clients' choices.

Another gender issue is the suitability of various types of therapy for women or men. Although women more often seek counseling and psychotherapy and tend to be better at the therapy tasks involved, their needs may not be met by the process itself. The gender bias in psychoanalytic approaches and the potential for gender bias in other therapies have presented important issues for therapy, and several alternative approaches have endeavored to correct these biases.

Recognizing the potential for bias in therapy has led to the notion that good therapy should be nonsexist (APA Task Force on Sex Bias..., 1978), and professionals have worked toward the principles underlying nonsexist therapy. Feminist alternatives to therapy arose from the belief that ignoring gender issues does not make therapy gender fair. The contention that nonsexist therapy is not an adequate answer to the gender bias in therapy prompted the development of therapies that are specifically feminist and oriented toward women's problems as well as practiced exclusively by women. "The sexism in so-called nonsexist brands of psychotherapy may be less blatant, but any approach to psychotherapy that conceptualizes women's social problems as personal pathology and promotes 'cures' for women's distress primarily through individual personal change strengthens the patriarchal status quo" (Rawlings, 1993, p. 90).

Feminist Therapy

A review of the history of feminist therapy (Enns, 1993, 1997) traced it to the early 1970s and the women's rights movement. Women, both inside and outside the mental health care professions, began to criticize therapy for its traditional goals and for its power in maintaining the status quo for women. Some women in professions that provide mental health care then responded by attempting to combine feminist goals with therapy; their results diverge from traditional therapy in several ways.

Two important principles underlie the practice of feminist therapy (Gilbert, 1980). The first principle is one borrowed from the feminist movement and states that "the personal is political." That is, personal experience is embedded within the social and political structure of the society, making the problems of any individual woman a reflection of the wider society.

Feminist therapy strives to enact this principle in several ways. Clients explore the influence of social roles on their individual behaviors, examining the difference between what they have been taught about appropriate behavior and what is actually appropriate. During feminist therapy women have a forum for validating their experiences as women, including the situations and problems that are unique to women, and "Feminist therapists help clients see that their problems have social as well as personal causes" (Cammaert & Larsen, 1988, p. 15).

Feminist therapy is political, striving to bring about change in society. The early feminist therapists were politically active in the women's movement, and indeed, such activity was a requirement for declaring oneself a feminist therapist. These therapists sought to bring about changes in the status of women and advocated political activism for their clients. Their position was that significant change was not possible in women's lives through personal changes in psychological adjustment; only change in society and in women's roles would lead to beneficial changes for women.

The second principle of feminist therapy states that therapists and clients should form an egalitarian relationship rather than the traditional therapeutic relationship in which therapists are powerful and dominant and clients are subordinate. This principle ensures that clients understand the types of therapy that they will receive and that they know about the options for other sources of assistance (Hare-Mustin, Marecek, Kaplan, & Liss-Levinson, 1979). This level of informed consent represents a consumer orientation to therapy, and feminist therapy tries to promote such an orientation.

The equal relationship between client and therapist also aims to "demystify" the therapist as a person who has special knowledge and power (Gilbert, 1980). The rationale for this position lies in the attempt to counter the typical subordinate position that women occupy and to promote the belief that feminist therapy is an appropriate place for women to begin to feel a sense of personal power.

Feminist therapists participate in therapy by modeling appropriate behaviors for their female clients and by sharing personal experiences with their clients. This degree of personal openness and the advocacy of political activity on the part of the therapist differentiates the role of feminist therapists from therapists in most traditional therapies. Feminist therapists consider these differences essential to their approach.

Theoretical Orientations of Feminist Therapy

Feminist therapists hold a variety of theoretical orientations. Indeed, feminist therapists have followed theories as diverse as psychoanalysis and behavior modification and all varieties of humanistic and cognitive therapies. The goals of feminist therapy differ somewhat, depending on the orientation of the therapist, but the feminist component has produced similarities in the goals of all feminist therapy: "The emphasis becomes growth rather than adjustment or remediation, development rather than blame or illness" (Cammaert & Larsen, 1988, p. 23).

Considering that psychoanalysis has been criticized for its sexism, it is ironic that psychoanalytic therapy is the orientation adopted by many feminist therapists. Yet revisions to traditional psychoanalytic theory now make it an appropriate basis for feminist therapy (Daugherty & Lees, 1988). These revisions retain the emphasis on early childhood development and the importance of unconscious forces in personality development and functioning but include the revised view from feminist psychoanalytic theorists (Chodorow, 1978; Dinnerstein, 1976).

The feminist psychoanalytic approach rejects the notion that a woman's personality is a variation on the male pattern; instead it attempts to explain both. These theorists have rejected the notion that women are developmentally inferior to men, specifically the beliefs that anatomy is destiny, that women unconsciously desire a penis, that female sexuality is oriented toward bearing sons, and that normal women are masochistic, dependent, narcissistic, and passive.

Feminist psychoanalytic therapy uses many of the techniques of traditional psychoanalysis, including "uncovering and exploring the traumatic memories and painful affects associated with childhood that develop into symptoms and psychological conflicts" (Daugherty & Lees, 1988, p. 78). Both versions of psychoanalysis have as their goal the process of uncovering unconscious conflicts and bringing this material to consciousness so that clients can make more reasonable decisions about their behaviors. Feminist psychoanalytic therapists share the principles of feminist therapy, conveying their feminist values to their clients and attempting to build egalitarian counseling relationships.

Feminist adaptations of cognitive, behavioral, and cognitive behavior therapy are more obvious than feminist adaptations of psychoanalysis. The development of behavior therapy and the inclusion of feminist goals in the family of cognitive and behavior therapies has now included the behavioral treatment of phobias (Fodor, 1988). This type of therapy was one of the earliest forms of behavior therapy, and women have become the most common clients for such treatment. Cognitive behavioral therapy is the integration of behavioral and cognitive therapy with research from cognitive and social psychology. During the 1970s, when feminist therapy arose, cognitive behavior therapy also gained prominence, and the goals of feminist theory were integrated into this therapy. The cognitive component of therapy was especially compatible with feminist therapy; the goals of analyzing the social system and restructuring thought processes are consistent with an understanding of the personal as political.

For example, a woman who is stressed by her work situation might be urged to consider her supervisor's sexism rather than blaming herself for her difficulty in obtaining promotions. Cognitive behavior therapy has social learning theory as its basis, with its view that the environment shapes behavior. This position is compatible with feminist therapy's view that the social context of behavior is essential to understanding the behavior.

Although behavior and cognitive behavior therapies are often selected for assertiveness and other skills training, these therapies are not the most ideal for feminist therapy. Both approaches to therapy view change as the responsibility of clients, so therapists must be vigilant to maintain a cooperative rather than dominant relationship with clients. Furthermore, these therapies originated and are used most successfully with White, middle-class clients.

Clients of Feminist Therapy

During the early years of feminist therapy, the majority of clients were White middle-class women—a demographic description that matches many of the clients who seek therapy.

Questions arose over the suitability of feminist therapy for all women: After all, some women who seek therapy do not endorse feminist goals, and many are not White or middle class. Is feminist therapy appropriate for all women? And is it ever appropriate for men?

A study of women in feminist and traditional therapy evaluated the relative effectiveness of each (Marecek, Kravetz, & Finn, 1979). The results indicated that women who identified themselves as members of the women's movement evaluated feminist therapy as more helpful than traditional therapy, but women who did not identify themselves as part of the women's movement found the two types of therapy to be equally helpful. Women with moderate views and conservative women were equally benefited by traditional and feminist therapy, but feminists did not find traditional therapy as helpful as feminist therapy. These results suggest that feminist therapy has the possibility for a wider appeal than traditional therapy.

Some women express a preference for feminist counselors, in particular college women seeking help for career counseling or sexual assault concerns (Enns & Hackett, 1990; Hackett, Enns, & Zetzer, 1992). In several studies, women showed some reluctance to see radical feminist therapists, and clients tended to prefer more moderate feminist therapists over traditional or nonsexist therapists, even those women with traditional gender role values.

As feminist therapy continued to expand, its clients became more diversified; the desire to include diverse clients became a goal for many feminist therapists (Comas-Díaz & Greene, 1994). This approach has advantages for a variety of ethnic minority clients (Mays & Comas-Díaz, 1988). The sensitivity to environmental factors and the recognition of the impact of social reality on psychological functioning make feminist therapy better suited to ethnic minority clients than therapies that conceptualize problems as personal and internal. Feminist therapy offers African American (Greene, 1994), Native American (LaFromboise, Berman, & Sohi, 1994), Asian American (Bradshaw, 1994), and Hispanic American (Vasquez, 1994) women a method to help them feel empowered, to give them skills to solve their problems, and to furnish opportunities to change society. By allowing these clients to center on family and community, feminist therapy can be useful to clients who are ethnic minorities.

The emphasis on the social environment as a factor in psychological problems makes feminist therapy "one of few models of behavior change that intentionally perceives the variability of sexual orientations in human beings as a simple fact, rather than a matter for concern and intervention" (Brown, 1988, p. 206). Thus, feminist therapy is an obvious choice for helping lesbians and gay men. Due to the homophobia they have internalized from society, gaining acceptance of their sexual orientation is a problem for many lesbians and gays, and dealing with homophobia can also create adjustment problems that are unique to lesbians and gay men. Feminist therapy offers these clients acceptance of their sexual orientation so that they may proceed to deal with problems related to sexual orientation as well as other personal concerns.

Although men may seem to be unlikely clients for feminist therapy, male clients can also benefit from this approach (Ganley, 1988). Feminist therapy may be the best approach for dealing with the problems of the masculine gender role. Traditional therapy holds a male model of mental health that views women as deficient for their femininity and that attempts to reconcile men with their role as breadwinners and competitors. Many feminist therapists adhere to a different model of mental health—an androgynous model. This view holds that both masculine and feminine characteristics are beneficial to mental health and that individuals who can combine these characteristics have many advantages.

A mixture of instrumental and expressive characteristics is related to positive mental health. In a study of masculine and feminine characteristics, the addition of expressiveness to instrumentality for men significantly added to the prediction of mental health (Sharpe, Heppner, & Dixon, 1995). That is, men who showed the expressiveness traditionally associated with femininity exhibited greater well-being than men who showed only the instrumentality traditionally associated with masculinity. This combination is also related to mental health in women (Hunt, 1993). The combination, however, is important. Extremes of instrumentality or expressiveness are negatively related to psychological well-being (Helgeson, 1994; Saragovi, Koestner, Di Dio, & Aubé, 1997). Therefore, the combination of characteristics and behaviors that feminist therapists encourage in women and men is related to psychological well-being and mental health.

By taking this approach with male clients, feminist therapists attempt to develop relationship skills, appropriate emotionality, empathy, and communication skills—skills that men often lack due to their masculine socialization. Feminist therapy with men also works toward altering views of gender roles and seeks to change men's attitudes concerning what is appropriate for both women and men. By examining and questioning traditional gender roles, feminist therapy with men upholds the principle that the personal is political, one of the basic principles of feminist therapy.

Feminist therapy with men differs from its practice with women. For one, traditional gender roles may make the attainment of an egalitarian relationship between therapist and client more difficult with male clients and female therapists. The attempts to give clients power in the therapeutic relationship may make men willing to take the dominant position, which is consistent with their traditional gender role but not with the goals of feminist therapy.

Feminist therapists should be models for the behavior their clients need to develop, but this aspect of feminist therapy is difficult when men are the clients. Men need to develop communication, nurturing, and nonviolent problem-solving skills (Ganley, 1988), but because these skills are stereotypically associated with women, observing women with these skills only reinforces the gender-traditional view. The obvious answer is for male therapists to practice feminist therapy and serve as role models for their male clients. Most feminist therapists, however, believe that the practice of feminist therapy is restricted to women. When male therapists adopt the principles of feminist therapy, they are labeled "profeminist." With either male or female therapists, men as clients in feminist therapy can find both appropriate modeling and support through participation in group therapy.

Therefore, feminist therapy is appropriate for a wide range of people. From its beginnings as a radical therapy for women discontent with traditional therapy (both as therapists and as clients), feminist therapy has broadened its scope and clientele. Studies have shown that women with both traditional and feminist beliefs can profit from feminist therapy and that feminists are likely to have problems with traditional therapy. Its emphasis on the political and social aspects of mental health makes feminist therapy well suited for people from other gender and ethic minority groups. In addition, men can benefit from feminist therapy by learning to develop communication and nurturing skills not associated with the masculine gender role. By adopting more androgynous behavior, both men and women can overcome gender role stereotyping and can gain greater flexibility in their lives.

Therapy with Men

Feminist therapy may be appropriate for men, but men rarely seek this type of therapy. Indeed, men are reluctant to seek even traditional types of psychotherapy. In seeking therapy, women outnumber men by a margin of two to one (Good, Dell, & Mintz, 1989). Men often encounter difficulties in counseling (Scher, 1981). Although therapy tends to uphold traditional gender roles, the format of therapy emphasizes behaviors associated with the feminine rather than the masculine role, and both clients and counselors experience difficulties in the counseling process due to male clients' stereotypically masculine behavior.

Male gender role expectations put men in situations of conflict and strain because those expectations hold that men should strive for power, control, and achievement (O'Neil, 1981; Pleck, 1981a, b). Men can become obsessed with competition and success, which requires dedication to these goals. In addition, these strivings require that men reject all aspects of femininity, resulting in restricted emotionality as well as distrust and fear of women. These attitudes create problems for men in forming intimate relationships and in fulfilling their full potential as humans and, in addition, present special problems for therapists in counseling men.

Investigations into the relationship between masculine gender role and attitudes toward seeking psychological counseling have revealed that stereotypical masculine beliefs negatively relate to willingness to seek help (Good, Dell, & Mintz, 1989). Furthermore, the emphasis on striving for success and restriction of emotional expression relate to depression, putting these men in greater need of help but with more reluctance to seek help (Good & Wood, 1995). Masculine socialization can keep men away from therapy (Robertson & Fitzgerald, 1992). Men who show emotion, express their vulnerability, and seek help from others fail to fit the masculine gender role, and all of these elements are necessary for psychotherapy. John Robertson and Louise Fitzgerald wrote, "Many approaches to personal counseling require that clients bring a sense of self-awareness to the counseling room; yet men appear to be socialized away from self-awareness and encouraged to control (or hide) their feelings" (1992, p. 240). The masculine gender role demands that men hide their vulnerabilities, whereas counseling calls for disclosing them. Counseling urges clients to share their problems with other persons, and men have been socialized to hide their problems and approach problem solving in an intellectual rather than an emotional way.

Thus, counseling is a process that men might avoid. Studies have shown a negative relationship between traditional masculine attitudes and the willingness to seek psychological counseling (Good et al., 1989; Robertson & Fitzgerald, 1992). Men who rigidly held to stereotypical masculinity were less willing to seek counseling that involved emotional expression than less traditional men (Wisch, Mahalik, Hayes, & Nutt, 1995). In addition, men who adhere to stereotypical masculinity found counseling more appealing when the process was presented in cognitive, problem-solving terms rather than as avenues of emotional expression.

One critic (Kipnis, 1991) maintained that some of men's reluctance to seek therapy comes from bias against men by mental health care professionals. This criticism contends that psychology has responded to women's needs by addressing women's problems, but no such changes have taken place for men. Examples of this bias included men who, along with their wives, had sought therapy and who had felt that the female therapists had aligned themselves with the wives but had failed to see the men's points of view. These comments are consistent with the contention that a female communication style has become the language of psychotherapy, and this situation may alienate some men (Tavris, 1992). Table 16.7 presents some of the barriers that can deter men from seeking and succeeding in counseling.

Psychological services can be made more approachable for men through changing the description of those services (Robertson & Fitzgerald, 1992). When traditionally oriented men in this study read a brochure describing psychological service offerings in terms of classes, workshops, seminars, and videotapes, they rated these services as more attractive than when the services were presented as belonging to a college counseling center. This study demonstrated that masculine values may be barriers to seeking counseling and that traditional men may be more willing to seek counseling services that are presented in a way that is compatible with their masculine values.

Counseling offers advantages for men: "Men need counseling because many of them are unhappy, dissatisfied with their lives, and damaged by their roles" (Scher, 1981, p. 199). Men need help in relinquishing some of the toxic elements of the masculine role so that they can learn to understand the value of being in touch with their emotions, ask for assistance when they need it, and encourage freedom from constraining gender roles in themselves and in others.

Gender Aware Therapy

Can therapy meet the needs of both women and men while not discriminating against either? Gender aware therapy (GAT) aims to integrate concepts of male and female gender development with the revised attitudes toward psychotherapy proposed by feminist therapists (Good, Gilbert, & Scher, 1990). This therapy approach has both similarities to and differences from nonsexist and feminist therapies. First, it acknowledges that society's conception of mental health is changing to a more androgynous standard in which conforming to traditional standards is no longer a desirable goal for either gender.

The originators of GAT (Good et al., 1990) claimed that five principles should be part of all types of therapy. Gender aware therapy has its foundation in feminist therapy, and its

TABLE 16.7 Barriers to Counseling Men

Help seeking is discouraged by elements of the masculine gender role:

- Men should not require help.
- Men should deny and suppress their emotion.
- Men should not express their vulnerability.

Therapy often takes a talk-based rather than action-based or intellectual approach to problem solution.

Emotional sharing is difficult for many men.

Men may believe that counselors are biased against men's needs.

Psychology has responded by addressing women's, not men's, needs.

Presentation of psychological services may not be in a format that does not appeal to men.

five principles distinguish it from feminist therapy by extending and enlarging that approach. The first of these principles urges therapists to consider gender an integral aspect of counseling and mental health. Gender aware therapy "incorporates an understanding of gender effects and sexism in its therapeutic strategies and goals" (Good et al., p. 377). Nonsexist therapy strives for equal treatment of men and women by ignoring gender. However, the differences in women's and men's lives make ignoring gender unrealistic, and many issues raised in therapy relate to gender and gender roles.

The second principle of gender aware therapy echoes "the personal is political" basis of feminist therapy in holding that consideration of the societal context of problems is essential. The third principle also incorporates the political activism of feminist therapy by urging therapists to question traditional gender roles, both for themselves and for their clients. The fourth principle urges gender aware therapists to form collaborative relationships with their clients, and the fifth principle directs therapists to respect their clients' freedom to choose. Table 16.8 presents these five points.

This freedom to choose includes the choice to adopt or reject traditional gender roles. Both traditional and nontraditional gender roles can be rigid and confining, and GAT urges therapists to allow their clients to find a combination that will enhance clients' full development. Gender aware therapy "eschews notions of political correctness" (Good et al., p. 377), urging clients to explore, find, and choose what is right for them. "In summary, GAT supports the notion that particular behaviors, preferences, and attributes need not be categorized as falling into the domain of traditional or nontraditional, male or female, gender roles. Rather, what GAT advocates is simply choice, despite gender conceptions or political correctness" (p. 377).

Research with counselors in training (Brems & Schlottmann, 1988) indicated that the aims of gender aware therapy may be feasible. By studying graduate students in counseling and clinical psychology (who would soon be therapists), these researchers found that gender-bound definitions of mental health have decreased; gender role stereotyping was almost entirely absent in the counselors in training. These findings present an optimistic picture that therapists are now being trained who are less bound by gender stereotypes, for both themselves and their clients. Such therapists are necessary for gender aware therapy.

Therefore, gender aware therapy is an extension of feminist therapy, which attempts to incorporate the awareness of gender and its far-reaching implications for people's lives and

TABLE 16.8 Five Principles of Gender Aware Therapy

1. Regard the conception of gender as an integral aspect of counseling and mental health
2. Consider problems within their societal context
3. Actively seek to change gender injustice experienced by women and men
4. Emphasize development of collaborative therapeutic relationships
5. Respect clients' freedom to choose

SOURCE: Based on Gender aware therapy: A synthesis of feminist therapy and knowledge about gender, 1990, (p. 377) by G. E. Good, L. A. Gilbert, & M. Scher, *Journal of Counseling & Development, 68.*

yet emphasize individual needs. Many therapists have acknowledged that gender-fair counseling and therapy are imperative, and this approach may fulfill those needs.

Sexual Exploitation in Therapy

As this chapter's headline story (Beck et al., 1992) detailed, the preponderance of women as clients and men as therapists poses a situation in which gender is nearly always either an overt or covert issue in the therapy process. The APA Task Force on Sex Bias and Sex-Role Stereotyping in Psychotherapeutic Practice (Brodsky & Holroyd, 1975) identified the treatment of clients as sex objects as a gender-related problem. Erotic or sexual behavior with clients is included in this category. As the headline story for this chapter suggested, sex between therapist and client is not unusual. Beginning with the founding fathers of psychoanalytic therapy and continuing today, clients are sexually exploited by the therapists to whom they come for help.

Most female clients consider sexual behavior on the part of therapists to be exploitation, but since professionals have begun to recognize this as a problem, they have found that not all of their colleagues consider erotic contact and sexual relationships with their clients completely unacceptable. During the 1970s, a survey of licensed psychologists in clinical practice (Holroyd & Brodsky, 1977) disclosed attitudes toward sexual and nonsexual physical contact with clients. Nonsexual physical contact was acceptable under some circumstances to 27% of the therapists, but a large majority of the therapists reported that erotic contact between clients and therapists would *not* be beneficial to clients. Significantly more female than male therapists (88% versus 70%) believed that such contact would not be a beneficial component of therapy.

A significant gender difference also appeared in the percentage of therapists who reported any type of sexual contact with clients—10.9% of male and 1.9% of female therapists. When considering only those therapists who admitted having intercourse with past or present clients, the survey found that 8.1% of the male and 1% of the female therapists acknowledged this behavior. Of those therapists who admitted at least one sexual relationship with a patient, 80% acknowledged more than one such relationship. This figure suggests that some therapists have formed a pattern of habitual sexual exploitation of their patients. Indeed, a small minority of therapists reported that they believed sexual contact between therapist and client to be beneficial to the client.

Subsequent research has investigated the effects of sexual intimacy between therapists and clients, detailing the factors that make such contact more likely on the part of professionals and the ways in which clients are harmed by sexual contact with their counselors (Pope, 1988). Among the factors that contribute to therapists' willingness to enter into sexual relationships with their clients are their lack of preparation for sexual attraction to clients and their denial of the harm that such relationships can exert.

The possibility of sexual attraction on the part of clients toward therapists and for therapists toward clients underlies the early theories on which psychoanalytic treatment and its variations are based, but this knowledge did not deter several prominent early psychotherapists from forming sexual relationships with their patients. Other theoretical orientations do not have reason to include this possibility, so it is not included in the training process.

GENDERED VOICES

Of Course I've Felt Attracted to My Clients

Both a counseling intern and a counselor with 30 years of experience told me, "Of course I've felt attracted to some of my clients. I think it's almost inevitable." Both reported that the attraction made them very aware of the nature of the counseling relationship and how inappropriate these feelings were. Both also became very conscious about behaving so as to conceal signs of their attraction, because it was considered professionally unacceptable.

"Part of our training includes the ethical unacceptability of any type of personal relationship with clients, especially any sexual relationship. It's completely unacceptable," the counseling intern said. "So feeling attracted to a client raised flags and made me aware that I needed to be very careful about what I did. I didn't want to convey my feelings to my client, and I didn't want to let my feelings affect my counseling. It's a difficult situation and an inevitable conflict, I think."

The veteran counselor agreed. "It's practically inevitable, although I have been sexually attracted to very few of my clients. When I felt attracted, those feelings made counseling more difficult. I tried to conceal how I felt, which is dishonest, while remaining honest in all other respects. And I tried very hard to do a good job in counseling the client. It made the counseling relationship more difficult."

"Nothing in our training taught me how to deal with these feelings," the intern said. "A great deal was oriented toward the ethics of counseling but not how to handle my feelings or situations in which clients express some attraction for me. It was all 'Don't do that,' but nothing about what to do. I wouldn't feel comfortable talking to my supervisor about my feelings because of the ethical prohibition. I know it's unreasonable to imagine that counselors won't feel attracted to clients, but it's so forbidden that I feel I shouldn't have or admit to the attraction. I know that I will think about how to avoid letting any client know about my attraction, but teaching me how to deal with such feelings and what to do—no, that was lacking in my training."

The experienced counselor said that his training included how to deal with clients' attraction to him but not his toward clients: "The whole issue of sexual exploitation of clients hadn't been publicized or addressed in counselor training, so those issues were not part of my training."

The failure to acknowledge this possibility and to prepare counselors with strategies to avoid sexual contact produces a gap in the training of counselors, leaving them unprepared to deal with the possibility that they may develop sexual feelings for their clients (Pope, 1988). Therapists receive training concerning ethics and the unacceptability of sexual contact with their clients, but most training programs devote very little time to discussions about what to do when therapists feel sexually attracted to clients, and a large majority of therapists experience such attraction. Without preparation, therapists are left with no strategies for dealing with the feelings that many of them develop for their clients.

Denial of the existence of therapist–client sex has been a substantial problem. Initially, journals were reluctant to publish articles, and conventions were unwilling to feature presentations on the topic (Pope, 1988). Widespread denial of the existence of this problem prevents therapists from having colleagues to consult when they feel sexually attracted to clients and brings forth a censorious attitude (but possibly no constructive action) from colleagues when they discover that counselors have exploited clients. In addition, the discovery of a sexual relationship typically leads to the dissolution of the therapy relationship, and thus few therapists become aware of the lasting harm that their clients experience as a result of the sexual relationship.

A variety of negative effects befall clients who have participated in sexual relationships with their therapists (Pope, 1988). Clients may not exhibit any immediate negative effects of sexual intimacy with their therapists, but evidence indicates that at least 90% will eventually experience negative effects. The effects are stronger when the relationship occurs concurrently with therapy, but clients who begin relationships with their therapists after the termination of therapy are still at risk.

The therapist–client relationship is one of trust and intimacy, but when sexual intimacy becomes part of the relationship, a betrayal of clients' trust has occurred. Thus, impaired ability to trust is a potential lifelong problem (Pope, 1988). This situation often leaves clients feeling ambivalent; they experience rage and a longing to escape combined with a fear of separation from the therapist. Sexually exploited clients may also feel guilt, isolation, emptiness, and sexual confusion. Some evidence also exists that sexually exploited clients are at heightened risk for emotional instability and suicide. Therefore, clients often experience a variety of serious problems after sexual involvement with their therapists.

The growing awareness of the sexual exploitation of clients by therapists has produced changes in the codes of ethics for all of the professions that provide mental health care (Vasquez & Kitchener, 1988). The ethical codes that govern psychiatrists, psychologists, social workers, and marriage and family therapists all specifically prohibit sexual activity between therapists and clients. In an attempt to inform the public, the Committee on Women in Psychology (1989) has published a brochure with information about the harmful effects of client–therapist sexual relationships and about client's rights to refuse such overtures.

Studies questioning psychologists, psychiatrists, and social workers about their sexual intimacies with clients found similar rates of sexual exploitation of clients (Pope, 1988). Studies completed during the 1970s indicated that over 10% of male therapists and between 2 and 3% of female therapists reported sexual intimacy with their clients. Later studies have shown lower rates of sexual exploitation of clients. These decreases suggest that the increased attention to this problem may be having positive effects, but an alternative possibility is that the publicity has sensitized therapists, who are no longer honest when surveyed about such relationships (Beck et al., 1992). In a national survey of psychiatrists, 65% reported that they had treated patients who had previously been sexually involved with their therapists (Gartrell, Herman, Olarte, Feldstein, & Localio, 1987). This figure suggests that a great majority of cases of sexual exploitation by therapists go unreported, though the patients continue to experience problems. Sexual exploitation of clients remains the most common of reported ethical violations by therapists, accounting for half of the complaints to state licensing boards (Marecek & Hare-Mustin, 1991).

The Self-Help Movement

A growing lack of confidence in psychotherapy, mounting awareness of sexual exploitation of clients, and increased cost have led to reluctance to seek therapy on the part of thousands of people with personal problems. A vast (and increasing) number of such people have dealt with a variety of problems without the assistance of mental health care professionals. These people have joined self-help groups, and the self-help movement constitutes a growing force in people's attempts to deal with personal problems. These people meet to share similar problems, and in the process, they receive emotional support as well as information that can assist in helping them cope with their problems.

Rather than consisting of therapists who direct the therapy and clients who take direction, self-help groups typically do not involve professional therapists and may have no designated leaders (Jacobs & Goodman, 1989). Trained professionals may not be necessary for therapeutic effects to occur (Christensen & Jacobson, 1994). The philosophy of the self-help approach is that people with similar problems can offer each other social support and information, which can be helpful and beneficial. "Member-governed self-help groups vary widely from tiny, freestanding gatherings to large, nationally networked assemblies and from formats that are laissez-faire to those that are thoroughly programmed by members or audiotape" (Jacobs & Goodman, 1989, p. 537). Although the concerns of people in these groups vary, the underlying philosophies are similar.

Self-help groups began to proliferate during the 1980s. The 1987 Surgeon General's Workshop on Self-Help and Public Health brought the benefits of self-help groups to the attention of an increased number of health care providers (Hedrick, 1995). In 1992, the number of self-help groups had grown to more than 500,000, and over 7 million people were involved, a number that equaled or exceeded those receiving professional therapy. Self-help groups exist in growing numbers in all industrialized countries and in most other countries in the world (Katz, 1993). The variety of problems around which the self-help groups form is vast, and Table 16.9 presents examples of these problems.

One of the reasons for the rapid growth in the self-help movement "lies in our stars—namely Oprah, Geraldo, Phil, and Ann Landers; also *New Woman, Cosmopolitan,* and other magazines; plus prime-time TV dramas, which refer, with increasing frequency, to self-help groups" (Baxter, 1993, p. 74). People who have experienced personal problems and who have found help from these groups have presented their stories on television talk shows; magazines have featured their stories; and TV dramatizations have shown the positive effects of self-help.

Television is not the only electronic medium involved in the growing self-help movement: Online self-help groups are proliferating (Spinney, 1995; Weinberg, Uken, Schmale, & Adamek, 1995). Internet sites are available for a number of problems, allowing people without easy access to groups in their hometowns to meet in cyberspace. Preliminary evidence (Weinberg et al., 1995) indicates that participants in online self-help groups receive some of the same benefits that other participants obtain.

The positive publicity about self-help has come at a time when traditional sources of help have disappeared or when these sources have become the targets of growing mistrust (Baxter, 1993; Jacobs & Goodman, 1989). Smaller families and increasing mobility have reduced the availability of social support to family members. In addition, families are often the *source* of problems for which people seek help. Many people have come to mistrust psychotherapy, partly as a result of the growing lack of confidence in public institutions and partly due to the negative publicity regarding sexual exploitation of clients.

The success of self-help groups is due in part to the comfort that people feel from being with others whose experience is similar (Jacobs & Goodman, 1989). Because individuals

TABLE 16.9 Examples of Self-Help Groups and Problems Served

Problem	Group	Problem	Group
Alcoholism	Alcoholics Anonymous	Alcoholic parent	Ala-Teen
Breast cancer survivors	Bosom Buddies	Overeating	Overeaters Anonymous
Gambling	Gamblers Anonymous	Divorced parents	Parents without Partners
Substance abuse	Narcotics Anonymous	Heart attack survivors	Mended Hearts
Parental bereavement	Compassionate Friends	Down syndrome	Parents of Children with Down Syndrome
Love addiction	Women Who Love Too Much		

Other Problems Served by Groups	
Cancer survivors	Incest survivors
Persons with AIDS	Adult children of alcoholics
Partners of persons with AIDS	Rape victims
Former dieters	Parents of children with cancer
Parents of children with diabetes	Parents of children with attention deficit hyperactive disorder
Heart transplant patients	Persons with multiple sclerosis
Anorexics	Persons with arthritis
Parents and families of anorexics	Medical and psychological problems associated with gays
People with disfigurements, including specific types such as burn victims, neurofibromatosis	Impotence
Chronic money management problems	Parents of children with schizophrenia
Psychological problems associated with retirement	Sexual addiction
Alopecia (radical hair loss)	Narcolepsy (sleep disorder)
Couples with fertility problems	Codependency
Agoraphobia	
Caretaker of Alzheimer's patients	

in these groups are similar, empathy is facilitated. People in self-help groups find that discussing their problems is easier because the other members of the group share important elements of their experience.

The financial advantages of self-help groups are another factor in the growth of this approach. These groups may charge participants a minimal fee, though many of them charge nothing. With the growing emphasis on cost containment, health care professionals have begun to promote cooperation between medicine and self-help groups (Baxter, 1993).

Free therapy is certainly cost-effective, but very little research has compared the effectiveness of self-help to traditional therapy (Christensen & Jacobson, 1994). Psychologists have biases against self-help groups, which may prevent them from conducting research on the effectiveness of these groups. Such research would be difficult, as members of self-help groups may concurrently be involved in individual therapy. This concurrent participation, combined with the lack of control over who participates in what type and in how many groups, makes research in this area difficult. Some evidence exists for the effectiveness for self-help groups, and with the cost difference, comparable effectiveness is certainly an important research question.

Self-help groups share the common philosophy of the power of social support from people with similar problems to heal. The variety of problems having corresponding support groups now number in the hundreds. One variety of support group, the consciousness raising group, specifically addresses problems related to gender roles.

Support Groups

People who have friends and family on whom they can depend for emotional and material help are healthier and better adjusted than people who are more socially isolated. That is, social support is a factor in both mental and physical health (Gartner, Gartner, & Ouellette Kobasa, 1988). Self-help groups allow people to form relationships with others with similar problems and to receive and give support. This format for increasing social support may be effective in helping people deal with problems.

The prototype for the self-help movement is Alcoholics Anonymous (AA). Founded in 1935 by two alcoholics who had stopped drinking, AA proclaimed that people with drinking problems could stay sober through the social support of others with similar problems (Robinson, 1979). The format is a meeting in which people acknowledge their alcoholism and their powerlessness over alcohol. To change their behavior, AA members seek the assistance of "a higher power" and attempt to abstain from drinking for a lifetime, one day at a time. The AA philosophy holds that alcoholics never recover, but instead spend their lives in recovery. AA meetings and the support of other recovering alcoholics are part of this process. This approach to dealing with problem drinking has been enormously influential and is included in most treatment programs for problem drinking, especially in the United States (Ogborne, 1996).

The format for AA has prompted the formation of other support groups for different problems. For example, addictions and other compulsive disorders were the concerns of early support groups such as Narcotics Anonymous, Gamblers Anonymous, and Overeaters Anonymous, but support groups now exist for a wider variety of problems. "There are groups for almost every serious medical problem and almost every presenting problem that clinicians confront, plus groups for dozens of conditions virtually unserved by therapists" (Jacobs & Goodman, 1989, p. 537). In addition, support groups have formed for problems in dealing with life transitions, such as menopause, and for people who care for others with problems, such as parents of children with mental disorders and caregivers for those with Alzheimer's disease.

Many support groups perform a valuable function for participants, but other groups have been the focus of a great deal of criticism, much of which has centered on groups formed around the concept of codependency. This concept originated with treatment involving the families of alcoholics, and it describes a pattern of pathological dependency among family members that combines with other behaviors that allow the alcoholic to continue with problem drinking. This notion of codependency then spread to people other than families with alcoholic members and now denotes "any person who is either a product of or a participant in a dysfunctional relationship involving abuse of any kind" (Lyons &

Greenberg, 1991, p. 436). This definition includes a great many people, the majority of whom are women concerned about their relationships with men.

The term *codependency* is recent, but the concept is not new—Karen Horney (1942) proposed the existence of morbid dependency in terms that were very similar to current descriptions of codependency. A contemporary study demonstrated that women with alcoholic fathers were more willing to assist exploitive experimenters significantly longer than nurturant experimenters, but women without alcoholic fathers showed the opposite pattern (Lyons & Greenberg, 1991). These results confirmed the notion of codependency, but results from other research (Loring & Cowan, 1997) suggested that codependency may be a situational rather than a personal characteristic. Codependency forms around situations of unequal power. The partner with less power may be self-sacrificing and deferential in response to relationship situations.

Self-sacrifice and deference are stereotypically feminine behaviors, and the concept of codependency labels them as pathological. This label has been the center of controversy and some argue that it has no place in mental health treatment. In one study, codependency showed a stronger relationship to the negative aspects of femininity (such as subservience, dependency, and complaining) than with having alcoholic fathers (Roehling, Koelbel, & Rutgers, 1994). Thus, codependency is a way to "pathologize" femininity, blaming women for the problems within families.

The central focus and possible origin for the criticism of support groups for codependency has been Robin Norwood's (1985) bestselling book, *Women Who Love Too Much.* In this book Norwood described women's "addiction" to relationships and borrowed the addiction framework from Alcoholics Anonymous as a model for providing advice to these women. Support groups that have formed for these "women who love too much" are similar to AA meetings, complete with a reliance on assistance from a "higher power" and an acceptance that complete recovery is not possible but the process of recovering lasts a lifetime.

Although Norwood's book promised to offer solutions for women's relationship difficulties, one critic (Tavris, 1989, p. 220) maintained that it delivered less than promised, providing only "friendly sermons that emphasize the healing power of love" rather than giving specific advice on how to produce changes. Accepting the blame for all negative aspects of one's life creates helplessness, and taking the blame for the behavior of others puts the burden of change on the woman rather than others (who may be behaving badly). This view leaves the women in these groups passively accepting rather than actively challenging the men with whom they have bad relationships. The assumptions of this approach are very similar to the gender bias in traditional psychotherapies—the notion that change is up to the individual and that women are to blame for the negative aspects of their lives. Critics believe that this form of support group repeats some of the most undesirable elements of traditional therapy for women.

Support groups offer emotional support and information to help people cope with a wide variety of problems. Some support groups, especially the ones for people with medical problems and for those who care for family members with medical problems, offer ways for people to help themselves without relying on professional assistance. Other support groups, especially the ones that promote the belief that codependency is the source of women's relationship problems, may harm their members by urging them to be passive and to accept the blame for others' behavior.

Consciousness Raising Groups

Consciousness raising groups originated as a way for women to share their unique experiences, explore the similarities of their lives, and increase interaction with other women (Morgan, 1970). These groups began to form in the mid-1960s as part of the women's movement, and as part of this movement, the aims were political as well as personal. The early consciousness raising groups consisted "primarily of radical feminists, and group discussions focused on political analyses and the development of feminist ideology" (Kravetz, 1980, p. 268).

An essential part of that ideology was the oppression of women as a class (Travis, 1988b). To recognize that their problems come from the shared experiences of being part of a group, women must accept that they are part of a class, and many women find this acceptance difficult. Humans tend to see themselves as unique and exceptions to the rule, so women often find it difficult to acknowledge that they have been the targets of discrimination or exploitation. Instead, they see their problems as personal instead of social. Consciousness raising aims to lead women to see themselves as members in the class of women and to see their similarities to other women's situations and problems.

The early emphasis on political ideology shifted to personal development, but increasing political activity was not among the goals for most women who joined consciousness raising groups (Kravetz, 1978). Instead, the most important goals were to share thoughts and feeling about being women, to learn about other women's experiences, to increase self-awareness, to get emotional support, and to examine the traditional gender role for women. Participants rated the groups as very successful in helping them to attain these goals, and the majority of participants encouraged other women to join groups.

The personal changes experienced by women during consciousness raising groups were likely to have been therapeutic, leading to these groups becoming substitutes for or

GENDERED VOICES

What Are These Groups Doing to You?

During one lecture on the tendency for bystanders to stand by rather than assist in emergency situations, I asked my class, "What would you do if someone fell out of his or her chair, unconscious? Would you wait for someone else to help, or would you feel comfortable in giving assistance, even to someone whom you might not know all that well?"

Most of my students expressed the indecision that is typical of such a question. After thinking for a moment, one middle-aged woman said, "I'm so codependent that I would probably help the person." I was shocked. I knew that she had been part of a self-help group for her drinking problems and possibly other groups as well, but I was stunned at her belief that rendering help to an unconscious person would be considered codependent. I told her, "Helping in a medical emergency isn't a sign of codependency. In my opinion, it's a sign of being a decent human. What are these groups doing to you?"

adjuncts to therapy (Enns, 1992). Although consciousness raising groups may have therapeutic effects, these groups differ from group therapy sessions in several ways (Kravetz, 1980). First, these groups seek to help women understand that their problems are not only personal but also social, whereas psychotherapy places the source of problems and potential for change within each individual. Second, the groups are explicitly political, whereas therapy is exclusively personal. Third, consciousness raising groups have no designated leaders and emphasize the equality of their members, whereas traditional therapists are the experts and clients seek their advice and direction. Fourth, consciousness raising groups take place in homes, churches, libraries, schools, and community centers rather than in therapists' offices or mental health centers.

The benefits of consciousness raising coupled with its differences from traditional therapy have highlighted the need for a closer examination of therapy. Indeed, consciousness raising groups formed the basis for feminist therapy, which adhered to two tenants of these groups—the political orientation and the concept of egalitarian relationships between therapists and clients.

The men's movement has also devised group meetings for men to share their concerns. In the 1970s, men's groups were similar to early women's consciousness raising groups, with the purpose of making members more sensitive to the politics and the disadvantages of their gender role. Both concentrated on the social inequities women had experienced and how rigid gender roles had harmed men as well as women. Men sought to understand how they had participated in and had been harmed by society's mandates for their behavior.

The men who adopted feminist goals sought to develop the qualities that their male gender role had prohibited, including sensitivity and the appropriate display of a range of emotions. In the 1980s the goals of the men's movement began to diverge from those of the women's movement (Faludi, 1991). Men's oppression became the theme of many men's groups during that decade. These groups concentrated on the gender inequity of divorce and custody laws as well as the emphasis on men's breadwinner role and the pressures on men to earn money and attain success. Similar to the political focus of women's consciousness raising groups, these men's groups tend to strive for political and legal changes to allow men more rights in divorce and custody cases. In contrast to the earlier profeminist men's groups, this variation of men's groups is often antifeminist, proclaiming that society has oppressed men and benefited women.

The gay male liberation movement is one branch of the men's movement that sought to gain political power and change laws in ways similar to the goals of the women's movement (Messner, 1997). These groups sought to bring social and legal acceptance for gay men. Concentrating on gay sexuality has been a frequent but not always successful strategy, and gay male liberation has not challenged fundamental conceptualizations of gender roles. Instead, the movement has glorified the characteristics associated with masculinity, striving to promote a positive image of gay men.

Men's groups have also originated a male counterpart to codependency—"men who give too much" (Kipnis, 1991). In this view, men have experienced economic exploitation in their relationships with women. Men feel that they must take care of women and that they are loved for this care rather than for themselves. This situation results in strivings for career, success, and money rather than attention to personal or relationship needs. The belief that they are needed for what they can provide rather than for who they are can lead men to give too much.

Another variety of men's consciousness raising groups followed the publication of Robert Bly's (1990) *Iron John.* This book remained on the *New York Times* bestseller list for weeks and captured the imagination of thousands of men. These men sought out experiences that would allow them to understand masculinity and how they could attain it by banding together with other men. Termed *mythopoetic,* these groups have focused on the anthropological, mythic, and poetic images of men in order to guide participants to positive images of masculinity.

Proponents of this approach (Kipnis, 1991; Moore & Gillette, 1990) have contended that men need to discover alternative styles of masculinity, because the current masculine gender role is immature as well as destructive to both society and to individual men. The mature masculinity they seek is not exploitive, violent, or lacking in emotion. They do not attempt to integrate feminine characteristics; rather, they consider these positive characteristics undiscovered masculine attributes.

The Promise Keepers is a fundamentalist Christian men's group that emphasizes traditional masculinity and urges men to reclaim the positions of responsibility and power in their families—to keep their promises to wives and family. This emphasis on masculinized Christianity is not recent, and a similar version appeared in the early years of the 20th century (Messner, 1997). The goal of Promise Keepers is religious, bringing men to Christianity as well as orienting them toward family. Their meetings are more like giant revivals than consciousness raising groups, taking place in stadiums. The group also has clearly political goals that are consistent with a conservative agenda, including restoring men to breadwinner and head of the household status.

Men's groups have a greater diversity than women's consciousness raising groups, but fewer men's groups exist. Women's groups tend to be oriented toward sensitizing women to the political goals of feminism, but men's groups have a variety of possible goals. Some of these groups have political goals, such as groups organized around gay rights, divorce, or custody rights; others supplement therapy for substance abuse; still others explore social conceptions of masculinity and ways to bring about positive personal and social changes.

These varieties of men's groups all share the social support and gender role focus that characterize consciousness raising groups. Both types of groups have also indulged in fixing blame; men's groups have blamed women for their problems, and women's groups have blamed men for the oppression of women. Some consciousness raising groups have tried to move beyond recrimination toward discovering how to enact greater flexibility of gender roles, but the focus on gender-specific inequities and support from others for expressing feelings make blaming easy. As yet, men's consciousness raising groups have not produced a radical therapy of their own based on men's needs, as women's consciousness raising groups have produced feminist therapy.

Although men's groups have a shorter history and a greater diversity than women's groups, both types of consciousness raising groups share the goals of reexamining gender roles and seeking possible avenues of change, unlike traditional psychotherapy. The women and men who join such groups may do so out of a need to explore their gender roles or to bond with others. Many women and men prefer the self-help approach to formal therapy due to prior negative experiences with or beliefs about therapy.

Summary

Psychoanalysis was an early form of treatment for mental disorders. Based on Freud's conceptualization of personality development and functioning, this therapy uses talk to help people bring unconscious material to consciousness. The pessimism of this view of humanity, combined with the length and expense of psychoanalysis, prompted others to develop alternative talk-based therapies. The humanistic approach to therapy includes client-centered and Gestalt therapies. Humanistic therapy attempts to help people accept their emotions and feelings, allowing them to progress toward fulfilling their potential.

Cognitive therapy focuses on thoughts as the basis for behavior and assumes that thoughts underlie behavior. The theory holds that irrational and self-defeating thoughts form the basis for psychological problems and that changes in behavior follow from changes in cognition. Behavior modification centers on overt behavior rather than cognitive processes, applying the principles of operant conditioning to alter undesirable behaviors. Cognitive behavior therapy is a blending of cognitive therapy and behavior modification that attempts to alter cognitions and establish different behaviors.

Medical therapies are also used to treat behavior problems. Psychoactive drugs have increased in use since the 1950s, and psychiatrists and other physicians prescribe a variety of such drugs for depression, anxiety disorders, and schizophrenia. Women receive more prescriptions for psychoactive drugs than men. The use of electroconvulsive therapy decreased during the 1970s but began to increase during the 1980s. Once used for many mental disorders, electroconvulsive therapy is now used largely for depression that has not responded to antidepressant drugs.

Charges of gender bias extend to all therapies. Psychoanalysis holds men as the standard for psychological development, a standard that women can never attain. Humanistic, cognitive, behavior modification, and cognitive behavior modification therapies are not inherently gender biased, but each offers a format in which therapists can impose their values. In addition, all concentrate on the individual and ignore the social and political aspects of problems. Research indicates that therapists focus on departures from traditional gender roles in their recommendations for treatment, and that therapy can be used to enforce traditional gender roles.

Nonsexist therapy was created in an attempt to remove the gender bias in therapy, but many female therapists believed that therapy should go further and even propose and promote feminist goals. Feminist therapists hold that personal problems are reflections of wider social problems, and they strive to maintain equality in the relationship between client and therapist. From its initial position of political activism, feminist therapy has expanded. Its emphasis on social context also makes feminist therapy appropriate for gays and lesbians as well as people from a variety of ethnic backgrounds.

Men are also clients of feminist therapists, but rarely so. In general, men are less often the clients of therapists than are women. Men's reluctance to seek therapy relates to the masculine gender role, and men with more traditional values are less willing to seek help than men with less traditional values. Men might be unwilling to discuss emotions or acknowledge their vulnerability, but they might also feel discriminated against in therapy. Research indicates that therapy tends to encourage men to adopt the traditional breadwinner role.

Gender aware therapy is an attempt to extend feminist therapy to a form that is applicable to the full range of clients. By integrating an awareness of the impact of gender with encouragements to men and women to find what is right for them, gender aware therapy concentrates on individual needs rather than political correctness.

A growing number of complaints of gender bias in therapy has led the American Psychological Association to survey female psychologists about their experiences. The results of this survey revealed four areas of concern: (1) using sexist psychoanalytic concepts, (2) fostering traditional gender roles, (3) diminished expectations for female clients, and (4) treating women as sex objects, including having sex with clients.

Surveys of therapists have revealed that the sexual exploitation of clients by therapists occurs with between 9 and 12% of male therapists and between 2 and 3% of female therapists. The prevalence of this problem has led professional associations to include prohibitions against sexual relationships with clients, but this section nevertheless remains the most commonly violated of any of the ethical codes. A growing body of evidence indicates that intimate relationships with therapists do long-lasting harm to clients.

Rather than seeking therapy from professionals, a growing number of people now join self-help groups. These groups mushroomed during the 1980s, and now over 7 million people in the United States participate in at least one self-help group. These groups offer emotional support and access to information from others who share the same type of problem. The low cost of self-help groups is attractive, and some research indicates that professional leaders may not be necessary for therapeutic effects to occur.

Substantial evidence exists concerning the benefits of social support, and groups that enlarge people's support networks can be helpful. Alcoholics Anonymous has provided a model for many support groups. A common theme that has recently become the focus of support groups based on the AA model is codependency. Although initially applied to children of alcoholics, the concept has now expanded to apply to anyone with a dysfunctional family background who becomes involved in a dependent relationship. Critics have accused groups organized around women's codependency ("women who love too much") of blaming women for the behavior of others and of "pathologizing" traditional feminine behavior.

Consciousness raising groups are a third type of support group. These groups are oriented toward understanding how the personal is political—how each person's experience reflects social more than personal circumstances. Although the focus of women's consciousness raising groups is political rather than therapeutic, research has indicated that women experience positive psychological changes from these groups. Feminist therapy derived its philosophy from women's consciousness raising groups. Men's consciousness raising groups have a shorter history but greater variety. These groups may have a feminist orientation but tend to concentrate on the social inequities of the male gender role. Other men's groups have attempted to redefine masculinity. They have searched for alternative means to achieve personal growth by seeking ways to attain genuine masculinity.

Glossary

behavior modification the application of principles of conditioning to behavior, with the goal of changing undesirable behavior to more acceptable alternatives.

electroconvulsive therapy the application to the brain of electric current sufficient to induce a convulsion, which for unknown reasons produces therapeutic effects.

psychoanalysis Freud's talk-based treatment for psychological problems that consists of attempts to bring unconscious material to consciousness.

repression a defense mechanism used to push troubling material from the conscious into the unconscious.

Suggested Readings

Baxter, Susan. (1993, March/April). The last self-help article you'll ever need. *Psychology Today,* pp. 70–71, 74–77, 94. This popular article goes beyond criticism into satire but presents the range of activities included in the self-help movement along with the opinions of experts in the area.

Enns, Carolyn Zerbe. (1997). *Feminist theories and feminist psychotherapies: Origins, themes, and variations.* New York: Harrington Park Press. For those who are interested in the history and variations on feminist therapy, this book details the history and development of liberal, radical, and cultural feminism and the therapies that have developed these social movements.

Marecek, Jeanne; & Hare-Mustin, Rachel T. (1991). A short history of the future: Feminism and clinical psychology. *Psychology of Women Quarterly, 15,* 521–536. For those who think that Enns's book is too long, this brief history of feminist criticism in clinical psychology will be easier to read. Marecek

their reliance on traditional gender roles. Although they had deliberately tried to escape those traditional roles, they had not succeeded well enough to be comfortable.

Multiple Roles Have Become the Rule

The traditional assumptions hold that women will choose jobs to support themselves until they marry but make marriage their primary careers, and that men will devote themselves to careers while remaining marginally involved in family life. The stereotypical assumptions about women's and men's careers no longer hold for many women and men. Like Susan and Alex in the headline story, a growing number of women pursue careers on a full-time, uninterrupted basis. As a result, many men are like Alex in that they no longer provide the sole support for their families. Also like this couple, many men and women are struggling with developing a way for both to have careers and be involved in family life.

Couples like Susan and Alex face problems stemming from social expectations. Despite joining the work force of paid employment, women still are expected (and expect themselves) to occupy the role of wife and mother, including performing a majority of family work. Men have experienced few changes in their roles: "Although there have been some change in attitudes toward a wife's roles there has been little or no change in preferences regarding the husband's roles" (Tittle, 1986, p. 1165). The increasing number of employed women has led to increased acceptance of women in the work force in addition to their role in the family, but men's roles have not undergone comparable changes and remain centered on the role of breadwinner. This expectation leaves men who want to be involved in household work and child care without social support for their choice.

Both men and women may be dissatisfied with the inequity in household work but have not managed to find a strategy for a more equitable division. Gender stereotypes push men away from household and child care work. Even when couples expect to share equally in household chores and child care, they often do not (Deutsch, Lussier, & Servis, 1993). Both husbands and wives expected husbands to participate in the care of their first child, but husbands actually participated very little—to the disappointment of both husbands and wives. Wives' work load from outside employment was a significant factor in the amount of child care their husbands performed, as were husbands' gender role attitudes. Not surprisingly, men with nontraditional gender role attitudes were more likely to participate in child care than men with more traditional attitudes. These results show that gender roles are a powerful force in determining who performs which tasks. Even when partners plan an equitable sharing of household work, they have difficulty implementing these plans.

Some jobs are especially problematic. High-level managerial and professional careers require long hours and extraordinary dedication. The corporate, male-dominated careers that women began entering in somewhat larger numbers during the 1970s did not change to accommodate women's family duties. Men provided the model for these careers—men who had wives to provide a support system for their husbands' careers. These wives offered not only emotional support at home but also social support in the public functions of the organization (Lopata, 1993). That is, the "corporate wife" joins auxiliaries, organizes social functions, and boosts her husband's career. Women too need "wives" to provide this support, but few husbands are willing to be homemakers who offer support to successful

GENDERED VOICES

I've Had This Conversation Before

Melinda was a single mother with a 2-year-old son who told me about her experiences with the woman she had hired to care for her son. She considered herself and her son extremely fortunate; the nanny was a retired pediatric nurse, ideally qualified to be a nanny, and a wonderful person. Like many mothers with careers, Melinda felt less than enthusiastic at the thought of leaving her son in the care of someone else, and she felt fortunate not only to be able to afford a full-time, live-in nanny but also to have found a great person. Indeed, they had become like a family.

Melinda's business career was demanding but fulfilling. She had worked as a secretary during the time that she was married, but she had divorced and pursued a sales and management career and had become successful. Like other women with demanding and fulfilling careers, she worked long and sometimes irregular hours. Her son's nanny took care of him and the house, cooking dinner for herself and the child. She said that she could easily cook for Melinda as well; she would be glad to do so, but Melinda needed to be home to eat with them.

Melinda explained that she didn't always know when she would need to work late, and she couldn't be sure about being home in time for dinner every night: "But that doesn't matter. If I'm late, just leave my dinner. It's no big deal." The nanny said that it was a big deal; she didn't want to cook dinner and have her be late and have cold food. It just wasn't right. Melinda thought, "I've had this conversation before—when I was married. Only this time I'm being the 'husband,' and last time I was the wife. My husband said all the things I'm saying and gave all the excuses I'm giving, and I said the words I'm hearing from my nanny." Melinda got to see how flexible gender roles can be because she had played both the husband and the wife.

female breadwinners. Job demands in two-career families have been the precipitating source of conflict leading either to divorce or to women dropping off the track to success in high-prestige careers (Campbell, 1986).

Pepper Schwartz (1994) studied couples who had managed to construct marriages in which each shared equitably in family life, and she contrasted these couples with more traditional marriages. One factor that distinguished these two types of couples was level of employment: Few fast track careers appeared among the marriages in which the partners shared equally. Schwartz found that these couples "maintain their relationship goals by folding work into the relationship rather than vice versa" (1994, p. 181). For both men and women, the relationship was more important than their careers. By making their relationship and home life primary, these couples have expanded the role for men, making them into full participants in their wives' and children's lives.

What are the consequences of role expansion for men and women? Three models hypothesize different consequences of multiple roles (Rodin, 1991). The *job stress model* holds that multiple roles lead to role conflict because people who try to fulfill many roles experience conflict when the multiple roles produce stress in their lives. This model proposes that role restriction would be healthier. An alternative model, the *health benefits model,* holds that employment offers direct benefits to women, such as feelings of control and self-esteem, social support from colleagues in the workplace, and financial gain. This model proposes that multiple roles are beneficial. The *role expansion model* emphasizes the indirect benefits of employment for women, proposing that the satisfaction of fulfilling several roles and the protection of occupying several different roles will be beneficial. Table 17.1 shows these models and the position of each on the benefits of multiple roles.

Research tends to support the advantages of multiple roles, especially the benefits that come from employment. Furthermore, a meta-analysis of job-related stress revealed no gender differences in experienced or perceived stress on the job (Martocchio & O'Leary, 1989). Employment may cause stress, but its impact is similar for men and women and does not harm women more than men. Indeed, multiple roles *decreased* psychological distress in business women, suggesting that the benefits of paid employment outweigh the stresses of fulfilling multiple roles (Abrams & Jones, 1994). Considering the economic and power benefits, women gain many advantages from paid employment: "Being at work protects women from the full impact of marriage" (Archer & Lloyd, 1982, p. 194).

Multiple roles benefit the health and happiness of both women and men. An analysis of the contributions of employment, marriage, and parenthood on health showed that employment had the strongest effect and parenthood the weakest (Verbrugge, 1983). The multiple roles of marriage, employment, and children were more positive for women than men, with a positive relationship between multiple roles and happiness (Gove & Zeiss, 1987). Thus, multiple roles offer health and happiness benefits for women and men, and employment is an important contributor to the gains.

Men tend to receive greater benefits from marriage than women (Barnett & Baruch, 1987) partially because their roles are less stressful than women's balance of career, household work, and child care. For men, participation in child care and family chores increased fathers' feelings of competence as parents, but these men were likely to feel that family responsibilities interfered with their careers. The men in this study saw their jobs as their core role and believed that their families enriched that role and made it meaningful, but they also believed that their families should not interfere with this core role. Social expectations support this view, exempting men from family involvement to concentrate on their careers. These careers are less essential to family income when wives are employed.

Although multiple roles have become the rule and evidence exists of the benefits of multiple roles, these changes may not be what women and men want. In the headline story, Susan was annoyed with Alex for being emotionally remote, but she was also irritated when he was "needy." Alex wanted Susan to take responsibility for tasks that men traditionally perform, yet he was angry when the salesman in a car dealership dealt with Susan rather than him because buying a car is an activity that Alex considered to be part of the man's

TABLE 17.1 Three Models of Multiple Roles

Model	Results of Multiple Roles	Benefits
Job stress model	Role conflict	None
Health benefits model	Feelings of control, increased self-esteem, social support from coworkers, financial benefits	Direct
Role expansion model	Feelings of success at occupying several roles and of protection of these roles	Indirect

job. What do women and men want from each other, and will getting those things help to formulate a peace plan for the gender wars?

What Do Women Want? What Do Men Want?

Questioning what women want became popular after Sigmund Freud asked the question of Marie Bonaparte in the 1930s (Jones, 1955). His version of the question, as many others have been, was an exasperated plea prompted by a genuine lack of understanding of women's motivations (Feist & Feist, 1998). Other men have contended that women's goals are unreasonable rather than mysterious. Are women's motives so troublesome and difficult to understand? And how different are the things that women and men want?

Men's motives have not been subject to the same degree of scrutiny, but the changes in women's roles have forced men to examine their own lives to consider what they want. Much of this examination has centered on what men want from women and the difficulties that changes in women's lives have created for men. Do men want traditional women, "new" women, or some combination?

Have Women Become More Like Men?

"Why can't a woman be more like a man?" was the title of a song in the musical play *My Fair Lady* (Lerner & Loewe, 1956). Henry Higgins sang about how unreasonable women were in comparison to men, and as he longed for women and men to be more similar, he was voicing the stereotypical belief that women and men differ in many ways. Although this view was common at the time the musical appeared (and for some people even now), the differences may have been exaggerations. Gender differences may not have been as large as people believed, but these beliefs have been perpetuated by focusing on the differences and maintaining the dichotomy by conceptualizing an "opposite" sex.

Women have begun to take the opportunity to pursue some of the goals that were reserved for men. If large differences once existed between men and women, perhaps the intervening years have allowed Higgins's wish to come true. Have women become more like men? And if this wish has come true, what do men think of these changes?

Higgins's wishes centered around emotionality; he listed negative emotions for women and positive ones for men. Of course, Higgins himself deviated from this ideal quite a bit, but his beliefs about differing emotionality in men and women may be partially correct. Women report more emotional intensity than men; they experience more positive as well as negative moods (Fujita, Diener, & Sandvik, 1991). This evidence offers some confirmation for the stereotype of emotional women, but other evidence suggests a more complex picture in which social rules for displaying emotion shape the gender differences in emotionality.

Rather than women becoming more like men, the opposite trend has appeared in relationships; the typical feminine style of intimacy has become the standard for both men and women (Cancian, 1986). Although men often feel uncomfortable in sharing emotions with others, especially with other men, a growing number of men are seeking this style of friendship. Pressure for men to become more emotionally intimate has also occurred in marriages and committed love relationships. Thus, women have not become more like men in this respect, but instead, men are in the process of becoming more like women.

Sexual behavior continues to show some gender differences. Some of those differences have decreased, but those that remain may be important. When Alfred Kinsey and his colleagues (Kinsey et al., 1948; Kinsey et al., 1953) conducted their surveys in the 1930s and 1940s, women reported more sexual activity and enjoyment than the popular image of women portrayed, but the double standard for sexual behavior constrained women from expressing their sexuality. Women were less likely to masturbate and to have intercourse outside marriage than men. Later surveys (Janus & Janus, 1993; Laumann et al., 1994) have shown a decrease in the differences.

Differences in sexuality may have a significant impact on heterosexual relationships (Hyde, 1996). Women now endorse a greater variety of sexual behaviors and are likely to have their first sexual intercourse at younger ages than in previous decades, but differences remain in the percentages of men and women who masturbate and in attitudes toward casual premarital sex. Men masturbate more and favor casual sex more than women. The implications of these differences may be larger than the differences themselves (Hyde, 1996).

For example, women's lower rate of masturbation may relate to their difficulties in having orgasms during sex with their partners, a problem that prompts many couples to seek therapy and many others to experience conflict in their sexual relationships (Hyde, 1996). (The advice of sex therapists often includes masturbation to learn how to have orgasms.) The difference in attitudes toward casual sex has a large influence on many relationships. When men and women bring different attitudes about commitment to their sexual relationships, their varying standards can result in jealousy and conflict.

Changes in sexual attitudes have allowed women to explore their sexuality (Ehrenreich, Hess, & Jacobs, 1986). Women made substantial changes in their sexual attitudes and behavior between the 1930s and the 1970s. The conservatism of the 1980s and the growing fear of AIDS produced some decrease in the willingness for sexual exploration in both men and women, but women's exploration of their sexuality has taken them in directions that were not necessarily compatible with men's sexual preferences. Indeed, increased acceptance of sexuality other than intercourse led women to be less sexually dependent on men. This decreased dependence has become a source of men's discontent. Women have become more sexual, but not like men and not necessarily to men's liking.

Women have become more like men in terms of their achievements; educational differences between men and women have decreased, with women and men receiving comparable numbers of college degrees. Differences still persist in several areas of training and in the advanced and professional degrees awarded, with men receiving more training for prestigious careers such as law, business, and medicine. Women have made gains, but men still dominate high-status, high-salary professions.

Interviews with women about their achievements in one study revealed a picture of women proud of their progress in careers who believe that they have fought and succeeded in gaining recognition (Sigel, 1996). Not only professional women but working-class women expressed pride in women's accomplishments. Talking to men provided a different view: Men saw the changes in terms of letting women have more opportunities. This difference in view is very revealing, with each gender taking credit for the changes in gender roles and seeing their own gender as in charge of the changes.

Employment gives women more economic advantages but also produces greater demands. Some women have sought employment out of a desire for personal fulfillment, whereas economic necessity is the reason for most women's employment. The degree to which women are satisfied with their employment varies according to the support they receive from their families. Women whose husbands provide little assistance and emotional support for their employment are less satisfied than women with more supportive families.

In needing and providing support, women and men are now similar, but these similarities represent changes in their traditional roles. Female homemakers were the traditional caregivers, but employed women need to receive support from as well as provide support to their families. In the past, male breadwinners could expect the support of their wives, but they are now expected to provide their wives with emotional support and also help with household work. Through these changes women and men have become more alike, but this change was probably not what men had in mind. In the past they have enjoyed the support of women without having to provide emotional support or share household work.

Both women and men need the support of the other to be able to fulfill their dependency needs (Eichenbaum & Orbach, 1983). Men and women have similar needs, but the chances of fulfillment are usually not the same. Despite the helplessness and passivity some women display, they do not have someone on whom they can rely for emotional support, leaving dependency needs unmet. The lack of compatibility between meeting dependency needs and adopting the male gender role can make men feel ashamed of their dependency needs. Although in the past men have been able to rely on women for emotional support, women's increasing requests for emotional support from men can be an unwelcome change for many men.

These decreases in gender differences support the notion that women and men have become more similar in education, employment, sexual attitudes and behavior, smoking rates, and athletic competition. The changes have occurred mostly in women. Whereas women have become more like men, men generally have not begun to adopt the positive aspects of women's behavior. This one-way change is not surprising when considering the situations that have produced the changes. Women have moved into the educational and employment worlds formerly occupied by men, but for the most part men have not made corresponding moves into women's worlds. Thus, men encounter few and women encounter many situations that encourage the adoption of a more flexible style.

Despite superficial endorsement of the virtues of the traditional feminine role of homemaker and mother, society has accorded little value to nurturing skills or other traditional feminine behaviors. Men's traditional masculine style of assertive, independent, agentic behavior has set the mold for behavior in a variety of situations. Women who enter these situations tend to adopt the style of the situation, which is usually agentic rather than communal. Society's value of masculine over feminine traits results in women receiving rewards for adopting such active, instrumental behaviors and men receiving little encouragement for becoming more expressive or communal in their behavior. Thus, women have more freedom to become androgynous by combining the positive aspects of masculinity with expressive, communal behaviors, but men have little encouragement to become more androgynous.

If they do, the outcome may not be entirely positive. Men who at age 12 expressed interests and traits more commonly associated with women showed poorer personal adjustment at ages 31 and 41 than men who had more traditionally masculine interests as children

(Aubé & Koestner, 1992). Women who had endorsed nontraditional masculine interests and traits experienced no similar negative outcomes. Indeed, masculine instrumental traits were positively related to adjustment during adulthood for both women and men. That is, an androgynous combination of interests was a negative factor for men's but not for women's adjustment. Another study (Orlofsky & O'Heron, 1987) indicated that both women and men show better adjustment when they endorsed masculine instrumental traits than when they endorsed feminine expressive traits. Both of these studies demonstrated society's emphasis on masculine values and suggested that women have found it easier to become more like men because they receive social rewards for these behaviors.

How do women feel about these changes? According to Susan Faludi (1991), a great deal of media attention has focused on the negative effects of the changes in women's lives. Faludi contended that the negative publicity about women's increased economic and sexual independence represents a reaction against these changes but that the stories misrepresent women's feelings; women would like more opportunities rather than a return to traditional gender roles. These media reports tend to focus on interviews with selected discontented women rather than presenting studies with more representative samples. Women in a survey and interview study (Sigel, 1996) confirmed this view. These women expressed pride in their workplace accomplishments and continued annoyance with discrimination, failures to be taken seriously, and lack of support and assistance from their husbands at home.

Has Henry Higgins's wish come true? Have women become more like men? And are the changes everything that he (and men like him) had hoped for? Men and women may have not been as different as Henry imagined, but women and men are now more alike than they once were. As women have entered male domains, their behavior has changed to accommodate the situation. Although some men have sought to adopt positive feminine behaviors, such as emotional expressiveness, men have not entered female domains to the same extent that women have entered the domain of men. Men are not encouraged or rewarded for feminine behavior, thus the changes have altered women's more than men's behavior.

These changes may not be what either women or men had in mind. Most people find change difficult and anxiety provoking, and changes in expectations for men and women have come about very rapidly. Indeed, the changes have occurred faster than social institutions have been able to change to accommodate them. People have few models to emulate in adopting new gender roles, and they live in a society that pressures them to be more traditional. When gender roles were narrowly defined, everyone knew what to do. Although the rules were unquestionably restrictive, which prevented people from performing gender-inappropriate activities, the roles were clear. Greater flexibility has produced uncertainty as well as options.

The power and privilege of men's gender role put them in a position of having more to lose through change, and men are less content than women with the changes that have occurred. Although some men have welcomed the opportunities to form more intimate relationships with friends and partners and to be involved in their children's lives, many others have resisted making changes or have found themselves not knowing how to enact the changes they want to make. The increased options have created opportunities for men that few of them want, such as careers as elementary school teachers or secretaries. Employed wives bring home income that may be very attractive, but few men welcome the prospect of having more household chores. Therefore, many men have not gotten what they wanted as women have become more like men.

Women too may not be entirely satisfied with the changes in their lives. As the many polls indicate, the majority of women favor more equal treatment in politics and jobs, but they too may resist making other changes in the roles and underlying assumptions about their relationships with men, their sexuality, and their children. Women become less interested in change when "it requires profound individual change as well, posing an unsettling challenge that well-adjusted people instinctively avoid. Why question norms of sex and character to which you've more or less successfully adapted?" (Kaminer, 1993, p. 51). Women do not want to lose their femininity in gaining equal rights, and they do not want to give up relationships with men (Sigel, 1996).

Some women long for a return to traditionalism, but that longing is stronger in men, who believe that changes in gender roles have caused them to lose more and gain less than women. Women tend to complain, not about what they have lost but about what they have gained—the equivalent of two full-time jobs. Men tend to complain about what they have lost—services and subservience (Gallagher, 1987). These "new" women are more independent and more difficult for men to control (Skovholt, 1978).

Why Can't a Man Be More Like a Woman?

The status of styles of masculinity can be analyzed into three categories that describe men and their reactions to the changes in women's roles (Skovholt, 1978). *Traditional men* regret the changes that have occurred, seeing no advantages for them in greater freedom for women. Indeed, these men feel the competition for grades and jobs and resent the presence of women in the workplace. Traditional men have stereotypical attitudes toward their own gender role and prefer women to adhere to traditional femininity. These men do not feel the appeal of expanding their gender role to include behaviors traditionally reserved for women, so they see nothing but disadvantages connected with changing gender roles.

Men in transition are able to accomplish the task of interacting with women as people as well as with women as romantic partners. Men in transition have the "cognitive capacity, to turn on and off the person–woman light bulb when interacting with a female" (Skovholt, 1978, p. 5). These men are not necessarily sympathetic with the goals of the feminist movement, but they are attempting to integrate the changes in women's role by changing their attitudes and behavior. Alex from this chapter's headline story fits into this category. He is able to interact with women as people as well as Susan as his romantic partner, and he is struggling to become more sensitive and responsive.

Alex, however, fails to recognize as problems many of the issues that Susan finds troubling. The men in one survey and interview study (Sigel, 1996) were much like Alex in failing to see the problem of gender discrimination. Some of these men were traditional men who longed for the "good old days" when men ruled the workplace and home, but most endorsed gender equality and sympathy with women's quest for fair treatment. However, this issue did not capture their interest and commitment. These men in transition were grappling with the changes in gender roles, but they were not actively working toward advancing women's equality.

The *male liberationists* embrace the feminist movement and extend the notion that gender roles are oppressive to men, highlighting the stresses of the male gender role and calling for changes for everyone. Table 17.2 summarizes these three categories of men.

TABLE 17.2 Three Categories of Contemporary Men

Approach	Characteristics	See Women As
Traditional	Wish to return to traditional gender roles for men and women	Subordinate
Men in transition	Attempt to adapt to the changes in gender roles	People as well as romantic partners
Male liberationists	See dangers of male gender role; embrace feminism	Equals

Women have become more like men, but more often men have declined than accepted opportunities to become more like women. That is, women have developed a more instrumental orientation, but many men have failed to develop their expressive skills. The asymmetry of these changes may have created a situation in which women want men to change. Women are asking Henry Higgins's question from their point of view: "Why can't a man be more like a woman?"

This question exists in two versions, one social and one personal. The first version applies to the question as a social one, challenging the wisdom of continuing to use men and masculine values as the preferred style. For example, what makes the hierarchical, directive (sometimes autocratic) style of leadership that men typically use preferable to the cooperative, democratic style women typically use? If differences in moral reasoning exist, why should the style dominant among women be considered inferior? Why can't men accept the value of the feminine style? Why are men considered the standard and women the exception (Bem, 1993b)? The second version of the question is more personal, challenging men to include more expressiveness in personal relationships and to participate more fully in "women's work"—that is, household work and child care. Women contend that in society at large as well as in their individual lives, all would profit from men accepting the value of expressive behaviors.

Some evidence exists to indicate that people have no problems accepting the value of the communal qualities associated with women. Alice Eagly and her colleagues (Eagly, 1994; Eagly, Mladinic, & Otto, 1991) investigated evaluations of men and women, finding that women received more positive personal evaluations than men. People think of women as a social category in very positive terms, a finding Eagly (1994) called the "Women are Wonderful" effect. These positive evaluations may signal a change in the social evaluation of women, allowing for a greater acceptance of feminine values.

However, these positive evaluations seem to contradict the disadvantages that women experience in so many realms. These positive evaluations were applied to women in traditional roles but failed to carry over to women who diverged from those traditional roles; that is, people saw women as wonderful mothers but not as business executives (Eagly, 1994). As Eagly et al. (1991) put it, "Although people evidently think that these qualities are wonderful human attributes, they may value them more in close relationships than in highly paid sectors of the work force" (p. 213). Thus, the evidence concerning positive attitudes about women does not ensure the social acceptance of their style in roles other than traditional ones.

Not only would women like for men to consider feminine behaviors as acceptable and appropriate, they would like for men to behave more expressively in their personal relationships. This wish has been the subject of a number of popular books oriented around communication between women and men. The places that these books have occupied on the bestseller lists speak to the strength of women's wish to have more expressive partners.

Some men have recognized the value of developing greater emotional expressiveness and have attempted to make changes in their behavior. Although these men believe that women and men should have equal power in relationships and equal access to education and careers, they may find these principles difficult to incorporate into their lives. Society offers few models for couples to develop equal relationships but many examples of traditional couples.

Marriages between feminist men and women do not always work as the partners envisioned (Campbell, 1986). The lack of social support for equitable marriages pushes men and women toward traditional gender roles. Even men who have agreed to share in household work and child care find these promises difficult to keep, and women's success can leave men feeling neglected and jealous of the time their wives spend on work. Pursuing demanding careers, the wives do not have time to do household work and child care without their husbands' help. When their husbands refuse to help, their marriages experience trouble. Marriages that begin with the men being liberationists sometimes end with both partners realizing that the men were more traditional than either had believed.

The motivation to make personal changes in ways of dealing with partners and children has been a focus in many of the men's movement groups; here men attempt to feel comfortable with emotional sharing and intimate disclosure. A growing number of men have accepted that the male gender role constrains their emotional expressiveness in ways that have harmed their relationships and possibly their well-being. This attitude has encouraged men to change.

What are the prospects for men becoming more like women? And how would women feel if they did? Currently, the rewards for men who adopt more expressive behaviors are not as great as for women who become more instrumental, which leads to the prediction that men may not change as much as women have. If the men who are involved in the men's movement provide any omen of changes to come, then men have little interest in adopting very many feminine qualities. Leaders in the men's movement, such as Sam Keen (1991) and Robert Bly (1990, 1994), have urged men to explore their masculinity and make changes in their attitudes and behavior, but their recommendations do not include listening to women to know what changes to make. The men's movement concept of authentic masculinity includes increased expressiveness and responsibility, making this view of what men should become correspond to the changes that many women want.

Will these views of masculinity influence men's attitudes and behavior? Although the vast majority of men are not involved in the men's movement, social changes become personal and affect people's lives (Sigel, 1996). The women's movement produced changes in the society, for women's lives, and for men's lives. The men's movement may have a parallel effect, and the discomfort may be similar, with women disliking some of the choices for change that men make in their lives.

Men and women may both want too much from each other, including things that appear to be contradictory. Each may want to be both independent and dependent, aggressive and passive, businesslike and romantic. These behaviors are not necessarily contradictory, but the rules that allow the display of both are more complex than the rules that allowed each gender only one pattern. Flexibility and acceptance of individual choices are goals for both the women's and men's movement, but both men and women are struggling with these new, more complicated rules.

Where Are the Differences?

One of the places where differences exist between the genders is in the theories used to explain psychological factors related to gender. The traditional dichotomy for theories of gender is the biological versus environmental view—attributing differences to nature or nurture. Although these opposing points of view have influenced research in gender, another approach now encompasses the nature–nurture debate in gender—the maximalist versus the minimalist positions.

The maximalist view holds that men and women have large differences, whereas the minimalist view holds that the differences between men and women are small compared to their similarities. The older versions of maximalist theory are biologically based, emphasizing gender differences and offering genetic or hormonal explanations for behavior as well as anatomy. These theorists tend to accept biological explanations as evidence of unchanging, fixed patterns of behavior. Thus, offering the biological explanation means accepting inevitable differences. These theorists tend to rationalize the disadvantaged social position of women (and often of ethnic minorities) by citing biological programming as the source of differences. Naomi Weisstein (1982, p. 41) summarized this position by saying, "Men are biologically suited to their life of power, pleasure, and privilege, and women must accept subordination, sacrifice, and submission. It's in the genes. Go fight city hall."

Not surprisingly, feminist scholars have disputed the biological basis of behavioral differences between men and women, proposing that social experiences produce differences in learning and thus in behavior. According to this view, social learning, not biology, forms the basis for psychological gender differences. This approach holds that behavior varies according to circumstances and surroundings, and these theorists attribute gender differences to the different situations that women and men typically encounter. Those who hold this view tend to be minimalists, accepting few essential differences between men and women.

Newer versions of the maximalist position also rely on social learning to explain gender differences. Although these theorists see the differences between women's and men's behavior as learned, they believe that the differences are large and persistent. Many of these maximalist theorists are also feminists, advocating the superiority of women's style and characteristics. Rather than accepting the differences as deficiencies, they promote the female version as the better alternative.

These theorists (including Gilligan, Chodorow, and Tannen) are appealing to some women because "they offer a flattering account of traits for which they have historically been castigated" (Pollitt, 1992, p. 802). This view is a modernized version of the Doctrine of the Two Spheres, the Victorian view that women were moral, pure, spiritual, emotional, and intellectually inferior. It is no longer possible to separate the more positive from the very negative characteristics of this view. The virtues that these maximalists idealize help rationalize the continued subordination of women. The popularity of this view is ironic, given that the roles of women and men are more similar than they have been at any time during the history of the West (Pollitt, 1992).

Both maximalists and minimalists look at the same research and find evidence to support their positions. The ability to maintain different interpretations of the same information highlights the constructed nature of theories; that is, those who support one view or the other have constructed their position in accordance with their beliefs about gender. Building and maintaining a theoretical position requires examining the research evidence, but theory goes beyond evidence. Therefore, it is possible for theorists to maintain discrepant positions with regard to gender differences, with some theorists holding maximalist and others minimalist positions.

Theories are not the only place that gender differences exist; gender-related differences also exist in behavior. The extent of gender-related differences, however, depends on the type of study considered. In considering studies on ability, few gender differences have appeared. In considering the choices that men and women have made about what to do in their lives, the gender differences are larger.

Differences in Ability

Considering the many comparisons of abilities of women and men, the gender differences are largest for physical strength. This difference relates to size and muscle mass, with men being significantly larger and stronger than women. The differences among individuals are also large; some women are stronger than other women, and some men stronger than other men. However, gender differences are larger than individual differences, making gender a good predictor of strength.

In the past, physical strength made a great deal of difference for a variety of activities, especially in the world of paid employment. Currently, few positions of prestige and power require strength, but the legacy of this position persists. In a survey and interview study of gender issues (Sigel, 1996), several men expressed the opinion that men should be paid more than women because men's jobs require more strength. Despite the high level of skills that secretaries might need, they should receive less money because their jobs do not require heavy labor. The requirements for physical labor were also mentioned as a reason why men should not be expected to share household work or child care—they had already done physical labor and should not be expected to do more at home.

Gender is a very poor predictor of mental abilities. In both verbal abilities and mathematical abilities, only small gender differences exist. Despite the widespread belief that men have superior mathematical and women superior verbal abilities, the technique of meta-analysis has revealed that the gender differences are small (Hyde, 1996; Hyde, Fennema, & Lamon, 1990; Hyde & Linn, 1988). The largest difference in cognitive abilities is on one type of spatial task, the mental rotation task. Men have a large advantage in this type of task, but other spatial tasks show a complex relationship with gender.

Research conducted in laboratory settings often shows few if any gender differences. When men and women are put into situations without gender-related cues, their behavior tends to be quite similar. For example, two studies of aggression, a literature review (Frodi,

Macaulay, & Thome, 1977) and a meta-analysis (Eagly & Steffen, 1986), showed that women and men are similar in their willingness to behave aggressively in laboratory situations, but outside the laboratory, gender differences appear.

Perhaps the laboratory setting minimizes behavioral differences, which makes this approach unsuited to demonstrating gender-related differences. Because laboratory settings have a tendency to demonstrate gender similarities, researchers may have to look at behavior in social settings in order to find differences. When examining the behavioral choices that men and women make, gender differences appear larger than when considering their abilities.

Differences in Choices

Women and men make different choices about important facets of their lives, and these choices reflect the behaviors that are encouraged for each gender. Although many barriers that prevented women and men from attempting some activities seem to have fallen away, constraints remain in the form of expectations and encouragement. Social expectations push each toward different options and thus toward different lives. These choices are more important than abilities in determining what happens in people's lives. The gender differences that exist in education, employment, family life, relationships, sexuality, emotionality, health-related behaviors, body image, and behavior problems reflect these different choices and the expectations that foster them.

Although men and women have similar mathematical abilities, young men are more likely than women to pursue careers that rely on math. Unlike the men enrolled in these courses, the women who enroll in advanced math courses tend not make such choices as their avenue to science careers. Even women who complete the math background do not choose science and engineering careers as often as men (AAUW, 1992). These discrepancies are larger than the differences in abilities would suggest: Fewer women enter mathematics and engineering than women who have the ability to do so (Hyde, 1996).

The expectation that men will pursue careers consistent with the breadwinner role and that women will seek careers compatible with family duties eliminates many choices for each. Men are limited in their family involvement by careers that require dedication and long hours. Men do not receive encouragement when they make different choices, such as allotting time to family life by choosing part-time employment or by choosing to be homemakers. Indeed, this choice is considered deviant, and men who have made such decisions are encouraged to reconsider (Robertson & Fitzgerald, 1990).

The movement of women into the paid work force has increased their options in some ways but not in others. Rather than giving women added choices concerning employment or homemaking, women now expect to be employed in addition to having a husband and children (Baber & Monaghan, 1988; Granrose & Kaplan, 1996). Women who have chosen to have a career and family experience the strains of juggling roles as they work to develop their careers, find adequate child care, and make time for children and husbands. Women who have chosen to be homemakers feel that their choice is not as well accepted or respected as the choice of pursuing paid employment, but they feel that the job they are doing is essential for their children's well-being. Women who have paid employment but would rather be homemakers and those who had expected to pursue careers but are homemakers face conflict between their expectations and their lives (Granrose & Kaplan, 1996). The change in patterns of employment for women has resulted in additional role responsibilities as well as additional options.

Men and women tend to choose different styles of friendships, and this difference is clearly a choice. That is, most women and men are capable of adopting the style of friendship more common in the other. A woman can be "one of the boys," and a man can adopt the emotionally intimate friendship pattern more common among women, but each tends to choose a gender-typical style of relating to others. This choice gives women more intimate friendships with other women than with men and prevents men from forming intimate friendships with other men (and possibly with women). Friendships are one source of social support that brings advantages for physical and mental health. Women's style of friendship tends to provide more emotional support, whereas men's style of friendship tends to offer more material support. The advantages of social support come from both types of support and extend to both women and men.

Women's choice of achieving intimacy through emotional sharing and talk has become the accepted style for love relationships (Cancian, 1986), and men can feel deficient if they are not adept at this type of relating. Men's attempts to establish intimacy through sexual activity are not entirely compatible with women's choice to create intimacy through talk and sharing feelings. Thus, sexuality may have different meanings for women and men. Even with comparable levels of desire, men and women make different choices concerning expressions of their sexuality.

Different choices also appear to be related to the varying life expectancies of men and women, with women choosing healthier and safer lifestyles in terms of their use of health care services, diet, alcohol intake, and seat belt use. On the other hand, men tend to make better choices concerning exercise and avoidance of unhealthy dieting. Both patterns match the interpretation that men's and women's health-related behaviors are oriented toward maintaining their gender roles. Women behave in healthy ways not because of their health concerns but due to their concern over thinness; likewise, men exercise and choose risky health-related behaviors in an effort to maintain a muscular appearance, which matches the Give 'Em Hell component of the masculine gender role.

Men's and women's strategies for handling negative feelings can lead to different methods of dealing with emotions they experience. These differences appear both in statistics on violence and rates of various types of psychopathology. The display rules for emotion allow (and perhaps even encourage) men to openly express anger, leading to more acts of violence and crime committed by men. Women are encouraged to restrict their displays of anger, leading not to a decrease in the experience but to differences in the expression of anger. One difference is that women often cry when they are angry, whereas men typically do not.

Different choices for dealing with negative feelings may be reflected in the statistics on psychiatric diagnosis. Women are more likely to receive the diagnosis of depression than men, but men are more likely to drink alcohol and use other illicit psychoactive substances than women. Some evidence exists that men use alcohol to cope with negative feelings (Berger & Adesso, 1991), whereas women ruminate over negative events and become depressed (Nolen-Hoeksema, 1987). These different choices produce apparent differences in psychopathology but may not indicate a difference in the experience of negative emotions.

The expression of psychopathology tends to fall along gender-stereotypical lines (Chesler, 1972; Rosenfield, 1982). The categories of psychopathology most common among women fall into the feminine gender role but are exaggerated versions of it: being dependent (dependent personality disorder), passive (major depression), self-sacrificing (self-defeating personality disorder), fearful (agoraphobia), and emotional (histrionic personality disorder). Men experience psychopathology that seems to have formed around elements of the masculine gender role and exaggerated these traits: being irresponsible, untruthful, and violent (antisocial personality disorder), recklessness (psychoactive substance abuse disorder), and inappropriately sexual (paraphilias). Although these patterns may not represent intentional choices, they exist as reflections of gender-typical differences.

The choices that men and women make tend to fall along the lines sanctioned by tradition. Women's choices and men's choices tend to keep men and women each in their own category, which creates male domain and female domains, with limited "visitation privileges" of one to the other. Yet these two domains are not different planets, as the bestselling book, *Men Are from Mars, Women Are from Venus,* suggested: "The truth is, there is only one culture, and it shapes each sex in distinct but mutually dependent ways in order to reproduce itself" (Pollitt, 1992, p. 806).

The freedom to make cross-gender choices is still limited. An argument has been made that there are benefits derived from perpetuating gender categories. Although such categorization may be convenient to each gender, it limits options to only two well-defined choices, and these choices ignore the inherent complexity of individual differences and fail to allow for the need for a wide range of individual choices. The range of abilities of men and women demand an equally wide range of choices—wider than are available in the bipolar classification of tradition.

Is a peace plan possible for the gender war? Have the forays into each others' worlds increased understanding and empathy? The current level of hostility would suggest not. Women's experiences in the world of work have had many positive attributes but have also shown to women that they are not treated equitably or taken seriously (Sigel, 1996). This continuing discrimination has escalated the hostility they feel toward their male counterparts rather than initiated a peace plan.

Recent controversies have "put the traditional male sense of entitlements under the microscope. On the simple level, men don't know where the line is. But on a deeper level, there is anxiety" (Levant in Gates, 1993, p. 50). Men's hostility has also increased, and women and ethnic minorities are sometimes the targets of their vehemence. Some men long for "the good old days" when men were privileged in the workplace and at home and women "knew their place." Relinquishing power and privilege is not easy, and men are not eager to do so. When they lose the favored status, men become angry and resentful. "There are many more men who are taking care of the children than there are men on the freeway going berserk" (Pleck in Gates, 1993, p. 53). But the resentment is there, which makes a peace plan difficult to formulate.

For society, peace in the gender war does not seem easily attainable. Several future scenarios are possible (Jones, 1996). Will the trend toward women as heads of households escalate into separatism in which women have exiled men? Will a male backlash prompt a super-patriarchy in which women are enslaved? Will technology create opportunities for people to do the work for which they are best suited, regardless of gender? Or will things continue as they have for the past 30 years, with women gaining rights, roles, and extra work while men struggle with changes in their own as well as women's roles? None of these future options promises a truce.

For individuals, a peace plan is possible (White & Tyson-Rawson, 1996). Indeed, many couples have worked out equitable plans for living together and have built satisfying personal relationships (Schwartz, 1994). Building such relationships often requires analyzing the underlying assumptions connected with gender roles and finding ways to overcome the roles that society dictates for women and men. Alex and Susan in this chapter's headline story underwent such an analysis, and it helped them understand their gender scripts and how to rewrite the parts that were not working. Not all relationships can be mended so easily, but failing to understand the importance of gender will almost certainly allow the wars to continue.

Summary

The roles that men and women occupy have undergone changes in the past three decades, allowing women to move into careers that had formerly been the province of men. As women began to acquire careers and salaries comparable with men's, some men began to imagine that women would become more like them, which would make relating to each other easier. Some of these men have been disappointed, because women have not always made the changes in their lives that many men had in mind.

The changes in women's employment have been additive rather than substitutive; that is, most women who are employed outside their homes also have family work to do when at home. Thus, most women are now employees, wives, and mothers. These multiple roles present stress in women's lives but also offer rewards. Research indicates that the rewards outweigh the stresses for most women. Men also occupy multiple roles as employees, husbands, and fathers, but men do less family work than women when at home, causing the breadwinner role in the family structure to be perpetuated. Research indicates that men find multiple roles rewarding, but they are less eager than women to allow family work to intrude on their employment obligations.

Men have long wondered what women want and have expressed the desire for women to behave in ways more similar to men. Gender differences may never have been as large as many people imagined, but men have gotten their wish in several respects: Women's behavior has changed to become more like men's behavior. These changes, however, have not resulted in the transformations that some men imagined. Men did not envision competition from women at work as a desirable outcome of gender similarity, but as women have moved into the world of paid employment, they have assumed roles and behaviors required by these situations. Men and women have become more alike in terms of education, employment, sexual attitudes and behavior, athletic competition, and rates of smoking. Few gender differences exist in experiencing emotion, but differences remain in how emotions are displayed. Men have become more like women in the style of forming close personal relationships and are beginning to explore the rewards of opening up to emotional sharing and talk.

Although the changes in women's lives have prompted men to change, these alterations have not been equal to the ones that women have experienced. A combination of the devaluation of traditionally feminine behaviors and the value placed on the activities that men perform has pushed women toward change. Some men dislike these changes, and long once again for traditional roles for both; some men are trying to make the transition; and some men have welcomed the increasing similarities. Women, however, are more pleased with the changes in their lives than are men.

Women also wish for changes in men; they want men to accept and adopt some of the characteristics typical of women. Women would like for men to accept the validity of the feminine approach and to feel comfortable in adopting positive behaviors traditionally associated with women. One of these desired changes has occurred to some extent—the change in ways to communicate in intimate relationships. Women would like for men to be more emotionally expressive and to communicate intimate thoughts and feelings to their partners. Women would also like for men to become more active with their families, sharing household work and child care. These changes may be difficult to accomplish. The devaluation of women's characteristics and work means that men have few incentives for behaving more like women.

If women have become more like men in a number of ways and men have become more like women in some ways, how many gender differences remain? Differences continue in theories, with maximalist theories advocating that differences exist between the genders and minimalist theories arguing along the lines of more similarities than differences.

Research on gender and ability has revealed relatively few differences. The largest of these differences in ability lies in men's strength advantage, but few differences exist when measuring other abilities in laboratory situations. When examining the choices that men and women make concerning how to live their lives, larger gender differences appear. Indeed, the difference in choices may promote the idea that greater differences exist than research has confirmed.

The choices that women and men make tend to preserve well-defined gender roles rather than allowing people to make freer choices and develop the most satisfying lives. Strict enforcement of gender-related behaviors may simplify rules of conduct, but preserving this dichotomy extracts a high price for individual women and men. On a societal level, the gender wars show no signs of diminishing in intensity, with many women wanting more changes and many men wanting a return to more traditional roles. On an individual level, peace between women and men is possible, and many couples have built relationships that allow them to participate fully in the work force, household work, child care, and each other's lives.

Suggested Reading

Kaminer, Wendy. (1993, October). Feminism's identity crisis. *Atlantic Monthly,* pp. 51–53, 56, 58–59, 62, 64, 66–68. Kaminer discusses the failure of most women to embrace feminism, despite their agreement with many of its goals, and she examines the implications of the maximalist and minimalist positions.

Schwartz, Pepper. (1994). *Peer marriage: How love between equals really works.* New York; Free Press. Schwartz examines couples' relationships, focusing on couples who have managed to construct marriage relationships in which both members are peers. Her report reveals the problems and advantages of working toward such relationships.

Sigel, Roberta S. (1996). *Ambition and accommodation: How women view gender relations.* Chicago: University of Chicago Press. Sigel conducted a survey and an interview study of men and women to determine their attitudes and experiences related to gender. Her book is an interesting mixture of quantitative results and personal experiences and opinions from these women and men. The book helps in developing an understanding of how the changes in gender roles have changed people's lives and how they are coping with the difficulties of living in a time of transition.

References

Abrams, Leslie R.; & Jones, Russell W. (1994, August). *The contribution of social roles to psychological distress in businesswomen.* Paper presented at the 102nd annual convention of the American Psychological Association, Los Angeles, CA.

Abramson, Paul R.; Goldberg, Philip A.; Greenberg, Judith H.; & Abramson, Linda M. (1977). The talking platypus phenomenon: Competency ratings as a function of sex and professional status. *Psychology of Women Quarterly, 2,* 114–124.

Adler, David A.; Drake, Robert E.; & Teague, Gregory B. (1990). Clinicians' practices in personality assessment: Does gender influence the use of DSM-III axis II? *Comprehensive Psychiatry, 31,* 125–133.

Adler, Jerry. (1996, June 17). Building a better dad. *Newsweek, 127*(25), pp. 58–64.

Akiyama, Hiroko; Elliott, Kathryn; & Antonucci, Toni C. (1996). Same-sex and cross-sex relationships. *Journals of Gerontology, Series B., 51,* 374–382.

Allen, Bem P. (1995). Gender stereotypes are not accurate: A replication of Martin (1987) using diagnostic vs. self-report and behavioral criteria. (Based on C. L. Martin's article, *Journal of Personality and Social Psychology, 52,* p. 489, 1987) *Sex Roles, 32,* 583–600.

Allmendinger, Jutta; & Hackman, J. Richard. (1995). The more, the better? A four-nation study of the inclusion of women in symphony orchestras. *Social Forces, 74,* 423–460.

Altman, Barbara Mandell. (1985). Disabled women in the social structure. In Susan E. Browne, Debra Connors, & Nanci Stern (Eds.), *With the power of each breath: A disabled women's anthology* (pp. 69–76). San Francisco: Cleis Press.

Altman, Lawrence K. (1997, June 22). Is the longer life the healthier one? *New York Times,* section 14 (Women's Health), p. 18.

American Association of University Women (AAUW). (1992). *The AAUW report: How schools shortchange girls.* Washington, DC: American Association of University Women Education Foundation and National Educational Association.

American Association of University Women (AAUW). (1993). *Hostile hallways: The AAUW survey on sexual harassment in America's schools.* Washington, DC: American Association of University Women Educational Foundation.

American Psychiatric Association. (1980). *Diagnostic and statistical manual of mental disorders* (3rd ed.). Washington, DC: American Psychiatric Association.

American Psychiatric Association. (1987). *Diagnostic and statistical manual of mental disorders* (3rd ed. rev.). Washington, DC: American Psychiatric Association.

American Psychiatric Association. (1994). *Diagnostic and statistical manual of mental disorders* (4th ed.). Washington, DC: American Psychiatric Association.

American Psychological Association Task Force on Sex Bias and Sex-Role Stereotyping in Psychotherapeutic Practice. (1978). Guidelines for therapy with women. *American Psychologist, 33,* 1122–1123.

Andersen, Arnold E.; & DiDomenico, Lisa. (1992). Diet vs. shape content of popular male and female magazines: A dose-response relationship to the incidence of eating disorders? *International Journal of Eating Disorders, 11,* 283–287.

Aneshensel, Carol S.; Frerichs, Ralph R.; & Clark, Virginia A. (1981). Family roles and sex differences in depression. *Journal of Health and Social Behavior, 22,* 379–393.

Aneshensel, Carol S.; & Pearlin, Leonard I. (1987). Structural contexts of sex differences in stress. In Rosalind C. Barnett, Lois Biener, & Grace K. Baruch (Eds.), *Gender and stress* (pp. 75–95). New York: Free Press.

Ankney, C. Davison. (1992). Sex differences in relative brain size: The mismeasure of woman, too? *Intelligence, 16,* 329–336.

Antill, John K. (1983). Sex role complementarity versus similarity in married couples. *Journal of Personality and Social Psychology, 45,* 145–155.

Archer, John; & Lloyd, Barbara. (1982). *Sex and gender.* Cambridge, England: Cambridge University Press.

Aries, Elizabeth. (1987). Gender and communication. In Phillip Shaver & Clyde Hendrick (Eds.), *Sex and gender* (pp. 149–176). Newbury Park, CA: Sage.

Aries, Elizabeth. (1996). *Men and women in interaction.* New York: Oxford University Press.

Ashel, Mark H. (1991). A psycho-behavioral analysis of addicted versus non-addicted male and female exercisers. *Journal of Sport Behavior, 14,* 145–154.

Ashton, Heather. (1991). Psychotropic-drug prescribing for women. *British Journal of Psychiatry, 158* (Suppl. 10), 30–35.

Astin, Helen S. (1984). The meaning of work in women's lives: A sociopsychological model of career choice and work behavior. *Counseling Psychologist, 12,* 117–126.

Astrachan, Anthony. (1986). *How men feel: Their response to women's demands for equality and power.* Garden City, NY: Anchor Press.

Attar, Beth K.; Guerra, Nancy G.; & Tolan, Patrick H. (1994). Neighborhood disadvantage, stressful life events, and adjustment in urban elementary-school children. *Journal of Clinical Child Psychology, 23,* 391–400.

Aubé, Jennifer; & Koestner, Richard. (1992). Gender characteristics and adjustment: A longitudinal study. *Journal of Personality and Social Psychology, 63,* 485–493.

Aubé, Jennifer; & Koestner, Richard. (1995). Gender characteristics and relationship adjustment: Another look at similarity–complementarity hypotheses. *Journal of Personality, 63,* 879–904.

Averill, James R. (1982). *Anger and aggression: An essay on emotion.* New York: Springer-Verlag.

Avery, Patricia G.; & Walker, Constance. (1993). Prospective teachers' perceptions of ethnic and gender differences in academic achievement. *Journal of Teacher Education, 44,* 27–37.

Ayanian, John Z.; & Epstein, Arnold M. (1991). Differences in the use of procedures between women and men hospitalized for coronary heart disease. *New England Journal of Medicine, 325,* 221–225.

Baber, Kristine M.; & Monaghan, Patricia. (1988). College women's career and motherhood expectations: New options, old dilemmas. *Sex Roles, 19,* 189–203.

Baenninger, Maryann; & Newcombe, Nora. (1989). A role of experience in spatial test performance: A meta-analysis. *Sex Roles, 20,* 327–343.

Bagley, Christopher; & King, Kathleen. (1990). *Child sexual abuse: The search for healing.* London: Tavistock/Routledge.

Bailey, William T.; Silver, N. Clayton; & Oliver, Kathleen A. (1990). Women's rights and roles: Attitudes among Black and White students. *Psychological Reports, 66,* 1143–1146.

Bakan, David. (1966). *The duality of human existence.* Chicago: Rand McNally.

Ball, Richard E.; & Robbins, Lynn. (1986). Marital status and life satisfaction among Black Americans. *Journal of Marriage and the Family, 48,* 389–394.

Balmary, Marie. (1982). *Psychoanalyzing psychoanalysis: Freud and the hidden fault of the father* (Ned Lukacher, Trans.). Baltimore: Johns Hopkins University Press. (Original work published 1979)

Bandura, Albert. (1986). *Social foundations of thought and action: A social cognitive theory.* Englewood Cliffs, NJ: Prentice-Hall.

Banks, Terry; & Dabbs, James M., Jr. (1996). Salivary testosterone and cortisol in delinquent and violent urban subcultures. *Journal of Social Psychology, 136,* 49–56.

Barak, Azy. (1997). Cross-cultural perspectives on sexual harassment. In William O'Donohue (Ed.),

Sexual harassment: Theory, research, and treatment (pp. 263–300), Boston: Allyn and Bacon.

Barak, Azy; Fisher, William A.; & Houston, Sandra. (1992). Individual difference correlates of the experience of sexual harassment. *Journal of Applied Social Psychology, 22,* 17–37.

Barnett, Rosalind C., & Baruch, Grace K. (1987). Social roles, gender, and psychological distress. In Rosalind C. Barnett, Lois Biener, & Grace K. Baruch (Eds.), *Gender and stress* (pp. 122–143). New York: Free Press.

Barnett, Rosalind C., Marshall, Nancy L., & Pleck, Joseph H. (1992). Men's multiple roles and their relationship to men's psychological distress. *Journal of Marriage and the Family, 54,* 358–367.

Baumeister, Roy F. (1988). Should we stop studying sex differences altogether? *American Psychologist, 43,* 1092–1095.

Baxter, Susan. (1993, March/April). The last self-help article you'll ever need. *Psychology Today,* pp. 70–71, 74–77, 94.

Baxter, Susan. (1994, March/April). The last word on gender differences. *Psychology Today, 27,* 50–53, 85–86.

Beal, Carole R. (1994). *Boys and girls: The development of gender roles.* New York: McGraw-Hill.

Beal, Carole R.; & Lockhart, Maria E. (1989). The effect of proper name and appearance changes on children's reasoning about gender constancy. *International Journal of Behavioral Development, 12,* 195–205.

Bechtel, Stefan; & Stains, Laurence R. (1995, December). The best sex you ever had. *Men's Health, 10*(10), 92–98.

Beck, Aaron T. (1985). *Anxiety disorders and phobias: A cognitive perspective.* New York: Basic Books.

Beck, Melinda; Springen, Karen; & Foote, Donna. (1992, April 13). Sex and psychotherapy. *Newsweek, 119,* 52–57.

Begley, Sharon. (1995, March 27). Gray matters. *Newsweek, 125,* 48–54.

Begley, Sharon. (1997, April 21). The science wars. *Newsweek, 129*(16), 54–57.

Belasco, Warren J. (1989, December). The two taste cultures. *Psychology Today,* 29–36.

Belenky, Mary Field; Clinchy, Blythe McVicker; Goldberger, Nancy Rule; & Tarule, Jill Mattuck. (1986). *Women's ways of knowing: The development of self, voice, and mind.* New York: Basic Books.

Belle, Deborah. (1990). Poverty and women's mental health. *American Psychologist, 45,* 385–389.

Bem, Sandra Lipsitz. (1974). The measurement of psychological androgyny. *Journal of Consulting and Clinical Psychology, 42,* 155–162.

Bem, Sandra Lipsitz. (1981). Gender schema theory: A cognitive account of sex-typing. *Psychological Review, 88,* 354–364.

Bem, Sandra Lipsitz. (1985). Androgyny and gender schema theory: A conceptual and empirical integration. In Theo B. Sonderegger (Ed.), *Nebraska symposium on motivation, 1984: Psychology and gender* (pp. 179–226). Lincoln, NE: University of Nebraska Press.

Bem, Sandra Lipsitz. (1987). Gender schema theory and its implications for child development: Raising gender-aschematic children in a gender-schematic society. In Mary Roth Walsh (Ed.), *The psychology of women: Ongoing debates* (pp. 226–245). New Haven, CT: Yale University Press.

Bem, Sandra Lipsitz. (1989). Genital knowledge and gender constancy in preschool children. *Child Development, 60,* 649–662.

Bem, Sandra Lipsitz. (1993a). Is there a place in psychology for a feminist analysis of the social context? *Feminism & Psychology, 3,* 230–234.

Bem, Sandra Lipsitz. (1993b). *The lenses of gender.* New Haven, CT: Yale University Press.

Ben-David, Sarah. (1993). The two facets of female violence: The public and the domestic domains. *Journal of Family Violence, 8,* 345–359.

Benbow, Camilla Persson. (1992). Academic achievement in mathematics and science of students between ages 13 and 23: Are there differences among students in the top one percent of mathematical ability. *Journal of Educational Psychology, 84,* 51–61.

Benbow, Camilla Persson; & Stanley, Julian C. (1980). Sex differences in mathematical ability: Fact or artifact? *Science, 210,* 1262–1264.

Benbow, Camilla Persson; & Stanley, Julian C. (1983). Sex differences in mathematical reasoning ability: More facts. *Science, 222,* 1029–1031.

Benderly, Beryl Lieff. (1987). *The myth of two minds.* New York: Doubleday.

Benderly, Beryl Lieff (1989, November). Don't believe everything you read.... *Psychology Today,* 67–69.

Benin, Mary Holland; & Angostinelli, Joan. (1988). Husbands' and wives' satisfaction with the division of labor. *Journal of Marriage and the Family, 50,* 349–361.

Berdahl, Jennifer L.; Magley, Vicki J.; & Waldo, Craig R. (1996). The sexual harassment of men? Exploring the concept with theory and data. *Psychology of Women Quarterly, 20,* 527–547.

Berenbaum, Sheri A.; & Snyder, Elizabeth. (1995). Early hormonal influences on childhood sex-typed activity and playmate preferences: Implications for the development of sexual orientation. *Developmental Psychology, 31,* 31–42.

Berger, Bertrand D.; & Adesso, Vincent J. (1991). Gender differences in using alcohol to cope with depression. *Addictive Behaviors, 16,* 315–327.

Berman, Phyllis W. (1980). Are women more responsive than men to the young? A review of developmental and situational variables. *Psychological Bulletin, 88,* 668–695.

Bernard, Jessie. (1972). *The future of marriage.* New York: World Publishing.

Bernard, Jessie. (1981). The good-provider role: Its rise and fall. *American Psychologist, 36,* 1–12.

Bernardo, Donna Hodgkins; Shehan, Constance L.; & Leslie, Gerald R. (1987). A residue of tradition: Jobs, careers, and spouses' time in housework. *Journal of Marriage and the Family, 49,* 381–390.

Berndt, Thomas J. (1982). The features and effects of friendship in early adolescence. *Child Development, 53,* 1447–1460.

Berndt, Thomas J.; & Perry, T. Bridgett. (1986). Children's perceptions of friendships as supportive relationships. *Developmental Psychology, 22,* 640–648.

Bernstein, Bianca L.; Hofmann, Barbara; & Wade, Priscilla. (1987). Preferences for counselor gender: Students' sex role, other characteristics, and type of problem. *Journal of Counseling Psychology, 34,* 20–26.

Bettencourt, B. Ann; & Miller, Norman. (1996). Gender differences in aggression as a function of provocation: A meta-analysis. *Psychological Bulletin, 119,* 422–447.

Betz, Nancy. (1993). Women's career development. In Florence L. Denmark & Michele A. Paludi (Eds.), *Psychology of women: A handbook of issues and theories* (pp. 627–684). Westport, CT: Greenwood Press.

Bickel, Janet. (1997). Gender stereotypes and misconceptions: Unresolved issues in physicians' professional development. *Journal of the American Medical Association, 277,* 1405–1406.

Biener, Lois. (1987). Gender differences in the use of substances for coping. In Rosalind C. Barnett, Lois Biener, & Grace. K. Baruch (Eds.), *Gender and stress* (pp. 330–349). New York: Free Press.

Biernat, Monica. (1991). Gender stereotypes and the relationship between masculinity and femininity: A developmental analysis. *Journal of Personality and Social Psychology, 61,* 351–365.

Biernat, Monica; & Kobrynowicz, Diane. (1997). Gender- and race-based standards of competence: Lower minimum standards but higher ability standards for devalued groups. *Journal of Personality and Social Psychology, 72,* 544–557.

Bigler, Rebecca S. (1997). Conceptual and methodological issues in the measurement of children's sex typing. *Psychology of Women Quarterly, 21,* 53–69.

Bigler, Rebecca S.; & Liben, Lynn S. (1993). A cognitive–developmental approach to racial stereotyping and reconstructive memory in Euro-American children. *Child Development, 64,* 1507–1518.

Bjorkqvist, Kaj. (1994). Sex differences in physical, verbal, and indirect aggression: A review of recent research, *Sex Roles, 30,* 177–188.

Blair, Sampson Lee; & Lichter, Daniel T. (1991). Measuring the division of household labor: Gender segregation of housework among American couples. *Journal of Family Issues, 12,* 91–113.

Blakeslee, Sandra. (1988, November 18). Female sex hormone is tied to ability to perform tasks. *New York Times,* A1, D20.

Blechman, Elaine A. (1980). Behavior therapies. In Annette M. Brodsky & Rachel Hare-Mustin (Eds.), *Women and psychotherapy* (pp. 217–244). New York: Guilford Press.

Blechman, Elaine A., Clay, Connie J.; Kipke, Michele D.; & Bickel, Warren K. (1988). The premenstrual experience. In Elaine A. Blechman & Kelly D. Brownell (Eds.), *Handbook of behavioral medicine for women* (pp. 80–91). New York: Pergamon Press.

Blier, Michael J.; Atkinson, Donald R.; & Greer, Carol A. (1987). Effect of client gender and counselor gender and sex roles on willingness to see the counselor. *Journal of Counseling Psychology, 34,* 27–30.

Block, Jeanne H. (1976). Debatable conclusions about sex differences [Book review of *The psychology of sex differences*]. *Contemporary Psychology, 21,* 517–522.

Blumenthal, Susan J.; & Wood, Susan F. (1997). Women's health care: Federal initiatives, policies, and directions. In Sheryle J. Gallant, Gwendolyn Puryear Keita, & Reneé Royak-Schaler (Eds.), *Health care for women: Psychological, social, and behavioral influences* (pp. 3–10). Washington, DC: American Psychological Association.

Blumstein, Philip; & Schwartz, Pepper. (1983). *American couples.* New York: Pocket Books.

Bly, Robert. (1990). *Iron John.* Reading, MA: Addison-Wesley.

Bly, Robert. (1994, August). *Where are men now?* Paper presented at the 102nd annual convention of the American Psychological Association, Los Angeles, CA.

Bohan, Janis S. (1996). *Psychology and sexual orientation: Coming to terms.* New York: Routledge.

Booth, Alan; Shelley, Greg; Mazur, Allan; Tharp, Gerry; & Kittok, Roger. (1989). Testosterone, and winning and losing in human competition. *Hormones and Behavior, 23,* 556–571.

Boston, Martha B.; & Levy, Gary D. (1991). Changes in differences in preschoolers' understanding of gender scripts. *Cognitive Development, 6,* 417–432.

Bradshaw, Carla K. (1994). Asian and Asian American women: Historical and political considerations in psychotherapy. In Lillian Comas-Díaz & Beverly Greene (Eds.), *Women of color: Integrating ethnic and gender identities in psychotherapy* (pp. 72–113). New York: Guilford Press.

Brannon, Linda. (1994). *No name required: Gender stereotyping based on passage content.* Paper presented at the 102nd annual convention of the American Psychological Association, Los Angeles, CA.

Brannon, Linda; & Feist, Jess. (1997). *Health psychology: An introduction to behavior and health* (3rd ed.). Pacific Grove, CA: Brooks/Cole.

Brannon, Robert. (1976). The male sex role: Our culture's blueprint of manhood and what it's done for us lately. In Deborah S. David & Robert Brannon (Eds.), *The forty-nine percent majority* (pp. 1–45). Reading, MA: Addison-Wesley.

Brecher, Edward M. (1969). *The sex researchers.* Boston: Little, Brown.

Breedlove, S. Marc. (1994). Sexual differentiation of the human nervous system. *Annual Review of Psychology, 45,* 389–418.

Brems, Christiane; & Schlottmann, Robert S. (1988). Gender-bound definitions of mental health. *Journal of Psychology, 122,* 5–14.

Bridge, M. Junior. (1995). What's news? In Cynthia M. Lont (Ed.), *Women and media: Content, careers, and criticism* (pp. 15–28). Belmont, CA: Wadsworth.

Britannica Book of the Year, 1992. (1992). Chicago: Encyclopedia Britannica.

Brodsky, Annette; & Holroyd, Jean (1975). Report of the Task Force on Sex Bias and Sex-Role Stereotyping in Psychotherapeutic Practice. *American Psychologist, 30,* 1169–1175.

Brooks-Gunn, Jeanne; & Furstenberg, Frank F., Jr. (1989). Adolescent sexual behavior. *American Psychologist, 44,* 249–257.

Broverman, Inge K.; Broverman, Donald M.; Clarkson, Frank E.; Rosenkrantz, Paul S.; & Vogel, Susan R. (1970). Sex-role stereotypes and clinical judgments of mental health. *Journal of Consulting and Clinical Psychology, 34,* 1–7.

Broverman, Inge K.; Vogel, Susan Raymond; Broverman, Donald M.; Clarkson, Frank E.; & Rosenkrantz, Paul S. (1972). Sex-role stereotypes: A current appraisal. *Journal of Social Issues, 28*(2), 59–78.

Brown, Laura S. (1988). Feminist therapy with lesbians and gay men. In Mary Ann Dutton Douglas & Lenore E. A. Walker (Eds.), *Feminist psychotherapies: Integration of therapeutic and feminist systems* (pp. 206–227). Norwood, NJ: Ablex.

Brown, Laura S. (1992). A feminist critique of personality disorders. In Laura S. Brown & Mary Ballou (Eds.), *Personality and psychopathlogy: Feminist reappraisals* (pp. 206–228). New York: Guilford Press.

Brown, Lyn Mikel; & Gilligan, Carol. (1992). *Meeting at the crossroads: Women's psychology and girls' development.* Cambridge, MA: Harvard University Press.

Brown, Lyn Mikel; & Gilligan, Carol. (1993). Meeting at the crossroads: Women's psychology and girls' development. *Feminism & Psychology, 3,* 11–35.

Brown, Susan L.; & Booth, Alan. (1996). Cohabitation versus marriage: A comparison of relationship quality. *Journal of Marriage and the Family, 58,* 668–678.

Browne, Angela; & Finkelhor, David. (1986). Impact of child sexual abuse: A review of the research. *Psychological Bulletin, 99,* 66–77.

Brownell, Kelly D., & Rodin, Judith. (1994). The dieting maelstrom: Is it possible and advisable to lose weight? *American Psychologist, 49,* 781–791.

Brownmiller, Susan. (1975). *Against our will: Men, women and rape.* New York: Simon & Schuster.

Bryant, Anne. (1995, March). Sexual harassment in school takes it toll. *USA Today Magazine, 123,* 40–41.

Buhrmester, Duane; & Furman, Wyndol. (1987). The development of companionship and intimacy. *Child Development, 58,* 1101–1113.

Bukowski, William M.; Gauze, Cyma; Hoza, Betsy; & Newcomb, Andrew F. (1993). Differences and consistency between same-sex and other-sex peer relationships during early adolescence. *Developmental Psychology, 29,* 255–263.

Burge, Penny L.; & Culver, Steven M. (1990). Sexism, legislative power, and vocational education. In Susan L. Gabriel & Isaiah Smithson (Eds.), *Gender in the classroom: Power and pedagogy* (pp. 160–175). Urbana, IL: University of Illinois Press.

Burnam, M. Audrey; Stein, Judith A.; Golding, Jacqueline M; Siegel, Judith M.; Sorenson, Susan B.; Forsythe, Alan B.; & Telles, Cynthia A. (1988). Sexual assault and mental disorders in a community population. *Journal of Consulting and Clinical Psychology, 56,* 843–850.

Burt, Martha R.; & Estep, Rhoda E. (1981). Apprehension and fear: Learning a sense of sexual vulnerability. *Sex Roles, 7,* 511–522.

Bush, Diane M.; & Simmons, R. G. (1987). Gender and coping with the entry into early adolescence. In Rosalind C. Barnett, Lois Biener, & Grace K. Baruch (Eds.), *Gender and stress* (pp. 185–217). New York: Free Press.

Buss, David M. (1991). Conflict in married couples: Personality predictors of anger and upset. *Journal of Personality, 59,* 663–688.

Buss, David M. (1994). *The evolution of desire.* New York: Basic Books.

Buss, David M. (1996). Sexual conflict: Evolutionary insights into feminism and the "battle of the sexes." In David M. Buss & Neil M. Malamuth (Eds.), *Sex, power, conflict: Evolutionary and feminist perspectives* (pp. 296–318). New York: Oxford University Press.

Buss, David M.; & Barnes, Michael. (1986). Preferences in human mate selection. *Journal of Personality and Social Psychology, 50,* 559–570.

Bussey, Kay; & Bandura, Albert. (1984). Influence of gender constancy and social power on sex-linked modeling. *Journal of Personality and Social Psychology, 47,* 1292–1302.

Bussey, Kay; & Bandura, Albert. (1992). Self-regulatory mechanisms governing gender development. *Child Development, 63,* 1236–1250.

Byne, William; Bleier, Ruth; & Houston, Lanning. (1988). Variations in human corpus callosum do not predict gender: A study using magnetic resonance imaging. *Behavioral Neuroscience, 102,* 222–227.

Cairns, Robert B. (1986). An evolutionary and developmental perspective on aggressive patterns. In Carolyn Zahn-Waxler, E. Mark Cummings, & Ronald Iannotti (Eds.), *Altruism and aggression: Biological and social origins* (pp. 58–87). Cambridge, England: Cambridge University Press.

Cairns, Robert B.; Cairns, Beverley D.; Neckerman, Holly J.; Ferguson, Lynda L.; & Gariépy, Jean-Louis. (1989). Growth and aggression: 1. Childhood to early adolescence. *Developmental Psychology, 25,* 320–330.

Caldwell, Mayta A.; & Peplau, Letitia Anne. (1982). Sex differences in same-sex friendship. *Sex Roles, 8,* 721–732.

Cameron, Oliver G.; & Hill, Elizabeth M. (1989). Women and anxiety. *Psychiatric Clinics of North America, 12,* 175–186.

Cammaert, Lorna P. (1985). How widespread is sexual harassment on campus? Special Issue: Women in groups and aggression against women. *International Journal of Women's Studies, 8,* 388–397.

Cammaert, Lorna P.; & Larsen, Carolyn C. (1988). Feminist frameworks of psychotherapy. In Mary Ann Dutton Douglas & Lenore E. A. Walker (Eds.), *Feminist psychotherapies: Integration of therapeutic and feminist systems* (pp. 12–36). Norwood, NJ: Ablex.

Campbell, Anne. (1993). *Men, women, and aggression.* New York: Basic Books.

Campbell, Bebe Moore. (1986). *Successful women, angry men: Backlash in the two-career marriage.* New York: Random House.

Cancian, Francesca M. (1986). The feminization of love. *Signs, 11,* 692–709.

Cancian, Francesca M. (1987). *Love in America: Gender and self-development.* Cambridge, England: Cambridge University Press.

Cann, Arnie; & Vann, Elizabeth D. (1995). Implications of sex and gender differences for self: Perceived advantages and disadvantages of being the other gender. *Sex Roles, 33,* 531–541.

Cannon, Walter B. (1927). The James–Lange theory of emotions: A critical examination and an alternative theory. *American Journal of Psychology, 39,* 106–124.

Caplan, Paula J. (1991). How *do* they decide who is normal? The bizarre, but true, tale of the DSM process. *Canadian Psychology, 32,* 162–170.

Caplan, Paula. J. (1993). Premenstrual syndrome DSM-IV diagnosis: The coalition for a scientific and responsible DSM-IV. *Psychology of Women: Newsletter of Division 35, American Psychological Association, 20*(3), 4–5, 13.

Caplan, Paula J.; & Caplan, Jeremy B. (1994). *Thinking critically about research on sex and gender.* New York: HarperCollins.

Caplan, Paula J.; MacPherson, Gael M.; & Tobin, Patricia. (1985). Do sex-related differences in spatial abilities exist? A multilevel critique with new data. *American Psychologist, 40,* 786–799.

Carli, Linda L. (1997). Biology does not create gender differences in personality. In Mary Roth Walsh (Ed.), *Women, men, & gender: Ongoing debates* (pp. 44–53). New Haven, CT: Yale University Press.

Carr, Judith G.; Gilroy, Faith D.; & Sherman, Martin F. (1996). Silencing the self and depression among women: The moderating role of race. *Psychology of Women Quarterly, 20,* 375–392.

Carr, Rey A. (1991). Addicted to power: Sexual harassment and the unethical behavior of university faculty. *Canadian Journal of Counselling, 25,* 447–461.

Carrier, Joseph. (1997). Miguel: Sexual life history of a gay Mexican American. In Maxine Baca Zinn, Pierrette Hondagneu-Sotelo, & Michael A. Messnser (Eds.), *Through the prism of difference: Readings on sex and gender* (pp. 210–220). Boston: Allyn and Bacon.

Carter, Stephen L. (1991). *Reflections of an affirmative action baby.* New York: Basic Books.

Casey, M. Beth; Nuttal, Ronald; Pezaris, Elizabeth; & Benbow, Camilla Persson. (1995). The influence of spatial ability on gender differences in mathematics college entrance test scores across diverse samples. *Developmental Psychology, 31,* 697–705.

Casper, Regina C.; Belanoff, Joseph; & Offer, Daniel. (1996). Gender differences, but no racial group differences, in self-reported psychiatric symptoms in adolescents. *Journal of the American Academy of Child and Adolescent Psychiatry, 35,* 500–508.

CDC news AIDS is top youth killer may prompt changes. (1995, February 4). *Lake Charles American Press,* p. 20.

Centers for Disease Control. (1992). Sexual behavior among high school students. *Journal of the American Medical Association, 267,* 628.

Central Intelligence Agency. (1992). *The world factbook 1992.* Washington, DC: U.S. Government Printing Office.

Chaiken, Shelly; & Pliner, Patricia. (1987). Women, but not men, are what they eat: The effect of meal size and gender on perceived femininity and masculinity. *Personality and Social Psychology Bulletin, 13,* 166–176.

Chartrand, Sabra. (1996, June 2). Gender gap splits views of glass ceiling. http://www.nytimes.com/search/daily/b...

Chehrazi, Shahla. (1986). Female psychology: A review. *Journal of the American Psychoanalytic Association, 34,* 111–162. Also in Mary Roth Walsh (Ed.). (1987). *The psychology of women: Ongoing debates* (pp. 22–38). New Haven: Yale University Press.

Chernin, Kim. (1978). *The obsession: Reflections on the tyranny of slenderness.* New York: Harper & Row.

Cherry, Frances; & Deaux, Kay. (1978). Fear of success versus fear of gender-inappropriate behavior. *Sex Roles, 4,* 97–101.

Chesler, Phyllis. (1972). *Women and madness.* New York: Avon.

Chess, Stella; & Thomas, Alexander. (1982). Infant bonding: Mystique and reality. *American Journal of Orthopsychiatry, 52,* 213–222.

Chodorow, Nancy. (1978). *The reproduction of mothering: Psychoanalysis and the sociology of gender.* Berkeley, CA: University of California Press.

Chodorow, Nancy. (1979). Feminism and difference: Gender, relation, and difference in psychoanalytic perspective. *Socialist Review, 46,* 42–64. Also in Mary Roth Walsh (Ed.). (1987). *The psychology of women: Ongoing debates* (pp. 249–264). New Haven, CT: Yale University Press.

Chodorow, Nancy J. (1994). *Femininities, masculinities, sexualities: Freud and beyond.* Lexington, KY: The University Press of Kentucky.

Christensen, Andrew; & Jacobson, Neil S. (1994). Who (or what) can do psychotherapy: The status and challenge of nonprofessional therapies. *Psychological Science, 5,* 8–14.

Christensen, Larry B. (1997). *Experimental methodology* (7th ed.). Boston: Allyn and Bacon.

Christian, Harry. (1994). *The making of anti-sexist men.* London: Routledge.

Chu, Chung-Chou; Abi-Dargham, Annissé; Ackerman, Bette; Cetingök, Maummer; & Klein, Helen E. (1989). Sex differences in schizophrenia. *International Journal of Social Psychiatry, 35,* 237–244.

Cicone, Michael V.; & Ruble, Diane N. (1978). Beliefs about males. *Journal of Social Issues, 34*(1), 1–15.

Cleary, Paul D. (1987). Gender differences in stress-related disorders. In Rosalind C. Barnett, Lois Biener, & Grace K. Baruch (Eds.), *Gender and stress* (pp. 39–72). New York: Free Press.

Cleary, Paul D.; & Mechanic, David. (1983). Sex differences in psychological distress among married people. *Journal of Health and Social Behavior, 24,* 111–121.

Cohen, Deborah (1992). Why there are so few male teachers in early grades. *Education Digest, 57*(6), 11–13.

Cohen, Jacob. (1969). *Statistical power analysis for the behavioral sciences.* New York: Academic Press.

Cohen, Laurie L.; & Shotland, R. Lance. (1996). Timing of first sexual intercourse in a relationship: Expectations, experiences, and perceptions of others. *Journal of Sex Research, 33,* 291–299.

Cohen, Theodore F. (1992). Men's families, men's friends: A structural analysis of constraints on men's social ties. In Peter M. Nardi (Ed.), *Men's friendships* (pp. 115–131). Newbury Park, CA: Sage.

Cohn, Barbara A.; Kaplan, George A.; & Cohen, Richard D. (1988). Did early detection and treatment contribute to the decline in ischemic heart disease mortality? Prospective evidence from the Alameda County Study. *American Journal of Epidemiology, 127,* 1143–1154.

Colby, Anne; & Damon, William. (1983). Listening to a different voice: A review of Gilligan's *A Different Voice. Merrill-Palmer Quarterly, 29,* 473–481. Also in Mary Roth Walsh (Ed.) (1987) *The psychology of women: Ongoing debates* (pp. 321–329). New Haven, CT: Yale University Press.

Collins, M. Elizabeth. (1991). Body figure perceptions and preferences among preadolescent children. *International Journal of Eating Disorders, 10,* 199–208.

Collins, Nancy L.; & Miller, Lynn Carol. (1994). Self-disclosure and liking: A meta-analytic review. *Psychological Bulletin, 116,* 457–475.

Coltrane, Scott; & Valdez, Elsa O. (1993). Reluctant compliance: Work–family role allocation in dual-earner Chicano families. In Jane C. Hood (Ed.), *Men, work, and family* (pp. 151–175). Newbury Park, CA: Sage.

Comas-Díaz, Lillian; & Greene, Beverly. (1994). Overview: An ethnocultural mosaic. In Lillian Comas-Díaz & Beverly Greene (Eds.), *Women of color: Integrating ethnic and gender identities in psychotherapy* (pp. 3–9). New York: Guilford Press.

Committee on Women in Psychology. (1989). If sex enters into the psychotherapy relationships. *Professional Psychology: Research and Practice, 20,* 112–115.

Condry, John; & Condry, Sandra. (1976). Sex differences: A study in the eye of the beholder. *Child Development, 47,* 812–818.

Condry, John C.; & Ross, David F. (1985). Sex and aggression: The influence of gender label on the perception of aggression in children. *Child Development, 56,* 225–233.

Connell, R. W. (1987). *Gender and power: Society, the person and sexual politics.* Cambridge, UK: Polity Press.

Connell, R. W. (1992). Masculinity, violence, and war. In Michael S. Kimmel & Michael A. Messner (Eds.), *Men's lives* (2nd ed.; pp. 176–183). New York: Macmillan.

Connell, R. W. (1995). *Masculinities.* Berkeley, CA: University of California Press.

Constantinople, Anne. (1973). Masculinity–femininity: An exception to a famous dictum. *Psychological Bulletin, 80,* 389–407.

Cook, Ellen Piel; Warnke, Melanie; & Dupuy, Paula. (1993). Gender bias and the DSM-III-R. *Counselor Education and Supervision, 32,* 311–322.

Cooperstock, Ruth (1970). A review of women's psychotropic drug use. *Canadian Journal of Psychiatry, 24,* 29–34.

Cowell, Patricia E.; Turetsky, Bruce I.; Gur, Ruben C.; Grossman, Robert I.; Shtasel, Derri L.; & Gur, Raquel E. (1994). Sex differences in aging of the human frontal and temporal lobes. *Journal of Neuroscience, 14,* 4748–4755.

Cowley, Geoffrey. (1996, September 16). Attention: Aging men. *Newsweek, 128*(12), pp. 68–75.

Crawford, June; Kippax, Susan; Onxy, Jenny; Gault, Una; & Benton, Pam. (1992). *Emotion and gender: Constructing meaning from memory.* London: Sage.

Crawford, Mary. (1989). Agreeing to differ: Feminist epistemologies and women's ways of knowing. In Mary Crawford & Margaret Gentry (Eds.), *Gender and thought: Psychological perspectives* (pp. 128–145). New York: Springer-Verlag.

Crawford, Mary; & Gressley, Diane. (1991). Creativity, caring, and context: Women's and men's accounts of humor preferences and practices. *Psychology of Women Quarterly, 15,* 217–231.

Crawford, Mary; & Marecek, Jeanne. (1989). Psychology reconstructs the female: 1968–1988. *Psychology of Women Quarterly, 13,* 147–165.

Crook, Thomas H.; Youngjohn, James R.; & Larrabee, Glenn J. (1993). The influence of age, gender, and cues on computer-simulated topographic memory. *Developmental Neuropsychology, 9,* 41–53.

Culbertson, Frances M. (1997). Depression and gender: An international review. *American Psychologist, 52,* 25–31.

Cutler, Susan E.; & Nolen-Hoeksema, Susan. (1991). Accounting for sex differences in depression through female victimization: Childhood sexual abuse. *Sex Roles, 24,* 425–438.

Dabbs, James M., Jr. (1992). Testosterone and occupational achievement. *Social Forces, 70,* 813–824.

Dabbs, James M., Jr.; Carr, Timothy S.; Frady, Robert L.; & Riad, Jasmin K. (1995). Testosterone, crime, and misbehavior among 692 male prison inmates. *Personality and Individual Differences, 18,* 627–633.

Dabbs, James M., Jr.; de la Rue, Denise; & Williams, Paula M. (1990). Testosterone and occupational choice: Actors, ministers, and other men. *Journal of Personality and Social Psychology, 59,* 1261–1265.

Dabbs, James M., Jr.; Hargrove, Marian F.; & Heusel, Colleen. (1996). Testosterone differences among college fraternities: Well-behaved vs. rambunctious. *Personality and Individual Differences, 20,* 157–161.

Dabbs, James M., Jr.; Hopper, Charles H.; & Jurkovic, Gregory J. (1990). Testosterone and personality among college students and military veterans. *Personality and Individual Differences, 11,* 1263–1269.

Dabbs, James M., Jr.; & Morris, Robin. (1990). Testosterone, social class, and antisocial behavior in a sample of 4,462 men. *Psychological Science, 1,* 209–211.

Dabbs, James M., Jr.; Ruback, R. Barry; Frady, Robert L.; Hopper, Charles H.; & Sgoutas, Demetrios S. (1988). Saliva testosterone and criminal violence among women. *Personality and Individual Differences, 9,* 269–275.

Darwin, Charles. (1872). *The expression of emotions in man and animals.* New York: Philosophical Library.

Daugherty, Cynthia; & Lees, Marty. (1988). Feminist psychodynamic therapies. In Mary Ann Dutton Douglas & Lenore E. A. Walker (Eds.), *Feminist psychotherapies: Integration of therapeutic and feminist systems* (pp. 68–90). Norwood, NJ: Ablex.

Davenport, Donna S.; & Yurich, John M. (1991). Multicultural gender issues. *Journal of Counseling and Development, 70,* 64–71.

Davis, Caroline; Elliott, Stuart; Dionne, Michelle; & Mitchell, Ian. (1991). The relationship of personality factors and physical activity to body satisfaction in men. *Personality and Individual Differences, 12,* 89–694.

Davis, Kathy. (1994). What's in a voice? Methods and metaphors. *Feminism & Psychology, 4,* 353–361.

Day, Randal D. (1992). The transition to first intercourse among racially and culturally diverse youth. *Journal of Marriage and the Family, 54,* 749–762.

Deaux, Kay. (1984). From individual differences to social categories: Analysis of a decade's research on gender. *American Psychologist, 39,* 105–116.

Deaux, Kay. (1987). Psychological constructions of masculinity and femininity. In June Machover Reinisch, Leonard A. Rosenblum, & Stephanie A. Sanders (Eds.), *Masculinity/Femininity: Basic perspectives* (pp. 289–303). New York: Oxford University Press.

Deaux, Kay. (1993). Commentary: Sorry, wrong number: A reply to Gentile's call. *Psychological Science, 4,* 125–126.

Deaux, Kay; & Lewis, Laurie. (1984). The structure of gender stereotypes: Interrelationships among components and gender label. *Journal of Personality and Social Psychology, 46,* 991–1004.

Deaux, Kay; White, Leonard; & Farris, Elizabeth. (1975). Skill versus luck: Field and laboratory studies of male and female preferences. *Journal of Personality and Social Psychology, 32,* 629–636.

Degler, Carl N. (1974). What ought to be and what was: Women's sexuality in the nineteenth century. *American Historical Review, 79,* 1467–1490.

DeHeer, N. Dean; Wampold, Bruce E.; & Freund, Richard D. (1992). Do sex-typed and androgynous subjects prefer counselors on the basis of gender or effectiveness? They prefer the best. *Journal of Counseling Psychology, 39,* 175–184.

de Lacoste-Utamsing; & Holloway, Ralph L. (1982). Sexual dimorphism in the human corpus callosum. *Science, 216,* 1431–1432.

de Monteflores, Carmen; & Schultz, Stephen J. (1978). Coming out: Similarities and differences for lesbians and gay men. *Journal of Social Issues, 34*(3), 59–72.

Denmark, Florence L. (1994). Engendering psychology. *American Psychologist, 49,* 329–334.

Derry, Paula S.; Gallant, Sheryle J.; & Woods, Nancy F. (1997). Premenstrual syndrome and menopause. In Sheryle J. Gallant, Gwendolyn Puryear Keita, & Reneé Royak-Schaler (Eds.), *Health care for women: Psychological, social, and behavioral influences* (pp. 203–220). Washington, DC: American Psychological Association.

Deutsch, Francine M.; Lussier, Julianne B.; & Servis, Laura J. (1993). Husbands at home: Predictors of paternal participation in childcare and housework. *Journal of Personality and Social Psychology, 65,* 1154–1166.

DiMatteo, M. Robin; & Kahn, Katherine L. (1997). Psychosocial aspects of childbirth. In Sheryle J. Gallant, Gwendolyn Puryear Keita, & Reneé Royak-Schaler (Eds.), *Health care for women: Psychological, social, and behavioral influences* (pp. 175–186). Washington, DC: American Psychological Association.

Dinnerstein, Dorothy. (1976). *The mermaid and the minotaur: Sexual arrangements and the human malaise.* New York: Harper & Row.

Dolan, Bridget. (1994). Why women? Gender issues and eating disorders: An introduction. In Bridget Dolan & Inez Gitzinger (Eds.), *Why women? Gender issues and eating disorders* (pp. 1–11). London: Athlone Press.

Doll, Richard; & Peto, Richard. (1981). *The causes of cancer.* New York: Oxford University Press.

Dollard, John; Doob, Leonard; Miller, Neal; Mowrer, O. Hobart; & Sears, Robert. (1939). *Frustration and aggression.* New Haven, CT: Yale University Press.

Dovidio, John F.; Ellyson, Steve L.; Keating, Caroline F.; Heltman, Karen; & Brown, Clifford E. (1988). The relationship of social power to visual displays of dominance between men and women. *Journal of Personality and Social Psychology, 54,* 233–242.

Dreher, George F.; & Cox, Taylor H., Jr. (1996). Race, gender, and opportunity: A study of compensation attainment and the establishment of mentoring relationships. *Journal of Applied Psychology, 81,* 297–308.

Drewnowski, Adam; & Yee, Doris K. (1987). Men and body image: Are males satisfied with their body weight? *Psychosomatic Medicine, 49,* 626–634.

Dreyfus, Colleen K. (1994, August). *Stigmatizing attitudes toward male victims.* Paper presented at the 102nd annual convention of the American Psychological Association, Los Angeles, CA.

Dubbert, Patricia M. (1992). Exercise in behavioral medicine. *Journal of Consulting and Clinical Psychology, 60,* 613–618.

Dubbert, Patricia M.; & Martin, John E. (1988). Exercise. In Elaine A. Blechman & Kelly D. Brownell (Eds.), *Handbook of behavioral medicine for women* (pp. 291–304). New York: Pergamon Press.

DuBois, David L.; & Hirsch, Barton J. (1990). School and neighborhood friendship patterns of Blacks and Whites in early adolescence. *Child Development, 61,* 524–536.

Duck, Steve (1991). *Understanding relationships.* New York: Guilford Press.

Dutton, Mary Ann; Haywood, Yolanda; & El-Bayoumi, Gigi. (1997). Impact of violence on women's health. In Sheryle J. Gallant, Gwendolyn Puryear Keita, & Reneé Royak-Schaler (Eds.), *Health care for women: Psychological, social, and behavioral influences* (pp. 41–56). Washington, DC: American Psychological Association.

Dweck, Carol S. (1986). Motivational processes affecting learning. *American Psychologist, 41,* 1040–1048.

Dwyer, Victor. (1997, May 19). Class action: Fighting homophobia in school. *Maclean's, 110,* 52–53.

Eagly, Alice H. (1987a). Reporting sex differences. *American Psychologist, 42,* 756–757.

Eagly, Alice H. (1987b). *Sex differences in social behavior: A social-role interpretation.* Hillsdale, NJ: Erlbaum.

Eagly, Alice H. (1994, August). *Are people prejudiced against women?* Paper presented at the 102nd annual convention of the American Psychological Association, Los Angeles, CA.

Eagly, Alice H. (1995). The science and politics of comparing women and men. *American Psychologist, 50,* 145–158.

Eagly, Alice H. (1997). Comparing women and men: Methods, findings, and politics. In Mary Roth Walsh (Ed.), *Women, men, and gender: Ongoing debates* (pp. 24–31). New Haven, CT: Yale University Press.

Eagly, Alice H.; & Johnson, Blair T. (1990). Gender and leadership style: A meta-analysis. *Psychological Bulletin, 108,* 233–256.

Eagly, Alice H.; Karau, Steven J.; & Makhijani, Mona G. (1995). Gender and the effectiveness of leaders: A meta-analysis. *Psychological Bulletin, 117,* 125–145.

Eagly, Alice H.; & Kite, Mary E. (1987). Are stereotypes of nationalities applied to both women and men? *Journal of Personality and Social Psychology, 53,* 451–462.

Eagly, Alice H.; Makhijani, Mona G.; & Klonsky, Bruce G. (1992). Gender and the evaluation of leaders: A meta-analysis. *Psychological Bulletin, 111,* 3–22.

Eagly, Alice H.; Mladinic, Antonio; & Otto, Stacey. (1991). Are women evaluated more favorably than men? An analysis of attitudes, beliefs, and emotions. *Psychology of Women Quarterly, 15,* 203–216.

Eagly, Alice H.; & Steffen, Valerie J. (1986). Gender and aggressive behavior: A meta-analytic review of the social psychological literature. *Psychological Bulletin, 100,* 309–330.

Eagly, Alice H.; & Wood, Wendy. (1985). Gender and influenceability: Stereotype versus behavior. In Virginia E. O'Leary, Rhoda Kesler Unger, & Barbara Strudler Wallston (Eds.), *Women, gender, and social psychology* (pp. 225–256). Hillsdale, NJ: Erlbaum.

Eccles, Jacquelynne S. (1987). Gender roles and achievement patterns: An expectancy value perspective. In June Machover Reinisch, Leonard A. Rosenblum, & Stephanie A. Sanders (Eds.), *Masculinity/Femininity: Basic perspectives* (pp. 240–280). New York: Oxford University Press.

Eccles, Jacquelynne S. (1989). Bringing young women to math and science. In Mary Crawford & Margaret Gentry (Eds.), *Gender and thought: Psychological perspectives* (pp. 36–58). New York: Springer-Verlag.

Eccles, Jacquelynne; & Bryan, James. (1994). Adolescence: Critical crossroad in the path of gender-role development. In Michael R. Stevenson (Ed.), *Gender roles through the life span: A multidisciplinary perspective* (pp. 111–147). Muncie, IN: Ball State University.

Eccles, Jacquelynne S.; & Jacobs, Janis E. (1986). Social forces shape math attitudes and performance. *Signs, 11,* 367–380.

Eccles, Jacquelynne S.; Wigfield, Allan; Harold, Rena D.; & Blumenfeld, Phyllis. (1993). Age and gender differences in children's self- and task-perceptions during elementary school. *Child Development, 64,* 830–845.

Eckhardt, Michael J.; Harford, Thomas C.; Kaelber, Charles T.; Parker, Elizabeth S.; Rosenthal, Laura S.; Ryback, Ralph S.; Salmoiraghi, Gian C.; Vanderveen, Ernestine; & Warren, Kenneth R. (1981). Health hazards associated with alcohol consumption. *Journal of the American Medical Association, 246,* 648–666.

Edmonds, Ed M.; & Cahoon, Delwin D. (1993). The "new" sexism: Females' negativism toward males. *Journal of Social Behavior and Personality, 8,* 481–487.

Ehrenreich, Barbara; & English, Deirdre. (1973). *Witches, midwives, and nurses: A history of women healers.* New York: Feminist Press.

Ehrenreich, Barbara; Hess, Elizabeth; & Jacobs, Gloria. (1986). *Re-making love: The feminization of sex.* Garden City, NY: Anchor Press.

Ehrhardt, Anke A.; & Meyer-Bahlburg, Heino F. L. (1981). Effects of prenatal sex hormones on gender-related behavior. *Science, 211,* 1312–1317.

Eichenbaum, Luise; & Orbach, Susie. (1983). *What do women want: Exploding the myth of dependency.* New York: Coward-McCann.

Eisenberg, Nancy; & Lennon, Randy. (1983). Sex differences in empathy and related capacities. *Psychological Bulletin, 94,* 100–131.

Ekman, Paul. (1984). Expression and the nature of emotion. In Klaus R. Scherer & Paul Ekman (Eds.), *Approaches to emotion* (pp. 319–343). Hillsdale, NJ: Erlbaum.

Ekman, Paul; Levenson, Robert W.; & Friesen, Wallace V. (1983). Autonomic nervous activity distinguishes among emotions. *Science, 221,* 1208–1210.

Ellenberger, Henri F. (1970). *The discovery of the unconscious.* New York: Basic Books.

Ellestad, Myrvin H. (1986). *Stress testing* (3rd ed.). Philadelphia: Davis.

Ellis, Albert. (1962). *Reason and emotion in psychotherapy.* New York: Stuart.

Enns, Carolyn Zerbe. (1992). Self-esteem groups: A synthesis of consciousness-raising and assertiveness training. *Journal of Counseling and Development, 71,* 7–13.

Enns, Carolyn Zerbe. (1993). Twenty years of feminist counseling and therapy: From naming biases to implementing multifaceted practice. *Counseling Psychologist, 21,* 3–87.

Enns, Carolyn Zerbe. (1997). *Feminist theories and feminist psychotherapies: Origins, themes, and variations.* New York: Harrington Park Press.

Enns, Carolyn Z.; & Hackett, Gail. (1990). Comparison of feminist and nonfeminist women's reactions to variants of nonsexist and feminist counseling. *Journal of Counseling Psychology, 37,* 33–40.

Entwisle, Doris R.; Alexander, Karl L.; & Olson, Linda Steffel. (1994). The gender gap in math: Its possible origins in neighborhood effects. *American Sociological Review, 59,* 822–838.

Epstein, Cynthia Fuchs. (1988). *Deceptive distinctions: Sex, gender and the social order.* New Haven, CT: Yale University Press.

Eron, Leonard D. (1987). The development of aggressive behavior from the perspective of a developing behaviorism. *American Psychologist, 42,* 435–442.

Eron, Leonard D.; Huesmann, L. Rowell; Brice, Patrick; Fischer, Paulette; & Mermelstein, Rebecca. (1983). Age trends in the development of aggression, sex typing, and related television habits. *Developmental Psychology, 19,* 71–77.

Eyer, Diane E. (1992). *Mother–infant bonding: A scientific fiction.* New Haven, CT: Yale University Press.

Faderman, Lillian. (1989). A history of romantic friendship and lesbian love. In Barbara J. Risman & Pepper Schwartz (Eds.), *Gender in intimate relationships* (pp. 26–31). Belmont, CA: Wadsworth.

Fagot, Beverly I.; & Hagan, Richard. (1991). Observations of parent reactions to sex-stereotyped behaviors: Age and sex effects. *Child Development, 62,* 617–628.

Fagot, Beverly I.; & Leinbach, Mary D. (1989). The young child's gender schema: Environmental input, internal organization. *Child Development, 60,* 663–672.

Fagot, Beverly I.; & Leinbach, Mary D. (1993). Gender-role development in young children: From discrimination to labeling. *Developmental Review, 13,* 205–224.

Fagot, Beverly I.; & Leinbach, Mary D. (1994). Gender-role development in young children. In Michael R. Stevenson (Ed.), *Gender roles through the life span: A multidisciplinary perspective* (pp. 3–24). Muncie, IN: Ball State University.

Fagot, Beverly I.; & Leinbach, Mary D. (1995). Gender knowledge in egalitarian and traditional families. *Sex Roles, 32,* 513–526.

Fagot, Beverly I.; Leinbach, Mary D.; & O'Boyle, Cherie. (1992). Gender labeling, gender stereotyping, and parenting behaviors. *Developmental Psychology, 28,* 225–230.

Fallon, April E.; & Rozin, Paul. (1985). Sex differences in perceptions of desirable body shape. *Journal of Abnormal Psychology, 94,* 102–105.

Faludi, Susan. (1991). *Backlash: The undeclared war against American women.* New York: Crown.

Farmer, Helen S.; & Sidney, Joan Seliger. (1985). Sex equity in career and vocational eduction. In Susan S. Klein (Ed.), *Handbook for achieving sex equity through education* (pp. 338–359). Baltimore: Johns Hopkins University Press.

Fausto-Sterling, Anne. (1985). *Myths of gender: Biological theories about women and men.* New York: Basic Books.

Fee, Elizabeth. (1986). Critiques of modern science: The relationship of feminism to other radical epistemologies. In Ruth Bleier (Ed.), *Feminist approaches to science* (pp. 42–56). New York: Pergamon Press.

Feingold, Alan. (1988). Cognitive gender differences are disappearing. *American Psychologist, 43,* 95–103.

Feingold, Alan. (1994). Gender differences in variability in intellectual abilities; A cross-cultural perspective. *Sex Roles, 30,* 81–92.

Feist, Jess; & Feist, Gregory J. (1998). *Theories of personality* (4th ed.). Boston: McGraw-Hill.

Feld, Scott L.; & Straus, Murray A. (1989). Escalation and desistance of wife assault in marriage. *Criminology, 27,* 141–161.

Felmlee, Diane H. (1994). Who's on top? Power in romantic relationships. *Sex Roles, 31,* 275–295.

Fennema, Elizabeth. (1980). Sex-related differences in mathematics achievement: Where and why. In Lynn H. Fox, Linda Brody, & Dianne Tobin (Eds.), *Women and the mathematical mystique* (pp. 76–93). Baltimore: Johns Hopkins University Press.

Ferree, Myra Marx; & Hess, Beth B. (1985). *Controversy and coalition: The new feminist movement.* Boston: Twayne.

Feyerherm, William. (1981). Measuring gender differences in delinquency: Self-reports versus police contact. In Marguerite O. Warren (Ed.), *Comparing female and male offenders* (pp. 46–54). Beverly Hills, CA: Sage.

Fields, Judith; & Wolff, Edward N. (1991). The decline of sex segregation and the wage gap, 1970–80. *Journal of Human Resources, 26,* 608–622.

Fine, Michelle. (1988). Sexuality, schooling, and adolescent females: The missing discourse of desire. *Harvard Educational Review, 58,* 29–53.

Finkelhor, David. (1980). Sex among siblings: A survey on prevalence, variety, and effects. *Archives of Sexual Behavior, 9,* 171–193.

Finkelhor, David. (1984). *Child sexual abuse: New theory and research.* New York: Free Press.

Finkelhor, David. (1990). Early and long-term effects of child sexual abuse: An update. *Professional Psychology Research and Practice, 21,* 325–330.

Finkelhor, David; & Baron, Larry. (1986). Risk factors for child sexual abuse. *Journal of Interpersonal Violence, 1,* 43–71.

Fischer, Agneta H. (1993). Sex differences in emotionality: Fact or stereotype? *Feminism & Psychology, 3,* 303–318.

Fischer, Ann R.; Good, Glenn E. (1994). Gender, self, and others: Perceptions of the campus environment. *Journal of Counseling Psychology, 41,* 343–355.

Fiske, Susan T. (1993). Controlling other people: The impact of power on stereotyping. *American Psychologist, 48,* 621–628.

Fiske, Susan T.; Bersoff, Donald N.; Borgida, Eugene; Deaux, Kay; & Heilman, Madeline E. (1991). Social science research on trial: Use of sex stereotyping research in *Price Waterhouse v. Hopkins. American Psychologist, 46,* 1049–1060.

Fitzgerald, Louise F. (1994, August). *Sexual harassment—A feminist perspective on the prevention of violence against women in the workplace.* Paper presented at the 102nd annual convention of the American Psychological Association, Los Angeles, CA.

Fitzgerald, Louise F.; Swan, Suzanne; & Magley, Vicki J. (1997). But was it really sexual harassment? Legal, behavioral, and psychological definitions of the workplace victimization of women. In William O'Donohue (Ed.), *Sexual harassment: Theory, research, and treatment* (pp. 5–28). Boston: Allyn and Bacon.

Fitzgerald, Louise F.; Weitzman, Lauren M.; Gold, Yael; & Ormerod, Mimi. (1988). Academic harassment: Sex and denial in scholarly garb. *Psychology of Women Quarterly, 12,* 329–340.

Flaskerud, Jacquelyn H. (1986). Diagnostic and treatment differences among five ethnic groups. *Psychological Reports, 58,* 219–235.

Flaskerud, Jacquelyn H.; & Hu, Li-tze. (1992). Relationship of ethnicity to psychiatric diagnosis. *Journal of Nervous and Mental Disease, 180,* 296–303.

Floyd, Kory. (1995). Gender and closeness among friends and siblings. *Journal of Psychology, 129,* 193–202.

Flynn, Clifton P. (1990). Relationship violence by women: Issues and implications. *Family Relations, 39,* 194–198.

Fodor, Iris Goldstein. (1988). Cognitive behavior therapy: Evaluation of theory and practice for addressing women's issues. In Mary Ann Dutton Douglas & Lenore E. A. Walker (Eds.), *Feminist psychotherapies: Integration of therapeutic and feminist systems* (pp. 91–117). Norwood, NJ: Ablex.

Folkman, Susan; & Lazarus, Richard S. (1980). An analysis of coping in middle-aged community sample. *Journal of Health and Social Behavior, 21,* 219–239.

Fontenot, Kathleen; & Brannon, Linda. (1991, August). *Gender differences in coping with workplace stress.* Paper presented at the 99th convention of the American Psychological Association, San Francisco, CA.

Ford, Clellan S.; & Beach, Frank A. (1951). *Patterns of sexual behavior.* New York: Harper.

Fowers, Blaine J. (1991). His and her marriage: A multivariate study of gender and marital satisfaction. *Sex Roles, 24,* 209–221.

Fowers, Blaine J.; Applegate, Brooks; Tredinnick, Michael; & Slusher, Jason. (1996). His and her individualisms? Sex bias and individualism in psychologists' responses to case vignettes. *The Journal of Psychology, 130,* 159–174.

Fox, Mary Frank. (1989). Women and higher education: Gender differences in the status of students and scholars. In Jo Freeman (Ed.), *Women: A feminist perspective* (4th ed.; pp. 217–235). Mountain View, CA: Mayfield.

Fox, Ronald C. (1996). Bisexuality in perspective: A review of theory and research. In Beth A. Firestein (Ed.), *Bisexuality: The psychology and politics of an invisible minority* (pp. 3–50). Thousand Oaks, CA: Sage.

Frankenhaeuser, Marianne. (1991). Psychophysiology of sex differences as related to occupational stress. In Marianne Frankenhaeuser, Ulf Lundberg, & Margaret Chesney (Eds.), *Women, work, and health: Stress and opportunities* (pp. 39–61). New York: Plenum Press.

Freiberg, Peter. (1991). Self-esteem gender gap widens in adolescence. *APA Monitor, 22*(4), 29.

Freud, Sigmund. (1925/1959). An autobiographical study. In James Strachey (Ed. and Trans.), *The standard edition of the complete psychological works of Sigmund Freud* (Vol. 20). London: Hogarth Press.

Freud, Sigmund. (1925/1989). Some psychical consequences of the anatomical distinction between the sexes. In Peter Gay (Ed.), *The Freud reader* (pp. 670–678). New York: Norton.

Freud, Sigmund. (1933/1964). Femininity. In James Strachey (Ed. and Trans.), *New introductory lectures on psychoanalysis* (p. 112–135). New York: Norton.

Frezza, Mario; di Padova, Carlo; Pozzato, Gabriele; Terpin, Maddalena; Baraona, Enrique; & Lieber, Charles S. (1990). High blood alcohol levels in women: The role of decreased gastric alcohol dehydrogenase activity and first-pass metabolism. *New England Journal of Medicine, 322,* 95–99.

Frodi, Ann M.; & Lamb, Michael E. (1978). Sex differences in responsiveness to infants: A developmental study of psychophysiological and behavioral responses. *Child Devleopment, 49,* 1182–1188.

Frodi, Ann M.; Macaulay, Jacqueline; & Thome, Pauline R. (1977). Are women always less aggressive than men? A review of the experimental literature. *Psychological Bulletin, 84,* 634–660.

Frye, Marilyn. (1997). Lesbian "sex." In Maxine Baca Zinn, Pierrette Hondagneu-Sotelo, & Michael A. Messner (Eds.), *Through the prism of difference: Readings on sex and gender* (pp. 205–209). Boston: Allyn and Bacon.

Fujita, Frank; Diener, Ed; & Sandvik, Ed. (1991). Gender differences in negative affect and well-being: The case for emotional intensity. *Journal of Personality and Social Psychology, 61,* 427–434.

Furman, Wyndol; & Bierman, Karen Linn. (1984). Children's conceptions of friendship: A multimethod study of developmental changes. *Developmental Psychology, 20,* 925–931.

Furstenberg, Frank F.; & Spanier, Graham B. (1984). *Recycling the family: Remarriage after divorce.* Beverly Hills, CA: Sage.

Galea, Lisa A.; & Kimura, Doreen. (1993). Sex differences in route-learning. *Personality and Individual Differences, 14,* 53–65.

Gallagher, Maggie. (1987, May 22). What men really want. *National Review,* 39–40.

Ganley, Anne L. (1988). Feminist therapy with male clients. In Mary Ann Dutton Douglas & Lenore E. A. Walker (Eds.), *Feminist psychotherapies: Integration of therapeutic and feminist systems* (pp. 186–205). Norwood, NJ: Ablex.

Garner, David M.; & Garfinkel, Paul E. (1980). Sociocultural factors in the development of anorexia nervosa. *Psychological Medicine, 10,* 647–656.

Garner, David M.; Garfinkel, Paul E.; Schwartz, Donald M.; & Thompson, Michael G. (1980). Cultural expectations of thinness in women. *Psychological Reports, 47,* 483–491.

Gartner, Alan; Gartner, Audrey J.; & Ouellette Kobasa, Suzanne C. (1988). Self-help. In Elaine A. Blechman & Kelly D. Brownell (Eds.), *Handbook of behavioral medicine for women* (pp. 330–342). New York: Pergamon Press.

Gartrell, Nanette; Herman, Judith L.; Olarte, Silvia; Feldstein, Michael; & Localio, Russell. (1987). Reporting practices of psychiatrists who knew of sexual misconduct by colleagues. *American Journal of Orthopsychiatry, 57,* 287–295.

Gates, David. (1993, March 29). White male paranoia. *Newsweek, 121,* 48–53.

Gay, Peter. (1988). *Freud: A life for our time.* New York: Norton.

Geer, James H.; & Broussard, Deborah Bice. (1990). Scaling heterosexual behavior and arousal: Consistency and sex differences. *Journal of Personality and Social Psychology, 58,* 664–671.

Gelles, Richard J. (1979). *Family violence.* Beverly Hills, CA: Sage.

Gelles, Richard J.; & Cornell, Claire Pedrick. (1990). *Intimate violence in families* (2nd ed.). Newbury Park, CA: Sage.

Gentile, Douglas A. (1993). Just what are sex and gender, anyway? A call for a new terminological standard. *Psychological Science, 4,* 120–122.

Gergen, Kenneth J. (1985). The social constructionist movement in modern psychology. *American Psychologist, 40,* 266–275.

Gerhart, Barry. (1990). Gender differences in current and starting salaries: The role of performance, college major, and job title. *Industrial and Labor Relations Review, 43,* 418–433.

Geschwind, Norman; & Galaburda, Albert S. (1987). *Cerebral lateralization.* Cambridge, MA: MIT Press.

Gibbons, Judith L.; Hamby, Beverly, A.; & Dennis, Wanda D. (1997). Researching gender-role ideologies internationally and cross-culturally. *Psychology of Women Quarterly, 21,* 151–170.

Gilbert, Lucia A. (1980). Feminist therapy. In Annette M. Brodsky & Rachel Hare-Mustin (Eds.), *Women and psychotherapy* (pp. 245–265). New York: Guilford Press.

Gilbert, Lucia A. (1984). Comments on the meaning of work in women's lives. *Counseling Psychology, 12,* 129–130.

Gilgun, Jane F. (1995). We shared something special: The moral discourse of incest perpetrators. *Journal of Marriage and the Family, 57,* 265–281.

Gilligan, Carol. (1982). *In a different voice: Psychological theory and women's development.* Cambridge, MA: Harvard University Press.

Gilligan, Carol; & Attanucci, Jane. (1988). Two moral orientations. In Carol Gilligan, Janie Victoria Ward, & Jill McLean Taylor, with Betty Bardige (Eds.), *Mapping the moral domain: A contribution of women's thinking to psychological theory and education* (pp. 73–86). Cambridge, MA: Harvard University Press.

Ginorio, Angela B.; Gutiérrez, Lorraine; Cauce, Ana Mari; & Acosta, Mimi. (1995). Psychological issues for Latinas. In Hope Landrine (Ed.), *Bringing cultural diversity to feminist psychology: Theory, research, and practice* (pp. 241–263). Washington, DC: American Psychological Association.

Ginsburg, Herbert; & Opper, Sylvia. (1969). *Piaget's theory of intellectual development: An introduction.* Englewood Cliffs, NJ: Prentice-Hall.

Glick, Peter; Zion, Cari; & Nelson, Cynthia. (1988). What mediates sex discrimination in hiring decisions? *Journal of Personality and Social Psychology, 55,* 178–186.

Golding, Jacqueline M.; Smith, G. Richard; & Kashner, T. Michael. (1991). Does somatization disorder occur in men? Clinical characteristics of women and men with multiple unexplained somatic symptoms. *Archives of General Psychiatry, 48,* 231–235.

Goldsmith, Ronald E.; & Matherly, Timothy A. (1988). Creativity and self-esteem: A multiple operationalization validity study. *Journal of Psychology, 122,* 47–56.

Goleman, Daniel. (1990, July 17). Aggression in men: Hormone levels are a key. *New York Times,* section C, p. 1.

Gonzalez, Judith Teresa. (1988). Dilemmas of the high-achieving Chicana: The double-bind factor in male/female relationships. *Sex Roles, 18,* 367–380.

Good, Glenn E.; Dell, Don M.; & Mintz, Laurie B. (1989). Male role and gender role conflict: Relations to help seeking in men. *Journal of Counseling Psychology, 36,* 295–300.

Good, Glenn E.; Gilbert, Lucia A.; & Scher, Murray. (1990). Gender Aware Therapy: A synthesis of feminist therapy and knowledge about gender. *Journal of Counseling & Development, 68,* 376–380.

Good, Glenn E.; & Wood, Phillip K. (1995). Male gender role conflict, depression, and help seeking: Do college men face double jeopardy? *Journal of Counseling and Development, 74,* 70–75.

Goodman, Lisa A.; Koss, Mary P.; Fitzgerald, Louise F.; Russo, Nancy Felipe; & Keita, Gwendolyn Puryear. (1993). Male violence against women: Current research and future directions. *American Psychologist, 48,* 1054–1058.

Gorelick, Sherry. (1994, November/December). The gender trap. *Ms. Magazine, 5*(3), 60–64.

Gorman, Christine. (1992, January 20). Sizing up the sexes. *Time,* 42–51.

Gorski, Roger A. (1987). Sex differences in the rodent brain: Their nature and origin. In June M. Reinisch, Leonard A. Rosenblum, & Stephanie A. Sanders (Eds.), *Masculinity/Femininity: Basic perspectives* (pp. 37–67). New York: Oxford University Press.

Gottman, John M. (1991). Predicting the longitudinal course of marriages. *Journal of Marriage and Family Therapy, 17,* 3–7.

Gottman, John, with Nan Silver. (1994). *Why marriages succeed or fail.* New York: Simon & Schuster.

Gould, Stephen Jay. (1996). *The mismeasure of man* (rev. ed.). New York: Norton.

Gove, Walter R. (1980). Mental illness and psychiatric treatment among women. *Psychology of Women Quarterly, 4,* 345–362.

Gove, Walter R. (1984). Gender differences in mental and physical illness: The effects of fixed roles and nurturant roles. *Social Science and Medicine, 19*(2), 77–84.

Gove, Walter R.; & Hughes, Michael. (1979). Possible causes of the apparent sex differences in physical health: An empirical investigation. *American Sociological Review, 44,* 126–146.

Gove, Walter R.; & Zeiss, Carol. (1987). Multiple roles and happiness. In Faye J. Crosby (Ed.), *Spouse, parent, worker: On gender and multiple roles* (pp. 125–137). New Haven, CT: Yale University Press.

Granrose, Cherlyn Skromme; & Kaplan, Eileen E. (1996). *Work–family role choices for women in their 20s and 30s.* Westport, CT: Praeger.

Gratch, Linda Vanden; Bassett, Margaret E.; & Attra, Sharon L. (1995). The relationship of gender and ethnicity to self-silencing and depression among college students. *Psychology of Women Quarterly, 19,* 509–515.

Gray, John. (1992). *Men are from Mars, women are from Venus.* New York: HarperCollins.

Green, Beth L.; & Russo, Nancy Felipe. (1993). Work and family roles: Selected issues. In Florence L. Denmark & Michele A. Paludi (Eds.), *Psychology of women: A handbook of issues and theories* (pp. 685–719). Westport, CT: Greenwood Press.

Green, Richard. (1987). *The "sissy boy syndrome" and the development of homosexuality.* New Haven, CT: Yale University Press.

Greenberger, Ellen; & O'Neil, Robin. (1993). Spouse, parent, worker: Role commitments and role-related experiences in the construction of adults' well-being. *Developmental Psychology, 29,* 181–197.

Greene, Beverly. (1994). African American women. In Lillian Comas-Díaz & Beverly Greene (Eds.), *Women of color: Integrating ethnic and gender identities in psychotherapy* (pp. 10–29). New York: Guilford Press.

Greene, Judith. (1987). Patterns of eating in normal men and women. *Psychology—A Quarterly Journal of Human Behavior, 24*(4), 1–14.

Greeno, Catherine G.; & Maccoby, Eleanor E. (1986). How different is the "different voice"? *Signs, 11*(2), 310–312.

Greenstein, Theodore N. (1996). Husbands' participation in domestic labor: Interactive effect of wives' and husbands' gender ideologies. *Journal of Marriage and the Family, 58,* 585–595.

Greenwald, Anthony G. (1975). Consequences of prejudice against the null hypothesis. *Psychological Bulletin, 82,* 1–20.

Gregory, Robert J. (1987). *Adult intellectual assessment.* Boston: Allyn and Bacon.

Groshen, Erica L. (1991). The structure of the female/male wage differential: Is it who you are, what you do, or where you work? *Journal of Human Resources, 26,* 457–472.

Grossman, Michele; & Wood, Wendy. (1993). Sex differences in intensity of emotional experience: A social role interpretation. *Journal of Personality and Social Psychology, 65,* 1010–1022.

Gupta, Nabanita Datta. (1993). Probabilities of job choice and employer selection and male–female occupational differences. *American Economic Review, 83*(2), 57–62.

Gur, Ruben C.; Mozley, Lyn Harper; Mozley, P. David; Resnick, Susan M.; Kapr, Joel S.; Alavi, Abass; Arnold, Steven E.; & Gur, Raquel E. (1995). Sex differences in regional glucose metabolism during a resting state. *Science, 267,* 528–531.

Gutek, Barbara A. (1985). *Sex and the workplace.* San Francisco: Jossey-Bass.

Gutek, Barbara A.; & Larwood, Laurie. (1989). Introduction: Women's careers are important and different. In Barbara A. Gutek & Laurie Larwood (Eds.), *Women's career development* (pp. 7–14). Newbury Park, CA: Sage.

Gutek, Barbara A.; & O'Connor, Maureen. (1995). The empirical basis for the reasonable woman standard. *Journal of Social Issues, 51*(1), 151–166.

Hackett, Gail; Enns, Carolyn Z.; & Zetzer, Heidi A. (1992). Reactions of women to nonsexist and feminist counseling: Effects of counselor orientation and mode of information delivery. *Journal of Counseling Psychology, 39,* 321–330.

Hahn, William Kerr. (1987). Cerebral lateralization of function: From infancy through childhood. *Psychological Bulletin, 101,* 376–392.

Halpern, Diane F. (1985). The influence of sex-role stereotypes on prose recall. *Sex Roles, 12,* 363–375.

Halpern, Diane F. (1992). *Sex differences in cognitive abilities* (2nd ed.). Hillsdale, NJ: Erlbaum.

Halpern, Diane F. (1994). Stereotypes, science, censorship, and the study of sex differences. *Feminism & Psychology, 4,* 523–530.

Halpern, Diane F. (1995). Cognitive gender differences: Why diversity is a critical research issue. In Hope Landrine (Ed.), *Bringing cultural diversity to feminist psychology: Theory, research, and practice* (pp. 77–92). Washington, DC: American Psychological Association.

Halpern, Diane F. (1997). Sex differences in intelligence: Implications for education. *American Psychologist, 52,* 1091–1102.

Hamilton, Sandra; & Fagot, Beverly I. (1988). Chronic stress and coping styles: A comparison of male and female undergraduates. *Journal of Personality and Social Psychology, 55,* 819–823.

Hamilton, Sandra; Rothbart, Myron; & Dawes, Robyn M. (1986). Sex bias, diagnosis, and DSM-III. *Sex Roles, 15,* 269–274.

Hampson, Elizabeth; & Kimura, Doreen. (1992). Sex differences and hormonal influences on cognitive function in humans. In Jill B. Becker, S. Marc Breedlove, & David Crews (Eds.), *Behavioral endocrinology* (pp. 357–398). Cambridge, MA: MIT Press.

Hancock, LynNell; & Kalb, Claudia. (1996, June 24). A room of their own. *Newsweek, 127,* 76.

Hantover, Jeffrey P. (1992). The Boy Scouts and the validation of masculinity. In Michael S. Kimmel & Michael A. Messner (Eds.), *Men's lives* (2nd ed.; pp. 123–131). New York: Macmillan.

Harding, Sandra. (1986). *The science question in feminism.* Ithaca: Cornell University Press.

Hare-Mustin, Rachel T. (1983). An appraisal of the relationship between women and psychotherapy: 80 years after the case of Dora. *American Psychologist, 38,* 593–601.

Hare-Mustin, Rachel T.; & Marecek, Jeanne. (1988). The meaning of difference: Gender theory, postmodernism, and psychology. *American Psychologist, 43,* 455–464.

Hare-Mustin, Rachel T.; Marecek, Jeanne; Kaplan, Alexandra G.; & Liss-Levinson, Nechama. (1979). Rights of clients, responsibilities of therapists. *American Psychologist, 34,* 3–16.

Harlow, Harry F. (1959). Love in infant monkeys. *Scientific American, 200*(6), 68–74.

Harlow, Harry F. (1971). *Learning to love.* San Francisco: Albion.

Harlow, Harry F.; & Harlow, Margaret Kuenne. (1962). Social deprivation in monkeys. *Scientific American, 207,* 136–146.

Harrison, James. (1978). Warning: The male sex role may be dangerous to your health. *Journal of Social Issues, 34*(1), 65–86.

Hassler, Marianne; Nieschlag, Eberhard; & de la Motte, Diether. (1990). Creative musical talent, cognitive functioning, and gender: Psychobiological aspects. *Music Perception, 8,* 35–48.

Hatfield, Elaine; & Rapson, Richard L. (1996). *Love and sex: Cross-cultural perspectives.* Boston: Allyn and Bacon.

Hedrick, Hannah L. (1995). The self-help sourcebook: Finding and forming mutual aid self-help groups (5th ed.) (Book review). *Journal of the American Medical Association, 274,* 847–849.

Heilman, Madeline E; Black, Caryn J.; Martell, Richard F.; & Simon, Michael C. (1989). Has anything changed? Current characterizations of men, women, and managers. *Journal of Applied Psychology, 74,* 935–942.

Helgeson, Vicki S. (1990). The role of masculinity in a prognostic predictor of heart attack severity. *Sex Roles, 22,* 755–776.

Helgeson, Vicki S. (1994). Relation of agency and communion to well-being: Evidence and potential explanations. *Psychological Bulletin, 116,* 412–428.

Helson, Ravenna; & Picano, James. (1990). Is the traditional role bad for women? *Journal of Personality and Social Psychology, 59,* 311–320.

Helzer, John E.; Robins, Lee N.; & McEvoy, Larry. (1987). Post-traumatic stress disorder in the general population: Findings of the Epidemiologic Catchment Area survey. *New England Journal of Medicine, 317,* 1630–1634.

Hendrick, Susan S.; Hendrick, Clyde. (1992). *Liking, loving, and relating* (2nd ed.). Pacific Grove, CA: Brooks/Cole.

Hendrick, Susan S.; Hendrick, Clyde; & Adler, Nancy L. (1988). Romantic relationships: Love, satisfaction, and staying together. *Journal of Personality and Social Psychology, 54,* 980–988.

Hendryx, Michael S.; & Ahern, Melissa M. (1997). Mental health functioning and community problems. *Journal of Community Psychology, 25,* 147–157.

Herdt, Gilbert H. (1981). *Guardians of the flutes: Idioms of masculinity.* New York: McGraw-Hill.

Herdt, Gilbert H. (1990). Mistaken gender: 5-alpha reductase hermaphorditism and biological reductionism in sexual identity reconsidered. *American Anthropologist, 92,* 433–446.

Herdt, Gilbert; & Boxer, Andrew. (1995). Bisexuality: Toward a comparative theory of identities and culture. In Richard G. Parker & John H. Gagnon (Eds.), *Concerning sexuality: Approaches to sex research in a postmodern world* (pp. 69–83). New York: Routledge.

Herman, Dianne F. (1989). The rape culture. In Jo Freeman (Ed.), *Women: A feminist perspective* (pp. 20–44). Mountain View, CA: Mayfield.

Herman, Judith Lewis. (1981). *Father–daughter incest.* Cambridge, MA: Harvard University Press.

Herrmann, Douglas J.; Crawford, Mary; & Holdsworth, Michelle. (1992). Gender-linked differences in everyday memory performance. *British Journal of Psychology, 83,* 221–231.

Herzog, David B.; Newman, Kerry L.; & Warshaw, Meredith. (1991). Body image and dissatisfaction in homosexual and heterosexual males. *Journal of Nervous and Mental Diseases, 179,* 356–359.

Hesselbrock, Victor M.; Hesselbrock, Michie N.; & Workman-Daniels, Kathryn L. (1986). Effect of major depression and antisocial personality on alcoholism: Course and motivational patterns. *Journal of Studies on Alcohol, 47,* 207–212.

Heusel, Colleen; & Dabbs, James M., Jr. (1996, August). *Testosterone predicts engineer employment status in an oilfield service company.* Paper presented at the 104th annual convention of the American Psychological Association, Toronto, Canada.

Hilgard, Ernest R. (1987). *Psychology in America: A historical survey.* San Diego: Harcourt Brace Jovanovich.

Hill, John P.; & Lynch, Mary Ellen. (1983). The intensification of gender-related role expectations during early adolescence. In Jeanne Brooks-Gunn & Anne C. Petersen (Eds.), *Girls at puberty: Biological and psychosocial perspectives.* New York: Plenum Press.

Hines, Melissa; & Collaer, Marcia L. (1993). Gonadal hormones and sexual differentiation of human behavior: Developments from research on endocrine syndromes and studies of brain structure. *Annual Review of Sex Research, 4,* 1–48.

Hiscock, Merrill; Inch, Roxanne; Jacek, Carolyn; Hiscock-Kalil, Cheryl; & Kalil, Kathleen M. (1994). Is there a sex difference in human laterality? I. An exhaustive survey of auditory laterality studies from six neuropsychology journals. *Journal of Clinical and Experimental Neuropsychology, 16,* 423–435.

Hiscock, Merrill; Israelian, Marlyne; Inch, Roxanne; Jacek, Carolyn; & Hiscock-Kalil, Cheryl. (1995). Is there a sex difference in human laterality? II. An exhaustive survey of visual laterality studies from six neuropsychology journals. *Journal of Clinical and Experimental Neuropsychology, 17,* 590–610.

Hochschild, Arlie, with Anne Machung. (1989). *The second shift: Working parents and the revolution at home.* New York: Viking.

Hochwarter, Wayne A.; Perrewe, Pamela L.; & Dawkins, Mark C. (1995). Gender differences in perceptions of stress-related variables: Do the people make the place or does the place make the people? *Journal of Managerial Issues, 7,* 62–74.

Hoffman, Curt; & Hurst, Nancy. (1990). Gender stereotypes: Perception or rationalization? *Journal of Personality and Social Psychology, 58,* 197–208.

Hoffman, Lorrie. (1982). Empirical findings concerning sexism in our schools. *Corrective and Social Psychiatry and Journal of Behavior Technology, Methods and Therapy, 28,* 100–108.

Holroyd, Jean Corey; & Brodsky, Annette M. (1977). Psychologists' attitudes and practices regarding erotic and nonerotic physical contact with patients. *American Psychologist, 32,* 843–849.

Holzbauer, Jerome J.; & Berven, Norman L. (1996). Disability harassment: A new term for a long-standing problem. *Journal of Counseling and Development, 74,* 478–483.

Holzer, Charles E.; Shea, Brent M.; Swanson, Jeffrey W.; Leaf, Philip J.; Myers, J.; George, L.; Weissman, M.; & Bednarski, P. (1986). The increased risk for specific psychiatric disorders among persons of low socioeconomic status. *American Journal of Social Psychiatry, 6,* 259–271.

Hopkin, Karen. (1995). Sugar 'n spice vs. puppy-dog tails: Sex differences in the brain. *Journal of NIH Research, 7,* 39–43.

Horner, Martina. (1969, November). Fail: Bright women. *Psychology Today,* 36–38, 62.

Horney, Karen. (1926/1967). The flight from womanhood: The masculinity complex in women as viewed by men and by women. In Harold Kelman (Ed.), *Feminine psychology* (pp. 54–70). New York: Norton.

Horney, Karen. (1932/1967). The dread of women: Observations on a specific difference in the dread felt by men and by women respectively for the opposite sex. In Harold Kelman (Ed.), *Feminine psychology* (pp. 133–146). New York: Norton.

Horney, Karen. (1939). *New ways in psychoanalysis.* New York: Norton.

Horney, Karen. (1942). *Self-analysis.* New York: Norton.

Horowitz, Allan V.; & White, Helene R. (1991). Becoming married, depression, and alcohol problems among young adults. *Journal of Health and Social Behavior, 32,* 221–237.

Hort, Barbara E.; Fagot, Beverly, I.; & Leinbach, Mary D. (1990). Are people's notions of maleness more stereotypically framed than their notions of femaleness? *Sex Roles, 23,* 197–212.

Hort, Barbara E.; Leinbach, Mary D.; & Fagot, Beverly I. (1991). Is there coherence among the cognitive components of gender acquisition? *Sex Roles, 24,* 195–207.

Hotelling, Kathy. (1991). Sexual harassment: A problem shielded by silence. *Journal of Counseling & Development, 69,* 497–501.

House, James S. (1984). Barriers to work stress: I. Social support. In W. Doyle Gentry, Herbert Benson, & Charles deWolff (Eds.), *Behavioral medicine: Work, stress, and health.* The Hague, Netherlands: Nijhoff.

Howard, Judith A.; Blumstein, Philip; & Schwartz, Pepper. (1987). Social or evolutionary theories? Some observations on preferences in human mate selection. *Journal of Personality and Social Psychology, 53,* 194–200.

Hoyenga, Katharine Blick; & Hoyenga, Kermit T. (1993). *Gender-related differences: Origins and outcomes.* Boston: Allyn and Bacon.

Hrdy, Sarah Blaffer. (1981). *The woman that never evolved.* Cambridge, MA: Harvard University Press.

Hrdy, Sarah Blaffer. (1986). Empathy, polyandry, and the myth of the coy female. In Ruth Bleier (Ed.), *Feminist approaches to science* (pp. 119–146). New York: Pergamon Press.

Hsu, L. K. George. (1990). *Eating disorders.* New York: Guilford Press.

Hubbard, Ruth. (1990). *The politics of women's biology.* New Brunswick: Rutgers University Press.

Hubbard, Ruth; & Wald, Elijah. (1993). *Exploding the gene myth.* Boston: Beacon Press.

Hudak, Mary A. (1993). Gender schema theory revisited: Men's stereotypes of American women. *Sex Roles, 28,* 279–293.

Huesmann, L. Rowell; Eron, Leonard D.; Lefkowitz, Monroe M.; & Walder, Leopold O. (1984). Stability of aggression over time and generations. *Developmental Psychology, 20,* 1120–1134.

Hughes, Diane L.; & Galinsky, Ellen. (1994). Gender, job and family conditions, and psychological symptoms. *Psychology of Women Quarterly, 18,* 251–270.

Humphreys, Ann P.; & Smith, Peter K. (1987). Rough and tumble friendship and dominancy in school children: Evidence for continuity and change with age in middle childhood. *Child Development, 58,* 201–212.

Hunt, Melissa G. (1993). Expressiveness does predict well-being. *Sex Roles, 29,* 147–169.

Hunt, Morton. (1974). *Sexual Behavior in the 1970s.* Chicago: Playboy Press.

Hyde, Janet Shibley. (1981). How large are cognitive gender differences? A meta-analysis using ω^2 and *d. American Psychologist, 36,* 892–901.

Hyde, Janet Shibley. (1984). How large are gender differences in aggression? A developmental meta-analysis. *Developmental Psychology, 20,* 722–736.

Hyde, Janet Shibley. (1986). Introduction: Meta-analysis and the psychology of gender. In Janet Shibley Hyde & Marcia C. Linn (Eds.), *The psychology of gender: Advances through meta-analysis* (pp. 1–13). Baltimore: Johns Hopkins University Press.

Hyde, Janet Shibley. (1990). *Understanding human sexuality* (4th ed.). New York: McGraw-Hill.

Hyde, Janet Shibley. (1994). Can meta-analysis make feminist transformations in psychology? *Psychology of Women Quarterly, 18,* 451–462.

Hyde, Janet Shibley. (1996). Where are the gender differences? Where are the gender similarities? In David M. Buss & Neil M. Malamuth (Eds.), *Sex, power, conflict: Evolutionary and feminist perspectives* (pp. 107–118). New York: Oxford University Press.

Hyde, Janet Shibley; Fennema, Elizabeth; & Lamon, Susan J. (1990). Gender differences in mathematics performance: A meta-analysis. *Psychological Bulletin, 107,* 139–155.

Hyde, Janet S.; Fennema, Elizabeth; Ryan, Marilyn; Frost, Laurie A.; & Hopp, Carolyn. (1990). Gender comparisons of mathematics attitudes and affect: A meta-analysis. *Psychology of Women Quarterly, 14,* 299–324.

Hyde, Janet Shibley; & Linn, Marcia C. (1988). Gender differences in verbal ability: A meta-analysis. *Psychological Bulletin, 104,* 53–69.

Idle, Tracey; Wood, Eileen; & Desmarais, Serge. (1993). Gender role socialization in toy play situations: Mothers and fathers with their sons and daughters. *Sex Roles, 28,* 679–691.

Ignico, Arlene A. (1989). Elementary physical education: Color it androgynous. *Journal OPERD,* 23–24.

Imperato-McGinley, Julianne; Guerrero, Luis; Gautier, Teofilo; & Peterson, Ralph E. (1974). Steroid 5 reductase deficiency in man: An inherited form of male pseudohermaphroditism. *Science, 186,* 1213–1215.

Jack, Dana Crowley. (1991). *Silencing the self: Women and depression.* Cambridge, MA: Harvard University Press.

Jacklin, Carol Nagy. (1989). Female and male: Issues of gender. *American Psychologist, 44,* 127–133.

Jacklin, Carol Nagy; & Maccoby, Eleanor E. (1978). Social behavior at thirty-three months in same-sex and mixed-sex dyads. *Child Development, 49,* 557–569.

Jacobs, Janis E.; & Eccles, Jacquelynne S. (1992). The impact of mothers' gender-role stereotypic beliefs on mothers' and children's ability perceptions. *Journal of Personality and Social Psychology, 63,* 932–944.

Jacobs, Jerry A. (1989). Long-term trends in occupational segregation by sex. *American Journal of Sociology, 95,* 160–173.

Jacobs, Jerry A. (1996). Gender inequality in higher education. *Annual Review of Sociology, 22,* 153–182.

Jacobs, Marion K.; & Goodman, Gerald. (1989). Psychology and self-help groups: Predictions on a partnership. *American Psychologist, 44,* 536–545.

Jacobs, Michael. (1992). *Sigmund Freud.* London: Sage.

Jacoby, Susan. (1995, July 18). Why are his feelings my responsibility? *Woman's Day,* 160.

James, William. (1890). *Principles of psychology* (Vols. 1–2). New York: Holt.

Janoff-Bulman, Ronnie; & Frieze, Irene H. (1987). The role of gender in reactions to criminal victimization. In Rosalind C. Barnett, Lois Biener, & Grace K. Baruch (Eds.), *Gender and stress* (pp. 159–184). New York: Free Press.

Janus, Samuel S.; & Janus, Cynthia L. (1993). *The Janus report on sexual behavior.* New York: Wiley.

Jeffery, Robert W.; Adlis, Susan A.; & Forster, Jean L. (1991). Prevalence of dieting among working men and women: The healthy worker project. *Health Psychology, 10,* 274–281.

Jet, (1997, September 22). Walt Whitman Community School, nation's first private school for gays opens in Dallas. *Jet, 92*(18), 12–13.

Johmann, Carol. (1985, May). Sex and morality. *Omni,* pp. 20, 80.

Johnson, D. Kay. (1988). Adolescents' solutions to dilemmas in fables: Two moral orientations—Two problem solving strategies. In Carol Gilligan, Janie Victoria Ward, & Jill McLean Taylor, with Betty Bardiger (Eds.), *Mapping the moral domain: A contribution of women's thinking to psychological theory and education* (pp. 49–71). Cambridge, MA: Harvard University Press.

Johnson, Michael P. (1995). Patriarchal terrorism and common couple violence: Two forms of violence against women. *Journal of Marriage and the Family, 57,* 283–294.

Johnson, Toni C. (1988). Child perpetrators—Children who molest other children: Preliminary findings. *Child Abuse and Neglect, 12,* 219–229.

Johnson, Toni C. (1989). Female child perpetrators: Children who molest other children. *Child Abuse and Neglect, 13,* 571–585.

Jones, Christopher B. (1996). Women of the future: Alternative scenarios. *The Futurist, 30,* 34–38.

Jones, Ernest. (1955). *The life and work of Sigmund Freud* (Vol. 2). New York: Basic Books.

Jones, James H. (1998). *Alfred C. Kinsey: A public/private life.* New York: Norton.

Jones, M. Gail. (1989). Gender issues in teacher education. *Journal of Teacher Education, 40,* 33–38.

Jussim, Lee; & Eccles, Jacquelynne S. (1992). Teacher expectations: II. Construction and reflection of student achievement. *Journal of Personality and Social Psychology, 63,* 947–961.

Jussim, Lee J.; McCauley, Clark R.; & Lee, Yueh-Ting. (1995). Why study stereotype accuracy and inaccuracy? In Yueh-Ting Lee, Lee J. Jussim, & Clark R. McCauley (Eds.), *Stereotype accuracy: Toward appreciating group differences* (pp. 3–27). Washington, DC: American Psychological Association.

Kaminer, Wendy. (1993, October). Feminism's identity crisis. *Atlantic Monthly,* 51–53, 56, 58–59, 62, 64, 66–68.

Kane, Penny. (1991). *Women's health: From womb to tomb.* New York: St. Martin's Press.

Kanter, Rosabeth Moss. (1975). Women and the structure of organizations: Explorations in theory and behavior. In Marcia Millman & Rosabeth M. Kanter (Eds.), *Another voice* (pp. 34–74). Garden City, NY: Anchor/Doubleday.

Kanter, Rosabeth Moss. (1977). *Men and women of the corporation.* New York: Basic Books.

Kantrowitz, Ricki E.; & Ballou, Mary. (1992). A feminist critique of cognitive–behavioral therapy. In Laura S. Brown & Mary Ballou (Eds.), *Personality and psychopathology: Feminist reappraisals* (pp. 70–87). New York: Guilford Press.

Kaplan, Alexandra G. (1980). Human sex-hormone abnormalities viewed from an androgynous perspective: A reconsideration of the work of John Money. In Jacquelynne E. Parsons (Ed.), *The psychobiology of sex differences and sex roles* (pp. 81–91). Washington, DC: Hemisphere.

Kaplan, Alexandra G.; & Yasinski, Lorraine. (1980). Psychodynamic perspectives. In Annette M. Brodsky & Rachel Hare-Mustin (Eds.), *Women and psychotherapy* (pp. 191–216). New York: Guilford Press.

Kaplan, Marcie (1983a). The issue of sex bias in DSM-III: Comments on the articles by Spitzer, Williams, and Kass. *American Psychologist, 38,* 802–803.

Kaplan, Marcie (1983b). A woman's view of the DSM-III. *American Psychologist, 38,* 786–792.

Kaplan, Robert M.; Anderson, John P.; & Wingard, Deborah L. (1991). Gender differences in health-related quality of life. *Health Psychology, 10,* 86–93.

Karabenick, Stuart A.; Sweeney, Catherine; & Penrose, Gary. (1983). Preferences for skill versus change-determined activities: The influence of gender and task sex-typing. *Journal of Research in Personality, 17,* 125–142.

Karlen, Amy; Hagin, Rosa A.; & Beecher, Ronnie. (1985). Are boys really more vulnerable to learning disability than girls? *Academic Psychology Bulletin, 7,* 317–325.

Karraker, Katherine Hildebrandt; Vogel, Dena Ann; & Lake, Margaret Ann. (1995). Parents' gender-stereotyped perceptions of newborns: The eye of the beholder revisited. *Sex Roles, 33,* 687–701.

Kaschak, Ellyn. (1992). *Engendered lives.* New York: Basic Books.

Kass, Frederic; Spitzer, Robert L.; & Williams, Janet B. W. (1983). An empirical study of the issue of sex bias in the diagnostic criteria of DSM-III axis II personality disorders. *American Psychologist, 38,* 799–801.

Katz, Alfred H. (1993). *Self-help in America: A social movement perspective.* New York: Twayne.

Katz, Phyllis A.; & Ksansnak, Keith R. (1994). Developmental aspects of gender role flexibility and traditionality in middle childhood and adolescence. *Developmental Psychology, 30,* 272–282.

Kaufman, Debra Renee. (1995). Professional women: How real are the recent gains? In Jo Freeman (Ed.), *Women: A feminist perspective* (5th ed.; pp. 287–305). Mountain View, CA: Mayfield.

Keen, Sam. (1991). *A fire in the belly: On being a man.* New York: Bantam.

Keller, Evelyn Fox. (1985). *Reflections on gender and science.* New Haven, CT: Yale University Press.

Kessler, Ronald C.; Brown, Roger L.; & Broman, Clifford L. (1981). Sex differences in psychiatric help-seeking: Evidence from four large-scale surveys. *Journal of Health and Social Behavior, 22,* 49–64.

Kessler, Ronald C.; & McRae, James A., Jr. (1983). Trends in the relationship between sex and attempted suicide. *Journal of Health and Social Behavior, 24,* 98–110.

Kidder, Louise. (1994, August). *All pores open.* Paper presented at the 102nd Annual Convention of the American Psychological Association, Los Angeles, CA.

Kiernan, Michaela; Rodin, Judith; Brownell, Kelly D.; Wilmore, Jack H.; & Crandall, Christian. (1992). Relation of level of exercise, age, and weight-cycling history to weight and eating concerns in male and female runners. *Health Psychology, 11,* 418–421.

Kilpatrick, Dean G.; Best, Connie L.; Saunders, Benjamin E.; & Veronen, Lois J. (1988). Rape in marriage and in dating relationships: How bad is it for mental health? *Annals of the New York Academy of Sciences, 528,* 335–344.

Kimball, Meredith M. (1995). *Feminist visions of gender similarities and differences.* New York: Haworth Press.

Kimmel, Michael S.; & Messner, Michael A. (1992). Introduction. In Michael S. Kimmel & Michael A. Messner (Eds.), *Men's lives* (2nd ed.; pp. 1–11). New York: Macmillan.

Kimura, Doreen. (1992, September). Sex differences in the brain. *Scientific American,* 119–125.

King, Abby C.; & Kiernan, Michaela. (1997). Physical activity and women's health: Issues and future directions. In Sheryle J. Gallant, Gwendolyn Puryear Keita, & Reneé Royak-Schaler (Eds.), *Health care for women: Psychological, social, and behavioral influences* (pp. 133–146). Washington, DC: American Psychological Association.

Kinsey, Alfred C.; Pomeroy, Wardell B.; & Martin, Clyde E. (1948). *Sexual behavior in the human male.* Philadelphia: Saunders.

Kinsey, Alfred C.; Pomeroy, Wardell B.; Martin, Clyde E.; & Gebhard, Paul H. (1953). *Sexual behavior in the human female.* Philadelphia: Saunders.

Kipnis, Aaron R. (1991). *Knights without armor: A practical guide for men in quest of masculine soul.* Los Angeles: Jeremy P. Tarcher.

Kirschstein, Ruth L. (1991). Research on women's health. *American Journal of Public Health, 81,* 291–293.

Kite, Mary E.; & Whitley, Bernard E., Jr. (1996). Sex differences in attitudes toward homosexual persons, behaviors, and civil rights: A meta-analysis. *Personality and Social Psychology Bulletin, 22,* 336–353.

Klaus, Marshall H.; & Kennell, John H. (1976). *Maternal infant bonding.* St. Louis: Mosby.

Kling, Kristen C.; & Hyde, Janet Shibley. (1996, August). *Gender differences in self-esteem: A meta-analysis.* Paper presented at the 104th annual convention of the American Psychological Association, Toronto, Canada.

Klonoff, Elizabeth A.; Landrine, Hope. (1992). Sex-roles, occupational roles, and symptom-reporting: A test of competing hypotheses of sex differences. *Journal of Behavioral Medicine, 15,* 355–364.

Klonoff, Elizabeth A.; & Landrine, Hope. (1997). *Preventing misdiagnosis of women.* Thousand Oaks, CA: Sage.

Knox, Sarah S.; & Czajkowski, Susan. (1997). The influence of behavioral and psychosocial factors on cardiovascular health in women. In Sheryle J. Gallant, Gwendolyn Puryear Keita, & Reneé Royak-Schaler (Eds.), *Health care for women: Psychological, social, and behavioral influences* (pp. 257–272). Washington, DC: American Psychological Association.

Koehler, Mary Schatz. (1990). Classrooms, teachers, and gender differences in mathematics. In Elizabeth Fennema & Gilah C. Leder (Eds.), *Mathematics and gender* (pp. 128–148). New York: Teachers College Press.

Koeske, Randi K.; & Koeske, Gary F. (1975). An attributional approach to moods and the menstrual cycle. *Journal of Personality and Social Psychology, 31,* 473–478.

Kohlberg, Lawrence. (1966). A cognitive–developmental analysis of children's sex-role concepts and attitudes. In Eleanor E. Maccoby (Ed.), *The development of sex differences* (pp. 52–173). Stanford, CA: Stanford University Press.

Kohlberg, Lawrence. (1981). *The philosophy of moral development.* San Francisco: Harper & Row.

Komarovsky, Mirra. (1982). Female freshmen view their future: Career salience and its correlates. *Sex Roles, 8,* 299–313.

Kopper, Beverly A.; & Epperson, Douglas L. (1991). Women and anger: Sex and sex-role comparisons in the expression of anger. *Psychology of Women Quarterly, 15,* 7–14.

Kopper, Beverly A.; & Epperson, Douglas L. (1996). The experience and expression of anger: Relationships with gender, gender role socialization, depression, and mental health functioning. *Journal of Counseling Psychology, 43,* 158–165.

Kortenhaus, Carole M.; & Demarest, Jack. (1993). Gender role stereotyping in children's literature: An update. *Sex Roles, 28,* 219–232.

Koss, Mary P. (1990). The women's mental health research agenda: Violence against women. *American Psychologist, 45,* 374–380.

Koss, Mary P. (1992). The underdetection of rape: Methodological choices influence incidence estimates. *Journal of Social Issues, 48*(1), 61–75.

Koss, Mary P. (1993). Rape: Scope, impact, interventions, and public policy responses. *American Psychologist, 48,* 1062–1069.

Koss, Mary P.; Gidycz, Christine A.; & Wisniewski, Nadine. (1987). The scope of rape: Incidence and prevalence of sexual aggression and victimization in a national sample of higher education students. *Journal of Consulting and Clinical Psychology, 55,* 162–170.

Kramarae, Cheris; & Treichler, Paula A. (1990). Power relationships in the classroom. In Susan L. Gabriel & Isaiah Smithson (Eds.), *Gender in the classroom: Power and pedagogy* (pp. 41–59). Urbana: University of Illinois Press.

Kravetz, Diane. (1978). Consciousness-raising groups of the 1970s. *Psychology of Women Quarterly, 3,* 168–186.

Kravetz, Diane. (1980). Consciousness-raising and self-help. In Annette M. Brodsky & Rachel Hare-Mustin (Eds.), *Women and psychotherapy* (pp. 267–283). New York: Guilford Press.

Kuhn, Deanna; Nash, Sharon C.; & Brucken, Laura. (1978). Sex role concepts of two- and three-year olds. *Child Development, 49,* 445–451.

Kuhn, Thomas S. (1962). *The structure of scientific revolutions.* Chicago: University of Chicago Press.

Kurdek, Lawrence A. (1993). The allocation of household labor in gay, lesbian, and heterosexual married couples. *Journal of Social Issues, 49*(3), 127–139.

Kurzweil, Edith. (1995). *Freudians and feminists.* Boulder, CO: Westview Press.

Lafavore, Michael. (1995, December). In the dark. *Men's Health, 10*(10), 71.

LaFromboise, Teresa D.; Berman, Joan Saks; & Sohi, Balvindar K. (1994). American Indian women. In Lillian Comas-Díaz & Beverly Greene (Eds.), *Women of color: Integrating ethnic and gender identities in psychotherapy* (pp. 30–71). New York: Guilford Press.

Lakoff, Robin. (1975). *Language and woman's place.* New York: Harper & Row.

Lancelot, Cynthia; & Kaslow, Nadine J. (1994). Sex role orientation and disordered eating in women: A review. *Clinical Psychology Review, 14,* 139–157.

Landau, Jacqueline; & Arthur, Michael B. (1992). The relationship of marital status, spouse's career status, and gender to salary level. *Sex Roles, 27,* 665–681.

Landrine, Hope. (1987). On the politics of madness: A preliminary analysis of the relationship between social roles and psychopathology. *Psychology Monographs, 113,* 341–406.

Landrine, Hope. (1989). The politics of personality disorder. *Psychology of Women Quarterly, 13,* 325–339.

Landrine, Hope; Bardwell, Stephen; & Dean, Tina. (1988). Gender expectations for alcohol use: A study of the significance of the masculine role. *Sex Roles, 19,* 703–712.

Landrine, Hope; & Klonoff, Elizabeth A. (1996). The Schedule of Racist Events: A measure of racial discrimination and a study of its negative physical and mental health consequences. *Journal of Black Psychology, 22,* 144–168.

Landrine, Hope; Klonoff, Elizabeth A.; & Brown-Collins, Alice. (1992). Cultural diversity and methodology in feminist psychology: Critique, proposal, empirical example. *Psychology of Women Quarterly, 16,* 145–163.

Landrine, Hope; Klonoff, Elizabeth A.; Gibbs, Jeannine; Manning, Vickie; & Lund, Marlene. (1995). Physical and psychiatric correlates of gender discrimination: An application of the Schedule of Sexist Events. *Psychology of Women Quarterly, 19,* 473–492.

Langley, Merlin R. (1994). The cool pose: An Africentric analysis. In Richard G. Majors & Jacob U. Gordon (Eds.), *The American Black male: His present status and his future* (pp. 231–244). Chicago: Nelson-Hall.

Larrabee, Glenn J.; & Crook, Thomas H. (1993). Do men show more rapid age-associated decline in simulated everyday verbal memory than do women? *Psychology and Aging, 8,* 68–71.

Larwood, Laurie; & Gutek, Barbara A. (1989). Working toward a theory of women's career development. In Barbara A. Gutek & Laurie Larwood (Eds.), *Women's career development* (pp. 170–183). Newbury Park, CA: Sage.

Laumann, Edward O.; Gagnon, John H.; Michael, Robert T.; & Michaels, Stuart. (1994). *The social organization of sexuality.* Chicago: University of Chicago Press.

Lavallee, Marguerite; & Pelletier, Rene. (1992). Ecological value of Bem's gender schema theory explored through females' traditional and nontraditional occupational contexts. *Psychological Reports, 70,* 79–82.

Lavin, Thomas J., III. (1987). Divergence and convergence in the causal attributions of married couples. *Journal of Marriage and the Family, 49,* 71–80.

Law, David J.; Pellegrino, James W.; & Hunt, Earl B. (1993). Comparing the tortoise and the hare: Gender differences and experience in dynamic spatial reasoning tasks. *Psychological Science, 4,* 35–40.

Lawton, Carol A. (1994). Gender differences in way-finding strategies: Relationship to spatial ability and spatial anxiety. *Sex Roles, 30,* 765–779.

Lazarus, Richard S. (1984). On the primacy of cognition. *American Psychologist, 39,* 124–129.

Lazarus, Richard S.; & Folkman, Susan. (1984). *Stress, appraisal, and coping.* New York: Springer-Verlag.

Leaf, Philip J.; & Bruce, Martha L. (1987). Gender differences in the use of mental health-related services: A re-examination. *Journal of Health and Social Behavior, 28,* 171–183.

Leaper, Campbell; Carson, Mary; Baker, Carilyn; Holliday, Heithre; & Myers, Sharon. (1995). Self-disclosure and listener verbal support in same-gender and cross-gender friends' conversations. *Sex Roles, 33,* 387–404.

Leder, Gilah C. (1990). Gender differences in mathematics: An overview. In Elizabeth Fennema & Gilah C. Leder (Eds.), *Mathematics and gender* (pp. 10–26). New York: Teachers College Press.

Lee, Valerie E.; & Burkam, David T. (1996). Gender differences in middle grade science achievement: Subject domain, ability level, and course emphasis. *Science Education, 80,* 613–650.

Lefkowitz, Monroe M.; Eron, Leonard D.; Walder, Leopold O.; & Huesmann, L. Rowell (1977). *Growing up to be violent: A longitudinal study of the development of aggression.* New York: Pergamon Press.

Leinbach, Mary D.; & Fagot, Beverly I. (1993). Categorical habituation to male and female faces: Gender schematic processing in infancy. *Infant Behavior and Development, 16,* 317–332.

Lenny, Ellen. (1977). Women's self-confidence in achievement settings. *Psychological Bulletin, 84,* 1–13.

Leong, Frederick T. L.; Snodgrass, Coral R.; & Gardner, William L., III. (1992). Management education: Creating a gender-positive environment. In Uma Sekaran & Frederick T. L. Leong (Eds.), *Womanpower: Managing in times of demographic turbulence* (pp. 192–220). Newbury Park, CA: Sage.

Lepowsky, Maria. (1994). Women, men, and aggression in an egalitarian society. *Sex Roles, 30,* 199–211.

Lerman, Hannah. (1992). The limits of phenomenology: A feminist critique of the humanistic personality theories. In Laura S. Brown & Mary Ballou (Eds.), *Personality and psychopathology: Feminist reappraisals* (pp. 8–19). New York: Guilford Press.

Lerman, Hannah. (1996). *Pigeonholing women's misery: A history and critical analysis of the psychodiagnosis of women in the twentieth century.* New York: Basic Books.

Lerner, Alan Jay; & Loewe, Frederick. (1956). *My fair lady: A musical play in two acts.* Based on *Pygmalion* by Bernard Shaw. New York: Coward-McCann.

Leslie, Leigh A.; Huston, Ted L.; & Johnson, Michael P. (1986). Parental reactions to dating relationships: Do they make a difference? *Journal of Marriage and the Family, 48,* 57–66.

Levant, Ronald F. (1990). Psychological services designed for men: A psychoeducational approach. *Psychotherapy, 27,* 309–315.

LeVay, Simon. (1991). A difference in hypothalamic structure between heterosexual and homosexual men. *Science, 253,* 1034–1037.

LeVay, Simon. (1996). *Queer science: The use and abuse of research into homosexuality.* Cambridge, MA: MIT Press.

Levenson, Robert W.; Carstensen, Laura L.; & Gottman, John M. (1994). The influence of age and gender on affect, physiology, and their interrelations: A study of long-term marriages. *Journal of Personality and Social Psychology, 67,* 56–68.

Levy, Gary D. (1989). Relations among aspects of children's social environments, gender schematization, gender role knowledge, and flexibility. *Sex Roles, 21,* 803–823.

Levy, Gary D.; & Boston, Martha B. (1994). Preschoolers' recall of own-sex and other-sex gender scripts. *Journal of Genetic Psychology, 155,* 369–371.

Levy, Gary D.; & Fivush, Robyn. (1993). Scripts and gender: A new approach for examining gender-role development. *Developmental Review, 13,* 126–146.

Levy, Jerre. (1969). Possible basis for the evolution of lateral specialization of the human brain. *Nature, 224,* 614–625.

Levy, Sandra M. (1985). *Behavior and cancer: Lifestyle and psychosocial factors in the initiation and progression of cancer.* San Francisco: Jossey-Bass.

Lewin, Miriam. (1984a). "Rather worse than folly?" Psychology measures femininity and masculinity: 1. From Terman and Miles to the Guilfords. In Miriam Lewin (Ed.), *In the shadow of the past: Psychology portrays the sexes* (pp. 155–178). New York: Columbia University Press.

Lewin, Miriam. (1984b). Psychology measures femininity and masculinity: 2. From "13 gay men" to the instrumental–expressive distinction. In Miriam Lewin (Ed.), *In the shadow of the past: Psychology portrays the sexes* (pp. 179–204). New York: Columbia University Press.

Lewin, Miriam. (1984c). The Victorians, the psychologists, and psychic birth control. In Miriam Lewin (Ed.), *In the shadow of the past: Psychology portrays the sexes* (pp. 39–76). New York: Columbia University Press.

Lewis, Carol D.; & Houtz, John C. (1986). Sex-role sterotyping and young children's divergent thinking. *Psychological Reports, 59,* 1027–1033.

Lewis, Shon. (1992). Sex and schizophrenia: Vive la difference. *British Journal of Psychiatry, 161,* 445–450.

Lewontin, R. C.; Rose, Steven; & Kamin, Leon J. (1984). *Not in our genes.* New York: Pantheon.

Liben, Lynn S.; & Golbeck, Susan L. (1984). Performance on Piagetian horizontality and verticality tasks: Sex-related differences in knowledge of relevant physical phenomena. *Developmental Psychology, 20,* 595–606.

Lindberg, Laura Duberstein; Sonenstein, Freya L; Ku, Leighton; & Martinez, Gladys. (1997). Age differences between minors who give birth and their adult partners. *Family Planning Perspectives, 29,* 61–66.

Linn, Marcia C.; & Petersen, Anne C. (1986). A meta-analysis of gender differences in spatial ability: Implications for mathematics and science achievement. In Janet Shibley Hyde & Maricia C. Linn (Eds.), *The psychology of gender: Advances through meta-analysis* (pp. 67–101). Baltimore: Johns Hopkins University Press.

Lips, Hilary M. (1989). Gender-role socialization: Lessons in femininity. In Jo Freeman (Ed.), *Women: A feminist perspective* (pp. 197–216). Mountain View, CA: Mayfield.

Livingston, Nancy. (1994, March 11). St. Paul, Minn., schools plan full-time coordinator for gay and lesbian students. *Knight-Ridder/Tribune News Service,* p. 0311 K2183.

Lloyd, Barbara; Duveen, Gerard; & Smith, Caroline. (1988). Social representation of gender and young children's play: A replication. *British Journal of Developmental Psychology, 6,* 83–88.

Locksley, Anne; Borgida, Eugene; Brekke, Nancy; & Hepburn, Christine. (1980). Sex stereotypes and social judgments. *Journal of Personality and Social Psychology, 39,* 821–831.

Long, J. Scott; & Fox, Mary Frank. (1995). Scientific careers: Universalism and particularism. *Annual Review of Sociology, 21,* 45–71.

Lont, Cynthia M. (Ed.). (1995). *Women and media: Content, careers, and criticism.* Belmont, CA: Wadsworth.

Lopata, Helena Znaniecka. (1993). The interweave of public and private: Women's challenge to American society. *Journal of Marriage and the Family, 55,* 176–190.

López, Steven Regeser. (1989). Patient variable biases in clinical judgment: Conceptual overview and methodological considerations. *Psychological Bulletin, 106,* 184–203.

Lorber, Judith. (1975). Women and medical sociology: Invisible professionals and ubiquitous patients. In Marcia Millman & Rosabeth M. Kanter (Eds.), *Another voice* (pp. 75–105). Garden City, NY: Anchor/Doubleday.

Lorber, Judith. (1989). Trust, loyalty, and the place for women in the informal organization of work. In J. Freeman (Ed.), *Women: A feminist perspective* (pp. 347–355). Mountain View, CA: Mayfield.

Lorber, Judith. (1997). Believing is seeing: Biology as ideology. In Maxine Baca Zinn, Pierrette Hondagneu-Sotelo, & Michael A. Messnser (Eds.), *Through the prism of difference: Readings on sex and gender* (pp. 13–22). Boston: Allyn and Bacon.

Loring, Marti; & Powell, Brian. (1988). Gender, race, and DSM-III: A study of the objectivity of psychiatric diagnostic behavior. *Journal of Health and Social Behavior, 29,* 1–22.

Loring, Susan; & Cowan, Gloria. (1997). Codependency: An interpersonal phenomenon. *Sex Roles, 36,* 115–123.

Lott, Bernice. (1997). Cataloging gender differences: Science or politics? In Mary Roth Walsh (Ed.), *Women, men, and gender: Ongoing debates* (pp. 19–23). New Haven, CT: Yale University Press.

Loury, Glenn C. (1996, January–February). Joy and doubt on the mall: The Million Man March and me. *Utne Reader, 73,* 70–73.

Loury, Linda Datcher. (1997). The gender earnings gap among college-educated workers. *Industrial and Labor Relations Review, 50,* 580–593.

Lueptow, Lloyd B. (1985). Conceptions of femininity and masculinity: 1974–1983. *Psychological Reports, 57,* 859–862.

Lye, Diane N. (1996). Adult child–parent relationships. *Annual Review of Sociology, 22,* 79–102.

Lyons, Deborah; & Greenberg, Jeff. (1991). Evidence of codependency in women with an alcoholic parent: Helping out Mr. Wrong. *Journal of Personality and Social Psychology, 61,* 435–439.

Lyons, Nona Plessner. (1988). Two perspectives: On self, relationships, and morality. In Carol Gilligan, Janie Victoria Ward, & Jill McLean Taylor, with Betty Bardige (Eds.), *Mapping the moral domain: A contribution of women's thinking to psychological theory and education* (pp. 21–48). Cambridge, MA: Harvard University Press.

Maccoby, Eleanor E. (1988). Gender as a social category. *Developmental Psychology, 24,* 755–765.

Maccoby, Eleanor E. (1990). Gender and relationships. *American Psychologist, 45,* 513–520.

Maccoby, Eleanor Emmons; & Jacklin, Carol Nagy (1974). *The psychology of sex differences.* Stanford, CA: Stanford University Press.

Majors, Richard G.; & Billson, J. M. (1992). *Cool pose: The dilemmas of Black manhood in America.* New York: Lexington.

Majors, Richard G.; Tyler, Richard; Peden, Blaine; & Hall, Ron. (1994). Cool pose: A symbolic mechanism for masculine role enactment and coping by Black males. In Richard G. Majors & Jacob U. Gordon (Eds.), *The American Black male: His present status and his future* (pp. 245–259). Chicago: Nelson-Hall.

Malamuth, Neil M. (1996). The confluence model of sexual aggression: Feminist and evolutionary perspectives. In David M. Buss & Neil M. Malamuth (Eds.), *Sex, power, conflict: Evolutionary and feminist perspectives* (pp. 269–295). New York: Oxford University Press.

Mancus, Dianne Sirna. (1992). Influence of male teachers on elementary school children's stereotyping of teacher competence. *Sex Roles, 26,* 109–128.

Mansnerus, Laura. (1992, January 5). Women take to the field. *New York Times,* Sec. 4A, pp. 40–41.

Marecek, Jeanne; & Hare-Mustin, Rachel. (1991). A short history of the future: Feminism and clinical psychology, *Psychology of Women Quarterly, 15,* 521–536.

Marecek, Jeanne; Kravetz, Diane; & Finn, Stephen. (1979). Comparison of women who enter feminist therapy and women who enter traditional therapy. *Journal of Consulting and Clinical Psychology, 47,* 734–742.

Martel, Richard F.; Lane, David, M.; & Emrich, Cynthia. (1996). Male–female differences: A computer simulation. *American Psychologist, 51,* 157–158.

Martin, Carol Lynn. (1987). A ratio measure of sex stereotyping. *Journal of Personality and Social Psychology, 52,* 489–499.

Martin, Carol Lynn. (1989). Children's use of gender-related information in making social judgments. *Developmental Psychology, 25,* 80–88.

Martin, Carol Lynn. (1995). Stereotypes about children with traditional and nontraditional gender roles. *Sex Roles, 33,* 727–751.

Martin, Carol Lynn; & Halverson, Charles. F., Jr. (1981). A schematic processing model of sex-typing and stereotyping in children. *Child Development, 52,* 1119–1134.

Martin, Carol Lynn; & Little, Jane K. (1990). The relation of gender understanding to children's sex-typed preferences and gender stereotypes. *Child Development, 61,* 1427–1439.

Martin, Carol Lynn; Wood, Carolyn H.; & Little, Jane K. (1990). The development of gender stereotype components. *Child Development, 61,* 1891–1904.

Martinko, Mark L; & Gardner, William L. (1983). A methodological review of sex-related access discrimination problems. *Sex Roles, 9,* 825–839.

Martocchio, Joseph J.; & O'Leary, Anne M. (1989). Sex differences in occupational stress: A meta-analytic review. *Journal of Applied Psychology, 74,* 495–501.

Masson, Jeffrey Moussaieff. (1984). *The assault on truth: Freud's suppression of the seduction theory.* New York: Farrar, Straus and Giroux.

Masters, William H.; & Johnson, Virginia E. (1966). *Human sexual response.* Boston: Little, Brown.

Masters, William H.; Johnson, Virginia E.; & Kolodny, Robert C. (1992). *Human sexuality* (4th ed.). New York: HarperCollins.

Matthews, Karen A. (1989). Are sociodemographic variables markers for psychological determinants of health? *Health Psychology, 8,* 641–648.

Matthews, Karen A.; Shumaker, Sally A.; Bowen, Deborah J.; Langer, Robert D.; Hunt, Julie R.; Kaplan, Robert M.; Klesges, Robert C.; & Ritenbaugh, Cheryl. (1997). Women's health initiative: Why now? What is it? What's new? *American Psychologist, 52,* 101–116.

Mays, Vickie M.; & Comas-Díaz, Lillian. (1988). Feminist therapy with ethnic minority populations: A closer look at Blacks and Hispanics. In Mary Ann Dutton Douglas & Lenore E. A. Walker (Eds.), *Feminist psychotherapies: Integration of therapeutic and feminist systems* (pp. 228–251). Norwood, NJ: Ablex.

Mazer, Donald B.; & Percival, Elizabeth F. (1989). Students' experiences of sexual harassment at a small university. *Sex Roles, 20,* 1–22.

Mazur, Allan. (1985). A biosocial model of status in face-to-face primate groups. *Social Forces, 64,* 377–402.

McCann, Nancy Dodd; & McGinn, Thomas A. (1992). *Harassed: 100 women define inappropriate behavior in the workplace.* Homewood, IL: Business One Irwin.

McCauley, Clark R. (1995). Are stereotypes exaggerated? A sampling of racial, gender, academic, occupational, and political stereotypes. In Yueh-Ting Lee, Lee J. Jussim, & Clark R. McCauley (Eds.), *Stereotype accuracy: Toward appreciating group differences* (pp. 215–243). Washington, DC: American Psychological Association.

McClelland, David C.; Atkinson, J. W.; Clark, R. W.; & Lowell, E. L. (1953). *The achievement motive.* New York: Appleton.

McCormick, Naomi B. (1994). *Sexual salvation: Affirming women's sexual rights and pleasures.* Westport, CT: Praeger.

McDonald, Karen; & Thompson, J. Kevin. (1992). Eating disturbance, body image dissatisfaction, and reasons for exercising: Gender differences and correlational findings. *International Journal of Eating Disorders, 11,* 289–292.

McDougall, William. (1923). *Outline of psychology.* New York: Scribners.

McFarlane, Jessica; Martin, Carol Lynn; & Williams, Tannis MacBeth. (1988). Mood fluctuations: Women versus men and menstrual versus other cycles. *Psychology of Women Quarterly, 12,* 201–223.

McFarlane, Jessica Motherwell; & Williams, Tannis MacBeth. (1994). Placing premenstrual syndrome in perspective. *Psychology of Women Quarterly, 18,* 339–373.

McGuiness, Diane; Olson, Amy; & Chapman, Julia. (1990). Sex differences in incidental recall of words and pictures. *Learning and Individual Differences, 2,* 263–285.

McHale, Susan M.; & Crouter, Ann C. (1992). You can't always get what you want: Incongruence between sex-role attitudes and family work roles and its implications for marriage. *Journal of Marriage and the Family, 54,* 537–547.

McHugh, Maureen C.; Koeske, Randi D.; & Frieze, Irene H. (1986). Issues to consider in conducting nonsexist psychological research: A guide for researchers. *American Psychologist, 41,* 879–890.

McKeever, Walter F. (1995). Hormone and hemisphericity hypotheses regarding cognitive sex differences: Possible future explanatory power, but current empirical chaos. *Learning and Individual Differences, 7,* 323–340.

McKinney, Kathleen; Olson, Carol V.; & Satterfield, Arthur. (1988). Graduate students' experiences with and responses to sexual harassment: A research note. *Journal of Interpersonal Violence, 3,* 319–328.

McLain, Susan June; & Perkins, Carol O. (1990). Disabled women: At the bottom of the work heap. *Vocational Educational Journal, 65*(2), 54–53.

McManus, I. C.; & Bryden, M. P. (1991). Geschwind's theory of cerebral lateralization: Developing a formal, causal model. *Psychological Bulletin, 110,* 237–253.

McWhirter, Ellen Hawley. (1994, August). *Perceived barriers to education and career: Ethnic and gender differences.* Paper presented at the 102nd annual convention of the American Psychological Association, Los Angeles, CA.

Meehan, Anita M.; & Janik, Leann M. (1990). Illusory correlation and the maintenance of sex role sterotypes in children. *Sex Roles, 22,* 83–95.

Melamed, Tuvia. (1996). Career success: An assessment of a gender-specific model. *Journal of Occupational and Organizational Psychology, 69,* 217–242.

Melson, Gail F.; & Fogel, Alan. (1988a). The development of nurturance in young children. *Young Children, 43,* 57–65.

Melson, Gail F.; & Fogel, Alan. (1988b, January). Learning to care: Boys are as nurturant as girls, but in different ways. *Psychology Today,* 39–45.

Mesquita, Batja; & Frijda, Nico H. (1992). Cultural variations in emotions: A review. *Psychological Bulletin, 112,* 179–204.

Messner, Michael A. (1997). *Politics of masculinities: Men in movements.* Thousand Oaks, CA: Sage.

Meyer-Bahlburg, Heino F. L. (1980). Sexuality in early adolescence. In Benjamin B. Wolman & John Money (Eds.), *Handbook of human sexuality* (pp. 61–82). Englewood Cliffs, NJ: Prentice-Hall.

Michael, Robert T.; Gagnon, John H.; Laumann, Edward O.; & Kolata, Gina. (1994). *Sex in America.* Boston: Little, Brown.

Middaugh, Anne. (1994, August). *Clinical psychology interns' attitudes and information about women.* Paper presented at the 102nd annual convention of the American Psychological Association, Los Angeles, CA.

Miller, Randi L.; & Gordon, Michael. (1986). The decline in formal dating: A study in six Connecticut high schools. *Marriage and Family Review, 10,* 139–156.

Miller, Ivan W.; Norman, William H.; & Dow, Michael G. (1988). Depression. In Elaine A. Blechman & Kelly D. Brownell (Eds.), *Handbook of behavioral medicine for women* (pp. 399–418). New York: Pergamon Press.

Mirowsky, John; & Ross, Catherine E. (1987). Belief in innate sex roles: Sex stratification versus interpersonal influence in marriage. *Journal of Marriage and the Family, 49,* 527–540.

Mischel, Walter. (1966). A social-learning view of sex differences in behavior. In Eleanor E. Maccoby (Ed.), *The development of sex differences* (pp. 56–81). Stanford, CA: Stanford University Press.

Mischel, Walter. (1993). *Introduction to personality* (5th ed.). Fort Worth: Harcourt Brace Jovanovich.

Mishkind, Marc E.; Rodin, Judith; Silberstein, Lisa R.; & Striegel-Moore, Ruth H. (1986). The embodiment of masculinity: Cultural, psychological, and behavioral dimensions. *American Behavioral Scientist, 29,* 545–562.

Mittwoch, Ursula. (1973). *Genetics of sex differentiation.* New York: Academic Press.

Money, John. (1986). *Venuses penuses: Sexology, sexosophy, and exigency theory.* Buffalo, NY: Prometheus Books.

Money, John. (1987a). Propaedeutics of diecious G-I/R: Theoretical foundations for understanding dimorphic gender-identity/role. In June Machover Reinisch, Leonard A. Rosenblum, & Stephanie A. Sanders (Eds.), *Masculinity/Femininity: Basic perspectives* (pp. 13–28). New York: Oxford University Press.

Money, John. (1987b). Sin, sickness, or status? Homosexual gender identity and psychoneuroendocrinology. *American Psychologist, 42,* 384–399.

Monroe, Judy. (1995, December). The great debate: Gender differences. *Current Health 2, 22,* 22–25.

Monsour, Michael; Harris, Bridgid; Kurzweil, Nancy; & Beard, Chris. (1994). Challenges confronting cross-sex friendships: "Much ado about nothing?" *Sex Roles, 31,* 55–77.

Montecinos, Carmen; & Nielsen, Lynn E. (1997). Gender and cohort differences in university students' decisions to become elementary teacher education majors. *Journal of Teacher Education, 48,* 47–54.

Mook, Douglas G. (1987). *Motivation: The organization of action.* New York: Norton.

Moore, Robert; & Gillette, Douglas. (1990). *King warrior magician lover: Rediscovering the archetypes of the mature masculine.* San Francisco: HarperSanFrancisco.

Morgan, Robin. (1970). Introduction: The women's revolution. In Robin Morgan (Ed.), *Sisterhood is powerful: An anthology of writings from the women's liberation movement* (pp. xv-xivi). New York: Vintage Books.

Mori, DeAnna; Chaiken, Shelly; & Pliner, Patricia. (1987). "Eating lightly" and the self-presentation of femininity. *Journal of Personality and Social Psychology, 53,* 693–702.

Mori, Lisa; Selle, Lynn L.; Zarate, Mylene G.; & Bernat, Jeffrey. (1994). *Asian American and Caucasian college students' attitudes towards rape.* Paper presented at the 102nd annual convention of the American Psychological Association, Los Angeles, CA.

Muehlenhard, Charlene L.; Friedman, Debra E.; & Thomas, Celeste M. (1985). Is date rape justifiable? The effects of dating activity, who initiated, who paid, and men's attitudes toward women. *Psychology of Women Quarterly, 9,* 297–309.

Muehlenhard, Charlene L.; & Hollabaugh, Lisa C. (1988). Do women sometimes say no when they mean yes: The prevalence and correlates of women's token resistance to sex. *Journal of Personality and Social Psychology, 54,* 872–879.

Muller, Charlotte F. (1990). *Health care and gender.* New York: Russell Sage Foundation.

Murphy, Declan G. M.; DeCarli, Charles; McIntosh, Andrew R; Daly, Eileen; Mentis, Marc J.; Pietrini, Pietro; Szczepanik, Joanna; Schapiro, Mark B.; Grady, Cheryl L.; Horwitz, Barry; & Rapoport, Stanley I. (1996). Sex differences in human brain morphometry and metabolism: An in vivo quantitative magnetic resonance imaging and positron emission tomography study on the effect of aging. *Archives of General Psychiatry, 53,* 585–594.

Murray, Kathleen. (1995, April). PMS: Is it for real? *Cosmopolitan, 218,* 208–211.

Nardi, Peter M. (1992a). "Seamless souls": An introduction to men's friendships. In Peter M. Nardi (Ed.), *Men's friendships* (pp. 1–14). Newbury Park, CA: Sage.

Nardi, Peter M. (1992b). Sex, friendship, and gender roles among gay men. In Peter M. Nardi (Ed.), *Men's friendships* (pp. 173–185). Newbury Park, CA: Sage.

National Center for Health Statistics. (1995, May 22). *National Economic, Social, and Environmental Data Bank* [Electronic Database]. Hyattsville, MD: Author.

Nelson, Katherine. (1981). Social cognition in a script framework. In John H. Flavell & Lee Ross (Eds.), *Social cognitive development: Frontiers and possible futures* (pp. 97–118). Cambridge, England: Cambridge University Press.

Netting, Nancy S. (1992). Sexuality in youth culture: Identity and change. *Adolescence, 27,* 961–976.

Neugebauer, D. D.; Dohrenwend, Bruce P.; & Dohrenwend, Barbara S. (1980). The formulation of hypotheses about the true prevalence of functional psychiatric disorders among adults in the United States. In Bruce P. Dohrenwend, Barbara S. Dohrenwend, M. S. Gould, B. Link, R. Neugebauer, & R. Wunsch-Hitzig (Eds.), *Mental illness in the United States* (pp. 45–94). New York: Praeger.

Newman, Leonard S.; Cooper, Joel; & Ruble, Diane N. (1995). The interactive effects of knowledge and constancy on gender-stereotyped attitudes. (Gender and Computers, part 2) *Sex Roles, 33,* 325–351.

Nieva, Veronica F.; & Gutek, Barbara A. (1981). *Women and work: A psychological perspective.* New York: Praeger.

Nikelly, Arthur G. (1994, August). *Drug advertisements and the medicalization of unipolar depression in women.* Paper presented at the 102nd annual convention of the American Psychological Association, Los Angeles, CA.

Noddings, Nel. (1991/1992, December/January). The gender issue. *Educational Leadership, 49*(4), 65–70.

Nolen-Hoeksema, Susan. (1987). Sex differences in unipolar depression: Evidence and theory. *Psychological Bulletin, 101,* 259–282.

Nolen-Hoeksema, Susan. (1994). *Rumination in response to depression.* Paper presented at the 102nd annual convention of the American Psychological Association, Los Angeles, CA.

Nordheimer, Jon. (1991, August 14). When a fellow needs a friend, not just a buddy. *New York Times,* pp. C1, C8.

Norwood, Robin. (1985). *Women who love too much: When you keep wishing and hoping he'll change.* New York: Pocket Books.

O'Brien, Edward J.; Jeffreys, Dorothy; Leitzel, Jeff; O'Brien, Jean P.; Mensky, Larissa; & Marchese, Marc. (1996, August). *Gender differences in the self-esteem of adolescents: A meta-analysis.* Paper presented at the 104th annual convention of the American Psychological Association, Toronto, Canada.

Ogborne, Alan. (1996). Professional opinions and practices concerning Alcoholics Anonymous: A review of the literature and a research agenda. *Contemporary Drug Issues, 23,* 93–104.

Okagaki, Lynn; & Frensch, Peter A. (1994). Effects of video game playing on measures of spatial performance: Gender effects in late adolescence. *Journal of Applied Developmental Psychology, 15,* 33–58.

Oliver, Mary Beth; & Hyde, Janet Shibley. (1993). Gender differences in sexuality: A meta-analysis. *Psychological Bulletin, 114,* 29–51.

Olson, Cheryl B. (1994, August). *Hostile environment: Gender, self-esteem and perception of sexual harassment.* Paper presented at the 102nd annual convention of the American Psychological Association, Los Angeles, CA.

O'Neil, James M. (1981). Patterns of gender role conflict and strain: Sexism and fear of femininity in men's lives. *Personnel and Guidance Journal, 60,* 203–210.

Orlofsky, Jacob L.; & O'Heron, Connie A. (1987). Stereotypic and nonstereotypic sex role trait and behavior orientations: Implications for personal adjustment. *Journal of Personality and Social Psychology, 52,* 1034–1042.

Ornstein, Robert. (1972). *The psychology of consciousness.* San Francisco: Freeman.

Osgood, D. Wayne; O'Malley, Patrick M.; Bachman, Jerald G.; Johnston, Lloyd D. (1989). Time trends and age trends in arrests and self-reported illegal behavior. *Criminology, 27,* 389–417.

Owen, Crystal L.; & Todor, William D. (1993). Attitudes toward women as managers: Still the same. *Business Horizons, 36*(2), 12–16.

Page, Jessica R.; Stevens, Heather B.; & Galvin, Shelley L. (1996). Relationships between depression, self-esteem, and self-silencing behavior. *Journal of Social and Clinical Psychology, 15,* 381–396.

Paludi, Michele A. (1984). Psychometric properties and underlying assumptions of four objective measures of fear of success. *Sex Roles, 10,* 765–781.

Parker, Louise. (1997). Causes of testicular cancer. *Lancet, 350,* 827–828.

Parlee, Mary Brown. (1973). The premenstrual syndrome. *Psychological Bulletin, 83,* 454–465.

Paskette, Electra D.; & Michielutte, Robert. (1997). Psychosocial factors associated with gynecological cancers. In Sheryle J. Gallant, Gwendolyn Puryear Keita, & Reneé Royak-Schaler (Eds.), *Health care for women: Psychological, social, and behavioral influences* (pp. 315–331). Washington, DC: American Psychological Association.

Pasman, Larry; & Thompson, J. Kevin. (1988). Body image and eating disturbances in obligatory runners, obligatory weightlifters, and sedentary individuals. *International Journal of Eating Disorders, 7,* 759–769.

Patterson, Charlotte J.; & Chan, Raymond W. (1997). Gay fathers. In Michael E. Lamb (Ed.), *The role of the father in child development* (3rd ed.; pp. 245–260). New York: Wiley.

Pearcey, Sharon M.; Docherty, Karen J.; & Dabbs, James M., Jr. (1996). Testosterone and sex role identification in lesbian couples. *Physiology & Behavior, 60,* 1033–1035.

Pearson, Judy C.; & West, Richard. (1991). An initial investigation of the effects of gender on student questions in the classroom: Developing a descriptive base. *Communication Education, 40,* 22–32.

Pennebaker, James W. (1982). *The psychology of physical symptoms.* New York: Springer-Verlag.

Pennebaker, James W.; & Roberts, Tomi-Ann. (1992). Toward a his and hers theory of emotion: Gender differences in visceral perception. *Journal of Social and Clinical Psychology, 11,* 199–212.

Peplau, Letitia Anne; & Campbell, Susan Miller. (1989). The balance of power in dating and marriage. In Jo Freeman (Ed.), *Women: A feminist perspective* (4th ed.; pp. 121–137). Mountain View, CA: Mayfield.

Peplau, Letitia Anne; Cochran, Susan; Rook, Karen; & Padesky, Christine. (1978). Loving women: Attachment and autonomy in lesbian relationships. *Journal of Social Issues, 34*(3), 7–27.

Peplau, Letitia Anne; & Conrad, Eva. (1989). Beyond nonsexist research: The perils of feminist methods in psychology. *Psychology of Women Quarterly, 13,* 379–400.

Peplau, Letitia Anne; & Gordon, Steven L. (1985). Women and men in love: Gender differences in close heterosexual relationships. In Virginia E. O'Leary, Rhoda Kesler Unger, & Barbara Strudler Wallston (Eds.), *Women, gender, and social psychology* (pp. 257–291). Hillsdale, NJ: Erlbaum.

Peplau, Letitia Anne; Hill, Charles T.; & Rubin, Zick. (1993). Sex role attitudes in dating and marriage: A 15-year follow-up of the Boston couples study. *Journal of Social Issues, 49*(3), 31–52.

Perlick, Deborah; & Silverstein, Brett. (1994). Faces of female discontent: Depression, disordered eating, and changing gender roles. In Patricia Fallon, Melanie A. Katzman, & Susan C. Wooley (Eds.), *Feminist perspectives on eating disorders* (pp. 77–93). New York: Guilford Press.

Perls, Frederick S. (1969). *Gestalt therapy verbatim.* Lafayette, CA: Real People Press.

Perry, David G.; Perry, Louise C.; & Weiss, Robert J. (1989). Sex differences in the consequences that children anticipate for aggression. *Developmental Psychology, 25,* 312–319.

Phillips, Roger D.; & Gilroy, Faith D. (1985). Sex-role stereotypes and clinical judgments of mental health: The Brovermans' findings reexamined. *Sex Roles, 12,* 179–193.

Phillips, Susan D.; & Imhoff, Anne R. (1997). Women and career development: A decade of research. *Annual Review of Psychology, 48,* 31–59.

Pickhardt, Irene. (1983, December). Sexist piglets: Studies show that sex-stereotyping is part of childhood. *Parents' Magazine,* 32–37.

Piirto, Jane. (1991). Why are there so few: (Creative women: Visual artists, mathematicians, musicians). *Roeper Review, 13,* 142–147.

Pinel, John P. J. (1997). *Biopsychology* (3rd ed.). Boston: Allyn and Bacon.

Pittman, Frank. (1992, January/February). Why the men's movement isn't so funny. *Psychology Today,* 84.

Plante, Thomas G.; & Rodin, Judith. (1990). Physical fitness and enhanced psychological health. *Current Psychology Research and Reviews, 9,* 3–24.

Pleck, Elizabeth H.; & Pleck, Joseph H. (1997). Fatherhood ideals in the United States: Historical dimensions. In Michael E. Lamb (Ed.), *The role of the father in child development* (3rd ed.; pp. 33–48). New York: Wiley.

Pleck, Joseph H. (1981a). *The myth of masculinity.* Cambridge, MA: MIT Press.

Pleck, Joseph H. (1981b, September). Prisoners of manliness. *Psychology Today,* 68–79.

Pleck, Joseph H. (1984). The theory of male sex role identity: Its rise and fall, 1936 to the present. In Miriam Lewin (Ed.), *In the shadow of the past: Psychology portrays the sexes* (pp. 205–225). New York: Columbia University Press.

Pleck, Joseph H. (1995). The Gender Role Strain paradigm: An update. In Ronald F. Levant & William S. Pollack (Eds.), *A new psychology of men* (pp. 11–32). New York: Basic Books.

Pleck, Joseph H. (1997). Parental involvement: Levels, sources, and consequences. In Michael E. Lamb (Ed.), *The role of the father in child development* (3rd ed.; pp. 66–103). New York: Wiley.

Pleck, Joseph H.; Sonenstein, Freya L.; & Ku, Leighton C. (1993). Masculinity ideology: Its impact on adolescent males' heterosexual relationships. *Journal of Social Issues, 49*(3), 11–29.

Pliner, Patricia; & Chaiken, Shelly. (1990). Eating, social motives, and self-presentation in women and men. *Journal of Experimental Social Psychology, 26,* 240–254.

Pliner, Patricia; Chaiken, Shelly; & Flett, Gordon L. (1990). Gender differences in concern with body weight and physical appearance over the life span. *Personality and Social Psychology Bulletin, 16,* 263–273.

Plutchik, Robert. (1984). Emotions: A general psychoevolutionary theory. In Klaus R. Scherer & Paul Ekman (Eds.), *Approaches to emotion* (pp. 197–219). Hillsdale, NJ: Erlbaum.

Poest, Catherine A.; Williams, Jean R.; Witt, David D.; & Atwood, Mary E. (1989). Physical activity patterns of preschool children. *Early Childhood Research Quarterly, 4,* 367–376.

Polivy, Janet; & Herman, C. Peter. (1983). *Breaking the diet habit: The natural weight alternative.* New York: Basic Books.

Polivy, Janet; & Thomsen, Linda. (1988). Dieting and other eating disorders. In Elaine A. Blechman & Kelly D. Brownell (Eds.), *Handbook of behavioral medicine for women* (pp. 345–355). New York: Pergamon Press.

Pollitt, Katha. (1992, December 28). Are women morally superior to men? *Nation,* 799–807.

Pollitt, Katha. (1995). Marooned on Gilligan's island: Are women morally superior to men? In Katha Pollitt, *Reasonable creatures: Essays on women and feminism* (pp. 42–62). New York: Knopf.

Pope, Kenneth S. (1988). How clients are harmed by sexual contact with mental health professionals: The syndrome and its prevalence. *Journal of Counseling and Development, 67,* 222–226.

Postman, Andrew. (1996, August). Big fat lies about men. *Mademoiselle, 102,* 152–155, 187.

Powlishta, Kimberly K. (1995). Gender bias in children's perceptions of personality traits. *Sex Roles, 32,* 17–28.

Powlishta, Kimberly K.; Serbin, Lisa A.; & Moller, Lora C. (1993). The stability of individual differences in gender typing: Implications for understanding gender segregation. *Sex Roles, 29,* 723–744.

Pryor, John B.; & Whalen, Nora J. (1997). A typology of sexual harassment: Characteristics of harassers and the social circumstances under which sexual harassment occurs. In William O'Donohue (Ed.), *Sexual harassment: Theory, research, and treatment* (pp. 129–151). Boston: Allyn and Bacon.

Ptacek, J. T.; & Millman, Wendy. (1996, August). *Sex differences in coping: Perceptions of differences in use and in willingness to report use.* Paper presented at the 104th convention of the American Psychological Association, Toronto, Canada.

Ptacek, J. T.; Smith, Ronald E.; & Dodge, Kenneth L. (1994). Gender differences in coping with stress: When stressor and appraisals do not differ. *Personality and Social Psychology Bulletin, 20,* 421–430.

Ptacek, J. T.; Smith, Ronald E.; & Zanas, John. (1992). Gender, appraisal, and coping: A longitudinal analysis. *Journal of Personality, 60,* 747–770.

Purifoy, Frances E.; & Koopmans, Lambert H. (1979). Androstenedione, testosterone, and free testosterone concentration in women of various occupations. *Social Biology, 26,* 179–188.

Quinn, Susan. (1987). *A mind of her own: The life of Karen Horney.* New York: Summit Books.

Ragins, Belle Rose; & Sundstrom, Eric. (1989). Gender and power in organizations: A longitudinal perspective. *Psychological Bulletin, 105,* 51–88.

Raichle, Marcus E. (1994, April). Visualizing the mind. *Scientific American, 270,* 58–64.

Rawlings, Edna I. (1993). Reflections on "Twenty years of feminist counseling and therapy." *Counseling Psychologist, 21,* 88–91.

Ray, William J. (1993). *Methods toward a science of behavior and experience* (4th ed.). Belmont, CA: Wadsworth.

Redman, Selina; Webb, Gloria R.; Hennrikus, Deborah J.; Gordon, Jill J.; & Sanson-Fisher, Robert W. (1991). The effects of gender upon diagnosis of psychological disturbance. *Journal of Behavioral Medicine, 14,* 527–540.

Regier, Darrel A.; Narrow, William E.; & Rae, Donald S. (1990). The epidemiology of anxiety disorders: The Epidemiologic Catchment Area (ECA) experience. *Journal of Psychiatric Research, 24* (Suppl. 2), 3–14.

Reid, Helen M.; & Fine, Gary Alan. (1992). Self-disclosure in men's friendships: Variations associated with intimate relations. In Peter M. Nardi (Ed.), *Men's friendships* (pp. 132–152). Newbury Park, CA: Sage.

Reid, Pamela T.; Tate, Carol S.; & Berman, Phyllis W. (1989). Preschool children's self-presentations in situations with infants: Effects of sex and race. *Child Development, 60,* 710–714.

Reinisch, June M.; Rosenblum, Leonard A.; Rubin, Donald B.; & Schulsinger, M. Fini. (1997). Sex differences emerge during the first year of life. In Mary Roth Walsh (Ed.), *Women, men, & gender: Ongoing debates* (pp. 37–43). New Haven, CT: Yale University Press.

Rejskind, F. Gillian; Rapagna, Socrates O.; & Gold, Dolores. (1992). Gender differences in children's divergent thinking. *Creativity Research Journal, 5,* 165–174.

Renzetti, Claire M.; & Curran, Daniel J. (1992). *Women, men, and society* (2nd ed.). Boston: Allyn and Bacon.

Resnick, Heidi S.; Kilpatrick, Dean G.; Best Connie L.; & Kramer, Teresa L. (1992). Vulnerability–stress factors in development of posttraumatic stress disorder. *Journal of Nervous and Mental Disease, 180,* 424–430.

Resnick, Heidi S.; Kilpatrick, Dean G.; Dansky, Bonnie S.; Saunders, Benjamin E.; & Best, Connie L. (1993). Prevalence of victim trauma and posttraumatic stress disorder in a representative national sample of women, *Journal of Consulting and Clinical Psychology, 61,* 984–991.

Ricciardelli, Lina A.; & Williams, Robert J. (1995). Desirable and undesirable gender traits in three behavioral domains. *Sex Roles, 33,* 637–655.

Riessman, Catherine Kohler. (1990). *Divorce talk: Women and men make sense of personal relationships.* New Brunswick: Rutgers University Press.

Riger, Stephanie. (1991). Gender dilemmas in sexual harassment policies and procedures. *American Psychologist, 46,* 497–505.

Riger, Stephanie. (1992). Epistemological debates, feminist voices: Science, social values, and the study of women. *American Psychologist, 47,* 730–740.

Risman, Barbara J. (1989). Can men "mother"? Life as a single father. In Barbara J. Risman & Pepper Schwartz (Eds.), *Gender in intimate relationships: A microstructural approach* (pp. 155–164). Belmont, CA: Wadsworth.

Riter, Robert N. (1997). I have breast cancer. *Newsweek, 130*(2), 14.

Roberts, Tomi-Ann. (1991). Gender and the influence of evaluations on self-assessments in achievement settings. *Psychological Bulletin, 109,* 297–308.

Roberts, Tomi-Ann; & Nolen-Hoeksema, Susan. (1994). Gender comparisons in responsiveness to others' evalutions in achievement settings. *Psychology of Women Quarterly, 18,* 221–240.

Robertson, John; & Fitzgerald, Louise F. (1990). The (mis)treatment of men: Effects of client gender role and life-style on diagnosis and attribution of pathology. *Journal of Counseling Psychology, 37,* 3–9.

Robertson, John; & Fitzgerald, Louise F. (1992). Overcoming the masculine mystique: Preferences for alternative form of assistance among men who avoid counseling. *Journal of Counseling Psychology, 39,* 240–246.

Robine, Jean-Marie; & Ritchie, Karen. (1991). Healthy life expectancy: Evaluation of global indicator of change in population health. *British Medical Journal, 302,* 457–460.

Robinson, David. (1979). *Talking out of alcoholism: The self-help process of Alcoholics Anonymous.* Baltimore: University Park Press.

Rodin, Judith. (1991). Foreword. In Marianne Frankenhaeuser, Ulf Lundberg, & Margaret Chesney (Eds.), *Women, work, and health: Stress and opportunities* (pp. vii–xi). New York: Plenum Press.

Rodin, Judith; & Ickovics, Jeannette R. (1990). Women's health: Review and research agenda as we approach the 21st century. *American Psychologist, 45,* 1018–1034.

Rodin, Judith; Silberstein, Lisa; & Striegel-Moore, Ruth. (1985). Women and weight: A normative discontent. In Theo B. Sonderegger (Ed.), *Nebraska symposium on motivation 1984: Psychology and gender* (Vol. 32, pp. 267–307). Lincoln, NE: University of Nebraska Press.

Roehling, Patricia V.; Koelbel, Nikole; & Rutgers, Christina. (1994, August). *Codependence: Pathologizing femininity?* Paper presented at the 102nd annual convention of the American Psychological Association, Los Angeles, CA.

Rogers, Carl R. (1951). *Client-centered therapy: Its current practice, implications, and theory.* Boston: Houghton Mifflin.

Rogers, Carl R. (1961). *On becoming a person: A therapist's view of psychotherapy.* Boston: Houghton Mifflin.

Rogers, Carl R. (1980). *A way of being.* Boston: Houghton Mifflin.

Rolls, Barbara J.; Fedoroff, Ingrid C.; & Guthrie, Joanne F. (1991). Gender differences in eating behavior and body weight regulation. *Health Psychology, 10,* 133–142.

Ronan, Colin A. (1982). *Science: Its history and development among the world's cultures.* New York: Facts On File Publications.

Roscoe, Bruce; Diana, Mark S.; & Brooks, Richard H., II. (1987). Early, middle, and late adolescents' views on dating and factors influencing partner selection. *Adolescence, 22,* 59–68.

Roscoe, Bruce; Kennedy, Donna; & Pope, Tony. (1987). Adolescents' views of intimacy: Distinguishing intimate from nonintimate relationships. *Adolescence, 22,* 511–516.

Roscoe, Will. (1993). How to become a berdache: Toward a unified analysis of gender diversity. In Gilbert Herdt (Ed.), *Third sex, third gender: Beyond sexual dimorphism in culture and history* (pp. 329–372). New York: Zone Books.

Rose, Suzanna; & Frieze, Irene Hanson. (1993). Young singles' contemporary dating scripts. *Sex Roles, 28,* 499–509.

Rosenfield, David; & Stephan, Walter G. (1978). Sex differences in attributions for sex-typed tasks. *Journal of Personality, 46,* 244–259.

Rosenfield, Sarah. (1982). Sex roles and societal reactions to mental illness: The labeling of "deviant deviance." *Journal of Health and Social Behavior, 23,* 18–24.

Rosenfield, Sarah. (1989). The effects of women's employment: Personal control and sex differences in mental health. *Journal of Health and Social Behavior, 30,* 77–91.

Rosenfield, Sarah. (1992). The costs of sharing: Wives' employment and husbands' mental health. *Journal of Health and Social Behavior, 33,* 213–225.

Rosenkrantz, Paul; Vogel, Susan; Bee, Helen; Broverman, Inge; & Broverman, Donald M. (1968). Sex-role stereotypes and self-concepts in college students. *Journal of Consulting and Clinical Psychology, 32,* 287–295.

Rosenthal, Patrice. (1996). Gender and managers' causal attributions for subordinate performance: A field story. *Sex Roles, 34,* 1–14.

Ross, Catherine E.; & Bird, Chloe E. (1994). Sex stratification and health lifestyle: Consequences for men's and women's perceived health. *Journal of Health and Social Behavior, 35*(2), 161–178.

Rothstein, Donna S. (1995). Do female faculty influence female students' educational and labor market attainments? *Industrial and Labor Relations Review, 48,* 515–530.

Rothstein, Edward. (1997, February 17). Software for girls: Glaring gender differences. *New York Times CyberTimes [online],* http://search.nytimes.com/search/daily.

Rubin, Linda J.; & Borgers, Sherry B. (1990). Sexual harassment in universities during the 1980s. *Sex Roles, 23,* 397–411.

Rubin, Robert T.; Reinisch, June M.; & Haskett, Roger F. (1981). Postnatal gonadal steroid effects on human behavior. *Science, 211,* 1318–1324.

Ruble, Diane N.; & Martin, Carol Lynn. (1998). Gender development. In Nancy Eisenberg (Ed.), *Handbook of child psychology, Vol. 3: Social, emotional, and personality development* (5th ed.; pp. 933–1016). New York: Wiley.

Rush, Florence. (1977). The Freudian cover-up. *Chrysalis, 1,* 31–45. (Reprinted in *Feminism & Psychology,* 1996, *6,* 261–276.)

Russell, Denise. (1995). *Women, madness and medicine.* Cambridge, UK: Polity Press.

Russell, Diana E. H. (1986). *The secret trauma: Incest in the lives of girls and women.* New York: Basic Books.

Russell, James A. (1991). Culture and the categorization of emotions. *Psychological Bulletin, 110,* 426–450.

Russell, James A. (1994). Is there universal recognition of emotion from facial expression: A review of the cross-cultural studies. *Psychological Bulletin, 115,* 102–141.

Russo, Nancy Felipe. (1990). Overview: Forging research priorities for women's mental health. *American Psychologist, 45,* 368–373.

Saal, Frank E.; Johnson, Catherine B.; & Weber, Nancy. (1989). Friendly or sexy? It may depend on whom you ask. *Psychology of Women Quarterly, 13,* 263–276.

Sadker, David; & Sadker, Myra. (1985). The treatment of sex equity in teacher education. In Susan S. Klein (Ed.), *Handbook for achieving sex equity through education* (pp. 145–161). Baltimore: Johns Hopkins University Press.

Sadker, Myra P.; & Sadker, David M. (1980). Sexism in teacher-education texts. *Harvard Educational Review, 50,* 36–46.

Sadker, Myra; Sadker, David; & Klein, Susan S. (1986). Abolishing misperceptions about sex equity in education. *Theory into Practice, 25,* 219–226.

Sadker, Myra; Sadker, David; & Steindam, Sharon. (1989). Gender equity and educational reform. *Educational Leadership, 46,* 44–47.

Saltzman, Amy. (1991, June 17). Trouble at the top. *U.S. News & World Report,* 40–48.

Sandomir, Richard. (1997, April 23). Prospects for Title IX expected to improve. *New York Times Cyber Times* [*online*], http://search.nytimes.com/search/daily.

Santrock, John W. (1993). *Adolescence: An introduction* (5th ed.). Madison, WI: Brown & Benchmark.

Saragovi, Carina; Koestner, Richard; Di Dio, Lina; & Aubé, Jennifer. (1997). Agency, communion, and well-being: Extending Helgeson's (1994) model. *Journal of Personality and Social Psychology, 73,* 593–609.

Sarason, Irwin G.; & Sarason, Barbara R. (1993). *Abnormal psychology: The problem of maladaptive behavior* (7th ed.). Englewood Cliffs, NJ: Prentice-Hall.

Savage, Robert M.; & Gouvier, W. Drew. (1992). Rey Auditory–Verbal Learning Test: The effects of age and gender, and norms for delayed recall and story recognition trials. *Archives of Clinical Neuropsychology, 7,* 407–414.

Savin-Williams, Ritch C. (1995). Lesbian, gay male, and bisexual adolescents. In Anthony R. D'Augelli & Charlotte J. Patterson (Eds.), *Lesbian, gay, and bisexual identities over the lifespan: Psychological perspectives* (pp. 165–189). New York: Oxford University Press.

Schachter, Stanley; & Singer, Jerome E. (1962). Cognitive, social, and psychological determinants of emotional state. *Psychological Review, 69,* 379–399.

Scher, Murray. (1981). Men in hiding: A challenge for the counselor. *Personnel and Guidance Journal, 60,* 199–202.

Scheibe, Gabriele; & Albus, Margot. (1992). Age at onset, precipitating events, sex distribution, and co-occurrence of anxiety disorders. *Psychopathology, 25,* 11–18.

Scherer, Klaus R.; Wallbott, Harald G.; & Summerfield, Angela B. (Eds.). (1986). *Experiencing emotion: A cross-cultural study.* Cambridge, England: Cambridge University Press.

Schiff, Debra. (1997). Give your daughters legos and erector sets, in addition to Barbies, if you want them to go into engineering. *Electronic Design, 45,* 79–80.

Schneer, Joy A.; & Reitman, Freida. (1990). Effects of employment gaps on the careers of M.B.A.'s: More damaging for men than for women? *Academy of Management Journal, 33,* 391–406.

Schneider, Beth F. (1987). Graduate women, sexual harassment, and university policy. *Journal of Higher Education, 58,* 46–65.

Schofield, Janet Ward. (1981). Complementary and conflicting identities: Images and interaction in an interracial school. In Steven R. Asher & John M. Gottman (Eds.), *The development of children's friendships* (pp. 53–90). Cambridge, England: Cambridge University Press.

Schratz, Marjorie M. (1978). A developmental investigation of sex differences in spatial (visual–analytic) and mathematical skills in three ethnic groups. *Development Psychology, 14,* 263–267.

Schultz, Duane P.; & Schultz, Sidney Ellen. (1992). *A history of modern psychology* (5th ed.). Fort Worth: Harcourt Brace Jovanovich.

Schutte, Nicola; Malouff, John; Curtis, Donna; Lowry, Manya; & Luis, Cheryl. (1996, August). *Women's acceptance of traditional roles and their career choice.* Paper presented at the 104th annual convention of the American Psychological Association, Toronto, Canada.

Schwartz, Pepper. (1994). *Peer marriage: How love between equals really works.* New York: Free Press.

Scully, Diana. (1990). *Understanding sexual violence: A study of convicted rapists.* London: HarperCollins Academic.

Segal, Julius; & Segal, Zelda. (1993, May). What five-year-olds think about sex: And when and how to give them the answers that they need to hear. *Parents' Magazine,* 130–132.

Seid, Roberta P. (1994). Too "close to the bone": The historical context of women's obsession with slenderness. In Patricia Fallon, Melanie A. Katzman, & Susan C. Wooley (Eds.), *Feminist perspectives on eating disorders* (pp. 3–16). New York: Guilford Press.

Seligmann, Jean, with Rogers, Patrick; & Annin, Peter. (1994, May 2). The pressure to lose. *Newsweek, 123*(18), 60–61.

Seligmann, Jean; & Gelman, David. (1993, March 15). Is it sadness or madness? Psychiatrists clash over how to classify PMS. *Newsweek, 121,* 66.

Sell, Randall L.; Wells, James A.; & Wypij, David. (1995). The prevalence of homosexual behavior and attraction in the United States, the United Kingdom and France: Results of national population-based samples. *Archives of Sexual Behavior, 24,* 235–248.

Sells, Lucy W. (1980). The mathematics filter and the education of women and minorities. In Lynn H. Fox, Linda Brody, & Dianne Tobin (Eds.), *Women and the mathematical mystique* (pp. 66–75). Baltimore: Johns Hopkins University Press.

Serbin, Lisa A.; Zelkowitz, Phyllis; Doyle, Anna-Beth; Gold, Dolores; & Wheaton, Blair. (1990). The socialization of sex-differentiated skills and academic performance: A mediational model. *Sex Roles, 23,* 613–628.

Serdula, Mary K.; Collins, Elizabeth; Williamson, David F.; Anda, Robert F; Pamuk, Elsie; & Byers, Tim E. (1993). Weight control practices of U.S. adolescents and adults. *Annals of Internal Medicine, 119,* 667–671.

Sharabany, Ruth; Gershoni, Ruth; & Hofman, John E. (1981). Girlfriend, boyfriend: Age and sex differences in intimate friendship. *Developmental Psychology, 17,* 800–808.

Sharpe, Mark J.; Heppner, Paul; & Dixon, Wayne A. (1995). Gender role conflict, instrumentality, expressiveness, and well-being in adult men. *Sex Roles, 33,* 1–17.

Sharps, Matthew J.; Price, Jana L.; & Williams, John K. (1994). Spatial cognition and gender: Instructional and stimulus influences on mental image rotation performance. *Psychology of Women Quarterly, 18,* 413–425.

Sharps, Matthew J.; Welton, Angela L.; & Price, Jana L. (1993). Gender and task in the determination of spatial cognitive performance. *Psychology of Women Quarterly, 17,* 71–83.

Shaywitz, Bennett A.; Shaywitz, Sally E.; Pugh, Kenneth R.; Constable, R. Todd; Skudlarski, Pawel; Fulbright, Robert K; Bronen, Richard A; Fletcher, Jac M.; Shankweiler, Donald P.; Katz, Leonard; & Gore, John C. (1995). Sex differences in the functional organization of the brain for language. *Nature, 373,* 607–609.

Shaywitz, Sally E.; Shaywitz, Bennett A.; Fletcher, Jack M.; & Escobar, Michael D. (1990, August 22–29). Prevalence of reading disability in boys and girls. Results of the Connecticut Longitudinal Study. *Journal of the American Medical Association, 264,* 998–1002.

Sherif, Carolyn W. (1982). Needed concepts in the study of gender identity. *Psychology of Women Quarterly, 6,* 375–398.

Sherman, Julia. (1971). *On the psychology of women: A survey of empirical studies.* Springfield, IL: Charles C. Thomas.

Sherman, Julia. (1978). *Sex-related cognitive differences: An essay on theory and evidence.* Springfield, IL: Charles C. Thomas.

Shields, Stephanie A. (1975a). Functionalism, Darwinism, and the psychology of women: A study in social myth. *American Psychologist, 30,* 739–754.

Shields, Stephanie A. (1975b). Ms. Pilgrim's progress: The contributions of Leta Stetter Hollingworth to the psychology of women. *American Psychologist, 30,* 852–857.

Shields, Stephanie A. (1984). "To pet, coddle, and 'do for'": Caretaking and the concept of maternal instinct. In Miriam Lewin (Ed.), *In the shadow of the past: Psychology portrays the sexes* (pp. 256–273). New York: Columbia University Press.

Shields, Stephanie A. (1987). Women, men, and the dilemma of emotion. In Phillip Shaver & Clyde Hendrick (Eds.), *Sex and gender* (p. 229–250). Newbury Park, CA: Sage.

Shields, Stephanie A. (1994, August). *Practicing social constructionism—Confessions of a feminist empiricist.* Paper presented at the 102nd annual convention of the American Psychological Association, Los Angeles, CA.

Shields, Stephanie A.; & Cooper, Pamela E. (1983). Stereotypes of traditional and nontraditional childbearing roles. *Sex Roles, 9,* 363–376.

Sibisi, Charles D. (1990). Sex differences in the age of onset of bipolar affective illness. *British Journal of Psychiatry, 156,* 842–845.

Sigel, Roberta S. (1996). *Ambition and accommodation: How women view gender relations.* Chicago: University of Chicago Press.

Signorella, Margaret L.; Bigler, Rebecca L.; & Liben, Lynn S. (1993). Developmental differences in children's gender schemata about others: A meta-analytic review. *Developmental Review, 13,* 147–183.

Signorella, Margaret L.; Frieze, Irene Hanson; & Hershey, Susanne W. (1996). Single-sex versus mixed-sex classes and gender schemata in children and adolescents: A longitudinal comparison. *Psychology of Women Quarterly, 20,* 599–607.

Silverstein, Brett; Carpman, Shari; Perlick, Deborah; & Perdue, Lauren. (1990). Nontraditional sex role aspirations, gender identity conflict, and disordered eating among college women. *Sex Roles, 23,* 687–695.

Silverstein, Brett; Perdue, Lauren; Wolk, Cordulla; & Pizzolo, Cecelia. (1988). Bingeing, purging, and estimates of parental attitudes regarding female achievement. *Sex Roles, 19,* 723–733.

Silverstein, Brett; & Perlick, Deborah. (1995). *The cost of competence: Why inequality causes depression, eating disorders, and illness in women.* New York: Oxford University Press.

Silverstein, Louise B. (1993). Primate research, family politics, and social policy: Transforming "cads" into "dads." *Journal of Family Psychology, 7,* 267–282.

Silverstein, Louise B. (1996). Fathering is a feminist issue. *Psychology of Women Quarterly, 20,* 3–37.

Simon, William; & Gagnon, John H. (1986). Sexual scripts: Permanence and change. *Archives of Sexual Behavior, 15,* 97–119.

Skovholt, Thomas M. (1978). Feminism and men's lives. *The Counseling Psychologist, 7*(4), 3–10.

Slade, Pauline. (1984). Premenstrual emotional changes in normal women: Fact or fiction? *Journal of Psychosomatic Research, 28,* 1–7.

Sleek, Scott. (1994, January). Girls who've been molested can later become molesters. *APA Monitor,* 34–35.

Smith, Thomas Ewin. (1997). Adolescent gender differences in time alone and time devoted to conversation. *Adolescence, 32,* 483–496.

Snodgrass, Sara E. (1985). Women's intuition: The effect of subordinate role on interpersonal sensitivity. *Journal of Personality and Social Psychology, 49,* 146–155.

Snodgrass, Sara E. (1992). Further effects of role versus gender on interpersonal sensitivity. *Journal of Personality and Social Psychology, 62,* 154–158.

Solomon, Alison. (1992). Clinical diagnosis among diverse populations: A multicultural perspective. *Families in Society, 73,* 371–377.

Spence, Janet T. (1985). Gender identity and its implications for the concepts of masculinity and femininity. In Theo B. Sonderegger (Ed.), *Nebraska symposium on motivation, 1984: Psychology and gender* (Vol. 32; pp. 59–95). Lincoln, NE: University of Nebraska Press.

Spence, Janet T.; & Hahn, Eugene D. (1997). The Attitudes Toward Women Scale and attitude change in college students. *Psychology of Women Quarterly, 21,* 17–34.

Spence, Janet T.; & Helmreich, Robert. (1978). *Masculinity and femininity: The psychological dimensions, correlates, and antecedents.* Austin: University of Texas Press.

Spence, Janet T.; Helmreich, Robert; & Stapp, Joy. (1974). The Personal Attributes Questionnaire: A measure of sex-role stereotypes and masculinity–femininity. *JSAS Catalog of Selected Documents in Psychology, 4,* 43 (Ms. no. 617).

Spinney, Laura. (1995, December 9). A virtual shoulder to cry on. *New Scientist, 148,* 36–40.

Sprecher, Susan; Hatfield, Elaine; Cortese, Anthony; Potapova, Elena; & Levitskaya, Anna. (1994). Token resistance to sexual intercourse and consent to unwanted sexual intercourse: College students' dating experiences in three countries. *Journal of Sex Research, 31,* 125–132.

Springer, Sally P.; & Deutsch, Georg. (1998). *Left brain, right brain* (5th ed.). New York: Freeman.

Sroufe, L. Alan; Bennett, Christopher; Englund, Michelle; & Urban, Joan. (1993). The significance of gender boundaries in preadolescence: Contemporary correlates and antecedents of boundary violation and maintenance. *Child Development, 64,* 455–466.

Stack, Carol B. (1997). Different voices, different visions: Gender, culture, and moral reasoning. In Maxine Baca Zinn, Pierrette Hondagneu-Sotelo, & Michael A. Messnser (Eds.), *Through the prism of difference: Readings on sex and gender* (pp. 51–57). Boston: Allyn and Bacon.

Stake, Jayne E.; & Lauer, Monica L. (1987). The consequences of being overweight: A controlled study of gender differences. *Sex Roles, 17,* 31–47.

Stangor, Charles; & Ruble, Diane N. (1987). Development of gender role knowledge and gender constancy. In Lynn S. Liben & Margaret L. Signorella (Eds.), *Children's gender schemata* (pp. 5–22). San Francisco: Jossey-Bass.

Stark, Ellen. (1989, May). Teen sex: Not for love. *Psychology Today,* 10–12.

Steele, Claude M. (1997). A threat in the air: How stereotypes shape intellectual identity and performance. *American Psychologist, 52,* 613–629.

Steele, Claude M.; & Aronson, Joshua. (1995). Stereotype threat and the intellectual test performance of African Americans. *Journal of Personality and Social Psychology, 69,* 797–811.

Steil, Janice M. (1989). Marital relationships and mental health: The psychic costs of equality. In Jo Freeman (Ed.), *Women: A feminist perspective* (pp. 138–148). Mountain View, CA: Mayfield.

Steil, Janice M. (1995). Supermoms and second shifts: Marital inequality in the 1990s. In Jo Freeman (Ed.), *Women: A feminist perspective* (5th ed.; pp. 149–181). Mountain View, CA: Mayfield.

Steinberg, Karen K.; Thacker, Stephen B.; Smith, Jay; Stroup, Donna F.; Zack, Matthew M.; Flanders, Dana; & Berkelmen, Ruth L. (1991). A meta-analysis of the effect of estrogen replacement therapy on the risk of breast cancer. *Journal of the American Medical Association, 265,* 1985–1990.

Steingart, Richard M.; Packer, Milton; Hamm, Peggy; Coglianese, Mary Ellen; Gersh, Bernard; Geltman, Edward M.; Sollano, Josephie; Katz, Stanley; Moyé, Lem; Basta, Lofty L.; Lewis, Sandra J.; Gottlieb, Stephen S.; Bernstein, Victoria; McEwan, Patricia; Jacobson, Kirk; Brown, Edward J.; Kukin, Marrick L.; Kantrowitz, Niki E.; & Pfeffer, Marc A. (1991). Sex differences in the management of coronary artery disease. *New England Journal of Medicine, 325,* 226–230.

Stephenson, P. Susan; & Walker, Gillian A. (1979). The psychiatrist-woman patient relationship. *Canadian Journal of Psychiatry, 24,* 5–16.

Sternberg, Robert J. (1986). A triangular theory of love. *Psychological Review, 93,* 119–135.

Sternberg, Robert J. (1987). Liking versus loving: A comparative evaluation of theories. *Psychological Bulletin, 102,* 331–345.

Stipp, David. (1996, May 13). The gender gap in cancer research. *Fortune, 133*(9), 74–76.

Stokes, Joseph; Riger, Stephanie; & Sullivan, Megan. (1995). Measuring perceptions of the working environment for women in corporate settings. *Psychology of Women Quarterly, 19,* 533–549.

Straus, Murray A.; & Gelles, Richard J. (1986). Societal change and change in family violence from 1975 to 1985 as revealed by two national surveys. *Journal of Marriage and the Family, 48,* 465–479.

Straus, Murray A.; Gelles, Richard J.; & Steinmetz, Suzanne K. (1980). *Behind closed doors:*

Violence in the American family. Garden City, NY: Anchor.

Strickland, Bonnie R. (1988). Sex-related differences in health and illness. *Psychology of Women Quarterly, 12,* 381–399.

Stroh, Linda K.; Brett, Jeanne M.; & Reilly, Anne H. (1992). All the right stuff: A comparison of female and male managers' career progression. *Journal of Applied Psychology, 77,* 251–260.

Stromquist, Nelly P. (1991). *Daring to be different: The choice of nonconventional fields of study by international women students.* New York: Institute of International Education.

Struckman-Johnson, Cindy. (1988). Forced sex on dates: It happens to men, too. *Journal of Sex Research, 24,* 234–241.

Struckman-Johnson, Cindy; & Struckman-Johnson, David. (1993). College men's and women's reactions to hypothetical sexual touch varied by initiator gender and coercion level. *Sex Roles, 29,* 317–385.

Struckman-Johnson, Cindy; & Struckman-Johnson, David. (1994). Men pressured and forced into sexual experience. *Archives of Sexual Behavior, 23,* 93–114.

Stumpf, Heinrich. (1993). Performance factors and gender-related differences in spatial ability: Another assessment. *Memory & Cognition, 21,* 828–836.

Stumpf, Heinrich; & Stanley, Julian C. (1996). Gender-related differences on the College Board's Advanced Placement and Achievement Tests, 1982–1992. *Journal of Educational Psychology, 88,* 353–364.

Subrahmanyam, Kaveri; & Greenfield, Patricia M. (1994). Effect of video game practice on spatial skills in girls and boys. *Journal of Applied Developmental Psychology, 15,* 13–32.

Suitor, J. Jill; & Reavis, Rebel. (1995). Football, fast cars, and cheerleading: Adolescent gender norms. *Adolescence, 30,* 265–272.

Swaab, D. F.; & Fliers, E. (1985). A sexually dimorphic nucleus in the human brain. *Science, 228,* 1112–1115.

Swaab, D. F.; Gooren, L. J. G.; & Hofman, M. A. (1995). Brain research, gender, and sexual orientation. *Journal of Homosexuality, 28,* 283–301.

Swain, Scott O. (1992). Men's friendships with women: Intimacy, sexual boundaries, and the informant role. In Peter M. Nardi (Ed.), *Men's friendships* (pp. 153–171). Newbury Park, CA: Sage.

Swim, Janet K. (1994). Perceived versus meta-analytic effect sizes: An assessment of the accuracy of gender sterotypes. *Journal of Personality and Social Psychology, 66,* 21–36.

Swim, Janet; Borgida, Eugene; Maruyama, Geoffrey; & Myers, David G. (1989). Joan McKay versus John McKay: Do gender stereotypes bias evaluations? *Psychological Bulletin, 105,* 409–429.

Tannen, Deborah. (1990). *You just don't understand: Women and men in conversation.* New York: William Morrow.

Tarkan, Laurie. (1995). Unequal opportunity. *Women's Sports and Fitness, 17,* 25–27.

Tavris, Carol. (1982). *Anger: The misunderstood emotion.* New York: Touchstone.

Tavris, Carol. (1989, December). Do codependency theories explain women's unhappiness—or exploit their insecurities? *Vogue,* 220, 224–226.

Tavris, Carol. (1992). *The mismeasure of woman.* New York: Simon & Schuster.

Tavris, Carol. (1994). Reply to Brown and Gilligan. *Feminism & Psychology, 4,* 350–352.

Tavris, Carol; & Wade, Carole. (1984). *The longest war: Sex differences in perspective* (2nd ed.). New York: Harcourt Brace Jovanovich.

Terman, Lewis M.; & Merrill, Maud A. (1937). *Measuring intelligence.* Boston: Houghton Mifflin.

Theberge, Nancy. (1991). A content analysis of print media coverage of gender, women, and physical activity. *Journal of Applied Sport Psychology, 3,* 36–48.

Thompson, Linda; & Walker, Alexis J. (1989). Gender in families: Women and men in marriage, work, and parenthood. *Journal of Marriage and the Family, 51,* 845–871.

Thorne, Barrie. (1993). *Gender play: Girls and boys in school.* New Brunswick, NJ: Rutgers University Press.

Tiefer, Lenore. (1995). *Sex is not a natural act and other essays.* Boulder, CO: Westview Press.

Tipton, Robert M.; Camp, Charissa C.; & Hsu, Katharine. (1990). The effects of mandatory seat belt legislation on self-reported seat belt use among male and female college students. *Accident Analysis and Prevention, 22,* 543–548.

Tittle, Carol Kehr. (1986). Gender research and education. *American Psychologist, 41,* 1161–1168.

Titus, Jordan J. (1993). Gender messages in education foundations textbooks. *Journal of Teacher Education, 44,* 38–43.

Tjaden, Patricia Godeke; & Tjaden, Claus D. (1981). Differential treatment of the female felon: Myth or reality? In Marguerite O. Warren (Ed.), *Comparing female and male offenders* (pp. 73–88). Beverly Hills, CA: Sage.

Tobin-Richards, Maryse H.; Boxer, Andrew M.; & Petersen, Anne C. (1983). The psychological significance of pubertal change sex differences in perceptions of self during early adolescence. In Jeanne Brooks-Gunn & Anne C. Petersen (Eds.), *Girls at puberty: Biological and psychosocial perspectives* (pp. 127–154). New York: Plenum Press.

Tomasson, Kristinn; Kent, D.; & Coryell, W. (1991). Somatization and conversion disorders: Comorbidity and demographics at presentation. *Acta Psychiatrica Scandinavica, 84,* 288–293.

Travis, Cheryl Brown. (1988a). *Women and health psychology: Biomedical issues.* Hillsdale, NJ: Erlbaum.

Travis, Cheryl Brown. (1988b). *Women and health psychology: Mental health issues.* Hillsdale, NJ: Erlbaum.

Turner-Bowker, Diane M. (1996). Gender stereotyped descriptors in children's picture books: Does "Curious Jane" exist in the literature? *Sex Roles, 35,* 461–488.

Twenge, Jean M. (1997). Attitudes toward women, 1970–1995. *Psychology of Women Quarterly, 21,* 35–51.

Ulibarri, Monica D.; Wilson, Cynthia; Grijalva, Annette; Hunt, William K.; & Seligman, Ross. (1994, August). *Acculturation and sexual behavior of Mexican-American adolescents.* Paper presented at the 102nd annual convention of the American Psychological Association, Los Angeles, CA.

Unger, Rhoda K. (1979). Toward a redefinition of sex and gender. *American Psychologist, 34,* 1085–1094.

Unger, Rhoda K. (1995). Conclusion: Cultural diversity and the future of feminist psychology. In Hope Landrine (Ed.), *Bringing cultural diversity to feminist psychology* (pp. 413–431). Washington, DC: American Psychological Association.

Unger, Rhoda K.; & Crawford, Mary. (1993). Commentary: Sex and gender—The troubled relationship between terms and concepts. *Psychological Science, 4,* 122–124.

Urberg, Katheryn A. (1979). Sex role conceptualizations in adolescents and adults. *Developmental Psychology, 15,* 90–92.

Uribe, Virginia; & Harbeck, Karen M. (1992). Addressing the needs of lesbian, gay, and bisexual youth: The origins of Project 10 and school-based intervention. In Karen M. Harbeck (Ed.), *Coming out of the classroom closet: Gay and lesbian students, teachers and curricula* (pp. 9–28). New York: Harrington Park Press.

U.S. Bureau of the Census. (1975). *Historical Statistics of the United States, Colonial Times to 1970.* Washington, DC: U.S. Government Printing Office.

U.S. Bureau of the Census. (1996). *Statistical abstracts of the United States, 1996* (116th ed.). Washington, DC: U.S. Government Printing Office.

U.S. Department of Education, National Center for Educational Statistics. (1995). *The condition of education, 1995.* Washington, DC: U.S. Government Printing Office.

U.S. Department of Health and Human Services. (1989). *Reducing the health consequences of smoking: Nicotine addiction. A report of the Surgeon General, 1988* (DHHS Publication no. DC 88–8406). Washington, DC: U.S. Government Printing Office.

U.S. Department of Health and Human Services. (1990). *Alcohol and health: Seventh special report to the U.S. Congress.* (DHHS Publication no. ADM 90–1656). Washington, DC: U.S. Government Printing Office.

U.S. Department of Health and Human Services. (1997). *Child maltreatment 1995: Reports from the states to the National Child Abuse and Neglect data system.* Washington, DC: U.S. Government Printing Office.

U.S. Department of Justice. (1996a). *Sourcebook of criminal justice statistics 1995.* Washington, DC: U.S. Government Printing Office.

U.S. Department of Justice, (1996b). *Uniform crime report for the United States, 1995.* Washington, DC: U.S. Government Printing Office.

U.S. Department of Labor, Women's Bureau. (1996, September). 20 facts on women workers. *Working Women,* No. 96–2.

Valdez, Jesse N. (1994, August). *Ethnic identity, sex roles, and sexual attitudes.* Paper presented at the 102nd annual convention of the American Psychological Association, Los Angeles, CA.

Vance, Carole S. (1984). Pleasure and danger: Toward a politics of sexuality. In Carole S. Vance (Ed.), *Pleasure and danger: Exploring female sexuality* (pp. 1–27). Boston: Routledge & Kegan Paul.

van Gelder, Sadie. (1996, November). It's who I am. *Seventeen,* 142–145, 149.

Vasquez, Melba J. T. (1994). Latinas. In Lillian Comas-Díaz & Beverly Greene (Eds.), *Women of color: Integrating ethnic and gender identities in psychotherapy* (pp. 114–138). New York: Guilford Press.

Vasquez, Melba J. T.; & Kitchener, Karen Strohm. (1988). Introduction to special feature: Ethics in counseling: Sexual intimacy between counselor and client. *Journal of Counseling and Development, 67,* 214–217.

Vasta, Ross; Knott, Jill A.; & Gaze, Christine E. (1996). Can spatial training erase the gender differences on the water-level task? *Psychology of Women Quarterly, 20,* 549–567.

Vazquez-Nuttall, Ena; Romero-Garcia, Ivonne; & De Leon, Brunilda. (1987). Sex roles and perceptions of femininity and masculinity of Hispanic women. *Psychology of Women Quarterly, 11,* 409–425.

Verbrugge, Lois M. (1983). Multiple roles and physical health of women and men. *Journal of Health and Social Behavior, 24,* 16–30.

Verbrugge, Lois M. (1985). Gender and health: An update on hypotheses and evidence. *Journal of Health and Social Behavior, 26,* 156–182.

Verbrugge, Lois M. (1986). From sneeze to adieu: Stages of health for American men and women. *Social Science Medicine, 22,* 1195–1212.

Verbrugge, Lois M. (1989). The twain meet: Emprical explanations of sex differences in health and mortality. *Journal of Health and Social Behavior, 30,* 282–304.

Vetter, Betty. (1992). Ferment: yes; Progress: maybe; Change: slow. *Mosaic, 23*(3), 34–41.

Voyer, Daniel. (1996). The relation between mathematical achievement and gender differences in spatial abilities: A suppression effect. *Journal of Educational Psychology, 88,* 563–571.

Voyer, Daniel; Voyer, Susan; & Bryden, M. Philip. (1995). Magnitude of sex differences in spatial abilities: A meta-analysis and consideration of critical variables. *Psychological Bulletin, 117,* 250–270.

Waber, Deborah. (1976). Sex differences in cognition: A function of maturation rate? *Science, 192,* 572–573.

Wagenheim, Jeff. (1996, January–February). Among the Promise Keepers: An inside look at the evangelical men's movement. *Utne Reader,* 73, 74–77.

Wainryb, Cecilia. (1993). The application of moral judgments to other cultures: Relativism and universality. *Child Development, 64,* 924–933.

Waldron, Ingrid. (1991). Effects of labor force participation on sex differences in mortality and morbidity. In Marianne Frankenhaeuser, Ulf Lundberg, & Margaret Chesney (Eds.), *Women, work, and health: Stress and opportunities* (pp. 17–38). New York: Plenum Press.

Walker, Betty A.; Reis, Sally M.; & Leonard, Janet S. (1992). A developmental investigation of the lives of gifted women. *Gifted Child Quarterly, 36,* 201–206.

Walker, Lenore E. (1989). Psychology and violence against women. *American Psychologist, 44,* 695–702.

Walker, William D.; Rowe, Robert C.; & Quinsey, Vernon L. (1993). Authoritarianism and sexual aggression. *Journal of Personality and Social Psychology, 65,* 1036–1045.

Wallace, Julia E. (1996). Gender differences in beliefs of why women live longer than men. *Psychological Reports, 79,* 587–591.

Wallston, Barbara Strudler. (1981). What are the questions in psychology of women? A feminist approach to research. *Psychology of Women Quarterly, 5,* 597–617.

Walsh, Mary Roth. (1985). Academic professional women organizing for change: The struggle in psychology. *Journal of Social Issues, 41*(4), 17–28.

Wark, Gillian R.; & Krebs, Dennis L. (1996). Gender and dilemma differences in real-life moral judgment. *Developmental Psychology, 32,* 220–230.

Warr, Mark. (1985). Fear of rape among urban women. *Social Problems, 32,* 238–250.

Warren, Marguerite O. (1981). Gender comparisons in crime and delinquency. In Marguerite O. Warren (Ed.), *Comparing female and male offenders* (pp. 7–16). Beverly Hills, CA: Sage.

Waterhouse, Ruth L. (1993). "Wild women don't have the blues": A feminist critique of "person-centered" counselling and therapy. *Feminism & Psychology, 3,* 55–71.

Weinberg, Nancy; Uken, Janet S.; Schmale, John; & Adamek, Margaret. (1995). Therapeutic factors: Their presence in a computer-mediated support group. *Social Work with Groups, 18*(4), 57–69.

Weinburgh, Molly. (1995). Gender differences in student attitudes toward science: A meta-analysis of the literature from 1970 to 1991. *Journal of Research in Science Teaching, 32,* 387–398.

Weisman, Claire V.; Gray, James J.; Mosimann, James E.; & Ahrens, Anthony H. (1992). Cultural expectations of thinness in women: An update. *International Journal of Eating Disorders, 11,* 85–89.

Weisner, Thomas S.; & Wilson-Mitchell, Jane E. (1990). Nonconventional family life-styles and sex typing in six-year-olds. *Child Development, 61,* 1915–1933.

Weiss, Maureen R.; & Barber, Heather. (1995). Socialization influences of collegiate male athletes: A tale of two decades. *Sex Roles, 33,* 129–140.

Weisstein, Naomi. (1970). "Kinde, küche, kirche" as scientific law: Psychology constructs the female. In Robin Morgan (Ed.), *Sisterhood is powerful: An anthology of writings from the women's liberation movement* (pp. 228–245). New York: Vintage Books.

Weisstein, Naomi. (1982, November). Tired of arguing about biological inferiority? *Ms.,* 41–46, 85.

Weitzman, Lenore. (1985). *The divorce revolution: The unexpected social and economic consequences for women and children in America.* New York: Free Press.

Welch-Ross, Melissa K.; Schmidt, Constance R. (1996). Gender-schema development and children's constructive story memory: Evidence or a developmental model. *Child Development, 67,* 820–835.

Wellman, Barry. (1992). Men in networks: Private communities, domestic friendships. In Peter M. Nardi (Ed.), *Men's friendships* (pp. 74–114). Newbury Park, CA: Sage.

Welter, Barbara. (1978). The cult of true womanhood: 1820–1860. In Michael Gordon (Ed.), *The American family in social–historical perspective* (2nd ed.; pp. 313–333). New York: St. Martin's Press.

West, Candace; & Zimmerman, Don H. (1987). Doing gender. *Gender and Society, 1,* 125–151.

Westkott, Marcia C. (1997). On the new psychology of women: A cautionary view. In Mary Roth Walsh (Ed.), *Women, men, and gender: Ongoing debates* (pp. 362–372). New Haven, CT: Yale University Press.

Wethington, Elaine; McLeod, Jane D.; & Kessler, Ronald C. (1987). The importance of life events for explaining sex differences in psychological distress. In Rosalind C. Barnett, Lois Biener, & Grace K. Baruch (Eds.), *Gender and stress* (pp. 144–156). New York: Free Press.

Wharton, Amy S.; & Baron, James N. (1987). So happy together? The impact of gender segregation on men at work. *American Sociological Review, 52,* 574–587.

Wharton, Amy S.; & Baron, James N. (1991). Satisfaction? The psychological impact of gender segregation on women at work. *Sociological Quarterly, 32,* 365–387.

Whatley, Marianne H. (1990). Sex equity in sex education. *Education Digest, 55*(5), 46–49.

Wheeler, Ladd; Reis, Harry; & Nezlek, John. (1983). Loneliness, social interaction, and sex roles. *Journal of Personality and Social Psychology, 45,* 943–953.

White, Mark B.; Tyson-Rawson, Kirsten J. (1996, March/April). A peace plan for the gender wars. *Psychology Today, 29*(2), 51–54, 74, 76, 78, 80, 85.

Whiting, Beatrice Blyth; & Edwards, Carolyn Pope. (1988). *Children of different worlds: The formation of social behavior.* Cambridge, MA: Harvard University Press.

Whitley, Bernard E., Jr. (1988). Masculinity, femininity, and self-esteem: A multitrait–multimethod analysis. *Sex Roles, 7/8,* 419–431.

Widiger, Thomas A.; & Settle, Shirley A. (1987). Broverman et al. revisited: An artifactual sex bias. *Journal of Personality and Social Psychology, 53,* 463–469.

Wieringa, Saskia E. (1994). The Zuni man–woman. *Archives of Sexual Behavior, 23,* 348–351.

Wilbur, Jerry. (1987). Does mentoring breed success? *Training & Development Journal, 41*(11), 38–41.

Wiley, Mary Glenn; & Eskilson, Arlene. (1985). Speech style, gender stereotypes, and corporate success: What if women talk more like men? *Sex Roles, 12,* 993–1007.

Williams, Christine L. (1992). The glass escalator: Hidden advantages for men in the "female" professions. *Social Problems, 39,* 253–267.

Williams, David R.; Takeuchi, David T.; & Adair, Russell K. (1992). Socioeconomic status and psychiatric disorder among Blacks and Whites. *Social Forces, 71,* 179–194.

Williams, Janet B. W.; & Spitzer, Robert L. (1983). The issue of sex bias in DSM-III: A critique of "A woman's view of DSM-III" by Marcie Kaplan. *American Psychologist, 38,* 793–801.

Williams, John E.; & Best, Deborah L. (1990). *Measuring sex stereotypes: A multination study* (rev. ed.). Newbury Park, CA: Sage.

Williams, Juanita H. (1983). *Psychology of women: Behavior in a biosocial context* (2nd ed.). New York: Norton.

Wilson, Robert A. (1966). *Feminine forever.* New York: M. Evans.

WIN News. (1997). Teen pregnancy a major problem in the U.S. *WIN News, 23*(3), 69.

Wisch, Andrew F.; Mahalik, James R.; Hayes, Jeffrey A.; & Nutt, Elizabeth A. (1995). The impact of gender role conflict and counseling techniques on psychological help seeking in men. *Sex Roles, 33,* 77–89.

Wiseman, Claire V.; Gray, James J.; Mosimann, James E.; & Ahrens, Anthony H. (1992). Cultural expectations of thinness in women: An update. *International Journal of Eating Disorders, 11,* 85–89.

Witelson, Sandra F. (1985). The brain connection: The corpus callosum is larger in left-handers. *Science, 224,* 665–668.

Witelson, Sandra F. (1991). Sex differences in neuroanatomical changes with aging. *New England Journal of Medicine, 325,* 211–212.

Witkin, Herman A.; Mednick, Sarnoff A.; Schulsinger, Fini; Bakkestrøm, Eskild; Christiansen, Karlo O.; Goodenough, Donald. R.; Hirschhorn, Kurt; Lundesteen, Claes; Owen, David R.; Philip, John; Rubin, Donald B.; & Stocking, Martha. (1976). Criminality in XYY and XXY men. *Science, 193,* 547–555.

Wooley, O. Wayne. (1994). ...And man created "woman": Representations of women's bodies in Western culture. In Patricia Fallon, Melanie A. Katzman, & Susan C. Wooley (Eds.), *Feminist perspectives on eating disorders* (pp. 17–52). New York: Guilford Press.

Worell, Judith. (1996). Opening doors to feminist research. *Psychology of Women Quarterly, 20,* 469–485.

Worell, Judith; & Etaugh, Claire. (1994). Transforming theory and research with women: Themes and variations. *Psychology of Women Quarterly, 18,* 443–450.

Wyatt, Gail E. (1985). The sexual abuse of Afro-American and White-American women in childhood. *Child Abuse and Neglect, 9,* 507–519.

Wyatt, Gail Elizabeth. (1992). The sociocultural context of African American and White American women's rape. *Journal of Social Issues, 48*(1), 77–91.

Wyatt, Gail Elizabeth. (1994). The sociocultural relevance of sex research: Challenges for the 1990s and beyond. *American Psychologist, 49,* 748–754.

Yama, Mark F.; Tovey, Stephanie L.; & Fogas, Bruce S. (1993). Childhood family environment and sexual abuse as predictors of anxiety and depression in adult women. *American Journal of Orthopsychiatry, 63,* 136–141.

Yee, Doris K.; & Eccles, Jacquelynne S. (1988). Parent perceptions and attributions for children's math achievement. *Sex Roles, 19,* 317–333.

Yoder, Janice D.; & Kahn, Arnold S. (1993). Working toward an inclusive psychology of women. *American Psychologist, 48,* 846–850.

Yoder, Janice D.; & Schleicher, Thomas L. (1996). Undergraduates regard deviation from occupational gender stereotypes as costly for women. *Sex Roles, 34,* 171–188.

Zajonc, R. C. (1984). On the primacy of affect. *American Psychologist, 39,* 117–123.

Zera, Deborah. (1992). Coming of age in a heterosexist world: The development of gay and lesbian adolescents. *Adolescence, 27,* 849–854.

Zimmer-Schur, Lori A.; & Newcomb, Michael D. (1994, August). *Dieting and exercise behaviors: Subscale development gender differences and depression.* Paper presented at the 102nd annual convention of the American Psychological Association, Los Angeles, CA.

Zinik, Cary. (1985). Identity conflict or adaptive flexibility? Bisexuality reconsidered. *Journal of Homosexuality, 11,* 7–19.

Zucker, Kenneth J.; Bradley, Susan J.; & Sanikhani, Mohammad. (1997). Sex differences in referral rates of children with gender identity disorder: Some hypotheses. *Journal of Abnormal Child Psychology, 25,* 217–227.

Zucker, Kenneth J.; Wilson-Smith, Debra N.; Kurita, Janice A.; & Stern, Anita. (1995). Children's appraisals of sex-typed behavior in their peers. *Sex Roles, 33,* 703–725.

Name Index

Abi-Dargham, Annissé , 400
Abrams, Leslie R., 441
Abramson, Linda M., 328
Abramson, Paul R., 328
Ackerman, Bette, 400
Acosta, Mimi, 177
Adair, Russell K., 390
Adamek, Margaret, 428
Adesso, Vincent, 397, 452
Adler, David A., 392
Adler, Jerry, 329
Adler, Nancy L., 243
Adlis, Susan A., 367
Ahern, Melissa M., 381
Ahrens, Anthony H., 365
Akiyama, Hiroko, 226
Albus, Margot, 399
Alexander, Karl L., 96
Allen, Bem P., 179, 180
Allmendinger, Jutta, 332
Altman, Barbara Mandell, 331
Altman, Lawrence K., 342, 355
American Association of University Women (AAUW), 289, 290, 291, 292, 293, 295, 298, 299, 300, 301, 310, 451
American Psychiatric Association (ApA), 374, 386, 387, 389, 390, 399, 404
American Psychological Association (APA), 8
American Psychological Association Division 35, 8
American Psychological Association Division 51, 11
American Psychological Association Task Force on Male Violence Against Women, 379
American Psychological Association Task Force on Sex Bias, 414, 415, 417, 425
Andersen, Arnold, 366
Anderson, John P., 364
Aneshensel, Carol S., 377
Angostinelli, Joan, 237
Ankney, C. Davison, 75
Antill, John K., 231
Antonucci, Toni C., 226
Applegate, Brooks, 416
Archer, John, 441
Aries, Elizabeth, 333
Aronson, Joshua, 182
Arthur, Michael B., 330
Ashel, Mark H., 371
Ashton, Heather, 413, 415
Association for Women in Psychology, 8
Astin, Helen S., 318
Astrachan, Anthony, 10
Atkinson, Donald R., 417
Atkinson, J. W., 308
Attanucci, Jane, 132, 134
Attar, Beth K., 380
Attra, Sharon L., 396
Atwood, Mary E., 370
Aubé, Jennifer, 231, 421, 445
Averill, James R., 190, 202, 203
Avery, Patricia G., 290
Ayanian, John Z., 346

Baber, Kristine M., 318, 319, 451
Bachman, Jerald, 208
Bacon, Francis, 39
Baenninger, Maryann, 103, 294
Bagley, Christopher, 265
Bailey, William T., 177
Bakan, David, 39, 40, 186
Baker, Carilyn, 226
Ball, Richard E., 234
Ballou, Mary, 411, 415
Balmary, Marie, 125, 126
Bandura, Albert, 140, 142, 143, 160
Banks, Terry, 67
Barak, Azy, 306, 337
Barber, Heather, 305
Bardwell, Stephen, 397
Barnes, Michael, 230
Barnett, Rosalind, C., 377, 378, 441
Baron, James N., 332
Baron, Larry, 267
Baruch, Grace K., 377, 441
Bassett, Margaret E., 396

Baumeister, Roy F., 13, 14, 15, 18
Baxter, Susan, 86, 113, 428, 429, 436
Beach, Frank A., 252, 277
Beal, Carole R., 143, 155, 156, 162
Beard, Chris, 226
Bechtel, Stefan, 251
Beck, Aaron T., 410, 411
Beck, Melinda, 406, 407, 425, 427
Bee, Helen, 172
Beecher, Ronnie, 92
Begley, Sharon, 20, 21, 39, 40, 73, 85, 86
Belanoff, Joseph, 396
Belasco, Warren J., 364
Belenky, Mary Field, 135, 136
Belle, Deborah, 380
Bem, Sandra Lipsitz, 3, 8, 14, 19, 144, 147, 148, 149, 150, 151, 162, 185, 391, 447
Ben-David, Sarah, 208
Benbow, Camilla Persson, 94, 95, 96, 298
Benderly, Beryl Lieff, xv, 81, 110, 201
Benin, Mary Holland, 237
Bennett, Christopher, 222
Benton, Pam, 203
Berdahl, Jennifer L., 338, 339
Berenbaum, Sheri A., 59
Berger, Bertrand D., 397, 452
Berman, Joan Saks, 365, 420
Berman, Phyllis W., 198, 199
Bernard, Jessie, 168, 228, 233, 377
Bernardo, Donna Hodgkins, 236, 238
Bernat, Jeffrey, 211
Berndt, Thomas J., 221, 224
Bernstein, Bianca L., 416
Bersoff, Donald N., 334
Berven, Norman L., 331
Best, Connie L., 379, 399
Best, Deborah L., 165, 176, 178
Bettencourt, B. Ann, 207, 208
Betz, Nancy, 318, 319, 329
Bickel, Janet, 357
Bickel, Warren K., 62
Biener, Lois, 397, 398
Bierman, Karen Lynn, 221
Biernat, Monica, 171, 327
Bigler, Rebecca S., 149, 158
Billson, J. M., 242
Binet, Alfred, 90
Bird, Chloe E., 354
Bjorkqvist, Kaj, 208, 209
Black, Caryn J., 327
Blakeslee, Sandra, 110
Blechman, Elaine A., 62, 64, 412, 415
Bleier, Ruth, 82
Blier, Michael J., 417
Block, Jeanne H., 16
Blumenfeld, Phyllis, 295
Blumenthal, Susan J., 358
Blumstein, Philip, 231, 238, 239, 240, 242, 243, 245, 248, 249, 254, 282, 283, 284, 285, 288
Bly, Robert, 11, 434, 448
Bohan, Janis S., 280, 281, 286
Booth, Alan, 65, 66, 232, 244
Borgers, Sherry B., 307
Borgida, Eugene, 16, 170, 334
Boston, Martha B., 152
Boxer, Andrew M., 286, 296
Bradley, Susan J., 157
Bradshaw, Carla K., 365, 420
Brannon, Linda, xiv, 356, 384
Brannon, Robert, 9, 10, 140, 168, 214, 354, 391
Brecher, Edward M., 253, 254, 259
Breedlove, S. Marc, 51, 53, 72, 75, 79, 82, 84, 280
Brekke, Nancy, 170
Brems, Christiane, 424
Brett, Jeanne M., 326
Brice, Patrick, 204
Bridge, M. Junior, 17
Britannica Book of the Year, 345, 351
Brodsky, Annette M., 414, 416, 425
Broman, Clifford L., 394
Brooks, Richard, 229, 269
Brooks-Gunn, Jeanne, 270
Broussard, Deborah Bice, 275
Broverman, Donald M., 172, 173, 391
Broverman, Inge K., 172, 173, 391, 392
Brown, Clifford E., 335
Brown, Laura S., 389, 420
Brown, Lyn Mikel, 135
Brown, Roger L., 394
Brown, Susan L., 232, 244
Brown-Collins, Alice, 41
Browne, Angela, 267
Brownell, Kelly D., 367, 369, 373
Brownmiller, Susan, 212
Bruce, Martha L., 394
Brucken, Laura, 146
Bryan, James, 296
Bryant, Anne, 300, 315
Bryden, M. Philip, 80, 100
Buhrmester, Duane, 221
Bukowski, William M., 221
Burge, Penny L., 299
Burkam, David T., 295
Burnam, M. Audrey, 379
Burt, Martha R., 269
Bush, Diane M., 295
Buss, David M., 230, 240, 275
Bussey, Kay, 142, 143, 160
Byne, William, 82

Cahoon, Delwin D., 176
Cairns, Beverly D., 205
Cairns, Robert B., 201, 205, 206, 208, 209
Caldwell, Mayta, 224
Cameron, Oliver G., 399
Cammaert, Lorna P., 307, 418
Camp, Charissa C., 352
Campbell, Anne, 206, 208
Campbell, Bebe Moore, 440, 448
Campbell, Susan Miller, 238, 239
Cancian, Francesca M., 218, 226, 227, 228, 232, 233, 234, 240, 245, 248, 442, 452
Cann, Arnie, 157
Cannon, Walter B., 190
Caplan, Jeremy B., 22, 42, 44, 99
Caplan, Paula J., 22, 42, 44, 99, 102, 375
Carli, Linda L., 53
Carpman, Shari, 368
Carr, Judith G., 396
Carr, Rey A., 306
Carr, Timothy S., 67
Carrier, Joseph, 33
Carson, Mary, 226
Carstensen, Laura L., 243
Carter, Stephen L., 327
Casey, M. Beth, 94
Casper, Regina C., 396
Cauce, Ana Mari, 177
Centers for Disease Control, 270
Cetingök, Maummer, 400

Chaiken, Shelly, 364, 366
Chan, Raymond W., 200
Chapman, Julia, 105
Chartrand, Sabra, 323
Chehrazi, Shahla, 126
Chernin, Kim, 365
Cherry, France, 309
Chesler, Phyllis, 392, 393, 415, 453
Chess, Stella, 198
Chodorow, Carol, 135
Chodorow, Nancy, 126, 127, 129, 130, 131, 135, 136, 137, 138, 419, 449
Christensen, Andrew, 428, 429
Christensen, Larry B., 30
Christian, Harry, 159, 319
Chu, Chung-Chou, 400
Cicone, Michael V., 173
Clark, R. W., 308
Clark, Virginia A., 377
Clarkson, Frank E., 173, 391
Clay, Connie J., 62
Cleary, Paul D., 376, 377, 399, 401
Clinchy, Blythe McVicker, 135
Cochran, Susan, 282
Cohen, Deborah, 291
Cohen, Jacob, 37
Cohen, Laurie L., 275
Cohen, Richard D., 346
Cohen, Theodore F., 225
Cohn, Barbara A., 346
Colby, Anne, 132
Collaer, Marcia L., 83
Collins, M. Elizabeth, 366
Collins, Nancy L., 224
Coltrane, Scott, 238
Comas-Díaz, Lillian, 420
Committee on Women in Psychology, 427
Condry, John C., 193
Condry, Sandra, 193
Confucius, 22
Connell, R. W. (Bob), 167, 168
Conrad, Eva, 41, 44
Constantinople, Anne, 181, 183, 187, 278
Cook, Ellen Piel, 388, 389
Cooper, Joel, 155
Cooper, Pamela, 29
Cooperstock, Ruth, 413, 415
Corder Bolz, Judy, 139
Cornell, Claire Pedrick, 241, 242
Cortese, Anthony, 26
Coryell, W., 401
Cowan, Gloria, 431
Cowell, Patricia E., 80, 85
Cowley, Geoffrey, 56
Cox, Taylor H., Jr., 327
Crandall, Christian, 369
Crawford, June, 203
Crawford, Mary, 4, 13, 31, 34, 105, 135, 136
Crook, Thomas H., 85, 105
Crouter, Ann, 237
Culbertson, Frances M., 395, 405
Culver, Steven M., 299
Curran, Daniel J., 382
Curtis, Donna, 319
Cutler, Susan, 379
Czajkowski, Susan, 346, 347

Dabbs, James M., Jr., 66, 67, 68, 70
Dalton, Katharina, 62
Damon, William, 132
Dansky, Bonnie S., 399
Darwin, Charles, 4, 5, 191, 194, 216
Daugherty, Cynthia, 419
Davenport, Donna S., 177
Davis, Caroline, 371
Davis, Kathy, 132, 134
Dawes, Robyn M., 392
Dawkins, Mark C., 332
Day, Randal D., 270
de la Motte, Diether, 106
de la Rue, Denise, 66
de Lacoste-Utamsing, Christine, 82
De Leon, Brunilda, 177
de Monteflores, Carmen, 280
Dean, Tina, 397
Deaux, Kay, 13, 16, 171, 188, 309, 312, 334
Degler, Carl N., 253
DeHeer, N. Dean, 417
Dell, Don M., 422
Demarest, Jack, 293
Denmark, Florence L., 15
Dennis, Wanda D., 179
Derry, Paula S., 363
Desmarais, Serge, 143
Deutsch, Francine M., 439
Deutsch, Georg, 77, 78, 79, 88, 110
Di Dio, Lina, 421
Diana, Mark, 229, 269
DiDomenico, Lisa, 366
Diener, Ed, 194, 442
DiMatteo, M. Robin, 360
Dinnerstein, Dorothy, 419
Dionne, Michelle, 371
Dixon, Wayne A., 421
Docherty, Karen J., 69
Dodge, Kenneth L., 385
Dohrenwend, Barbara S., 380
Dohrenwend, Bruce P., 380
Dolan, Bridget, 367
Doll, Richard, 350, 351
Dollard, John, 202
Doob, Leonard, 202
Dovidio, John F., 335
Dow, Michael G., 394
Doyle, Anna-Beth, 293, 315
Drake, Robert E., 392
Dreher, George F., 327
Drewnowski, Adam, 366
Dreyfus, Colleen K., 211
Dubbert, Patricia M., 304, 371
DuBois, David L., 223
Duck, Steve, 244, 247
Dupuy, Paula, 388
Dutton, Mary Ann, 378
Duveen, Gerald, 25
Dweck, Carol S., 311
Dwyer, Victor, 301

Eagly, Alice H., 13, 14, 16, 18, 19, 174, 175, 179, 207, 214, 235, 328, 334, 447, 450
Eccles, Jacquelynne S., 94, 96, 97, 111, 295, 296
Eckhardt, Michael J., 352
Edmonds, Ed M., 176
Edwards, Carolyn Pope, 178
Ehrenreich, Barbara, 357, 359, 443
Ehrhardt, Anke A., 59
Eichenbaum, Luise, 444
Eisenberg, Nancy, 214
Ekman, Paul, 191
El-Bayoumi, Gigi, 378
Ellenberger, Henri F., 116
Ellestad, Myrvin H., 346
Elliott, Kathryn, 226
Elliott, Stuart, 371
Ellis, Albert, 408, 410
Ellis, Henry Havelock, 252, 253
Ellyston, Steve L., 335
Emrich, Cynthia, 108

English, Deirdre, 357, 359
Englund, Michelle, 222
Enns, Carolyn Zerbe, 417, 420, 433, 436
Entwisle, Doris R., 96
Epperson, Douglas, 203
Epstein, Arnold M., 346
Epstein, Cynthia Fuchs, 2, 135
Eron, Leonard D., 202, 204, 205
Escobar, Michael D., 92
Eskilson, Arlene, 333
Estep, Rhoda E., 269
Etaugh, Claire, 41
Eyer, Diane E., 197, 198, 217

Faderman, Lillian, 282
Fagot, Beverly I., 143, 150, 153, 154, 161, 175, 384
Fallon, April E., 366
Faludi, Susan, 433, 445
Farmer, Helen S., 317
Farrakhan, Louis, 12
Farris, Elizabeth, 312
Fausto-Sterling, Anne, 62, 72, 109
Fedoroff, Ingrid C., 364
Fee, Elizabeth, 22
Feingold, Alan, 92, 94, 95, 100, 103, 111
Feist, Gregory J., 116, 120, 409, 442
Feist, Jess, 116, 120, 356, 409, 442
Feld, Scott L., 241
Feldstein, Michael, 427
Felmlee, Diane H., 238, 243
Fennema, Elizabeth, 94, 96, 97, 450
Ferguson, Lynda L., 205
Ferree, Myra Marx, 7
Feyerherm, William, 208
Fields, Judith, 332
Fine, Gary Alan, 226
Fine, Michelle, 269
Finkelhor, David, 264, 267
Finn, Stephen, 420
Fischer, Agneta H., 191, 214, 217
Fischer, Ann R., 305
Fischer, Paulette, 204
Fisher, William A., 306
Fiske, Susan T., 179, 181, 334
Fitzgerald, Louise F., 307, 335, 336, 337, 341, 379, 416, 422, 423, 451
Fivush, Robyn, 151, 152, 156
Flaskerud, Jacquelyn H., 390
Fletcher, Jack M., 92
Flett, Gordon L., 366
Fliers, E., 83
Floyd, Kory, 225
Flynn, Clifton P., 379
Fodor, Iris Goldstein, 412, 419
Fogas, Bruce S., 379
Fogel, Alan, 198
Folkman, Susan, 381, 383, 384
Fontenot, Kathleen, 384
Foote, Donna, 406
Ford, Clellan S., 252, 277
Forster, Jean L., 367
Fowers, Blaine J., 377, 416
Fox, Mary Frank, 302, 303, 306, 323
Fox, Ronald C., 285
Frady, Robert L., 67, 68
Frankenhaeuser, Marianne, 348
Freiberg, Peter, 297
Frensch, Peter A., 102
Frerichs, Ralph R., 377
Freud, Anna, 120
Freud, Martha, 120
Freud, Sigmund, 5, 6, 7, 115, 116, 117, 118, 119, 120, 121, 122, 123, 124, 125, 126, 127, 130, 135, 136, 138, 202, 263, 407, 408, 414, 435
Freund, Richard D., 417
Frezza, Mario, 397
Friedman, Debra E., 271
Friesen, Wallace V., 191
Frieze, Irene H., 12, 42, 148, 229, 290
Frijda, Nico H., 192, 193
Frodi, Ann M., 207, 214, 450
Frost, Laurie A., 97
Frye, Marilyn, 283, 284
Fujita, Frank, 194, 442
Furman, Wyndol, 221
Furstenberg, Frank F., 248, 270

Gagnon, John H., 212, 257, 258, 274
Galaburda, Albert, 80
Galea, Liisa, 105
Galinsky, Ellen, 377
Gallagher, Maggie, 11
Gallant, Sherlye J., 363
Galvin, Shelley L., 396
Ganley, Anne L., 420, 421
Gardner, William L., III, 321, 326
Garfinkel, Paul E., 365, 368
Gariépy, Jean-Louis, 205
Garner, David M., 365, 368
Gartner, Alan, 430
Gartner, Audrey J., 430
Gartrell, Nanette, 427
Gates, David, 453
Gault, Una, 203
Gautier, Teofilo, 60
Gauze, Cyma, 221
Gay, Peter, 119, 120
Gaze, Christine E., 102
Gebhard, Paul H., 253, 254
Geer, James H., 275
Gelles, Richard J., 241, 242
Gelman, David, 374, 389
Gentile, Douglas A., 13
Gergen, Kenneth J., 21
Gerhart, Barry, 321
Gershoni, Ruth, 224
Geschwind, Norman, 80
Gibbons, Judith L., 179
Gibbs, Jeannine, 381
Gidycz, Christine A., 210
Gilbert, Lucia A., 318, 418, 423
Gilgun, Jane F., 265
Gillette, Douglas, 434
Gilligan, Carol, 114, 130, 131, 132, 133, 134, 135, 136, 137, 449
Gilroy, Faith D., 392, 396
Ginorio, Angela B., 177, 178
Ginsburg, Herbert, 145
Glick, Peter, 322
Golbeck, Susan L., 102
Gold, Dolores, 106, 293, 315
Gold, Yael, 307
Goldberg, Philip A., 328
Goldberger, Nancy Rule, 135
Golding, Jacqueline M., 401
Goldsmith, Ronald E., 106
Goleman, Daniel, 46, 65, 70
Gonzalez, Judith Teresa, 309, 310
Good, Glenn E., 305, 422, 423, 424
Goodman, Gerald, 428, 430
Goodman, Lisa A., 379
Gooren, L. J. G., 84
Gordon, Jill J., 393
Gordon, Michael, 229
Gordon, Steven L., 233, 234, 239
Gorelick, Sherry, 164, 165
Gorman, Christine, 1
Gorski Roger A., 83
Gottfried, Kurt, 21

Gottman, John M., 243, 249
Gould, Stephen Jay, 5, 23, 76
Gouvier, W. Drew, 105
Gove, Walter R., 363, 376, 382, 441
Granrose, Cherlyn Skromme, 451, 452
Gratch, Linda Vanden, 396
Gray, James J., 365
Gray, John, 234
Green, Beth L., 324
Green, Judith, 364
Green, Richard, 157
Greenberg, Jeff, 431
Greenberg, Judith H., 328
Greenberger, Ellen, 378
Greene, Beverly, 420
Greenfield, Patricia M., 102
Greeno, Catherine G., 132
Greenstein, Theodore N., 236
Greenwald, Anthony G., 38
Greer, Carol A., 417
Gregory, Robert J., 91
Gressley, Diane, 31, 34
Grijalva, Annette, 270
Groshen, Erica L., 332
Grossman, Michele, 194
Guerra, Nancy G., 380
Guerreo, Luis, 60
Gupta, Nabanita Datta, 320
Gur, Raquel E., 74
Gur, Ruben C., 85
Gutek, Barbara A., 317, 318, 320, 330, 333, 335, 336, 337, 338, 339
Guthrie, Joanne F., 364
Gutiérrez, Lorraine, 177

Hackett, Gail, 420
Hackman, J. Richard, 332
Hagan, Richard, 143
Hagin, Rosa A., 92
Hahn, Eugene D., 175
Hahn, William Kerr, 79
Hall, Ron, 242
Halpern, Diane F., 13, 14, 41, 91, 102, 104, 105, 106, 111, 112, 113
Halverson, Charles F., Jr., 148, 149, 179
Hamby, Beverly A., 179
Hamilton, Sandra, 384, 392
Hampson, Elizabeth, 110
Hancock, LynNell, 289, 290
Hantover, Jeffrey P., 9
Harbeck, Karen M., 301
Harding, Sandra, 22
Hare-Mustin, Rachel T., 21, 414, 418, 427, 436
Hargrove, Marian F., 67
Harlow, Harry F., 195, 196, 216
Harlow, Margaret Kuenne, 195, 196
Harold, Rena D., 295
Harris, Bridgid, 226
Harrison, James, 347, 363
Haskett, Roger F., 60, 62
Hassler, Marianne, 106
Hatfield, Elaine, 26, 133, 134, 227, 233, 249, 258, 273, 279
Hayes, Jeffrey A., 422
Haywood, Yolanda, 378
Hedrick, Hannah L., 428
Heilman, Madeline E., 327, 334
Helgeson, Vicki S., 348, 421
Helmreich, Robert, 186
Helson, Ravenna, 364
Heltman, Karen, 335
Helzer, John E., 388
Hendrick, Clyde, 243, 245
Hendrick, Susan S., 243, 245
Hendryx, Michael S., 381
Hennrikus, Deborah J., 393
Henri, Victor, 90
Hepburn, Christine, 170
Heppner, Paul, 421
Herdt, Gilbert H., 60, 61, 277, 286
Herman, C. Peter, 369
Herman, Dianne F., 212, 267
Herman, Judith L., 427
Herrmann, Douglas J., 105
Hershey, Susanne W., 290
Herzog, David B., 369
Hess, Beth B., 7
Hess, Elizabeth, 443
Hesselbrock, Michie N., 397
Hesselbrock, Victor M., 397
Heusel, Colleen, 67
Hilgard, Ernest R., 194, 195
Hill, Charles T., 231
Hill, Elizabeth M., 399
Hill, John P., 296
Hines, Melissa, 83
Hirsch, Barton J., 223
Hiscock, Merrill, 79
Hochschild, Arlie, 236
Hochwarter, Wayne A., 332
Hoffman, Curt, 180
Hoffman, Lorrie, 293, 299
Hofman, John E., 224
Hofman, M. A., 84
Hofmann, Barbara, 416
Holdsworth, Michelle, 105
Hollabaugh, Lisa C., 271
Holliday, Heithre, 226
Hollingworth, Leta Stetter, 4
Holloway, Ralph, 82
Holroyd, Jean Cory, 414, 416, 425
Holzbauer, Jerome J., 331
Holzer, Charles E., 390
Hopkin, Karen, 88
Hopkins, Ann, 334
Hopp, Carolyn, 97
Hopper, Charles H., 67, 68
Horner, Martina, 308, 309
Horney, Karen, 115, 119, 120, 121, 122, 124, 126, 136, 408, 431
Horowitz, Allan V., 397
Hort, Barbara E., 161, 175
Hotelling, Kathy, 306, 307
House, James S., 382
Houston, Lanning, 82
Houston, Sandra, 306
Houtz, John C., 106
Howard, Judith A., 231
Hoyenga, Katharine Blick, 87
Hoyenga, Kermit T., 87
Hoza, Betsy, 221
Hrdy, Sarah Blaffer, 195, 201, 276
Hsu, Katharine, 352
Hsu, L. K. George, 365, 368, 369
Hu, Li-tze, 390
Hubbard, Ruth, 40, 57
Hudak, Mary A., 159, 176
Huesmann, L. Rowell, 204, 205
Hughes, Diane L., 377
Hughes, Michael, 363
Humphreys, Ann P., 221
Hunt, Earl B., 102
Hunt, Melissa G., 421
Hunt, Morton, 256, 257
Hunt, William K., 270
Hurst, Nancy, 180
Huston, Ted L., 243
Hyde, Janet Shibley, 36, 38, 42, 93, 94, 97, 100, 107, 108, 113, 204, 254, 258, 259, 275, 276, 288, 310, 363, 443, 450, 451

Ickovics, Jeannette R., 353, 361
Idle, Tracey, 143
Ignico, Arlene A., 292
Imhoff, Anne R., 318, 319, 341
Imperato-McGinley, Julianne, 60

Jack, Dana Crowley, 396
Jacklin, Carol Nagy, 15, 16, 37, 91, 93, 96, 105, 204, 214, 220, 293
Jacobs, Gloria, 443
Jacobs, Janis E., 97
Jacobs, Jerry A., 302, 315, 320, 330
Jacobs, Marion K., 428, 430
Jacobs, Michael, 6
Jacobson, Neil S., 428, 429
Jacoby, Susan, 218, 219, 225, 227
James, William, 190
Janik, Leann M., 170
Janoff-Bulman, Ronnie, 148
Janus, Cynthia L., 257, 443
Janus, Samuel S., 257, 443
Jeffery, Robert W., 367
Johmann, Carol, 114, 132, 134
Johnson, Blair T., 334
Johnson, Catherine B., 337
Johnson, D. Kay, 132
Johnson, Michael P., 128, 243
Johnson, Toni C., 267
Johnson, Virginia E., 252, 259, 260, 263, 276, 286
Johnston, Lloyd D., 208
Jones, Christopher B., 453
Jones, Ernest, 442
Jones, James H., 255
Jones, M. Gail, 291
Jones, Russell W., 441
Jung, Carl, 406
Jurkovic, Gregory, 67
Jussim, Lee J., 97, 179

Kahn, Arnold S., 14
Kahn, Katherine L., 360
Kalb, Claudia, 289, 290
Kamin, Leon, 5
Kaminer, Wendy, 446, 455
Kane, Penny, 346, 355, 356, 358, 359, 360, 373, 394
Kanter, Rosabeth Moss, 326, 327
Kantrowitz, Ricki E., 411, 415
Kaplan, Alexandra G., 48, 409, 418
Kaplan, Eileen E., 451, 452
Kaplan, George A., 346
Kaplan, Marcie, 388
Kaplan, Robert M., 364
Karabenick, Stuart A., 312
Karau, Steven J., 334
Karlen, Amy, 92
Karraker, Katherine Hildebrandt, 143
Kaschak, Ellyn, 126, 127, 128, 129, 130, 137, 138
Kashner, T. Michael, 401
Kaslow, Nadine J., 367, 368
Kass, Frederic, 391
Katz, Alfred H., 428
Katz, Phyllis A., 151, 158, 160
Kaufman, Debra Renee, 330
Keating, Caroline F., 335
Keen, Sam, 11, 448
Keita, Gwendolyn Puryear, 379
Keller, Evelyn Fox, 39, 79
Kennedy, Douglas, 270
Kennell, John, 198
Kent, D., 401
Kessler, Ronald C., 353, 376, 394, 405
Kidder, Louise, xiii
Kiernan, Michaela, 369, 371
Kilpatrick, Dean G., 379, 399
Kimball, Meredith M., 96, 97
Kimmel, Michael S., 15
Kimura, Doreen, 81, 86, 103, 105, 110
King, Abby C., 371
King, Kathleen, 265
Kinsey, Alfred C., 252, 253, 254, 255, 256, 257, 263, 265, 270, 276, 278, 285, 286, 443
Kipke, Michele D., 62
Kipnis, Aaron R., 422, 433, 434
Kippax, Susan, 203
Kirschstein, Ruth L., 358
Kitchener, Karen Strohm, 427
Kite, Mary E., 175, 282
Kittok, Roger, 65
Klaus, Marshall H., 198
Klein, Helen E., 400
Klein, Susan S., 299
Kling, Kristen C., 310
Klonoff, Elizabeth A., 41, 354, 381, 401
Klonsky, Bruce G., 334
Knott, Jill A., 102
Knox, Sarah S., 346, 347
Kobrynowicz, Diane, 327
Koehler, Mary Schatz, 99
Koelbel, Nikole, 431
Koeske, Gary F., 64
Koeske, Randi K., 12, 42, 64
Koestner, Richard, 231, 421, 445
Kohlberg, Lawrence, 131, 132, 133, 144, 145, 146, 147
Kolata, Gina, 258
Kolodny, Robert C., 263
Komarovsky, Mirra, 319
Koopmans, Lambert H., 69
Kopper, Beverly A., 203
Kortenhaus, Carole M., 293
Koss, Mary P., 210, 212, 271, 378, 379
Kramarae, Cheris, 306
Kramer, Teresa L., 379
Kravetz, Diane, 420, 432, 433
Krebs, Dennis L., 132, 134
Ksansnak, Keith R., 151, 158, 160
Ku, Leighton C., 229, 272
Kuhn, Deanna, 146
Kuhn, Thomas S., 34, 39
Kurdek, Lawrence A., 237
Kurita, Janice A., 156
Kurzweil, Edith, 116, 120, 123, 124
Kurzweil, Nancy, 226

Lafavore, Michael, 251, 268, 269
LaFromboise, Teresa D., 365, 420
Lake, Margaret Ann, 143
Lakoff, Robin, 332, 333
Lamb, Michael, 214
Lamon, Susan J., 94, 450
Lancelot, Cynthia, 367, 368
Landau, Jacqueline, 330
Landrine, Hope, 41, 354, 381, 390, 392, 393, 397, 399, 401, 405
Lane, David M., 108
Langley, Merlin R., 242
Larrabee, Glen J., 85, 105
Larsen, Carolyn C., 418
Larwood, Laurie, 317, 318
Lauer, Monica L., 365
Laumann, Edward O., 212, 257, 258, 271, 274, 276, 278, 286, 443
Lavallee, Marguerite, 161
Lavin, Thomas J., III, 240
Law, David J., 102

Lawton, Carol A., 105
Lazarus, Richard S., 190, 381, 383, 384
Leaf, Philip J., 394
Leaper, Campbell, 226
Leder, Gilah C., 97
Lee, Valerie E., 295
Lee, Yueh-Ting, 179
Lees, Marty, 419
Lefkowitz, Monroe M., 204
Leinbach, Mary D., 150, 153, 154, 161, 175
Lennon, Randy, 214
Lenny, Ellen, 310
Leonard, Janet S., 298
Leong, Frederick T. L., 326
Lepowsky, Maria, 209
Lerman, Hannah, 386, 388, 389, 405, 415
Lerner, Alan Jay, 442
Leslie, Gerald R., 236
Leslie, Leigh A., 243
Levant, Ronald F., 414, 453
LeVay, Simon, 84, 280, 281
Levenson, Robert W., 191, 243
Levitskaya, Anna, 26
Levy, Gary D., 151, 152, 156, 158
Levy, Jerre, 81
Levy, Sandra M., 351
Lewin, Miriam, 90, 165, 166, 181, 183, 186, 187, 188, 278
Lewis, Carol D., 106
Lewis, Laurie, 171
Lewis, Shon, 400
Lewontin, R. C., 5
Liben, Lynn S., 102, 149, 158
Lichter, Daniel, 236
Lindberg, Laura Duberstein, 272
Linn, Marcia C., 94, 100, 450
Lips, Hilary M., 143
Liss-Levinson, Nechama, 418
Little, Jane K., 147, 154, 155, 156, 169
Livingston, Nancy, 301
Lloyd, Barbara, 25, 441
Localio, Russell, 427
Lockhart, Maria, 155
Locksley, Anne, 170
Loewe, Frederick, 442
Long, J. Scott, 323
Lont, Cynthia M., 142
Lopata, Helena Znaniecka, 341, 439
López, Steven Regreser, 393, 394
Lorber, Judith, 21, 195, 326, 354
Lorenz, Konrad, 197, 198
Loring, Marti, 390
Loring, Susan, 431
Lott, Bernice, 13, 14, 15, 18, 19
Loury, Glenn C., 12
Loury, Linda Datcher, 325
Lowell, E. L., 308
Lowry, Manya, 319
Lueptow, Lloyd B., 174
Luis, Cheryl, 319
Lund, Marlene, 381
Lussier, Julianne B., 439
Lye, Diane N., 225
Lynch, Mary Ellen, 296
Lyons, Deborah, 430, 431
Lyons, Nona Plessner, 132

Macaulay, Jacqueline, 207, 450
Maccoby, Eleanor E., 13, 15, 16, 37, 91, 93, 105, 132, 181, 204, 214, 220, 221, 222, 250, 293
MacPherson, Gael M., 99
Magley, Vicki J., 335, 338, 341
Mahalik, James R., 422
Majors, Richard G., 242
Makhijani, Mona G., 334
Malamuth, Neil M., 212
Malouff, John, 319
Mancus, Dianne Sirna, 291
Manning, Vicki, 381
Mansnerus, Laura, 297
Marecek, Jeanne, 4, 21, 418, 420, 427, 436
Marshall, Nancy L., 378
Martel, Richard F., 108, 327
Martin, Carol Lynn, 62, 147, 148, 149, 154, 155, 156, 163, 169, 170, 174, 179, 180
Martin, Clyde E., 253, 254
Martin, John E., 304, 371
Martinez, Gladys, 272
Martinko, Mark L., 321
Martocchio, Joseph, 441
Maruyama, Geoffrey, 16
Masson, Jeffrey Moussaief, 125, 126
Masters, William H., 252, 259, 260, 263, 264, 276, 286
Matherly, Timothy A., 106
Matthews, Karen A., 347, 358, 363
Mays, Vickie M., 420
Mazer, Donald B., 307
Mazur, Allan, 65, 66
McCann, Nancy Dodd, 332, 336
McCauley, Clark R., 179, 180
McClelland, David C., 308
McCormick, Naomi B., 269, 275, 288
McDonald, Karen, 371
McDougall, William, 190, 202
McEvoy, Larry, 388
McFarlane, Jessica, 62, 63, 64
McGinn, Thomas, 332, 336
McGuiness, Diane, 105
McHale, Susan M., 237
McHugh, Maureen C., 12, 42
McKeever, Walter F., 110
McKinney, Kathleen, 307
McLain, Susan June, 331
McLeod, Jane D., 376, 405
McManus, I. C., 80
McRae, James A., Jr., 353
McWhirter, Ellen Hawley, 320
Mechanic, David, 377
Meehan, Anita M., 170
Melamed, Tuvia, 325
Melson, Gail F., 198
Mermelstein, Rebecca, 204
Merrill, Maud A., 90
Mesquita, Batja, 192, 193
Messner, Michael A., 11, 15, 347, 433, 434
Meyer-Bahlburg, Heino F. L., 55, 59
Michael, Robert T., 212, 257, 258
Michaels, Stuart, 212, 257
Michielutte, Robert, 362
Middaugh, Ann, 389
Miles, Catherine Cox, 183
Miller, Ivan W., 394
Miller, Lynn Carol, 224
Miller, Neal, 202
Miller, Norman, 207, 208
Miller, Randi L., 229
Millman, Wendy, 385
Mintz, Laurie B., 422
Mirowsky, John, 233
Mischel, Walter, 141
Mishkind, Marc E., 365
Mitchell, Ian, 371
Mittwoch, Ursula, 57
Mladinic, Antonio, 174, 328, 447
Moller, Lora C., 156
Monaghan, Patricia, 318, 319, 451
Money, John, 59, 60, 280

Monroe, Judy, 89, 90, 105
Monsour, Michael, 226
Montecinos, Carmen, 291
Mook, Douglas G., 308
Moore, Robert, 434
Morgan, Robin, 432
Mori, Lisa, 211, 364
Morris, Robin, 67, 68
Morton, George, 76
Mosher, Clelia Duel, 253
Mosimann, James E., 365
Mowrer, O. Hobart, 202
Muehlenhard, Charlene L., 271
Muller, Charlotte F., 355
Murphy, Declan G., 85
Murray, Kathleen, 45, 61, 62, 64, 65
Myers, David G., 16
Myers, Sharon, 226

Naditch, S. F., 102
Nardi, Peter M., 220, 224, 282
Narrow, William E., 398
Nash, Sharon C., 146
National Center for Health Statistics, 353
National Council of Women Psychologists, 8
National Opinion Research Council, 270, 286
Neckerman, Holly J., 205
Nelson, Cynthia, 322
Nelson, Katherine, 151
Netting, Nancy S., 272, 273, 288
Neugebauer, D. D., 380
Newcomb, Andrew F., 221
Newcomb, Michael D., 367
Newcombe, Nora, 103, 294
Newman, Kerry L., 369
Newman, Leonard S., 155
Nezlek, John, 224
Nielsen, Lynn E., 291
Nieschlag, Eberhard, 106
Nieva, Veronica F., 333
Nikelly, Arthur G., 413
Noddings, Nel, 298
Nolen-Hoeksema, Susan, 311, 379, 395, 396, 398, 452
Nordheimer, Jon, 220
Norman, William H., 394
Norwood, Robin, 431
Nutt, Elizabeth A., 422
Nuttal, Ronald, 94

O'Boyle, Cherie, 154
O'Brien, Edward J., 310
O'Connor, Maureen, 336
O'Heron, Connie A., 174, 445
O'Leary, Anne M., 441
O'Malley, Patrick M., 208
O'Neil, James M., 422, 437
O'Neil, Robin, 378
Offer, Daniel, 396
Office of Research on Women's Health, 358
Ogborne, Alan, 430
Okagaki, Lynn, 102
Olarte, Silvia, 427
Oliver, Kathleen A., 177
Oliver, Mary Beth, 258, 259, 275, 276, 288
Olson, Amy, 105
Olson, Carol V., 307
Olson, Cheryl B., 306
Olson, Linda Steffel, 96
Onxy, Jenny, 203
Opper, Sylvia, 145
Orbach, Susie, 444
Orlofsky, Jacob L., 174, 445
Ormerod, Mimi, 307
Ornstein, Robert, 78
Osgood, D. Wayne, 208
Otto, Stacey, 174, 328, 447
Ouellette Kobasa, Suzanne C., 430
Owen, Crystal L., 328

Padesky, Christine, 282
Page, Jessica R., 396
Paludi, Michele A., 309
Parker, Louise, 362
Parlee, Mary Brown, 62
Paskette, Electra D., 362
Pasman, Larry, 371
Patterson, Charlotte J., 200
Pearcey, Sharon M., 69
Pearlin, Leonard I., 377
Pearson, Judy C., 305
Peden, Blaine, 242
Pellegrino, James W., 102
Pelletier, Rene, 161
Pennebaker, James W., 190, 356
Penrose, Gary, 312
Peplau, Letitia Anne, 41, 44, 224, 231, 233, 234, 238, 239, 282
Percival, Elizabeth F., 307
Perdue, Lauren, 368
Perkins, Carol O., 331
Perlick, Deborah, 368
Perls, Frederich (Fritz) S., 409
Perrewe, Pamela L., 332
Perry, David G., 206
Perry, Louise C., 206
Perry, T. Bridgett, 221
Petersen, Anne C., 100, 296
Peterson, Ralph E., 60
Peto, Richard, 350, 351
Pezaris, Elizabeth, 94
Phillips, Roger D., 392
Phillips, Susan D., 318, 319, 341
Piaget, Jean, 145, 147
Picano, James, 364
Pickhardt, Irene, 139, 140, 142, 146, 149, 150
Piirto, Jane, 106
Pinel, John P. J., 48, 50, 65, 72, 74, 86
Pittman, Frank, 11
Pizzolo, Cecelia, 368
Plante, Thomas G., 371
Pleck, Elizabeth H., 201
Pleck, Joseph H., 167, 168, 188, 201, 229, 378, 422, 453
Pliner, Patricia, 364, 366
Plutchik, Robert, 202
Poest, Catherine A., 370
Polivy, Janet, 365, 367, 369
Pollitt, Katha, 138, 449, 450, 453
Pomeroy, Wardell B., 253, 254
Pope, Kenneth S., 425, 426, 427, 437
Pope, Tony, 270
Postman, Andrew, 189, 214
Potapova, Elena, 26
Powell, Brian, 390
Powlishta, Kimberly K., 156, 157
Price, Jana L., 102
Pryor, John B., 339
Ptacek, J. T., 384, 385
Purifoy, Frances, E 69

Quinn, Susan, 121, 122
Quinsey, Vernon L., 212

Rae, Donald S., 398
Ragins, Belle Rose, 334
Raichle, Marcus E., 85
Rank, Otto, 406
Rapagna, Socrates O., 106

Rapson, Richard L., 133, 134, 227, 233, 249, 258, 273, 279
Rawlings, Edna I., 417
Ray, William J., 23
Reavis, Rebel, 297
Redman, Selina, 393
Regier, David A., 398
Reid, Helen M., 226
Reid, Pamela T., 198
Reilly, Anne H., 326
Reinisch, June M., 53, 60, 62
Reis, Harry, 224
Reis, Sally M., 298
Reitman, Freida, 326
Rejskind, F. Gillian, 106
Renzetti, Claire M., 382
Resnick, Heidi S., 379, 388, 399
Riad, Jasmin K., 67
Ricciardelli, Lina A., 186
Riessman, Catherine Kohler, 245, 246, 247, 248
Riger, Stephanie A., 22, 40, 42, 44, 130, 326
Risman, Barbara J., 201, 217
Ritchie, Jean-Marie, 371
Ritchie, Karen, 343
Riter, Robert, 350
Robbins, Lynn, 234
Roberts, Tomi-Ann, 190, 311
Robertson, John, 416, 422, 423, 451
Robine, Jean-Marie, 343
Robine, Karen, 371
Robins, Lee N., 388
Robinson, David, 430
Rodin, Judith, 353, 361, 365, 367, 369, 371, 373, 440
Roehling, Patricia V., 431
Rogers, Carl R., 408, 409
Rolls, Barbara J., 367, 369
Romero-Garcia, Ivonne, 177
Ronan, Colin A., 22
Rook, Karen, 282
Roscoe, Bruce, 229, 230, 269, 270
Roscoe, Will, 284
Rose, Robert, 46
Rose, Steven, 5
Rose, Suzanna, 229
Rosenblum, Leonard A., 53
Rosenfield, David, 312
Rosenfield, Sarah, 377, 393, 453
Rosenkrantz, Paul S., 172, 173, 174, 391
Rosenthal, Patrice, 328
Ross, Catherine E., 233, 354
Ross, David T., 193
Rothbart, Myron, 392
Rothstein, Edward, 370
Rowe, Robert C., 212
Rozin, Paul, 366
Ruback, R. Barry, 68
Rubin, Donald B., 53
Rubin, Linda L., 307
Rubin, Robert T., 60, 62
Rubin, Zick, 231
Ruble, Diane N., 147, 148, 154, 155, 163, 173
Rush, Florence, 124, 125, 126
Russell, Denise, 407, 413
Russell, Diana E. H., 267
Russell, James A., 191, 192
Russo, Nancy Felipe, 324, 378, 379
Rutgers, Christina, 431
Ryan, Marilyn, 97

Saal, Frank E., 337
Sadker, David M., 291, 293, 298, 299
Sadker, Myra P., 291, 293, 298, 299
Saltzman, Amy, 316, 324
Sandomir, Richard, 305
Sandvik, Ed, 194, 442
Sanikhani, Mohammad, 157
Sanson-Fisher, Robert W., 393
Santrock, John W., 229
Saragovi, Carina, 421
Sarason, Barbara R., 385, 386, 387, 413, 414
Sarason, Irwin G., 385, 386, 387, 413, 414
Satterfield, Arthur, 307
Saunders, Benjamin E., 379, 399
Savage, Robert M., 105
Savin-Williams, Rich C., 281
Schachter, Stanley, 190, 215
Scheibe, Gabriele, 399
Scher, Murray, 422, 423
Scherer, Klaus R., 192, 202
Schiff, Debra, 294
Schleicher, Thomas L., 309
Schlottmann, Robert S., 424
Schmale, John, 428
Schmidt, Constance R., 158
Schneer, Joy A., 326
Schneider, Beth F., 307
Schofield, Janet Ward, 223
Schratz, Marjorie M., 100
Schulsinger, M. Fini, 53
Schultz, Duane P., 3, 6, 90, 115
Schultz, Sidney Ellen, 3, 6, 90, 115
Schultz, Stephen J., 280
Schutte, Nicola, 319
Schwartz, Donald M., 365
Schwartz, Pepper, 231, 238, 239, 240, 242, 243, 245, 248, 249, 254, 282, 283, 284, 285, 288, 329, 440, 454, 455
Scully, Diana, 33, 211, 212
Sears, Robert, 202
Segal, Julius, 264
Segal, Zelda, 264
Seid, Roberta P., 366
Seligman, Ross, 270
Seligmann, Jean, 369, 374, 389
Sell, Randall L., 278
Selle, Lynn L., 211
Sells, Lucy W., 96, 97, 100
Serbin, Lisa A., 156, 293, 294, 315
Serdula, Mary K., 367
Servis, Laura J., 439
Settle, Shirley, 392
Sgoutas, Demetrious S., 68
Sharabany, Ruth, 224
Sharpe, Mark J., 421
Sharps, Matthew J., 102
Shaywitz, Bennett A., 85, 92
Shaywitz, Sally E., 92
Shehan, Constance L., 236
Shelley, Greg, 65
Sherif, Carolyn W., 13
Sherman, Julia, 5, 102, 115
Sherman, Martin F., 396
Shields, Stephanie A., 3, 4, 19, 29, 90, 193, 194, 197, 198, 214
Shotland, R. Lance, 275
Sibisi, Charles D., 401
Sidney, Joan Seliger, 317
Sigel, Roberta S., 318, 341, 443, 445, 446, 448, 450, 453, 455
Signorella, Margaret L., 158, 159, 290
Silberstein, Lisa R., 365
Silver, N. Clayton, 177
Silver, Nan, 249
Silverstein, Brett, 368
Silverstein, Louise B., 195, 201
Simmons, R. G., 295

Simon, Michael C., 327
Simon, Théodore, 90
Simon, William, 274
Singer, Jerome E., 190, 215
Skinner, B. F., 140
Skovholt, Thomas M., 446
Slade, Pauline, 64
Sleek, Scott, 267
Slusher, Jason, 416
Smith, Caroline, 25
Smith, G. Richard, 401
Smith, Peter K., 221
Smith, Ronald E., 384, 385
Smith,Thomas Ewin, 224
Snodgrass, Coral R., 326
Snodgrass, Sara E., 106
Snyder, Elizabeth, 59
Sohi, Balvindar K., 365, 420
Solomon, Alison, 390
Sonenstein, Freya L., 229, 272
Spanier, Graham B., 248
Spence, Janet T., 175, 186
Spinney, Laura, 428
Spitzer, Robert L., 389, 391
Sprecher, Susan, 26
Springen, Karen, 406
Springer, Sally P., 77, 78, 79, 88, 110
Sroufe, L. Alan, 222
Stack, Carol B., 135
Stains, Laurence R., 251
Stake, Jayne E., 365
Stangor, Charles, 147, 148
Stanley, Julian C., 95, 96
Stapp, Joy, 186
Stark, Ellen, 271
Steele, Claude M., 182
Steffen, Valerie, 207, 214, 450
Steil, Janice M., 239, 329
Steinberg, Karen K., 363
Steindam, Sharon, 293, 299
Steingart, Richard M., 347, 357
Steinmetz, Suzanne, 241
Stephan, Walter G., 312
Stephenson, P. Susan, 389
Stern, Anita, 156
Sternberg, Robert J., 219, 220, 221, 222, 228, 233, 243, 244
Stevens, Heather B., 396
Stipp, David, 358, 362
Stokes, Joseph, 326
Straus, Murray A., 241
Strickland, Bonnie R., 373
Striegel-Moore, Ruth H., 365
Stromquist, Nelly P., 319
Struckman-Johnson, Cindy, 211
Struckman-Johnson, David, 211
Stumpf, Heinrich, 96, 100
Subrahmanyam, Kaveri, 102
Suitor, J. Jill, 297
Sullivan, Megan, 326
Summerfield, Angela B., 192, 202
Sundstrom, Eric, 334
Swaab, D. F., 83, 84
Swain, Scott O., 226
Swan, Suzanne, 335, 341
Sweeney, Catherine, 312
Swim, Janet K., 16, 180

Takeuchi, David T., 390
Tannen, Deborah, 234, 235, 449
Tarkan, Laurie, 303
Tarule, Jill Mattuck, 135
Tate, Carol S., 198
Tavris, Carol, 3, 6, 64, 88, 120, 135, 157, 202, 203, 217, 276, 357, 388, 396, 398, 423, 431
Teague, Gregory B., 392
Terman, Lewis M., 90, 183
Tharp, Gerry, 65
Theberge, Nancy, 304
Thomas, Alexander, 198
Thomas, Celeste M., 271
Thome, Pauline R., 207, 450
Thompson, J. Kevin, 371
Thompson, Linda, 200, 236, 237, 239, 241, 367
Thompson, Michael G., 365
Thomsen, Linda, 365, 367
Thorndike, Edward, 4
Thorne, Barrie, 32, 143, 222, 223, 268
Tiefer, Lenore, 260, 263
Tipton, Robert M., 352
Tittle, Carol Kehr, 439
Titus, Jordan J., 291
Tjaden, Claus D., 209
Tjaden, Patricia Godeke, 209
Tobin, Patricia, 99
Tobin-Richards, Maryse H., 296
Todor, William D., 328
Tolan, Patrick H., 380
Tomasson, Kristinn, 401
Tovey, Stephanie L., 379
Travis, Cheryl Brown, 350, 353, 354, 357, 394, 432
Tredinnick, Michael, 416
Treichler, Paula A., 306
Turner-Bowker, Diane M., 293
Twenge, Jean M., 175
Tyler, Richard, 242
Tyson-Rawson, Kristen J., 438, 454

U.S. Bureau of the Census, 242, 303, 343, 351, 353, 362
U.S. Department of Education, 298, 302, 303
U.S. Department of Health and Human Services, 208, 350, 353
U.S. Department of Justice, 208, 209, 210
U.S. Department of Labor, 318, 320
U.S. Supreme Court, 305
Uken, Janet S., 428
Ulibarri, Monica D., 270
Unger, Rhoda K., 12, 13, 14, 176
Urban, Joan, 222
Urberg, Kathryn A., 157, 158
Uribe, Virginia, 301

Valdez, Jesse N., 238, 270
Van Gelder, Sadie, 301
Vance, Carole S., 277
Vann, Elizabeth D., 157
Vasquez, Melba J. T., 420, 427
Vasta, Ross, 102
Vazquez-Nuttall, Ena, 177, 178
Verbrugge, Lois M., 356, 364, 371, 373, 441
Veronen, Lois J., 379
Vetter, Betty, 108
Vogel, Dena Ann, 143
Vogel, Susan Raymond, 172, 173, 391
Voyer, Daniel, 94, 100, 102, 103
Voyer, Susan, 100

Waber, Deborah, 80
Wade, Carole, 6, 120, 157
Wade, Priscilla, 417
Wagenheim, Jeff, 11

Wainryb, Cecelia, 133
Wald, Elijah, 57
Walder, Leopold O., 204
Waldo, Craig R., 338
Waldron, Ingrid, 351, 353
Walker, Alexis J., 200, 236, 237, 239, 241
Walker, Betty A., 298
Walker, Constance, 290
Walker, Gillian A., 389
Walker, Lenore E. A., 378
Walker, William D., 212
Wallace, Julia E., 342, 363
Wallbott, Harald G., 192, 202
Wallston, Barbara Strudler, 35
Walsh, Mary Roth, 8
Wampold, Bruce E., 417
Wark, Gillian R., 132, 134
Warnke, Melanie, 388
Warr, Mark, 209
Warren, Marguerite O., 208
Warshaw, Meredith, 369
Waterhouse, Ruth L., 415
Webb, Gloria R., 393
Weber, Nancy, 337
Wechsler, David, 91
Weinberg, Nancy, 428
Weinburgh, Molly, 298
Weisner, Thomas S., 150, 151
Weiss, Maureen R., 305
Weiss, Robert J., 206
Weisstein, Naomi, xiv, 8, 19, 201, 449
Weitzman, Lauren M., 307
Weitzman, Lenore, 247
Welch-Ross, Melissa K., 158
Wellman, Barry, 225
Wells, James A., 278
Welter, Barbara, 166, 167, 228
Welton, Angela L., 102
West, Candace, 16
West, Richard, 305
Westkott, Marcia C., 408
Wethington, Elaine, 376, 382, 405
Whalen, Nora J., 339
Wharton, Amy S., 332
Whatley, Marianne H., 269
Wheaton, Blair, 293, 315
Wheeler, Ladd, 224
White, Helene R., 397
White, Leonard, 312
White, Mark B., 438, 454
Whiting, Beatrice Blyth, 178
Whitley, Bernard E., Jr., 27, 282
Widiger, Thomas A., 392
Wieringa, Saskia E., 284
Wigfield, Allan, 295
Wilbur, Jerry, 306, 327
Wiley, Mary Glenn, 333
Williams, Janet B. W., 391
Williams, Christine L., 324
Williams, David R., 390
Williams, Janet B., 389
Williams, Jean R., 370
Williams, John E., 165, 176, 178
Williams, John K., 102
Williams, Juanita H., 120
Williams, Paula M., 66
Williams, Robert J., 186
Williams, Tannis MacBeth, 62, 63, 64
Wilmore, Jack H., 369
Wilson, Cynthia, 270
Wilson, Robert A., 359
Wilson-Mitchell, Jane E., 150, 151
Wilson-Smith, Debra N., 156
Wingard, Deborah L,. 364
Wisch, Andrew F., 422
Wiseman, Claire V., 365
Wisniewski, Nadine, 210
Witelson, Sandra F., 82, 83
Witkin, Herman A., 58
Witt, David D., 370
Wolff, Edward N., 332
Wolk, Cordulla, 368
Wood, Carolyn H., 156, 169
Wood, Eileen, 143
Wood, Phillip K., 422
Wood, Susan F., 358
Wood, Wendy, 194, 235
Woods, Nancy F., 363
Wooley, O. Wayne, 365
Woolley, Helen Thompson, 4
Worell, Judith, 41
Workman-Daniels, Kathryn L., 397
Wundt, Wilhelm, 3
Wyatt, Gail Elizabeth, 211, 267, 272
Wypij, David, 278

Yama, Mark F., 379
Yasinski, Lorraine, 409
Yee, Doris K., 97, 366
Yoder, Janice D., 14, 309
Youngjohn, James R., 105
Yurich, John M., 177

Zajonc, R. C., 190
Zanas, John, 384
Zarate, Mylene G., 211
Zeiss, Carol, 441
Zelkowitz, Phyllis, 293, 315
Zera, Deborah, 281, 282
Zetzer, Heidi, 420
Zimmer-Schur, Lori A., 367
Zimmerman, Don H., 16
Zinik, Cary, 285
Zion, Cari, 322
Zucker, Kenneth J., 156, 157

Subject Index

AA. *See* Alcoholics Anonymous
Abuse. *See* Domestic violence; Sexual abuse
Accidents, as cause of death, 343, 345, 351–353, 363, 372
Achievement, 308–313
  as part of Male Sex Role Identity, 168, 173, 183, 187, 201, 290, 293, 368, 422
  definitions of, 308
  educational, gender differences in, 38, 74, 87, 97–100, 106, 107, 109, 111–112, 113, 295–298, 313–314, 443
  ethnicity as a factor in, 5, 182, 291, 324–327
  fear of success and, 308–310
  gender role changes and, 41
  internal vs. external explanations for, 311–313
  need for, 308
  occupational, gender differences in, 324–328
  self-confidence and, 295–298, 310–311
  testosterone as a factor in, 67
  See also Educational achievement
Acquaintance or date rape, 210–214, 269, 271, 379
Acquired immunodeficiency syndrome (AIDS), 351, 362
  homophobia and, 280
  impact on behavior of, 443
  risk factors for, 280, 284, 351, 362
Addiction to exercise, 371
Addictions, support groups for, 429–431
  See also Substance abuse
Adolescents
  aggression among, 205–206, 209
  dating, 229–231
  eating disorders in, 367–369
  eating patterns in, 364
  educational issues for, 98, 100
  exercise patterns in, 370–371
  friendships among, 223–224
  gender development in, 157–159
  gender stereotyping by, 179, 181
  health services use by, 351
  heterosexual behavior among, 268–272
  homosexual behavior among, 281–282, 286, 301
  physiological changes in, 53–56
  sexual activity by, 264, 267, 277
  See also College students
Adrenal gland, in endocrine system, 48, 54, 56, 58–60
Adrenogenital syndrome, 58–60
Adulthood
  aggression during, 206–208
  brain changes during, 80, 84
  friendships during, 224–226
  gender development in, 153, 157–159
  gender stereotyping during, 171, 173–176
  heterosexual behavior during, 272–277
  homosexual behavior during, 282–285
African Americans
  careers and gender, 319, 324
  college degrees, 303, 327
  eating disorders in, 365
  educational achievement among, 99, 100, 182
  gender and ethnic segregation in school, 223
  gender differences in self-esteem, 310
  gender stereotyping and, 177–178
  marital power among, 239
  marital satisfaction among, 234
  moral judgments, 135
  psychiatric diagnoses and, 390
  racist discrimination directed toward, 381
  rape reporting and, 211
  relationship problems for men, 242
  risk of violence among, 351–352, 353
  sexuality and, 253, 270, 272
African culture
  science and, 22
  Thonga sexual practices, 277
Age
  body image concerns and, 366
  eating disorders and, 367

Agentic traits, 39–40, 444
Aggression, 201–213
anger and, 191, 192, 193, 194, 202–203
definition of, 202
developmental trends for, 203–207
display rules and, 191, 214–215
in Freudian theory, 116–117
frustration and, 202
gender differences in provocations to, 207
gender stereotypes and, 193–194, 195
hormones and, 45–46, 65–70
indirect, 208, 209, 214, 215
as instinctive behavior, 190, 194, 201, 202
in laboratory vs. social settings, 208, 451
longitudinal studies of, 204–206
in Male Sex Role Identity, 167–168, 187, 214, 348, 391
physical vs. social, 208, 209
power and, 208
sexual, 210–213
social standards for expressions of, 206
Agoraphobia, 398, 400, 453
AIDS. *See* Acquired immunodeficiency syndrome
Alcoholics Anonymous (AA), 429, 430, 431
Alcohol use, 33
depression and, 397–398
experience of violence and, 352–353
gender and, 353, 379, 397
marital relationship and, 240
mental disorders and, 67, 390, 396–397
mortality and, 452
PMS symptom, 62
self-help groups for, 429, 430
Alternative medicine, gender and use of, 356
Alzheimer's patients, support groups for caretaker of, 430
American Psychiatric Association (ApA)
diagnostic category controversy in, 374–375, 388–390
DSM classification system, 386–388
American Psychological Association (APA)
Division 35, Psychology of Women, 8–9
Division 51, Society for the Psychological Study of Men and Masculinity, 11
Task Force on Male Violence against Women, 379
Task Force on Sex Bias and Sex-Role Stereotyping in Psychotherapeutic Practice, 414, 415, 417, 425
Anal stage, in Freudian theory, 116
Androcentric bias, 14
Androgen insensitivity syndrome, 59–60
Androgens, 47–48, 49–50, 55, 56, 69, 80
Androgyny, 181, 185–186
as feminist therapy model, 420–421
as gender aware therapy model, 423
societal values and, 444
Anger
aggression and, 191, 192, 193, 194, 202–203, 206
differences in expression of, 192, 214
gender and, 193–194, 202–203
gender role and, 214
Anorexia nervosa, 367–369, 372
Anterior commisure, 76, 82, 84
Antigone phase, 127–129
Antisocial behavior, testosterone levels and, 66–70
Antisocial personality disorder, 387–391, 392, 393, 453
Anxiety disorders, 267, 377, 379, 387, 389, 393, 398–400, 435
APA. *See* American Psychological Association
Appearance
concerns about, 297, 366–367
gender stereotyping and, 176
romantic partner's, 229, 278
Artistic ability, gender and, 106
Asian Americans
enrollment in college, 303
enrollment in mathematics courses, 99, 100
eating disorders, 365
psychiatric diagnoses and, 390
rape reporting and, 211
Association for Women in Psychology, 8, 10
Athletes, eating disorders among, 369
Athletics
financial support for women's, 302–303
gender and, 297, 314, 370
women's participation in, 302–304, 314
See also Title IX of the Education Amendments of 1972
Attachment
nurturing behavior and, 197–198
primate studies, 195
Attitude Interest Analysis Survey, 183

Balinese, sexual practices of, 277
Bedouins, emotional experience among, 192
Behaviorism, 5
theory of instincts vs., 195
Behavior modification, 411–412
in feminist therapy, 418
gender bias and, 415
Bem Sex Role Inventory (BSRI), 185–186
Bias of researchers, xi, 4, 8, 13, 35–36
emphasis on differences, 39
evaluation of emotions and, 193–194, 214
feminist theory and, 40–42
for race as well as gender, 5
inevitability of, 20–21, 40–41
PMS research and, 62
in stages of research, 35–36, 39
strategies for reducing, 40–42
Bias of survey respondents, 26, 252
Biological determinism, 108–111
bias in favor of, 1–3, 5
arguments against, 31, 38, 53, 87, 108–111
maternal instinct and, 194–195
model and alternatives, 86

Biologically based gender differences
as an alternative schema, 150
depression and, 395
in Freudian theory, 121
in the functionalist view, 4
media views of, 1–3, 90
mental abilities and, 90, 96, 108–111
minimalist vs. maximalist views of, 2, 449–450
sexual orientation and, 84, 270–281
social roles and, 13
Biosocial theory, testosterone levels and, 66
Bipolar disorder, 395, 400–401, 402
Birth control
adolescent sexual behavior and, 272
health services used for, 342, 355, 359–360
struggle for women's access to, 7
Bisexuality, 59, 285–286, 301
Body image
eating disorders and, 366–367
eating patterns and, 369
exercise patterns and, 366–367, 371
gender differences in, 365–367, 451
Bonding
infants and caregivers, 197–198
male, 11
Borderline personality disorder, 391
Boys
aggressive behavior in, 203–204, 206, 209
careers information directed toward, 298–299
emotional behavior in, 193–194
friendships between, 220–222, 224, 248, 452
gender development in, 6, 116–119, 127, 142–143, 156–157
gender identity disorder in, 157
mathematics achievement, 37–38, 94–96, 99, 100, 295–296
nurturing and, 198, 200
portrayed in children's books, 291–292
self-confidence during elementary and high school, 297–298
sex education for, 268, 287
as sexual abuse victims, 265–267, 379
sexual behavior, 269–272, 277
sexual harassment in school perpetrated by, 299–300
spatial abilities advantage, 80, 101–102
Boy Scouts, 9
Brain, 73–88
cerebral hemispheres and lateralization in, 75, 77–81
and differences in mental abilities, 109–111
endocrine system and, 46
gender-related functional differences in, 73–74, 81–84
gender-related structural differences in, 53, 75, 80, 84–86, 280
Breadwinner role
gender role changes and, 340, 439–440, 444, 451
as source of stress, 376, 378, 380, 433, 434
as the traditional marital role, 177, 201, 416, 420, 434, 454
Breast cancer, 363
death rates from, 349–350, 362
in men, 349, 350
risk factors, 350–351, 363
survivors' self-help groups, 429
BSRI (Bem Sex Role Inventory), 185–186
Buddhism, science and, 22

Cancer, 348–351
defined, 348
mortality and, 345–346, 349, 362
risk factors, 349–351, 353, 363
socioeconomic conditions and, 346
Cardiovascular disease (CVD), 343, 345–348
defined, 343
gender differences in treatment of, 346–347
mortality and, 347, 372
risk factors, 347–348
Careers, 317–330
balancing family and, 329–330, 439–442
barriers to advancement in, 319, 323–329
educational preparation for, 298–299
gender-atypical, 317, 320, 340
gender differences in choice of, 317–320, 451
gender roles and, 320
gender stereotypes and, 321–322, 324, 328
glass ceiling in, 317, 323–324
glass escalator in, 323–325
opportunities for, 320–330
See also Employment, Occupation
Caregivers, support groups for, 430
Care giving, 444
for children, 198–201, 329, 380
for the elderly, 226, 430
as maternal instinct, 194
among nonhuman primates, 195–197
for pets, 198–199
See also Nurturing
Care vs. justice moral orientation, 131–132
Castration complex, 117
Casual sex
gender differences in acceptance of, 259, 275–276, 443
as homosexual pattern, 284–285
Causality
correlation vs., 28
experimental studies and, 29
ex post facto studies and, 30–31
Celibacy
among college students, 273–274
among the elderly, 274
patterns of, 273–274
Cerebral cortex, 75
Cerebral hemispheres, 77–82, 84, 109–110
gender-related differences in, 79–82, 84, 85
Cervical cancer, 351
Childbirth
as cause of death, 346
as a factor in seeking healthcare, 346, 359, 360
medicalization of, 354
Child care
gender roles and, 329, 438–439, 441, 448, 450, 455
as source of stress, 375–378, 380, 451

women as primary providers, 200–201, 235–236, 238, 340
Child custody, men's movement and, 11
Childhood experiences
in Freudian theory, 6, 116–119
in Horney's theory, 121
Children
adult, friendships between parents and, 225
aggressive behavior by, 203–206, 209
body image concerns in, 366
cerebral lateralization in, 79–80
cross-gender interactions by, 221–222
eating disorders in, 366
educational experiences of, 291–295
ethnic and racial self-segregation by, 223
exercise patterns in, 370–371
friendship patterns in, 220–223
gender identity in, 145–146, 152–157
gender identity disorder in, 157
gender segregation by, 143, 220–223, 226, 268
gender stereotyping by, 139–140, 150–151, 157–159, 169–171
health services use by, 360
morbidity and mortality in, 345
multicultural study of, 178–179
nurturing behavior by, 214
play activity differences in, 220–222
sexual activity by, 255, 263–264, 268, 277
sexual molestation of, 264–268
See also Boys; Girls
Chinese culture, science and, 22
Chlamydia, 361
Choice, gender and, 11, 96, 99, 100, 107, 109, 111–112, 295–297, 301–306, 320, 325, 334, 363, 385, 451–454
Chromosomal abnormalities, 57–58
Chromosomes, sexual differentiation and, 48–49
Chronic diseases, defined, 343, 346
Cigarette smoking, cancer risk and, 349–350
Classroom issues. *See* School-related factors; Teacher attitudes
Client-centered therapy, 408–409
gender bias and, 415
Clothing, as a clue to gender, 145–146, 154
gender stereotyping and, 184
Codependency, controversy about, 430–431
Cognition
experience of emotions and, 190
in structuralist view, 3
Cognitive ability
biologically based theory of, 109–110
environment and, 97–98
gender differences in, 81, 85, 104–105, 107–109, 111–112, 450
hormones and, 110
See also specific cognitive abilities
Cognitive behavior therapy, 412
in feminist therapy, 419
Cognitive development
gender identity and, 145–146
gender schemata and, 147–150
moral development and, 131
Piaget's theory of, 145
in social learning theory, 143
stereotypes and, 170–171
Cognitive developmental theory, 144–147, 153
gender schema theory vs., 147–148, 150, 152, 153, 160–161
gender script theory vs., 161
social learning theory vs., 152, 153, 160
Cognitive labeling, emotional expression and, 190
Cognitive theory of depression, 395–396
Cognitive therapy, 410–411
in feminist therapy, 418–419
gender bias and, 415–416
Cohabitation,
as alternative to marriage, 231–232, 248
balance of power in, 239, 341
dissolution of, 247
stability of relationship in, 242, 244–245
College students
athletic participation by, 303–305, 370
career expectations of, 318–319
coping strategies of, 384
cross-cultural studies of, 26–27, 175, 177, 178
dating behavior by, 229–230, 269
eating disorders in, 367–368
educational patterns of, 100, 301–304, 306
friendships among, 224
gender schemata among, 148
gender stereotyping by, 170–171, 172, 173, 175–176
as predominant participants in research, 14, 41, 112
sexual behavior among, 210–211, 272–274
sexual harassment of, 271, 306–307
See also Adolescents
Coming out, 281–282
Commitment
in Sternberg's triangular theory, 219, 222, 228, 233
Cancian's blueprints and, 228, 232
relationship stability and, 243–244
in sexual relationships, 275, 282, 443
Committed relationships, 231–232
See also Cohabitation; Gay and lesbian relationships; Love relationships; Marriage
Communal traits, femininity and, 39–40, 186, 444, 447
Communication
male–female differences in, 234–235, 448, 455
marital dissolution and, 246
in marriage, 234–235
nonverbal, 106–107
about sex, 271
workplace issues, 332–335
Communion. *See* Communal traits
Companionate love, 219
Companionship blueprint, 228–229, 232–233
ideal of marriage as, 245–247
Competition
achievement and, 309,
for jobs, men vs. women, 446, 454
in Male Sex role identity, 168, 293, 422
testosterone levels and, 65–67

Compulsive personality disorder, 378–379, 398–400
Computer games, 296
  for girls, 370
Concepts, operational definitions of, 25, 27
Conditioning. *See* Operant conditioning
Condom use, adolescent sexual behavior and, 272
Confidence. *See* Self-confidence
Conflict
  aggression as a style of managing, 209
  differing sexual values as a source, 270–271, 275
  in love relationships, 234, 237–241
  parental, as a risk for sexual abuse, 267
  stability of relationship and, 241–244
Confucianism, science and, 22
Congruence, in client-centered therapy, 409–410
Conscience, in Freudian theory, 6, 119
Consciousness-raising groups, 10–11, 432–434
Consequences, in social learning theory, 141–142, 144
Constructionists, 21, 40
Consummate love, in Sternberg's triangular theory, 219, 228, 233
Contraception. *See* Birth control
Conversion disorder, 401
Coping resources
  gender and, 381–382
  social support, 382–383
Coping strategies, 383–385
  among African American men, 242
  and mental disorders, 396, 398
Corpus callosum, 76–78
  gender-related differences in, 82–83, 84, 109
Correlational studies, 27–28, 30
  statistical significance in, 35–36
Correlation coefficient, Pearson product-moment, 27
Counseling, gender bias in, 299, 414–416
  for disabled, 331
  feminist therapy and, 416–421
  gender issues in, 416–425
  for men, 421–423
  See also Psychotherapy
Craniometry, 76
Creativity, gender and, 105–107
Criminal behavior
  gender and, 208–213
  psychological effects on victims of, 379–380
  testosterone levels and, 68–70
  and XYY chromosome pattern, 57–58
Critical periods in development, 53, 58, 80, 197–198
Cross-cultural studies
  of cognitive abilities, 100, 111
  of emotional expression, 192–193
  of gender stereotyping, 178–179
  of life expectancy, 345–346
  of psychiatric diagnoses, 390
  of romantic relationships, 227–228
  of sexual behavior, 277
  See also Culture; Ethnic background
Crying, as expression of anger, 216
Cult of True Womanhood, 166–168, 171, 172, 173, 176
Cultural relativism, 133–134
Culture
  depression and, 395–396
  experience of emotions and, 191
  friendships and, 220
  in gender schema theory, 148
  gender stereotypes and, 150, 175–179
  homosexual behavior and, 284, 290
  life expectancy and, 345–346
  masochism and, 122
  psychiatric diagnoses and, 390
  psychoanalytic theory and, 120
  reflected by the media, 17
  research influenced by, 76
  sexual activity and, 252, 258, 268, 270, 277–279, 284
  sexual development and, 60
  sexual violence and, 212
Cunnilingus, 257, 283
CVD. *See* Cardiovascular disease

Data, 24
Date or acquaintance rape, 211–213, 255, 267, 271
Dating, 228–231, 243, 269, 271
Dependency needs, gender role changes and, 444
Dependent personality disorder, 387, 393, 453
Dependent variables, 28
  in ex post facto studies, 30, 32
Depression
  alcohol use and, 397–398
  cognitive therapy for, 410
  described, 394–395
  dieting and, 367, 368
  drug therapy for, 413
  drug use and, 397–398
  electroconvulsive therapy for, 413
  ethnic background and, 390
  exercise and, 371
  experience of violence and, 267, 378–379, 387, 389
  family roles and, 377, 380
  gender differences in, 332, 393, 395–396, 452–453
  major, 395
  in PMS, 62, 65
  silencing the self and, 396
Descriptive research methods, 24–28
  correlational study, 27–28
  naturalistic observation, 24–26
  surveys, 26–27
  See also Qualitative research
"Developmental sexism," 139–140
Developmental stages
  in Freudian theory, 116–118
  friendships and, 248
  of sexual dimorphism, 48
  versus continuous development, 146–147
Diagnosis
  advantages and disadvantages of, 384–385
  defined, 384
  of mental disorders, 385–388
Diagnostic and Statistical Manual of Mental Disorders (American Psychiatric Association)
  ethnic stereotypes and, 390
  gender inequities in, 388–394
  PMS controversy and, 374–375
"Dichotomania," 110
Diet
  cardiovascular risk and, 347
  cancer risk and, 350
Dieting
  as eating disorder, 367
  weight loss problems with, 367

Differential Aptitude Test (DAT), gender-related differences in, 94, 111
Digestive tract cancers
 death rates from, 349
 diet and, 350
Dimorphism, sexual, 48, 60, 70
 brain structure and, 74–77, 82, 83–84, 109
Disabilities
 conversion disorder as an erroneous diagnosis for, 401
 gender differences and, 343
Disability harassment, 331
Discrimination
 in education, 290
 gender stereotypes and, 14, 324, 328
 in hiring, 321–323
 mental health and, 381
 sexual harassment as, 335
Display rules, 191
 expressions of emotion and, 191, 214–215
Diversity issues
 aggression in an egalitarian society, 208
 "cool pose" in African American men, 242
 disability and employment, 331
 emphasis on similarities vs. differences, 14
 expression of emotions, 192–193
 gender and mental abilities across cultures, 100
 gender roles in Native American culture, 284
 invisibility of discrimination to the privileged, 15
 life expectancy, 345–346
 mental disorders and ethnicity, 390
 morality and cultural relativity, 133–134
 nationality stereotypes, 175
 nonwestern cultures and science, 22
 race and brain capacity, 76
 race/gender research and, 5
 racial stereotyping and achievement, 327
 schemata and race, 149
 school and sexual orientation, 301
 self-segregation in school and, 222
 in sexual activity, 277
 socioeconomic status and testosterone, 68
 stereotypes as threat, 182
 a third sex, 61
Division 35, 8–9, 10
Division 51, 10, 11
Divorce, 244–248
 coping resources in, 247–248
 increase in, 228, 245
 medical care issues in, 355–356
 men's movement and, 11, 433–434
 predictors of, 243–244
 psychological problems and, 378, 380, 382
 standard of living and, 247
Doctrine of the Two Spheres, 165–167
 love relationships and, 228
 maximalist view of gender and, 449
Dolls, gender roles and, 60, 139, 142, 169, 221, 290
Domesticity, in Cult of True Womanhood, 166–167
Domestic violence
 gender differences in, 208, 210
 mental disorders and, 378–380, 403–404, 452
 stability of relationship and, 241–243
Dominican Republic, pseudohermaphoroditism in, 61
Double standard for mental health, 392
Double standard for sexual behavior, 256
 adolescent sexuality and, 269, 270, 271
 adult sexuality and, 275–276, 443
 childhood sexuality and, 264
 communication difficulties and, 271
 gender differences in acceptance of, 258, 259
 Playboy Foundation survey and, 257
Dress, gender stereotyping and, 145–146, 160, 193–194
Drug therapy, for mental disorders, 413–414
Drug use
 childhood sexual abuse and, 379
 gender differences in, 397–398, 413
 mental disorders related to, 396–398
 and testosterone level, 67–69
DSM classification system, 386–388
 controversy about, 374–375
 ethnic stereotypes and, 390, 393
 gender inequities in, 388–394
Dysfunctional relationships, codependency controversy, 430–431
Dysthymia, 394–396

Eating behaviors, 364–369
 body image and, 365–367
 gender and, 129, 364–365
Eating disorders, 367–369
 behavior modification therapy for, 412
 exercise and, 371
Education, gender differences in, 290–308, 443, 444
 fields of study, 303–304
 historical background, 166, 289–290
 Male Sex Role Identity and, 168
 See also Teacher attitudes
Educational achievement
 and ethnicity, 177–178
 gender differences in, 298–299
 sexual harassment and, 299–301
Ego, in Freudian theory, 119, 408
Electroconvulsive therapy, 413–414
Embedded figures test, 100, 102, 103
Embryonic and fetal development, 49–53
Emotions, 189–217
 and brain function, 85
 cognition and, 190–191
 culture and, 192–193
 differences in expression of, 189–190, 191, 193–194, 214–215, 218–219, 391, 422–423, 441–442, 445, 448, 449, 451, 454
 emotional support, 221, 224, 225, 276, 382–383, 403, 430, 432, 439, 444, 452
 "his and hers" theory of, 190–191
 marital communication and, 227, 233, 242–243, 455
 physiological aspects of, 190
 PMS and, 61–62, 64–65
 stereotypes and, 193–194
 suppression of, 242
 See also specific emotions
Empirical observation, 23, 28, 39

Employed women
  choice issues for, 451–452
  ethnic differences in, 177–178
  in field of psychology, 8
  increases in number of, 320, 439
  health advantages for, 329, 377
  household work and, 236, 238–239, 329
  love relationships and, 232
  management style of, 334
  marital power of, 239
  relationship changes and, 439
  role expansion and, 441
  role overload and, 377, 441
  testosterone levels and, 69
Employment
  disabled women and, 331
  discrimination in hiring, 321–322
  gender differences in, 320–321
  gender segregation in, 330–331
  glass ceiling issues, 316–317
  glass escalator issues, 324, 325
  male vs. female leadership styles in, 333–334
  multiple role concerns, 376–378, 439–440, 454
  sexual harassment issues, 338–340
  social support in, 444
  wage gap, 317, 323, 325, 330, 332, 340
  workplace interaction issues, 335–339
  See also Careers; Occupation
Empty love, in Sternberg's triangular theory, 219
Endocrine glands, 46
Endocrine system, 46–48
  developmental abnormalities in, 58–59
  in puberty, 53–56
  in reproductive cycle, 54–55
  sexual activity and, 55–56
Endometrial cancer, 362
Engineering, gender and, 108–109, 303, 304, 307, 323, 324, 451
Environment
  and biology interact, 86–87
  in feminist therapy, 420
  in gender schema theory, 148, 149
  mathematical abilities and, 97
  in social learning theory, 140, 141–142
  See also Culture
Essentialist view, 2, 13, 281
Estradiol, 47
  premenstrual syndrome and, 62
  in reproductive cycle, 55
Estrogen replacement therapy, 363
Estrogens, 47–48, 54–56
  mental ability and, 110
  premenstrual syndrome and, 62
  sexually dimorphic nucleus and, 83
Ethical issues
  ex post facto studies and, 29
  sexual exploitation in psychotherapy, 426–427
Ethnic background
  adolescent sexual behavior and, 270
  career advancement and, 317, 323
  career expectations and, 309–310, 319–320
  coping resources and, 383
  educational achievement and, 303
  fear of success and, 309–310
  feminist therapy and, 420
  gender stereotypes and, 177–178
  life expectancy and, 343–344, 351–352
  mathematical achievement and, 100
  mental disorder diagnoses and, 390
  mortality and, 351–352
  poverty effects and, 380
  schemata based on, 149
  self-segregation by, 223
  sexist discrimination in, 381
  token status and, 326
Europeans, emotional expression by, 192–193
Evaluation
  bias in, 36
  meta-analysis, 36
  statistical significance, 35
  statistical vs. practical significance, 35
Evolution, theory of
  aggression and, 210
  cerebral lateralization and, 81
  expression of emotions and, 191
  functionalism influenced by, 4
  maternal instinct and, 216
Evolutionary psychology, 212
  gender differences in sexual selectivity, 275–276
  mate selection and, 230–231
Excitement phase in sexual response, 260
Exercise, 369–371
  addiction to, 371
  gender differences in, 292, 369–372
  psychological health and, 370
  sports vs., 370
  as weight control strategy, 366
Expectations
  career opportunities and, 290, 314, 317, 318–320
  educational achievement and, 97
  emotional responses and, 189–190, 193–194
  mathematical achievement and, 38, 99, 143
  occupational achievement and, 318–320, 329
  research results and, 36, 62
  spatial abilities and, 102
Experiment, defined, 28
Experimental research methods, 28–29
  ex post facto methods vs., 29–30
  gender research limitations, 34
  meta-analysis of, 35–37
Expert power, 334–335
Ex post facto studies, 29–32
  interpretation limitations, 30–32
Expressive qualities, 183, 214–215
  femininity and, 186, 187
  in mates, 231
  marital satisfaction and, 243
  men's adoption of, 214, 416, 421, 444–445
External genitalia, 48, 50, 52, 55, 57, 58, 60
Extramarital sex
  gender differences and, 258, 259
  in NORC survey, 255
  in Kinsey survey, 254, 255 256
  in Playboy Foundation survey, 255, 257

Failure, internal vs. external explanations for, 311–313
Family Duty blueprint, 228,
Family roles
  gender differences in, 228–229, 329–330, 376–378, 382, 439–441, 451, 454
  self-help groups as substitute for, 430
  as source of stress, 330, 376–378, 395
  as source of support, 382–383

Family work. *See* Household work
Fathers
  absent, masculine identity problems and, 11
  bonding by, 197
  gender role development and, 143, 159, 319
  gender stereotypes and, 140
  involved in child care, 200–201, 441
  sexual molestation by, 128, 267–268
Fatuous love, in Sternberg's triangular theory, 219
Fear of success, 308–310
Fellatio, 257, 277, 284
Female reproductive cycle, 55
Females. *See* Femininity; Girls; Women
Female sexual differentiation, 49–53
Feminine identity, social learning theory of, 142–144
Femininity
  in Chodorow's theory, 127
  codependency concept and, 431
  communal traits and, 39–40
  Cult of True Womanhood, 166–167
  cultural variations in, 176–179
  expressive traits and, 186–187
  in Freudian theory, 7
  gender schema and concepts of, 148, 150
  gender stereotypes, 165–168
  in Horney's theory, 122–123
  leadership style associated with, 334
  measurement of, 181–186
  mental health concepts and, 420–422
  psychoanalytic view of, 119–120, 123
  religion and, 165–166
  science and, 39
  sexual orientation and, 278
Feminist empiricists, 40–42
Feminist movement
  and biological theories of gender differences, 449
  consciousness-raising groups in, 432
  influence of, 7–8
  maximalist theories of gender and, 134–136
  men's responses to, 10–12, 446–447
  psychoanalytic theory and, 120, 123–124, 126–130
  scientific method criticized by, 22, 40–42
  scientific methods proposed by, 40–42
Feminist standpoint epistemologies, 40–42
Feminist standpoint theory, 130–136
Feminist therapy, 417–421
  clients of, 419–421
  consciousness-raising groups and, 433
  gender aware therapy and, 423–424
  gender and practice of, 420–421
  goals of, 418–419
  principles of, 417–418
  theoretical orientations of, 418–419
Fetal development. *See* Prenatal development
A Fire in the Belly: On Being a Man (Keene), 11
Fitness, gender and, 296, 369–372
  See also Athletics; Exercise
Follicle-stimulating hormone (FSH), 54–55, 62
  in female reproductive cycle, 54–55, 62
  in male reproductive cycle, 55
  premenstrual syndrome and, 62
Freudian theory of personality, 115–120
  basic concepts, 116–119
  feminist revisions of, 123–124, 126–130
  historical background, 5–7, 115–116
  on moral development, 119
  on women, 118–120, 123–124
Freudian therapy, 407–408, 414
Friendships
  among children, 220
  among college students, 224
  among the elderly, 226
  among married people, 224–225
  among men, 220
  between parents and adult children, 225
  changes over life span, 223–226
  companionate love, 219
  as coping resource, 382
  cross-gender, 223
  homosexuality fears and, 224, 226–227
  interracial, 223
  self-disclosure in, 223–225
  styles of, 224, 226–227
  triangular theory of love and, 219, 243
Frontal lobe, 75–76, 80
Frustration
  aggression and, 202
  anger and, 202
FSH. *See* Follicle-stimulating hormone
Functional magnetic resonance imaging (FMRI), 73–74, 85
Functionalism, 3–4, 7, 15
Fungal disease, sexually transmitted, 361–362

Gamblers Anonymous, 429, 430
GAT (gender aware therapy), 423–425
Gay, defined, 254
Gay and lesbian experiences
  culture and, 277, 279
  gay liberation movement, 433
  in school, 301
Gay and lesbian relationships, 277–285
  attitudes toward, 279–280
  balance of power in, 239
  coming-out issues, 281–282
  division of household labor in, 237
  friendships, 282
  gender differences in, 282–284
  in Kinsey survey, 254–255
  in NORC survey, 278
  in Playboy Foundation survey, 256
  stability of, 245
Gay fathers, 200
Gender
  approaches to study of, 15–16, 40–42
  choice and, 451–454
  definition of, 13
  differences in ability and, 450–451
  as "hot" topic, xi, 17
  maximalist view drawbacks, 135–136, 449–450
  reasons for studying, 12–13
  research limitations, 34–39
  sex differences vs. gender differences, 12–13
  theory vs. reality, 450
Gender aware therapy (GAT), 423–425

Gender bias. *See* Gender stereotypes; Sexism
Gender constancy
  in cognitive developmental theory, 145–147
  development of, 153–156
  genital knowledge and, 150
Gender flexibility, development of, 158–159
Gender harassment form of sexual harassment, 336
Gender identity, 145
  in adolescence and adulthood, 157–159
  in childhood, 146, 153–157
  cognitive development and, 146–147, 161
  development of, 152–159
  in infancy, 152–153
  psychoanalytic view of. *See* Personality theory
  sexually dimorphic nucleus and, 83
  stereotype development, 146, 149, 154
  See also Femininity; Male Sex Role Identity; Masculinity
Gender identity disorder, 157
Gender labeling, 145–146, 154, 156, 160, 161
Gender roles
  athletic activities and, 296, 370
  cardiovascular disease risk and, 348
  career expectations and, 319–320, 329
  changes in, 443–452
  consciousness-raising groups and, 432–434
  dating behavior and, 229–230
  defined, 140
  depression symptoms and, 395–396
  eating and, 367–368
  emotions and, 191–215. *See also* Emotions
  experience of emotions and, 194
  expression of emotions and, 218
  expressions of anger and, 203
  gender stereotypes and, 154, 164–165, 179, 180–181, 187, 194
  health risks and, 347, 364, 372
  health services use and, 354–359
  household work and, 235–238, 438–439
  men's movement and, 11
  mental disorder diagnoses and, 389, 391–392, 393, 396–397, 399, 402–403
  mental disorder treatment and, 415–417, 420–424, 430
  multiple role models, 439–442
  Native American berdache, 284
  nurturing behavior and, 198, 200
  power and, 238–239, 241
  romantic attraction and, 228, 231, 232–233, 243
  traditional assumptions about, 11, 16, 132, 157, 238
  workplace issues, 333, 335
Gender schema theory, 147–151
  cognitive developmental theory vs., 160
  gender script theory vs., 161
  social learning theory vs., 160
Gender script theory, 151–152
Gender segregation
  by children, 221–222, 226, 268, 281
  in employment, 317, 320, 330–332
  in housework, 236
Gender similarities, xii
Gender stereotypes, 164–188
  achievement perceptions and, 312–313
  advantages of, 180–181
  anxiety disorders and, 393
  career advancement and, 323–324, 327–329
  childhood play activities and, 220–221
  in children's books, 292–293
  in classrooms, 290–291
  college experiences and, 298–300
  compatibility in relationships and, 231
  counselor gender choice and, 416
  cultural variations in, 175, 176–179
  in dating behavior, 230–231
  defined, 165
  development of, 168–171
  education and, 290–291
  emotional expression and, 191–193, 442–443
  fear of success, 309
  feminist reaction to, 8
  function of, 179–181
  gender roles and, 154, 164–165, 179, 180–181, 187, 194
  health care and, 347–348, 356–357
  hiring practices and, 321–322
  historical background, 165–167
  homosexuality and, 183
  household work and, 236, 439
  interactions of, 171–172
  judgments based on, 171–176
  maintenance of, 170–171
  mental disorder diagnoses and, 389, 391–392, 393, 396–397, 399, 402–403
  mental disorder treatment and, 415–417, 420–424, 430
  nationality stereotypes and, 175
  nurturing behavior and, 200, 203
  perceptions influenced by, 171–176
  power and, 187
  relationships and, 230–233
  self-perceptions and, 170–171
  teacher attitudes and, 290–291
  See also Stereotyping
Genetic stage of development, 48
Genitalia
  development of, 49–50
  internal vs. external, 48, 49–50
Genital stage, in Freudian theory, 118
Genital system cancers
  death rates from, 349
  risk factors for, 351
Genital warts, 362
Gestalt therapy, 409–410
Girls
  aggression in, 204–206
  childhood play activities of, 220–222
  development of aggression in, 203–206
  dieting and body image problems among, 366–368
  friendships among, 221–223
  gender development in, 156–157
  sexual abuse of, 265–267
  social aggression by, 206
  See also Femininity; Women
"Give 'Em Hell." *See* Male Sex Role Identity
Glass ceiling, 316–317, 323–324
Glass escalator, 325
Gonadal hormones, 47–48
Gonadal stage of development, 48
Gonadotropins, 46
  in puberty, 54
Gonads, in endocrine system, 46

Gonorrhea, 361
Good Provider role, 167, 228, 329
Gross motor skills, gender and, 221
Groups, interaction styles in, 221
Guns, male relationships with, 117

Health
  eating behaviors and, 364–369
  exercise patterns, 369–371
  gender roles and, 347, 354–359, 364, 372, 452
  life expectancy patterns, 342–343, 344, 345–346
  lifestyle choices and, 452
  marital status and, 233–234
  survival and gender, 342–354
Health care system, 354–363
  gender bias in, 357–358
  gender differences in use of, 354–356
  gender stereotypes and, 346–347, 356–357
  mental disorder diagnosis concerns, 374–375
  mental disorder treatments. *See* Psychotherapy
  reproductive health and, 354, 359–363
Health insurance, 355–356
Heart disease. *See* Cardiovascular disease
Hegemonic masculinity, 168
Hepatitis, as viral STD, 362
Hermaphroditism, 59–60
Herpes, genital, 362
Heterosexuality, 268–277
  in adolescence, 268–272
  in adulthood, 272–277
Hispanic Americans
  adolescent sexual behavior among, 270, 272
  in blue-collar occupations, 324
  college enrollment, 303
  eating disorders among, 365
  feminist therapy with, 420
  gender stereotyping and, 177–178
  housework sharing among, 238
  marital power among, 239
  mathematical and spatial ability and, 100
Historical background, 3–4
  behaviorism, 4
  body image, 365
  brain research, 74, 75
  educational patterns, 302, 303
  Freudian theory, 5–7, 115–116, 124
  functionalism, 4
  gender stereotypes, 165–168, 177
  household division of labor, 329
  intelligence testing, 90–91
  life expectancy, 344
  love relationships, 227–229
  men's friendships, 220
  men's movement, 9–12
  mental disorder diagnoses, 386
  psychoanalysis, 5–7
  scientific method, 21–23
  sexual behavior and, 280
  structuralism, 3–4
  women's studies, 7–9
Histrionic personality disorder, 387, 391, 392, 393
HIV. *See* Human immunodeficiency virus
Homicide. *See* Violence
Homophobia, 226
  AIDS and, 280
  formation of intimacy in men's friendships and, 226–227
  in school, 301
Homosexual experiences. *See* Gay and lesbian experiences
Homosexuality, 254, 277–285
  in adolescence, 280–282
  in adulthood, 282–285
  biological basis for, 280–281
  gender stereotypes and, 172,
  masculinity/femininity scales and, 183
  See also Gay and lesbian experiences; Gay and lesbian relationships
Homosexual relationships. *See* Gay and lesbian relationships
Honor, cultural differences and, 192
Hormonal stage of development, 48
Hormone replacement therapy, 359
Hormones
  behavior and, 44–45, 60–70
  cerebral lateralization and, 80–81
  defined, 46
  in embryonic development, 49–50, 53
  in endocrine system, 46–48
  mental abilities and, 90, 110
  popular beliefs about, 45–46, 64–65
  prenatal abnormalities, 46, 48, 49, 57–58
  in puberty, 53–56
  in reproductive cycle, 54–56
  sex differences and, 47–48
  sexual activity and, 56
  sexually dimorphic nucleus and, 83–84
Hostile environment sexual harassment, 336–337
Household work
  conflict in couples over, 237–238
  gender role changes and, 438–439, 441, 445, 447
  in marriage, 236–238
  as source of stress, 376–378
Housewife
  as low-power role, 377
  as supporting role, 439
Human immunodeficiency virus (HIV), 362
  condom use and, 272
  homophobia and, 280
  risk factors for, 280, 284, 351
Humanistic therapies, 409–410
  gender bias and, 415
Human Sexual Response (Masters and Johnson), 260
Hypothalamus, 46
  in endocrine system, 55
  gender-related differences in, 53, 82, 83
Hypothesis, 35, 36
Hysteria (conversion disorder), 401

Id, in Freudian theory, 119
Identification
  in Chodorow's theory, 127
  in Freudian theory, 119, 122, 123
Identity. *See* Cult of True Womanhood; Femininity; Gender identity; Male Sex Role Identity; Masculinity
Illusory correlation, gender stereotypes and, 170
Imprinting, 197–198
Incest, 265, 267
Income, marital power and, 239
Independence blueprint, 232, 248–249
Independent variables, 28, 30
Indian culture
  Lepcha sexual practices, 277
  science and, 22
  son preference, 133
In a Different Voice (Gilligan), 130
Indirect aggression, 208, 209

Individual differences, as alternative schema, 150
Industrial Revolution
gender stereotypes and, 165
household work and, 235
love relationships and, 228
Infant development
Chodorow's theory and, 127
of gender identity, 152–153
sexuality and, 263
Infatuation, in Sternberg's triangular theory, 219
Infectious disease
as cause of death, 345–346
sexually transmitted, 361–362
Informed consent, in feminist therapy, 418
Initiation ceremonies, in men's movement, 11
Instincts
behaviorist theory vs., 195
emotions and, 194
in Freudian theory, 6, 116
See also Aggression; Maternal instinct
Instrumental characteristics
marital satisfaction and, 243
and mental health, 421
women's adoption of, 319, 444–445, 447
Instrumental-expressive distinction
gender role changes and, 444–445, 447
for masculinity/femininity, 183, 186
Intelligence
concept of, 90–91
gender differences in, 76, 90, 450
See also Mathematical ability; Spatial abilities; Verbal ability
Intelligence testing
functionalism and, 4
historical background, 90–91
Interdependence blueprint, 232, 249
Internal genitalia, 48, 59, 70
Intersexuality, 59–60
Intimacy
among adolescents, 224
between parents and adult children, 225
childhood relationships and, 221, 222
in Companionship blueprint, 228
gender differences in, 224, 226–227, 270
gender role trends and, 442–443, 452
in marital communication, 225, 234–235
marital dissolution and, 246
in psychotherapy, 406, 425, 427
relationship stability and, 243
in same-sex relationships, 283
in Sternberg's triangular theory, 219, 221, 228
in women's friendships, 220, 233
Introspection, as research method, 3
"Intuition," gender and, 110
Iron John (Bly), 10
Italians, emotional expression by, 192

Justice vs. care moral orientation, 132, 134

Kaposi's sarcoma, 351
Kinsey surveys, 253–256
on extramarital sex, 254
gender role changes and, 443
NORC survey and, 257
Playboy Foundation survey and, 256–257
on same-gender sexual experiences, 254, 255
on sexual molestation, 255
social standards and, 253
Klinefelter's syndrome, 57–58

Language ability, gender and, 79, 80, 91–94
Late luteal phase dysphoric disorder (LLPD), 374–375
Latency stage, in Freudian theory, 118
Lateralization
cerebral hemispheres and, 75–82
defined, 77
gender-related cognitive differences and, 109–110
gender-related differences in, 79–82
Latino Americans. *See* Hispanic Americans
Learning, gender and, 103, 105
Leisure time, active vs. sedentary, 370
Lepchas of India, sexual practices of, 277
Lesbian, defined, 254
Lesbian relationships, 254, 278–279, 282–284
See also Gay and lesbian relationships
Leukemia, death rates from, 349
LH. *See* Luteinizing hormone
Life expectancy
historical background, 344
lifestyle choices and, 452
male vs. female, 343, 344, 345–346
worldwide patterns of, 345–346
Lifestyle
exercise patterns and, 370–372
gender differences in choice of, 452
health risks and, 363–364
psychological health and, 376–381
Liking, in Sternberg's triangular theory of love, 219
LLPDD (late luteal phase dysphoric disorder), 374–375
Loneliness, friendship and, 224
Longitudinal research, on aggression, 204–206
Love
concepts of, 233–234
Companionship blueprint and, 228–229, 232
Family Duty blueprint and, 228
Independence blueprint and, 232
stability of relationships and, 241–244
Sternberg's triangular theory of, 219, 228, 233
Love relationships, 227–244
balance of power in, 238–241
characteristics valued in, 229–231, 448–449
companionate, 219
conflict in, 240–244
dating, 229–231
dissolution of, 244–248
gender role restrictions and, 226–227
historical background, 227–229
male and female concepts of, 233–234
similarities among, 285
stability of, 241–245
working women and, 228–229, 232–233, 235–239, 438–441
See also Cohabitation; Gay and lesbian relationships; Marriage
Lung cancer, death rates from, 349
Luteinizing hormone (LH), 55–56

in female reproductive cycle, 55
in male reproductive cycle, 55
premenstrual syndrome and, 62
Lymphatic cancers, death rates from, 349

Machismo, marital power and, 249
Major depression, 394, 395. *See also* Depression
Males. *See* Boys; Men; Masculine identity; Masculinity
Male Sex Role Identity, 167–168, 172–173, 176
aggressive behavior and, 65–68, 204–216
display rules and, 191, 214–216, 452
health-related behaviors and, 451–452
health services use and, 354, 359
perceptions based on, 346
personality disorders and, 386–387, 389–393, 399, 404–405
Male sexual differentiation, 48, 72
Map use, gender and, 89
Marriage, 231–249, 253, 256–257
communication in, 234–235
Companionship blueprint in, 228, 232, 245, 248
concepts of, 231–238
conflict in, 233–234, 237, 240–242
dissolution of, 246–247
division of household labor in, 237–242, 249
Family Duty blueprint in, 228
friendships in, 224
gender differences in benefits from, 233–234, 240
Good Provider role in, 228, 329
health of partners and, 233
Independence blueprint in, 232
Interdependence blueprint in, 232, 248
power issues in, 233, 235–238
remarriage patterns, 232
satisfaction in, 247
sexual activity in, 270, 272
sexual freedom vs., 273
stability of, 231, 233, 237, 241–249
Masculine identity
men's movement and, 9, 11–12
social learning theory on, 140–141, 143–146
See also Male Sex Role Identity
Masculinity
agentic traits and, 186–188, 444
cerebral lateralization and, 79
in Chodorow's theory, 126
cultural variations in, 113
in Doctrine of the Two Spheres, 166–167, 228, 341, 449
emotional sharing and, 225, 423, 448, 452, 454
in Freudian theory, 5–7, 115
gender schema and concepts of, 140, 147–151
gender stereotypes, 163–165, 169, 171–180, 187
guns and, 117, 353
in Horney's theory, 123
instrumental traits and, 444–445
measurement of, 27, 166, 185–187
men's movement and, 9, 11–12
psychoanalytic view of, 7
psychotherapy and, 422–423
of science, 39–40
Sex Role Strain and, 378
sexual orientation vs., 183–184, 248, 278, 280
styles of, 168, 434, 436
Masculinity complex, 121–123
Masochism, in Freud's vs. Horney's theory, 121–122
Massa intermedia of thalamus, 76, 82
gender-related differences in, 82, 84
Masters and Johnson studies, 259–263
Masturbation
by children, 116, 256–257, 263, 268, 286
defined, 255
Freudian view of, 116, 119
gender differences in, 275, 286, 443
in Kinsey survey, 255–256
in NORC survey, 257
in Playboy Foundation survey, 256
in same-sex relationships, 283–284
Maternal instinct, 189, 194–195
attachment and, 197–198, 216
gender roles and, 209
primate studies, 195, 276
Mathematical ability, 37, 94–100
environment and, 419
gender and, 142–148
parents' beliefs about, 97, 98, 99
Mathematics performance
as meta analysis example, 36, 94, 97, 103, 109
self-confidence and, 310–311
Matriarchy, myth of, 238
Maximalist view of gender differences, 2, 134–135, 449
Media
emphasis on gender in, 16–18
sensationalism in, 17
stereotyping perpetuated by, 97
Medical care. *See* Health care system
Medical treatment, for mental disorders, 413–414
gender bias and, 413
Memory, gender and, 90, 103, 105
Men
aggressive behavior in, 65, 68
body image concerns of, 365–367, 369–371
communication styles of, 245
counseling for, 422–424
display rules for, 214–215
eating disorders among, 365–366
eating patterns of, 365–366
emotional expression and, 191, 192, 422
emotional stereotypes and, 192
exercise patterns in, 366, 369–370
expressions of anger by, 203, 206
feminist therapy for, 420–423
friendships between, 220
gender role changes and, 444, 446, 448, 452
health risks and lifestyle of, 397
health services treatment of, 354–356
health services use by, 354–356, 358–359
hormonal abnormalities in, 46, 56–57, 61
hormonal regulation in, 56–57
life expectancy in, 343–347
love and marriage concepts of, 233–234
mental disorder diagnosis in. *See* Mental disorders
mental disorder treatment and, 414–416, 430
morbidity and mortality in, 360, 372
as rape victims, 210–212
reproductive systems in, 359–360
romantic beliefs of, 233

Men *(continued)*
as sexual abuse victims, 210–212
sexual violence by, 211–212
stress and coping patterns in, 363, 375–378
violence and, 378–379
See also Boys, Masculine identity, Masculinity
Menarche, 54
Men Are from Mars, Women Are from Venus (Gray), 234, 453
Menopause, 359, 361–363, 430
fitness needs and, 370–371, 373
medicalization of, 354
power and, 184
support groups for, 430
Men's movement, 9–11
consciousness-raising groups in, 432–434
development of, 11
different orientations within, 9–11
relationships and, 211, 219, 227
Menstrual cycle, 55–56
hormonal changes in, 62–63
Mental disorders, 374–396
anxiety disorders, 398–399
bipolar disorder, 400–402
coping resources and, 403–404, 408
coping strategies and, 403–404, 408
discrimination in, 381
DSM diagnostic categories, 373–375, 386–391
ethnic background and, 389–390
gender bias in treatment of, 414–416
gender and diagnosis of, 388–389, 391–394
overdiagnosis and underdiagnosis of, 393–394
poverty and, 380–381
premenstrual syndrome controversy, 374–375
schizophrenia, 387, 400, 402
self-help groups for, 427–430
sexual disorders, 401–402
socioeconomic status and, 380–381, 390
somatoform disorders, 401, 402
stress and, 376–381
substance-related, 396–398
treatment for. *See* Psychotherapy
violence and, 378–380
See also Depression
Mental rotation, 100, 102, 103
Mentoring relationships, 306, 326–327
ethnicity and, 327
gender and, 306, 326–327
Meta-analysis, 36–38
Mexican Americans. *See* Hispanic Americans
Miles and Terman Attitude Interest Analysis Survey, 183
Million Man March, 10, 12
Minimalist view of gender differences, 2, 449–450
Minnesota Multiphasic Personality Inventory, MF scale, 183,
Models, in social learning theory, 142–143
Monogamy, 273–274
Mood
day of the week and, 64
hormones and, 60–65
Mood disorders. *See* Anxiety disorders; Bipolar disorder; Depression; Drug use, mental disorders related to
Mood swings, in PMS, 60–61
Moral development
Gilligan's theory of, 130–132, 134
Kohlberg's theory of, 131
Moral reasoning
gender and, 114–115, 131–133, 134
relativism vs. universality in, 133–134
Moral superiority of women, 166
Morbidity
gender and, 342–343, 354–359
gender roles and, 363–364
Mortality
accidents and, 351–352
cancer and, 348–351
cardiovascular disease and, 343, 346–348
gender factors in, 342–343, 345–354
violence and, 351–354
worldwide patterns of, 345–346
Mothering
bonding and, 197–198
in Chodorow's theory, 126–127
experience required for, 195–197
gender stereotypes and, 195
See also Maternal instinct; Nurturing
Motor systems, 74
Müllerian system, 49, 51
Musical ability, gender and, 106
My Fair Lady (Lerner and Loewe), 442
Myth of the Coy Female, 276

Narcissistic personality disorder, 391
Narcotics Anonymous, 429, 430
National Council of Women Psychologists, 8, 10
National Institute of Mental Health, on poverty and mental health, 380–381
Nationality stereotypes
emotional expression and, 192–193
gender stereotypes and, 175
National Opinion Research Council (NORC) sex survey, 257–258, 263
bisexuality reports in, 286
celibacy reports in, 274
conservative attitudes expressed in, 257, 258, 274
discrepancy between media portrayals and findings from, 258
forced sex reports in, 258, 271
gay and lesbian sexuality in, 278, 279
gender differences in sexuality, 258
liberal sexual attitudes in, 257
National Organization to Change Men, 11
National Organization for Men, 11
Native American culture
the berdache in, 284
science and, 22
Native American women
as feminist therapy clients, 420
weight concerns in, 365
Naturalistic observation, 24–26
Nature–nurture controversy, 1–2
functionalist vs. behaviorist views, 4
maximalist theory and, 449
in mental abilities, 112
social learning theory and, 140
Nervous system, physiology of brain and, 74
Neurons, 74
New Guinea
pseudohermaphroditism in, 61
sexual activity in, 277

Nonverbal communication, gender and, 106–107
Nonwestern cultures, science in, 22
"No Sissy Stuff." *See* Male Sex Role Identity
Nurturing
  boys and pets, 215
  in Chodorow's theory, 126–127
  experience required for, 195–197
  gender stereotypes and, 194–195, 199–200
  pleasure and dissatisfaction with, 200–201
  primate studies, 195–197
  social roles and, 199–201
  as source of stress, 376–378
  See also Care giving

Objectivity, scientific bias vs., 20–21, 39–40
Observation
  naturalistic, 24–26
  in scientific method, 22–23
  in social learning theory, 141–142
Obsessive-compulsive disorder, 399, 400
Occipital lobe, 75
Occupation
  accident risk and, 353
  cancer risk and, 349
  career planning bias, 299
  eating disorders and, 368, 369
  fear of success and, 308–310
  gender-atypical choices in, 317, 319, 320
  gender differences in, 317–318, 320
  gender distribution by, 321
  gender segregation in, 330–332
  gender stereotyping and, 150, 158, 171, 172, 321–323
  maximalist view and, 135
  physical activity and, 370, 450
  testosterone levels and, 66–67
  See also Careers; Employment
Oedipus complex, 116–118
  Antigone phase and, 128–129
  contemporary views of, 126–130
  Freud's revision of, 124–126
  moral development and, 118, 119
  pre-Oedipal period, 126–127
Office of Research on Women's Health, 358
One-way mirrors, 25
Operant conditioning, 140
  behavior modification and, 411–412
  in learning theory, 140–141
Operational definition, 25
Opinion polls. *See* Surveys
Oral–genital sexual activity
  among gay men, 284
  among lesbians, 283
  in NORC survey, 157
  in Playboy Foundation survey, 257
Oral stage, in Freudian theory, 116
Orgasm
  female type of, 263
  gender differences in, 262
  in Kinsey survey, 254, 255
Orgasm phase, in sexual response, 262
Osteoporosis
  fitness and, 371
  in aging women, 358, 363
Ovarian cancer, 362
Overeaters Anonymous, 429, 430

Panic Attacks, 398–399, 400
PAQ (Personal Attribute Questionnaire), 186
Paranoid personality disorder, 391
Paraphilias, 401
Parenting
  aggressive behavior and, 204, 205, 206
  friendships and, 225
  and gay or lesbian children, 281
  gender identity and, 143–144, 151, 154, 157
  gender roles and, 200
  gender schemata and, 150
  gender stereotyping and, 158, 159
  mathematical abilities and, 96
  for sexism prevention, 150
  sexuality concerns, 263–264
  social learning theory and, 142, 160
  as source of stress, 377–378
Parietal lobe, 75–76
Passion
  as danger, 227
  in Sternberg's triangular theory of love, 219, 233
  Companionship blueprint and, 233
  relationship stability and, 244
Passivity, female myth of, 201
Pearson product–moment correlation coefficient, 27
Peers
  gender identity and, 143
  social development and, 196
Penis envy
  in Freudian theory, 117–118
  in Horney's theory, 121
Personal Attribute Questionnaire (PAQ), 186
Personality
  gender and, 115
  masculinity/femininity measurement, 181, 183, 185–187
  traditional approaches to, 115–126
  See also Personality theory
Personality disorders, gender bias and, 389, 391
Personality theory,
  of Chodorow, 126–127
  contemporary psychoanalytic, 126–130
  cultural influences on, 123–123
  feminist, 126–132, 134–136
  of Freud, 114–120
  Freud and Horney compared, 123
  historical background, 5–7, 123–126
  of Horney, 120–123
  of Kaschak, 127–129
  males as standard for, 14
Phallic stage, in Freudian theory, 116, 118
Phobias, 399, 400
  behavior modification therapy for, 411–412
Physical appearance, gender stereotyping and, 171–172
Physical strength, gender differences in, 450
Physiology
  brain and nervous system, 74
  emotional expression and, 190, 199, 200, 214–215
  endocrine system, 46–48
  fetal development, 49–53
  in Freudian theory, 6
  puberty, 53–56
  of sexual response, 260–263
Piaget's water-level problem, 101, 103
Piety, in Cult of True Womanhood, 166, 167
Pituitary gland, in endocrine system, 46, 47
Plateau phase, in sexual response, 260–262

Play activities, gender differences in, 220–221
Playboy Foundation survey, 256–257
  NORC survey and, 257
PMDD (premenstrual dysphoric disorder), 374–375
PMS. *See* Premenstrual syndrome
Politics
  consciousness-raising groups and, 432
  constructionist view of science and, 20–21
  feminist therapy and, 417–418
Positron emission tomography (PET), 73–74, 85
Posttraumatic stress disorder (PTSD), 387–388, 399, 400
  criminal violence and, 379
  diagnosis of, 387
  as DSM category, 399, 400
Poverty, as source of stress, 380–381
Power
  communication styles and, 235
  conflict management and, 240–241
  expert, 334–335
  expression of aggression and, 208, 213
  femininity and, 184
  gender stereotyping and, 181
  in marital relationships, 238–241
  psychological health and, 377
  role models and, 142
  sexual abuse and, 267–268
  sexual harassment and, 339
  workplace issues, 334–335
Practical significance, 35–36
Pregnancy
  adolescent, 271–272
  health services use and, 355, 359–363
  mortality and, 345–346
Preliminary Scholastic Aptitude Test (PSAT). *See* Scholastic Aptitude Test
Premarital sex
  changes in patterns of, 255, 256–257, 270
  gender differences in, 255, 258
  in Kinsey survey, 256
  in NORC survey, 257–258
  in Playboy Foundation survey, 256–257
Premenstrual dysphoric disorder (PMDD), 374–375
Premenstrual syndrome (PMS)
  diagnostic controversy on, 45–46, 64–65, 374–375
  popular beliefs about, 45–46, 60–62
  research findings on, 62–65
Prenatal development
  abnormalities and, 56–60
  cerebral lateralization and, 80
  sex differentiation, 49–53
Pre-Oedipal period, 126–127
Primacy of relationship, marital dissolution and, 245, 246
Primate studies
  on nurturing behavior, 195–197
  on sexual behavior, 276
Prisons, suppression of emotions in, 215
Progesterone, 48
  premenstrual syndrome and, 62
  in reproductive cycle, 55, 63
Progestins, 48
Promise Keepers, 10, 11–12, 434
Prostate cancer, 358, 362
PSAT (Preliminary Scholastic Aptitude Test). *See* Scholastic Aptitude Test
Pseudohermaphroditism, 59–60
Psychoactive drugs, in psychotherapy, 413–414
  gender and, 413, 415
Psychoactive substances, disorders related to, 396–398
Psychoanalysis, 407–408
  cultural influences on, 6–7, 123–124
  feminist theories and, 123–124, 126–130
  in feminist therapy, 418–419
  Freudian personality theory, 115–119
  gender bias in, 414
  Horney's personality theory, 120–123
  influence of, 5–7, 9, 129–130
  sexual abuse of patients by, 406
Psychological disorders. *See* Mental disorders
Psychological health, fitness and, 371
Psychology, Freud's influence on, 115–116
The Psychology of Sex Differences (Maccoby and Jacklin), 15
Psychopathology
  gender-atypical behavior and, 393, 415–416
  gender stereotypes and, 415, 453
  overdiagnosis concerns, 393–394
  premenstrual syndrome controversy, 374–375, 389
  See also Mental disorders
Psychosexual stages, in Freudian theory, 116
Psychotherapy
  approaches to, 407–414
  behavior modification, 411–412
  cognitive therapy, 410–411
  feminist, 417–421
  gender aware therapy (GAT), 423–425
  gender bias in, 414–416
  gender stereotyping in, 414, 416, 417
  humanistic therapies, 409–410
  medical therapies, 413–414
  nonsexist, 417
  psychoanalysis, 407–408
  self-help movement as alternative to, 427–430
  sexual exploitation in, 406–407, 425–427
Puberty
  academic accomplishment and, 296
  physiological changes in, 53–56
Punishment
  in learning theory, 140–141
  social learning theory and, 141–143

Qualitative research, 32–33
Quantitative ability. *See* Mathematical ability
Quasi-experimental studies. *See* Ex post facto studies
Questionnaires, in descriptive research, 26
Quid pro quo form of sexual harassment, 335–336

Race
  parallels between gender and, 5
  schema based on, 149
  See also Ethnic background
Racism
  brain research and, 76
  sexism and, 5
  as a source of stress, 381

Rape
date or acquaintance, 212, 258, 271, 379
males as victims of, 211, 258
psychological aftermath of, 379
unreported, 211
Rational-emotive therapy, 410
Reinforcement
in learning theory, 140–141
in social learning theory, 141–144
Relationships, 218–250
"addiction" to, 431
Antigone phase and, 128–129
codependency controversy, 431
dating, 229–231
gender asymmetry in, 218–219, 223–224
gender and goals for, 447–449
gender role changes and, 442–443
men's movement and, 11–12, 453–454
moral development and, 131–132
See also Cohabitation; Friendships; Gay and lesbian Relationships; Love Relationships; Marriage
Releasing hormones, 46
Religion, Cult of True Womanhood and, 166
Remarriage, 248
Representative sample, sexuality research and, 252, 253, 256, 257
Repression, in psychoanalysis, 408
Reproductive health
cancers, 349, 351, 362
health care services use and, 355, 359–363
sexually transmitted diseases, 361–362
Reproductive system
female, 360
male, 361
Research
bias in. See Bias of researchers; Bias of survey respondents
cultural influences on, 21, 22, 39–40
Division 35 and, 8–9
expectations and, 64, 76
feminist orientation for, 8–9
gender as object of, 15–17
historical background of. *See* Historical background
interpretation problems, 30–32, 34–36
limitations of, 34–39
representative sample for, 252
on sexual behavior, 252–263
speculation vs. result, 34
stereotyping and, xiv
Resolution phase, in sexual response, 262
Right and left brain. *See* Lateralization
Risk factors, defined, 347
Rod-and-frame test, 101, 102
Role models
in feminist therapy, 420
in social learning theory, 142–144
Role overload, 377–378, 441–442
Roles, in social science, 140
Romantic love
childhood relationships and, 222–223
gender and, 233–234
in Sternberg's triangular theory, 219

Satisfaction, life
marriage and, 234
multiple roles and, 441
SAT. *See* Scholastic Aptitude Test
Schema, defined, 147
Schizoid personality disorder, 389, 391
Schizophrenia, 401–402
drug therapy for, 413
Scholastic Aptitude Test (SAT), gender-related differences in, 94–95
School-related factors
counselor bias, 299
gender segregation, 221–231
mathematical abilities, 94–99
prejudice against gays and lesbians, 301
sexual harassment, 299–300, 306–307
See also Education; Teacher attitudes
Science
bias vs. objectivity in, 20–21, 39–40
gender differences in study of, 295, 296, 298
historical background, 21–23
methods used in, 23–33
in nonwestern cultures, 22
See also Scientific method
Scientific method
data collection in, 23–24
descriptive research methods, 24–28
experimental research methods, 28–29
ex post facto studies, 29–32
feminist standpoint epistemologies, 40–42
feminist standpoint theory and, 130–136
gender images in, 39–40
gender research limitations, 34–39
historical background, 21–23
limitations and concerns, 34–39
psychoanalytic theory and, 129
qualitative methods, 32–35
theories vs. speculations, 34
variables in, 24
SDN (sexually dimorphic nucleus), 83–84
Seduction theory, 124
Freud's abandonment of, 124–126
Self-concept
gender identity and, 145–146
in gender schema theory, 148
gender stereotypes and, 3, 172
Self-confidence
ability and, 310–311
educational achievement and, 290, 295, 296
gender differences in, 310–311
Self-esteem
childhood sexual abuse and, 379
gender stereotypes and, 172
physical fitness and, 371
Self-fulfilling prophecies, mathematical ability and, 97
Self-help movement, 427–434
advantages and drawbacks of, 429–430, 431–432
consciousness-raising groups, 432–434
self-help group examples, 429
support groups, 430–432
Self-image. *See* Self-concept
Sensory systems, 75–76
Sex
gender vs., 12–13
physiology of, 261–262
Sexism
brain research and, 74
"developmental," 139–140
gender schemata and, 150
in mental health diagnoses, 388–389, 391–394

Sexism *(continued)*
parenting to prevent, 150
in psychotherapy, 414–416
racism and, 5, 381
in scientific methods, 39–40
as a source of stress, 381
Sex role spillover, 333–334
harassment and, 335
Sex roles. *See* Gender roles
Sex Role Strain, 168
Sexual abuse, 263–268
incidence of, 265–267
Kinsey survey on, 255
long-term effects of, 267, 379
patterns of, 265–267
Sexual activity
diversity in, 277
intimacy and, 234, 235
marital dissolution and, 246–247
power and, 268, 271
relationship satisfaction and, 283, 285
in same-gender relationships, 283–285
See also Sexual behavior
Sexual attitudes, gender differences in, 258–259
Sexual Behavior in the 1970s (Hunt), 256
Sexual behavior
in adolescence, 268–272, 281–282, 286
in adulthood, 272–276, 282, 285, 286
birth control use, 272, 355
cancer risk and, 351
celibacy, 273–274
bisexual, 285–286
by college students, 272–274
double standard. *See* Double standard for sexual behavior
gender and, 258–259, 268–271, 276. *See also specific types of behavior*
gender role changes and, 443
heterosexual, 268–276
in Horney's theory, 121–122
incest, 265
monogamy, 272–274
pregnancy and, 271–272
primate studies on, 276
same-sex, 277–285
sexually transmitted diseases and, 269, 272
study methods, 251–252
surveys on, 252–258
in therapeutic relationships, 406–407, 425–427
See also Sexual activity
Sexual Behavior in the Human Female (Kinsey, Pomeroy, Martin, & Gebhard), 254
Sexual Behavior in the Human Male (Kinsey, Pomeroy, & Martin), 254
Sexual dimorphism, 48
brain structure and, 75, 82–83
Sexual disorders, 401–402
Sexual dysfunctions, 401–402
Sexual exploitation, in psychotherapy, 406–407, 425–427
Sexual freedom, as heterosexual pattern, 272–274
Sexual harassment
of college students, 306–307
educational achievement and, 300
gender differences in, 307, 337–339
of high school students, 299–300, 306
in mentoring relationships, 306
"reasonable woman" standard and, 336
types of, 335–337
by women, 338
in workplace, 335–340
Sexuality
in children, 263–268
in Freudian theory, 116–119
gender and, 258–259
gender role changes and, 443
laboratory studies of, 259–260
methods of studying, 251–252
Myth of the Coy Female, 276
negative messages about, 251, 263–264, 268–269, 279–280
research sample problems, 252
surveys on, 252–258
See also Heterosexuality; Homosexuality; Sexual activity; Sexual behavior
Sexually dimorphic nucleus (SDN), 283–284
Sexually transmitted diseases (STDs), 361–362
health services use and, 361
Sexual molestation. *See* Sexual abuse
Sexual orientation
biological basis for, 280–281
defined, 268
eating disorders and, 369
feminist therapy and, 420
gender stereotypes and, 184
masculinity/femininity scales and, 183, 277–278
Sexual violence, 210–214
Shame, cultural differences in, 192
Shock therapy. *See* Electroconvulsive therapy
Siblings, sexual activity between, 264
Significance, statistical vs. practical, 35–36
Silencing the self, depression and, 396
Single mothers, mental health risks to, 377, 378, 380–381
"Sissies," 156–157, 168, 174
Smoking, cancer risk and, 349–350
Social aggression
gender differences in, 208
sexual violence and, 210–214
See also Indirect aggression
Social categories
gender stereotypes and, 165, 328, 447
gender studied as, 16–17, 31–32
Social class
division of household work, 237–238
eating disorders and, 368
marital dissolution and, 246
marital power and, 238–239
psychiatric diagnoses and, 390, 393
See also Socioeconomic status
Socialization view, of coping strategies, 384
Social learning theory, 140–144
cognitive behavior therapy and, 419
cognitive developmental theory vs., 146, 160
criticisms of, 144
gender schema theory vs., 160
maximalist theory of gender and, 449
Social roles
in feminist therapy, 418, 420–421
nurturing behavior and, 200–201
Social support
as coping resource, 382–383
self-help groups as, 428, 430–432
wife role as, 448
Socioeconomic conditions
mortality and, 343, 346

Socioeconomic status
division of household labor and, 237–238
divorce and, 247
mental disorder risk and, 380, 381
psychiatric diagnoses and, 390
school achievement and, 97–98, 293–294
testosterone and, 67, 68, 70
See also Social class
Somatization disorder, 401, 402
Somatoform disorders, 401, 402
Spatial abilities
definitions of, 99
ethnic background and, 100
gender and, 99, 101, 102, 103, 105, 107, 108, 109, 111
types of, 93, 99–102, 104
Spatial perception, 100–102
Spatial visualization, 102
Spatiotemporal ability, 102
Speech, localization of in brain, 79, 87
Spheres of influence, gender stereotypes on, 165–167
Splenium, gender-related differences in, 82–83
Sports. *See* Athletics
Spousal abuse. *See* Domestic violence
Stanford-Binet intelligence test, 90, 91
Statistically significant results, 35–36
Statistics, in correlational study, 27
STDs. *See* Sexually transmitted diseases
Stepfathers, sexual abuse by, 267
Stereotyping
by adolescents, 157–158
by adults, 159
by children, 139–140, 143, 154, 156, 158,
cognitive ability and, 102, 107
in cognitive developmental theory, 146
ethnic, 149
gender schemata and, 149–150
gender scripts and, 151
on mathematics and gender, 94, 97, 99
media and, 142
memory performance and, 105
of nationalities, 175
in social learning theory, 142, 144
spatial ability testing and, 102
See also Gender stereotypes
Steroid hormones, 46–48
Stress
coping resources for, 381–383
coping strategies for, 383–385
gender differences in responses to, 384–385
multiple roles and, 439–440
physiological responses to, 348
sources of, 376–381
Stroke. *See* Cardiovascular disease
Structuralist school of psychology, 3
Structural view, of coping strategies, 384
"Sturdy Oak." *See* Male Sex role Identity
Subject variable, gender studied as, 15–16, 17, 30, 31, 32, 34, 38
Submissiveness, in Cult of True Womanhood, 166–167
Substance abuse. *See* Drug use
Success
fear of, 308–310
internal vs. external explanations for, 311–313
self-confidence and, 310–311
Suicide, gender and, 353
Superego, in Freudian theory, 119
Support groups, 430–432
Support systems. *See* Social support
Surveys, 26–27
representative samples for, 252
of sexual behavior, 252–258
of sexual abuse, 265
Swiss, emotional expression by, 192
Syphilis, 361

Taosim, science and, 22
Teacher attitudes
ethnic bias, 291
gender bias, 290, 291, 298–299, 305–306
gender stereotyping, 292–293, 298, 299
mathematical abilities and, 97, 98, 99
mentoring relationships and, 306
Teenagers. *See* Adolescents
Television, influence of
on aggressive behavior, 204, 205
on physical activity, 370
Temporal lobe of brain, 75
Terminology
issues in science, 39
sex vs. gender, 12–13
Testosterone
aggression and, 65–70
in brain development, 50
cerebral lateralization and, 80
sexually dimorphic nucleus and, 83–84
spatial ability and, 80
Thalamus, gender-related differences in, 82
Theories
constructionist view of, 21, 39–40
speculation vs., 34
Therapeutic relationship
in feminist therapy, 418
in humanistic therapy, 409
sexual exploitation in, 406–407, 425–427
Title IX of the Educational Amendments of 1972, 290, 300
athletic participation and, 303–305, 370
Token, of minority group, 326
"Tomboys," 59, 156, 174, 221–222
Traits, gender stereotyping and, 171–173
Tranquilizer use, 397, 413
Triangular theory of love, 219, 228, 233, 243
childhood relationships and, 220, 221
Trichomoniasis, 361
Trobriand Islanders, sexual practices of, 277
Tropic hormones, 46
Turner's syndrome, 57

Unconscious, in Freudian theory, 116
Underemployment, among disabled, 331
Unemployment
among disabled, 331
as source of stress, 380
Urinary tract cancers, death rates from, 349
Utku Eskimos, emotional experiences among, 192

Validation
defined, 183
MMPI and, 183

Values
in Freudian theory, 6
in media, 17
in research design, 21, 29, 35, 36, 37, 39–40, 41, 42
Vanatinai of New Guinea, aggression in, 209
Variables
in ex post facto studies, 30
independent vs. dependent, 28
in scientific method, 24
Venereal disease. *See* Sexually transmitted diseases
Verbal ability
environment and, 112
gender and, 80, 86, 91–94, 100, 104, 108, 110, 450
methods of study, 93
Verbal learning, gender and, 105
Violence
as cause of death, 351–354
expression of emotions as, 202, 452
gender and, 208–214, 351–354, 452
male mortality and, 352–354
psychological aftermath of, 378–380
as source of stress, 378–380
XYY chromosome pattern and, 57–58
See also Domestic violence
Viral infections, sexually transmitted, 362. *See also* Human immunodeficiency virus
Virginity, in Cult of True Womanhood, 166
Visual-spatial abilities. *See* Spatial abilities
Vocational education, gender bias in, 299

Wage gap, 316
for disabled, 331
discrimination in hiring and, 323, 325
gender segregation and, 330, 332
Warts, genital, 362
Water-level problem, 101, 102, 105
Wechsler intelligence tests, 91, 92
Weight concerns, gender and, 365–367
Weight control strategies, 367, 369, 371
Wife battering. *See* Domestic violence
Wife role
lower power in, 376–377
as support, 439, 444
Wolffian system, 49, 51
"Womanless" psychology, behaviorism as, 4
Womb envy, in Horney's theory, 121
Women
aggression in, 203, 206–209, 211
as athletes, 297, 303–305, 370–371
body image concerns of, 365–367
communication styles of, 234–235, 332–333
depression in, 395–396
display rules for, 215
eating disorders among, 367–368
eating patterns of, 364–365
emotional expression and, 214–215, 442
emotional stereotypes and, 191, 193–194, 442
emotions suppressed by, 203
fear of crime among, 209–210
fear of success among, 308–310
in feminist psychoanalytic theory, 123–124, 126–130
fitness needs of, 371–372
friendships among, 224, 225, 227
gender role changes and, 442–446, 453–454
health risks and lifestyle of, 363–364
health services treatment of, 354–356
health services use by, 356–359, 360–361
hormonal abnormalities in, 57, 58, 59
life expectancy in, 342–343, 344, 345–346
love and marriage concepts among, 233–234
mental disorder diagnosis in. *See* Mental disorders
mental disorder treatment and, 413–416, 417–418
morbidity and morality in, 342–354
myth of passivity in, 201
poverty effects and, 380–381
reproductive health concerns of, 358–363
reproductive system in, 360
sexual abuse by, 267
sexual harassment by, 300, 338–339
sexual violence against, 210–214
social aggression by, 206, 208
stress and coping patterns in, 381–385
testosterone levels and behavior of, 68–69
See also Girls; Femininity
Women's movement
consciousness-raising groups in, 432–433
feminist therapy and, 417–418
Women's Research Agenda, poverty and mental health on, 380–381
Women's studies, development of, 7–9
Women Who Love Too Much (Norwood), 431
Work. *See* Careers; Employment; Occupation
Working women. *See* Employed women

X chromosome, 49
XO chromosome pattern, 57
XXX chromosome pattern, 57

Yeast (*Candidias albicans*) infection, 361–362